GLOBAL AGRICULTURAL TRADE AND DEVELOPING COUNTRIES

GLOBAL AGRICULTURAL TRADE AND DEVELOPING COUNTRIES

Editors
M. Ataman Aksoy and John C. Beghin

THE WORLD BANK
Washington, D.C.

Library of Congress Cataloging-in-Publication Data

Global agricultural trade and developing countries / editor M. Ataman Aksoy, John C. Beghin.
        p. cm. – (Trade and development)
    Includes bibliographical references and index.
    ISBN 0-8213-5863-4
        1. Produce trade—Developing countries. 2. Produce trade—Government
policy—Developing countries. 3. International economic relations. I. Aksoy, M.
Ataman, 1945- II. Beghin, John C. (John Christopher), 1954- III. Trade and
development series

HD9018.D44G565 2004
382'.41'091724—dc22   2004058811

CONTENTS

List of Boxes

List of Figures

List of Tables

ACKNOWLEDGMENTS

This book is a joint effort by the Prospects Group in DEC and the Trade Group in PREM. Support has been given by the trade group in DECRG and through the Knowledge for Change (KCP) trust funds. Supporting donors for KCP include Canada, Finland, Norway, Sweden, Switzerland, the United Kingdom, and the European Commission.

The completion of this book would not have been possible without the help of numerous colleagues inside and outside of the World Bank. Colleagues in the Development Prospects Group and throughout the Development Economics Vice Presidency and the World Bank's operational units provided critical help and feedback. Support by the former and current Chief Economists, Nicholas Stern and Francois Bourguignon was instrumental. Bernard Hoekman supported this project in all its stages, and without his support this book would not have happened. We are particularly grateful for the ideas and insights of Uri Dadush, Hans Timmer, Richard Newfarmer, Will Martin, Yvonne Tsikata, John Redwood, Kutlu Somel, Tercan Baysan, and especially to John Nash, Kevin Cleaver, Sushma Ganguly, Cornelis Van Der Meer, and their colleagues in the Agricultural and Rural Development Department that reviewed the manuscript and helped to improve it.

We also benefited from presentations and feedback at the 2003 World Bank ABCDE Conference in Paris; to the board of Executive Directors of the World Bank; at the World Bank's international trade workshop, the WTO, UNCTAD, FAO, the 2003 World Outlook Conference at the OECD in Paris, the 2003 American Agricultural Economics Meetings in Montreal, the European Commission, the French Ministry of Agriculture; and at the University of California at Berkeley. Outside the Bank, we would like to particularly thank Bruce Babcock, Pierre Bascou, Jean Christophe Bureau, Tassos Haniotis, Chad Hart, David Roland-Holst, Daniel Sumner, Peter Timmer, and Pat Westhoff for discussions and comments that helped to shape our views.

Finally, we would like to thank Baris Sivri who carried out most of the data work for the book, to Meta de Coquereaumont and Steven Kennedy for editing the manuscript and making it readable, to Awatif Abuzeid and Cathy Rollins for preparing the manuscript in record time, and to Santiago Pombo-Bejarano and Mary Fisk for managing the publishing process.

CONTRIBUTORS

M. Ataman Aksoy has recently retired from the Prospects Group of Development Economics at the World Bank and is now a Consultant at the World Bank in Washington, D.C.

John Baffes is Senior Economist in the Prospects Group of Development Economics at the World Bank in Washington, D.C.

John C. Beghin is Professor, and Martin Cole Endowed Chair for the Department of Economics and Center for Agricultural and Rural Development at Iowa State University in Ames.

Paul Brenton is Senior Economist in the Trade Department of the World Bank in Washington, D.C.

Tom Cox is Professor in the Agricultural and Applied Economics Department at the University of Wisconsin in Madison.

Ndiame Diop is Economist in the Trade Department of the World Bank in Washington, D.C.

Harry de Gorter is Associate Professor of Agricultural Economics at Cornell University in Ithaca, New York.

Spencer Henson is Professor of Economics in the Department of Agriculture, Economics, and Business at the University of Guelph in Canada.

Takako Ikezuki is Junior Professional Associate Economist in the Trade Department of the World Bank in Washington, D.C.

Steven M. Jaffee is Senior Economist in the Trade Department of the World Bank in Washington, D.C.

Bryan Lewin is Consultant in the Agriculture and Rural Development Department of the World Bank in Washington, D.C.

Myles Mielke is Senior Commodity Specialist in Basic Foodstuffs Service at Commodities and Trade Division of the Food and Agriculture Organization of the United Nations in Rome, Italy.

Donald O. Mitchell is Lead Economist in the Prospects Group of Development Economics at the World Bank in Washington, D.C.

Cathy A. Roheim is Professor of Economics in the Department of Environmental and Natural Resource Economics at the University of Rhode Island.

Mirvat Sewadeh is Consultant in the Trade Department of the World Bank in Washington, D.C.

Baris Sivri is Consultant in the Development Economics Group of the World Bank in Washington, D.C.

Dominique van der Mensbrugghe is Lead Economist in the Prospects Group of Development Economics at the World Bank in Washington, D.C.

Panos Varangis is Lead Economist in the Agriculture and Rural Development Department of the World Bank in Washington, D.C.

Eric J. Wailes is the L. C. Carter Professor in the Department of Agricultural Economics and Agribusiness at University of Arkansas in Fayetteville.

Yong Zhu is a Research Associate in the Agricultural and Applied Economics Department at University of Wisconsin in Madison.

ACRONYMS AND ABBREVIATIONS

ABARE	Australian Bureau of Agricultural and Research Economics
ACP	Africa, Caribbean, and Pacific
ACPC	Association of Coffee-Producing Countries
AFIPEK	Kenya Fish Processors and Exporters Association
AGOA	African Growth and Opportunity Act
AGRM	Arkansas Global Rice Model
AMAD	Agricultural Market Access Database
APEC	Asia Pacific Economic Cooperation
APTA	Andean Trade Preference Act
BAAC	Bank for Agriculture and Agricultural Cooperatives
BULOG	Nacional Logistics Agency (Indonesia)
CAP	Common Agricultural Policy (EU)
CBERA	Caribbean Basin Economic Recovery Act
CIMMYT	Internacional Maite and Wheat Improvement Center
CMO	Common Market Organization
Conasupo	Compania Nacional de Subsistencias Populares (Mexico)
CTE	Committee on Trade and the Environment (WTO)
EBA	Everything But Arms (EU)
EEZ	exclusive economic zones
EPA	economic partnership agreements
EU	European Union
EVSL	early, voluntary sector-liberalization
FAIR	Federal Agricultural Improvement and Reform Act (U.S.)
FAPRI	Food and Agricultural Policy Research Institute
FAO	Food and Agriculture Organization of the United Nations

FSU	Former Soviet Union
FTA	free trade agreement
GAP	good agriculture practice
GATT	General Agreement on Tariffs and Trade
GBC	Guatemalan growers association
GDP	gross domestic product
GSP	generalized system of preferences
GTAP	Global Trade Analysis Project
HACCP	hazard analysis and critical control point
HFCS	high-fructose corn syrup
HS	harmonized system
IADB	Inter-American Development Bank
ICAC	International Cotton Advisory Committee
ICO	International Coffee Organization
LDC	least-developed countries
MAFF	Ministry of Agriculture, Forestry, and Fisheries (Japan)
MFN	most-favored nation
MPS	market price support
NAFTA	North American Free Trade Agreement
ODA	official development assistance
OECD	Organisation for Economic Co-operation and Development
OPEC	Organization of Petroleum Exporting Countries
PIPAA	Integrated Program for Agricultural and Environmental Protection
PROCAMPO	Programa de Apoyos Directos al Campo
PROMPEX	Peruvian Commission for Export Promotion
PS&D	Production supply and distribution
PSE	producer subsidy equivalents
SACU	Southern Africa Customs Union
SAM	social accounting matrix
SMP	skim milk powder

TCK	*tilletia controversa kuhn* fungus	USFDA	United States Food and Drug Administration
TRQ	tariff rate quota		
UKP	UzKhlopkoprom/ UzPakhtasanoitish	USGAO	United States General Accounting Office
UNCTAD	United Nations Conference on Trade and Development	USDA	United States Department of Agriculture
UNEP	United Nations Environment Programme	USITC	United States International Trade Commission
URAA	Uruguay Round Agreement on Agriculture	UW-WDM	University of Wisconsin-Madison World Dairy Model
USAID	United States Agency for International Development	VAT	value-added tax
		WTO	World Trade Organization

INTRODUCTION AND OVERVIEW

M. Ataman Aksoy and John C. Beghin

In recent years, agricultural protection and its impact on developing countries have attracted growing attention. While manufacturing protection has declined worldwide following substantial reforms of trade policies, especially in developing countries, most industrial and many developing countries still protect agriculture at high levels. Agricultural protection continues to be among the most contentious issues in global trade negotiations, with high protection in industrial countries being the main cause of the breakdown of the Cancún Ministerial Meetings in 2003.

Why Highlight Agriculture?

What happens in the global agricultural market is important for developing countries beyond the price changes triggered by global reforms. For countries with a small urban population, increasing agricultural exports can accelerate growth more than expanding domestic market demand can. Although food production for home consumption and sale in domestic markets accounts for most agricultural production in the developing world, agricultural exports and domestic food production are closely related. Export growth contributes significantly to the growth of agriculture overall by generating cash income for modernizing farming practices. For

those leaving the farm, growth and modernization of agriculture create jobs in agricultural processing and marketing, as well as the expansion of other nonfarm jobs.

Although most successful developing countries have not relied on agriculture for export expansion and growth, growth in agriculture has a disproportionate effect on poverty because more than half of the populations in developing countries reside in rural areas and poverty is much higher in rural areas than in urban areas. Some 57 percent of the developing world's rural population lives in lower-middle-income countries, and 15 percent lives in the least-developed countries. Even though historical trends show that agriculture's importance diminishes over time and the share of population in rural areas declines, there will still be more poor people in rural areas than in cities for at least a generation.

Why This Book?

This book explores the outstanding issues in global agricultural trade policy and evolving world production and trade patterns. Its coverage of agricultural trade issues ranges from the details of cross-cutting policy issues to the highly distorted agricultural trade regimes of industrial countries and detailed studies of agricultural commodities of economic importance to many developing countries. The book brings together the background issues and findings to guide researchers and policymakers in their global negotiations and domestic policies on agriculture. The book also explores the key questions for global agricultural policies, both the impacts of current trade regimes and the implications of reform. It complements the recent agricultural trade handbook that focuses primarily on the agricultural issues within the context of the World Trade Organization (WTO) negotiations (Ingco and Nash 2004).

The first part of the book replies to the broad, cross-cutting questions raised by researchers and policymakers about agricultural trade regimes and trade performance. What has happened to the structure of agricultural trade over the last two decades? What is the level of protection across commodities and countries? Do tariff preferences make a big difference in the levels of protection facing developing-country agricultural products? Has the move toward decoupling agricultural support from production reduced the effects of agricultural support? Do stricter food safety standards constitute a new barrier to market access by developing countries? How big are the potential gains from global liberalization, and how sensitive are estimates to various assumptions? While these topics have been analyzed before, much of the work here relies on new information. The answers to these questions give a clearer picture of global agricultural policies and reforms.

However, broad answers to these questions typically do not convince the critics and, more important, provide little implementable guidance on specific policy issues. Micro details and partial equilibrium analyses at country and commodity levels are necessary to ensure that these broad results are credible and specific enough to be a basis for policies. The second part of the book complements the broad answers with detailed studies of commodities that are of considerable economic importance to many developing countries and that are representative of the export bundle of developing countries. The commodities selected are sugar, dairy, rice, wheat, groundnuts, fruits and vegetables, cotton, seafood, and coffee. Most of the products selected have highly distorted policy regimes in industrial and some developing countries. The

general issues of competition, entry, and exit, which are major issues for products with distorted policies, are equally important for the less-protected traditional export products such as coffee, tea, and cocoa. Exporters of such products still face long-term price declines, price volatility, and other problems usually associated with products with distorted policy regimes. Seafood also faces fewer trade distortions but is included as representative of the problems facing new, expanding sectors in the presence of domestic subsidies in industrial countries.

The commodity studies analyze the current trade regimes in key producing and consuming countries, document the magnitude of distortions in these markets, and assess the distributional impacts (across countries and across groups of consumers, taxpayers, and producers within countries) of trade and domestic policy reforms in developing and industrial countries. These assessments are based on rigorous quantitative analyses of various reform scenarios and disaggregated partial equilibrium models. The impacts of current agricultural trade policies and of policy reforms vary substantially across commodities, and different reforms result in very different gainers and losers.

Some Key Findings

Despite the diversity of the cross-cutting analyses and commodity studies, it is possible to draw some general conclusions. First, these commodity markets exhibit a complex political economy, both domestically and internationally. The arcane nature of many policy interventions in these commodity markets and the many heterogeneous interests exacerbate this complexity. Identifying superior policy options is not difficult, but the feasibility of reform depends on the power of vested interests and the ability of governments to identify tradeoffs and possible linkages that will allow them to pursue multiple goals (food security, income transfers, expansion of domestic value added) more efficiently.

Second, a narrow sectoral or product approach is unlikely to be fruitful in WTO negotiations. The commodity studies illustrate why. They also illustrate that potential tradeoffs exist even within agriculture, as interests differ across commodities.

Third, and perhaps most important, the studies reveal the importance of microanalysis for identifying both the key policy instruments that distort competition and the likely winners and losers from global reforms (producers, consumers, taxpayers within and across countries). Knowing who is likely to gain or lose from reform is critical for sequencing reforms and putting in place complementary policies, including assistance to reduce the cost of adjustment in noncompetitive sectors.

Fourth, the studies identify trade distortions (border protection) and domestic subsidies as major factors affecting world markets and thus developing-country consumers and producers. A common theme is that border protection is more distorting in most markets, with the notable exceptions of cotton and seafood (corroborating the findings of Hoekman, Ng, and Olarreaga 2002). Both domestic subsidies and border protection contribute to making commodity markets artificially thin, with small trade volumes and a small number of agents, in turn leading to high variability in prices and trade flows. Large trade distortions impede trade flows, depress world prices, and discourage market entry or delay exit by noncompetitive producers. Border barriers are high in most of the commodity markets studied (the exceptions are cotton, coffee, and seafood), including industrial countries and many developing countries. For example, the global trade-weighted average tariff for all types of rice is 43 percent and reaches 217 percent for Japonica rice. Many Asian countries remain bastions of protectionism in their agricultural and food markets.

Subsidies have similar effects, depressing world prices and inhibiting entry by inducing procyclical surplus production by noncompetitive (often large) producers. In dairy and sugar markets, the effects of export subsidies have been smaller than those of tariffs and tariff rate quota schemes, partly because of the export subsidy disciplines introduced in the Uruguay Round Agreement on Agriculture. Many domestic subsidies in Organisation for Economic Co-operation and Development (OECD) countries, such as cotton subsidies in the United States, are countercyclical.

Domestic support and protection policies have substantial negative effects on producers in developing countries, because of the sheer size of the subsidies relative to the size of the market. Cotton subsidies in the United States and European Union (EU), for example, reached $4.4 billion in a $20 billion market. Such large subsidies shield noncom-

petitive producers from exit decisions, making decoupling of these policies a moot point. If U.S. cotton subsidies were abolished, revenues for cotton farmers in West and Central Africa would increase by some $250 million. Total official development assistance (ODA) to the region in 1999 was $1.9 billion, 15–25 percent of which typically goes to agricultural assistance, not all of it directly reaching producers. One can see the incompatibility between ODA and farm policy in donor countries that subsidize their rich farmers.

Fifth, a development strategy based on agricultural commodity exports is likely to be impoverishing in the current agricultural policy environment in which policymakers in many countries have mercantilist and protectionist reflexes that, when aggregated, compromise world trade in agricultural and food products. The emergence of competitive producers in developing countries does not lead to a rationalization of production among noncompetitive producers as it would in a liberalized market. Instead, noncompetitive producers remain in business, buffered by extensive protection and support.

Potential Winners and Losers from Trade Liberalization

Agricultural trade liberalization would create winners and losers. The studies conclude that reform would reduce rural poverty in developing economies, both because in the aggregate they have a strong comparative advantage in agriculture and because the agricultural sector is important for income generation in these countries.

Resource reallocation within agriculture would be substantial. For example, production of groundnut products in India would likely contract as would vegetable oil production in China, but dairy production and exports would expand in India, and rice production and exports would expand in China. Liberalization of value-added activities is crucial for expanding employment and income opportunities beyond the farm gate. Such findings illustrate the importance of a multicommodity approach to reform, as gains and losses will differ by market. They also illustrate the importance of social safety nets and other complementary policies.

Consumers in highly protected markets will benefit greatly from trade liberalization as domestic (tariff-inclusive) prices fall and product choice expands. Consumers in poor, net-food-importing countries could face higher prices if these markets were not protected before liberalization, because of higher import unit costs. In practice, however, such concerns have often been exaggerated. For example, dairy consumption in the Middle East and North Africa would be little affected by trade liberalization because, while world prices would rise, high import tariffs would be removed, so that the net impact on dairy consumer prices would be negligible. Consumer prices would rise for rice, however, since the removal of low tariffs would not offset the increase in border prices.

Other winners and losers would also emerge. Multilateral trade liberalization erodes the benefits from preferential bilateral trade agreements and pits low-cost producers in some developing countries (such as sugar producers in Brazil and Thailand) against less efficient producers in the least-developed countries who are currently helped by preferential access. The actual gains from such preferences, however, have been smaller than expected because of efficiency differences.

How these reforms occur will have important consequences for developing countries. The best approach is coordinated global liberalization of policies. This approach would yield the largest price increases to offset some of the lost rents. For example, world sugar price increases alone would offset about half the lost quota rents, or about $0.45 billion, for countries with preferential access. The analysis shows that losses in rents would be much less than is commonly expected, because high production costs eat up much of the potential benefit from preferential access to the high-price markets. Moreover, the cost to the European Union and the United States of each $1 in preferential access is estimated at more than $5, a very inefficient way to provide development assistance. Global liberalization of primary commodity markets should be accompanied by further effective opening of value-added markets, along with some targeted assistance to overcome supply constraints. Supply constraints are particularly acute in Africa and some Latin American countries but are not insurmountable, as success stories in horticultural and seafood markets in Kenya show.

Although the commodity case studies provide evidence that higher market prices would prevail in traditional agricultural commodity markets (sugar, cotton, dairy, groundnuts, rice, and to a lesser extent, wheat) if trade and domestic distortions were removed, prospects of continuing high prices are limited because of the nature of these markets (a large number of low-cost competitors and inelastic demand). The bulk-commodity route to export expansion requires low-cost conditions and achievement of economies of scale. These markets face a long-term decline in prices as economies of scale and competitive pressures yield lower costs and margins. Domestic farm subsidies in industrial countries have exacerbated this low-price tendency by fostering production beyond what free markets would demand, with dramatic immiserizing consequences in some cases, such as cotton.

Better opportunities exist in new markets such as horticulture and seafood and in more differentiated products (niche coffee markets, confectionary peanuts). The high-quality differentiated-product alternative requires quality upgrades and the necessary infrastructure and institutions to certify products. These new markets imply increased costs to meet quality standards and higher rewards. Producers have to be able to demonstrate quality, an institutional challenge in many countries. This second strategy can be successful only when supply constraints are alleviated. Trade barriers also exist in these new markets, especially with higher safety standards. However, while the findings show that food safety standards are becoming more stringent, the view that standards are simply new barriers to trade has been somewhat oversold.

What the Book Covers

Part 1 contains six chapters on cross-cutting issues, and Part 2 includes nine commodity studies. While the chapters in Part 1 are sequenced to provide a detailed picture of cross-cutting issues in global agricultural trade, they can be read individually as self-contained pieces. The accompanying CD-ROM contains detailed supplementary tables and annexes.

Changes in Agricultural Trade Flows

Chapter 2, "The Evolution of Agricultural Trade Flows," by Ataman Aksoy, gives a bird's-eye view of the changes in global agricultural trade flows since the early 1980s and contrasts these with the progressive global integration of manufacturing. World trade in agriculture, broadly defined throughout the book to include seafood, processed foods, and some agro-processing such as wine and tobacco products, was $467 billion in 2001–01, up from $243 billion in 1980–81. During the 1980s real manufacturing and agriculture exports expanded at similar rates of 5.7 and 4.9 percent a year. However, during the 1990s real agricultural export growth decelerated to 3.7 percent a year, falling well behind the 6.7 percent annual growth in manufacturing.

Developing countries increased their share in manufacturing exports during the 1990s but saw little expansion in agricultural exports, barely maintaining their share of around 36 percent after losing market shares during the 1980s. All of their gains in agriculture during the 1990s came from expansion of their exports to other developing countries. More than 48 percent of world agricultural trade is still accounted for by trade between industrial countries—about the same share as in 1980–81.

This stability of trade shares comes as a surprise, since it was during the 1990s that Uruguay Round commitments in agriculture began to be implemented and rapid trade reforms were introduced in developing countries. More than a third of world agricultural exports are traded within EU member nations and among the three signatories of the North American Free Trade Agreement (NAFTA).

Low-income countries' agricultural trade surpluses against both middle-income and industrial countries has increased. Low-income developing countries now export more to middle-income countries than they do to the European Union, their largest export market in the early 1980s. The agricultural trade surpluses of middle-income countries have diminished. Among industrial countries, Japan has the largest agricultural trade deficit (almost $50 billion in 2000–01); the European Union, once the largest net buyer of agricultural commodities, has seen its deficits decline; and NAFTA's trade surplus has shrunk considerably. Developing-country regions, after losing market shares during the 1980s, regained most of them by the end of 1990s. The only exception is Sub-Saharan Africa, which lost market shares during the 1980s and did not regain them during the 1990s.

The structure of world trade has changed, especially for developing countries. Nontraditional products, especially seafood and fruits and vegetables, now constitute almost half their exports. Also,

exports of temperate-climate products (grains, meats, dairy products, edible oils and seeds, and animal feed) have surpassed exports of traditional tropical products (coffee, tea, cocoa, textile fibers, sugar, and nuts and spices). More important, exports of fruits and vegetables are now greater than total exports of traditional products. Seafood exports are larger still, with a growing portion of exports coming from aquaculture.

State of Agricultural Protection

Chapter 3, "Global Agricultural Trade Policies," by Ataman Aksoy, summarizes the state of agricultural protection, using data on domestic support policies from the OECD and tariff data from the WTO for a large set of developing and industrial countries. The analysis of experience with the new rules on market access, export subsidies, and domestic support indicates that the effects of implementation of the Uruguay Round Agreement on Agriculture have been modest. Within OECD countries, producer support in agriculture was about $230 billion in 2000–02, or almost 46 percent of production value (evaluated at world prices), down from approximately 63 percent in 1986–88, but still very high. Of producer support, 63 percent came through higher prices associated with border protection (so-called Market Price Support or MPS) and 37 percent from direct subsidies.

While protection remained high in industrial countries, many developing countries have significantly liberalized their agricultural sectors since the early 1980s. Average agricultural tariffs, the main source of protection in developing countries, declined from 30 percent to 18 percent during the 1990s. In addition, these countries eliminated import restrictions, devalued exchange rates, abandoned multiple exchange rate systems that penalized agriculture, and eliminated almost all export taxes. As overall taxation of agriculture declined in developing countries, reactive protection in response to industrial-country support to agricultural producers increased, especially in food products. All these measures increased incentives for agricultural production in many developing countries. However, without compensating reductions in protection in industrial and some middle-income countries, the result was overproduction (beyond competitive and undistorted market levels) and price declines for many commodities, reducing opportunities for competitive developing countries to expand exports and rural incomes.

The structure of agricultural tariffs is complicated and nontransparent. More than 40 percent of the agricultural tariff lines in the European Union and the United States contain specific duties, which make it difficult to calculate average tariffs, obscure true levels of protection, and penalize developing countries that supply cheaper products. Specific duties, which are rare in manufacturing, are also used to hide high rates of protection in agriculture. The ad valorem equivalents of specific duties, when they can be measured, are much higher than the average ad valorem duties. Also, a much higher proportion of tariff lines in final products than in raw and intermediate products have specific rates. Low-income countries have more transparent tariff regimes and tend to use ad valorem tariffs.

Average agricultural tariffs in industrial countries, when they can be measured, are some two to four times higher than manufacturing tariffs. Developing-country exports confront tariff peaks as high as 500 percent in some industrial countries. High variance and high peaks make it difficult to measure the real impact of protection on key products, whose high tariff rates are buried in lower average tariffs. This is why the OECD measure of protection, market price support, which compares local and international prices, shows much higher rates of protection than do average tariffs. Tariffs also increase by the degree of product processing, creating an escalating tariff structure that impedes access to processed food markets. In addition, almost 30 percent of domestic production in OECD countries is protected by tariff rate quotas.

Trade Preferences

Industrial countries have established tariff preference schemes to create market access opportunities for developing countries, especially for low-income countries. In chapter 4, "The Impact of Agricultural Trade Preferences on Low-Income Countries," Paul Brenton and Takako Ikezuki examine the impacts of these preferences. For most developing countries, preferences have provided limited gains at best. Many agricultural products exported from developing countries, especially traditional tropical products, are subject to zero duties in industrial

countries, so tariff preferences are irrelevant. Although duties on other primary agricultural products and processed products are often very high, few of these products receive preferences. Nevertheless, for a small number of products substantial preferences are available for certain countries, usually within strict quantitative limits. Countries that produce sugar and tobacco, for example, have received large transfers as a result of these preferences.

Comparison of different preference schemes is difficult because the schemes differ substantially. They differ in the group of eligible countries, the products covered, the size of the preferences granted, and administrative requirements, especially rules of origin. These differences are a major weakness of the current system of preferences. Differences between preference schemes constrain the ability of developing-country suppliers to develop global market strategies.

In general, preferences are unilateral concessions by industrial countries. The agreements require renewal, and specific products can be withdrawn at short notice. This uncertainty has impeded new investment. The most highly protected products, which would have the highest potential margins of preference, are often excluded or preferences are small. Rules of origin for processed products often constrain the ability of countries to expand into these products.

The value of preferences is largest in the EU market, driven mainly by the very high EU prices for sugar. For some countries, such as Mauritius, preferences seem to explain at least part of the relatively strong economic performance and economic diversification. For the majority of low-income countries, however, EU, Japanese, and U.S. preferences have had little impact and have done little to stimulate the export of a broader range of products.

Decoupling Agricultural Support

One key challenge is to lower the effect of domestic subsidies on world production and prices. Although official export subsidies may be small and shrinking, implicit export subsidies created by domestic support are increasing, lending unfair advantage to producers in industrial countries. More generally, there is a move toward supporting agriculture through direct subsidies rather than through border barriers. Some domestic support to agriculture has moved away from being directly linked to production to being partially decoupled, with payments made based on historical production levels and other mechanisms. Decoupling should reduce the output effects of support and thus increase world prices for the exports of developing countries. The move to decoupled agricultural support policies is therefore a step in the right direction.

How much has the world actually moved to decoupled payments? What has been the net effect on resource use, efficiency, and trade distortions? In chapter 5, "Experience with Decoupling Agricultural Support," John Baffes and Harry de Gorter evaluate the impact of decoupling measures in industrial and developing countries. From 1986–88 to 2000–02, domestic subsidies paid to farmers in OECD countries increased 60 percent. Output and input subsidies ("large" impact programs) increased moderately compared with the substantial increases in payments linked to land area or number of animals, decoupled historical entitlements, or input use and overall farm income ("smaller" impact programs). Payments based on area planted and number of animals have increased most, followed by historical entitlements.

The United States took the first step toward decoupling in the 1985 Farm Bill, which shifted the base of support from current yields to historical yields. In the 1996 Farm Bill the United States replaced deficiency payments with decoupled support. The European Union partially replaced intervention prices with decoupled payments following the Common Agricultural Policy reform of 1992. Mexico replaced price supports with decoupled payments in 1994 with the introduction of the National Program for Direct Assistance to Rural Areas (Programa de Apoyos Directos al Campo [PROCAMPO]). More recently, Turkey replaced some price supports and input subsidies with decoupled payments. In addition to broad decoupling attempts, there have been numerous one-time buyouts, including New Zealand's exit grant in 1984, the buyout of Canada's grain transportation subsidy in 1995, and the buyout of the U.S. peanut marketing quota under the 2002 Farm Bill.

Experience designing and implementing these programs has been mixed. Although decoupling has led to a reallocation of resources in agriculture, its effects have been modest. In many cases, overpro-

duction has continued. One-time buyouts have had greater success in eliminating very inefficient arrangements, but their range is limited. More attention should be given to constraints on input use, government credibility, other support programs, and time limits. Unless these aspects are addressed, decoupled support is likely to have the same kinds of undesirable effects as other subsidy programs. Payments should be time limited, provided only to help producers adjust. The European Union and Turkey have no time limit. The United States had (at least implicitly) a time limit in the 1996 Farm Bill but violated it three years later. Mexico has a time limit and has complied with it so far.

The coexistence of coupled and decoupled programs means that incentives to overproduce remain. In the four decoupling cases examined, all either left some coupled support programs in place or added new ones. Eligibility rules need to be fixed and clearly defined. Updating the bases for payment of subsidies and adding crops results in a government credibility problem and reduces the effect of the decoupling programs.

Food Product and Safety Standards

With the decline in traditional barriers to trade, attention has focused on the potential role of standards as technical barriers to trade. Zero-duty access means little if countries cannot meet product standards. Chapter 6, "Agro-Food Exports from Developing Countries: The Challenges of Standards," by Steven M. Jaffee and Spencer Henson, provides an overview of the impact of food safety and agricultural health standards on developing country agro-food exports. Standards have become an increasingly important influence on the international competitiveness of developing countries, especially in the context of high-value agricultural and food products. Some well-established sectors that are highly export dependent have been hurt by new and stricter standards. In several cases, developing countries have faced restrictions because of their inability to meet food safety or agricultural health requirements. At the same time, other developing countries have gained access to high-value markets in industrial countries despite these stricter standards.

The evidence in this chapter suggests a less pessimistic picture for developing countries than that commonly presented, which sees standards as barriers to developing-country trade. Rising standards accentuate underlying supply chain strengths and weaknesses and thus have different effects on the competitive position of different countries. In this perspective, food safety measures must be viewed within the context of more general capacity constraints.

Much of the impetus for stricter food safety and agricultural health standards is coming from consumer and commercial interests, magnified by advances in technology and new security concerns. Thus prospects are slim for slowing this movement or allowing poorer countries to meet lower standards. Developing countries need to find ways to develop and improve food safety and agricultural health management systems to meet these standards.

A crucial need is for management capacity, not only to comply with the different requirements in different markets but also to demonstrate that compliance has been achieved. While many countries have struggled to meet ever-stricter standards, even some very poor countries have managed to implement the necessary capacity, especially where the private sector is well organized and the public sector supports the efforts of exporters. Many poor countries have successfully entered the demanding seafood and fresh fruit and vegetable markets. Most violations reported at border controls involve failures to meet simple hygiene standards.

There is no single model for all countries striving to meet the challenges posed by standards. Institutional frameworks are required, however, to overcome the problems associated with being poor or small. These can include outgrower[1] programs for smallholder farmers, systems of training and oversight for small and medium-size enterprises established through associations and other groups, and twinning and regional networking for small countries. Such efforts undoubtedly need to be improved and refined, but they offer useful guidance on effective ways to proceed.

The chapter clearly demonstrates the need for developing countries to be proactive when facing new food safety and agricultural health standards. By thinking strategically, countries can program capacity enhancement into wider and longer-term efforts to enhance domestic food safety and agricultural health management systems and export

competitiveness. Failing this, countries face the need for potentially large-scale investments over long periods of time to remedy violations of standards as they arise. In all of this, the public and private sectors need to work together to identify the most efficient and effective ways to develop capacity. Food safety and agricultural health controls must be seen as a collaborative effort in a system that is only as strong as its weakest link.

Welfare Gains from Global Agricultural Reform

Given the magnitude of the distortions in agricultural sectors in all countries, an obvious question concerns the net impact of status quo policies and of global reform. Models of global trade and domestic policy reforms often yield very large welfare gains for both industrial and developing countries. Critics argue that many of the assumptions of these studies are exaggerated and that their results should be treated with caution. In chapter 7, "Global Agricultural Reform: What Is at Stake?" Dominique van der Mensbrugghe and John C. Beghin look beyond the estimates of aggregate welfare gains to structural changes that would emerge from multilateral trade liberalization in agricultural and food markets, including cross-regional patterns of output and trade. They address some of the common criticisms of these aggregate models and explore the implications for welfare, trade, output, and value added of changing key modeling assumptions. The real gains often amount to 1 percent or less of base income, whereas the structural changes (resource reallocation) can be greater than 50 percent. The chapter decomposes the impacts of partial reforms both regionally and across instruments to determine the share of the global gains that comes from reform in industrial countries and the share from reform in developing countries. It also examines the extent to which border protection and various forms of domestic support drive global gains.

The second part of the chapter addresses some of the issues raised by critics of trade reform—notably, that the estimated gains for developing countries are too optimistic and that the transitional costs for industrial-country farmers are high and too often ignored. The analysis looks at three assumptions that could influence the level of gains: the consequences of lowering agricultural productivity growth in developing countries, the impact of constraining output supply response in low-income countries, and the assumptions on the magnitude of trade elasticities. The chapter also examines the impact of lowering the rate of exit of industrial-country farmers, including adjustments to transition.

The results are broadly robust to the range of sensitivity analyses undertaken, but trade elasticities are the most important. Assuming low productivity gains in agriculture in developing countries leads to a reversal in the estimated impact of global liberalization for industrial countries, with an increase in the net food trade surplus. If productivity grows slowly in developing countries, they become much larger importers of food and agricultural products, and trade reform accentuates this tendency. Low-income developing countries experience an increase in net food trade surplus that is much smaller than under the higher productivity assumption. Thus different assumptions about productivity could lead to different conclusions about the direction of food self-sufficiency in the aftermath of reform. Supply constraints do not qualitatively affect the estimated impact of trade reform on agricultural output, although estimated changes tend to be smaller. Higher trade elasticities dampen the adverse terms-of-trade shocks from reforms, leading to larger income gains and higher variations at the country level.

Commodity Studies

Nine chapters analyze the impact on global markets of policies for selected commodity groups. The commodity groups were selected to provide a broad range of policy environments, to deal with different groups of countries, and to show the diversity of gainers and losers.

Sugar Chapter 8, "Sugar: Opportunity for Change," by Donald O. Mitchell, looks at the sugar market, one of the most distorted markets in the world. The European Union, United States, and Japan together protect sugar at some $6.4 billion a year, about the value of total developing-country exports. On average, domestic producers in these countries receive more than triple the world price for their output. Among middle-income countries, Mexico, Poland, Turkey, and almost all beet-producing, northern developing countries also provide significant

support to their producers. Thus 80 percent of world production and 60 percent of world trade take place at prices much higher than world prices.

There are pressures on the European Union and the United States to reform their sugar markets because of internal market changes and international commitments already made under NAFTA, the EU Everything but Arms Program, and the Uruguay Round Agreement on Agriculture. Their protectionism is unravelling, another case of border opening forcing domestic policy discipline. Needed reforms could be carried out in conjunction with scheduled reviews of the EU Common Agricultural Policy in 2006 and expiration of the U.S. Farm Bill in 2007, which could provide a target period for getting reforms agreed on and in place. Japan remains a bastion of protectionism, with tariffs, price surcharges, and trade management by state agencies.

Preferential and regional agreements often bar low-cost producers from entering the internal markets covered by the agreements. Quota allocations are concentrated in a few, often high-cost countries, which are generally not the poorest. For example, Mauritius has 38 percent of EU quotas. Thailand, a very low-cost producer, is limited to a 15,000 ton quota in the United States, whereas the Philippines has a quota 10 times larger that often goes unfilled.

Multilateral negotiations provide an opportunity to rationalize the proliferation of preferential agreements, by phasing in multilateral liberalization and allowing markets to allocate access on a competitive basis. Reforms would result in a contraction of output in both industrial countries and beet-producing developing countries. World prices would rise by about 40 percent. The big gainers would be producers in Thailand, Latin America, and southern Africa among developing countries and Australia among industrial countries. Consumers would gain in almost every country, since even competitive producers cover their export losses with higher-price domestic sales. The losses to quota holders, many of them very high-cost producers, would be much smaller because of the world price increases.

Dairy In chapter 9, "Dairy: World Markets and the Implications of Policy Reform for Developing Countries," Tom Cox and Yong Zhu analyze the dairy market, which is the most distorted of all the markets examined in this volume. The sector is distorted by a complex system of domestic and international trade barriers, including surplus disposal in the Quad countries (Canada, Japan, the European Union, and the United States) and the Republic of Korea. OECD support totaled $41 billion in 2002, and tariff rates are above 30 percent worldwide. The Quad countries and Australia and New Zealand dominate the export market. Although Australia and New Zealand are competitive exporters, with few distortions, dairy interest groups in the Quad countries are strongly entrenched. Prospects for policy reforms appear dim, especially in the European Union and Japan. Domestic price discrimination schemes in the European Union, the United States, and Canada rely on the ability to close borders, suggesting that the emphasis in the Doha Round negotiations should be on commitments to lower border protection.

Despite high distortion levels, the global dairy market is dynamic, with much growth potential. Dairy consumption in Asia has been expanding dramatically with income growth, urbanization, and the westernization of diets. Innovations in food processing also contribute to the sector's dynamism, with new value-added opportunities such as dry whey and lactose, for which trade barriers are low. Innovations have also expanded trade opportunities for traditional milk products such as milk powder and butter-oil, which are transformed into final products after importation to circumvent protection on finished products. Concentration and vertical integration in industrial countries are also important sources of economies in procurement, processing, and logistics and lead to high levels of foreign direct investment. Global reforms could raise prices by 20–40 percent and lead to production declines in the Quad countries and increases in Australia, New Zealand, Latin America, and India.

Rice   In chapter 10, "Rice: Global Trade, Protectionist Policies, and the Impact of Trade Liberalization," Eric J. Wailes analyzes rice, the most important food grain in the world. On average, consumers in low-income food-deficit countries get 28 percent of their calories from rice. Production and consumption are concentrated in Asia (China, India, and Indonesia). The rice market is a mature market, with static demand in industrial countries and growing demand in developing economies

driven by demographics rather than by income growth. Prospects for growth in trade therefore rely on policy reforms.

Tariff and related border protection are very high, averaging about 40 percent globally and rising to 200 percent in some markets. Support in OECD countries is almost $25 billion. Support in Japan, expressed in ad valorem form, is a staggering 700 percent of world prices. Tariff escalation is systematically practiced (from paddy to milled rice) in many countries. In the European Union the tariff on milled rice (80 percent) is prohibitive, except for small preferential import quotas granted to a few countries. Tariff escalation is also prevalent in Central and South America. Mexico has a 10 percent tariff on paddy rice and a 20 percent tariff on brown and milled rice. This pattern of protection depresses world prices for milled high-quality long grain rice relative to prices for brown and rough rice, creating economic hardship for millers of high-quality long grain rice in exporting countries such as Thailand, the United States, and Vietnam.

Net rice consumers would be negatively affected by trade liberalization if the new consumer price rises with reform. Prices would rise wherever current ad valorem tariffs are lower than the potential world price increase following liberalization, such as in the Middle East.

Wheat   In chapter 11, "Wheat: The Global Market, Policies, and Priorities," Donald O. Mitchell and Myles Mielke analyze the world wheat market, which has become less distorted since 1990. A number of countries have undertaken reforms unilaterally or as a consequence of commitments under the Uruguay Round. The European Union and the United States have ended their export subsidies, but other surplus-disposal programs, such as nonemergency food aid and export credits, are still in place. Most importing countries have reduced their tariffs on wheat or allowed duty-free imports from regional trading partners and thus benefit from low world market prices. A few importers, such as Japan, continue with high levels of protection that raise internal prices to more than five times world market levels.

While wheat trade has become less distorted, tariff escalation is high. Tariffs on flour are well above those on wheat, and tariffs on bakery and pasta products are even higher. Consequently, trade in wheat products is confined largely to free-trade areas such as the European Union and NAFTA.

A major concern for wheat-importing countries is the lack of assured access to wheat markets in periods of high prices. In the 1970s the United States imposed an export embargo on wheat, to protect domestic consumers from high world prices. In 1995 the European Union imposed an export tax on wheat for a similar reason. Such actions increase international price volatility and reinforce the desire for self-sufficiency in importing countries. Importing countries need to pressure exporting countries for assured market access as part of the Doha Round of multilateral trade negotiations.

OECD countries still provide substantial support to wheat producers, but the production effects have been partially offset by land set-aside programs and by the way support is provided. Global liberalization is expected to raise world wheat prices by a relatively small amount (5–10 percent) because of large surplus capacity in major exporters. This capacity could return to production following policy reforms, preventing prices from rising significantly. Big gainers would be Argentina, Kazakhstan, and Ukraine, with some output reduction by the United States and the European Union. Further reforms of the global wheat market should focus on ensuring access to wheat exports during price spikes, reducing producer support in OECD countries, reducing protection in the few remaining highly protected markets, and reducing tariff escalation on wheat products.

Groundnuts In chapter 12, "Groundnuts: Policies, Global Trade Dynamics, and the Impact of Trade Liberalization," Ndiame Diop, John C. Beghin, and Mirvat Sewadeh analyze groundnuts, an important product for many low-income producers and consumers. There are two main groundnut markets, one for edible groundnuts (confectionary, processed butter and paste) and one for crushed groundnuts (oil and cakes) used in livestock feed. The peanut oil market is declining because of the availability of lower-priced vegetable oils, but the confectionary nuts market is expanding. African producers have considerable potential in this sector, but supply volatility, inefficient processing, and uneven quality are challenges to their becoming dependable exporters of confectionary products.

The policy dimension of international groundnut markets is a challenge largely for developing countries. India and, to a lesser extent, China are large, protected groundnut markets, and low-cost producers in Argentina and Sub-Saharan Africa are potential gainers from global reforms. The United States, which once strongly supported the peanut sector, eliminated major distortions with a one-time buyout in 2002, but a now-redundant tariff of 160 percent remains. Liberalization would make India and China net importers of some peanut products. With trade liberalization, the bulk of world welfare gains would occur with groundnuts rather than with derivative products, although liberalization of the value-added markets (groundnut oil and meal) would lead to larger welfare gains and higher rural incomes for African countries ($72 million in aggregate welfare and $124 million in farm profits). Consumers in OECD countries would pay higher prices for these products, but there would be little effect on poverty. Consumers in India and southern China, who pay for heavy and inefficient government intervention in the sector, would be better off.

The major challenge in successful negotiations to open groundnut product markets is to overcome entrenched interests in India and China. Except for the United States, industrial countries have limited interests at stake in these markets and should not be an impediment to reform. Moreover, U.S. producers would benefit from the higher world prices that would prevail under free trade, helping to offset reductions in U.S. tariffs.

Fruits and vegetables In chapter 13, "Fruits and Vegetables: Global Trade and Competition in Fresh and Processed Products," Ndiame Diop and Steven M. Jaffe look at another dynamic product group, which now constitutes almost 21 percent of developing-country exports. World imports of fruits and vegetables grew 2–3 percent a year during the 1990s, a slowdown over the 1980s. Low population and income growth in the European Union, where product markets were already mature and saturated, had much to do with the slowdown. Adverse price movements for fresh and processed products from the mid-1990s onward also contributed to the deceleration. Trade growth remained robust among NAFTA countries, for exports to high-income Asian countries and for trade between developing countries.

Although many developing-country suppliers have entered this market, relatively few countries have achieved significant success on a sustained basis. This is a highly competitive and rapidly changing industry, with multiple influences on competitiveness.

Unlike the case in many other agricultural sectors, production and export subsidies are not pervasive in horticulture. Border controls are the main instrument of protection. The United States, the European Union, and Japan use a range of complex tools, including highly dispersed ad valorem tariffs, specific duties, seasonal tariffs, tariff escalation, and preferential access with tariff rate quotas. Many industrial countries have set up complex systems of preferential access to provide a few privileged trade partners with favorable entry without undermining protection of domestic producers. The product coverage of preferential access schemes is wide, but entry is often limited by quotas for "sensitive products." Tariff escalation is widespread, although its extent varies significantly across countries.

Further tariff liberalization would be needed to reduce tariff peaks, especially in the European Union and the Republic of Korea. Changes in domestic support will not affect the sector significantly because most countries have low levels of direct government intervention. Reductions in tariffs and other import restrictions are thus critical for determining the impact of trade agreements and policies on world horticultural trade. Still, as experience suggests, the main beneficiaries of such reforms will be a limited number of middle-income countries that have developed strong production, post-harvest processing, logistical marketing, and sanitary and phytosanitary management systems and that continue to attract new investment. With few exceptions, low-income countries still face substantial supply-side challenges in taking advantage of existing and future international market opportunities.

Cotton   In chapter 14, "Cotton: Market Setting and Policies," John Baffes explores cotton, a market with minimal border restrictions but considerable domestic support. Cotton production is an important source of rural income and exports in Africa and Central Asia. In 1998–99, cotton accounted for more than 30 percent of merchandise exports in Benin, Burkina Faso, Chad, Mali, Togo, and Uzbekistan, and 15 percent in Tajikistan. Cotton faces intense competition from synthetic fibers,

especially following the technological improvements of the early 1970s that brought prices down to those for cotton. Since 1975 polyester and cotton have traded at roughly the same price levels. Cotton's share of total fiber consumption has dropped from 68 percent in 1960 to 40 percent in 2001–02. Cotton demand has grown at the same rate as population growth during the last 40 years.

The major challenge for cotton is to cut back support policies, particularly in the United States, which subsidized cotton at a cost of $3.7 billion in 2001–02, and the European Union (Greece and Spain), which provided subsidies of almost $1 billion. These are extremely high subsidies in a market in which production was valued at $20 billion in 2001–02. At this level of support, U.S. and EU cotton producers receive prices that are 87 percent and 160 percent, respectively, above world prices. China has also supported its cotton sector. Many cotton-producing developing countries have reacted to low world prices by introducing offsetting support. Support in Brazil, Egypt, India, Mexico, and Turkey totaled $0.6 billion in 2001–02.

Cotton support policies reduce world prices by some 10–15 percent, cutting the incomes of poor farmers in West Africa and Central and South Asia. Cotton has important implications for poverty reduction in these countries as it is one of the most important sources of cash in these economies. If support were removed completely, Africa would increase production by 6 percent and Uzbekistan by 4 percent, while the United States would reduce production by 7 percent and the European Union by 10 percent.

Seafood   In chapter 15, "Seafood: Trade Liberalization and Impacts on Sustainability," Cathy A. Roheim looks beyond global trade policies to examine the complementary issues of management and sustainability. Seafood is one of the most traded food commodities in the world. Developing countries account for more than 50 percent of the global fish product trade by value. This trade now constitutes 20 percent of their agricultural and food processing exports, more than tropical beverages (coffee, cocoa, and tea), nuts and spices, cotton, and sugar and confectionary combined. Aquaculture has expanded to 30 percent of world seafood production. The most valuable component of the seafood trade is shrimp, with total world trade of more than $10 billion in 2000.

Capture fisheries still supply the majority of fish production, but 60 percent of the world's fisheries are either overused or fully used. Even with the establishment of the 200-mile exclusive economic zones in 1977, which brought a third of the world's oceans under the jurisdiction of coastal states, most fisheries management plans have not achieved their stated goal of maintaining sustainable fisheries.

Most seafood product trade flows from developing countries to industrial countries. In several developing countries, fish products are a primary source of export earnings. Trade barriers may have significant potential for harm for these countries. Among trade barriers, tariffs are low compared with the effects of sanitary and phytosanitary measures and, increasingly, countervailing and antidumping measures. Many industrial countries heavily subsidize their fishing sector, including buying access to the waters of developing nations. These subsidies and other fishing arrangements mean that industrial countries capture a significant portion of fishing value added. Many developing countries do not have management policies or lack the resources to enforce them, with the result that capture fisheries are being depleted. Increased aquaculture production in developing countries, particularly of shrimp, has had adverse environmental impacts along coastal areas.

The effects of trade liberalization will differ by country, depending on domestic policies for fisheries and aquaculture. If trade liberalization in fish products leads to higher prices for exporters, fish catches may decline as already overstressed resources are pushed past sustainable levels. This in turn will lead to a decline in food security and, ultimately, to unsustainable international seafood markets.

Coffee   In chapter 16, "Coffee: Market Setting and Policies," John Baffes, Bryan Lewin, and Panos Varangis look at a traditional tropical product, one that does not have major trade distortions. Tariffs are low, and there is only slight tariff escalation on processed coffee. Yet despite this, coffee prices have been highly volatile. This volatility reflects mainly weather-related conditions (and to a lesser extent currency fluctuations) in Brazil.

Coffee consumption has been stagnant (common among primary commodities), in part because of competition from the soft drink industry. Except in Brazil, Colombia, Ethiopia, and Mexico, little coffee is consumed in developing countries. Efforts to expand coffee consumption in developing countries are likely to come at the expense of tea, a commodity produced by the same countries that produce coffee.

Although a few large producers produce most of the coffee, several small countries depend heavily on coffee. In Burundi, Ethiopia, and Rwanda, coffee accounts for more than half of total merchandize exports. The coffee market had supply controls in place longer than any other important commodity. In addition to stabilizing (and perhaps raising) prices in the short term, these agreements brought new entrants into the coffee market. With the exception of Colombia, Ethiopia, and, to a lesser degree, Côte d'Ivoire, Kenya, and Tanzania, the marketing regimes in coffee-producing countries are liberal. Some 6–8 percent of coffee output is traded outside of traditional marketing channels, as organic, fair-trade, gourmet specialty, and eco-friendly products. These new markets provide higher prices to producers.

During the 1990s, Brazil expanded its coffee production to areas less subject to frost, reducing weather-induced supply disruptions. Vietnam emerged as the dominant supplier of robusta coffee, currently producing as much coffee as Colombia. New technologies on the demand side have enabled roasters to be more flexible in switching quickly among coffee types, implying that premiums for certain types of coffee cannot be retained for long. Thus the so-called coffee crisis is more a case of new entry, faster technological change, and so far, little exit.

Note

1. *Outgrower* refers to farmers producing for a larger processor under some contractual arrangement and technical advice or oversight.

References

Hoekman, Bernard, Francis Ng, and Marcelo Olarreaga. 2002. "Reducing Agricultural Tariffs versus Domestic Support: What's More Important for Developing Countries?" World Bank Policy Research Working Paper 2918. Washington, D.C.

Ingco, Merlinda, and John D. Nash, eds. 2004. *Agriculture and the WTO: Creating a Trading System for Development.* Washington, D.C.: World Bank.

PART I

GLOBAL PROTECTION AND TRADE IN AGRICULTURE

THE EVOLUTION OF AGRICULTURAL TRADE FLOWS

M. Ataman Aksoy

Despite tremendous change in the past 20 years in global specialization and trade in manufacturing, remarkably little structural change has occurred in global agricultural trade flows. This chapter examines the growth and structure of agricultural trade since the 1980s, looking at the performance of industrial and developing countries and of specific commodity groups. To place arguments about agricultural policies in perspective, it also presents basic statistics on rural income and poverty.

Agriculture and Rural Income

The share of agriculture in global trade has been shrinking, as has its share in global gross domestic product. Most successful developing countries have not relied on agriculture for their exports. Yet for most developing countries, growth in agriculture has a disproportionate effect on poverty because more than half of the people in developing countries reside in rural areas.[1] Some 57 percent of the developing world's rural population lives in lower-middle-income countries, and 15 percent lives in the least-developed countries (table 2.1). Although most of the world's poor countries are in Sub-Saharan Africa, the region accounts for only about 12 percent of the developing world's rural population. Asia accounts for 65 percent.

Although the share of the population in rural areas is declining, more poor people will live in rural areas than in cities in developing countries for at least a generation. With urbanization, the rural share of poor households will decline, but based on current trends that share will not fall below 50 percent before 2035 (Ravallion 2001).

Poverty

By the international $1-a-day poverty line, most of the world's poor live in China, India, and "other low-income" countries (see table 2.1). Least-developed countries constitute 15 percent of the world's population but almost 24 percent of the world's poor. National poverty data, which disaggregate information by rural and urban households but are not available for all countries, yield similar results. They

Research support for this chapter was supplied by Baris Sivri, Tarek Souweid, Konstantin Senyut, and Zeynep Ersel. The author would like to thank John Beghin, Donald Mitchell, John Baffes, Steve Jaffee, Ndiame Diop, Sushma Ganguly, Harry De Gorter, and anonymous reviewers for their comments. Some of the preliminary findings of this chapter have been incorporated into Beghin and Aksoy (2003) and World Bank (2003).

TABLE 2.1   Distribution of Poor People in Developing Countries, 1999

| Country Category | Population 2001 (millions) | | | | Percentage of Developing World's Rural Population | Poverty Headcount (under $1/day) | |
	National	Rural	Urban			Rate (percent)	Number of Poor People (millions)
Least-developed countries	596	443	153	74	15	49	292
Other low-income countries excluding India	839	501	338	60	17	26	218
Middle-income countries excluding China	1,435	478	957	33	16	8	114
China	1,272	805	467	63	27	18	226
India	1,032	745	288	72	25	35	358
Total	5,175	2,972	2,203	57	100	23	1,209

Source: World Bank data.

TABLE 2.2   Rural Population and Poverty for a Sample of 52 Developing Countries
(percent)

| Income Group | Sample Countries | | All Developing Countries |
	Share of Rural Dwellers	Share of Poor in Rural Areas	Share of Rural Dwellers
Upper-middle-income countries	19	37	22
Lower-middle-income countries	64	72	61
Low-income countries	65	74	60
Least-developed countries	76	82	68
All developing countries	63	73	56

Note: Sample consists of 52 countries for which separate rural and urban income data are available.
Source: World Bank data.

show that four countries—Bangladesh, China, India, and Indonesia—account for 75 percent of the world's rural poor. It is in Asia, therefore, that rural income growth will have the greatest impact on poverty.

In the 52 countries for which separate rural and urban income data are available, 63 percent of the population lives in rural areas, slightly more than the 56 percent for developing countries as a whole (table 2.2). Some 73 percent of poor people live in rural areas and the incidence of poverty is higher in rural areas in all groups of developing countries, whatever their income level. In the least-developed countries, 82 percent of the poor live in rural areas.

On average, farmers are poorer than nonfarmers in developing countries but are better off than non-farmers in industrial countries. In almost all devel-

oping countries, rural households have lower average incomes than nonrural households (figure 2.1). The ratio of rural incomes to nonrural incomes ranges from 40 to 75 percent, a relationship that remains consistent across groups of developing countries. The same relationship holds for the middle-income OECD (Organisation for Economic Co-operation and Development) countries, such as Greece, the Republic of Korea, and Turkey.[2] Farm household incomes are around 75–80 percent of nonfarm incomes.

The opposite is true in many high-income OECD countries. Average farm household incomes are higher than average household incomes (figure 2.2). Average farm household incomes are almost 275 percent of average household incomes in the Netherlands, 175 percent in Denmark, 160 percent in France, and 110 percent in the

FIGURE 2.1   Ratio of Farm Household Income to Nonfarm Household Income for Selected Developing Countries, Various Years

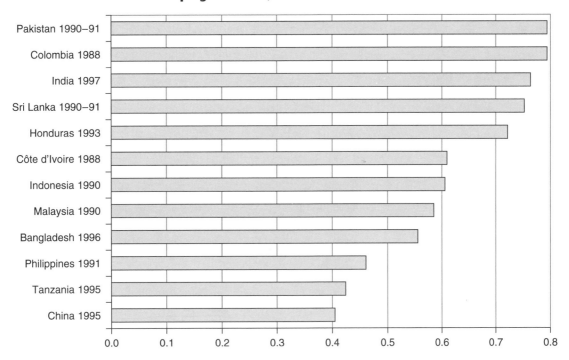

Source: Eastwood and Lipton 2000.

FIGURE 2.2   Ratio of Farm Household Income to All Household Income for Selected High-Income Countries

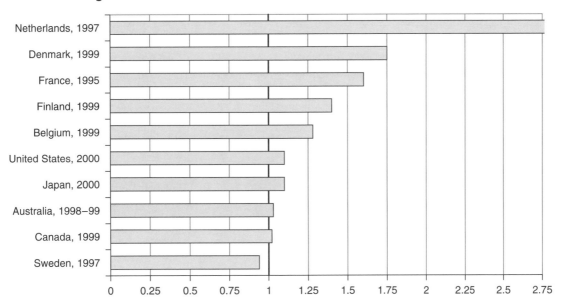

Note: The ratio is for farm household income to all households except in Japan, where it is farm household income to workers' household income.

Source: OECD 2002 and 2003.

United States and Japan. In most other high-income countries, average farm incomes are either equal to or very slightly lower than the average household income (OECD 2002).

Structure of Income Sources

In addition to these differences in relative rural and nonrural income levels between developing and industrial countries, the two groups of countries have different structures of income sources. Most rural households in poor countries are dependent on agriculture. Rural households in Ethiopia, Malawi, and Vietnam, for example, derive about three-quarters of their income from agricultural activities, mainly subsistence farming (table 2.3). Wages are the second-largest income source, with some of the wage income originating in agriculture. For example, in Malawi, where 8 percent of total income is from wages, 3 percentage points of that income is from agriculture. In Mexico, where 40 percent of total income is from wages and only 26 percent is directly from agriculture, 24 percentage points of wage income is from agriculture, bringing agriculture's contribution to almost 50 percent.

As countries develop, the share of nonfarm income in rural households increases, so that agricultural price and output variations have a smaller direct impact on rural households (figure 2.3).[3] In most industrial countries, the share of farm income in total household income declines even further, as other sources of income gain a larger share (salaries and wages from other activities; investment income;

and social transfers from health, pension, unemployment, and child-allowance schemes). While ratios of farm to nonfarm income are higher for some European countries, definitional differences make reliable comparisons across countries very difficult (OECD 2002).

Income Distribution

It is often argued that income distribution in rural areas of developing countries is highly unequal and that the gains from global reforms could accrue primarily to the well-to-do rather than to the rural poor. Gini coefficients for a group of developing and industrial countries indicate that despite claims to the contrary, income distribution in most developing countries is more equitable in rural households than in nonrural households (table 2.4). This is true for both low- and middle-income countries. The opposite is true in industrial countries.

In industrial countries the largest farm operations, generally the most profitable and wealthiest, receive most of the benefits of support systems. Subsidy programs are not intended to keep small, struggling family farms in business but to provide large rents to large-scale farmers. Current production-based policies, by increasing land prices, also encourage the creation of larger farms and the elimination of small family farms. The unintended spillover effects of these policies on other countries and on global markets are large and negative.

Agricultural protection in rich countries would appear to worsen global income distribution. Farmers in industrial countries earn more on average

TABLE 2.3   Structure of Rural Household Incomes, Selected Developing Countries
(percent)

Type of Income	Ethiopia 2000	Malawi 1997	Vietnam 1993	Pakistan 1989	Mexico 2000
Total agricultural income	77	76	63	45	26
Agricultural cash income	18	16	—	—	22
Subsistence farming	59	60	—	—	4
Transfers	16	7	1	9	23
Wages	3	8	21	31	40
Other	4	9	15	15	11
Total	100	100	100	100	100

— Not available.

Source: World Bank household data.

FIGURE 2.3   Ratio of Farm Income to Total Income of Farm Households, Selected Countries and Years

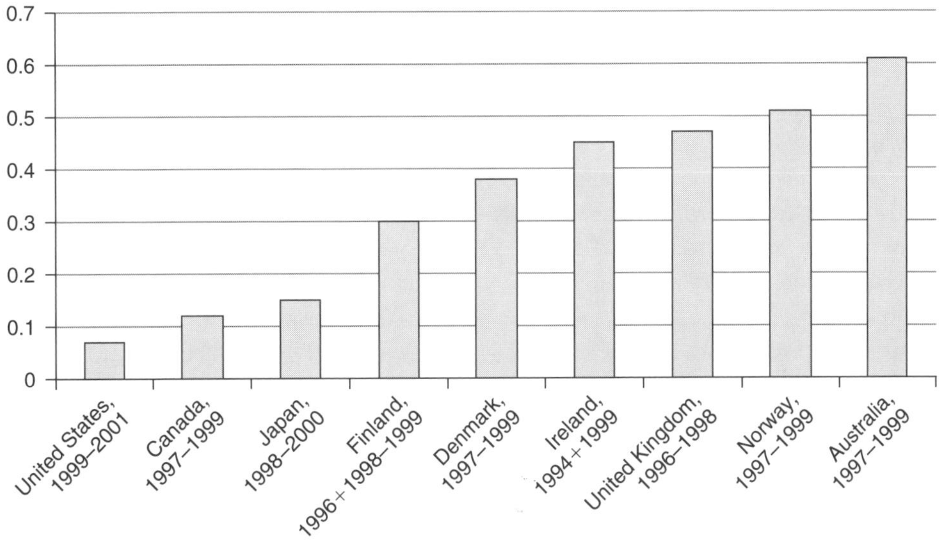

Note: Data are averages of three most recent years available.
Source: OECD 2002.

TABLE 2.4   Urban and Rural Income Inequality, Selected Countries and Years

Low-Income Countries	Rural Gini	Urban Gini	Middle-Income Countries	Rural Gini	Urban Gini	High-Income Countries	Rural Gini	Urban Gini
Bangladesh 1996	0.26	0.36	Mexico 1996	0.34	0.40	Australia 1994/95	0.36	0.31
Pakistan 1991	0.41	0.39	Turkey 1994	0.46	0.58	Canada 1994	0.30	0.29
Sri Lanka 1990/91	0.28	0.35	Colombia 1988	0.47	0.49	Denmark 1992	0.32	0.23
Indonesia 1990	0.26	0.35	Costa Rica 1984	0.41	0.48	Finland 1995	0.26	0.22
Lesotho 1993	0.55	0.58	Peru 1994	0.37	0.35	France 1994	0.29	0.29
Madagascar 1980	0.44	0.49	India 1997	0.30	0.36	Ireland 1987	0.37	0.32
Tanzania 1993	0.35	0.42	China 1995	0.34	0.28	Italy 1995	0.43	0.34
Uganda 1992	0.35	0.44	Rep. of Korea 1987	0.12	0.42	Netherlands 1994	0.31	0.26
Malawi 1997–98	0.33	0.52	Thailand 1986	0.45	0.46	Norway 1995	0.20	0.24
Nigeria 1996	0.42	0.50	Malaysia 1987	0.42	0.43	Spain 1990	0.28	0.31
Burkina Faso 1995	0.40	0.45	Philippines 1991	0.39	0.47	United States 1994	0.37	0.37

Source: OECD 1999 for the high-income countries; National Statistics Office for Malawi; World Bank data for Nigeria; Ozmucur and Silber 2000 for Turkey; and Eastwood and Lipton 2000 for the remaining countries.

than the national income average, and most farm aid goes to the largest and wealthiest farmers. At the other end of the global income spectrum, more poor people in developing countries tend to live in rural areas. Agricultural support in industrial countries tends to depress world prices and demand for the agricultural products of developing countries and to lower rural incomes. Global trade reforms, to the extent that they transfer resources from well-to-do farmers in industrial countries to poorer farmers in developing countries, will thus improve global income distribution while reducing global poverty.

Broad Trends in Agricultural Trade

The last two decades have been a period of very rapid export growth from developing countries, aided by the growth of the world economy and the lowering of trade barriers, as well as by increasing supply capabilities in developing countries. The resulting increased import and export shares in total output have been a key source of growth in many developing countries. This growth has been fastest in manufacturing, where global levels of protection have been reduced significantly. Growth has been slower in agriculture, where significant protection still remains.[4]

While the 1990s were a period of rapid trade reform in developing countries and of implementation of Uruguay Round commitments, the Uruguay Round seems not to have yielded any meaningful reduction in protection in industrial countries (see chapter 3). Protection in OECD countries increased during the 1960s and 1970s, reaching its peak in the late 1980s. There is little evidence that protection decreased significantly in the 1990s. In many cases, protection might even have increased in the 1990s through "dirty tariffication" (Nogues 2002; Ingco 1997).

Growth in Agricultural Trade

World agricultural trade in 2000–01 was $467 billion, up from $243 billion in 1980–81.[5] Real manufacturing and agriculture trade expanded at similar rates during the 1980s (5.7 and 4.9 percent a year), but real manufacturing export growth accelerated to 6.7 percent a year during the 1990s, while agricultural export growth decelerated to 3.4 percent (table 2.5).

The picture is similar for developing countries. Their manufacturing export growth accelerated and agricultural export growth stagnated during the 1990s. Manufacturing export growth rates increased both to other developing countries and to industrial countries, while agricultural export growth rates increased to other developing countries but decreased to industrial countries.

These differential growth rates are reflected in the shares of exports in world trade in developing countries (table 2.6). Their share in manufacturing exports rose dramatically, from 19 percent in 1980–81 to 33 percent in 2000–01, with higher exports to both developing countries and industrial countries. In agricultural trade, developing countries lost market shares during the 1980s and barely recovered during the 1990s to their 1980–81 level of around 36 percent. All of this gain in the 1990s came from expansion of exports to other developing countries. Despite these changes in the shares, nearly half of world agricultural trade takes place among industrial countries.

The deceleration in growth of world agricultural trade reflects the decline in real import growth rates of industrial countries, from 4.8 percent a year in the 1980s to 2.3 percent in the 1990s.[6] Over that same period, real import growth rates for developing countries accelerated from 4 percent to 6.1 percent a year.

Two explanations have been proposed for the decline in import growth in industrial countries: a lower elasticity of demand for agricultural products in industrial countries and the decline in commodity prices in the 1990s. Gross domestic product (GDP) growth slowed from 3.0 percent a year in the 1980s to 2.3 percent a year during the 1990s in industrial countries, while rising from 3.1 percent to 3.7 percent in developing countries. Unless there

TABLE 2.5 Average Annual Real Export Growth Rates, 1980s and 1990s
(percent)

| | World | | Total | | Developing Countries | | | |
| | | | | | Developing to Developing Countries | | Developing to Industrial Countries | |
Sector	1980–81/ 1990–91	1990–91/ 2000–01	1980–81/ 1990–91	1990–91/ 2000–01	1980–81/ 1990–91	1990–91/ 2000–01	1980–81/ 1990–91	1990–91/ 2000–01
Agriculture	4.9	3.4	5.3	5.3	4.2	7.2	5.9	4.4
Manufacturing	5.7	6.7	7.4	10.9	7.1	12.1	7.5	10.3

Note: Manufacturing imports are adjusted by the manufactures' unit value. World agricultural trade is adjusted by commodity price index with world trade weights, and developing country exports are adjusted by the same index with developing country trade weights.
Source: COMTRADE.

TABLE 2.6 Shares of Developing and Industrial Countries in World Exports, 1980–81 to 2000–01
(percent)

Sector by Destination	Developing Countries			Industrial Countries		
	1980–81	1990–91	2000–01	1980–81	1990–91	2000–01
Agriculture						
Total	37.8	33.0	36.1	62.2	67.0	63.9
To developing countries	13.4	10.5	13.7	18.9	14.5	15.6
To industrial countries	24.3	22.4	22.4	43.4	52.5	48.3
Manufacturing						
Total	19.3	22.7	33.4	80.7	77.3	66.6
To developing countries	−6.6	7.5	12.3	21.7	15.2	19.0
To industrial countries	12.7	15.2	21.1	59.0	62.1	47.6

Source: COMTRADE.

TABLE 2.7 Changes in Agriculture Price Indices, 1980s and 1990s
(percent)

Item	1980–81/1990–91	1990–91/2000–01
U.S. farm products (producer price index)	4.7	−6.8
Raw commodities (world trade weights)	−8.3	−6.6
Raw commodities (developing countries' weights)	−22.7	−15.2

Source: World Bank.

was a significant change in income elasticities between 1980s and 1990s, however, these changes in GDP growth rates are not large enough to explain the declines in real import growth rates. Faster liberalization in developing countries can explain some of the increases in their faster import growth rates. However, experience in the last two decades also shows that the correlation between demand and trade growth is not very high over the medium and short run, when changes in trade regimes and competitiveness will have bigger impacts (box 2.1 shows the relationship between demand and import growth for selected products in industrial countries).

As for the decline in commodity prices, these were greater during the 1980s than the 1990s and so could not have been the cause of the decline in growth rates (table 2.7).

In the absence of specialization, slowing demand growth will lead to slowing import growth if output growth does not also slow. Agricultural production indexes show a slight acceleration of production

growth rates for industrial countries and no change for developing countries (table 2.8). Thus the deceleration in import growth rates is not reflected in a deceleration in supply, and a significant component of demand is met by domestic supply.

Agricultural Trade Shares

The evidence that the agricultural trade shares of developing countries have not increased is

TABLE 2.8 Average Annual Agricultural Output Growth Rates, 1980s and 1990s
(percent)

Period	Industrial Countries	Developing Countries
1980–81/1990–91	0.88	3.67
1990–91/2000–01	1.13	3.68

Source: FAO Agriculture Production Index.

BOX 2.1   Role of Demand and Changes in Market Share

Low income elasticities for agricultural products, especially in industrial countries, are identified as the primary reason for the slowdown in global agricultural trade growth. These low income elasticities are contrasted with higher income elasticities for manufactured products. While trade and demand growth are highly correlated in the long run, it is not clear whether they are in the medium run. Variables such as level and changes in protection and the degree of comparative advantage play an important role.

If world trade expands primarily because of increases in demand, then slower agricultural trade can be explained by lower income elasticities and lower income growth in industrial countries. But if the primary cause of trade expansion over the medium run is restructuring of production and changes in both imports and exports, without commensurate changes in total demand,

then changes in trade regimes can explain a significant part of trade growth. Since the mid-1970s merchandise trade has expanded much faster than demand, showing the importance of production restructuring. Unfortunately, the systemic information that is necessary to decompose the determinants of export growth exists only for manufacturing. The information for agriculture is very limited.

When manufacturing (including food processing) import growth to industrial countries (Canada, Germany, Japan, and the United States) is decomposed between demand and market share changes, demand growth accounted for 32 percent of import growth and changes in market share for 68 percent. For imports from developing countries, growth contributed only 21 percent while changes in market share contributed 79 percent (Aksoy, Ersel, Sivri 2003).

Demand and Import Growth in Selected Industrial Countries, 1991–99
(percent)

Sectors	Industrial Country Demand Growth[a]	Import Growth from the World	Import Growth from Developing Countries	1991 Market Shares	
				World	Developing Countries
Food processing	15.82	26.65	14.46	6.41	2.42
Garments	14.35	57.29	73.08	43.19	33.80
Glass products	13.06	63.54	71.99	14.24	4.30

a. Includes Canada, Germany, Japan, and the United States.
Source: Aksoy, Ersel, Sivri 2003.

The examples of food processing, garments, and glass products illustrate the lack of a strong relationship between import and demand growth. The three subsectors have similar demand growth rates but very different import growth rates. The import growth rates are differ-

ent not only for imports from developing countries but for imports from the rest of the world as well. Depending on policy regimes and changes in policy regimes, trade growth rates can be very different from growth rates in demand.

consistent with other partial findings. Within a narrower definition of agriculture, and focusing mostly on key commodities, OECD (2001) data show that import shares of these agricultural commodities in key industrial countries have not increased since 1986. For many agricultural commodities, imports as a share of world consumption stagnated. For some commodities, such as sugar and wheat, there has been significant import substitution since the 1960s and 1970s, when the OECD countries greatly increased their protection.

A trade flow matrix for the years 1980–81, 1990–91, and 2000–01 shows the details of nominal agricultural trade flows among different groups of countries (table 2.9). The European Union is the largest trader, with exports of $181 billion and imports of $197 billion. Developing countries as a block are the second largest trader, with exports of $162 billion and imports of $128 billion.

Trade among industrial countries dominates global agricultural trade, most of it within the trade blocs such as the European Union and NAFTA

TABLE 2.9   Global Agricultural Trade Flows
(US$ billion)

Importers \\ Exporters		Low-Income Countries	Middle-Income Countries[a]	Developing Countries	EU-15	Japan	NAFTA	Other Industrial Countries	Total Imports
Low-income countries	1980–81	0.86	2.16	3.03	2.19	0.20	1.42	0.63	7.47
	1990–91	0.81	2.52	3.33	1.17	0.06	1.22	0.73	6.52
	2000–01	1.50	4.48	5.98	2.01	0.06	1.99	1.78	11.82
Middle-income countries[a]	1980–81	3.05	25.73	28.78	14.55	1.02	20.03	6.51	70.88
	1990–91	4.05	29.72	33.77	17.41	1.32	19.30	7.18	78.99
	2000–01	9.20	48.44	57.64	22.85	1.74	23.42	10.71	116.36
Developing countries	1980–81	3.91	27.89	31.80	16.74	1.21	21.45	7.14	78.34
	1990–91	4.85	32.25	37.10	18.59	1.39	20.52	7.92	85.51
	2000–01	10.70	52.92	63.63	24.86	1.80	25.41	12.49	128.18
EU-15	1980–81	7.20	22.89	30.09	53.82	0.24	15.44	5.55	105.15
	1990–91	7.66	33.76	41.42	116.81	0.28	9.99	9.42	177.92
	2000–01	9.65	37.81	47.46	131.33	0.15	9.57	9.38	197.89
Japan	1980–81	1.13	6.64	7.77	1.22	—	9.20	2.56	20.74
	1990–91	1.85	14.61	16.47	3.78	—	14.65	4.32	39.23
	2000–01	2.52	19.21	21.73	4.83	—	17.61	5.11	49.28
NAFTA	1980–81	2.62	11.67	14.30	4.42	0.37	8.86	2.78	30.73
	1990–91	2.06	15.02	17.08	7.96	0.42	15.52	3.54	44.53
	2000–01	3.72	21.95	25.67	12.60	0.54	34.80	4.77	78.38
Other industrial countries	1980–81	0.47	1.68	2.14	3.79	0.06	1.53	0.62	8.15
	1990–91	0.40	2.31	2.71	7.01	0.07	1.66	1.09	12.54
	2000–01	0.54	3.24	3.79	7.22	0.08	2.15	1.70	14.94
Total exports	1980–81	15.33	70.77	86.10	79.99	1.89	56.48	18.64	243.10
	1990–91	16.81	97.95	114.77	154.16	2.15	62.35	26.29	359.72
	2000–01	27.14	135.13	162.27	180.84	2.57	89.55	33.45	468.67

— Not available.

Note: All data are import-based and all the exports and imports are evaluated at c.i.f. (cost, insurance, and freight) prices.

a. Includes China and India.

Source: COMTRADE.

(North American Free Trade Agreement). This intrabloc trade accounts for more than a third of global agricultural trade. In 2000–01 industrial country agricultural exports to other industrial countries totaled $226 billion. Of that, $131 billion was intra-EU trade (almost 58 percent) and $35 billion was intra-NAFTA trade. Agricultural trade among industrial countries excluding intra-EU and intra-NAFTA was only $60 billion.

Agricultural trade within trade blocs as a share of total trade is not only high, but it has increased during the last 20 years. Intra-EU agricultural imports increased from 51 percent of total agricultural imports in 1980–81 to 66 percent in 2000–01; intra-NAFTA imports rose from 29 percent to 44 percent. This increase shows how removing tariff barriers can stimulate trade.

Trade among developing countries is also increasing, with more than 50 percent of their agricultural imports coming from other developing countries. Only 39 percent of their agricultural exports are to other developing countries, however, showing the continuing importance of industrial-country markets for their exports. Other developing countries accounted for 39 percent of exports from low-income countries and 51 percent of imports in 2000–01, increases from 26 percent and 41 percent, respectively, in 1980–81. Shares for middle-income countries were similar, with other developing countries accounting for 39 percent of their exports and 50 percent of their imports in 2000–01. Developing countries have become major players in the world agricultural trade, especially if intra-EU and intra-NAFTA trade is excluded.

TABLE 2.10   Agricultural Trade Flows (excluding Intra-EU and Intra-NAFTA Trade), 1980–81 to 2000–01
(US$ billion)

Country Group and Period	Exports	Imports	Net Imports
Low-income developing countries			
1980–81	15.33	7.47	−7.86
1990–91	16.81	6.52	−10.30
2000–01	27.14	11.82	−15.32
Middle-income developing countries[a]			
1980–81	70.77	70.88	0.11
1990–91	97.95	78.99	−18.96
2000–01	135.13	116.36	−18.77
EU-15			
1980–81	26.17	51.32	25.16
1990–91	37.34	61.10	23.76
2000–01	49.51	66.56	17.06
NAFTA			
1980–81	47.62	21.86	−25.75
1990–91	46.83	29.01	−17.82
2000–01	54.75	43.57	−11.17
Japan			
1980–81	1.89	20.74	20.74
1990–91	2.15	39.23	39.23
2000–01	2.57	49.28	49.28
Other industrial countries			
1980–81	18.64	8.15	−10.49
1990–91	26.29	12.54	−13.76
2000–01	33.45	14.94	−18.51

a. India and China are included under the middle-income developing countries.
Source: COMTRADE and computations by the author.

Since 1980–81 the biggest change in net agricultural trade flows has been the relative decline in EU imports from the rest of the world and the increase in its export share (table 2.10). In 1980–81 the European Union was the largest importer in the world, accounting for 32 percent of world imports. By 2000–01 its import share had dropped to 23 percent and its export share had increased to 16 percent (from 13 percent). Its trade deficit declined as well, from $25 billion in 1980–81 to $19 billion in 2000–01. The opposite has happened in NAFTA, whose trade surplus has decreased. Japan has been the world's largest net importer of agricultural products since 1990–91, and Australia and New Zealand combined have surpassed NAFTA as net exporters.

The combined trade surplus of developing countries increased to $34 billion in 2000–01, from $8 billion in 1980–81. They have a trade surplus with all groups of countries except Australia and New Zealand.

Distribution of the Trade Expansion

A contentious issue in the literature has been the trade performance of low-income countries. Many analysts have argued that the low-income countries have not benefited from the expansion in global trade. This is only partially true in agriculture. Low-income countries' share of world exports fell from 6.3 percent in 1980–81 to 4.3 percent in 1990–01 and barely recovered to 5.8 percent in 2000–01.

However, if intra-EU and intra-NAFTA trade are excluded, their share increases from 8.5 percent in 1980–81 to 8.9 percent in 2000–01. As measured by export and import performance, the 1980s were a period of decline for low-income countries, while the 1990s were a period of major expansion.

Their overall trade surpluses, however, have risen throughout the period, from $7.8 billion in 1980–81 to $15 billion in 2000–01. Low-income developing countries have a trade surplus with industrial countries and with middle-income developing countries, and both of these surpluses have increased since 1980. Their exports have increased as well, primarily to other developing countries. In 2000–01 low-income countries exported more to other developing countries than to the European Union, while in 1980–81 they exported only half as much. Some analysts have argued that it is primarily small low-income countries that have performed poorly, but the results do not change if the low-income countries are divided into small and large countries. Trade expanded for both groups during the 1990s, and both have increased their trade surpluses in agriculture (table 2.11). Smaller low-income countries did perform much worse than large low-income countries during the 1980s, however, when their exports and imports declined.

TABLE 2.11   Agricultural Trade Flows of Developing Countries, by Groups, 1980–81 to 2000–01
(US$ billion)

Group and Period	Exports	Imports	Net Imports
Low-income, small			
1980–81	10.63	3.26	−7.37
1990–91	10.06	2.39	−7.67
2000–01	14.95	4.45	−10.5
Low-income, large[a]			
1980–81	4.7	4.21	−0.49
1990–91	6.75	4.13	−2.62
2000–01	12.19	7.38	−4.81
Middle-income, large exporters[b]			
1980–81	20.26	17.73	−2.53
1990–91	25.94	18.47	−7.47
2000–01	38.4	18.11	−20.29
Middle-income, Asian importers[c]			
1980–81	5.28	12.62	7.34
1990–91	9.54	22.77	13.23
2000–01	7.22	28.49	21.27
China and India			
1980–81	7.14	5.87	−1.27
1990–91	15.13	6.56	−8.57
2000–01	23.67	14.12	−9.55
Other middle-income			
1980–81	38.09	34.65	−3.44
1990–91	47.34	31.19	−16.15
2000–01	65.85	55.64	−10.21

a. Bangladesh, Ethiopia, Indonesia, Nigeria, and Pakistan.
b. Argentina, Brazil, and Thailand.
c. Republic of Korea, Hong Kong (China), Singapore, Taiwan (China).
Source: COMTRADE and World Bank calculations.

Middle-income countries, however, performed worse during the 1990s, becoming smaller net exporters, with a shrinking trade surplus with the rest of the world. There are large differences in agricultural trade performance among the middle-income countries. Argentina, Brazil, and Thailand are becoming major exporters (see table 2.11). These countries, which do not have highly distorted agricultural trade regimes, are frequently cited as potential gainers from global liberalization. The upper-middle-income manufacturing exporters in East Asia, another group of developing countries, are becoming major importers of agricultural commodities, along with Japan. Of these, the Republic of Korea and Taiwan (China) have distorted trade regimes, while Hong Kong (China) and Singapore have liberal trade regimes. With liberalization, China and India, with one-third of the world's population, could emerge as major global exporters and importers. While they have trade surpluses, the surpluses did not increase significantly during the 1990s. The remaining middle-income countries experienced rapid trade growth during the 1990s, but their trade surpluses shrank considerably during this period. The significant trade liberalization among developing countries since the 1980s, especially among middle-income countries, could explain some of the expanding imports of these countries.

Disaggregated Export and Import Performance

To get an accurate sense of changes in trade, it is important to measure the contributions of different product groups to those changes.[7] Many analysts argue that the markets for traditional exports to industrial countries are static because of both low income elasticities and product substitution. For example, coffee and tea have been partially displaced by soft drinks, cotton by synthetic fibers, and sugar by high-fructose corn syrup (see commodity chapters).

To examine the detailed flows, agricultural products were separated into four groups. One group consists mainly of developing-country tropical products, such as coffee, cocoa, tea, nuts, spices, textile fibers (mostly cotton), and sugar and confectionary products. A second is made up of highly protected temperate zone products of industrial countries, such as meats, milk and milk products,

grains, animal feed, and edible oil and oilseeds. A third category consists of dynamic nontraditional products, such as seafood, fruits, vegetables, and cut flowers, for which global protection rates are lower. A fourth group consists of other products, including processed agricultural products such as tobacco and cigarettes, beverages, and other processed foods.

Import growth rates in industrial countries have declined across all these agricultural product groups (table 2.12). The decline does not originate with price declines, which were greater during the 1980s than the 1990s, or with slower import growth of tropical products, whose share was only 16 percent in 1990–91. Industrial countries' growth in imports from both developing and other industrial countries declined during the 1990s, while developing countries' import growth rates accelerated in all four product groups. Again, the differences in import growth rates of developing countries between the 1980s and the 1990s are striking, suggesting a significant role for the trade liberalization of the late 1980s and 1990s (see chapter 3).

Changes in Trade Structure

The structure of world trade in agriculture has changed since the 1980s along with overall trade growth rates. Expanding groups include fruits and vegetables, which now have the largest share of world exports at 19 percent; fish and seafood, at 12 percent; and alcoholic and nonalcoholic beverages, at almost 9 percent (table 2.13). While these product groups tend to have high income elasticities, they also have low rates of protection in industrial and large developing countries.

Product groups that show significant declines are grains, from 17 percent to 10 percent; coffee, cocoa, and tea, from 8.5 percent to 5.4 percent; sugar and confectionary products, from 6.4 percent to 3.1 percent; and textile fibers, from 5.9 percent to 2.8 percent. These declines result from a combination of price declines, low demand elasticities, and, in the case of sugar and grains, expanded production in industrial countries.

For developing countries the biggest decline in export shares has come in their traditional tropical products, such as coffee and cocoa, while the biggest gains have come in nontraditional exports, such as seafood and fruits and vegetables. For protected products, such as grains, the increase in export

TABLE 2.12   Annual Import Growth Rates for Four Classifications of Agricultural Products, 1980s and 1990s
(percent)

Product Classification	Developing Countries		Industrial Countries	
	1980–81/ 1990–91	1990–91/ 2000–01	1980–81/ 1990–91	1990–91/ 2000–01
Tropical products				
Coffee, cocoa, and tea, raw and processed	1.9	5.1	−0.6	1.6
Nuts and spices	1.4	4.7	5.0	3.8
Textile fibers	3.8	0.8	0.2	−5.9
Sugar and confectionary	−5.7	3.7	0.4	0.2
Subtotal	−0.3	2.9	0.2	0.1
Temperate products				
Meats, fresh and processed	2.2	2.9	6.1	1.2
Milk and milk products	1.9	3.0	6.3	1.8
Grains, raw and processed	−1.3	1.6	0.4	1.8
Animal feed	5.3	5.9	3.8	1.2
Edible oil and oil seeds	2.0	6.8	1.3	1.0
Subtotal	0.7	3.5	3.6	1.4
Seafood, fruits, and vegetables				
Seafood, fresh and processed	8.8	7.7	10.4	3.3
Fruits and vegetables, fresh and processed	2.8	6.4	8.3	1.9
Subtotal	4.4	6.8	9.0	2.4
Other processed products				
Tobacco and cigarettes	8.5	4.1	6.6	3.3
Beverages, alcoholic and nonalcoholic	4.9	6.6	8.8	4.6
Other processed food	5.6	11.9	13.6	4.9
Other	−2.0	2.6	0.2	0.6
Subtotal	3.9	6.0	7.4	4.0
Total	1.4	4.3	5.1	2.0

Source: COMTRADE.

[handwritten margin note: "dynamic nontraditional"]

shares during the 1990s are due exclusively to expanding trade among developing countries; these products lost shares in industrial-country markets and gained them in developing-country markets. Market share gains for beverages come primarily from expanding exports of wine and beer to both developing- and industrial-country markets.

Whatever the causes for these changes, analysis of agricultural trade for developing countries now needs to focus on the new commodities, such as seafood, fruits, vegetables, and cut flowers, and on

other processed products, which together constitute almost 50 percent of the exports of developing countries. Temperate zone products constitute another 28 percent, while the traditional products that have received most of the attention in the literature now constitute only 19 percent of the exports of developing countries. Attention also has to be placed on further expanding trade within developing countries in temperate zone products such as milk, grains, and meats, whose trade within developing countries has already increased significantly.

[handwritten margin note: "true for LICs too?"]

TABLE 2.13   The Structure of Agricultural Exports, 1980–81 to 2000–01
(percent of total world trade)

Product Classification	Developing-Country Exports			Industrial-Country Exports			World Exports		
	1980 –81	1990 –91	2000 –01	1980 –81	1990 –91	2000 –01	1980 –81	1990 –91	2000 –01
Tropical products									
Coffee, cocoa, and tea, raw and processed	18.3	11.0	8.5	2.5	2.9	3.6	8.5	5.6	5.4
Nuts and spices	2.4	2.7	2.8	0.7	0.7	0.8	1.3	1.3	1.5
Textile fibers	8.0	6.2	3.3	4.5	3.9	2.6	5.9	4.7	2.8
Sugar and confectionary	10.5	4.6	4.3	3.9	2.8	2.3	6.4	3.4	3.1
Subtotal	39.2	24.4	18.9	11.6	10.3	9.3	22.0	14.9	12.7
Temperate products									
Meats, fresh and processed	7.2	8.3	6.0	14.8	15.7	15.4	11.9	13.2	12.0
Milk and milk products	0.3	0.7	1.1	7.9	7.9	7.6	5.0	5.5	5.2
Grains, raw and processed	9.3	4.9	7.0	21.6	13.8	11.6	16.9	10.9	9.9
Animal feed	7.5	7.9	8.5	7.7	5.1	5.3	7.7	6.0	6.4
Edible oil and oil seeds	4.6	5.7	5.5	4.8	4.4	4.4	4.7	4.8	4.8
Subtotal	28.8	27.5	28.1	56.9	46.8	44.2	46.3	40.4	38.3
Seafood, fruits, and vegetables									
Seafood, fresh and processed	6.9	15.9	19.4	5.5	8.2	8.0	6.0	10.8	12.2
Fruits, vegetables, and cut flowers	14.7	22.2	21.5	13.1	17.2	17.3	13.7	18.9	18.9
Subtotal	21.6	38.2	41.0	18.7	25.5	25.4	19.8	29.7	31.0
Other processed products									
Tobacco and cigarettes	2.6	3.1	3.3	3.0	4.2	4.8	2.8	3.8	4.2
Beverages, alcoholic and nonalcoholic	1.1	1.8	3.6	6.9	9.5	11.5	4.7	6.9	8.6
Other products and processed food	6.7	5.0	5.2	3.0	3.8	5.0	4.4	4.2	5.1
Subtotal	10.4	9.9	12.1	12.8	17.5	21.2	11.9	15.0	17.9
Total	100.0	100.0	100.0	100.0	100.0	100.0	100.0	100.0	100.0

Source: COMTRADE.

These developments show that many developing countries can compete in the product categories historically dominated by industrial countries and that trade reforms in industrial sectors could lead to a large expansion of exports from these developing countries.

Industrial-country export structures have also changed, with a decline in exports of protected products and expansion in exports of beverages and fruits and vegetables (including intra-EU trade). Greater domestic production of sugar, grains, and other protected products has made many industrial countries more self-sufficient and reduced their exports to each other.

Degree of Processing

Despite significant tariff escalation in processed products, trade has moved toward processed (final) agricultural products and away from raw material and intermediate products.[8] In 1980–81 final products made up slightly more than a quarter of world exports, and raw and intermediate products made up two-thirds. By 2000–01 the share of final products had increased to 38 percent of total exports (table 2.14). The share of final products in exports increased for both developing and industrial countries, but in 2000–01 final products still constituted only 10 percent of the exports from low-income

TABLE 2.14 Share of Agricultural Final Products in Exports, 1980–81 to 2000–01
(percent)

Years	World	Developing Countries	Developing Low-Income Countries	Developing Middle-Income Countries[a]	Industrial Countries
1980–81	27.3	15.5	6.6	17.4	33.8
1990–91	33.2	19.1	7	21.2	39.8
2000–01	38.3	24.8	10.4	27.8	45.6

a. Includes China and India.
Source: COMTRADE.

countries, compared with 46 percent from industrial countries.

Tariff escalation has slowed the growth of trade in final products. Shares of final products are much higher within trading blocs, where there are no tariffs, than as shares of exports to the rest of the world. For example, in 2000–01 final products constituted 49 percent of intra-EU exports but 39 percent of EU exports to the rest of the world. For NAFTA final products constituted 38 percent of intra-NAFTA exports but 32 percent of NAFTA exports to the rest of the world. For developing countries, however, the share of final products in 2000–01 exports was the same (around 25 percent) for exports to developing countries and to industrial countries (table 2.15).

More detailed disaggregation of export flows by degree of processing does not yield much more information than the aggregate flows. The export share of final products increased for tropical and temperate product groups. For seafood and fruits and vegetables, the shares of final product stayed the same because of the higher value of fresh produce. In tropical products trade among industrial countries is now primarily trade in final products.

Export Shares by Product and Region

Developing countries lost agricultural market shares during the 1980s, mainly because the increase in their shares of seafood and fruit and vegetable exports was not great enough to compensate for the decline in tropical product exports (table 2.16). During the 1990s developing countries increased their export shares for most product groups, while the loss of market share in tropical products slowed.

The geographical structure of developing-country exports has changed little since the 1980s.

Sub-Saharan Africa is the only region that has not made up the market share losses of the 1980s. Despite preferential access, Africa's export share in industrial-country markets has halved. The other regions made a comeback in the 1990s.

Conclusion

The incidence of poverty is much higher in rural areas than in urban areas in developing countries, the average incomes are much lower, and even with rapid urbanization, the rural share of the poor will not fall below 50 percent before 2035. In industrial countries average farm household incomes are higher than average household incomes. The shares of nonfarm income in total farm household incomes are much higher in industrial countries than in developing countries, partially shielding farmers from price and supply shocks. Finally, the distribution of income is more equitable in rural areas in developing countries than in urban areas, while the opposite is true for industrial countries.

Remarkably little structural change has occurred in global agricultural trade since the early 1980s, unlike the significant changes in global specialization and trade in manufacturing. Unlike the case with manufacturing, developing countries have not been able to increase their export shares in agriculture. They have maintained their global trade shares by expanding exports to other developing countries. Again unlike the case with manufacturing and services, trade-to-output ratios in agriculture have not increased. Import growth rates accelerated in developing countries and decelerated in industrial countries during the 1990s. These results are consistent with significant trade liberalization in manufacturing in both developing and industrial countries and reforms in agricultural trade regimes only in developing countries. Developing countries

TABLE 2.15   Export Shares by Level of Processing, 1980–81 to 2000–01
(percent of world trade)

Product	Industrial to Developing Countries			Industrial to Industrial Countries			Developing to Developing countries			Developing to Industrial Countries			Total Exports		
	1980–81	1990–91	2000–01	1980–81	1990–91	2000–01	1980–81	1990–91	2000–01	1980–81	1990–91	2000–01	1980–81	1990–91	2000–01
Tropical products															
Raw	1.45	1.31	1.33	3.02	2.74	1.61	3.77	2.14	2.16	8.86	4.83	3.39	17.10	11.03	8.49
Final	0.96	0.56	0.50	1.40	1.91	2.09	0.65	0.38	0.48	1.09	0.17	0.26	4.10	3.02	3.33
Total	2.41	1.87	1.83	4.42	4.64	3.69	4.42	2.52	2.64	9.95	5.01	3.66	21.20	14.05	11.82
Temperate products															
Raw	10.10	6.73	5.68	15.31	14.64	12.53	4.79	3.62	4.45	4.67	3.72	3.19	34.88	28.71	25.85
Final	2.61	2.07	2.74	7.40	7.90	7.22	0.56	0.69	1.30	0.86	1.05	1.23	11.44	11.71	12.49
Total	12.71	8.80	8.42	22.72	22.54	19.75	5.36	4.31	5.75	5.53	4.78	4.42	46.32	40.42	38.34
Seafood, fruits, and vegetables															
Raw	1.11	1.18	1.87	7.62	11.81	10.23	1.56	1.89	2.56	5.21	8.19	9.15	15.50	23.07	23.81
Final	0.65	0.39	0.63	2.61	4.05	3.82	0.44	0.47	0.76	1.39	2.56	2.91	5.08	7.47	8.12
Total	1.75	1.58	2.50	10.22	15.86	14.05	2.00	2.36	3.32	6.60	10.75	12.05	20.58	30.54	31.93
Other processed products															
Raw	0.60	0.39	0.49	1.39	1.32	0.96	1.33	0.84	0.99	1.89	1.41	1.05	5.22	3.96	3.49
Final	1.37	1.85	2.42	4.63	8.16	9.67	0.33	0.51	1.04	0.36	0.51	1.29	6.69	11.03	14.42
Total	1.97	2.24	2.91	6.02	9.49	10.63	1.66	1.35	2.03	2.25	1.92	2.35	11.91	14.99	17.91
Total food and agriculture															
Raw	13.26	9.61	9.36	27.35	30.51	25.33	11.45	8.49	10.16	20.63	18.16	16.78	72.69	66.77	61.63
Final	5.59	4.87	6.29	16.03	22.01	22.80	1.98	2.05	3.58	3.70	4.29	5.69	27.31	33.23	38.37
Total	18.85	14.48	15.65	43.38	52.52	48.12	13.43	10.54	13.75	24.33	22.45	22.47	100.00	100.00	100.00

Note: "Raw" includes both raw and intermediate goods, because their movements are highly correlated.
Source: COMTRADE.

TABLE 2.16   Export Shares by Product and Region, 1980–81 to 2000–01
(percent of world trade)

Item	Exports to Developing Countries			Exports to Industrial Countries			Total Exports		
	1980 –81	1990 –91	2000 –01	1980 –81	1990 –91	2000 –01	1980 –81	1990 –91	2000 –01
Tropical products									
Industrial countries	2.4	1.9	1.8	4.4	4.6	3.7	6.8	6.5	5.5
Developing countries	4.4	2.5	2.6	10.0	5.0	3.7	14.4	7.5	6.3
Americas	1.8	0.7	0.8	4.9	2.2	1.5	6.7	2.9	2.4
East Asia And Pacific	1.1	0.7	0.6	1.5	0.9	0.8	2.5	1.6	1.3
Europe and Central Asia	0.4	0.1	0.3	0.3	0.2	0.2	0.7	0.4	0.5
Middle East and North Africa	0.1	0.1	0.2	0.1	0.1	0.1	0.3	0.1	0.2
South Asia	0.5	0.5	0.3	0.4	0.2	0.2	0.9	0.8	0.5
Sub-Saharan Africa	0.5	0.3	0.5	2.8	1.4	0.9	3.2	1.7	1.4
Subtotal	**6.8**	**4.4**	**4.5**	**14.4**	**9.6**	**7.4**	**21.2**	**14.0**	**11.8**
Temperate products									
Industrial countries	12.7	8.8	8.4	22.7	22.5	19.8	35.4	31.3	28.2
Developing countries	5.4	4.3	5.8	5.5	4.8	4.4	10.9	9.1	10.2
Americas	2.2	1.3	2.7	2.1	2.3	2.2	4.3	3.7	4.9
East Asia And Pacific	1.7	1.9	1.7	2.0	1.4	1.2	3.7	3.2	3.0
Europe and Central Asia	0.7	0.5	0.5	0.7	0.7	0.6	1.3	1.2	1.2
Middle East and North Africa	0.1	0.2	0.2	0.1	0.1	0.1	0.2	0.3	0.3
South Asia	0.4	0.3	0.4	0.1	0.1	0.1	0.5	0.4	0.6
Sub-Saharan Africa	0.3	0.1	0.1	0.5	0.2	0.1	0.8	0.3	0.3
Subtotal	**18.1**	**13.1**	**14.2**	**28.2**	**27.3**	**24.2**	**46.3**	**40.4**	**38.3**
Seafood, fruits, and vegetables									
Industrial countries	1.8	1.6	2.5	10.2	15.9	14.0	12.0	17.4	16.5
Developing countries	2.0	2.4	3.3	6.6	10.7	12.1	8.6	13.1	15.4
Americas	0.4	0.4	0.8	2.2	3.8	4.3	2.6	4.1	5.1
East Asia And Pacific	0.8	1.3	1.4	2.3	3.8	4.3	3.0	5.1	5.7
Europe and Central Asia	0.2	0.2	0.4	0.7	1.2	1.3	0.9	1.4	1.7
Middle East and North Africa	0.3	0.2	0.3	0.4	0.6	0.5	0.7	0.9	0.8
South Asia	0.2	0.2	0.2	0.4	0.5	0.6	0.6	0.6	0.8
Sub-Saharan Africa	0.1	0.1	0.2	0.7	0.8	1.0	0.8	0.9	1.2
Subtotal	**3.8**	**3.9**	**5.8**	**16.8**	**26.6**	**26.1**	**20.6**	**30.5**	**31.9**
Other processed products									
Industrial countries	2.0	2.2	2.9	6.0	9.5	10.6	8.0	11.7	13.5
Developing countries	1.7	1.4	2.0	2.3	1.9	2.3	3.9	3.3	4.4
Americas	0.1	0.1	0.5	0.4	0.5	0.9	0.5	0.6	1.4
East Asia And Pacific	1.2	0.9	1.0	1.3	0.8	0.8	2.5	1.7	1.8
Europe and Central Asia	0.2	0.1	0.2	0.2	0.3	0.2	0.4	0.4	0.4
Middle East and North Africa	0.1	0.1	0.2	0.0	0.0	0.0	0.1	0.1	0.2
South Asia	0.1	0.1	0.1	0.1	0.1	0.1	0.2	0.2	0.1
Sub-Saharan Africa	0.0	0.1	0.1	0.2	0.2	0.2	0.3	0.3	0.4
Subtotal	**3.6**	**3.6**	**4.9**	**8.3**	**11.4**	**13.0**	**11.9**	**15.0**	**17.9**
Total									
Industrial countries	18.9	14.5	15.7	43.4	52.5	48.1	62.2	67.0	63.8
Developing countries	13.4	10.5	13.7	24.3	22.4	22.5	37.8	33.0	36.2
Americas	4.6	2.6	4.8	9.5	8.8	9.0	14.1	11.4	13.8
East Asia And Pacific	4.7	4.8	4.8	7.1	6.9	7.1	11.8	11.7	11.9
Europe and Central Asia	1.4	0.9	1.4	2.0	2.4	2.4	3.4	3.3	3.7
Middle East and North Africa	0.7	0.6	0.9	0.6	0.8	0.7	1.3	1.4	1.5
South Asia	1.2	1.1	1.0	0.9	0.9	1.0	2.1	2.0	2.0
Sub-Saharan Africa	0.9	0.7	0.9	4.2	2.6	2.3	5.1	3.3	3.3
Total	**32.3**	**25.0**	**29.4**	**67.7**	**75.0**	**70.6**	**100.0**	**100.0**	**100.0**

Source: COMTRADE.

lost export market shares during the 1980s, mainly because of the collapse in the value of tropical products, and made up the loss during the 1990s by increasing their shares of other commodities.

Trade among industrial countries still dominates world agricultural trade flows, with much of the trade taking place within trading blocs, such as the European Union and NAFTA. Trade among developing countries has expanded, especially during the 1990s, when most developing countries grew faster than they had in the past and liberalized their trade regimes. The middle-income developing countries have now become the biggest single market for the exports of low-income developing countries. Despite the belief of many to the contrary, low-income countries have increased their trade surplus in agricultural commodities over the last two decades, especially during the 1990s.

Some change has taken place in the product mix of global agricultural trade. The shares of nontraditional products, such as seafood, fruits, and vegetables, have increased, and the shares of traditional tropical products have decreased. Seafood, fruits, and vegetables, and processed foods now constitute about 50 percent of the agricultural exports of developing countries. Temperate zone products, such as grains, dairy, and meats, constitute another 28 percent. Traditional exports, such as tea, coffee, cocoa, sugar, cotton, nuts, and spices, now constitute a very small share of exports. This suggests the need for more attention to global and country policies for nontraditional product groups.

There is also a move toward greater trade in final products. However, most of this trade takes place within trade blocs, such as the European Union and NAFTA, primarily because of steeply escalating tariffs. Despite significant reforms, the European Union has become more self-sufficient in agriculture, and its net trade deficit has shrunk. During the 1990s, Japan became the biggest net importer of agricultural commodities, followed by the Asian Tigers: the Republic of Korea, Taiwan (China), Hong Kong (China), and Singapore. Sub-Saharan Africa is the only developing-country region that has not regained the market share lost during the 1980s.

Although linking this lack of change to trade policies is not straightforward, the next chapter shows that agricultural trade policies tend to be much more restrictive than manufacturing policies. This very high protection in agriculture has slowed the move-ment of production to more competitive producers and created much more static global trade flows.

Notes

1. Global poverty rates estimated on a consistent international poverty line of $1 a day are not disaggregated by rural and urban populations. Such disaggregated data are available only for national poverty rates, which vary across countries, and the country coverage of these surveys is limited. Data here are from 52 country household surveys conducted between 1990 and 2001.

2. The information and data are not identical, however. There is a difference between rural households and farm households. One is a locational definition, while the other is defined by the sources of income.

3. Of course, in most regions where agriculture is the primary activity, income from nonfarm sources is also related to agriculture. In regions where there are other nonfarm-related activities, or other transfers, the relationship between off-farm income and farm income will not be so close.

4. Annex 2 in the attached CD-ROM has detailed product coverage by degree of processing, description of the commodity groups, the concordance between nomenclatures, the country coverage, country income and geographic classifications, and detailed trade flows by more detailed commodity groups.

5. This study uses a broad definition of the agricultural sector that includes fisheries as well as raw agricultural commodities and processed food products. This classification includes all stages of processing and results in economically consistent data series. See the CD-ROM for the details of the coverage and definition of subgroups. Data for the European Union-15 have been used for all periods. Mexico is included in NAFTA and not in developing countries. For comparability over time, trade within the Commonwealth of Independent States is excluded from developing-country trade data for 1990–2001, as is trade within the former Yugoslavia and within the Southern African Customs Union. Data on imports are used in most cases, but export data are used for the following countries and years: United Arab Emirates 2000–01, Bulgaria 1980–81 and 1990–91, German Democratic Republic 1980–81, Iran 1980–81 and 1990–91, Kuwait 2000–01, Lebanon 1980–81 and 1990–91, Libya 2000–01, Romania 1980–81, Sudan 1990–91, Soviet Union 1980–81, South Africa 1990–91, China 1980–81, and intra-EU flows for 2000–01.

6. The deceleration of the world trade growth rates was not caused by price declines in the 1990s. In nominal terms, import growth declined from 5.1 percent a year in the 1980s to 2.1 percent in the 1990s in industrial countries, while rising from 1.4 percent to 4.3 percent in developing countries.

7. The price series are not consistent with the trade categories so the disaggregated flows discussed in this section are based on nominal trade data.

8. To have consistent data going back to 1980, this analysis uses Standard International Trade Classification (SITC 1), which is not as precise as the Harmonized System in separating the products by degree of processing. Thus the results are not as precise as they are under the Harmonized System classification.

References

Aksoy, M. Ataman, Z. Ersel, and B. Sivri. 2003. "Demand Growth versus Market Share Gains: Decomposing Export Growth in the 1990s." World Bank, Washington, D.C.

Beghin, John C., and M. Ataman Aksoy. 2003. "Agricultural Trade and the Doha Round: Preliminary Lessons From the Commodity Studies." Paper presented at the Annual World Bank Conference on Development Economics Europe Conference, May 15–16, Paris.

Eastwood, R., and M. Lipton. 2000. "Rural-Urban Dimensions of Inequality Change." University of Sussex, Brighton, United Kingdom.

Ingco, M. 1997. "Has Agricultural Trade Liberalization Improved Welfare in the Least-Developed Countries? Yes." Policy Research Working Paper 1748. World Bank, Washington, D.C.

Nogues, Julio J. 2002. "Comment to 'Trade, Growth, and Poverty—A Selective Survey' by Andrew Berg and Anne Krueger, and 'Doha and the World Poverty Target' by L. Alan Winters." Commentary presented at the Annual World Bank Conference on Development Economics, May 10–11, Brussels.

OECD (Organisation for Economic Co-operation and Development). 1999. "Low Incomes in Agriculture in OECD Coun-tries." Directorate for Food, Agriculture, and Fisheries, Committee for Agriculture, Paris.

———. 2001. *The Uruguay Round Agreement on Agriculture: An Evaluation of Its Implementation in OECD Countries.* Paris.

———. 2002. "Farm Household Income Issues in OECD Countries: A Synthesis Report." Directorate for Food, Agriculture, and Fisheries, Committee for Agriculture, Paris.

———. 2003. *Farm Household Income: Issues and Policy Responses.* Paris.

Ravallion, Martin. 2001. "On the Urbanization of Poverty." World Bank, Country Economics Department, Washington, D.C.

Silber, J., and S. Ozmucur. 2000. "Decomposition of Income Inequality: Evidence from Turkey." Topics in Middle Eastern and North African Economics, Electronic Journal 2. Economic Association and Loyola University, Chicago.

World Bank. 2003. *Global Economic Prospects 2004: Realizing the Development Promise of the Doha Agenda.* Washington, D.C.

3

GLOBAL AGRICULTURAL TRADE POLICIES

M. Ataman Aksoy

Agricultural protection continues to be the most contentious issue in global trade negotiations.[1] The high protection in industrial countries was the main cause of the breakdown of the Cancún Ministerial Meetings in 2003. Although protection for manufacturing products in both industrial and developing countries has declined significantly and overall trade reforms have been adopted in developing countries, agricultural protection in industrial countries has changed very little.

Until the 1990s industrial countries generally protected agriculture while developing countries generally taxed it (Krueger, Schiff, and Valdes 1992; World Bank 1986). Industrial countries supported their agricultural sectors through subsidies to producers, high tariffs, and other nontariff measures such as import restrictions and quotas. While this protection was acknowledged in the economic literature and in global discussions, its implication for developing countries received much less attention.

Until the late 1980s and 1990s many developing countries generated a large portion of their agricultural gross domestic product (GDP) in lower-efficiency production for the domestic market, supplying the world market with tropical commodities that industrial countries could not easily produce. Some countries exported limited amounts of products, such as sugar and beef, in which they competed with industrial countries under preferential-access programs. Many governments levied export taxes on agricultural products to generate revenues while protecting manufacturing through high tariffs and other import restrictions. These countries also used price controls, exchange rate policies, and other restrictions to keep agricultural prices low for urban consumption. Thus, many policy analysts focused more on the taxation of agriculture and its negative effects on supply in developing countries than on protection in industrial countries.[2] In industrial countries the higher returns created by protection led to capital-intensive and supposedly efficient agricultural sectors, creating the impression that their higher yields reflected comparative advantage rather than public support.

This pattern of incentives began to change with the reforms in developing countries. Over the last two decades many developing countries have moved from taxing agriculture to protecting it.

Research support for this chapter was supplied by Baris Sivri and Konstantin Senyut. The author would like to thank John Beghin, Donald Mitchell, John Baffes, Harry de Gorter, and the reviewers for their comments. Some of the findings of this chapter have been incorporated into Beghin and Aksoy (2003) and World Bank (2003).

Most of this change has come not through increasing protection on agricultural products but through eliminating import restrictions and lowering tariffs on manufactured products, devaluing exchange rates, abandoning multiple exchange rate systems that penalized agriculture, and eliminating export taxes (World Bank 2001; Jansen, Robinson, and Tarp 2002; Quiroz and Opazo 2000).

Meanwhile, reforms in most industrial countries have been modest—despite the inclusion of agriculture under the World Trade Organization (WTO) Uruguay Round of international trade negotiations. Increasing the incentives for agricultural production in many developing countries without lowering the incentives in industrial countries led to overproduction and price declines for many commodities, reducing opportunities for many developing countries to expand exports and rural incomes (see chapter 2).

This chapter evaluates both the broad trends in agricultural protection and the structure of protection in key industrial and developing countries. Specific issues, such as the impact of preferences, decoupled support, and other forms of protection, are covered in the following chapters, as are the structure and levels of protection for selected individual commodities.

Uruguay Round Agreement on Agriculture

Since the 1980s major reforms have been made in protection regimes around the world, both through unilateral reform of tariffs and quantitative import restrictions and through undertakings within the Uruguay Round of multilateral trade negotiations. Most developing countries have eliminated export taxes; average tariffs have declined rapidly; and other import restrictions, such as foreign exchange allocations for import, have effectively disappeared (World Bank 2001).

Industrial countries have also started to reduce distortions in their agricultural trade policies. Agricultural trade policies were brought into the global trade negotiations for the first time in the 1994 Uruguay Round Agreement on Agriculture (URAA). Before then, import barriers in agriculture were coupled with the widespread use of production-related subsidies, such as price supports, which in some countries increased production above the competitive market equilibrium level.

With the intention of aligning agricultural trade rules with the rules applying to trade in other goods, negotiators agreed that all barriers to imports, other than those in place for health and safety reasons, should be subject to tariffs only. Before agreeing on tariff reductions, countries had to convert all border measures to their tariff equivalents—a process called tariffication—by calculating the difference between domestic and world market prices (the price-gap method). Once tariff equivalents were established, reductions were applied to bound tariffs. Developed countries were to reduce tariffs by an average of 36 percent and a minimum of 15 percent over 6 years. Developing countries had lower targets of a 20 percent reduction and a minimum of 10 percent over 10 years.[3] For cases of very high tariffs or import quotas that had allowed in some imports, minimum and current market access opportunities were also negotiated. Usually, a minimal tariff rate (called a tariff rate quota, or TRQ) was set for a limited volume of imports.

With the removal of nontariff measures, some countries were concerned about not being able to prevent sudden surges in imports. To allay these concerns, negotiators agreed that a special agricultural safeguard could be applied to certain products.

The URAA offered limited opportunities for undertaking minimum import commitments for certain products rather than adopting tariffs for them. This option was taken by Japan, the Republic of Korea, and the Philippines for rice and by Israel for certain sheep and dairy products. Japan and Korea have now tariffed their rice imports.

Similar efforts were made to reduce the distorting effect of subsidies. Subsidies were classified by degree of distortion: a Red Box for prohibited subsidies, an Amber Box for subsidies that had to be reduced, and a Green Box for nondistorting subsidies. The negotiators decided to treat export subsidies separately, so the Red Box disappeared, and the Amber Box became the core of the negotiations. A new Blue Box was created to cover direct payments to producers under production-limiting programs that were considered to be less trade distorting than pure market price supports (Ingco and Nash 2004).

Amber Box

To measure domestic support and establish a basis for reductions, a total aggregate measure of support was created based on support to agriculture during the base period, 1986–88. The measure covered market price support and production-related subsidies to farmers. Each country agreed to reduce its supports on the basis of this measure. Industrial countries committed to reduce support by 20 percent by 2000, and developing countries committed to a 13.3 percent reduction by 2004. Countries with no Amber Box supports agreed not to use supports over a de minimis level of 5 percent (10 percent for developing countries) of the total value of agricultural production.

Green Box

To qualify as a Green Box measure, requiring no reduction, a subsidy must have no or almost no trade-distorting effect and must be provided through publicly funded government programs. Despite these general requirements, the Green Box covers a wide range of programs.

Blue Box

A special exemption from reduction commitments covers payments made under production-limiting programs, provided that the payments are based on fixed areas, crop yields, livestock numbers, or, if the payments are variable, on 85 percent of the base level of production. These payments replaced traditional market support payments in the European Union (EU) and elsewhere that had led to overproduction or had become too expensive to maintain.

Evolution of Agricultural Protection in Industrial and Developing Countries

Review of the experience with the new rules on market access, export subsidies, and domestic support shows only modest effects. One reason is that support levels were at historically high levels during the base period selected (1986–88). In some countries, such as the United States, reforms undertaken before the negotiations were adequate to achieve compliance with the new rules on reducing domestic support (OECD 2001).

OECD Countries

Two different sets of data are available to estimate the degree of protection in agriculture. The most comprehensive coverage is for OECD (Organisation for Economic Co-operation and Development) countries: all the industrial countries and a few middle-income developing countries. The focus is on selected agricultural commodities that constitute 60–70 percent of domestic agricultural output. Food processing and seafood are generally not covered.

Agricultural protection in OECD countries is measured using three instruments. One is market price support, the difference between domestic and international prices caused by border barriers such as tariffs and quantitative restrictions. It measures the total impact of border barriers on the prices of domestic production and is equivalent to border protection weighted by domestic production. Border barriers are the major tool of protection and account for about 70 percent of total protection in OECD countries. A second instrument is direct support, the direct production-related subsidies given to farmers. A third is the general support given to agriculture through research, training, marketing support, and infrastructure. This instrument is not usually included in overall production support estimates. In addition, many countries have subsidies for consumers. These subsidies generally do not affect production and so are not included in producer support estimates.

The second measure of support is the border protection measured by average tariffs, a measure available for all countries. Both the market support price and the average tariff rate are used to compare protection across time and across countries. Both measures have limitations. Average tariffs measure protection on all agricultural commodities, including products that are not produced domestically, while the market price support measures show only the protection rate for locally produced commodities. In countries such as the United States that produce a large number of agricultural commodities and have a diversified agricultural sector or in which the degree of protection on locally produced and imported commodities is similar, these two measures tend to be very close (figure 3.1). In countries such as Japan where local production is highly specialized or locally produced commodities have different rates of protection from imported commodities, the two measures will differ much more. Average tariffs also fail to give a clear picture of real protection for domestic producers when the variances in tariff rates are large

FIGURE 3.1   **Market Price Support and Average Tariffs for Selected OECD Countries**
(percent)

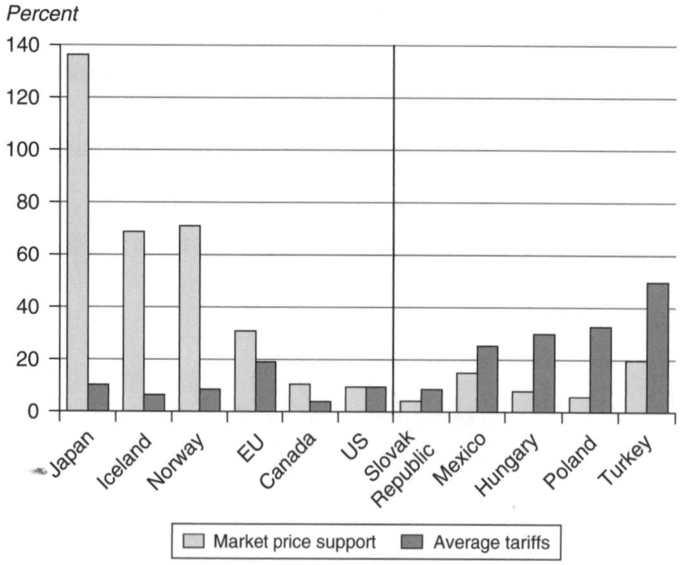

Note: Market price support figures are calculated using the 2000 and 2001 average except for the Slovak Republic, which uses just the 2000 average.
Source: Organisation for Economic Co-operation and Development and World Trade Organization Integrated Database.

and the peaks on key domestically produced commodities are very high.

Average tariffs underestimate the real degree of protection given to local producers in industrial countries and overestimate protection in the OECD developing countries (see figure 3.1). Thus the low average tariffs in industrial countries, which are compared with higher average tariffs in developing countries, are highly misleading. Industrial countries protect commodities produced domestically much more than commodities that are not produced locally. Developing countries, in contrast, seem to protect commodities that are not produced locally more than commodities that are.

Most of the analysis of protection in OECD countries covers the post-1986 period because systemic data have been collected since then. Other estimates, though not exactly comparable over time, indicate that the 1986–88 baseline was a period of peak protection levels in the OECD (figure 3.2) and that the significant increase in protection took place during the 1960s and 1970s.

Since 1986–88, when data become more consistent, overall protection (total support) for agricultural producers in the OECD, including border protection and direct subsidies, fell from 63 percent

of gross agricultural output at world prices to 45 percent in 2000–02 (table 3.1). The contribution of border barriers to total protection came down from 77 percent to about 63 percent. If the 1960s and 1970s are used as the base, however, protection has risen in most OECD countries.

The overall protection rate, which declined rapidly after 1986 to a low of 42 percent in 1995–97, began to rise after 1997 as world agricultural prices declined (figure 3.3). This recent increase is driven both by higher domestic prices compared with international prices and by increases in direct support. This overall cyclical movement is observed in most major countries and groups (European Union, Japan, and the United States). The counter-cyclical movement of border protection indicates that the concept of full ad valorem tariffication is not complete and that the instruments for increasing protection as global prices decline are still operative. Direct subsidies also increased as world prices declined because most direct subsidies are tied to the differences between a floor and a world price and increase when world prices decline.

The European Union and the United States marginally reduced their overall support during 1986–2002. In the European Union the prices

FIGURE 3.2 Nominal Rates of Agricultural Support in OECD Countries 1965–2002
(percent of total value of production evaluated at world prices)

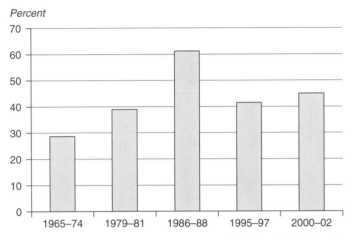

Source: OECD PSE database, except ABARE (1999) for 1965–74 and author's calculation for 2000–02.

TABLE 3.1 Percentage of Farm Gate Prices Attributable to Border Protection and Direct Subsidies by Country and Group, 1986–2002, Evaluated at World Prices

Country or Group	Market Price Support (Border Protection)			Direct Subsidies			Total Producer Support Estimate		
	1986–88	1995–97	2000–02	1986–88	1995–97	2000–02	1986–88	1995–97	2000–02
OECD	48.2	28.2	28.1	4.3	13.3	16.7	62.5	41.5	44.9
European Union	65.3	28.3	30.3	10.5	20.4	23.1	75.8	48.8	53.4
United States	16.0	7.5	9.3	18.3	7.4	16.9	34.3	14.9	26.2
Japan	145.4	131.7	131.5	16.8	13.0	14.4	162.1	144.7	146.0
Eastern European countries[a]	45.2	8.7	14.1	18.3	4.8	8.0	63.6	13.5	22.1
Australia and New Zealand	4.2	2.8	0.3	6.4	3.9	3.2	10.6	6.8	3.6
Canada	53.1	42.6	10.9	11.1	12.8	12.1	64.2	55.4	23.0
Other developing OECD[b] countries	31.4	38.1	44.2	6.4	8.0	8.4	37.8	46.1	52.6

a. Czech Republic, Hungary, Poland, and the Slovak Republic.
b. Republic of Korea, Mexico, and Turkey.
Source: OECD. PSE Database.

received by farmers were 65 percent higher than international prices in 1986–88 and 30 percent higher in 2000–02. Similarly, in the United States domestic prices declined from 16 percent higher than international prices to 9.3 percent higher. In the United States the primary source of support is direct subsidies to farmers. The level of subsidy stayed around 17 percent, much higher than the level of border barriers. The prices are set at world

or close to world levels. During the 1990s the European Union also lowered many domestic prices and moved to support farmers through direct subsidies, some coupled and some partially decoupled. Thus, direct production-related payments to farmers increased from 10.5 percent to 23 percent, partially compensating for the decline in border barriers. So, while the type of support changed from border measure to different forms of

FIGURE 3.3 Rates of Agricultural Support in OECD Countries and Real U.S. Agricultural Price Index

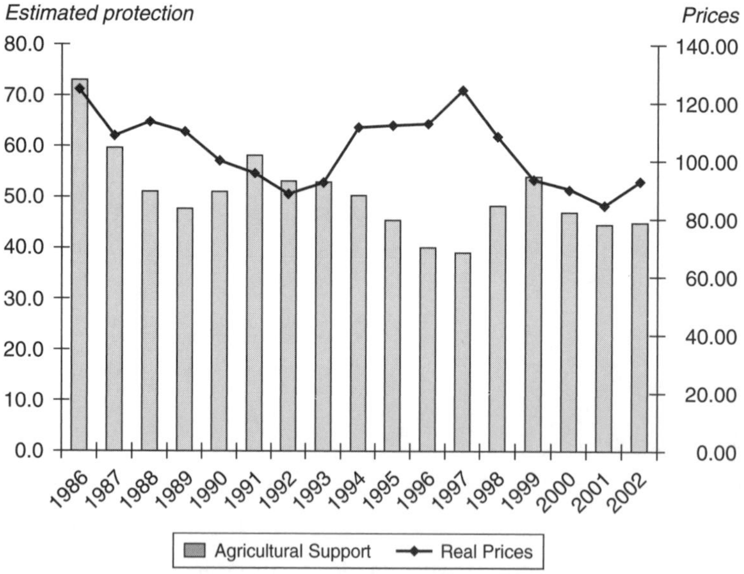

Source: OECD for 1986–2001; author's calculation for 2002. Agricultural price data is from the U.S. Department of Agriculture and is deflated by the manufacturing unit value index.

direct support, there was very little reduction in overall protection (see chapter 5).

Among the middle-income countries of the OECD, the Eastern European countries had the largest reductions in protection, from about 64 percent in 1986–88 to 18 percent in 2000–02. The Republic of Korea always had very high protection, and it has stayed high, with small variations. Mexico and Turkey, which started with low protection, increased it over this period, mainly through higher border protection.

These numbers support the hypothesis that the Uruguay Round did not have a significant impact on the levels of agricultural support in OECD countries, especially the large industrial countries (Ingco 1997; Messerlin 2002; Nogues 2003; OECD 2001). Thus, despite the implicit promise by industrial countries that agriculture would follow the path of manufacturing, with protection rates continuously declining—one of the reasons developing countries embraced trade liberalization—this has not happened.

Other Developing Countries

In contrast to the modest changes in agricultural protection in OECD countries, changes in protec-

tion in most developing countries have been significant. From the 1960s to the 1980s, despite high tariffs on agricultural products, most developing countries had negative total protection rates on agriculture, a result of both direct protection, including tariffs and taxes on agricultural products, and indirect protection caused by protection of industry and exchange rate overvaluation (Schiff and Valdes 1992; World Bank 1986). In a sample of 15 developing countries studied by Schiff and Valdes (1992), all but the 3 OECD middle-income countries had negative direct protection rates and negative total protection rates on agriculture. Of the 3 OECD middle-income countries, the total protection rate was marginally positive for the Republic of Korea and Portugal (table 3.2).

The average agricultural tariff in developing countries declined from 30 percent in 1990 to 18 percent in 2000, a significant drop (figure 3.4).[4] These reductions were complemented by elimination of import licensing, most export taxes, and many quantitative restrictions (World Bank 2001). Overvaluation of exchange rates, the main source of the bias against agriculture, decreased or was eliminated during the 1990s in most developing countries. On average, tariffs are now much higher in agriculture than in manufacturing, a reversal of

TABLE 3.2 Agricultural Protection Rates in Selected Developing Countries

Group	Direct Protection	Tax Due to Industrial Protection	Total Protection
Developing countries[a]	−13.0	−27.8	−35.7
OECD middle-income countries[b]	17.8	−28.4	−3.6

a. Argentina, Brazil, Chile, Colombia, Côte d'Ivoire, Dominican Republic, Egypt, Ghana, Malaysia, Morocco, Pakistan, Philippines, Sri Lanka, Thailand, and Zambia.

b. Republic of Korea, Portugal, and Turkey.

Source: Schiff and Valdes 1992, table 2-1.

FIGURE 3.4 Average Most-Favored-Nation Applied Tariffs for Agricultural and Manufacturing Products in Developing Countries, 1990–2000
(percent)

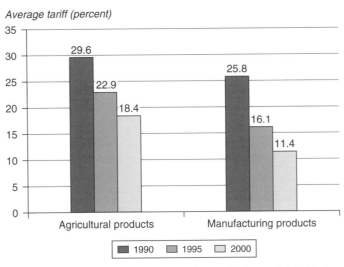

Average tariff (percent)

Legend: 1990, 1995, 2000

Note: Tariff rates are simple averages of countries' unweighted tariffs.

Source: TRAINS.

the tendency during the 1980s of greater protection for the industrial sector.

A study of 15 developing countries by Jansen, Robinson, and Tarp (2002) also concludes that the bias against agriculture had been largely eliminated. They find that by the end of the 1990s the economywide system of indirect taxes, including tariffs and export taxes, significantly discriminated against agriculture in only one country, was largely neutral in five, provided a moderate subsidy to agriculture in four, and strongly favored agriculture in five. Quiroz and Opazo (2000), updating Schiff and Valdes (1992) for Latin America, also conclude that direct protection and protection due to higher tariffs in manufacturing have fallen but that exchange rates appreciated, reversing some of the lower protection for exportable commodities.

Current Structure of Agricultural Protection

The overall support given to agricultural producers in OECD countries through higher domestic prices and direct production-related subsidies was $228 billion during 2000–02 (table 3.3). About 63 percent, or $143 billion, of this came from border barriers and market price support, and 37 percent from direct subsidies to farmers. The bulk of the support went to temperate-climate products such as milk, meats, grains, and sugar.

Aggregate support levels in OECD countries vary significantly. Iceland, Norway, and Switzerland have very high levels of support, through both high border protection and high direct payments. At the other extreme, Australia and New Zealand have very low

TABLE 3.3 Agricultural Support in OECD Countries, 2002–02
(billions of U.S. dollars)

Support	United States	European Union	Japan	Emerging Supporters[a]	Eastern European Countries[b]	Total OECD
Who receives support						
Producers	46.97	92.19	47.50	30.49	4.41	227.54
General services	24.29	8.02	12.25	5.98	0.57	53.08
Consumers	22.24	3.64	0.42	0.97	0.06	34.26
Total	93.50	103.85	60.17	37.44	5.05	314.88
Products that receive support						
Milk	11.25	16.11	4.63	2.53	1.03	40.14
Beef and pork	1.99	25.05	3.50	2.63	0.73	36.65
Rice	0.92	0.25	16.47	7.21	na	25.00
Wheat	3.99	8.97	0.89	0.36	0.31	15.31
Corn	6.80	2.41	na	1.32	−0.10	10.64
Other	22.02	39.40	22.00	16.46	2.45	99.81
Source of producer support						
Border measures[c]	16.63	52.24	42.80	25.60	2.81	142.66
Domestic measures[d]	30.34	39.95	4.70	4.89	1.60	84.89

na – not applicable.
a. Republic of Korea, Mexico, and Turkey.
b. Czech Republic, Hungary, Poland, and Slovak Republic.
c. Tariffs and tariff equivalents of other border measures.
d. Direct payments to producers.
Source: OECD 2003 and authors' calculations.

support levels. Japan and the Republic of Korea have high support levels mainly through higher tariffs and quantitative restrictions. In between are the European Union toward the higher end and Canada toward the lower end.

This section evaluates tariff regimes for agricultural products for 6 industrial and 24 developing countries within the context of the objectives of the Uruguay Round. The selection of countries was constrained by the lack of recent detailed tariff schedules for most countries.[5]

The countries are placed in four groups for analysis: the Quad countries (Canada, the European Union, Japan, and the United States); eight large middle-income countries with significant agricultural sectors (Brazil, China, India, the Republic of Korea, Mexico, South Africa, Russian Federation, and Turkey); eight other middle-income countries, to ensure regional balance (Bulgaria, Costa Rica, Hungary, Jordan, Malaysia, Morocco, Philippines, and Romania); and eight low-income countries

(Bangladesh, Guatemala, Indonesia, Kenya, Malawi, Togo, Uganda, and Zimbabwe). The analysis focuses on tariffs because they are the only comparable measure of protection and support across countries and because lower, more transparent tariff structures were a key objective of the Uruguay Round.

Tariff Transparency

The objective of achieving greater transparency of protection levels through tariffication has not been fully realized, especially in the key industrial countries and some middle-income countries. Many tariffs are still specific, compound, or mixed, making it almost impossible to estimate real protection levels, since these will change with the price of imports. Protection rates rise as the world prices of products decline, increasing protection levels for lower-priced products originating from developing countries.[6]

Transparency in agriculture is significantly greater in developing countries than in industrial

FIGURE 3.5 **Non-Ad-Valorem Tariff Lines as a Share of Total**
(percent)

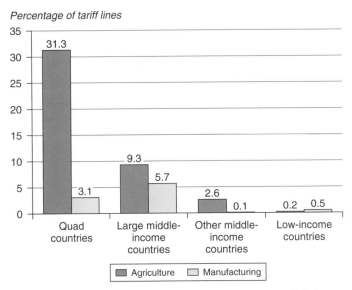

Percentage of tariff lines

Note: Covers tariff lines with specific, compound, or mixed duties.
Source: World Trade Organization Integrated Database (most-favored-nation applied duties).

countries (figure 3.5). Of the 24 developing countries in the sample, only 4 have non-ad-valorem rates in more than 5 percent of tariff lines—Bulgaria (13.5 percent), South Africa (25 percent), Russian Federation (31 percent), and Turkey (6 percent)—all of them middle-income countries. Of the remaining 20 countries, 4 have them in less than 5 percent of tariff lines, 5 in less than 1 percent; 11 have none. Within the Quad, Japan has specific, compound, or mixed rates in 15 percent of its tariff lines, Canada in 24 percent, the United States in 40 percent, the European Union in 44 percent, and Norway, with the highest share of any industrial country, in 54 percent. The European Union also has duties that vary according to the content of the products in 4 percent of its tariff lines, and the United States in 1 percent of its tariff lines. Thus, transparency of tariff rates is consistently weaker for industrial countries and a few middle-income countries than for most developing countries.

The pattern of specific duties varies across countries. In the United States almost all categories of products have non-ad-valorem rates between 30 and 60 percent of tariff lines. In the European Union some product groups, such as milk, grains, sugar, and beverages have non-ad-valorem duties in more than 90 percent of tariff lines. In the developing countries that have specific duties, they are clustered within a few product groups. For example, in Malaysia they are on tobacco and alcohol products, in Mexico on chocolate and confectionary products, sugar, nuts, and spices.

Specific duties are found almost exclusively in agriculture. For example, in the United States, which has the highest percentage of non-ad-valorem duties in manufacturing, only 8 percent of tariff lines in manufacturing are non-ad-valorem, compared with 43 percent in agriculture. The European Union has almost no non-ad-valorem duties in manufacturing, but 44 percent of its tariff lines in agriculture have non-ad-valorem rates. Thus the use of specific duties is not a general administrative arrangement but is limited to agriculture.

More detailed analysis of the incidence of specific duties suggests that they are being used primarily as an instrument of disguised protection. First, the average ad valorem equivalents of specific duties, where available, are much higher than the average ad valorem rates, as shown for four countries that reported the ad valorem equivalents of non-ad-valorem rates (table 3.4). This suggests that reported average duties are seriously underestimated for countries with a large proportion of non-ad-valorem duties.

TABLE 3.4   Average Ad Valorem and Specific Duty Rates
(percent)

Country or Group	Average ad Valorem Tariff	Average ad Valorem Tariff Equivalent of Specific Duties	Share of Non-ad-Valorem Lines
Australia	1.2	5.0	0.9
United States	10.6	35.2	43.6
European Union	21.6	58.0	40.4
Jordan	8.1	11.7	0.8

Note: Average applied, out-of-quota, ad valorem, and ad valorem equivalents of non-ad-valorem tariffs for which equivalents are reported.
Source: World Trade Organization Integrated Database (most-favored-nation applied duties).

TABLE 3.5   Proportion of Non-Ad-Valorem Tariff Lines by Degree of Processing
(percent)

Country or Group	Raw	Intermediate	Final
Norway	41.39	58.84	68.53
European Union	22.05	45.27	57.54
United States	37.91	43.05	41.34
Canada	17.14	23.01	30.20
Russian Federation	11.79	9.74	53.06
Turkey	0	5.22	12.70

Note: Tariff Lines containing specific, compound, or mixed duties, as a percentage of all lines.
Source: World Trade Organization Integrated Database (most-favored-nation applied duties).

Second, the share of tariff lines with non-ad-valorem duties increases with the degree of processing and is highest in final products, which are generally classified under food-processing industries. For example, in the European Union, the share of non-ad-valorem tariff lines is 22 percent for raw materials but 43 percent and 58 percent for intermediate and final products (table 3.5). In the Russian Federation the share of non-ad-valorem duties in tariff lines is 12 percent for raw materials but 53 percent for final products.

Levels of Tariff Protection

The conversion of nontariff barriers to tariffs under the Uruguay Round Agreement on Agriculture was an important step forward, but in most industrial and developing countries average agricultural tariffs are much higher than average tariffs for nonagricultural products and continue to restrict trade (table 3.6).

The tariff data presented here, especially for industrial and some middle-income countries, seriously underestimates actual border protection for domestic producers. Specific duties are not reflected in the averages, and they are generally higher than ad valorem rates (see table 3.4). The reported ad valorem equivalents of specific duties for the European Union and the United States are much higher than the ad valorem rates. Assuming the same pattern for Canada and Japan, which have non-ad-valorem rates for 25 percent and 15 percent of their tariff lines, respectively, Quad average tariffs are being significantly underestimated. The degree of bias is indicated by the third column in table 3.6 showing the proportion of tariff lines to which the average tariffs apply.

Except for Canada, which has a large proportion of non-ad-valorem tariffs without equivalents, average tariffs are much higher in agriculture than in manufacturing. The difference is especially pronounced in the European Union, where the

TABLE 3.6   Average Agricultural Tariffs, Selected Country Groups and Years
(percent)

Country or Group	Agriculture	Manufacturing	Share of Lines Covered in Agriculture
Quad countries	10.7	4.0	86.7
Canada (2001)	3.8	3.6	76.0
Japan (1999)	10.3	3.7	85.5
United States (2001)	9.5	4.6	99.4
European Union (1999)	19.0	4.2	85.9
Large middle-income countries[a]	26.6	13.1	91.3
Other middle-income countries[b]	35.4	12.7	97.7
Lower-income countries[c]	16.6	13.2	99.8

Note: Most-favored-nation, applied ad valorem, out-of-quota duties.

a. Brazil (2001), China (2001), India (2000), the Republic of Korea (2001), Mexico (2001), Russian Federation (2001), South Africa (2001), and Turkey (2001).

b. Bulgaria (2001), Costa Rica (2001), Hungary (2001), Jordan (2000), Malaysia (2001), Morocco (1997), Philippines (2001), and Romania (1999).

c. Bangladesh (1999), Guatemala (1999), Indonesia (1999), Kenya (2001), Malawi (2000), Togo (2001), Uganda (2001), and Zimbabwe (2001).

Source: World Trade Organization Integrated Database (most-favored-nation applied duties).

average tariff is 19 percent in agriculture and 4.2 percent in manufacturing. Among developing countries the results are similar, with a few exceptions such as Brazil and Indonesia, whose manufacturing tariffs are marginally higher (less than 1 percentage point). Only in Malaysia are tariffs much higher in manufacturing (9.7 percent) than in agriculture (2.8 percent).

Developing countries in the sample have higher agricultural tariffs than industrial countries, with Morocco (64 percent), the Republic of Korea (42.2 percent), and Turkey (49.5 percent) having the highest average tariff rates, and Indonesia (8.5 percent) and Malaysia the lowest (2.8 percent). Again, it is important to recall that average tariffs in countries with a high share of non-ad-valorem rates in tariff lines are seriously underestimated; examples are the Russian Federation (a non-ad-valorem rate in tariff lines of 31 percent), South Africa (25 percent), Bulgaria (14 percent), and Turkey (6 percent).

In addition, average tariffs are not reflective of protection because the tariffs have wide dispersion and very high peaks. While tariffs on average are lower in industrial countries, significant tariff peaks indicate high rates of protection for specific products—almost 1,000 percent in the Republic of Korea, 506 percent in the European Union, and 350 percent in the United States.[7] Many low-income countries have lower peaks and variance than many of the middle-income coun-

tries (table 3.7). Furthermore, actual protection for local producers is much higher than these average tariffs in industrial countries and much lower than the average tariffs in selected developing countries, as shown previously (see figure 3.1).

The difference between average rates and maximum tariff rates and the relative domestic price differences for local production measured by market price support data from the OECD indicate that protection is very uneven, with domestic production being protected much more significantly. Japan, with an average tariff of 10 percent and a maximum ad valorem tariff of 50 percent, has estimated market price support of 130 percent. The difference can only be attributed to specific duties not included in the data set. The situation is similar for the European Union, with an average tariff of about 19 percent and market price support of 30 percent. For both Japan and the European Union, tariffs for many locally produced items are very high. For example, in the European Union average tariffs are 34.6 percent for grains, 54.6 percent for milk and milk products, and 32.5 percent for meats.

Another issue is the product coverage of the tariffs presented here and included in the market price support measures used by the OECD. The tariffs reported here include seafood, tobacco and cigarettes, wine, and tropical products, none of which is included in the market price support measures for

TABLE 3.7   Tariff Peaks and Variance in Selected Countries
(percent)

Country or Group	Average Tariff	Maximum Tariff	Standard Deviation	Share of Lines Covered
Canada	4.1	238.0	13.5	74.2
Japan	10.9	50.0	10.1	84.8
United States	9.9	350.0	26.5	99.5
European Union	19.0	506.3	27.3	85.9
Republic of Korea	39.9	917.0	107.9	97.9
Brazil	13.2	55.0	5.6	100.0
Costa Rica	14.2	154.0	18.0	100.0
Morocco	67.4	376.5	70.6	100.0
Indonesia	8.9	170.0	25.6	100.0
Malawi	16.5	25.0	8.5	100.0
Togo	15.6	20.0	6.1	99.9
Uganda	13.6	15.0	3.2	100.0

Note: Most-favored-nation, out-of-quota, applied tariffs.
Source: World Trade Organization Integrated Database.

TABLE 3.8   Tariff Rate Escalation in Agriculture, Selected Country Groups and Years
(percent)

Country or Group	Raw	Intermediate	Final	Average	Share of Lines Covered
Quad countries	6.1	9.3	14.8	10.7	86.7
Canada	1.4	3.4	6.5	3.8	76.0
Japan	4.2	10.2	15.9	10.3	85.5
United States	5.5	7.1	12.6	9.5	99.3
European Union	13.2	16.6	24.3	19.0	85.9
Large middle-income countries[a]	21.9	23.3	34.4	26.6	91.3
Other middle-income countries[b]	21.6	31.7	49.0	35.4	97.7
Lower-income countries[c]	13.2	14.8	23.0	16.6	99.8

Note: Most-favored-nation applied, ad valorem, out-of-quota duties.
a. Brazil (2001), China (2001), India (2000), the Republic of Korea (2001), Mexico (2001), Russian Federation (2001), South Africa (2001), and Turkey (2001).
b. Bulgaria (2001), Costa Rica (2001), Hungary (2001), Jordan (2000), Malaysia (2001), Morocco (1997), Philippines (2001), and Romania (1999).
c. Bangladesh (1999), Guatemala (1999), Indonesia (1999), Kenya (2001), Malawi (2000), Togo (2001), Uganda (2001), and Zimbabwe (2001).
Source: World Trade Organization Integrated Database (most-favored-nation applied duties).

the OECD countries. If seafood, beverages, tobacco, and noncompetitive tropical products are excluded, the average tariff rises from 3.8 percent to 10.4 percent in Canada and from 10.7 percent to 24.7 percent in Japan (excluding specific tariffs). This supports the hypotheses that the low average tariffs are misleading and that protection is uneven and focused primarily on selected domestically produced commodities.

Tariff Escalation

Protection escalates with the level of processing in almost all countries and across all products (table 3.8). Escalation slows diversification into value added and processed products. The manufacturing component of agriculture and food processing have very high rates of protection.

TABLE 3.9 Tariff Escalation in Selected Agricultural Product Groups
(percent)

Product	European Union	United States	Japan
Traditional tropical products			
Coffee			
Raw	7.3	0.1	6.0
Final	12.1	10.1	18.8
Cocoa			
Raw	0.5	0.0	0.0
Intermediate	9.7	0.2	7.0
Final	30.6	15.3	21.7
New expanding products			
Fruits			
Raw	9.2	4.6	8.7
Intermediate	13.3	5.5	13.2
Final	22.5	10.2	16.7
Vegetables			
Raw	9.9	4.4	5.0
Intermediate	18.5	4.4	10.6
Final	18.0	6.5	11.6
Seafood			
Raw	11.5	0.6	4.9
Intermediate	5.1	3.2	4.3
Final	16.2	3.5	9.1

Note: Most-favored-nation applied, ad valorem, out-of-quota duties.
Source: World Trade Organization Integrated Database.

Tariff escalation occurs in all types of products, not just those produced in industrial countries. Data on products with low tariffs on raw commodities, both traditional products (coffee and cocoa) and new products (fruits and vegetables, seafood), show that tariff escalation is common to both (table 3.9). Tariffs are extremely low on the raw stages of traditional products, whereas the final stages and processed products have extremely high tariffs. Similar tariff escalation is apparent in fruits and vegetables, which are supposed to be less protected and in which developing country exports have expanded.

In addition, these averages mask very high peaks on individual products. In the United States maximum tariffs are 136 percent on final fruit products and 186 percent on cocoa products. In the European Union the maximum rates are 98 percent and 146 percent on processed fruits and vegetables and 63 percent on cocoa products. And again, many of the final product tariffs are non-ad-valorem, meaning that the averages underestimate the full extent of high tariffs.

Tariff Rate Quotas

Tariff rate quotas, designed to ensure some degree of market access despite protection, have resulted in more complex tariff regimes. While the number of tariff lines under tariff rate quotas is small, these lines cover some of the main commodities produced in OECD countries. According to OECD data, almost 28 percent of domestic agricultural production is protected by tariff rate quotas. Rates range from a high of 68 percent in Hungary to 38 percent in the European Union and 26 percent in the United States to 13 percent in Japan (figure 3.6). Australia and New Zealand have no tariff rate quotas.

Export Subsidies

Although lower tariffs and the move toward direct production subsidies are beginning to reduce the need for export subsidies in agriculture (they have been illegal on nonagricultural products since

FIGURE 3.6   **Share of Output under Tariff Rate Quotas**
(percent)

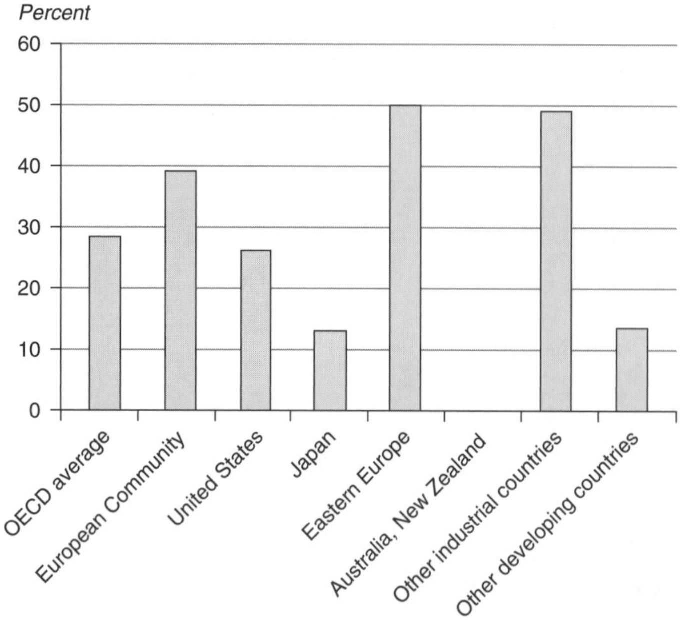

Source: OECD, Agricultural Market Access Database (AMAD).

1955), export subsidies continue to distort world markets. The European Union accounts for almost 90 percent of all OECD export subsidies. The Uruguay Round Agreement on Agriculture placed limits on export subsidies for individual commodities but allowed some flexibility. With usage levels low early in the implementation period, when world prices were high, several countries carried forward unused export subsidy credits for later use. Circumvention, through the subsidy elements of export credits, export restrictions, and revenue-pooling arrangements in major products, is a concern.

Even if tariffs were eliminated altogether along with the official export subsidies, current agricultural production subsidies would keep the domestic and export price of many commodities lower than their costs of production in industrial countries. By lowering production costs, production subsidies favor industrial-country producers over developing-country producers, who do not receive direct subsidies. Consider cotton subsidies in the European Union and the United States. Tariffs are zero, and domestic prices are the same as world or export prices (Baffes 2004; Watkins 2003). Yet in the United States in 2001, production subsidies effectively increased the prices farmers received (or reduced

their costs of production) by 51 percent, leading to increased production that depressed the world price. U.S. export prices were 58 percent of the average costs of production for wheat, 67 percent for corn, and 77 percent for rice (Watkins 2003). The move toward replacing border barriers with direct subsidies in industrial countries will increase the importance of these implicit export subsidies.[8]

Implications of Reform

One trade reform proposal that would have cut agricultural tariffs substantially was put up by Stuart Harbinson, chairman of the agricultural negotiations in the Doha Round of the WTO trade negotiations (DRIFE 2003). The proposal was rejected by industrial-country trade ministers as too radical, however, and brought the Cancún Ministerial Meetings to a close. The implications of this proposal in terms of actual tariff outcomes is presented below as an illustration.

Harbinson proposed that industrial countries cut average agricultural tariffs 60 percent on bound tariffs above 90 percent, 50 percent on bound tariffs between 15 and 90 percent, and 40 percent on bound tariffs below 15 percent.[9] For developing

TABLE 3.10   Tariffs in the European Union and the United States Before and After Average Reduction from Applied Tariffs under the Harbinson Proposal
(percent)

| | United States | | | | European Union | | | |
| | Before Harbinson | | After Harbinson | | Before Harbinson | | After Harbinson | |
Product	Average	Peak	Average	Peak	Average	Peak	Average	Peak
Raw	5.5	350.0	2.7	140.0	13.2	131.8	6.9	52.7
Intermediate	7.1	159.3	3.8	63.8	16.6	284.8	8.3	113.9
Final	11.7	180.8	6.2	72.3	26.8	506.3	13.1	202.5
Overall	8.8	350.0	4.6	140.0	19.7	506.3	9.9	202.5

Note: The analysis excludes cigarettes and alcoholic drinks.
Source: World Trade Organization Integrated Database.

TABLE 3.11   Tariffs in Selected Developing Countries Before and After Average Reductions from Bound Rates
(percent)

| | Costa Rica | | India | | Jordan | | Korea, Rep. of | |
Category	Average	Peak	Average	Peak	Average	Peak	Average	Peak
Before Harbinson	49.0	245.0	115.3	300.0	21.5	180.0	50.8	917.0
After Harbinson	33.8	147.0	72.3	180.0	14.9	108.0	33.2	550.2
Current applied rates	13.1	154.0	36.7	115.0	18.5	120.0	42.7	917.0

Note: The analysis excludes cigarettes and alcoholic drinks.
Source: World Trade Organization Integrated Database.

countries and for products that are not considered strategic, average tariffs would be cut 40 percent for bound tariffs above 120 percent, 35 percent for tariffs between 60 percent and 120 percent, 30 percent for tariffs between 20 percent and 60 percent, and 25 percent for tariffs below 20 percent. These cuts would be implemented over 5 years for industrial countries in equal installments and over 10 years for developing countries (WTO 2003).

While the proposed cuts look significant—some groups have called them radical—their impact would not be as great as might appear. For developing countries the key issue is reductions from the bound, not the applied, rates. Most developing countries have bound their tariffs at relatively high rates, but applied rates are much lower. If cuts are made to the bound rates, countries would get credit for the unilateral reforms, but the reductions would not lead to significant actual reductions in tariffs.

For the United States and the European Union, average effective tariffs would be halved by the end

of the reform process under an optimistic scenario in which all tariffs are cut by the average rate from the applied rates (table 3.10).[10] EU tariffs would come down from 20 percent to about 10 percent, while U.S. tariffs would drop from 9 percent to below 5 percent. Even so, the average agricultural tariffs in both areas would remain significantly higher than the average manufacturing tariffs of 4.2 percent in the European Union and 4.6 percent in the United States. Tariff peaks would remain above 200 percent in the European Union and above 140 percent in the United States.

For developing countries the optimistic scenario lowers all the bound rates by the amount of the average cut. Cuts from bound rates do not significantly lower protection in most developing countries. At the end of 10 years the Harbinson reform would leave bound tariffs significantly above the currently applied rates in Costa Rica and India and only marginally below the current applied rates in Jordan and the Republic of Korea (table 3.11).

Because these results would hold for most developing countries, existing levels of protection in the developing world would not be significantly reduced under the Harbinson proposals or under any other proposals that start with bound rates.

Thus even significant cuts in tariffs by industrial and developing countries will leave agricultural sectors with highly distorted tariff structures. In addition to average cuts, however designed, there has to be an agreement on tariff peaks, which should be capped at reasonably low rates.

Conclusion

Within OECD countries, budgetary subsidies and subsidies from consumers (through high tariffs and quantitative restrictions on domestic production of selected commodities) to agricultural producers totaled about $228 billion in 2000–02, or 45 percent of farm revenues. That was down from 62 percent in 1986–88 but is still very high. Some 63 percent of this support was through the higher prices associated with border protection and 37 percent through direct subsidies. In developing countries almost all support is generated through border barriers.

Average agricultural tariffs in industrial countries, when they can be measured, are two to four times higher than average manufacturing tariffs. Even at that, these averages seriously underestimate the actual level of protection to local producers. Almost 30 percent of domestic production in OECD countries is protected by tariff rate quotas. More than 40 percent of the tariff lines in the European Union and the United States include specific duties, which make it difficult to calculate average tariffs, obscure actual levels of protection, and penalize developing countries that supply cheaper products. Tariff peaks as high as 500 percent confront imports from developing countries. Tariffs also rise by degree of processing, creating a highly escalating tariff structure that limits access to processed food markets.

Developing countries, too, have maintained high border protection and have higher average agricultural tariffs than industrial countries. What is worse, many of the protectionist developing countries are middle-income economies, where the demand for agricultural products is growing rapidly. These countries are beginning to resemble industrial countries in their structure of protection. More generally, as taxation of agriculture diminishes in developing countries, reactive protection in response to industrial-country agricultural support is increasing. Many developing countries have increased protection of domestic food products against cheaper, subsidized exports from industrial countries.

Although official export subsidies may be small and shrinking, implicit export subsidies resulting from domestic support are increasing, lending unfair advantage to industrial-country producers. In the United States and the European Union, domestic and export prices of cotton are the same—but those prices are less than half the average cost of production. Similar differences exist for many other products, a gap that will increase as industrial countries move from protection through border barriers and high support prices to support through coupled or partially decoupled subsidies.

Two other dynamics complicate protection. First, many agricultural policies are anticyclical, with protection increasing when agricultural prices are low. Thus protection levels fell as commodity prices increased in the early 1990s and then rose again as prices declined in the late 1990s. Second, rapid and sustained technical progress in agriculture has lowered the costs of production and thus lowered prices. Countries that have been able to enjoy the benefits of technological change have managed to maintain their production and compete with subsidized production.

Significant reforms are needed to make a dent in rural poverty in most developing countries (see chapter 2). Given the magnitude of the distortions in the agricultural sectors in all countries, the proposals for reform have been quite modest. Yet even the modest proposals have not been accepted by the key industrial countries.

A few simple issues stand out. Given the complexity of the protection regimes, all non-ad-valorem tariffs should be converted into ad valorem tariffs. Variances in tariff rates are so high that the only way to reduce protection significantly is through binding ad valorem, nonseasonal tariff caps that are gradually reduced to zero or to very low levels. Otherwise, high tariffs on selected products will continue under all modalities of reform. Finally, direct support programs have to be fully decoupled from production in industrial and middle-income countries (see chapter 5), and other instruments have to be used to support the rural sector in these countries.

Notes

1. Annex 3 in the attached CD-ROM contains detailed tariff tables for 31 countries.

2. For example, most of the policy work on agricultural policies in the World Bank in the 1970s and 1980s focused on supply enhancement and the elimination of taxation of agriculture.

3. These were simple averages and were not weighted for the volume of trade. Thus some countries made large reductions in tariffs that were already low (from 2 percent to 1 percent, for example, for a 50 percent reduction), while making only the minimum reduction in sensitive product groups with high tariffs.

4. It has not been possible to generate consistent agricultural manufacturing and agricultural tariffs for earlier years.

5. The annex in the attached CD-ROM presents the detailed structure of tariffs for the individual countries and the year for which the tariff information applies for each country. The years are also presented in table 3.6.

6. For example, EU duties on wine are 13 euros a hectoliter, or about $0.15 a bottle. For a $1 (c.i.f.) bottle of wine from developing countries such as Bulgaria and Moldova, that gives a high tariff rate of 15 percent. For a $10 dollar bottle of wine from California, the tariff rate would be just 1.5 percent, a very low one.

7. Peaks for the European Union and the United States are all specific tariffs, whereas the variance and peaks for Canada and Japan probably do not reflect the real peaks because specific duties are excluded.

8. Elimination of the Peace Clause, which effectively prohibited legal action against implicit export subsidies, could change the legality of having domestic costs much higher than export prices. Decoupling payments to producers from production levels is another alternative that would allow income support to farmers but eliminate its link with production decisions (see chapter 5).

9. These are average cuts, so actual cuts in each line could be lower.

10. The European Union and United States were selected because there are tariff equivalents for the specific duties. The data for the European Union are for 1999, the last year for which the tariff equivalents were available. The difference between bound and effective rates is very small in most industrial countries and for ease of presentation, the reductions were taken from the effective rates.

References

ABARE (Australian Bureau of Agricultural and Resource Economics). 1999. "Reforming World Agricultural Trade Policies." Research Report 99.12. Canberra.

Baffes, John. 2004. "Cotton: Market Setting and Policies." Chapter 16 in this volume. World Bank, Washington D.C.

Beghin, John C., and M. Ataman Aksoy. 2003. "Agricultural Trade and the Doha Round: Preliminary Lessons From the Commodity Studies." Paper presented at the Annual World Bank Conference on Development Economics Europe Conference, May 15–16, Paris.

DRIFE (Danish Research Institute of Food Economics). 2003. "Note on the Harbinson Draft on Modalities in the WTO Agriculture Negotiations." Agricultural Policy Research Division, Frederiksberg, Denmark.

Ingco, Merlindo. 1997. "Has Agricultural Trade Liberalization Improved Welfare in the Least-Developed Countries? Yes." Policy Research Working Paper 1748. World Bank, Washington, D.C.

Ingco, Merlindo, and John D. Nash. 2004. *Agriculture and the WTO: Creating a Trading System for Development.* Washington, D.C.: World Bank.

Jansen, H. Tarp, Sherman Robinson, and Finn Tarp. 2002. "General Equilibrium Measures of Agricultural Policy Bias in Fifteen Developing Countries." Discussion Paper 105. International Food Policy Research Institute, Trade and Macroeconomics Division, Washington, D.C.

Krueger, Anne, M. Schiff, and A. Valdes. 1992. *The Political Economy of Agricultural Pricing Policy.* A World Bank Comparative Study. Baltimore: Johns Hopkins University Press.

Messerlin, Patrick A. 2002. "Agriculture in the Doha Round." Paper presented at the World Bank Roundtable on Policy Research in Preparation for the 5th WTO Ministerial Meeting, May 20–21, Cairo.

Nogues, Julio J. 2003. "Agricultural Exports in a Protectionist World: Assessing Trade Strategies for MERCOSUR." Inter-American Development Bank, Trade and Integration Division, Washington, D.C.

OECD (Organisation for Economic Co-operation and Development). 2001. *The Uruguay Round Agreement on Agriculture: An Evaluation of Its Implementation in OECD Countries.* Paris.

————. 2003. *Agricultural Policies in OECD Countries: Monitoring and Evaluation.* Paris.

Quiroz, J., and L. Opazo. 2000. "The Krueger-Schiff-Valdés Study 10 Years Later: A Latin American Perspective." *Economic Development and Cultural Change* 49(1): 181–96.

Schiff, M., and A. Valdes. 1992. *The Political Economy of Agricultural Pricing Policy: A Synthesis of the Economics in Developing Countries.* Baltimore: Johns Hopkins University Press.

Watkins, Kevin. 2003. "Northern Agricultural Policies and World Poverty: Will the Doha 'Development Round' Make a Difference?" Oxfam. Paper presented at the Annual World Bank Conference on Development Economics Europe Conference, May 15–16, Paris.

World Bank. 1986. *World Development Report 1986.* Washington, D.C.

————. 2001. *Global Economic Prospects and the Developing Countries 2001.* Washington, D.C.

————. 2003. *Global Economic Prospects 2004: Realizing the Promise of the Doha Agenda.* Washington, D.C.

WTO (World Trade Organization). 2003. "Negotiations on Agriculture First Draft of Modalities for the Further Commitments." WTO Document TN/AG/W/1/Rev.1. Geneva.

4

THE IMPACT OF AGRICULTURAL TRADE PREFERENCES, WITH PARTICULAR ATTENTION TO THE LEAST-DEVELOPED COUNTRIES

Paul Brenton and
Takako Ikezuki

Improving the ability of the least-developed countries (LDCs) to participate fully in world markets can accelerate development and poverty reduction. Their dependence on agriculture, together with the high duties levied on many agricultural imports by industrial countries, suggests that preferences on agricultural products could help boost exports and growth in developing countries.

In practice, however, preferences have had little impact for most developing countries. First, many agricultural products produced in developing countries are subject to zero duties in industrial countries, and therefore no trade preference can be given. Usually these are tropical products that are not produced in industrial countries. Second, the primary agricultural products and processed products with very high duties are typically excluded from preferences or the preference margin is very small. For a small number of products, however, preference margins are substantial, although usually within strict quantitative limits and only for certain countries. Countries that have been granted preferential access for sugar and tobacco, for example, have received large transfers because of preferences. These factors, together with restrictive rules

of origin for many processed products, have severely limited the role of trade preferences in encouraging agricultural diversification in developing countries. Many countries remain dependent on the export of staple products, for which world prices have fluctuated wildly.

While the United States, the European Union (EU), and Japan all offer preference schemes, comparing them is difficult since each scheme differs in important respects: the group of eligible countries, the products covered, and the magnitude of the preference granted. Administrative requirements, especially rules of origin, also vary across schemes and across products. These differences are a major weakness of the current system of preferences.

This chapter reviews these schemes, concentrating on the preferences offered to least-developed countries, and discusses some of the key problems with preferences:

- They are unilateral concessions from industrial countries that must be renewed, and specific products can be withdrawn at short notice, creating too much uncertainty to stimulate new investment.

The authors are grateful for the comments of M. Ataman Aksoy and Harry de Gorter.

exclusions

- The most highly protected products, with the highest potential margins of preference, are often excluded or receive only small preference margins.

ROOs

- Rules of origin for processed products constrain the ability of countries to expand into these products.

complexity

- Differences and inconsistencies between preference schemes prevent developing-country suppliers from developing global market strategies.

If trade preferences are to assist developing countries,

- The schemes should be made permanent and comprehensive, with no product exclusions.
- They should be harmonized, preferably at the World Trade Organization (WTO), with common and simple rules of origin.
- The domestic investment environment in beneficiary countries must be improved so that producers and investors can exploit the opportunities that arise from trade preferences to develop competitive businesses that will survive once those preferences are eroded.
- Developing countries need to diversify into a broader range of exports and not become dependent on the preferential access granted for a narrow range of products.
- Beneficiaries should ensure preferences are integrated as one element of a strategy for broad-based export expansion.
- Preferences for a small group of developing countries should not act as a brake on the multilateral liberalization of agricultural products under the WTO. Many developing countries receive little or nothing from preferences but would gain from a reduction of subsidies in rich countries (which, for example, would benefit cotton producers in Western Africa) and from multilateral tariff reductions in all countries. Such liberalization can be achieved only through negotiations at the WTO.

Trade Preferences in Principle and in Practice

Trade preferences allow products from developing countries to enter industrial-country markets with lower import duties than are applied to other countries' products under the importing country's most-favored-nation (MFN) tariffs. The principal scheme governing such preferences is the Generalized System of Preferences (GSP), which originated in the work of the United Nations Conference on Trade and Development (UNCTAD) in the 1960s to introduce a harmonized preference scheme across donor countries (UNCTAD 2001). Because preferences for particular countries are at odds with the fundamental nondiscrimination principle of the General Agreement on Tariffs and Trade (GATT) and the WTO, the Decision on Differential and More Favorable Treatment, Reciprocity, and Fuller Participation of Developing Countries (called the Enabling Clause) was adopted under the GATT in 1979 to allow industrial countries to offer more favorable treatment to developing countries on a nonreciprocal basis.

Potential Benefits of Trade Preferences

Tariffs introduce a wedge between the world price of a product and the price in the domestic market. Tariff preferences give suppliers in beneficiary developing countries access to part or all of this price premium that normally accrues to the importing-country government as tariff revenue. The acquisition of these rents raises returns in the developing country and, depending on the nature of competition in domestic product and factor markets, stimulates expansion of the activity concerned, with implications for wages and employment.

The arguments underlying trade preferences are that the small scale of industry and the low level of development in developing countries lead to high costs, which reduce the ability to compete in global markets, and to lack of diversification, which increases risks. Developing countries, especially least-developed countries, face much higher trade-related costs than other countries in getting their products into international markets. Some of these costs may reflect institutional problems within the countries themselves, such as inefficient practices and corruption, and these problems require a domestic policy response. But some costs also reflect weak transportation infrastructure in many countries and firms' lack of access to standard trade-facilitating measures such as insurance and trade finance.

Trade preferences can provide the premium over the normal rate of return that is required to encourage investment in these economies. The increase in trade attributable to preferences leads to more output and, if there are scale economies, to lower costs, which stimulate further trade.[1] It is important, however, that the sectors that receive preferences and investment are those in which the country has a comparative advantage in the long term and that investment not be based on a false comparative advantage based on the margin of preference.

Why Do Trade Preferences Fall Short of Their Potential?

Assessments of the impact of trade preferences suggest that they have not transformed the export and growth performance of most developing-country beneficiaries, although performance may have been worse without them and a few countries may have benefited substantially. Trade preferences have not enabled beneficiaries as a group to increase their market shares in the main preference-granting markets.[2] Why?

UNCTAD's objectives of harmonizing preference regimes across countries and making preferences general and nondiscriminatory among developing countries were never achieved. Industrial countries have often excluded the most heavily protected products, many of which offer the greatest scope for gains by developing countries. The segmented markets for preferential-access goods make the program a weak mechanism for integrating developing countries into the world economy.

Industrial countries that grant preferences unilaterally determine which countries and which products are included in their schemes and what rules govern the provision of preferences—and graduation from the program. Preference schemes typically are not permanent programs but require legislative renewal. And preference-granting countries have the discretion to remove countries and products from the program, creating uncertainty and discouraging investment in developing countries to exploit available opportunities. Recently, however, the European Union introduced the Everything but Arms program for the least-developed countries, introducing an element of permanency into preference schemes for the first time.

Most highly protected products are excluded from preference schemes. When preferences are granted on some products for which domestic prices in industrial countries are much higher than world prices, such as sugar in the European Union, traded quantities are limited to avoid undermining the distortionary policies that generate the large divergence between domestic and world prices. Nevertheless, in these instances preferential access can lead to substantial gains for preferred suppliers.

How much of the available rents are actually obtained by suppliers in developing countries depends on the nature of competition in the industry and the rules and regulations governing the granting of preferential access, among other factors. If there is little effective competition among buyers, then exporters may be unable to acquire much of the price premium. Ozden and Olarreaga (2003) find that only a third of the available rents for African exports of clothing to the United States under the African Growth and Opportunity Act (AGOA) actually accrue to exporters. Furthermore, satisfying the rules governing preferences raises costs and reduces the extent to which the preferences raise actual returns. The cost of satisfying the rules of origin in preferences schemes is a major reason for low rates of utilization (UNCTAD 2001; Brenton and Imagawa 2004).[3]

Undesirable Effects of Preference Schemes

Tariff preferences can lead to several adverse effects. Negotiations under the Doha Round have shown that preferences can be used to bolster external support for highly protectionist policies in industrial countries and to weaken proposals that would substantially reduce such levels of protection. Preferences can also create a degree of dependence that constrains flexibility and diversification and results in high-cost production of preferred products (Topp 2001). And the beneficiaries of trade preferences are not always the poorest constituents in developing countries. When rents do accrue to the developing country, they tend to accrue to the owners of the most intensively used factors. With agricultural preferences, the main beneficiaries are the owners of land. Preferences could have a strong impact on poverty if the landowners are poor or, when they are not poor, if policies for redistribution are in place. So even when preferences create substantial transfers for producers in developing countries, they may not necessarily stimulate the long-term growth of exports or reduce poverty, and they can lead to a less-diversified export base.

The Nature and Impact of Preferences Offered by the United States, the European Union, and Japan

The impact of a particular scheme of trade preferences on individual countries is determined by several factors:

- The scope of preferences in terms of the range of products covered.
- The importance of products eligible for preferences in the export and production structure of the beneficiary country.
- The margins of preference, determined by the height of the MFN tariff and the size of the preference.
- Actual utilization of preferences. To a large extent this reflects the costs of satisfying the rules, mainly the rules of origin, governing preferences. If the costs of compliance exceed the margin of preference, the preference will not be used.
- The extent to which preferences facilitate diversification into a broader range of products. This is determined by the coverage of the scheme, the margins of preference on products not currently exported, and the rules of origin relating to these products.

Whether such preference opportunities are actually exploited depends on the domestic investment environment in the beneficiary country and the extent to which legal characteristics of the preference scheme constrain investment decisions. The economic impact of the preferences offered by the United States, the European Union, and Japan vary enormously across beneficiary countries. For some countries exports are dominated by products that do not receive preferences, and there has been little success in diversification. This is especially the case for countries dependent on products that are currently subject to zero import duties in developed countries, such as coffee and cocoa. For other countries, however, all exports are eligible for prefer-

ences to a particular market and the potential impact of preferences is much greater. The actual utilization of preferences, from very low rates to full utilization, also varies substantially across countries. Also of importance is that utilization rates tend to be lower for processed products.

The Scope of Preferences

Whether trade preference schemes assist the integration of developing countries into world markets depends on the breadth of the preferences offered in terms of the number and importance of eligible products.

Products subject to tariff quotas complicate the assessment of the impact of trade preferences. During the Uruguay Round of world trade negotiations, industrial countries agreed to reduce tariffs on a range of sensitive agricultural products but only for limited quantities of imports, often creating two or more tariff lines for each product: the duty on in-quota quantities and the duty (often very high) on additional out-of-quota imports. Preferences are offered on the in-quota quantities only, and once the quota is reached, preferences are no longer available. Quotas can be global (available to all eligible countries) or bilateral (limits are specified for a particular country). With bilateral limits, quantities may not be sufficient to induce investments in raising capacity, whereas for preferences based on global tariff quotas, uncertainty over when the quota will be filled dampens interest in investment or even in exporting.

Thus the lack of preferences for out-of-quota quantities is important in assessing the impact of preference schemes. The analysis here includes out-of-quota rates in calculating the average duty on products not covered by preferences even if the quotas are not exceeded, because of the discouraging impact of the tariff quotas. This approach differs from that of preference-giving countries, which typically assume that if exports from a preference-receiving country or group of countries do not exceed the preferential quota, the product is fully covered by the scheme and the out-of-quota rates are not relevant. Of course, the obvious response is that if the out-of-quota rates are not relevant, there is no reason not to offer full duty- and quota-free access.

U.S. Preferences under the GSP and AGOA

The United States has offered preferences under the Generalized System of Preferences (GSP) since the mid-1970s, with a significant increase in coverage for low-income countries in 1997. The current GSP program expires at the end of 2006. In 2003, 143 developing countries were eligible for preferences under the GSP. There are no partial preferences, so the preferential rate on all included products is zero. However, the preferences can be withdrawn at any time. In addition, the GSP contains safeguards in the form of benefit ceilings for each product and country, known as competitive need limitations (these do not apply to LDCs). A country loses its GSP eligibility for a product if it supplies more than 50 percent of U.S. imports of that product or if its exports exceed a certain dollar value.[4]

The African Growth and Opportunity Act of 2000 offers improved market access to 48 Sub-Saharan African countries subject to certain criteria regarding basic human rights and the rule of law. The competitive needs limitations of the GSP do not apply to AGOA preferences. The current scheme expires in 2015. So far, 38 countries have been granted eligibility for AGOA preferences.

The average duty on agricultural goods from countries that do not receive preferences in the United States is 7.3 percent (table 4.1). The preferences available under the GSP for non-LDCs reduce the average tariff to 6.2 percent. The impact of the GSP on LDCs is more substantial, reducing the average tariff to just under 4 percent. AGOA has little impact on the LDCs, reducing the average tariff by just 0.2 percentage points, but it offers non-LDCs enhanced preferences similar to those available to LDCs under the GSP. All these average tariffs include the out-of-quota duties for tariff quota products.

Comparing MFN duties on the products covered by preferences and average duties on products excluded from preferences shows that the average margin of preference on products under the GSP is 3.6 percent for non-LDCs and 5 percent for LDCs (table 4.2). AGOA enhances the preferences available for non-LDCs by including products subject to an average duty of 7 percent. However, the average tariff on products excluded from preferences is more than 30 percent. The GSP and AGOA do not affect the maximum duty that can be applied to imports from LDCs (more than 160 percent for groundnuts, an important product for a number of African countries).

The duties shown in tables 4.1 and 4.2 are unweighted averages. They do not capture actual duties being levied on developing-country exports but rather the duties that would apply if developing countries exported a completely diversified bundle of agricultural products. In practice, the duties actually levied on many countries are close to zero since these countries export a bundle of exports

TABLE 4.1 Average Unweighted Tariffs on Agricultural Products in the United States, 2003
(percent)

Category	Non-LDC	LDC
MFN rates	7.3	7.3
GSP beneficiaries	6.2	3.9
AGOA beneficiaries	3.8	3.7

Note: Because of the potential effect on decisions to export and invest, average tariffs include out-of-quota tariffs on tariff quota products even if quotas are not filled.

Source: Calculated using data from U.S. International Trade Commission dataweb.

TABLE 4.2 Average Unweighted MFN Tariffs on Agricultural Products Covered by GSP and AGOA in the United States, 2003
(percent)

Category	Non-LDC	LDC
Total GSP	3.6	5.4
GSP	3.6	3.6
GSP LDC	—	7.0
Total AGOA	7.0	9.4
Excluded lines	32.5	32.8

— Not available

Note: Data for calculated duties and customs value for the GSP group were used to derive ad valorem equivalents for specific duties. When there are zero duties from the GSP group of countries, data for total imports were used to calculate the ad valorem equivalent.

Source: Calculated using data from U.S. International Trade Commission dataweb.

TABLE 4.3   Number of Agricultural Tariff Lines Liberalized under GSP and AGOA Programs in the United States, 2003

Category	Non-LDCs		LDCs	
Total tariff lines	1,723		1,723	
Total GSP	519		1,038	
GSP LDC	519	(38)	547	(158)
AGOA	541	(120)	26	
Duty-free lines	440		440	
Dutiable lines (MFN)	223		219	

Note: The numbers in parentheses are the number of product lines relating to in-quota duty rates for products subject to tariff quotas.
Source: Calculated using data from U.S. International Trade Commission dataweb.

concentrated on zero or low-duty products. Developing countries in Africa currently export almost no products that are subject to tariff quotas—the main exceptions are sugar and tobacco. But this may simply reflect the fact that very high duties can be levied once the quota is reached.[5] Liberalization of many of these products under AGOA or GSP is unlikely to have a substantial impact on trade in the short term, but it could encourage investment in future capacity in certain countries.

Data on the number of tariff lines liberalized under U.S. preference programs show that a quarter of tariff lines already have zero MFN duties (table 4.3). For the LDCs, AGOA liberalizes only an additional 26 agricultural tariff lines, or less than 2 percent of the total number of agricultural lines and just under 12 percent of the remaining dutiable lines (those lines for which the MFN duty is not zero). The main products liberalized under AGOA have already been liberalized for LDCs under the GSP. For non-LDCs, AGOA adds 541 products to the 519 products already eligible for duty-free preferences for developing countries under the GSP. Hence, the potential impact is much greater for non-LDCs.[6]

Under AGOA more than 200 agricultural tariff lines have MFN duties but no preferences. These amount to 17 percent of the number of dutiable agricultural tariff lines in the U.S. schedule, although they protect much more than 17 percent of U.S. agricultural production. More than 150 of these lines relate to the over-quota rates for products subject to tariff rate quotas. These products include certain meat and dairy products, many

sugar products, chocolate, prepared foodstuffs, and tobacco products.

EU Preferences under the GSP and Cotonou Agreement

The current GSP scheme of the European Union, which runs to the end of December 2004, has two categories of products: nonsensitive, for which duties are suspended; and sensitive, which face a flat rate reduction of 3.5 percentage points from the MFN rate. A number of products, including meats, dairy products, certain vegetables, cereals, some prepared foodstuffs, and wine are entirely excluded from the scheme. Among eligible products, proportionate reductions are high for most industrial products, for which the average MFN tariff is 4 percent, but relatively low for many agricultural products, for which the average MFN tariff is almost 20 percent. The EU tariff structure for agricultural products is extremely complicated, with more than 45 percent of product lines subject to non-ad-valorem duties. This complexity is reflected in similar complexity in preferences granted.

Specific duties, those based on physical rather than monetary values, are reduced by 30 percent, except when they are combined with ad valorem duties (as in a range of processed agricultural products of interest to developing countries), when they are not reduced. Typically, the specific duties provide the greatest part of the protection on these products. For a number of products, primarily fruits and vegetables, the European Union applies a system of minimum reference prices that vary by season, despite the dubious compatibility of the approach with WTO rules. This can lead to a very complex structure of preferences (box 4.1). Minimum duties specified in the European Union's Common Customs Code do not apply to products covered under the GSP.

Within the GSP, the European Union discriminated in favor of the least-developed countries. All imports of industrial products and a range of agricultural products from these countries entered duty free, but a significant number of agricultural products still faced some market access barriers. These were removed under the Arms initiative introduced in 2001, which grants duty-free access, without any quantitative restrictions, to imports of all products from the least-developed countries, except arms and munitions. Liberalization was immediate except for three products (fresh bananas, rice, and sugar), for which tariffs gradually will be reduced to zero (in 2006 for bananas and in 2009 for rice and sugar). The effect of the Arms initiative will be limited in the short run since the LDCs were not exporting the products that were immediately liberalized (Brenton 2003).

Because preferences for the least-developed countries are granted for an unlimited period and are not subject to periodic review, the Everything but Arms program should provide greater certainty of market access and therefore stimulate a greater production response by existing products and a conducive environment for exports of a wider range of products. This is a crucial aspect of the program. The challenge for developing countries is to create a climate that allows investment to take place in activities in which a comparative advantage can be sustained in the long run.

However, these changes may be partly undermined by the inclusion of a new reason for suspending preferences: "massive increases in imports of products *relative to the usual levels of production and export capacity*" (our emphasis). This could constrain large-scale investment to transform the production capacity in a particular country and discourage diversification into new products.[7]

The European Union offers enhanced preferences beyond those of the GSP to Sub-Saharan African, Caribbean, and Pacific countries (the ACP countries) under the Cotonou Agreement. There are individual protocols for bananas, beef, veal, and sugar. These products accounted for three-quarters

TABLE 4.4 Average Unweighted Tariffs on Agricultural Products in the European Union, 2002
(percent)

Category	Average Tariff
MFN rates	17.3
GSP beneficiaries	15.3
ACP beneficiaries	6.9

Note: For seasonal rates, the duty applied on July 1 is used, the high season for most fruits and vegetables. For products for which it is not possible to calculate an ad valorem equivalent of the complex duties that are applied (for example, for chocolate the duty depends on the milk and sugar content), an ad valorem duty of 30 percent was assigned for the MFN rate and 20 percent for the ACP rate. These are conservative assumptions since many of these complex duties are likely to be prohibitive. In 2002 there were 161 lines for which the ad valorem equivalent could not be computed.
Source: Calculated from EU Commission data and World Trade Organization Integrated Data Bank.

of the value of ACP preferences in the late 1990s, including industrial products, which are all eligible for duty-free access (McQueen 1999).

The average duty in the European Union is very high, at more than 17 percent. Countries eligible for GSP benefits on agricultural products face a slightly lower average duty of 15.3 percent, and ACP countries face a much lower average duty of about 7 percent (table 4.4). The average duty that would be levied on products covered by the GSP if those preferences were removed is about 14 percent (table 4.5). Full preferences tend to be granted on agricultural products with lower MFN rates, whereas those with higher MFN rates tend to receive only partial preferences. Products not granted preference under the GSP scheme tend to be very-high-duty products, with an average tariff of more than 25 percent.

The average duty on products covered by the Cotonou Agreement is more than 21 percent, and the preferences available are much deeper than those under the GSP. And while very-high-duty products tend to receive only partial preferences, many high-duty products excluded from the GSP receive preferences under Cotonou. The average duty on excluded products is just under 10 percent. Nevertheless, preferences do not reduce the

Box 4.1   The EU System of Entry Prices: The Example of Tomatoes

The EU entry price system for imports of vegetables such as tomatoes consists of two sets of tariffs that vary according to the price and season. If the import price is higher than a specified level (which varies by season), only an ad valorem duty is applied. If the import price is lower than this level, then a specific duty is applied as well, which varies by price and season. No preferences are granted under the GSP. For African, Caribbean, and Pacific (ACP) countries, preferences are granted from January to April and in the final 10 days in December. The preference takes the form of a reduction in the ad valorem duty; there is no reduction in the specific duty. This form of entry price system is applied to 34 agricultural products, mainly fruits and vegetables.

Entry Prices and Duties for Tomatoes

Time	Entry Price (euros per 100 kg)	MFN	ACP	GSP	GSP LDC
Jan–Mar	84.6	8.8	3.5	No preference	0
April	112.6	8.8	3.5	No preference	0
May 1–14	72.6	8.8	No preference	No preference	0
May 15–31	72.6	14.4	No preference	No preference	0
June–Sept	52.6	14.4	No preference	No preference	0
Oct	62.6	14.4	No preference	No preference	0
Nov 1– Dec 20	62.6	8.8	No preference	No preference	0
Dec 21–Dec 31	67.6	8.8	3.5	No preference	0

Specific Duties When Import Price Falls below Set Levels

Import Price (euros per 100 kg)	MFN Duty	ACP Duty
January		
82.9 to 84.6	8.8% + 1.7 euro/100 kg	3.5% + 1.7 euro/100 kg
81.2 to 82.9	8.8% + 3.4 euro/100 kg	3.5% + 3.4 euro/100 kg
79.5 to 81.2	8.8% + 5.1 euro/100 kg	3.5% + 5.1 euro/100 kg
77.8 to 79.5	8.8% + 6.8 euro/100 kg	3.5% + 6.8 euro/100 kg
0 to 77.8	8.8% + 29.8 euro/100 kg	3.5% + 29.8 euro/100 kg
July		
51.5 to 52.6	14.4% + 1.1 euro/100 kg	14.4% + 1.1 euro/100 kg
50.5 to 51.5	14.4% + 2.1 euro/100 kg	14.4% + 2.1 euro/100 kg
49.4 to 50.5	14.4% + 3.2 euro/100 kg	14.4% + 3.2 euro/100 kg
48.4 to 49.4	14.4% + 4.2 euro/100 kg	14.4% + 4.2 euro/100 kg
0 to 48.4	14.4% + 29.8 euro/100 kg	14.4% + 29.8 euro/100 kg

For example, an ACP exporter of tomatoes that tries to sell in the EU market in January at a price of, say, 67 euros per 100 kilograms would face an ad valorem equivalent duty of 49.8 percent with the MFN rate being 53.3 percent. A higher cost non-ACP producer who sells at 80 euros per 100 kilograms would face a duty of 13 percent. The duty-inclusive price of the low-cost supplier, even with preferences, is higher than the duty-inclusive price of the high-cost supplier. Hence, specific duties act as an implicit preference toward high-cost suppliers and against lower-cost developing countries, although in this case, if sufficient information is available, there is an opportunity for the low-cost ACP supplier to raise its price and pay a lower duty.

maximum duty that can be applied (a duty of more than 200 percent on milk and cream).

Cotonou preferences cover 81 percent of agricultural tariff lines (table 4.6). Of the remaining lines, 14 percent have zero MFN duties, and 5 percent cover products excluded from preferences. Again, this 5 percent of lines will be protecting much more than 5 percent of EU agricultural output.

put. Cotonou provides full preferences (100 percent duty reduction) for 50 percent of the total number of tariff lines and partial reductions for 31 percent of products (typically removal of the ad valorem component but not the specific duty). Most of the products are highly sensitive and highly taxed imports. The ad valorem equivalent of these specific duties is often very high (see table 4.5).

Japan's GSP Scheme

Japan offers GSP preferences to 164 developing countries. The current scheme expires in 2011. The scheme provides enhanced preferences for LDCs, with partial preferences deepened to 100 percent cuts and (since April 2003) greater product coverage (which is not captured here). There are no explicit quantitative ceilings on preferences, although there are safeguard mechanisms and a country's exports are excluded if they exceed 25 percent of Japan's total imports and 1 billion yen in value.

The average MFN tariff on Japanese imports of agricultural products in 2002 was 15.6 percent (table 4.7). GSP preferences reduced this to 15.1 percent for non-LDCs, an average preference margin of 0.5 percentage point. The average margin for the slightly deeper preferences for LDCs was 1.4 percentage points. Again, it must be noted that

TABLE 4.5 Average Unweighted MFN Tariffs on Agricultural Products Covered by GSP and Cotonou Agreement, 2002
(percent)

Category	Average Tariff
Total GSP	14.1
Lines with full preferences	7.0
Lines with partial preferences	15.2
Excluded GSP lines	26.3
Total Cotonou	21.3
Lines with full preferences	13.7
Lines with partial preferences	33.0
Excluded Cotonou lines	9.6

Source: Calculated using data from EU Commission and World Trade Organization Integrated Data Bank.

TABLE 4.6 Number of Tariffs Lines Liberalized under EU Preferences for ACP Countries, 2002

Category	Tariff Lines Number	Share of Total (percent)
Total lines	2,354	
MFN duty-free	334	14
Total ACP	1,905	81
Full reduction preferences	1,181	50
Partial reduction preferences	724	31
Dutiable MFN lines	115	5
Main sectors containing products excluded from preferences	Wine	
Main sectors containing products subject to partial preferences	Meat, dairy, fruits and vegetables, grains and flour, prepared food stuffs	

Source: Calculated using data from EU Commission.

TABLE 4.7   Average Unweighted Tariffs on Agricultural Products in Japan, 2002
(percent)

Category	Non-LDCs	LDCs
Average MFN	15.6	15.6
Average applied preferential duty	15.1	14.2

Note: Specific duties were converted to ad valorem equivalents based on the total value and quantity of imports from developing countries. When that information was not available, the value and quantity of imports from all sources was used. For tariff lines for which there were no imports, an ad valorem equivalent of 30 percent was assumed—probably an underestimate since these duties are likely to be prohibitive.

Source: Calculated using data from United Nations Conference on Trade and Development TRAINS.

TABLE 4.8   Average Unweighted MFN Tariffs on Agricultural Products Covered by GSP in Japan, 2002
(percent)

Category	Non-LDCs	LDCs
Total GSP	10.4	9.8
Full preference	7.3	9.8
Partial preference	12.0	
Excluded lines (MFN)	20.8	21.5

Source: Calculated using data from United Nations Conference on Trade and Development (TRAINS).

TABLE 4.9   Tariffs Lines Liberalized under Japan's GSP Preferences, 2002

Category	Non-LDCs		LDCs	
	Number of Tariff Lines	Share of Total (percent)	Number of Tariff Lines	Share of Total (percent)
Total lines	2,014		2,014	
MFN duty-free	393	20	393	20
Total GSP	221	11	298	15
Full preferences	80	4	298	15
Partial preferences	141	7	0	
Dutiable lines (MFN)	1,400	70	1,323	66
Main sectors containing products excluded from preferences	Meat, fish, dairy, cereals, prepared meat and fish, sugar, cocoa, prepared food products			

Source: Calculated using data from the United Nations Conference on Trade and Development (TRAINS).

these are not average duties paid since few imports are in the high-duty categories.

The average duty on products covered by the GSP was 10.4 percent for non-LDCs and 9.8 percent for the LDCs (table 4.8). The duty on products excluded from preferences is high relative to duties on products covered by preferences, even when conservatively estimated, at about 21 percent (see note to table 4.7).

Some 20 percent of agricultural tariff lines in Japan are subject to zero duties, while preferences under the GSP cover 11 percent of agricultural products for non-LDCs and 15 percent for LDCs (table 4.9). The 2003 reform of the GSP added an additional 198 products (or 10 percent of total tariff lines) to preferences for LDCs. For non-LDCs most products under preferences receive only a partial reduction in duties, and 71 percent of agricultural products are excluded from preferences, while preferences were not available for 67 percent of tariff lines for LDCs in 2002 (falling to 57 percent in 2003).

Proportion of Trade Covered by Preferences

U.S. Preferences

Examination of the proportion of developing-country exports covered by U.S. preference programs shows that (table 4.10)

- Exports of processed agricultural products are much smaller than exports of primary agricultural products.
- For a large proportion of primary product exports (more than 70 percent for the three groups of countries), there are no preferences since the MFN duty is zero. A much larger proportion of processed exports is eligible for preferences.
- Preference use is high for primary products (more than 80 percent) and higher than the rate of preference use for processed products.
- Products not eligible for preferences constitute a small proportion of current exports.

EU Preferences

Several findings stand out in an examination of the proportion of exports covered by EU

preferences (table 4.11) and show the following:

- The value of agricultural exports to the European Union is much larger than that of exports to the United States, for both processed and primary products. Again, the value of exports is smaller for processed products than for primary products.
- A much larger proportion of exports are eligible for preferences than in the United States because fewer export products have MFN duties of zero. Two-thirds or more of exports are eligible for preferences.
- Products not eligible for preferences constitute a very small proportion of current exports.

Japanese Preferences

An examination of the proportion of developing country exports covered by GSP exports to Japan shows the following: (table 4.12)

- As a market for the exports of agricultural products of African LDCs, Japan is smaller than the European Union and about the same size as the United States.
- Exports from other LDCs, including those in Asia, are considerably smaller than those from

TABLE 4.10   Exports to the United States under AGOA and by other LDCs under the GSP, 2002
(US$ millions)

Category	GSP and AGOA Preferences		
	GSP+AGOA Non-LDCs	GSP+AGOA LDCs	GSP LDCs
Basic agricultural commodities			
Total exports to United States	600	247	122
Exports duty free	431 (72)	190 (77)	114 (93)
Exports for which preferences requested	149 (25)	47 (19)	7 (6)
Exports eligible, but preferences not requested	15 (1)	11 (4)	1 (1)
Exports not eligible for preferences	6 (1)	0 (0)	0 (0)
Processed agricultural products			
Total exports to United States	133	51	2.3
Exports duty free	55 (41)	9 (18)	0.9 (41)
Exports for which preferences requested	61 (46)	31 (61)	0.6 (29)
Exports eligible, but preferences not requested	11 (8)	10 (20)	0.7 (30)
Exports not eligible for preferences	5 (4)	0	0

Note: Numbers in parentheses are shares of exports for each category of agricultural exports.
Source: Calculated using data from U.S. International Trade Commission dataweb.

TABLE 4.11   Exports to the European Union from ACP Beneficiaries, 2002
(US$ millions)

Category	Africa Africa LDC	Africa Non-LDC	Caribbean	Pacific
Basic agricultural commodities				
Total exports to the European Union	1,904	5,159	1,018	310
Exports duty free	533 (28)	2,065 (40)	55 (5)	68 (22)
Exports for which preferences requested ACP+GSP	1,188 (62)	2,623 (51)	874 (86)	223 (72)
Exports eligible, but preferences not requested	183 (10)	471 (9)	89 (9)	19 (6)
Exports not eligible for preferences	0.2 (0)	0.5 (0)	0.18 (0)	0 (0)
Processed agricultural products				
Total exports to the European Union	303	1,414	455	15
Exports duty free	30 (10)	16 (1)	8 (2)	1 (10)
Exports for which preferences requested ACP+GSP	235 (78)	1,186 (84)	416 (92)	8 (57)
Exports eligible, but preferences not requested	37 (12)	212 (15)	30 (7)	5 (34)
Exports not eligible for preferences	0.1 (0)	0 (0)	0.1 (0)	0 (0)

Note: Numbers in parentheses are shares of exports for each category of agricultural exports.
Source: Calculated using data from EU Commission.

TABLE 4.12   Exports to Japan from LDCs in 2002
(US$ millions)

Category	All LDCs	African LDCs	Other LDCs
Basic agricultural commodities			
Total exports to Japan	381	241	140
Exports duty free	131 (34)	124 (51)	8 (5)
Exports for which preferences requested	62 (16)	52 (22)	10 (7)
Exports eligible, but preferences not requested	3.7 (1)	3 (1)	0 (0)
Exports not eligible for preferences	184 (48)	62 (26)	122 (87)
Processed agricultural products			
Total exports to Japan	40.8	39.4	1.4
Exports duty free	36.7 (90)	36.2 (92)	0.5 (35)
Exports for which preferences requested	3.5 (9)	2.8 (7)	0.6 (44)
Exports eligible, but preferences not requested	0.3 (0.8)	0.3 (0.7)	0.1 (3.8)
Exports not eligible for preferences	0.3 (0.7)	0.1 (0.2)	0.2 (16.5)

Note: Numbers in parentheses are shares of exports for each category of agricultural exports.
Source: Calculated using data from Ministry of Finance, Japan.

African LDCs. This may reflect the structure of protection and preferences in Japan.

- For African LDCs, more than 50 percent of exports of basic agricultural products enter the Japanese market at zero duty MFN rates. Of the remaining exports to Japan, 23 percent are eligible for preferences, and 26 percent are excluded from preferences. For other LDCs, only 5 percent of exports of basic agricultural products enter duty free under zero percent MFN rates, just 7 percent are eligible for preferences and 87 percent are excluded from preferences.

- Exports of processed products to Japan are a very small share for African LDCs and are non-existent for non-African developing countries.

Within the overall figures for each preference-granting market, there are large variations across countries. For example, while the value of exports eligible for preferences exceeds 20 percent of total exports to the European Union for non-LDC African countries, it is less than 20 percent for 11 LDC African countries and higher than 80 percent for 11 other LDC African countries. There are also important differences across schemes for the same country. For example, 90 percent of Guinea-Bissau's exports to the European Union are eligible for preferences, yet none of its current exports to the United States receive preferences because the exports are subject to an MFN rate of zero. For Mozambique, by contrast, 97 percent of exports to the European Union and 86 percent of exports to the United States are eligible for preferences.

There are also substantial variations across countries in their use of available preferences. For example, in 2002, only 10 percent of Ethiopia's exports to the European Union that were eligible

for preferences made use of those preferences, while 85 percent of eligible exports to the United States did. Botswana used 99 percent of available preferences in the European Union but only 22 percent of those in the United States.

The Value of Preferences

An estimate of the value of trade preferences to the exporting countries was also calculated, using the amount of exports actually receiving preferences and the margin of preference to derive the tariff revenue that would have been paid without preferences. This overstates the actual transfers to developing countries because some of the rent will be acquired by importers in the preference-granting country, especially if there is a single buyer, and because of the administrative costs incurred by exporters, such as compliance with rules of origin.[8]

Average transfers to LDCs under AGOA and the GSP amount to less than 1 percent of their agricultural exports to the United States in 2002 (figure 4.1). For most countries, preferences have a negligible impact under the current structure of exports. Preferences of this magnitude will not encourage additional investment in these countries and will do little to mitigate the high transaction costs these countries

FIGURE 4.1 The Value of Preferences Requested under GSP and AGOA Programs of the United States, as a Share of Agricultural Export to the United States (percent)

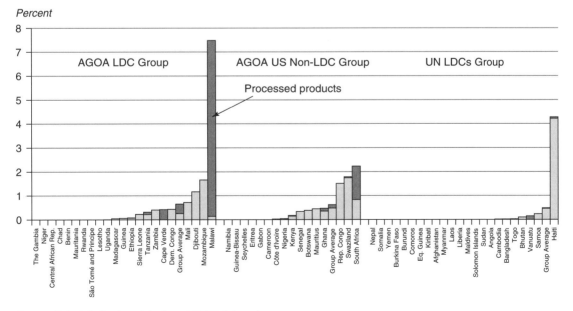

Source: Calculated using data from USITC dataweb.

face in accessing world markets. Malawi may be an exception. It receives a transfer equivalent to just over 7 percent of the value of exports to the United States, thanks largely to exports of processed products (mainly tobacco). Haiti is the only other LDC to receive significant preferences. It is granted more favorable treatment than the GSP under the Caribbean Basin Initiative, mainly for exports of tropical fruits such as mangoes. Preferences for non-LDCs in the United States are also small, with the average transfer being less than 1 percent of the value of exports to the United States.

Under the Cotonou and GSP preference schemes, the highest transfers go to non-LDCs, mainly as rents on sugar exports (figure 4.2). Mauritius, for example, is a major beneficiary receiving transfers in 2002 equivalent to more than 52 percent of the value of its agricultural exports to the European Union in that year. The value of preferences for sugar accounted for more than 30 percent of the value of exports for Fiji, the Republic of Congo, Swaziland, and a number of Caribbean countries. Among LDCs, preferences on sugar resulted in substantial transfers to Burkina Faso, Malawi, and Mozambique.

While transfers to a small number of LDCs under the Cotonou Agreement are substantial, the average transfer across all LDC beneficiaries

amounts to 6 percent of the value of their exports to the European Union. A large number of countries receive little or no benefit from EU preferences on agricultural products. For 10 of the LDCs, including Chad, Niger, and Rwanda, the value of EU preferences amounts to less than 2 percent of the value of exports.

As with the U.S. and EU programs, Japanese preferences for a few countries under the GSP program in 2002 are substantial, primarily for fish products (figure 4.3). For the majority of LDCs, however, transfers due to preferences are zero. Only 6 of the 46 LDCs receive a transfer greater than 1 percent of the value of agricultural exports to Japan in 2002.

Preferences and Export Diversification

A key problem for the least-developed countries has been their export reliance on a small number of agricultural commodities. This export concentration leaves them vulnerable to external shocks and the downward trend in commodity prices. Preferences could provide incentives for investment in sectors in which countries have a comparative advantage but that are not being exploited because of difficulties in accessing export markets.

FIGURE 4.2   The Value of Preferences Requested under Cotonou and GSP Programs of the EU, as a Share of Agricultural Export to the EU
(percent)

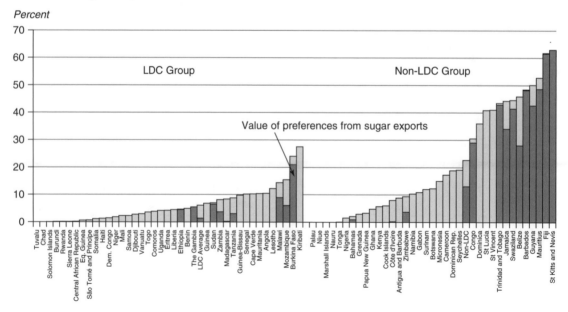

Source: Calculated using data from EU Commission.

FIGURE 4.3   The Value of Preferences for LDCs under the GSP Program of Japan, as a Share of Agricultural Export to Japan
(percent)

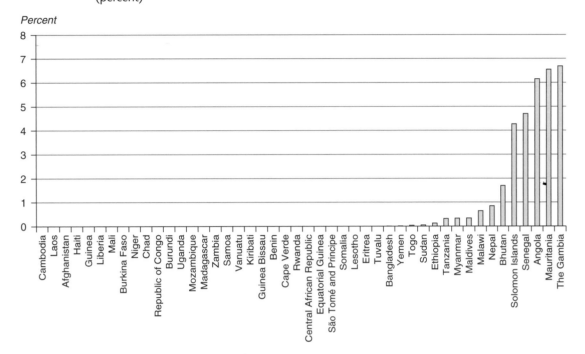

Source: Calculated using data from Ministry of Finance, Japan.

Preferences have done little to increase the diversification of agricultural exports. Only 4 of the 38 countries eligible for preferences under AGOA have significantly diversified their exports of agricultural products over the last 20 years (Ghana, Nigeria, South Africa, and Tanzania). For the other 34 countries, five or fewer products accounted for more than 90 percent of their agricultural exports in both 1982 and 2002.[9] The same pattern holds for African exports to the European Union. In 1982, for 37 of the 44 African ACP countries, five or fewer products accounted for more than 90 percent of exports to the European Union. By 2002 only two of these countries had diversified their exports to the European Union to reduce the importance of the main five export products. None of the LDCs had diversified exports to Japan. In 2002 the five top products accounted for 90 percent or more of every country's exports.

Much of this failure to stimulate export diversification likely results from several features of the programs. The uncertain duration of the preferences granted, the exclusion of many products with the largest preference margins, and the inadequacy of preference margins for making investments in new activities attractive, given the high transaction costs of operating in the least-developed countries. Also

possibly contributing are the administrative rules governing the granting of preferences, described below. However, the main factor constraining diversification is likely to be the poor domestic investment climate in most of the beneficiary countries.

Constraints on Preferences and Diversification: Rules of Origin

Rules of origin are essential to ensure that preferences are granted only to exporters from eligible countries. The nature of the rules of origin, however, are a key element determining the extent to which countries are able to take advantage of the preferences available to them. For a product produced in a single stage or wholly obtained in one country, origin is relatively easy to establish. Primary agricultural products typically fall into this category. Proof that the product was produced or obtained in the preferential trade partner is normally sufficient. The process of proving conformity, however, may incur costs that reduce the value of the preferences.

For processed manufactured products, rules of origin stipulate how much or what kind of domestic processing must take place. The U.S. GSP scheme has a value-added requirement of 35 percent for all products. The U.S. scheme also allows for cumulation between selected countries, so that value added in those countries can be counted toward the overall value-added requirement for the product exported to the United States. AGOA permits such cumulation among all Sub-Saharan preference trade partners. In practice, many processed food products are excluded from the GSP and AGOA.

EU rules of origin are product specific and sometimes complex. Some products require a change of tariff heading, some have a value-added requirement, and some are subject to a specific manufacturing process requirement. In some cases these methods are combined. For certain industrial products, a choice among alternative methods is permitted—for example, either a change of tariff heading or satisfaction of a value-added requirement. This more flexible approach is not available for agricultural products.

For many products, the EU rules require a change of chapter, which is even more restrictive than a change of heading. Some of the EU rules exclude some changes in tariff classification by proscribing the use of certain imported inputs. For example, the rule of origin for bakery products such as bread, pastry, cakes, and biscuits requires a change of tariff heading except for any heading in chapter 11 (products of the milling industry), meaning that bakery products cannot use imported flour, a restrictive requirement for countries without a competitive milling industry. Products that include sugar have to demonstrate that the value of any imported sugar does not exceed a certain proportion of the price of the product.

While the European Union has sought to harmonize the processing requirements for each product across preference programs, a number of general rules vary substantially across different schemes, particularly those on the nature and extent of cumulation and the tolerance rule. There are important differences in the rules of origin among the Everything but Arms program, the GSP, and the Cotonou Agreement. For example, the Cotonou Agreement permits full cumulation. The GSP has more limited partial cumulation that can take place only within four regional groupings (Association of South-East Asian Nations, Central American Common Market, the Andean Community, and South Asian Association for Regional

Cooperation), but it excludes the ACP countries. Hence LDC members of the ACP that are eligible to export to the EU under Everything but Arms may often prefer to continue exporting under the Cotonou Agreement because of the more liberal rules of origin (Brenton 2003).

The rules of origin for the Japanese GSP require a change of tariff heading to demonstrate that a substantial transformation has taken place, although there is a list of products for which specific criteria are defined. Thus, for example, flour or similar products cannot be produced from imported grains. Cumulation is allowed among a limited group of Southeast Asian countries (Indonesia, Malaysia, Philippines, Thailand, and Vietnam).

An important feature of these preferential trade schemes is the requirement of direct consignment or direct transport. This stipulates that goods for which preferences are requested be shipped directly to the destination market. If they are in transit through another country, documentary evidence may be required to show that the goods remained under the supervision of the customs authorities of the country of transit, did not enter the domestic market there, and did not undergo operations other than unloading and reloading. In practice, it can be very difficult to obtain the necessary documentation from foreign customs.

In general, preferences are more effective when the rules of origin are simple and easy to apply. Further, the value of OECD (Organisation for Economic Cooperation and Development) preferences would be enhanced by greater uniformity in the way given products are treated in the different schemes. Thus a product that qualifies for preferences in one market should be granted preferential access to all other OECD countries. The WTO would be an appropriate forum for discussing and agreeing on a common set of rules of origin.

Preference Erosion by Multilateral Tariff Reductions

As multilateral tariff reductions are negotiated at the WTO, the margins of preference available to developing countries decline. Whether developing countries lose overall from multilateral liberalization depends on the extent of negotiated tariff reductions on products that currently receive preferential access and on the importance of products excluded from preferences or not using current preferences. The analysis here makes clear that the impact of reducing tariffs will vary substantially across countries but that most countries will not lose because they currently gain very little from preferences.[10] For the countries that receive substantial transfers from preferences, the commodity impact of tariff liberalization is crucial. For example, significant reductions in EU tariffs and internal prices for sugar would have a significant impact on a number of countries, especially if existing quotas were maintained.

The impact of reducing tariffs on products excluded from preferences will tend to be positive for the least-developed countries. These products have very high tariffs, and a reduction in protection would stimulate exports from countries with a comparative advantage in these products. Whether the least-developed countries would gain more from the inclusion of these very-high-duty products under preferences and the continuation of high levels of protection is difficult to assess, but the uncertain duration of many nonreciprocal schemes and the difficulties of satisfying rules of origin are likely to limit the value of preferences on these products.

Wainio and Gibson (2003) estimate that, as a group, countries receiving nonreciprocal trade preferences on agricultural products in the United States would gain from multilateral trade liberalization because losses from preference erosion would be exceeded by gains on products on which these countries pay the MFN tariff. Within this group, a country will tend to lose on balance from multilateral liberalization only if more than 80 percent of its exports to the United States receive preferences, while it would tend to gain if less than 50 percent of its exports benefit from preferences. For countries in between, whether there was a net gain or a loss from reducing MFN tariffs would depend on the particular tariff-cutting formula and the structure of exports.

Conclusion

In principle, trade preferences can assist development if they provide temporary margins of preference to enable industries to adjust and compete more effectively in global markets. Multilateral trade liberalization contributes to this outcome by ensuring that preferences have a short "half-life"[11] and that inefficient, high-cost industries with entrenched lobbies do not constrain flexibility and adjustment. Multilateral liberalization is also important for limiting the long-term trade diverting impact of preferences on other countries (typically these will be other developing countries).

In practice, only a small number of countries receive large transfers as a result of preferences in OECD markets. The values of preferences are largest in the EU market, driven by a narrow range of products and the very high EU price for sugar. In a few countries, such as Mauritius, preferences appear to have contributed to a relatively strong economic performance and economic diversification (Subramanian 2001). In other countries, even though preferences have led to large transfers, domestic industries have experienced rising costs and declining output and have accumulated large debts.[12] Nevertheless, the majority of beneficiaries of U.S., EU, and Japanese preferences have experienced little or no impact. Preferences have done nothing to stimulate the export of a broader range of products.

The key issues for improving trade preference schemes are as follows:

- How to enhance the value of preferences under current export structures, which would be facilitated by
  - Extending coverage to all agricultural products.
  - Liberalizing the rules of origin and simplifying the process of certifying compliance.
  - Removing sources of uncertainty concerning product and country coverage and the duration of preference schemes.
- How to strengthen the impact of existing preferences on developing countries, which would be facilitated by
  - Improving the domestic investment environment.
  - Addressing the internal barriers that raise the costs of trade for developing countries—inadequate and high-price transport services, reflecting lack of infrastructure and lack of effective competition in many countries, inefficient and corrupt customs practices, and lack of trade-supporting financial and telecommunications services.[13]

- How to ensure that preferences do not interfere with multilateral liberalization, which would be facilitated by
  - Developing mechanisms for helping countries that incur significant losses from preference erosion adjust.
  - Not using fear of preference erosion to maintain high levels of protection in industrial countries.

The challenge is to find preference schemes that complement the domestic reforms that developing countries must undertake to improve the returns to exports without stifling diversification and multilateral trade liberalization. Trade preferences are not a panacea for success but rather should be seen as just one part of a strategy to boost export-led growth and development. Realizing the full potential of trade also requires improving customs clearance procedures, reducing the costs of transportation and other trade-related services, ending corruption, and removing other disincentives to investment. Addressing these issues will permit broad-based export growth and will ensure that as preferences decline with multilateral liberalization, the economic structure needed for continued export expansion is in place. The Integrated Framework for Trade-Related Technical Assistance, when incorporated into poverty reduction strategies, provides a vehicle for addressing these issues, defining appropriate policy responses, and mobilizing relevant resources.

Notes

1. By providing a stimulus to increased trade, preferences can lead to lower transportation costs, which in turn lead to a further trade impact. Hummels and Skiba (2002) discuss how economies of scale in transportation can lead to a virtuous circle involving increased trade and lower transportation costs.

2. For example, the share of Sub-Saharan African countries in U.S. imports of agricultural products fell from 4.3 percent in 1982 to 2.5 percent in 2002. Similarly, the share of the African, Caribbean, and Pacific countries in total EU agricultural imports fell from 11.7 percent in 1982 to 7.8 percent in 2002. And the share of low-income countries in Japanese imports fell from 1.2 percent to 0.5 percent over the same period. More systematic empirical studies of the impact of trade preferences are rare and seldom separate out the impact on agricultural products.

3. The rate of utilization of preferences is the proportion of exports from developing countries to the European Union, the United States, and Japan that are recorded at the border as requesting preferences. Therefore, the underutilization of preferences (the fact that some exports do not request and therefore are not granted the preferential access for which they are in principle eligible) cannot reflect the inability to meet other requirements to access the relevant market, such as health and safety or sanitary requirements or deficiencies in their infrastructure, as is sometimes suggested. Lack of infrastructure might explain a muted response from trade to preferences but cannot explain why, at the border, some products that are eligible for preferences do not request those preferences.

4. For a comprehensive description of U.S. preferences for agricultural products, see Wainio and Gibson (2003)

5. Many of the tariff quota products are also subject to safeguard measures. Once quantities exceed the quota, exports to the United States are subject to both the high MFN duty and an additional, often high, safeguard duty.

6. A number of lines shown as AGOA products are likely to be economically meaningless. These are lines that refer to General Note 15 of the U.S. tariff schedule, which excludes from the in-quota quantity for a product subject to a tariff rate quota and to safeguard amounts that are imported by the U.S. government, by individuals in quantities of less than five kilograms, and samples for exhibition or for display at trade fairs. If such products are imported from AGOA countries, they are eligible for zero duty access. In the 2002 tariff schedule, 85 agricultural lines designated as AGOA products referred to General Note 15, or 14 percent of AGOA-designated agricultural tariff lines. In 2002 imports from AGOA countries were recorded in only one of these categories, and the amount was negligible. For a more accurate representation of the impact of AGOA, these lines are excluded from the analysis.

7. This clause was initially discussed in the context of combating fraud. However, this is not made clear in the legislation, and it appears that the clause could be invoked in more general circumstances.

8. The value of preferences will also be overstated for products for which there are no nonpreferential imports and for which the duty exceeds the prohibitive level—the gap between the internal price in the importing country and the world price.

9. The analysis was undertaken at the 5-digit level of the Standard International Trade Classification (SITC). There are around 250 agricultural products in this classification. The 34 countries include 3 that did not export any agricultural products to the United States in 2002.

10. Stevens (2003) notes that the flip side of the preference coin is agricultural protectionism in OECD countries, which has led to cheaper imports for African countries of a number of agricultural products, such as cereals. There are two impacts: preferences increase export receipts to pay for imports, and OECD protectionism reduces the prices of those imports. Even countries that gain little from preferences may lose from multilateral trade reform.

11. Taken from Schott (2004), who presented the notion in terms of free trade agreements.

12. Mitchell (2004) shows that the sugar industry in the Caribbean is dominated by high-cost producers, few of which can profitably export to the European Union, even at four times world prices. Sugar production has been declining, and efforts to diversify away from sugar have generally been unsuccessful. A serious problem in a number of countries is the high level of accumulated debt of the state-owned sugar industries, which can amount to a substantial proportion of gross domestic product.

13. These issues are highlighted in diagnostic trade studies undertaken in the context of the Integrated Framework for Trade-Related Technical Assistance for the least-developed countries (see www.integratedframework.org).

References

Brenton, P. 2003. "Integrating the Least Developed Economies into the World Trading System: The Current Impact of EU Preferences under Everything but Arms." *Journal of World Trade* 37: 623–46.

Brenton, P., and H. Imagawa. 2004. "Rules of Origin, Trade and Customs." In J. Sokol and L. de Wulf, eds., *The Customs Modernisation Handbook*. Washington, D.C.: World Bank.

Hummels, D., and Alexandre Skiba. 2002. "A Virtuous Circle? Regional Tariff Liberalization and Scale Economies in Transport." Purdue University, West Lafayette, Ind., www.mgmt.purdue.edu/faculty/hummelsd.

McQueen, M. 1999. "After Lome IV: ACP-EU Trade Preferences in the 21st Century." *Intereconomics* 34: 223–32.

Mitchell, D. 2004. "Sugar in the Caribbean: Policies and Diversification Strategies to Cope with Declining Preferences." World Bank, Washington, D.C.

Ozden, C., and M. Olarreaga. 2003. "AGOA and Apparel: Who Captures the Tariff Rent in the Presence of Preferential Market Access?" World Bank, Washington, D.C.

Schott, J. 2004. "Free Trade Agreements: Boon or Bane of the World Trading System?" In J. Schott, ed., *Free Trade Agreements: US Strategies and Priorities*. Washington, D.C.: Institute for International Economics.

Stevens, C. 2003. "Agricultural Reform and Erosion of Preferences." Institute of Development Studies, Brighton, U.K.

Subramanian, A. 2001. "Mauritius: A Case Study." *Finance and Development* 38(4): 22–25.

Topp, V. 2001. "Trade Preferences: Are They Helpful in Advancing Economic Development in Poor Countries?" Australian Bureau of Agricultural and Resource Economics, Canberra.

UNCTAD. 2001. "Improving Market Access for LDCs." UNCTAD/DITC/TNCD/4, http://www.unctad.org/en/docs//poditctncd4.en.pdf.

Wainio, J., and P. Gibson. 2003. "The Significance of Nonreciprocal Trade Preferences for Developing Countries." Paper presented at the International Conference "Agricultural Policy Reform and the WTO: Where Are We Heading?" June 23–26, Capri, Italy.

5

EXPERIENCE WITH DECOUPLING AGRICULTURAL SUPPORT

John Baffes and Harry de Gorter

For most of the past half century industrial countries have had high levels of agricultural protection, provided by import tariffs, quantitative restrictions, and domestic subsidies. Among the many claimed objectives of these policies, boosting the income of small family farms is by far the most frequently cited (Winters 1989–90). Because most of this support is based on current output, input use, and prices, it also induces overproduction. Given the weight of industrial countries in the global trading system, the aggregate effect of such support is to depress world commodity prices, reducing the export shares of countries that do not protect their agricultural sectors. Such support is costly and often goes to unintended recipients, thus exacerbating rather than eliminating the presumed income inequalities that justified support in the first place.

Considering the harmful effects of such support on world markets and the mismatch between stated objectives and ultimate outcomes, its outright elimination is sometimes advocated. But societies have the right to transfer income to groups as they deem necessary. Perhaps the only effective way to achieve socially acceptable and politically feasible reform is to decouple payments from current production levels, input use, and prices. Thus, the relevant question is how support can be given without creating negative effects for the rest of the world—how to increase farmers' incomes without distorting production and consumption.

This chapter analyzes the experience with decoupling, making a clear distinction between decoupling that replaces domestic support and decoupling that replaces border support. It reviews a number of one-time buyouts, the best form of decoupling, and looks at the externalities of decoupling, especially for middle- and low-income countries, in reducing poverty, instituting land title reform, and providing credit.

What Is Decoupling?

Decoupling has different meanings to economists, policymakers, and trade negotiators. Some see it as a transition mechanism to a fully competitive sector.

The authors would like to thank Ataman Aksoy, John Beghin, Uri Dadush, Gaston Gohou, Bernard Hoekman, John Nash, and Marcelo Olarreaga for helpful comments on earlier drafts. Comments received from the participants at the 2003 Annual World Bank Conference on Development Economics–Europe and several World Bank seminars are greatly appreciated.

Others see it as another support program, with fewer production- and trade-distorting effects. Some use decoupling only to refer to programs for transferring income to producers; others use the term much more broadly, to include, for example, programs to improve the environment. Sometimes decoupling is assessed according to the policy's long-run impact on output through such factors as uncertainty, investment, and expectations.

Decoupling was discussed in the literature as early as 1945, when the American Farm Economic Association announced 18 awards for papers on "a price policy for agriculture, consistent with economic progress, that will promote adequate and more stable income from farming." Nicholls and Johnson (1946)—recipients of the first- and second-place awards—summarized the main findings of the award-wining papers. Several recommendations closely resembled decoupled support. For example (p. 281),

> Cochrane presents a special formula for progressively smaller income payments for aiding producers in adjusting their operations from a support level to a free market situation. These declining payments would be based on production during 1939–41, so that the producer would not be "tied to commodity in surplus to receive a payment benefit." Thus, he could shift to some other product during the payment period without losing the specified payments.

Perhaps the first analyst to explicitly advocate decoupled support in U.S. agriculture was Swerling (1959). Two characteristics of Swerling's proposal are especially interesting. First, he advocated a safety net mechanism for agriculture, similar to safety nets in other sectors of the economy (such as unemployment insurance). Second, he proposed linking the benefits of the decoupled support to income declared in tax returns during the recent past (not to historical production or area). Specifically (pp. 179–80), he wrote:

> Removal of this price stimulus is long overdue.... An income-insurance plan for farm-operators [should be in place] that include[s] the following elements: (1) ... benefits will be related to income experience of the particular individual during the recent past; (2) the purpose would not be to support income at artificially high levels but to prevent a severe temporary decline in individual income; (3) the right to benefits would attach to the person, not to farm land or the farm enterprise, and would accordingly not be transferable; (4) the benefit to be enjoyed by any individual would not exceed a modest maximum; (5) benefits would not be conditioned upon the production of particular commodities or even upon continued employment in agriculture....

Another early decoupling proposal was put forward by Nash in Europe (1961, p. 188):

> Instead of obstructing the withdrawal of farmers from an industry which cannot adequately reward them, ... an unconditional payment [could be made] to all those at present engaged in farming, or to those of them deemed to be in need of compensation, calculated by the reference to the difference between the incomes now earned under the protective system and those capable of being earned under a system of free market prices. An annuity calculated in this way and payable for life to all engaged in farming, but not transferable to their successors, would, in theory at least, make it possible to bring the protective system to an end while fully making good the loss of income to its present beneficiaries. There is no doubt that compensation of this kind is feasible.

The proceedings of the workshop "Decoupling: The Concept and Its Future in Canada" contains numerous definitions of decoupling (Finkle and Cameron 1990). Consider the following two rather contrasting views. Van Donkersgoed (1988, p. 40), of the Christian Farmers Foundation of Ontario, defined decoupling as "a program in which eligibility is not linked to production, the production potential of resources or the production effort of a farm entrepreneur; rather eligibility is linked to stewardship farming practices, marketing, the maintenance of rural communities, diversified ownership of the assets of production, moderate-sized family enterprises and other rural, non-production valuables that add to the quality of Canadian life." Spriggs and Sigurdson (1988, p. 93), in contrast, simply stated: "In fact, a program to eliminate subsidies would be the ultimate in decoupling. It is the only truly decoupled program that there is."

Cahill (1997, p. 351) defines as fully decoupled from production a policy that "does not influence production decisions of farmers receiving payments, and that permits free market determination of prices (facing all farmers, whether or not receiving income support)." A policy is effectively fully decoupled if "the provision of the compensatory payment package results in production that, for any crop, does not exceed that level that would exist without compensation." The Organisation for Economic Co-operation and Development (OECD 2000a) defines decoupling in a similar way.

Hennessy (1998) includes as decoupling payments triggered by ex post market or production conditions, as long as the payment level is not conditioned on an individual's specific level of production. Disaster relief measures, for example, would be considered decoupled because they are not affected by the individual's level of production.

Goodwin and Mishra (2002) argue that a fully decoupled payment must be fixed and guaranteed and thus is not influenced by ex post realizations of market conditions (such as low prices or area yields). This is the narrowest definition because neither payments nor the rules of eligibility and the base criteria can be changed. If a time limit is added to this definition, then decoupling simply implies a number of annual payments to producers. Where financial markets function efficiently, these bonds can be converted into a single payment. In such a setting, decoupling would consist of an administrative decision to remove distortions followed by a single payment—a radical policy initiative. In fact, a number of analysts have advocated a fundamental reform of the European Union's Common Agricultural Policy (CAP), with the last step consisting of payment of a bond (see, for example, Beard and Swinbank 2001, Swinbank and Tangermann 2001, and Tangermann 1991).

The Politics of Decoupling

Politicians are reluctant to subsume all agricultural policies into a universal social welfare program, including job retraining and the like, even though these types of programs to help small farmers would be ideal and truly compatible with World Trade Organization (WTO) policy in being minimally trade distorting (as Swerling originally suggested in 1959). It is very difficult to end farm subsidy programs, however; there is always a bias to maintain current policies because politicians lose more support if they take away subsidies than they gain if they introduce new ones. Furthermore, governments like to concentrate the benefits of subsidies and diffuse the costs to as many people as possible in order to maximize political support. And small groups are better able to organize and control free riders. All this appears to make it inevitable that governments will favor commodity- or sector-based policies over all other forms of agricultural support. So, fully decoupled payments and one-time buyouts, even more than universal programs, have the political disadvantage of not being able to continue to favor incumbent farmers. They also look like corporate welfare, whereas trade barriers and price supports reduce visible taxpayer costs and hide the fact that large farms get most of the transfers. Politicians also lack the commitment mechanism to keep such policies in place—politicians are tempted to reintroduce support later in its original form or with new distorting programs.

Under many current systems, a complex web of policies, including payments not to produce, subsidies, and production controls, help to obfuscate the policies' true nature in terms of who benefits and to what extent. Another class of subsidy programs, the whole farm insurance program used in Canada and the revenue stabilization programs used in the past, has the economic advantage of not singling out specific sectors. And because all farms are eligible, taxpayer constraints dilute the per farm benefits thereby reducing the political support for such programs. Thus Canada has eliminated perfectly functioning revenue insurance programs, and other countries are not rushing to adopt wholesale farm income insurance programs.

Politicians and farm lobbies capitalize on the fact that most voters know of at least one farmer, often a family member, who experienced severe adjustments in the past 50 years. Thus it is much easier to maintain the status quo of subsidies in agriculture. Politicians also play on insecurities related to food self-sufficiency in case of war, food safety issues arising because of new technologies and genetically modified organisms, and the multifunctional benefits of farms in providing landscape amenities and rural livelihoods.

The Economics of Decoupling

Decoupling can be viewed as two distinct transition mechanisms: one replacing domestic support and one replacing border measures. The key variable driving this distinction is the source of financing for the original support measures: consumers, taxpayers, or a combination.

Replacing domestic support measures such as production subsidies with decoupled support is straightforward in the small country case and can be shown to be Pareto improving. Instead of providing output-based subsidies, the government makes lump-sum payments to producers based on some historical criteria without any constraint or requirement on the current use of their resources. Under the lump-sum scheme, producers can receive higher payments because welfare losses (the so-called Harberger triangles) disappear. Taxpayers can also be better off if part of the efficiency gains is translated into lower taxes. Because both producers and taxpayers can be made better off, decoupling in the production subsidy case is clearly a Pareto-improving move.

Decoupling in the case of an import tariff, however, is more complicated as it involves eliminating tariffs, raising additional taxes, and distributing the tax revenues to producers. Producers are no worse off (they receive the same amount of support), consumers are better off (they pay lower prices), but taxpayers are worse off because they lose the tariff revenue and must finance the decoupled support. Assuming that welfare losses arising from border measures are higher than welfare losses arising from domestic subsidies, decoupling of border measures is welfare improving. It is not a Pareto improvement, however. Furthermore, while the removal of the import tariff implies welfare gains, introduction of the tax to finance decoupled support implies welfare losses. Alston and Hurd (1990, p. 155) contend the following:

> Currently it is fashionable to argue for "decoupling" farm programs in the sense that income transfers should be achieved with minimal consequences for commodity markets. Along with the benefits from transparency, the benefits

from decoupling may be illusory. The issue here is whether the costs of distortions in commodity markets are necessarily greater than the costs of distortions introduced elsewhere in the economy to finance "decoupled" transfers.

Moschini and Sckokai (1994) claim that the welfare losses of raising new taxes to finance decoupling are unlikely to be larger than the welfare gains from decoupling. Beghin, Bureau, and Park (2003) estimate that in the Republic of Korea it costs taxpayers $1.61 for every $1 transferred to producers. Using a general equilibrium model, Parry (1999) finds that the efficiency cost of taxpayer-financed lump-sum transfers to agriculture equals 27 percent of the amount of the income transfer.

Since most of the support is at the border, decoupling is likely to be a complicated exercise with mixed outcomes. Although the costs of taxpayer-financed programs are shown to be significant, welfare gains depend on how decoupled programs are financed. But the general result from the public finance literature is that trade taxes have much higher inefficiencies relative to other forms of taxation or sources of revenue for farmers.

Experience with Broad Decoupling Attempts

Early attempts at decoupling failed. The 1949 Brannan Plan in the United States, which proposed cash payments to farmers whose overall income fell below a certain level, was defeated in the U.S. Congress. Similarly in Europe, the Mansholt Plan of 1968, which advocated support in order to finance mandatory retirement for older farmers, also failed.

The first attempt at decoupling came in the United States with the 1985 Farm Bill, which shifted the base of support from current yields to historical yields (see timeline in table 5.1). The European Union (EU) partially replaced intervention prices with direct payments following the Common Agricultural Policy reform of 1992. Mexico replaced price supports with direct payments in 1994 with the introduction of the National Program for Direct Assistance to Rural Areas (Programa de Apoyos Directos al Campo, or Procampo). The United States replaced deficiency payments with decoupled support in the 1996

TABLE 5.1   Chronology of Broader Decoupling and Recoupling Episodes, 1985–2004

Year	Country	Policy change
1985	United States	1985 Farm Bill introduces "frozen" government payment yields per acre.
1992	European Union	Mac Sharry reforms of the Common Agricultural Policy reduce price supports and introduce direct payments linked to historical area planted (with "frozen" government payments for the output per hectare) or number of animals (but farmers still need to produce to receive payments).
1994	Mexico	Procampo introduces payments based both on historical acres and yields up to 2008 with a phase-out of import barriers under the North American Free Trade Agreement, input subsidies, and activities of the state trading monopoly.
1996	United States	1996 Farm Bill eliminates target prices, replacing them with decoupled historical entitlements, the so-called production flexibility contract payments, to end in 2002.
1996	Mexico	Base acres can be switched to other crops or enterprises, and rural development policy is launched to foster productivity.
1998	United States	Emergency market loss assistance payments effectively reverse the 1996 Farm Bill.
2000	European Union	Agenda 2000 extends, deepens, and widens the Mac Sharry reforms.
2001	Turkey	Direct income support program reduces some administered prices and input subsidies. Only minor changes in border policies.
2002	United States	2002 Farm Bill extends production flexibility contracts, formalizes emergency payments as countercyclical payments, adds new crops to production flexibility contracts program, allows base acres and payment yields to be updated, increases price supports for coupled subsidies, and introduces three new crops to the coupled subsidy program.
2002	Mexico	Target prices and input subsidies are reintroduced. Procampo remains largely unchanged.
2002	European Union	Mid-term review, resulting in June 2003 agreement to switch most direct payments to decoupled payments, with entitlements sold with or without land; level of payments and some support prices to decline in 2005–07.
2004	European Union	Decoupled payments are introduced for the so-called Mediterranean products (cotton, olive oil, and tobacco).

Source: Authors' compilations.

Farm Bill. More recently, Turkey replaced some price support and input subsidies with direct payments. In addition to broad decoupling programs, there have been numerous one-time buyouts, including New Zealand's exit grant in 1984, the buyout of Canada's grain transportation subsidy in 1995, and the buyout of the U.S. peanut marketing quota under the 2002 Farm Bill.

Decoupling Efforts in the United States

The budgetary outlays for most U.S. commodity programs are authorized by Congress (and subsequently approved by the president) every few years through farm bills. There have been 20 such bills since the first one in 1929. The central feature of the New Deal farm programs of the 1930s was price supports achieved through taxpayer-funded production subsidies and supply controls (acreage set-asides, accumulation, maintenance, and disposal of public stocks). Payments were based on the difference between the target price set by the government and the higher of the market price or the price at which the government would value crops used as collateral for loans made by a public corporation. The total payment was equal to the yield per acre multiplied by a farm's eligible payment acreage (the amount of land devoted to cultivation of the crop

TABLE 5.2   Composition of Agricultural Support in the United States, 1986–88 to 1999–2001
(US$ millions)

Category	1986–88	1989–92	1993–95	1996–98	1999–2001
Value of production	113,537	168,615	184,239	199,990	192,417
Total support estimate	68,540	72,779	79,060	81,715	95,455
Producer support estimate	41,839	34,326	31,091	36,384	51,256
Market price support	19,533	17,825	16,969	17,864	18,662
Budgetary support	22,306	16,501	14,123	18,519	32,594
Output	2,919	510	241	1,644	9,285
Input use	6,516	6,574	6,003	6,088	6,877
Area	11,313	6,897	5,396	1,247	2,722
Historical entitlements	0	0	0	6,647	10,085
Input constraints	637	1,776	1,963	1,940	1,844
Overall farm income	912	743	520	954	1,780

Source: OECD database.

in question). This portfolio of policy instruments was the primary means of price support for the major field crops for decades until the 1980s.

The Food Security Act of 1985 set a new trend for major field crops by reducing the role of acreage set-asides and public stockholding and moving toward decoupling, with a "freeze" on payment yields (farmers were paid on the basis of fixed output per acre regardless of what was actually produced). Payment yield was established for each farm by the Department of Agriculture, based on average yields in 1981–85.

Acreage set-asides and public stockholding were largely abandoned by the mid-1990s and eliminated soon thereafter with the introduction of the Federal Agricultural Improvement and Reform (FAIR) Act in 1996. FAIR also banished the target price used in calculating deficiency payments but maintained the lower fixed price, called the loan rate, which had triggered public stock purchases in the past. In place of the links between support, prices, and production, production flexibility contract payments were introduced. Participating producers received payments in proportion to what they had received during 1990–95 or would have received had they been enrolled. These historical benefits were in turn determined by a farmer's historical production levels. Each participating producer received a fixed schedule of payments, which was to decline gradually through 2002. Although not specifically stated, it was implicitly assumed that the payments would end by 2002.

The effect of the 1996 Farm Bill on the structure of budgetary outlays is shown in table 5.2. It breaks the producer support estimate down into market price support (a measure of border protection) and budgetary support (a measure of domestic support). Budgetary support is further decomposed into support based on output and input use (considered as having a large impact on production and trade, or fully coupled support) and support based on area, historical entitlements, input constraints, and overall farm income (considered as having a smaller impact on production and trade, or partially decoupled support; for further details and definitions, see OECD 2000b).

Historical entitlements, which did not exist before 1996, represented more than a third of total budgetary support in 1996–98. They are exempt from disciplines in the WTO (they are in the Green Box; see chapter 3). Area payments declined from $5.4 billion in 1993–95 to $1.2 billion in 1996–98 and are also exempt from reduction commitments in the WTO (they are in the Blue Box). During these two periods, output payments under discipline in the WTO (in the Amber Box) also increased, from $0.2 billion to $1.6 billion, a reflection primarily of declining commodity prices and consequently increased loan rate payments.

Although payments were made on a crop-by-crop basis, planting was not required or restricted to any particular crop. Payments were tied to 85 percent of the fixed-base area (average of acres planted or prevented from being planted for covered crops of wheat, feed grains, rice, and cotton) and fixed-payment yields. Because the payments were independent of current production, farmers had far greater flexibility to make planting decisions (or to not plant at all). Farmers were free to allocate their land to any crops on the "contract acres" except fruits and vegetables, but they had to maintain their land in "agricultural use." Thus producers were to depend more heavily on the market and also bear greater risk from increased price variability.

The FAIR Act was meant to be a transition toward a new policy environment with a diminished government role in commodity markets. Commodity prices declined sharply in the late 1990s, however, triggering three major policy events that reversed much of what had been accomplished by the FAIR Act. First, emergency payments were introduced, approximately equal to 50 percent of decoupled payments in 1998 and 100 percent of decoupled payments in 1999, 2000, and 2001. These were designated as non-product-specific support and so escaped reduction under the de minimis proviso of the WTO. Second, when market prices fell below the loan rate, the government extended the marketing loan program by issuing loan deficiency payments, which had the same economic effects as the previous deficiency payment scheme. Third, the 2002 Farm Bill was introduced, increasing several loan rates, introducing three more crops into the loan rate scheme, and allowing base acres and payment yields to be updated and soybean acreage to be added to the base. The bill formalized the emergency payments into a new countercyclical scheme in which payments vary with price but not with quantity.

The emergency measures introduced in 1998 (and later the 2002 Farm Bill) changed the structure of the budgetary outlays considerably. Between 1996–98 and 1999–2001, historical entitlements increased by more than 50 percent (from $6.6 billion to $10.1 billion, area payments increased twofold, and payments based on output increased more than fivefold (see table 5.2), implying that support is less decoupled now than it was after 1996.

Decoupling Efforts in the European Union

The principal vehicle of support in the European Union has been the Common Agricultural Policy.

Following the Spaak Report of 1956, which suggested that agriculture requires special treatment, the Stresa Conference of 1958 outlined CAP's three guiding principles: free flow of agricultural commodities within the common market, preference to member states, and common financing. CAP, formally put in place in 1962, had multiple objectives: increase agricultural production, ensure a fair standard of living for the agricultural community, stabilize markets, guarantee a regular supply of agricultural commodities, and ensure reasonable prices for consumers. The objectives were to be achieved through domestic price supports, export subsidies, and common trade barriers. The first and last objectives were fully met within a few years, but concerns were soon raised about excess production and the unsustainable level of CAP budgetary requirements if policies did not change.

Reform of the CAP was attempted in 1972, following the recommendations of the 1968 Mansholt Plan. The plan proposed, among other reforms, lump-sum transfers to 5 million farmers to retire them from farming and reduce active farmland by 5 percent. The Mansholt Plan, the first attempt to decouple, was never implemented.

The first major reinstrumentation of the CAP took place in 1992. The reform, known as the Mac Sharry reform after the EU's Commissioner for Agriculture, together with the Blair House Accord of the United States, paved the way for the signing of the Uruguay Round Agreement on Agriculture in 1994. For cereal, oilseed, and protein crops and for beef and veal, price supports provided by import levies or export refunds were reduced, and farmers were compensated with direct payments. For crops, payments were based on 85 percent of historical plantings (with a paid minimum area set-aside requirement, a further paid voluntary set-aside of up to 30 percent of historical area, and a base acre limit for payments set at the national or regional level). The area-payment rates varied by crop type, and the set-aside payments were initially higher but are now equal. The only requirement is the land had to be set aside or planted in crops or temporary grass. Small-scale farmers producing less than 92 tons of cereals annually are exempt from set-asides and receive "all cereals" payments irrespective of crop planted (representing 25 percent of area but 70 percent of farmers).

TABLE 5.3   Composition of Agricultural Support in the European Union, 1986–88 to 1999–2001
(US$ millions)

Category	1986–88	1989–92	1993–95	1996–98	1999–2001
Value of production	214,849	275,770	286,658	291,427	237,990
Total support estimate	109,654	138,927	133,050	129,328	112,628
Producer support estimate	93,719	117,097	116,519	111,966	99,343
Market price support	80,257	93,282	76,084	64,989	60,863
Budgetary support	13,446	23,327	40,279	47,468	38,693
Output	5,009	6,769	2,999	3,945	3,644
Input use	5,025	7,135	8,133	8,446	6,540
Area	2,701	6,987	24,326	29,419	24,733
Historical entitlements	0	559	1,466	1,007	597
Input constraints	711	1,877	3,356	4,650	3,178
Overall farm income	0	0	0	2	0

Source: OECD database.

Between 1986–88 and 1993–95, budgetary support in the EU increased threefold, from $13.4 billion to $40.3 billion, while border support declined from $80 billion to $76 billion (table 5.3). Most of the increase in budgetary support was attributable to area payments and, to a more limited extent, to historical entitlements and input constraints (designated Blue Box payments and so exempt from reductions in the WTO).

Following the 1992 reforms, the level of support remained unchanged, but its structure changed considerably. For example, while estimated producer support averaged $117 billion for 1989–92 and 1993–95, border protection support declined from $93 billion in 1989–92 to $76 billion in 1993–95. Support based on output declined from $7 billion to $3 billion, and area payments increased from $7 billion to $24 billion. Thus the 1992 CAP reform was a good step toward decoupling.

Under Agenda 2000, price support to crops declined, direct payments increased and were realigned across all crops, and reference yields were changed in some countries. A push toward more investment in rural development was also made. A large transformation has occurred away from border protection and input subsidies to direct payments. Total support has been declining, especially in grains and oilseeds. More than the increase in budgetary allocations, which remains moderate compared with other expenditures, the growing importance of rural development seems to follow from the official reference to it as the "second pillar of the CAP."

The European Union now has greater flexibility to overhaul any policy element in light of changes in market developments, costs, enlargement, WTO (and other) trade negotiations, food crises, and other pressure for reform. The budget for Agenda 2000 did not include any provision for extending direct payments to farmers in Eastern Europe, making reform a requirement. Meanwhile, the European Union has launched free trade negotiations with Mercosur, and it established the Everything but Arms initiative with low-income developing countries. Because Mercosur includes some major agricultural exporting nations and the Everything but Arms program will increase imports, especially for sugar, rice, and bananas, further reform of the CAP is necessary.

Recent food crises underline the need for reform, sometimes for more regulation and controls over production practices, including animal welfare. Against this background, the European Commission's midterm review of Agenda 2000 proposed a set of reforms that include further decoupling, continuing set-asides, and more cross-compliance rules with statutory environmental, food safety, and animal health and welfare standards.

Current EU compensatory payments still influence farmers' decisions on how much land to plant.

This results not only because farmers are obligated to produce cereals on the base acres to receive the payments, but also because area payments in the European Union are made on an aggregate, fixed-area basis that is set at the national or regional level. Individual farmers do not have a base area—just eligible acres for which they receive payments and have area set-asides. If the regional base area is exceeded, the per-unit subsidy is prorated downward proportionately for all farmers in the region.

Because the prorating occurs on the total area planted ex post, farmers have an incentive to over-plant in order to maximize their share of fixed budget outlays or to defend against share erosion due to overplanting by other producers. This means that the area payments are fully coupled to plantings because individual farmers are not penalized for their own decisions to overplant. Area payments with a national base area are therefore not a limit on total acres planted.

For EU cattle, the headage payments under "production-limiting" arrangements are anything but production limiting because farmers are allowed to keep more cattle than are eligible for payments, so there is no absolute production control, and the number of eligible animals is not limited to the number on farms prior to the introduction of payments in 1992. Where numbers of animals are below the maximum that could be claimed per farm, farmers have an incentive to expand their stock up to the limits on which payments are made. Thus incentives in the program have been to encourage initial expansion of animal numbers and then to lock production in at around the levels that are consistent with the maximum number of animals eligible for payments. Those numbers reflect the very high levels of support for several decades as well as the incentives inherent in the headage payments.

The CAP reform agreement of June 2003 requires decoupling at least 75 percent of payments in the arable sector and at least 50 percent in the beef and sheep sectors. Dairy premiums will be added into the single farm payment after 2007. The decoupled single farm payment will be based on average payments claimed over the three-year reference period, 2000–02, and will be paid per eligible hectare of land. Entitlements can be sold with or without land. Member states are offered some flexibility in the year they begin and in fully or partially decoupling within the limits for each sector. They may also give up to 10 percent of the payments for environmentally friendly farming and restrict entitlement trading within a region. All payments are to be reduced 3 percent in 2005, 4 percent in 2006, and 5 percent in 2007. Support prices will also decline. Payments will be conditional on compliance with various measures, including environmental and acreage set-asides.

Decoupling Efforts in Mexico

About a quarter of Mexico's population depends on agriculture, which contributes 5 percent to gross domestic product (GDP), down from 9 percent in the early 1980s. According to the OECD, total transfers to agriculture averaged $7 billion annually during 1999–2001, $5.7 billion of which went to producer support. This support corresponds to $1,000 per full-time farmer equivalent and $53 per hectare, both considerably lower than the OECD averages of $11,000 per farmer and $192 per hectare. About 29 percent of producer support went to maize, 21 percent to milk, and 13 percent to sugar.

Traditionally, Mexico's state agricultural enterprise, Conasupo (Compania Nacional de Subsistencias Populares), has been heavily involved in the marketing, transportation, storage, and processing of most agricultural commodities. Maize, beans, and wheat, by far the most important agricultural commodities, have been heavily subsidized through a system of guaranteed prices. The government also set prices, which were usually announced before planting decisions were made and were uniform across the country and across seasons. Conasupo bought unlimited quantities at the guaranteed prices. Hence, producers knew in advance the price they would receive and shifted production to crops with the highest degree of relative protection rather than with the highest profitability according to world prices. The poorest peasants did not benefit from guaranteed prices since they formally marketed little or none of their production.

In 1994 Mexico introduced Procampo, a decoupled support program to provide income support to grain and oilseed producers—about 90 percent of all Mexican farmers. Procampo replaced the old scheme of guaranteed prices. By supporting farmers' incomes rather than production of specific commodities, Procampo was expected to make production and trade less distorted. It is also distributionally more attractive than the earlier guaranteed price program because poor subsistence farmers are eligible for payments and there is a ceiling of 100 hectares on the amount of land that a single farmer can use to claim payments.

Government credibility became a major issue for Procampo. Initially, some producers did not believe that the government would actually implement the program. Fearing increased taxation, they underreported land allocated to eligible commodities. The government's turnaround, requiring that land be allocated to eligible crops after initially delinking payments from the current use of land, likely further discredited the government. (In 1996 the government increased the number of eligible crops.) The macroeconomic environment also played an important role. When Procampo was in the design phase, most commodities were highly protected, but the 1994 devaluation of the peso sharply reduced protection rates.

Despite these shortcomings the program has at least two features that improve income distribution (sometimes at the cost of more inefficiency). First, decoupled area payments are given for a minimum of one hectare, even if the actual size of a farm is less than one hectare. Second, land reforms allow small farms to rent approximately 10 percent of their land to larger farmers. These features can have a significant positive impact on income distribution compared with historical guaranteed prices.

Few small farmers benefited from that system because they were often net buyers, sold products at distress prices at harvest, or could not take advantage of price supports because they were not integrated with market price centers because of high transaction costs.

Just as the United States did, however, Mexico reintroduced its price support in 2002. New countercyclical payments, similar to those that the United States introduced in its 2002 Farm Bill, took effect with the 2002–03 marketing year. The payments were to equal the difference between the target price and the sum of the market price and Procampo payments. The payments would apply to eight commodities. In addition, a new common subsidized price for electricity used for agricultural production was introduced (estimated to cost $0.6 billion annually.)

The most visible change in Mexican agricultural policies has been the move from support based on input use to support based on historical entitlements, under Procampo (table 5.4). Border measures are still the dominant component of support, accounting for 64 percent of producer support during 1999–2001.

Mexico's decoupled payment program encountered several problems. The program was announced well in advance of the registration of eligible producers. The lag allowed many farmers to increase the amount of land in production of the eligible commodities and thus to increase their future payments. So rather than moving resources

TABLE 5.4   Composition of Agricultural Support in Mexico, 1986–88 to 1999–2001
(US$ millions)

Category	1986–88	1989–92	1993–95	1996–98	1999–2001
Value of production	15,412	25,209	26,186	27,033	30,328
Total support estimate	1,287	8,121	7,558	4,858	6,999
Producer support estimate	−266	5,718	5,060	3,190	5,694
Market price support	−1,710	4,025	2,918	1,495	3,625
Budgetary support	1,444	1,692	2,142	1,695	2,068
Output	1	26	52	4	110
Input Use	1,442	1,663	1,308	676	721
Area	0	3	6	62	61
Historical entitlements	0	0	776	925	1,112
Input constraints	0	0	0	0	0
Overall farm income	0	0	0	27	63

Source: OECD database.

to more efficient uses, the scheme, initially at least, moved more resources into production that was already inefficient. Moreover, because land rights among landowners, tenants, and sharecroppers were unclear, it was difficult to determine who was entitled to payment.

Decoupling Efforts in Turkey

The agricultural sector in Turkey employs 43 percent of the labor force and contributes 16 percent to GDP, down from 26 percent in 1980. Total agricultural support in Turkey reached an annual average of $9.7 billion during 1999–2001, $6.5 billion of it in direct producer support, according to the OECD (table 5.5). Of that amount, $5.1 billion was transferred through border measures, the dominant component of agricultural support in Turkey. At 5.1 percent of GDP, Turkey's agricultural support rate is the highest of all OECD countries and almost four times the OECD average of 1.3 percent. This support corresponds to $162 per hectare, compared with the $192 per hectare average for OECD. Sugar accounts for 13 percent of estimated producer support, milk for 11 percent, and wheat for 10 percent. The main policy instruments for agricultural support have been border measures, administered prices, input subsidies, and budgetary payments. With a per capita GDP of a little over $3,000, this support imposes considerable budgetary strains on the economy.

Responding to the high cost of support and its distortionary effects, Turkey embarked on a major agricultural policy reform program in 2001 with World Bank assistance (World Bank 2001). A main component of the reform was to replace administered prices and input subsidies with annual direct income support payments. In addition, farmers were granted a one-time payment to cover the cost of transition from overproduced and highly subsidized commodities to other commodities.

Income support payments were set at $100 per hectare, but even this low level of transfer implied an eventual annual expenditure of $1.9 billion. The upper limit, initially set at 20 hectares, was raised to 50 hectares in 2002. As in Mexico, to allow small subsistence farmers (who otherwise received no support) to benefit from the program, a minimum payment was set for farmers cultivating below a certain threshold.

A number of hard choices had to be made following the decision to implement direct income support payments. A key decision related to records (as was the case in Mexico). A pilot program was set up in several districts in four provinces to test two methods of developing a registry for producers. One method, applied in two provinces, used the existing land registry records. A second method, applied in the other two provinces, was based on certifications by the chief of the village, the council, and the local farmers associations. Payments were

TABLE 5.5 **Composition of Agricultural Support in Turkey, 1986–88 to 1999–2001**
(US$ millions)

Category	1986–88	1989–92	1993–95	1996–98	1999–2001
Value of production	18,343	26,859	29,158	34,068	29,458
Total support estimate	3,092	7,212	6,027	10,705	9,649
Producer support estimate	2,779	6,127	4,675	7,791	6,522
Market price support	1,884	4,784	2,712	5,710	5,093
Budgetary support	895	1,344	1,962	2,081	1,429
Output	11	30	242	104	337
Input Use	885	1,314	1,720	1,978	957
Area	0	0	0	0	0
Historical entitlements	0	0	0	0	136
Input constraints	0	0	0	0	0
Overall farm income	0	0	0	0	0

Source: OECD database.

made on a per hectare basis in two installments for up to two hectares.

While the pilot benefited 9,681 farmers including many small farmers, at a cost of $2.3 million, numerous problems were encountered during implementation. Land registries contained unclear descriptions, shared titles did not specify the amount of land that each person owned, and many landowners who had inherited their land did not possess deeds. Registration procedures were also unclear, and various "producer certificates" were issued without uniform standards. Many share-croppers were declared ineligible for participation because they lacked official documents. There were also cases of false claims, for nonfarm land or land not in agricultural use.

Other problems were related to the design and implementation of the pilot. Farmers received inadequate information about the program, and consequently many failed to apply for benefits (especially in remote villages). The agencies involved in the pilot also received inadequate training and information. And farmers were not given enough time to apply for the program.

Experience with One-Time Buyouts

In addition to broad decoupling attempts, countries have conducted numerous one-time buyouts in the last two decades. These buyouts have been much more successful than the broader decoupling efforts.

The 2002 U.S. Peanut Quota Buyout

The U.S. peanut program goes back to 1934, when peanut producers agreed to reduce their acreage in return for payments. The program failed to reduce output and was revised in 1941 by introducing individual acreage allotments and penalties for farmers who exceeded the allotments. The allotments were not enforced, however. The Agricultural Act of 1949 established support prices for peanuts, and until 1978 all peanuts from approved allotments were guaranteed the support price. The program again ran into financial difficulties primarily because of the introduction of high-yielding varieties. Beginning in 1978 peanut quotas were set annually and producers received support for quota peanuts only. During 1979–82 farmers had to have

both quantity and acreage allotments to be eligible for payments. The acreage allotment was abandoned in 1982. Quantity quotas were tradable, with some exceptions. Imports were banned.

The program again ran into trouble as the costs of the program grew enormously. Peanut manufacturers pressed for reforms because they wanted access to lower-priced peanuts, while the introduction of the North American Free Trade Agreement (NAFTA) allowed peanut products to enter duty free from Mexico and Canada.

Some modifications were made in 1996, but the biggest change came with the 2002 Farm Bill, with the government deciding to buy out the marketing quotas created in 1978. Eligible quota holders are to be compensated for the lost value of the marketing quota during fiscal years 2002–06. Quota holders can elect to receive payment in five equal installments of $0.11 a pound per year times the actual quota allotment for the 2001 marketing year or to receive the undiscounted sum of all the payments in the first year, equal to $0.55 a pound. Given that an average effective quota for 1998–2000 is 5.6 million tons, the buyout is expected to cost $181 million a year, or $1.4 billion for the five-year period. During the same period, the annual value of U.S. peanut production was $3.1 billion (8.79 million tons times $355 per ton). In addition to the quota buyout, peanut producers will be compensated by receiving support from the other provisions of the 2002 Farm Bill (decoupled and countercyclical payments). Several factors led to this change in the existing peanut program: pressure from imports under NAFTA, opposition by other industry groups, and enormous increases in the fiscal costs of the program (see chapter 12 in this volume).

Canada's Buyout of the Railway Subsidy ("Crow Rate") for Grain Shippers

Canada's Crow Rate program (named for Crowsnest Pass in the Rocky Mountains) goes back to 1897, when Canadian Pacific Railway was given a subsidy of $3.4 million to build a line between Alberta and British Columbia. In exchange for the subsidy, Canadian Pacific agreed to charge grain farmers 20 percent less than the (then) prevailing rates. The 1925 Railway Act made the subsidized rates statutory. Over the years the Crow subsidies were extended to numerous commodities. Because of the higher prices received by western grain farmers created by the transportation subsidies, value-added industries (especially livestock production), moved to central and eastern Canada where grain prices were lower (Klein and Kerr 1995).

In 1995 the Canadian government decided to terminate the program, which was becoming fiscally unsustainable. To ease the transition, a one-time payment of C$1.6 billion was made to eligible farmers. An additional C$300 million was invested in a more efficient grain handling and transportation system. The one-time payment was spread over two fiscal years and made to owners of prairie farmland with eligible crops grown in 1994 and summer fallow land in 1993, adjusted for a productivity factor, distance factor, and provincial allocation factor. Eligible crops were those that were eligible for subsidies under the Western Grains Transportation program. There were no restrictions on how the payments were used, and they were treated as a capital gain rather than as current income, a concession valued by the OECD at an estimated $0.6 billion.

The outcome has been positive overall. The lower grain prices lifted a constraint on value-added industries, encouraging entrepreneurship and innovation; led to diversification into specialty crops; lowered land prices; and exposed the industry to trade challenges. The change also brought Canada into compliance with international trade agreements.

The 1984 New Zealand Exit Grant

Before 1984 New Zealand's farmers were receiving generous support—in some years as high as 40 percent of the value of production. In 1984 the government abolished the subsidies. With the economy almost on the brink of bankruptcy and facing deteriorating external markets, inflation, and historically high interest rates, the government eliminated almost 30 different production subsidies. Although the end of agricultural subsidies took place in conjunction with overall deregulation of the economy and reduced input costs, currency appreciation and low commodity prices during 1985–87 made the transition stressful.

To ease the transition, the government provided one-time exit grants to farmers leaving the land, equivalent to about 66 percent of their previous annual income. Farmers with extremely low incomes were temporarily entitled to social welfare income support. Farmers were also offered limited financial advice. There was no substantive effort to soften the effects of the change. Despite early predictions that large numbers of farmers would leave the land, only 1 percent of farms failed, with significant adjustments occurring in the form of off-farm employment and changes in input use and output mix.

Land prices, which had been kept artificially high by the subsidies, plummeted with their removal. Marginal land reverted to bush, and subsidy-driven land management problems ended. Now farmland values have more than recovered as farm profitability has been restored. Farmers reduced costs and focused on producing higher-value products, where profitable. Many farmers restructured their debts and continued farming, adjusting farm practices to reduce input costs. With investment decisions now subject to commercial and good farming disciplines, agricultural input suppliers were forced to become more competitive, also improving the competitiveness of the agricultural sector.

Since 1986–87 the value of economic activity in New Zealand's farm sector has grown by more than 40 percent in constant dollar terms, and agriculture's contribution to the economy has risen from 14.2 percent of GDP in 1986–87 to 16 percent in 1999–2000. With the removal of farm subsidies, GDP growth went from 1 percent in 1986 to the current annual average of 5.9 percent. New Zealand has around 80,000 farm holdings. Sheep and beef farms account for 20 percent of the number of farms, and dairy farms for 18 percent. Horticulture, forestry, cropping, and rural tourism also contribute to the rural sector, which employs 11.4 percent of the work force. About 80 percent of New Zealand's farm outputs are exported, accounting for more than half of New Zealand's merchandise exports.

Assessing Decoupling

The movement toward decoupled agricultural policies is undeniably a step in the right direction, reducing trade distortions and increasing world prices for developing countries' exports. But how much movement has actually occurred? And what have been the net effects on resource use, efficiency, and trade distortions?

The rate of agricultural protection in OECD countries has declined, while the share of domestic support has increased. Total direct support to agricultural producers as measured by estimated producer support averaged $235 billion in 2000–02, 63 percent of it from border measures. Most support is concentrated in a few sectors (milk, meats, and sugar).

Although the absolute level of producer support has remained fairly constant, taxpayer-financed subsidies paid directly to farmers have increased significantly. From 1986–88 to 2000–02, domestic subsidies to farmers rose 60 percent, with large-impact programs (output and input subsidies) increasing moderately compared with the substantial increases in so-called smaller-impact programs (subsidies for land area and number of animals, decoupled historical entitlements, and payments based on input use restrictions and overall farm income). Payments based on area planted and number of animals have increased the most, followed by historical entitlements. Several countries, however, have made little progress in reforming the composition of support away from border support to domestic support (among them Japan and Switzerland), while others have not needed substantial reforms (many members of the CAIRNS Group).

As for reductions in trade distortions, experience in the decoupled programs described above has been mixed. The few countries studied here have moved away from border support to domestic support and to less distorting domestic support. Although there is evidence of a reallocation of resources across agriculture as a result, the decline in total output and increase in world prices have been modest.

In addition to the uneven distribution of "coupled" subsidies (less in major field crops, more in sugar and livestock), other factors help to explain the lack of significant reductions in output. Eligibility rules have changed, and expectations about future policies and dynamic considerations affect current production decisions because producers develop expectations about future assistance based on past government actions. Experience shows that imperfect decoupled programs still distort trade, especially when decoupled payments are substantial. Large payments can have risk reduction effects that lead to increased output. Direct payments also help cover fixed costs, allowing farmers to cross-subsidize production at market prices. Direct payments can affect farmers' investment and exit decisions if they are facing constraints in capital and labor markets. Direct payments allow banks to make loans that they otherwise would not and allow farmers with specialized skills to stay in agriculture.

The primary motivation for decoupling is to compensate farmers for the move to free markets by providing transitional adjustment assistance. This also makes the programs politically more palatable and transparent. Ideally, compensation programs would be universal (open to all sectors in the economy, not just agriculture) or at least non-sector-specific within agriculture. A simple and minimally distorting scheme would be a one-time unconditional payment to everyone engaged in farming or deemed in need of compensation that is nontransferable, along the lines of the one-time buyouts discussed earlier.

However, because a one-time buyout is an unlikely outcome (unless it is well-targeted in one sector), specific attention should be given to time limits, harmonization with other support programs, government credibility, and constraints on input use (Baffes and de Gorter 2003 provide a detailed discussion of these conditions along with WTO's potential role on decoupling). Unless these aspects are properly addressed, decoupled programs are likely to have the same detrimental effects as other subsidy programs.

Most important, programs should be strictly limited in duration. The European Union and Turkey have no limit: the United States had (at least implicitly) one in the 1996 Farm Bill but violated it three years later. Mexico's reform had a time limit, which so far has not been extended. A time limit helps to ensure that payments are made for adjustment purposes only.

If there are other (coupled) support programs, the decoupled program may not eliminate the incentives to overproduce. All four decoupling cases examined here either left other coupled support programs in place or added new ones.

To maintain government credibility and reduce uncertainty, eligibility rules need to be clearly defined and not allowed to change. The time period on which payments are based, the level of payments, and the sectors covered should all remain fixed. Updating bases and adding crops create a government credibility problem, making the decoupling policy inconsistent over time. If governments have the discretion to change eligibility criteria and payments as market conditions change, these commitments will not be viewed as binding. Farmers, meanwhile, will change their production decisions to reflect this, thus undermining decoupling.

Support to specific sectors within agriculture should be in the form of taxpayer-funded payments. There should be no requirement of production. Land, labor, and any other input should not have to be in "agricultural use."

Experience shows the difficulty of designing effective decoupling schemes. But strict criteria are required to minimize direct trade distortions because sector-specific decoupled support can still affect output indirectly, through wealth effects and lessened constraints in credit and labor markets. One way to improve the performance of decoupling schemes might be to have the WTO specify the conditions; this approach would avoid countervailing duties by other countries.

References

Alston, J. M., and B. H. Hurd. 1990. "Some Neglected Social Costs of Government Spending in Farm Programs." *American Journal of Agricultural Economics* 72.

Baffes, John, and Harry de Gorter. 2003. "Decoupling Support to Agriculture: An Economic Analysis and of Recent Experience." Paper presented at the Annual World Bank Conference on Development Economics–Europe, May 15–16, Paris.

Baffes, John, and Jacob Meerman. 1998. "From Prices to Incomes: Agricultural Subsidization without Protection?" *World Bank Research Observer* 13(2): 191–211.

Beard, Nick, and Alan Swinbank. 2001. "Decoupled Payments to Facilitate CAP Reforms." *Food Policy* 26: 121–46.

Beghin, John C., Jean-Christophe Bureau, and Sung Joon Park. 2003. "Food Security and Agricultural Protection in South Korea." *American Journal of Agricultural Economics* 85: 618–32.

Cahill, Sean, A. 1997. "Calculating the Rate of Decoupling for Crops under CAP/Oilseeds Reforms." *Journal of Agricultural Economics* 48: 349–78.

Finkle, Peter, and Duncan Cameron. 1990. *Decoupling: The Concept and Its Future in Canada.* Ottawa: Agriculture Canada.

Goodwin, Barry K., and Ashok K. Mishra. 2002. "Are 'Decoupled' Farm Program Payments Really Decoupled? An Empirical Evaluation." Ohio State University, Columbus, http://departments.agri.huji.ac.il/economics/kenes-goodwin2.pdf.

Hennessy, David A. 1998. "The Production Effects of Agricultural Income Support Policies under Uncertainty." *American Journal of Agricultural Economics* 80(1): 46–57.

Klein, K. K., and W. A. Kerr. 1995. "The Crow Rate Issue: A Retrospective on the Contributions of the Agricultural Economics Profession in Canada." *Canadian Journal of Agricultural Economics* 44(1): 1–18.

Moschini, G., and P. Sckokai (1994), "Efficiency of Decoupled Farm Programs under Distortionary Taxation," *American Journal of Agricultural Economics* 76.

Nash, Eric Francis. 1961. "Agriculture." In Arthur Selton, ed., *Agenda for a Free Society: Essays on Hayek's "The Constitution of Liberty."* London: The Institute of Economic Affairs.

Nicholls, William H., and D. Gale Johnson. 1946. "The Farm Price Policy Awards, 1945: A Topical Digest of the Winning Essays." *Journal of Farm Economics* 27(1): 267–83.

OECD (Organisation of Economic Co-operation and Development). 2000a. "Decoupling: A Conceptual Overview." COM/AGR/APM/TD/WP 14. Paris.

———. 2000b. "Methodology for the Measurement of Support and Use in Policy Evaluation." Paris.

Parry, Ian W. H. 1999. "Agricultural Policies in the Presence of Distorting Taxes." *American Journal of Agricultural Economics* 81.

Spriggs, John, and Dale Sigurdson. 1988. "The Economics of Decoupling and Targeting Canada's Grain and Livestock Stabilization Programs." In Peter Finkle and Duncan Cameron, eds., *Decoupling: The Concept and Its Future in Canada.* Ottawa: Agriculture Canada.

Swerling, Boris G. 1959. "Income Protection for Farmers: A Possible Approach." *Journal of Political Economy* 64(2): 173–86.

Swinbank, Alan, and Stefan Tangermann. 2001. "The Future of Direct Payments under the CAP: A Proposal." *EuroChoices* 1(1): 28–35.

Tangermann, Stefan. 1991. "A Bond Scheme for Supporting Farm Incomes." In J. Marsh, B. Green, B. Kearney, L. Mahé, S. Tangermann, and S. Tarditi, eds., *The Changing Role of the Common Agricultural Policy: The Future of Farming in Europe.* London: Belhaven.

Van Donkersgoed, Elbert. 1988. "Decoupling: A Family Farm and Stewardship Approach." In Peter Finkle and Duncan Cameron, eds., *Decoupling: The Concept and Its Future in Canada.* Ottawa: Agriculture Canada.

Winters, L. Alan. 1989–90. "The So-Called 'Non-Economic' Objectives of Agricultural Support." *OECD Economic Studies* 13: 238–66.

World Bank. 2001. "Turkey—Agricultural Reform Implementation Project." Project Appraisal Document. Europe and Central Asia Region, Turkey Country Unit, Washington, D.C.

6

AGRO-FOOD EXPORTS FROM DEVELOPING COUNTRIES: THE CHALLENGES POSED BY STANDARDS

Steven M. Jaffee and
Spencer Henson

Food safety and agricultural health standards can impede trade, especially for developing countries, through explicit bans on imports of particular products or through the high cost of compliance with stringent standards, which can diminish competitiveness. In certain circumstances, however, the new landscape of proliferating and increasingly stringent food safety and agricultural health standards can be a basis for the competitive repositioning and enhanced export performance of developing countries. Key to this is the ability of developing countries to upgrade capacity and make necessary adjustments in the structure and operation of their supply chains. In an attempt to rebalance much of the dialogue in this area, this chapter explores the nature of the new standards landscape and the related capacity requirements, before looking at the impacts on trade. In addition to the traditional approach using quantitative measures of changes in trade that are related to the evolution of standards, the chapter presents a number of illustrative case studies that relate losses or gains in trade to food safety and agricultural health requirements within the context of wider supply chain challenges.

Standards: Barrier or Catalyst?

The expansion of global trade in perishable agricultural products and high-value foods has highlighted the great divergence in national standards for food safety and animal and plant health and in the capacities of public authorities and commercial supply chains to manage the risks associated with trade in these products. For many higher-value foods, including fruits and vegetables, fish, beef, poultry, and herbs and spices, the challenges of international competitiveness have moved well beyond price and basic quality to food safety and agricultural health concerns.[1] There is increasing attention to the risks associated with microbial pathogens; residues from pesticides, veterinary medicines, and other agricultural inputs; and environmental or naturally occurring toxins. And there is greater scrutiny of the production and processing techniques employed along supply chains (Buzby 2003).

There are several reasons why food safety and agricultural health standards, referred to as sanitary and phytosanitary measures within the World Trade Organization (WTO), differ across countries

(Unnevehr 2003; Henson 2004). Differences in tastes, diets, income levels, and perceptions influence people's tolerance of these risks. Differences in climate and available technology (from refrigeration to irradiation) affect the incidence of food safety and agricultural health hazards. Standards reflect the feasibility of implementation, itself influenced by legal and industry structures as well as technical, scientific, administrative, and financial resources. Some food safety risks tend to be greater in developing countries because of weaknesses in physical infrastructure and the higher incidence of certain infectious diseases. Tropical and subtropical climates may be more conducive to the spread of certain pests and diseases that pose risks to health.

Thus the intrinsic risks associated with the production, transformation, and sale of high-value and perishable food products, combined with different standards and institutional capabilities, can pose major challenges for international trade. And food safety and agricultural health standards are changing rapidly, along with increased public awareness of food safety in high-income countries following a series of highly publicized food scares or scandals (bovine spongiform encephalopathy, or BSE, in beef in the United Kingdom, *E. coli* in hamburgers in the United States, dioxins in animal feed in Belgium). In response, there have been significant institutional changes in food safety oversight and reform of laws and regulations. For long-held concerns such as pesticide residues, there has been a tightening of standards in many countries. And new standards are being applied to address previously unknown or unregulated hazards, such as BSE, genetically modified organisms, and environmental contaminants.

As official standards and public oversight have changed, the private sector has moved rapidly to address food safety risks and the concerns and preferences of consumers, resulting in a proliferation of private codes of practice and other forms of supply chain governance. Private systems of food safety governance are also being applied more widely in middle-income and some low-income countries, in part through investments by multinational supermarket and restaurant chains and competitive responses by local firms (Reardon and Berdegue 2002). In addition, new food safety standards in industrial countries are shaping the expectations of developing-country consumers, especially those with higher incomes and in urban areas.

The proliferation and enhanced stringency of food safety and agricultural health standards are a growing concern among many developing countries and those promoting their increased integration into the world trading system. Reflecting wider changes in the trade regime for various agricultural and food products, there is a presumption that food safety and agricultural health measures will be used as protectionist tools, providing "scientific" justification for prohibiting certain imports or applying higher standards to imports than to domestic supplies. Even if standards are not intentionally used to discriminate, their growing complexity and lack of harmonization could still impede the trading efforts of developing countries.

There is also a concern that many developing countries lack the administrative, technical, and scientific capacities to comply with emerging requirements. The investment and recurrent costs of compliance could undermine the competitive position of developing countries or otherwise compress the profitability of high-value food exports. The combined effects of institutional weaknesses and rising compliance costs could contribute to the further marginalization of weaker economic players, including poor countries, small businesses, and smallholder farmers.

A less pessimistic view emphasizes the opportunities provided by evolving standards, which some developing countries can use to their competitive advantage. Many of the emerging public and private standards can serve as a bridge between increasingly demanding consumers and distant suppliers. The standards can provide a common language within the supply chain and promote consumer confidence in food product safety.

From this standards-as-catalyst perspective, food safety and agricultural health standards may provide a powerful incentive for modernizing developing-country export supply chains and giving greater clarity to the management functions of government. Further, there may be spillovers into domestic food safety and agricultural health, to the benefit of the local population and domestic producers. Part of the costs of compliance could be considered necessary investments, while an array of foreseeable and unforeseeable benefits might arise from the adoption of different technologies and management systems. Rather than degrading the comparative advantage of developing countries, enhancement of capacity to meet stricter standards could create new forms of competitive advantage, providing the basis for more sustainable and profitable trade over the long term.

This rather crude dichotomy between standards as barriers and standards as catalysts suggests a complex reality in which close attention is needed to the specifics of particular markets, products, and countries to understand how the changing food safety and agricultural health standards environment is providing challenges and opportunities for developing countries. This chapter draws on the literature and work in progress to examine the underlying evidence on the changing standards environment and its implications for developing-country exporters of high-value agricultural and food products. Drawing on both systematic and anecdotal evidence, the chapter presents a varied picture, partially supporting both perspectives.

The Sanitary and Phytosanitary Agreement: An End to Disguise and Discrimination?

During the Uruguay Round of multilateral trade negotiations, agricultural exporters voiced concerns that sanitary and phytosanitary measures were being used to restrict foreign competition and that such protectionist measures would likely increase as the use of more traditional trade barriers declined. The Agreement on the Application of Sanitary and Phytosanitary Measures provided a set of multilateral rules recognizing the need of countries to adopt such measures and creating a framework to reduce their trade distorting effects.

The agreement, built on the Standards Code of the 1947 General Agreement on Tariffs and Trade, permitted measures "necessary to protect human, animal, or plant life and health," yet required that regulators base measures on a scientific risk assessment, recognize that different measures can achieve equivalent safety outcomes, and allow imports from particular regions in an exporting country when presented with evidence of the absence or low incidence of pests or diseases. The agreement encouraged the adoption of international standards, making explicit reference to those of the Codex Alimentarius Commission for food safety,

the International Office of Epizootics for animal health, and the International Plant Protection Convention for plant health. The agreement protects the rights of countries to choose their own "appropriate level of protection," yet guides members to "take into account the objective of minimizing negative trade effects."

Important underlying objectives are minimization of protectionist and unjustified discriminatory use of standards and promotion of greater transparency and harmonization. In both regards, experience has been mixed. The difficulties encountered are probably due less to specific shortcomings of the Sanitary and Phytosanitary Agreement itself than to the intrinsic complexities of managing food safety and agricultural health protection and the rapidly evolving markets for agricultural and food products. Further, it is evident that WTO members vary widely in their understanding of the agreement and their ability to take advantage of the rights and responsibilities it defines.

The agreement has not brought an end to the differential application of standards—nor should it. Differentiation is a necessary part of any risk-based food safety and agricultural health control system. The hazards to be monitored and the control measures to be implemented need to be prioritized at the country, industry, and enterprise levels. Political factors as well as scientific evidence influence priorities, focusing, for example, on issues of greatest concern to consumers and other interest groups (Henson 2001). As resources are limited and implementation may be costly, an effective risk management system will go beyond prioritizing potential hazards to differentiate explicitly among alternative sources of supply based on conditions of production, experience, and assessments of risk management capabilities in the supply chain.

Separating Legitimate and Illegitimate Standards Differentiation

When regulators and others have wide discretion and differentiation is required for cost-effective management of food safety and agricultural health, there remains ample scope for mischief. Yet separating legitimate differentiation from illegitimate discrimination is problematic. Even more difficult is clearly attributing standards to protectionist intentions, considering that in most circumstances at least partially legitimate food safety or agricultural health issues are involved. For example, in two widely referenced cases of assumed protectionist motivation—restrictions on exports of Mexican avocados and Argentine citrus fruits to the United States—there was scientific justification for measures to prevent the spread of plant disease, though less-trade-restricting measures were available (Roberts and Orden 1997). In other cases, trade partners have different perspectives on the state of scientific knowledge and the need to make allowance for uncertainty. A prominent case is the dispute between the European Union (EU) and United States over the use of hormones in beef cattle (Pauwelyn 1999; Bureau, Marette, and Schiavina 1998).

Thus, questions remain about whether there is systematic discrimination against imports in the application of food safety and agricultural health controls. One question is whether foreign suppliers must comply with higher standards than domestic suppliers. No systematic research has been done on this subject, although a great deal of anecdotal evidence is presented by those who purport to have been adversely affected by such discrimination. And WTO members raised 241 complaints in the Sanitary and Phytosanitary Committee from 1995 to 2002 (Roberts 2004).

General impressions suggest that many countries, both industrial and developing, have a lower tolerance for certain animal and plant health risks from imports than from domestic sources. There have been cases when countries have restricted imports from countries experiencing a plant pest or animal disease that is also prevalent domestically. Similar observations can be made for some food safety controls. For example, the United States has long argued that, like itself, a broad array of countries has a near-zero tolerance for salmonella in imported poultry products yet this pathogen is widely present in domestic supply chains. Countries can also apply discriminatory measures to different importing countries. For example, the Philippines complained that Australia prohibited imports of Philippine sauces containing benzoic acid while permitting imports from New Zealand of similar products containing that additive.

Private and Public Oversight and Monitoring

High-value food exporters in developing countries frequently claim that they face more rigorous controls than do domestic suppliers in certain industrial countries. But this intensive oversight and monitoring often come from private entities, especially supermarkets and their buying agents, rather than from official systems. And the methods of control that exporters face are more visible in their effects, in that compliance for exporters is assessed at the border, with entry possibly denied on this basis, whereas domestic suppliers are regulated through inspection of processing facilities, with a focus on system-based controls and market surveillance.

Yet, there is anecdotal evidence that regulatory oversight is substantially more stringent on domestic supplies in certain products and markets. For example, there is no official requirement in the United States for border testing of cereals or nuts for the presence of aflatoxin. Private-sector testing for aflatoxin levels in cereals is commonplace in the domestic market, however, with frequent price discounts being applied by buyers. Over a typical three-year period the U.S. Food and Drug Administration's (FDA) Center for Food Safety and Applied Nutrition inspects all domestic firms that produce low-acid canned foods, yet only 3 percent of foreign facilities that export such products to the United States market undergo such inspection.[2] The FDA inspects only 1–2 percent of the more than 6 million consignments of food (and cosmetic products) imported each year. For relatively high-risk products (for example, fish and meat products), a higher proportion of domestic than imported supplies is inspected. In both the United States and the European Union compliance monitoring for pesticide residues pays considerably more attention (absolute and proportional) to domestic suppliers than to imports.[3]

There is also little research comparing the intensity with which private buyers and distributors enforce their own standards among domestic suppliers and foreign suppliers, especially in developing countries. With less opportunity to observe directly the food safety and agricultural health control systems employed by developing-country suppliers, private buyers would likely emphasize end-product testing or third-party certification of quality management systems. This is certainly a clear trend among buyers in the United Kingdom and the Netherlands, for example, yet it is doubtful that such requirements are being imposed on developing-country suppliers at the same rate as on their industrial-country competitors.[4]

Increased Complexity of the Standards Environment

The overall picture for food safety and agricultural health requirements in trade is becoming increasingly complex and fast moving as standards are promulgated in multiple spheres at both public and private and national and international levels. The complexity of this issue stems from the variability of the standards themselves and from differences in how and with what intensity standards are monitored and enforced, which is also changing over time.

The transparency of official regulatory measures in the application of food safety and agricultural health requirements has clearly improved since the Sanitary and Phytosanitary Agreement entered into force. Some 85 percent of WTO members have established an "enquiry point" for obtaining information on proposed food safety and agricultural health requirements. Between 1995 and 2002 WTO members submitted some 3,220 notifications indicating the nature and objectives of proposed measures, the products they applied to, whether they were based on an international standard, and when the measure was to come into force. These notifications provide advance warning of new or modified measures and an opportunity for trading partners to raise questions about the proposed measures, both bilaterally and through the Sanitary and Phytosanitary Committee. An increasing proportion of WTO members, including developing countries, has been taking advantage of this opportunity to raise concerns (Roberts 2004).

While the transparency of many food safety and agricultural health measures has increased, considerable variation remains in standards across countries. And there is widespread uncertainty about how certain countries are implementing their standards. Roberts, Josling, and Orden (1999) note the paucity of international standards for many agrofood products and indicate that the vast majority of food safety and agricultural health measures notified to the WTO during 1995–99 had no international standard.[5] With specific reference to horticultural products, Roberts and Krissoff (2003) found that over the same period two-thirds of notifications involved measures for which there was no recognized international standard and that many involved maximum pesticide residue levels. Jaffee (2003) notes that despite EU efforts to harmonize maximum pesticide residue levels in

imported fresh fruit and vegetables, wide variations remain in operative standards due to countries' different approaches to surveillance and enforcement.

Variations in standards are also common in other sectors. Henson and Mitullah (2004) note the varied standards that developing countries must meet to gain and maintain access to the U.S., EU, and Japanese markets for fish products. While some requirements overlap, differences remain in both regulatory and technical requirements. Likewise, Mathews, Bernstein, and Buzby (2003) highlight the range of product and process standards countries require to minimize the risk of salmonella contamination in poultry products. Dohlman (2003) and Otsuki, Wilson, and Sewadeh (2001) discuss the significant differences in the maximum permitted level for aflatoxin in cereals and nuts and in the sampling methods used. This lack of harmonization of standards and conformity assessment procedures raises production and transaction costs for developing-country suppliers, necessitating duplicative testing and reducing their ability to achieve economies of scale in production and in food safety and agricultural health management functions.

Also contributing to the increased complexity of the standards environment is the expansion of risk-based process standards relating to production, postharvest, and other procedures, and the proliferation of private standards. Roberts (2004) notes that the major international standards organizations have devoted more of their attention and resources over the past decade to the development of common approaches to risk identification, assessment, and management than to international standards themselves. This reflects both the inefficiency and the inefficacy of end-product testing, particularly in view of the levels of risk deemed acceptable today and the emergence of new or newly prominent food-borne pathogens.

With respect to private standards, there have been attempts to harmonize standards formerly applied by individual private companies, yet a plethora of private standards are still simply communicated through individual supply chains and can vary widely in their specific requirements. Examples of private protocols that have been codified and are available to the public include food safety and food hygiene protocols, such as the British Retail Consortium Technical Food Standard and the EUREPGAP Fruit and Vegetable Standard, which combines food safety, environmental, and social dimensions. Other standards focus on social or environmental issues, such as Social Accountability 8000, the Ethical Trading Initiative, and the Marine Stewardship Initiative.

Variations in food safety and agricultural health requirements together with the progressive shift toward process-based measures have enhanced the importance of "equivalence" of national standards and systems. Currently, there is no systematic recording of equivalence agreements. Most appear to be between industrial countries. Certain developing countries, including successful agricultural exporters, have highlighted the difficulties in gaining recognition for the equivalency of their food safety and other controls to those of their major trading partners (WTO 2001). A successful and wide-ranging example of equivalence, however, is the recognition by the European Union that many developing and industrial countries have established systems of hygienic control for fish and fishery products that offer a level of protection at least comparable to its own legislation (see discussion below).

A parallel trend, reflecting the proliferation of private standards, is the heightened importance of certification of compliance with defined standards, which is typically undertaken by a third-party agency that the buyer recognizes as "competent." A crucial issue for developing countries is the establishment of certification capacity and parallel institutions for accrediting certification bodies. Exporters in countries that lack an accreditation certification system may be forced to use the services of an accredited body in another country, at considerable cost (El-Tawil 2002).

What Capacity Is Needed?

Countries frequently require guarantees that imports come from areas that are free of certain pests or diseases; that minimum standards of hygiene have been applied in manufacture, packaging, and distribution; and that products are free of excessive residues of pesticides, medicines, and other contaminants. The exporting country must have the capacity to comply with these requirements and to demonstrate compliance. Among the required capacities are:

- Detecting the presence or demonstrating the absence of biological, chemical, and physical hazards and having an information system to inform decision-making processes.
- Employing emergency procedures in the event of emerging hazards or outbreaks.
- Certifying that traded products meet established food safety risks.
- Undertaking scientific analysis of hazards in agricultural inputs and food products.
- Establishing and maintaining the identity of agricultural products through the supply chain.
- Establishing and maintaining systems for hygienic practices in agro-food product handling and transformation.
- Registering the production, distribution, and use of agricultural inputs that may pose risks to human, animal, or plant health.

Administrative and technical capacities for food safety and agricultural health management are embodied in institutional structures and procedures, physical infrastructure, and human capital. It is frequently assumed that managing food safety and agricultural health is predominantly a public-sector responsibility. While some crucial regulatory, research, and management functions are normally carried out by governments, and importing countries may require that certain functions be performed by a designated public-sector "competent authority," the private sector also has important roles:

- Because it is typically well informed about technical options and hazard management systems, it should contribute to standard setting.
- Compliance with food safety and agricultural health standards requires specific actions by individual producers and processors.
- Capacity building in the private sector can complement (or substitute for) public-sector capacity, as through investment in accredited laboratory testing facilities.

Development of food safety and agricultural health management systems is closely related to the availability of wider technical, administrative, and scientific capacities that reflect broader patterns of economic development as much as specific demands for food safety and agricultural health controls. Unnevehr and Hirschhorn (2001) highlight the capacity needs for food safety management at different stages of economic development.

Export-oriented agriculture gives rise to a new set of challenges because foreign food safety and agricultural health requirements may differ sharply from domestic requirements, especially in the case of low-income countries (Dong and Jensen 2004).

Some regulatory, technical, and administrative capacities represent a greater constraint on developing-country exports of agricultural and food products than do others.[6] In general, weaknesses in the management of plant and animal health issues are more likely to be an absolute barrier to trade than is lack of food safety controls. For many food safety hazards there is an array of effective technologies or approaches, some of which do not require sophisticated equipment or expertise. Even where management of food safety hazards is well within the capacities of producers and processors, systems of conformity assessment require testing and certification of food safety management systems and end products. Many developing countries lack the capability to undertake the rigorous epidemiological surveillance and risk assessments demanded by trading partners. They lack the accredited laboratories and internationally recognized systems for certification (El-Tawil 2002). Thus, regardless of private-sector capacity to meet the food safety and quality requirements of foreign customers, the country as a whole will be unable to gain market access.

While many developing countries have widespread weaknesses in food safety and agricultural health management capacity, there is evidence that even low-income countries can establish the regulatory, technical, and administrative arrangements to meet demanding standards in high-income export markets. The European Commission has recognized a relatively large—and growing—number of low- and lower-middle-income countries as having standards of hygiene in the capture, processing, transportation, and storage of fish and fishery products that are at least equivalent to those of the European Union. Their shipments benefit from reduced physical inspection at the border.

How Significant Are Compliance Costs?

Developing countries can incur significant "costs of compliance" whenever changes are made in international standards or those of their trading partners. These costs can come in various forms, including fixed investments in adjusting production and processing facilities and practices, recurrent personnel and management costs to implement food and other control systems and the public- and private-sector costs of conformity assessment.

Typically there are a variety of technological and administrative ways in which to achieve compliance with a certain standard. For this and other reasons the level and relative significance of compliance costs can vary enormously from industry to industry and between countries.[7] Important variables include the structure and conditions of the supply chain, the extent of administrative and scientific capacities, the degree of cooperation within industries and between the public and private sectors, and the strength of technical service industries. Where the export industry is mature and reasonably well developed, changes in food safety and agricultural health standards may require only incremental adjustments by producers and exporters and modest changes in public-sector oversight arrangements. Where the supply chain is makeshift, however, or uses multipurpose facilities and when new requirements (or levels of enforcement) necessitate major upgrades, some firms may need to redirect their products to less-demanding markets, while others will need to undertake significant fixed investments.

Consider the differences in adjustment costs associated with investments in the upgrading of hygiene controls in the shrimp industries in Bangladesh and Nicaragua (table 6.1). In Bangladesh major investments had to be made in the mid-1990s to upgrade fish-processing facilities, product-testing laboratories, and other areas in response to repeated quality and safety detentions of products entering the United States and a ban in 1997 on shrimp imports into the European Union. These investments equaled 2.3 percent of the value of the country's shrimp exports in 1996–98. Annual maintenance costs for hazard analysis and critical control point (HACCP) and regulatory systems equaled 1.1 percent of exports. The Nicaraguan shrimp industry needed to make adjustments during 1997–2002 to hygiene controls to ensure compliance with modified U.S. fish safety regulations, including requirements to implement a HACCP program. But many Nicaraguan factories were

TABLE 6.1   Costs of Compliance with Export Food Safety Requirements in the Shrimp Processing Industry in Bangladesh and Nicaragua
(millions of US$)

Cost	Bangladesh 1996–98	Nicaragua 1997–2002
Industry facility upgrading	17.55	0.33
Government	0.38	0.14
Training programs	0.07	0.09
Total	18.01	0.56
Annual maintenance of HACCP program	2.43	0.29
Shrimp exports during focal periods	775.00	92.60
Average annual shrimp exports	225.00	23.20
Ratio of upgrade costs to focal year export (%)	2.3	0.61
Ratio of maintenance costs to annual exports (%)	1.1	1.26

Source: Based on Cato and Lima dos Santos 2000, and Cato, Otwell, and Coze 2003.

relatively new and modern, so only modest incremental investments were needed, equivalent to 0.6 percent of the value of exports.

Many technological and organizational changes involve shifts in levels and structures of operating costs. The costs associated with these changes are often controversial. The changes are sometimes perceived to be unjustified, because they lack scientific basis or replace simpler, less costly procedures that might provide similar outcomes. Another complaint is that suppliers obtain little or no benefit beyond continued market access, while the opportunity cost of the required investments can be considerable. This complaint is more difficult to sustain, often reflecting a lack of appreciation of the frequently intangible or indirect benefits that can result from enhancement of food safety controls, for example. Improved control systems can reduce waste, improve product-cost accounting, and enhance staff morale. Thus, changes in product and process technologies can generate substantial increases in efficiency, reducing production costs and promoting competitiveness.

The expenditures related to standards compliance can have other beneficial, multiplier effects. Some of the needed investments may require labor, especially skilled and supervisory workers, creating additional job opportunities. Other expenditures may go toward building materials, contractors, and technical services, much of which could be sourced locally. Only where upgrading relies primarily on imported equipment or expertise would there be few multiplier effects.

The enhancement of food safety capacity can also have more dynamic and wide-ranging impacts on private-sector suppliers. For example, implementing an HACCP system and gaining third-party certification can send positive signals to existing and potential customers, enabling firms to reposition themselves in the marketplace or access new markets. Indian fish-processing plants that have invested in sophisticated systems of hygiene control are seeking to access higher-value markets for processed and semi-processed products. Sometimes, when problems are experienced in complying with requirements in a particular market, producers and exporters will shift to markets with lower or different food safety requirements. Kenyan fish exporters, which have been highly dependent on European markets, have attempted to diversify their exports to Australia, Japan, and the United States.

But even where the administrative, technical, and financial burdens of compliance are manageable at the country or industry level, the burdens may be too great at the firm level. There is a general concern that the challenge of rising standards is marginalizing smaller players, especially producers, traders, and processors, as well as smaller industries as a whole. There is, however, little empirical evidence to support this argument. In part, this is because of the difficulties of disentangling the specific role of standards compliance in the consolidation processes of agro-food systems.

In many cases, compliance requirements exacerbate other factors that threaten the status quo in established supply chains. For example, both the Indian and Kenyan fish-processing sectors were facing longer-term challenges when forced to comply with enhanced hygiene standards for exports. Indian exporters were facing intense price competition from other suppliers such as Thailand and Vietnam. The Kenyan fish-processing sector suffered from chronic excess capacity because of raw material shortages. In both cases the costs of compliance with stricter food hygiene standards have induced consolidation of the industry that likely would have occurred anyway, albeit over a longer period. In Nicaragua the decline in the production share of small-scale shrimp producers had more to do with Hurricane Mitch and its aftermath than with the tightening of standards (Cato, Otwell, and Coze 2003).

A particular concern is that smaller players can be disadvantaged where there are economies of scale or scope in the implementation of particular technologies or administrative systems. Studies of compliance with labor and environmental standards in the United States suggest that costs are proportionately higher for smaller firms (Crain and Johnson 2001). In some cases the necessary investments have elements of lumpiness, for example, in laboratory equipment and cold-storage facilities, which are economically viable only for large-scale operations or require collective action. Likewise, smaller firms may find it more difficult to hire certain types of skilled personnel. More generally, smaller firms can be overwhelmed by the sheer number of changes needed to comply with new food safety requirements, even when the cash investments required are not substantial.

Sometimes certifying that the standards have been met is more difficult for small producers than complying with food safety and agricultural health requirements. For example, Kenyan vegetable exporters face considerable oversight costs in demonstrating compliance to their major European buyers.[8] In turn, this generates pressure for rationalizing supply chains. Changes in the product composition of trade may also affect structural patterns.[9] Further, in a competitive environment, exporters find it difficult to control the volume and continuity of smallholder supplies due to side-selling by farmers. Where export supply commitments are firm and specific, exporters need more effective control, and this can induce backward integration into production.

A frequent presumption when discussing the marginalization of suppliers is that standards compliance is a do-or-die situation. In reality, however, there is rarely just a single market for a particular product. Suppliers need to seek out markets (and market segments) where they have advantages rather than disadvantages. For example, there may be opportunities in domestic or regional markets for the same or similar products, with lower prices offset by the absence of compliance challenges and costs. Directing attention to these markets may be one way to avoid marginalization. Thus, the development of high-value agricultural and food products sectors in the future is likely to be bimodal, with some firms upgrading and adapting and others targeting other markets and raising their capacity at a slower pace.

What Impact Are Standards Having on Exports of High-Value Agro-Food Products?

The application of food safety and agricultural health standards by governments and the private sector can significantly affect international trade. While most standards are designed in pursuit of the legitimate goals of maintaining human, plant, and animal health, they can also serve as technical barriers to trade. Roberts, Josling, and Orden (1999) classify technical trade barriers associated with agricultural and food products into three categories: full or partial import bans; technical specifications, including product and process standards; and information remedies, including packaging and labeling requirements and controls on voluntary (health and other) claims. Full or partial bans are the most trade restricting. Total bans are typically used when great risks are associated with certain plant and animal health problems and where cost-effective measures are not available. Partial bans may permit trade only in certain seasons or from certain countries or regions. Technical specifications and informational remedies will normally apply to both imports and domestic supplies. Their effects on trade will derive from the relative abilities of different suppliers to comply with these measures, the incidence of compliance costs, and how each affects the relative competitiveness of different suppliers.

While there is general agreement that food safety and agricultural health measures strongly affect international agro-food trade, there is no consensus on the importance of individual measures, their impact compared with other trade-distorting measures, or their aggregate net effect. Testing the empirical impact of such standards on trade is enormously difficult. First, it requires assumptions about how the broad array of measures is actually enforced and how enforcement deters or encourages potential export suppliers, depending on whether suppliers need to make major or modest adjustments. This variable cannot be aggregated and differs across countries and industries. Second, food safety and agricultural health standards may have secondary effects, for example, leading to shifts in sourcing, the production of complementary and competitive goods, and the spread of regulations and restrictions to other countries. Third, a specific measure may not be a dominant or even important determinant of observed trade flows. There is a risk of ascribing agro-food standards to shifts in trade that are driven by other economic or technical factors. Fourth, there are problems in defining the counterfactual. Without the measure, would trade have been unimpeded, or would distributors and consumers have sought the product from other suppliers instead? In the absence of a (trade-restricting) measure, might overall demand have declined for a product for which certain problems were identified? Finally, many food safety and agricultural health measures will affect domestic suppliers as well, with varied outcomes in terms of shifts in the relative competitiveness and market share of the different players.

These and other empirical problems have led researchers to devote more attention to specific cases and to attempt to highlight the role played by (changing) food safety and agricultural health requirements on bilateral or broader multicountry patterns of trade. Some of the cases are discussed below. Only one study, however, has attempted to provide an aggregate measure of the level of agricultural and food trade constrained or blocked by technical barriers. In 1996 the U.S. Department of Agriculture, drawing on the expert opinions of staff and other regulatory personnel, found that "questionable" technical barriers (measures judged to have no scientific basis) were inhibiting U.S. exports of agricultural and food products to some 62 countries. More than 300 market restrictions

were identified as constraining exports valued at $5 billion, equal to around 7 percent of U.S. agricultural, food, and forestry trade in 1996. Two-thirds of the identified measures, including nearly all full or partial import bans, addressed risks for animal or plant health (Roberts, Josling, and Orden 1999).

This type of broad estimate of trade effects has not been made for any other country. Other approaches have provided insights into the subject, however. Most commonly, researchers have looked to the only two available multicountry sources of data on the subject, official listings of agricultural and food product detentions and rejections by industrial countries and the growing number of complaints recorded by the Sanitary and Phytosanitary Committee. Though incomplete, both are useful proxies for the trade-inhibiting effects of food safety and agricultural health standards.

Border Detentions and Rejections of Agricultural and Food Products

Information is available for a limited number of countries (through periodic reports and web-based databases) on the incidence of detention or rejection of imported agricultural and food products for reasons associated with quality, safety, labeling, or other technical issues. The most widely available and cited data are for the European Union and the United States.[10] The data provide a reasonable picture of the incidence of product rejections over time by country of origin but do not specify the volume or value of rejected consignments.

Several patterns emerge from product rejection data for the European Union and United States:

- *Rising incidence.* In the European Union the number of notifications or alerts increased more than sixfold between 1998 (230 cases) and 2002 (1,520). This increased incidence of rejections reflects a combination of factors, including the tightening or harmonizing of standards, application of standards for formerly unregulated hazards, and substantially increased capacity for inspection and enforcement. In the United States there was a sixfold increase in the number of product inspections by the FDA, in part because of heightened concerns about bioterrorism.[11]

- *Product concentration.* Most detentions and rejections occurred in a few product categories: fish and crustaceans (35 percent of rejections in 2002), meat products, and fruits and vegetables. For the European Union there was also a high incidence of rejections for nuts, while for the United States there were many rejections of low-acid canned foods. Comparatively few rejections were issued on quality or safety grounds for beverage crops, cereal products, feedstuffs, or spices.

- *Country of origin concentration.* A few countries accounted for the bulk of rejections. Among developing countries most of the rejections were from countries that have been dominant suppliers of "sensitive" products for many years (for example, Brazil, Mexico, Thailand, and Turkey) or newly emerging large exporters of such products (for example, China, India, and Vietnam). In 2002 five countries (Brazil, China, Thailand, Turkey, and Vietnam) accounted for nearly 60 percent of EU rejections of agricultural and food products from outside Europe. Some of these countries, however, are simultaneously increasing their EU market share for such products, suggesting that border rejections are more of an irritant than a major problem for larger exporters.

- *Minimal interception of products from low-income countries.* Exports from low-income countries account for a very small proportion of product rejections. For example, in 2002 the European Union rejected only 26 consignments from low-income Sub-Saharan African countries, with most countries experiencing only one or two rejections. Most of these countries are exporting less sensitive products in terms of food safety or agricultural health risks, or they have been recognized as being fully harmonized with EU requirements for more sensitive products such as fish and thus are subject to lower levels of border inspection.

- *Leading reasons for product rejections.* For the European Union the largest (and growing) proportion of rejections concerns chemical and other contaminants in food, especially veterinary drug residues, pesticide residues, and mycotoxins. Chemical contaminants accounted for nearly two-thirds of rejections in 2002, up from 55 percent in 2000. Microbial pathogens were implicated in 30 percent of rejections,

down from 41 percent. This pattern reflects the growing harmonization of EU standards for an array of chemical contaminants and the increased political and technical attention to these issues within the European Union. For the United States a large proportion of border rejections in the late 1990s was due to the presence of filth or foreign bodies (32 percent), microbial pathogens (17 percent), or problems associated with the packaging or labeling of canned food products for which botulism is a risk (13 percent). A smaller proportion of rejections was due to chemical contaminants (12 percent).

Neither the European Union nor the United States systematically reports on the volume or value of trade that is affected by border inspections and rejections. To obtain a rough notion of the value of trade interrupted by technical measures, data were collected (from official sources and consultations with private traders) on the proportion of trade in particular products that was likely to have been detained or rejected in 2000–01. These estimates were then applied to overall trade in these products to estimate the value of interrupted trade (table 6.2). For simplicity, the proportion of trade for particular products that is subject to rejections is assumed to be the same for products flowing between low-, middle-, and high-income countries. This is unlikely to be so in practice, but data are not available to provide more refined estimates.

The value of world agro-food trade affected by official product rejections at the import level is estimated at $3.8 billion in 2000–01.[12] This is almost certainly an overestimate since similar levels of rejection are assumed for products entering developing countries as for those entering industrial countries, even though levels of standards and enforcement capacities are typically lower in developing countries. Reflecting the dominant share of high-income countries in certain product groups for which detention or rejection levels are high (for example, meat and dairy products, other processed foods, and processed fruit and vegetables), these countries are estimated to account for 53 percent of rejected exports, while they account for some 63 percent of world agricultural and food product exports. The estimated value of developing-country agro-food border rejections is $1.8 billion, 74 percent of it accounted for by middle-income

TABLE 6.2 Estimated Value of World Agricultural and Food Trade Directly Affected by Import Border Rejections Based on Technical Standards, 2000–01
(millions of US$)

Product Group	Estimated Proportion of Trade (%)[a]	High-Income Countries	Middle-Income Countries[b]	Low-Income Countries	China	Total Trade Affected
Meat and dairy products	1.25	811	142	8	21	982
Fish and fishery products	1.00–2.00	232	417	145	90	884
Fruit and vegetables	0.75–1.50	367	439	44	61	911
Grains	0.50	160	40	6	8	214
Animal feed	0.50	65	39	4	2	110
Tropical beverages	0.25	25	18	16	0	59
Nuts and spices	0.75–1.50	16	33	30	1	80
Other processed food	1.00–2.00	122	53	3	6	184
All other categories[c]	0.25	199	112	19	6	307
Total		1,997	1,332	275	195	3,799
Proportion of trade affected		0.70	1.10	0.93	1.25	0.84

a. Where there are two numbers the first relates to exports of high-income countries and the second to those of middle- and low-income countries.

b. Excluding China.

c. Includes oilseeds, textile fibers, drinks, tobacco/cigarettes, and sugar/confectionery.

Source: Authors' computation based on official data and consultations with private traders.

countries. For low-income countries the estimated $275 million in agricultural and food product trade rejected at the importing-country border represents less than 1 percent of their agricultural and food exports. The product composition of the rejected exports is broadly consistent with the data presented earlier on EU and U.S. rejections. For middle-income countries, the dominant products are fruits and vegetables and fish, followed by livestock products. For low-income countries, fish is the dominant category, accounting for more than half the estimated rejections.

Until recently, border rejections for food safety or related technical reasons have had only a modest impact on overall trade in agricultural and food products, including that of developing countries. An estimated 1 percent of this trade was directly affected in 2000–01. Further, only a small proportion of rejected consignments is actually destroyed at the point of import. Some (perhaps significant) proportion of the product is reshipped, reconditioned, or otherwise managed for sale whether in the domestic market of the exporter or in some other international market. Indeed, for most food categories the proportion of agro-food trade that encounters official rejection is probably substan-

tially lower than the proportion of sales that are subjected to price discounts by private buyers because of quality defects, lack of timeliness, and poor presentation. The products with the highest estimated proportion of rejections are also those with the highest rates of growth in international agricultural trade.

Thus while undoubtedly an irritant to exporters, border rejections are not a major impediment to trade. Still, they are costly, both in the value of lost product and in adverse reputation effects on the supplier and the country of origin. Some importing countries will list for automatic detention particular suppliers or the entire country following repeated violations of food safety and other standards. Subsequent shipments are detained, inspected, and tested at the expense of the exporter or importer until a record of compliance has been (re)established. This can take a long time, and the costs can be considerable (Lamb, Velez, and Barclay 2004). Further, during this period exporters may lose customers who are unwilling to incur the costs and delays associated with enhanced border formalities.

In addition, there are some indications for certain high-income countries that increased attention is being given to border inspections of products deemed "sensitive" in relation to new regulatory concerns about food safety and agricultural health risks. If the patterns described above are indicative, an increasing level of border interceptions of products would be expected in coming years. This will either increase the transaction costs for certain developing-country suppliers or induce them to make adjustments in production, postharvest, and product monitoring and testing arrangements.

Border rejections attributable to food safety concerns represent only a small part of the constraint on international trade in agricultural and food products associated with food safety and agricultural health measures. For example, although meat and dairy products may be subject to the highest level of rejections in global trade, these are not significant for low-income countries and are probably of secondary importance for most middle-income countries. In terms of the impact on aggregate trade, far more inhibiting are the broad array of measures related to animal and plant health that render large numbers of countries ineligible to supply many livestock products and food crops to other countries (Sumner 2003).

While this pattern undoubtedly reflects traditional trade protections and subsidies in industrial countries that distort world trade, animal disease controls exclude many developing countries from world markets for these products altogether.[13] In part this reflects the prevalence of endemic infectious diseases of animals in many low- and middle-income countries. Indeed, the high costs of establishing and maintaining disease-free areas can be beyond the means of many of the poorest countries. Many developing countries lack the surveillance and risk assessment capacity to demonstrate that they have areas that are disease-free and to get these areas recognized as such by the International Office of Epizooties.[14] And even where developing countries have established disease-free areas, they face the risk that trade will be disrupted should outbreaks of disease occur. A recent example is the restrictions applied to exports of poultry from Thailand and Vietnam because of an outbreak of avian flu. The overall impact of animal disease issues, therefore, is to enhance the risks associated with trade in livestock products and put a great onus on public authorities to invest in disease controls and to ensure their continued efficacy.

Because of an inability to meet a broad array of food safety and agricultural health requirements pertaining to livestock disease and hygiene controls, most low-income countries are restricted to trade in live animals rather than livestock products. This avoids the need for attention to hygienic slaughter in an abattoir, meat inspection, and refrigerated transport.[15] Even if animal disease and hygiene capacity could be enhanced, however, low-income countries would need to compete with well-established livestock product exporters such as Argentina and Australia, which are more reliable producers with fewer animal health problems and more standardized production. However, the benefits from access to high-value markets could be considerable for developing countries that invest in animal disease controls, as a case study of foot and mouth disease controls in Zimbabwe shows (Perry and others 2003).

Disputes and Complaints through the WTO

Complaints and counter-notifications made through the Sanitary and Phytosanitary Committee within the WTO also provide an indication of the nature and breadth of the standards challenge for developing countries (table 6.3). While the counter-notification database and the information provided in most counter-notifications do not permit quantifying the levels of developing-country trade that has or might be affected by the contested measures, it does provide some insights. A summary of complaints by regulatory goal and country group suggests that (at least some) developing countries have actively used this formal review and complaint process to register their concerns about a significant number of notified measures by both industrial and developing countries. A more detailed look at the individual complaints, indicates that:

- Complaints by developing countries are dominated by a handful of countries—Argentina, Brazil, Chile, and Thailand. Each of these countries has issued or supported more than a dozen complaints, with Argentina being involved in more than a quarter of all developing-country complaints. Only a handful of other countries, including Ecuador, India, the Philippines, South Africa, and Uruguay, have been involved in

TABLE 6.3 Number of Counter-Notifications to the Sanitary and Phytosanitary Committee Relating to Reported Measures, 1995–2002

Complaints	Regulatory Goal of Contested Measure				
	Plant Health	Animal Health	Human Health	Other[a]	Total
By industrial countries against:					
Industrial countries	16	7	44	3	70
Developing countries	17	11	41	4	73
Multiple countries	—	2	—	—	2
Subtotal	33	20	85	7	145
By developing countries against:					
Industrial countries	12	12	34	2	60
Developing countries	8	17	7	2	34
Multiple countries	—	2	—	—	2
Subtotal	20	31	41	4	96
Total	53	51	126	11	241

— Not available

a. Includes complaints about horizontal regulations (such as those regulating products of modern biotechnology) that reference human, animal, and plant health as objectives.
Source: Roberts 2004.

multiple cases. This pattern of participation reflects the prominence of certain countries in trade in a few product categories, especially beef and horticultural products, rather than the overall structure of developing country agricultural and food trade.

• These data alone provide little information about the extent to which food safety and agricultural health measures are inhibiting exports of low-income countries. Low-income countries are weakly represented in counter-notifications, issuing or supporting complaints in only five cases. This could reflect the structure of their exports (concentrated in commodities for which food safety and agricultural health measures are of lesser importance) or their limited capacity to participate in the formal review process. This lack of formal complaints does not mean that they have been able to resolve their concerns bilaterally.

• Among the seemingly large number of developing-country complaints are a limited number of repeated concerns, with slight variations. Most complaints about animal health issues relate to what are claimed to be overly restrictive (and nonscientifically based) measures

dealing with foot and mouth disease and beef products or bovine spongiform encephalopathy and animal by-products for pet food, animal feed, and cosmetics. Similarly, most complaints about plant health issues relate to claims of overly restrictive measures for plant diseases or pests or for horticultural products. Complaints related to food safety are a mixture of specific concerns, with no large clustering around particular themes. Surprisingly, given the huge importance for developing-country trade, there are few complaints about measures governing fish products.

• The reasons for developing-country complaints are varied, yet most involve concerns about the lack of scientific evidence in relation to food safety, the absence of risk assessments in relation to plant health, and inconsistencies between country and international standards in animal health.

• Among industrial countries, the European Union has been the subject of the largest number of complaints by developing countries. There were more than three times as many complaints against the European Union as against the United States. Several factors might account for this. Harmonization of food safety and agricultural health measures within the European Union has often resulted in the adoption of the most stringent standards previously applied by individual member states. The European Union has more frequently and most visibly embraced the precautionary principle when adopting certain standards, sometimes giving rise to controversies over the scientific basis for the measures. And because of the complex administrative structure of the European Union, some countries find it difficult to resolve concerns through bilateral discussions and therefore more readily turn to the Sanitary and Phytosanitary Committee for concerns related to the European Union than for other countries.

Thus, the growing number of recorded complaints or counter-notifications by developing countries provides only a crude indicator of the extent to which food safety and agricultural health measures impede their trade in high-value agricultural and food products. These complaints probably represent only the tip of the iceberg as most concerns and disputes are raised bilaterally, and the majority of negotiations are handled by technical organizations rather than country trade representatives. Some of the complaints have occurred in the context of expanding trade ties, which can increase the seriousness of previously minor effects.

There is little basis for associating the growing number of complaints with deliberate protectionism. Many of the concerns seem to be related more to inadequate (scientific) information rather than to discrimination. Further, the apparatus of formal complaints relates only to mandatory standards set by public agencies. A growing array of standards are being set privately, either through consensus within particular industries or by the gatekeepers of the dominant supply chains. While many such standards are ostensibly voluntary, they are becoming the de facto standards to gain or maintain access to particular buyers or market segments.

Some Illustrative Case Studies

Because the data on agricultural and food product rejections and disputes related to food safety and agricultural health measures provide an incomplete picture of the effects on developing countries,

analysts are using case studies to examine the effects of specific standards on the trade of particular countries and products. Earlier work emphasized the potential disruptive impact of food safety and agricultural health measures on exports from developing countries (Otsuki, Wilson, and Sewadeh 2001; Wilson and Otsuki 2003). More recent work by the U.S. Department of Agriculture (Buzby 2003) and the International Food Policy Research Institute (Unnevehr 2003) point to more varied experiences. Other case study analyses have been undertaken by the United Nations Conference on Trade and Development (UNCTAD), the United Nations Environment Programme (UNEP), and the World Bank.[16]

This section draws on selected examples to illustrate the complex ways in which sanitary and phytosanitary measures can affect developing-country exports. Three of the most prominent concerns raised in the literature are emphasized in the selection of case studies: fish trade bans and their wider supply chain effects, limits on mycotoxins as trade barriers, and the strengthening of horticultural product and process standards.

Fish Bans and Their Wide Supply-Chain Effects

Since 1990 developing-country exports of fish and fishery products have increased at an average annual rate of 6 percent (Delgado and others 2003). A major challenge faced by developing countries in seeking to maintain and expand their share of global markets is the progressively stricter food safety requirements, particularly in major industrial countries. Previous studies suggested that some exporters experienced considerable problems in complying with these requirements.

The European Union lays down harmonized requirements governing hygiene throughout the supply chain for fish and fishery products. Processing plants are inspected and approved individually by a specified "competent authority" in the country of origin, whether an EU member state or a third country, to ensure compliance. Imports from third countries are required to have controls that are at least equivalent to those of the European Union.[17] Exports from countries for which local requirements have been recognized as equivalent are subject to reduced physical inspection at the border. Countries that have not yet met these requirements but that have provided assurances that their controls are at least equivalent to those of the European Union are permitted to export but are subject to higher rates of border inspection. The current deadline for all countries to be fully harmonized with the EU's hygiene standards is December 31, 2005.

Kenya is an example of longer-term efforts to comply with the European Union's food safety requirements, overlaid with the need to overcome restrictions on trade relating to immediate food safety concerns. Kenya's major fish export is Nile perch from Lake Victoria. Until the mid-1980s this was a relatively minor species in the Lake Victoria fishery, but with a shift in focus from local to export markets, Nile perch came to account for more than 90 percent of Kenya's exports of fish and fishery products by the mid-1990s, with a value of around $44 million in 1996. Most exports were destined for the European Union. Through the 1980s there was significant investment in industrialized fish-processing facilities, and 15 facilities were in operation by the mid-1990s. At the landing beaches, however, there was little or no change in fishing methods or marketing facilities.

Initially, Nile perch exports were extremely profitable. Processing capacity soon exceeded the supply of fish, however, a situation that sets the competitive environment in which all levels of the chain operate. Although food safety requirements in their major export markets were evolving, most processors made little attempt to upgrade their facilities and systems of procurement, processing, and marketing. Likewise, the legislative framework of food safety controls remained largely unchanged, despite the fact that the structure and focus of the supply chain had shifted to exports. The picture was of a supply chain that had not been upgraded in line with the growth in exports and was unable to implement effective controls within the context of rapidly evolving standards overseas. Thus, both the public authorities and exporters were in the position of continuous problem solving.

In recent years exporters of Nile perch have faced a catalogue of restrictions on trade with the European Union. In 1996 salmonella was detected in a number of consignments of Nile perch from Kenya (and Tanzania and Uganda) at the Spanish border, and Spain immediately prohibited imports. In April 1997 the European Commission introduced a requirement for salmonella testing of all consignments of Nile perch from the region. Following an outbreak of cholera across East Africa, testing was extended to all fish and to cover *Vibrio cholerae* and *Vibrio parahaemoliticus*. These requirements were lifted in June 1998. In March 1999 a suspected case of fish poisoning with pesticide was identified in Uganda. The European Union subsequently imposed a ban on exports of Nile perch in April 1999 that was not lifted for Kenya until December 2000. In each case, the impact was immediate. Exports declined, although over time declines were partially offset by increased sales to other markets. Fish-processing plants, most already operating at less then 50 percent capacity, reduced their production, and some closed. In turn, the landed price of Nile perch fell.

Both the Kenyan government and the private sector tried to upgrade food safety controls. Responsibility for regulatory controls was split between the Ministry of Health and the Fisheries Department of the Ministry of Agriculture and Rural Development, creating significant coordination problems. To improve compliance, the Fisheries Department was made the sole "competent authority," and legislation was quickly revised in line with the European Union's requirements.

Fish-processing plants upgraded their facilities and implemented an HACCP system, at an estimated average cost per plant of about $40,000 and a total cost of $557,000. These costs were prohibitive for several processing facilities, which closed, helping to reduce excess capacity. Simultaneously, fish-processing companies began to cooperate to present a united voice to the government and European Commission. The Kenya Fish Processors and Exporters Association (AFIPEK), formed in 2000, has developed a code of good manufacturing practice for the sector.

A remaining weakness in the Nile perch supply chain is standards of hygiene at landing beaches. Most attempts by the government to implement effective management of the fishery resource and marketing arrangements have failed. Only recently have efforts been made to provide toilets, paved and fenced landing areas, potable water, and covered markets. This is the biggest compliance issue facing the sector in the short to medium term for access to EU markets.

The efforts of the Kenyan government and private sector eventually paid off, and in December 2003 the European Commission recognized the controls in place as equivalent to those in the European Union. The European Union's hygiene requirements for fish and fishery products have had profound effects on the Nile perch sector in Kenya. Whereas the export supply chain had developed with a sole focus on EU markets, today most exporters have diversified their export base and have major markets in Australia, Japan, and the United States. Compliance with EU requirements helped Kenyan exporters to access and maintain these markets.

This case illustrates the significant impact that stricter food safety requirements can have on a supply chain that is almost entirely export oriented and dependent on a single market. It also demonstrates how such requirements can exacerbate pressures for restructuring and reform, while prevailing supply and capacity issues constrain how various levels of the chain are able to respond. The case also illustrates the interdependencies between levels of the supply chain and between the public and private sectors in meeting food safety requirements in export markets. And it demonstrates the importance of responding quickly to emerging food safety and agricultural health standards. The periods of restrictions faced by Kenyan exporters of Nile perch very much reflect the fact that little had been done in response to the implementation of stricter food safety requirements in the country's most important export market. Rather, most of the concerted effort to comply with these requirements was stimulated by the sudden loss of market access, in very much a crisis management mode of operation.

Limits on Mycotoxins as Trade Barriers

Mycotoxins are toxic by-products of mold infestations, affecting as much as a quarter of global food and feed crop output (Dohlman 2003; Reddy and others 2002). They commonly occur in the production of corn, wheat, and peanuts, causing considerable crop losses (Bhat and Vasanthi 1999). Their incidence is affected by weather and insect infestation, although proper production and postharvest (especially storage) practices can strongly mitigate occurrence.[18] Consuming foods with very high levels of mycotoxins can be fatal, and long-term consumption of foods with lower levels has been linked to liver cancer. Since the discovery of mycotoxins in the 1960s, regulatory limits have been established

in 77 countries to protect consumers (Egmond 1999). There are wide differences in national standards, however, linked to different susceptibilities and different perceptions of acceptable health risks. For example, acceptable tolerances for aflatoxin in food range from zero to 50 parts per billion.

There are indications that mycotoxin problems have disrupted developing-country trade. Thailand was once a leading world exporter of corn. Because of persistent aflatoxin problems, however, Thai corn regularly sold at a discount, costing the country an estimated $50 million a year in reduced export revenue.[19] Similarly, India was historically a significant supplier of peanut meal to the European Union, but this trade declined sharply in the early 1980s because of problems meeting stricter standards for aflatoxin. Otsuki, Wilson, and Sewadeh (2001), in a widely cited study, examine the process of harmonization of the European Union's standards for aflatoxin and the potential impact on exports of selected products, including cereals and dried fruit and nuts, from African countries.[20] In 1997 the European Union proposed a set of harmonized standards for aflatoxin for member states, which had developed their own standards, and a uniform sampling procedure for testing. In response to the European Union's notification to the WTO, developing countries raised a series of objections to the proposed standards and sampling methods. The proposed standards were to be far more stringent than the proposed Codex standard, without proper scientific justification.[21]

Otsuki, Wilson, and Sewadeh (2001) argue that these standards are unnecessarily stringent given the estimated risk reduction that would be achieved. Their work is widely cited for its econometric estimation of the potential loss of African trade that could be attributed to the change in the European Union's standard. Using a gravity model, which incorporates a number of variables assumed to affect bilateral trade flows, they compare existing levels of African exports to the European Union with likely levels following implementation of the new standards and likely levels had the European Union adopted the Codex standard (15 parts per billion) across all product categories. They estimate that annual African exports to the European Union of cereals and nuts and dried fruit would decline from $770 million to $372 million following adoption of the EU standard but would rise to slightly more than $1 billion under the Codex standard.

Hence, the decision by the European Union to adopt the more stringent standards was estimated to have cost Africa some $667 million.

The conclusions of this work were headline grabbing but widely misinterpreted. Many subsequent commentators have mistakenly referred to the estimates as if they were actual losses rather than the results of an econometric simulation. Several shortcomings of this method need to be taken into account when interpreting the results.[22] The major focus here relates to the value of exports before and after the adoption of the standard and the lessons that stakeholders take from the example.

The trade data used to establish the baseline put African exports to the European Union (in 1998) at $472 million for dried fruit and nuts and $298 million for cereals, with the bulk of this trade occurring with France. These figures seem implausible, especially for cereals, given Africa's lack of competitiveness in this sector relative to Europe. Statistics from the United Nations COMTRADE database show much lower European imports from Africa in 1998 of $104 million for dried fruit, $45 million for groundnuts, $27 million for other edible nuts, and less than $14 million for cereals and cereal products.[23] This suggests that the baseline against which the impact of the standards should have been assessed was $190 million (c.i.f.—cost, insurance, and freight—value) rather than $770 million.

What about the evidence on impact? Most of the region's dried fruit trade is accounted for by two North African countries—Tunisia and Algeria—whose exceptionally dry climate contributes to a very low incidence of aflatoxin. The only other African country with any history and recent strength in exports of dried fruit is South Africa. The new EU standards came into full force in April 2002. Both in the year proceeding and the year following that date there were no cases of dried fruit consignments from Africa being detained on entry to the European Union. In fact, while total EU imports of dried fruit declined somewhat in 2002, imports from Africa increased, boosting Africa's share from 9.8 percent in 2001 to 10.3 percent in 2002. Competing countries with more humid conditions (especially Turkey) incurred higher levels of product rejections during 2003. For dried fruit, the more stringent EU standards and enforcement at the border worked to the competitive advantage of Africa's leading suppliers.

What about groundnuts? Africa's groundnut exports are dominated by South Africa, although Egypt, The Gambia, Sudan, and Senegal have maintained small exports of confectionery nuts. Various supply-side constraints have inhibited the competitiveness of many African countries in the international market for groundnuts (see chapter 12).[24] In 2002 South Africa had 12 consignments of groundnuts rejected by EU member states because of aflatoxin. Only 3 of the 12 would have met the less stringent Codex standard or the standards applied previously by the individual member states. The rejected consignments were returned to South Africa, presumably for sale elsewhere, rather than destroyed. Probably a few hundred thousand dollars of business was affected, although the probable sale of these nuts in other markets would have substantially mitigated these losses. No evidence was found that Africa's limited exports to the European Union of either cereals or tree nuts have been adversely affected since the adoption of the new standards. Thus the near-term loss of African trade because of the more stringent EU standards has likely been in the hundreds of thousands of dollars rather than in the hundreds of millions.

While the case for significant African trade losses is weak, compliance with the EU aflatoxin standards remains a challenge for some developing countries. Between 2000 and 2002 the number of border rejections of nuts, nut products, and other snacks increased threefold (from 92 to 251). In 2002 some 235 consignments of nuts and dried fruit were rejected on grounds of excessive levels of aflatoxin. Most of the rejected shipments were from Turkey (77 cases involving hazelnuts and dried fruit), Brazil (51 cases, mainly Brazil nuts), and Iran (50 cases, mainly pistachios). Other countries with more than a few rejections were China (18), South Africa (12), the United States (7), and Argentina (5).

Although the data are incomplete, the EU notifications and alerts database reports the actual test results for levels of aflatoxin for many months. In most cases of rejection, the measured levels of aflatoxin are substantially higher (sometimes many times higher) than the Codex standard and also significantly above the domestic standards of the exporting countries. For example, of the 15 nut and dried fruit consignments rejected in January 2002, only 3 were above the EU standard but below the Codex standard. In October 2002, one country source of nuts had 38 individual consignments rejected, 15 involving aflatoxin levels of 100 parts per billion or more.[25] This suggests that suppliers, especially those producing in humid conditions, are having considerable difficulty controlling aflatoxin contamination.

It is still unclear, however, how much EU standards on aflatoxin have affected developing-country trade. For example, Iran has been experiencing problems with aflatoxin for several years. Its exports of edible nuts declined from $452 million in 1996 to less than $210 million in 2002. Further analysis is needed to determine how much of this decline can be attributed to problems with aflatoxin contamination and of that, how much to regulatory measures rather than to a more general loss of buyer confidence. Exports from Turkey, however, seem to have been little affected by the increased stringency of EU standards and enforcement. In 2002 the volume of products rejected by the European Union constituted less than 1 percent of Turkish exports of nuts and dried fruit to that market. Any rejected product is reexported to countries with less strict standards (or enforcement) or sold domestically, reducing losses.

Proliferation of Horticultural Product Standards

The regulatory and private governance systems for international fresh produce markets are becoming increasingly complex. This changing regulatory environment appears to be raising the bar for new entrants and throwing new challenges in the path of existing developing-country suppliers. Concern is mounting about the ability of small and low-income countries to meet rising public and private standards and thus their ability to remain competitive in international fresh produce markets (Dolan and Humphrey 2000; Chan and King 2000; Buurma and others 2001). High-profile food scares and highly publicized instances of pesticide residue violations have created an impression of extreme vulnerability of developing-country suppliers. Yet experiences are mixed, and most countries and industries that have run into standards-related barriers have also been struggling with other supply-chain problems that have inhibited their profitability and competitiveness. Consider the contrasting experiences of two low-income countries, Guatemala and Kenya.

Guatemalan raspberries: a cautionary tale?   In the late 1980s several firms began exporting raspberries from Guatemala to the United States during months when U.S. domestic supplies were limited (Calvin 2003; Calvin, Flores, and Foster 2003). By 1996 these exports had reached $3 million, with some 85 growers participating. In that year, however, the U.S. Centers for Disease Control and Prevention and Health Canada received reports of some 1,465 cases of food-borne illness associated with the parasite *Cyclospora*. Raspberries from Guatemala were identified as the most likely source of the contamination.

The FDA sent a team to Guatemala to investigate, amid considerable scientific uncertainty and great difficulty identifying the likely source of the contamination. The association of Guatemalan growers (GBC) remained unconvinced that its raspberries were the source of the problem. It attempted to put in place a limited program to screen out potentially high-risk farms, but the program had no effective enforcement mechanism. After another large outbreak of *Cyclospora*-related illnesses in the spring of 1997, the GBC voluntarily agreed to stop exports of raspberries to the United States. Despite the fact that the Guatemalan government created a food safety commission with enforcement powers in late 1997, the FDA was unconvinced and essentially imposed an import ban on Guatemalan raspberries.

During the next two years many organizations in the United States and Canada worked with the Guatemalans to solve the problem. A Model Plan of Excellence was put in place in 1999, involving the application of food safety practices by growers, mandatory inspection by government, and a system of product traceability back to individual growers. The United States lifted the ban on imports of Guatemalan raspberries. In 2000, however, there were two further *Cyclospora* outbreaks, which were traced back to a single Guatemalan farm. The grower was removed from the program, and there have been no further outbreaks.

While the Model Plan of Excellence was technically successful, it came too late to save the industry. Facing consumer concerns, several supermarkets in the United States sought alternative sources of raspberries. Recognizing the enormous challenge of rehabilitating the reputation of Guatemalan raspberries in the eyes of both consumers and distributors, several leading firms (both Guatemalan and international firms) shifted their operations to Mexico. By 2001 only four growers of raspberries for export remained in Guatemala, with exports of less than $200,000. Meanwhile, Mexico's exports of raspberries grew from $2.9 million in 1998 to $8.9 million in 2002 and now account for the largest share of an expanding U.S. import market.

Although the Guatemalan raspberry industry never recovered, other parts of the fresh produce industry built on the institutional capacity building that had taken place. For example, the inspection agency, the Integrated Program for Agricultural and Environmental Protection (PIPAA), has been working closely with local blackberry growers, a leading local supermarket chain, and others to enhance food safety management systems. PIPAA is also collaborating with the Animal and Plant Health Inspection Service and the FDA in the United States on a program for Guatemalan exports of mangoes and papayas.

Calvin, Flores, and Foster (2003) draw several lessons from Guatemala's experience. Delays in addressing food safety and agricultural health problems may hurt an industry's exports and reputation. An effective traceability system allows focusing on particular growers or exporters rather than needing to enhance standards in an entire industry. Finally, strong grower organizations can improve an industry's ability to respond to food safety challenges. There is also a wider lesson from Guatemala's experience. Small countries and niche products are probably far more vulnerable to loss of markets and collapse of reputation in the face of food safety problems than are larger countries and more mainstream or generic products. Both international buyers and consumers would likely be more tolerant and patient with core, long-standing suppliers that have established a "brand" in which they have confidence.

Kenyan fresh produce exports: some success. Kenya's fresh produce trade dates to the mid-1950s, when small quantities of temperate-climate vegetables and tropical fruits were supplied in the European winter off-season to up-market stores in London.[26] This off-season trade was later joined by year-round supplies of high-quality green beans and a broad array of vegetables that are part of the traditional diets of UK immigrant populations from South Asia. Most of the products were air-freighted in two-kilogram boxes for sale through wholesale markets or to distributors and caterers.

For years the industry functioned with simple supply chains, involving little investment in infrastructure, product development, or management systems. Around a dozen medium-size firms plus large numbers of small, part-time operators handled the exports, frequently trading with relatives or similar small-scale companies in Europe. Fresh produce was purchased from large numbers of growers. Produce was generally collected in cardboard boxes from farms or along roadsides and brought to a central warehouse, sifted through and regraded if necessary, cooled a little, and trucked to the airport for evening shipment. Ministry of Agriculture officials at the airport conducted limited inspections. This was the model from the 1960s to the mid-1980s. The industry remained competitive in some markets and for some products, but not for others. The Kenyan fresh produce export trade grew slightly in the 1970s but stagnated in the 1980s.

Since the early 1990s the industry has been reshaped and transformed in response to—and in anticipation of—commercial, regulatory, and private governance changes within its core external markets. Commercial pressures came from saturated markets for certain products and increased competition from suppliers that had improved their supply capabilities and had less expensive sea or air-freight costs than did Kenya. Commercial changes within Europe also required a shift in the Kenyan approach. In many countries large supermarket chains were in ascendancy while wholesale markets were declining. Consolidation was also occurring among importers, packers, and distributors. The growing segments of the fresh produce market were being managed by fewer players. On the regulatory front a steady wave of activity was geared toward strengthening and harmonizing EU and member state regulations and monitoring systems for food safety, quality conformity, and plant health. Also emerging were progressively refined private-sector standards or codes of practice governing food safety, plant health, and other issues.

Several leading Kenyan exporters caught an early glimpse of this new fresh produce environment and began to reorient their operations. With the encouragement of several UK supermarkets, they began to experiment with new crops, new consumer packaging, and new combinations of vegetables. An increasing proportion of products was directed to selected supermarket chains, which began to send "audit" teams to Kenya to check hygiene and other conditions on farms and pack-houses. Improvements and investments were recommended and in some cases required. With renewed confidence in the future of the industry, several exporters invested heavily in new or upgraded pack-houses and related food safety management systems for packing ready-to-eat and semi-prepared products. Mixed salads, stir-fry mixes, vegetable kebabs, and other value-added products now account for more than 40 percent of what has been a burgeoning trade over the past decade. Between 1991 and 2003 Kenya's fresh vegetable exports increased from $23 million to $140 million.[27]

Rising public- and private-sector standards have posed challenges to the Kenyan fresh produce industry, yet they have also thrown a lifeline to the industry. Because of Kenya's location and relatively high air-freight costs, its fresh produce sector cannot compete with many other players on a unit-cost basis. Margins have been squeezed in the market for mainstream, commodity-type vegetables. With rising labor costs in Europe, however, the Kenyan industry has positioned itself as a slicer, dicer, and salad-maker, all labor-intensive functions. Thus far, this market segment has grown fastest in the United Kingdom, although there is increased buyer interest and consumer demand on the European continent as well. This suggests that well-organized industries in low-income countries can use stricter standards as a catalyst for change—and profit in the process.

Conclusions

There are now a number of documented cases in which developing countries have faced restrictions because of their inability to meet food safety or agricultural health requirements. In some of these, well-established export-dependent sectors have been compromised by the implementation of new, stricter standards, with negative repercussions for the livelihoods of those involved. At the same time, other countries have managed to gain access to high-value markets in industrial countries despite the exacting standards. Clearly, the situation is not as black and white as some commentators suggest. What cannot be disputed, however, is that stan-

dards have become an increasingly important influence on the international competitiveness of developing countries, especially for high-value agricultural and food products.

The evidence presented in this chapter, while admittedly incomplete, suggests that the picture for developing countries as a whole is much less pessimistic than that widely presented by the standards-as-barriers perspective. Indeed, rising standards accentuate underlying supply-chain strengths and weaknesses and thus affect the competitive positions of countries and distinct market participants, making it important to view the effects of food safety and agricultural health measures in the context of wider capacity constraints. The key question for developing countries is how to exploit their strengths and overcome their weaknesses to emerge as gainers rather than losers.

Still, by raising the bar for new entrants and placing a premium on effective safety management and logistical coordination, higher official and private standards can weaken the competitive position of small and poorer countries and the ability of small enterprises and farmers to remain active and profitable in export supply chains. But food safety and agricultural health standards are here to stay, and there is no slowing down their rate of change or applying for special and differential treatment. Much of the impetus for standards comes from consumer and commercial interests, magnified by advances in technology and added security concerns.

The answer for developing countries is to develop and improve food safety and agricultural health management systems. This requires simultaneous attention to legal systems, human capital, and physical infrastructure, among other things. Management capacity is required not only to comply with different requirements in different markets, but also to demonstrate compliance with standards. Although many countries have struggled to meet ever stricter standards, even some very poor countries have managed to implement the necessary capacity. This has most commonly occurred where the private sector is well organized and the public sector is well focused and supports the efforts of exporters. To meet the challenges posed by standards in international markets for high-value agricultural and food products, developing countries need institutional frameworks to help them overcome the problems associated with being poor or small. These can include outgrower programs for smallholder farmers, systems of training and oversight for smaller enterprises organized through associations and other groups, and twinning and regional networking for small countries.

An overarching message is the need for developing countries (and their exporters) to be proactive on food safety and agricultural health issues. It is important not to be pushed into action by a major crisis. By thinking strategically, countries, producers, and exporters can program capacity enhancement into wider and longer term efforts to enhance domestic food safety and agricultural health management systems and export competitiveness. The alternative is that large investments will be required over a long period just to "put out fires." In all of this, there is a need for the public and private sectors to work together to identify the most efficient and effective ways to develop capacity, viewing food safety and agricultural health controls as a collaborative effort.

Notes

1. For the more traditional food exports of developing countries, such as beverage crops, fiber crops, tobacco, and sugar, international trade is still largely governed by price and quality and by traditional forms of trade protection and preferences (see chapters 3 and 4).

2. According to a source at the Food and Drug Administration, while 99 percent of domestic facilities are found to be in compliance, some 30 percent of inspected foreign facilities have significant system defects.

3. See www.cfsan.fda.gov and europa.eu.int/comm/food/fs/ inspections/fnaoi/reports/annual_eu/index_en.html.

4. For example, as of August 2003, two countries—the Netherlands and the United Kingdom—accounted for more than two-thirds of the area certified as being EUREPGAP-compliant. EUREPGAP is a set of good agricultural practices (GAP) based on accepted standards and promoted by the European retailer produce group (EUREP). Only a small proportion of the area in developing countries on which fresh produce is grown for the European market was so certified, the bulk of it in South Africa. Recognizing these constraints, extended deadlines have been given to many developing-country exporters and producers to adopt and gain certification against the EUREPGAP protocol.

5. Only 20 percent of the notifications by low-income countries and 22 percent of those of high-income countries involved applications of international standards.

6. An array of capacity assessment instruments are used to gauge strengths and weaknesses of food safety and agricultural health management capacity. Some instruments focus on specific dimensions of capacity, while others provide a broader overview.

7. In practice, it is rather difficult to measure "costs of compliance." Food safety is very often achieved in combination with other business functions and is thus a joint product with those functions. Thus, there are questions over what investments and which management systems are put in place strictly to ensure compliance with particular standards and which service a multiplicity of functions. In practice, it is often difficult to make this separation. For example, cold-store facilities may be needed to prevent the multiplication of bacteria in fresh produce, yet such facilities are also critical for achieving a quality characteristic or extended shelf-life.

8. One leading Kenyan firm estimated that the costs of its small farmer oversight arrangements represented about 12 percent of its costs of raw materials. These transaction costs represent 6 percent of the f.o.b. (free on board) value of French beans, which is equivalent to the exporter's profit on the product and about 60 percent of the grower's profit.

9. Some new products may not require as much farm labor as previously traded products or may require more capital investment. In either scenario the comparative advantage of smallholders may be reduced.

10. Data for the United States can be found at www.fda.gov/ ora/oasis/ora_oasis_ref.html, and for the European Union at www.europa.eu.int/comm/food/fs/sfp/ras_index_en.html. The data exclude certain agricultural and food products for which the FDA has no jurisdiction, most notably meat and poultry. Until 2002 these data referred to border detentions regardless of whether the product was eventually permitted to enter. Since then they have recorded border rejections. The European Union has made disaggregated data on import alerts available only since 2002, although annual reports with broad summary statistics were published previously.

11. Between 2002 and 2003 the number of ports at which the FDA has assigned inspection staff increased from 40 to 90. During this period, a $96 million increase in the FDA's budget for food security work enabled it to hire 655 new field personnel. In the Bush administration's proposed 2005 budget, the FDA would receive a 9 percent increase in funding to expand its "food defense" program. The fiscal 2005 budget calls for 97,000 import inspections, seven times the number undertaken in 2001. Similarly large increases were proposed for the Department of Agriculture's work on food safety.

12. To put this number into perspective, the estimated total costs to the United Kingdom alone from BSE-related market losses and for the various cull and disposal schemes was more than $5 billion (Mathews, Bernstein, and Buzby 2003). This does not take any account of the adverse impact on the country's tourism industry.

13. For example, the United States currently permits imports of beef from only 33 countries and imports of chicken from only 4 countries.

14. Currently, the International Office of Epizooties recognizes only 57 countries as being totally free of foot and mouth disease without vaccination, of which 26 are developing countries—only 3 of them low-income countries. For further information, see www.oie.int.

15. Indeed, more widespread cases of both new and well-established animal diseases have led to heightened concerns about the role of international trade in the spread of such diseases. In the case of BSE, widespread restrictions have been applied to trade in live animals, meat, animal feed, and an array of by-products used in the cosmetics, pharmaceutical, and other industries.

16. For the case studies produced by UNCTAD, see r0.unctad.org/trade_env/test1/openF1.htm. For the case studies produced by UNEP, see www.unep.ch/etu/publications/ Ctry_studies.htm.

17. The European Commission has presented its controls on hygiene for imports of fish and fishery products as a practical example of the application of equivalence (WTO 2001). Thus, rather than laying down specific requirements, the European Commission focuses on the conditions under which products will be equivalent to those produced in the European Union.

18. Although the growth of mycotoxin-producing molds is an endemic problem in humid areas, management of this problem need not involve very sophisticated or costly measures. See Boutrif (1997), Park, Njapau, and Boutrif (1999), and Dimanche and Kane (2002) for examples of practical and low-cost measures.

19. There, most of the problem occurred during postharvest as the harvested maize was typically stored in moist if not wet conditions for one to two months before sale and processing (Tangthirasunan, T. n.d.).

20. This is probably the most widely cited study on the potential or actual impact of rising food safety standards on exports of agricultural and food products from developing countries.

21. In response to objections, the European Union revised some of its proposed measures. In its 1998 Directive, it established a limit for total aflatoxin in groundnuts subject to further processing at 15 parts per billion, and a limit for aflatoxin B1 at 8 parts per billion, which was consistent with the proposed Codex standard. For other nuts and dried fruit subject to further processing, more stringent limits were set at 10 parts per billion for total aflatoxin and 5 parts per billion for aflatoxin B1. There was no equivalent Codex standard. The strictest standard was set for cereals, dried fruits and nuts intended directly for human consumption with maximum levels of 4 parts per billion for total aflatoxin and 2 parts per billion for aflatoxin B1. Again, there was no equivalent Codex standard.

22. See, for example the discussions about gravity models and other approaches to estimating the trade impacts of standards in Beghin and Bureau (2001), OECD (2003), and Wilson (2003).

23. In that year, African exports of cereals totaled $105 million, with Egypt accounting for $70 million. The vast majority of this trade was conducted with countries of the Near East and Middle East.

24. In the 1960s and 1970s Africa was a major world supplier of groundnuts, with large exporters in Malawi, Nigeria, Senegal, and other countries. For reasons unrelated to aflatoxin, these exports lost their international competitiveness, and most production went to serve domestic markets or for use in oil crushing. Over the years, research activity and the commercial trade in Africa moved away from confectionery-type varieties preferred in world markets, and recent attempts to revive confectionery nut exports have encountered major problems attributable to inadequate seed, basic quality control and price incentives for farmers.

25. Moonen (2004) reports on testing results from the Dutch import control authority. It is common that groundnut shipments from developing countries have levels of aflatoxin contamination of between 50 and 800 parts per billion. Also cited by Moonen are toxicological surveys in Senegal for groundnuts sold in the domestic market. Some 90 percent of sampled groundnuts were contaminated with aflatoxin with the average level being 230 parts per billion.

26. The discussion in this section draws on Jaffee (2003).

27. Systems for crop procurement have also been transformed, with many leading companies investing in their own farms or inducing changes in the practices of outgrowers. There has been an array of joint public-private initiatives to train growers in all aspects of good agricultural practice. But not all of the industry has transformed itself. Some 25 smaller exporters lack the financial resources to invest in modern pack-houses and continue to supply loose produce to commission agents and others in European wholesale markets and the Middle East.

References

Beghin, J., and J. C. Bureau. 2001. "Quantitative Policy Analysis of Sanitary, Phytosanitary and Technical Barriers to Trade." *Economie Internationale* 87(3): 107–30.

Bhat, Ramesh, and S. Vasanthi. 1999. "Mycotoxin Contamination of Foods and Feeds." Paper presented at the Third Joint FAO/WHO/UNEP International Conference on Mycotoxins, March 3–6, Tunis.

Boutrif, E. 1997. "Aflatoxin Prevention Programmes." Food and Agriculture Organization, Rome.

Bureau, J. C., S. Marette, and A. Schiavina. 1998. "Non-Tariff Trade Barriers and Consumers' Information: The Case of the EU–US Trade Dispute over Beef." *European Review of Agricultural Economics* 25(4): 437–62.

Buurma, J. S., M. J. B. Mengelers, A. J. Smelt, and E. Muller. 2001. "Developing Countries and Products Affected by Setting New Maximum Residue Limits of Pesticides in the EU." Agricultural Economics Research Institute, The Hague.

Buzby, J., ed. 2003. *International Trade and Food Safety: Economic Theory and Case Studies.* Agricultural Economic Report 828. U.S. Department of Agriculture. Washington, D.C.

Calvin, L. 2003. "Produce, Food Safety, and International Trade: Response to U.S. Foodborne Illness Outbreaks Associated with Imported Produce." In J. Buzby, ed., *International Trade and Food Safety: Economic Theory and Case Studies.* Agricultural Economic Report 828. U.S. Department of Agriculture. Washington, D.C.

Calvin, L., L. Flores, and W. Foster. 2003. "Case Study: Guatemalan Raspberries and Cyclospora." In L. Unnevehr, ed., *Food Safety in Food Security and Food Trade.* Washington, D.C.: International Food Policy Research Institute.

Cato, J., and C. Lima dos Santos. 2000. "Costs to Upgrade the Bangladesh Frozen Shrimp Processing Sector to Adequate Technical and Safety Standards and to Maintain a HACCP Program." In L. Unnevehr, ed., *HACCP: New Studies of Costs and Benefits.* St. Paul: Eagen Press.

Cato, J., S. Otwell, and A. Coze. 2003. "Nicaragua's Shrimp Subsector: Developing a Production Capacity and Export Market during Rapidly Changing Worldwide Safety and Quality Regulations." Case study prepared as part of a World Bank program on The Challenges and Opportunities Associated with International Agro-Food Standards. Washington, D.C.

Chan, M., and B. King. 2000. "Review of the Implications of Changes in EU Pesticides Legislation on the Production and Export of Fruits and Vegetables from Developing Country Suppliers." Natural Resources and Ethical Trade Programme, London.

Crain, W., and J. Johnson. 2001. "Compliance Costs of Federal Workplace Regulations: Survey Results from U.S. Manufacturers." George Mason University, Regulatory Studies Program, Arlington, Va.

Delgado, C. L., N. Wada, M. W. Rosegrant, S. Meijer, and M. Ahmed. 2003. *Fish to 2020: Supply and Demand in Changing Global Markets.* Washington, D.C.: International Food Policy Research Institute.

Dimanche, P., and A. Kane. 2002. "Senegal's Confectionery Peanut Supply Chain: The Challenge of Controlling Aflatoxin Levels." In *Food Safety Management in Developing*

Countries. Proceedings of the International Workshop, CIRAD-FAO, December 11–13, Montpellier, France.

Dohlman, E. 2003. "Mycotoxin Hazards and Regulations: Impacts on Food and Animal Feed Crop Trade." In J. Buzby, ed., *International Trade and Food Safety: Economic Theory and Case Studies.* Agricultural Economic Report 828. U.S. Department of Agriculture. Washington, D.C.

Dolan, C., and J. Humphrey. 2000. "Governance and Trade in Fresh Vegetables: The Impact of UK Supermarkets on the African Horticulture Industry." *Journal of Development Studies* 37(2): 147–76.

Dong, F., and H. Jensen. 2004. "The Challenge of Conforming to Sanitary and Phytosanitary Measures for China's Agricultural Exports," MATRIC Working Paper 04-MWP 8, Iowa State University, Ames, Iowa.

Egmond, Hans. 1999. "Worldwide Regulations for Mycotoxins." Paper presented at the Third Joint FAO/WHO/UNEP International Conference on Mycotoxins, March 3–6, Tunis.

El-Tawil, A. 2002. "An In-Depth Study of the Problems by the Standardizers and Other Stakeholders from Developing Countries." Paper presented at the ISO/WTO regional workshops: Part 1. International Organization for Standardization, Geneva.

Henson, S. J. 2001. "Appropriate Level of Protection: A European Perspective." In K. Anderson, C. McRae, and D. Wilson, eds., *The Economics of Quarantine and the SPS Agreement.* University of Adelaide, Centre for International Trade Studies, Australia.

———. 2004. "National Laws, Regulations, and Institutional Capabilities for Standards Development." Paper prepared for a World Bank training seminar on Standards and Trade, January 27–28, Washington, D.C.

Henson, S. J., and W. Mitullah. 2004. "Kenyan Exports of Nile Perch: Impact of Food Safety Standards on an Export-Oriented Supply Chain." Case study for a World Bank program on the Challenges and Opportunities Associated with International Agro-Food Standards. Policy Research Working Paper 3349. World Bank, Washington, D.C.

Jaffee, S. 2003. *From Challenge to Opportunity: Transforming Kenya's Fresh Vegetable Trade in the Context of Emerging Food Safety and Other Standards in Europe.* Agriculture and Rural Development Discussion Paper 1. World Bank, Washington, D.C.

Lamb, J., J. Velez, and R. Barclay. 2004. "The Challenge of Compliance with SPS and Other Standards Associated with the Export of Shrimp and Selected Fresh Produce Items to the United States Market." Paper submitted to the World Bank. Washington, D.C.

Mathews, K, J. Bernstein, and J. Buzby. 2003. "International Trade of Meat/Poultry Products and Food Safety Issues." In J. Buzby, ed., *International Trade and Food Safety: Economic Theory and Case Studies.* Agricultural Economic Report 828. U.S. Department of Agriculture, Washington, D.C.

Moonen, I. 2004. "The Aflatoxin Case: Process and Impact Evaluation of the EU Regulation on Aflatoxin." Paper submitted to the Netherlands Ministry of Foreign Affairs, Policy Coherence Unit, The Hague.

OECD (Organisation for Economic Co-operation and Development). 2003. "Trade Effects of the SPS Agreement." Joint Working Party on Agriculture and Trade, Paris.

Otsuki, T., J. Wilson, and M. Sewadeh. 2001. "Saving Two in a Billion: Quantifying the Trade Effect of European Food Safety Standards on African Exports." *Food Policy* 26(5): 495–514.

Park, D., H. Njapau, and E. Boutrif. 1999. "Minimizing Risks Posed by Mycotoxins Utilizing the HACCP Concept." Paper presented at the Third Joint FAO/WHO/NEP International Conference on Mycotoxins, March 3–6, Tunis.

Pauwelyn, J. 1999. "The WTO Agreement on Sanitary and Phytosanitary (SPS) Measures as Applied in the First Three SPS Disputes." *Journal of International Economic Law* 2(94): 641–49.

Perry, B. D., T. F. Randolph, S. Ashley, R. Chimedza, T. Forman, J. Morrison, C. Poulton, L. Sibanda, C. Stevens, N. Tebele, and I. Yngstrom. 2003. "The Impact and Poverty Reduction Implications of Foot and Mouth Disease Control in Southern Africa." International Livestock Research Institute, Nairobi.

Reardon, T., and J. A. Berdegue. 2002. "The Rapid Rise of Supermarkets in Latin America: Challenges and Opportunities for Development." *Development Policy Review* 20(4): 371–88.

Reddy, D., K. Thirumala-Devi, S. Reddy, F. Waliyar, M. Mayo, K. Devi, R. Ortiz, and J. Lenne. 2002. "Estimation of Aflatoxin Levels in Selected Foods and Feeds in India." In *Food Safety Management in Developing Countries,* Proceedings of the International Workshop, CIRAD-FAO, December 11–13, Montpellier, France.

Roberts, D. 2004. "The Multilateral Governance Framework for Sanitary and Phytosanitary Regulations: Challenges and Prospects." Paper prepared for a World Bank training seminar on Standards and Trade, January 27–28, Washington, D.C.

Roberts, D., and B. Krissoff. 2003. "The WTO Agreement on the Application of Sanitary and Phytosanitary Barriers." U.S. Department of Agriculture, Economic Research Service, Washington, D.C.

Roberts, D., and D. Orden. 1997. "Determinants of Technical Barriers to Trade: The Case of U.S. Phytosanitary Restrictions on Mexican Avocados, 1972–1995." In D. Orden and D. Roberts, eds., *Understanding Technical Barriers to Trade.* Minneapolis-St. Paul: University of Minnesota, International Agricultural Trade Research Consortium.

Roberts, D., T. Josling, and D. Orden. 1999. "A Framework for Analyzing Technical Trade Barriers in Agricultural Markets." U.S. Department of Agriculture, Economic Research Service. Washington, D.C.

Sumner, D. A., ed. 2003. *Exotic Pests and Diseases: Biology and Economics for Biosecurity.* Ames, Iowa: Iowa State Press.

Tangthirasunan, T. n.d. "Mycotoxin Economic Aspects." Food and Agriculture Organization. Rome.

Unnevehr, L. 2003. "Food Safety in Food Security and Food Trade: Overview." In L. Unnevehr, ed., *Food Safety in Food Security and Food Trade.* Washington, D.C.: International Food Policy Research Institute.

Unnevehr, L., and N. Hirschhorn. 2001. "Designing Effective Food Safety Interventions in Developing Countries." World Bank, Washington, D.C.

Wilson, J., and T. Otsuki. 2003. "Balancing Risk Reduction and Benefits from Trade in Setting Standards." In L. Unnevehr, ed., *Food Safety in Food Security and Food Trade.* Washington, D.C.: International Food Policy Research Institute.

Wilson, N. 2003. "A Review of Empirical Studies of the Trade and Economic Effects of Food Safety Regulations." In A. Velthuis, ed., *New Approaches to Food Safety Economics.* Boston: Kluwer Academic Publishers.

WTO (World Trade Organization). 2001 "Equivalence: Note by the Secretariat." G/SPS/W/111. Geneva.

7

GLOBAL AGRICULTURAL REFORM: WHAT IS AT STAKE?

Dominique van der Mensbrugghe
and John C. Beghin

This chapter uses a global, dynamic applied general equilibrium model (LINKAGE) to assess how the multifarious trade and support policies in agriculture affect income, trade, and output patterns at the global level.[1] Such models have become a standard tool for assessing policy reforms because they capture linkages across sectors and regions (through trade) and because, by their nature, they have adding-up constraints so that supply and demand are in equilibrium in all markets. The analysis provides order-of-magnitude estimates of the potential consequences of policy changes, rather than a single point or "best" estimate. It also looks at the induced structural changes, including cross-regional patterns of output and trade, which tend to be much larger than the more familiar gains to real income. Whereas income gains typically amount to 1 percent of base income or less, structural changes—for example, in sectoral output or trade—can be greater than 50 percent.

Two sets of simulations are used to create a deeper picture of what drives the key results. One set decomposes the aggregate results by looking at the impacts of partial reforms—both regionally and across instruments—to identify what share of the global gains derives from reform in industrial countries and what from reform in developing countries and what share is driven by border protection and what by domestic support. The second set of simulations addresses issues raised by critics of trade reform—notably that the predicted gains for developing countries are too optimistic and that the transition costs for industrial-country farmers are high and too often ignored. Concerns have also been raised about the ability of developing countries to respond to reforms and to achieve consistently high productivity gains. To answer the questions about the impacts on developing countries, three assumptions are explored: the consequences of assuming differential and lower agricultural productivity in some developing countries, the impacts of constraining output supply response in selected low-income countries, and estimates of trade elasticities. The chapter also assesses the impacts of

With great appreciation from the authors, the underlying work in this chapter has benefited over several years from useful comments and suggestions from the following colleagues: Ataman Aksoy, Jonathan Brooks, Bill Cline, Uri Dadush, Bernard Hoekman, Jeff Lewis, Will Martin, John Nash, Richard Newfarmer, David Roland-Holst, Josef Schmidhuber, and Hans Timmer as well as participants at seminars at the OECD and the University of California at Berkeley.

slower exit by industrial-country farmers and how this would affect transition adjustments.

Some of the main findings:

- Reform of agricultural and food trade policy provides 70 percent of the global gains from merchandise trade reform—$265 billion of a total of $385 billion.
- The global gains are shared roughly equally between industrial and developing countries, but developing countries gain significantly more as a share of initial income. Significant income gains occur in developing-country agriculture, where poverty tends to be concentrated.
- Developing countries gain more from reforming their own support policies than from improved market access in industrial countries. Likewise, industrial countries also gain relatively more from their own reform.
- Notwithstanding the overall benefits from greater openness, structural changes are important and transition adjustments need to be addressed.
- Productivity and supply assumptions affect impact assessment, but their influence is small, and they do not alter the main aggregate findings. Trade elasticities, however, are key in determining the overall level of the income gains. Higher elasticities dampen terms-of-trade effects and increase trade and real income gains more than proportionally, while the opposite is true for lower elasticities. These effects can be very large for individual countries.

The Modeling Framework

The LINKAGE model is based on a standard neo-classical general equilibrium model with firms maximizing profit in competitive markets and consumers maximizing well-being under a budget constraint. The model has added features related to its dynamic nature. It is global, with the world decomposed into 23 regions, and multisectoral, with economic activity aggregated into 22 sectors (see annex A in the report on the CD-ROM). Seven of the 23 regions are classified as high-income (or industrial) including Canada, Western Europe (European Union-15 plus the European Free Trade Association countries), Japan, and the United States—the so-called Quad countries. The develop-

ing countries include some of the large countries that are important in agricultural markets as producers or as consumers (Argentina, Brazil, China, India, and Indonesia). The remaining developing countries are grouped into regional aggregations.[2] The sectoral decomposition is concentrated in the agricultural and food sectors (15 of the 22 sectors).

The LINKAGE model is dynamic, with scenarios spanning 1997 to 2015. The dynamics include exogenously given labor and land growth rates, savings-driven investment and capital accumulation, and exogenous productivity growth. Structural changes over time are driven by differential growth rates and supply and demand parameters. Trade is modeled using the Armington assumption. Goods are differentiated by region of origin using a two-nested structure (domestic absorption first allocated across domestic and aggregate import goods, then aggregate imports allocated across different regions of origin).

Overview of Baseline Simulation

Assessing the impacts of policy reforms requires two steps in the dynamic framework of the LINKAGE model, a baseline (or reference) simulation and a reform simulation. The baseline involves running the model forward from its 1997 base year to 2015, with exogenous assumptions about labor and population growth rates, productivity, and demand behavior parameters including savings, which determines the rate of capital accumulation (adjusted exogenously for depreciation).

The baseline simulation can also incorporate changes in base year policies—to take into account known changes in policies (between 1997 and the present) or anticipated changes. The baseline described below assumes no changes in base year policies, however; they are held at their 1997 levels. Thus the reform simulations reflect changes from their 1997 levels, not changes that would be anticipated from 2004 levels.[3] It is unclear in which direction some past and anticipated changes would affect the global trade reform results. Some changes clearly reflect further opening—for example, China's accession to the World Trade Organization (WTO) and some bilateral free trade agreements. Others would go in the opposite direction—for example, the changes to the U.S. farm support programs.

Agriculture and Food Trends in the Baseline Scenario

Trends in agriculture and food supply and demand across the globe as determined in the baseline scenario are driven in part by the macroeconomic environment (as described in annex B on the CD-ROM). But they are also driven by microeconomic assumptions about the mobility of factors, production technologies, income and price elasticities, and trade elasticities, among others.

For agriculture and food between 2000 and 2015, both demand and production grow at 1.0–1.2 percent a year in industrial countries and at a much higher 2.9–3.4 percent in developing countries (tables 7.1 and 7.2 summarize the results; tables on the CD-ROM provide details for individual countries). On a per capita basis there is more demand growth in developing countries, largely because of higher income elasticities for food. Thus the baseline assumes that demand growth will be lower than output growth in industrial countries and higher than output growth in developing countries.

With higher output growth than demand, industrial countries will see an increase in their exportable surplus. On aggregate their net

TABLE 7.1 Trends in Agriculture, 2000–15

Country Grouping	Average Annual Growth (percent)				Net Trade (billions of 1997 US$)	
	Output	Demand	Imports	Exports	2000	2015
High-income countries	1.2	1.1	1.9	3.0	−24.3	−3.1
Low-income countries	3.6	3.5	4.4	5.5	9.9	21.6
Middle-income countries	3.2	3.3	8.3	5.4	14.4	−18.5
Low-income countries, excluding India	3.7	3.4	3.6	6.6	7.2	22.4
Middle-income countries, including India	3.2	3.4	8.3	5.1	17.1	−19.3
Developing countries	3.3	3.4	7.8	5.4	24.3	3.1
World total	2.6	2.6	4.4	4.2	0.0	0.0

Note: Net trade is measured at f.o.b. prices (imports exclude international trade and transport margins).
Source: World Bank simulations with LINKAGE model, based on release 5.4 of the GTAP data.

TABLE 7.2 Trends in Processed Foods, 2000–15

Country Grouping	Average Annual Growth (percent)				Net Trade (billions of 1997 US$)	
	Output	Demand	Imports	Exports	2000	2015
High-income countries	1.2	1.0	1.3	2.4	7.7	53.5
Low-income countries	3.3	3.4	3.9	2.2	3.6	1.8
Middle-income countries	2.9	3.1	4.5	2.0	−11.3	−55.3
Low-income countries, excluding India	3.1	3.3	3.8	2.2	1.8	−0.2
Middle-income countries, including India	2.9	3.1	4.5	2.0	−9.5	−53.4
Developing countries	2.9	3.2	4.5	2.1	−7.7	−53.5
World total	1.8	1.8	2.4	2.3	0.0	0.0

Note: Net trade is measured at f.o.b. prices (imports exclude international trade and transport margins).
Source: World Bank simulations with LINKAGE model, based on release 5.4 of the GTAP data.

agricultural and food trade will improve dramatically from a deficit of $17 billion in 2000 to a surplus of $50 billion in 2015 (at 1997 prices). The opposite occurs in developing countries, where a net positive balance in agriculture and food turns into a large deficit of $50 billion, due mostly to a ballooning deficit in processed food. Agriculture and food balances are positive for low-income countries in 2000 and 2015.

Developing a baseline of the future world economy requires nuanced analysis. The country and regional growth rates used here are in line with consensus views, given stronger demographic trends and income elasticities for agriculture and food in developing economies. World and regional totals may be skewed by several factors. The weights are biased toward industrial countries because of the use of base year (1997) value shares. Volume shares would yield different figures. Demand growth in developing countries may be overstated because income elasticities are held constant at their base year levels. It is plausible to argue that income elasticities would converge toward those of high-income countries as developing countries grow. The growth numbers are also broadly consistent with Food and Agriculture Organization (FAO) historical trends. The discrepancy between agricultural growth and food processing originates in the growth in intermediate demand for agricultural products as food processing grows. A more meat-intensive future world would also exhibit a slight acceleration in agricultural growth relative to food because of the feed input in the livestock sector. So, while the baseline scenario is plausible, aggregate growth rates should be used with caution for all these reasons.

The biggest mover among developing countries is China, where the food deficit of $8 billion in 1997 would swell to somewhere around $120 billion by 2015. Demand is expected to outpace output by about 1 percentage point a year.[4] In agriculture this provides new opportunities for Sub-Saharan Africa and Latin America, with both seeing a large rise in agricultural surplus (on an aggregate basis). Sub-Saharan Africa will nonetheless see a slight deterioration in its processed-food balance. The aggregate net trade balances may mask more detailed sectoral shifts. For example, Sub-Saharan Africa will continue to be a net importer of grains through the baseline scenario time horizon, and therefore a rise

in world prices induced by trade reform could lead to a negative terms-of-trade shock since the agricultural commodities they tend to export—for example, coffee and cocoa—already have relatively free access.

With relatively low demand growth in industrial countries and relatively high output growth, the exportable agricultural surplus will increase substantially, particularly from North America and Oceania. Europe and Japan are the exceptions, with output growth expected to be anemic.

The Impacts of Agricultural Reform

The impacts of agricultural trade reform are examined first in the context of global merchandise trade reform, and then the results are decomposed by type of reform and region, to assess the relative importance for developing countries of reforms in industrial countries and in developing countries.

Results of Global Merchandise Trade Reform

Global reform involves removing protection in all (nonservice) sectors, in all regions, and for all instruments of protection (leaving other taxes unchanged, although lump-sum taxes (or transfers) on households adjust to maintain a fixed government fiscal balance). The model contains six instruments of protection:

- Import tariffs, eliminated only if they are positive
- Export subsidies, eliminated only if they are negative[5]
- Capital subsidies, with direct payments converted into subsidies on capital
- Land subsidies, with some payments also converted to subsidies on land
- Input subsidies
- Output subsidies

The overall measure of reform, referred to as real income, measures the extent to which households are better off in the post-reform scenario than in the baseline scenario in the year 2015.[6] The world gain (measured in 1997 U.S. dollars) is $385 billion, an increase from baseline income of some 0.9 percent (table 7.3). The gains are relatively

TABLE 7.3 **Real Income Gains and Losses from Global Merchandise Trade Reform: Change from 2015 Baseline**

Country Grouping	All Instruments	Tariffs Only	Export Subsidies Only	Capital Subsidies Only	Land Subsidies Only	Input Subsidies Only	Output Subsidies Only
Change in value (billions of 1997 US$)							
High-income countries	188.3	160.4	1.4	1.1	−4.8	−0.3	9.0
Low-income countries	31.9	34.6	−1.1	−0.1	−0.7	−0.3	0.2
Middle-income countries	164.7	187.7	−7.0	−1.2	−7.3	−3.8	−6.4
Low-income countries, excluding India	19.9	21.5	−0.9	−0.1	−0.6	−0.2	0.9
Middle-income countries, including India	176.7	200.8	−7.3	−1.2	−7.4	−3.9	−7.0
Developing countries	196.5	222.3	−8.2	−1.3	−8.1	−4.1	−6.2
World total	384.8	382.7	−6.8	−0.2	−12.8	−4.4	2.8
Percentage change							
High-income countries	0.6	0.5	0.0	0.0	0.0	0.0	0.0
Low-income countries	1.6	1.7	−0.1	0.0	0.0	0.0	0.0
Middle-income countries	1.8	2.0	−0.1	0.0	−0.1	0.0	−0.1
Low-income countries excluding India	1.9	2.1	−0.1	0.0	−0.1	0.0	0.1
Middle-income countries including India	1.7	1.9	−0.1	0.0	−0.1	0.0	−0.1
Developing countries	1.7	1.9	−0.1	0.0	−0.1	0.0	−0.1
World total	0.9	0.9	0.0	0.0	0.0	0.0	0.0

Source: World Bank simulations with LINKAGE model, based on release 5.4 of the GTAP data.

evenly divided between industrial countries ($188 billion) and developing countries ($197 billion), but developing countries are considerably better off as a share of reference income, with a gain of 1.7 percent compared with 0.6 percent for industrial countries.

Caveats. A few caveats about the basic global reform scenario. First, there are known deficiencies in the base year policies, which are taken from release 5.4 of the Global Trade Analysis Project (GTAP) database. Most preferential arrangements—including the Generalized System of Preferences and some regional trading agreements—are not incorporated.[7] Alternative scenarios could be undertaken to test their overall importance especially regarding the utilization rates of the preferences. Second, the reference scenario assumes no changes in the base year policies between the base and terminal years. Thus changes in trading regimes since 1997, such as China's accession to the WTO, or antic-

ipated changes, such as the elimination of the Multifiber Arrangement, are not taken into account.[8]

Third, changes to some key assumptions or specifications could generate higher benefits. For example, raising the trade elasticities—as some have argued—dampens the negative terms-of-trade effects. Increasing returns to scale can generate greater efficiency improvements, depending on the structure of product markets and scale economies to be achieved. Reform of services could have economywide impacts to the extent that cheaper and more efficient services can lower production costs as well as improve real incomes. Changes in investment flows—not modeled here—have proven to be as important (sometimes more) as lowering trade barriers in many regional agreements. In a global model, the net change would be zero. Therefore, any reallocation of capital would lead some countries to be better off, all else remaining the same, and others worse off (abstracting from the benefits of future repatriated profits).

Gross flows could have a greater impact than net capital flows to the extent that they raise productivity if they are associated with technology-laden capital goods. Finally, dynamic effects can also lead to a boost in the overall gains from reform.

The global scenario captures some of the inherent dynamic gains, notably changes from savings and investment behavior. These can sometimes have a substantial impact, to the extent that imported capital goods are taxed. Assuming that savings rates are unchanged, a sharp fall in the price of capital goods can lead to a significant rise in investment (more bang per dollar invested). The scenario does not incorporate changes to productivity, however. The channels and magnitudes of trade-related changes to productivity are as yet poorly validated by solid empirical evidence, and attempts to incorporate these effects are by and large simply illustrative of potential magnitudes. Recent World Bank reports suggest that these effects could be large, but the reports are really an appeal for more empirical research.[9]

Decomposition by instrument. The key finding on instruments of protection is the predominant role of tariffs. Removal of tariffs accounts for virtually all of the gains. The other instruments have much smaller impacts on real income—slightly positive on average for industrial countries and negative in aggregate for developing countries. For example, elimination of export subsidies negatively affects Africa—both North and Sub-Saharan—and the Middle East, although it provides a positive benefit for Europe. Elimination of domestic protection also tends to be negative for developing countries, and at times for industrial countries as well. The rest of Sub-Saharan Africa is a notable exception, with an income gain of 0.6 percent. This could reflect the removal of significant output subsidies on cotton in some of the major producing countries (China and the United States).

The ambiguity of the welfare impact is in part driven by the nature of partial reforms. Removal of one form of protection may exacerbate the negative effects of other forms of protection. For example, removal of output subsidies may worsen the impact of tariffs if removal of the subsidies leads to a reduction in output and an increase in imports. There are no robust theoretical arguments to determine which is more harmful. There are also other general equilibrium effects inherent in multisectoral global models.

While the aggregate measure of gain often garners the most attention—at least from policy makers and the media—more relevant for most players are the detailed structural results. By and large, it is the structural results that influence the political economy of reforms, particularly since the losers from reforms tend to be concentrated and a well-identified pressure group, whereas the gainers are typically diffuse and harder to identify. For example, a 10 percent decline in the price of wheat could have a major impact on a farmer's income, but an almost imperceptible effect on the average consumer.

With reform, aggregate agricultural output of industrial countries declines—by more than 11 percent when all forms of protection are eliminated (table 7.4). Removal of tariff protection generates the greatest change to production in industrial countries, but unlike the case with the welfare impacts, the other forms of protection have measurable, if smaller, impacts on output. Removal of output subsidies results in the next greatest change in agricultural output, driven largely by the nearly 5 percent output decline in the United States—although land and export subsidies have nearly the same aggregate impact. The detailed results for the Quad countries confirm several points of common wisdom regarding the patterns of protection. First, the United States makes more use of output subsidies than do Europe and Japan. Europe makes greater use of export subsidies and direct payments (capital and land subsidies). Japanese protection is mostly in the form of import barriers.

Results of Agricultural Reform

Full merchandise trade reform provides a benchmark from which to judge the maximal effects from reform. This section focuses on the agricultural and food sectors.

Real income gains. If all regions remove all protection in agriculture and food, the global gains in 2015 amount to $265 billion—nearly 70 percent of the gains from full merchandise trade reform (table 7.5). This is remarkable considering the small size of agriculture and food in global output (figure 7.1).[10] Agriculture represents less than

TABLE 7.4   Agricultural Output Gains and Losses from Global Merchandise Trade Reform: Change from 2015 Baseline

Country Grouping	All Instruments	Tariffs Only	Export Subsidies Only	Capital Subsidies Only	Land Subsidies Only	Input Subsidies Only	Output Subsidies Only
Change in value (billions of 1997 US$)							
High-income countries	−109.7	−56.2	−9.5	−1.6	−10.4	−7.4	−12.0
Low-income countries	14.8	11.5	1.1	0.0	0.7	0.4	2.0
Middle-income countries	41.8	18.1	8.2	−0.2	8.5	0.5	9.3
Low-income countries, excluding India	13.7	10.5	0.9	0.0	0.5	0.3	2.8
Middle-income countries, including India	42.9	19.2	8.4	−0.2	8.7	0.6	8.6
Developing countries	56.6	29.7	9.3	−0.1	9.2	0.9	11.3
World total	−53.1	−26.6	−0.2	−1.7	−1.2	−6.5	−0.7
Percentage change							
High-income countries	−11.1	−5.7	−1.0	−0.2	−1.1	−0.7	−1.2
Low-income countries	2.4	1.8	0.2	0.0	0.1	0.1	0.3
Middle-income countries	2.4	1.0	0.5	0.0	0.5	0.0	0.5
Low-income countries, excluding India	4.1	3.1	0.3	0.0	0.2	0.1	0.8
Middle-income countries, including India	2.1	0.9	0.4	0.0	0.4	0.0	0.4
Developing countries	2.4	1.2	0.4	0.0	0.4	0.0	0.5
World total	−1.6	−0.8	0.0	−0.1	0.0	−0.2	0.0

Source: World Bank simulations with LINKAGE model, based on release 5.4 of the GTAP data.

TABLE 7.5   Real Income Gains from Agricultural and Food Trade Reform: Change from 2015 Baseline
(billions of 1997 US$)

Country Grouping	Global Merchandise Trade Reform — Global	Agricultural and Food Trade Reform — Global	Agricultural and Food Trade Reform — High-Income Countries	Agricultural Trade Reform Only — High-Income
High-income countries	188.3	136.6	92.0	29.3
Low-income countries	31.9	10.3	3.0	1.1
Middle-income countries	164.7	118.2	6.9	−4.9
Low-income countries, excluding India	19.9	8.4	3.6	1.6
Middle-income countries, including India	176.7	120.1	6.4	−5.3
Developing countries	196.5	128.6	10.0	−3.8
World total	384.8	265.2	102.0	25.5

Source: World Bank simulations with LINKAGE model, based on release 5.4 of the GTAP data.

FIGURE 7.1   Output Structure in Base Year, 1997

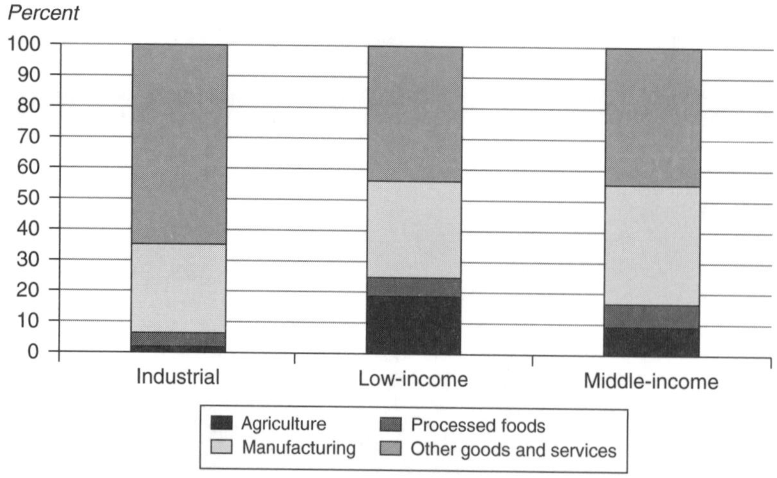

Percent

Legend:
- ■ Agriculture
- □ Manufacturing
- ▨ Processed foods
- ▤ Other goods and services

Source: GTAP release 5.4.

2 percent of output for industrial countries and 10.5 percent for developing countries, while processed foods represent 4.5 percent for industrial countries and 7.5 percent for developing countries. Agriculture is still a relatively high 19 percent of output in the low-income developing countries. Clearly, protection tends to be higher in agriculture and food than in other sectors, particularly in industrial countries, but in middle-income countries as well. Protection is more uniform in low-income countries.

For low-income countries the gains from global free trade in agriculture and food amount to around one-third of the gains from global free trade in all merchandise. This is a consequence of their dependence on imports of the most protected food items—such as grains—while they are net exporters of commodities with little or no protection. The middle-income countries gain 71 percent from global free trade in agriculture and food, nearly as much as industrial countries, which gain 72 percent as compared with full merchandise trade reform.

If reforms are limited to high-income countries—a super-version of special and differential treatment—with perhaps an agreement by middle-income countries to bind at existing levels of protection, global gains drop to $102 billion, indicating that a significant portion of the global gains is generated by removal of agricultural barriers in developing countries (see table 7.5).[11] The drop in gains is particularly striking for middle-income countries, where the gains from their own agricultural and food reform would be quite substantial. On a percentage basis, this is less so for low-income countries. The industrial countries reap gains of $92 billion, implying that agricultural reform in developing countries could generate gains of about $45 billion for the industrial countries.

The final decomposition scenario is to assess the impacts of reform in agriculture alone in industrial countries—leaving protection unchanged for processed foods. This lowers the gains substantially for industrial countries—from $92 billion to $29 billion (see table 7.5). Protection is high in both sectors, and the processed foods sector is more than twice as large as the agricultural sector. Furthermore, in a partial reform scenario, the efficiency gains in agriculture could be offset to some extent by further losses in processed foods. Output will expand in the processed food sector as resources are moved around—and the lower costs of inputs will also provide incentives to increase output. Middle-income countries could lose from an agriculture-only reform in industrial countries. They would benefit little from improved market access in agriculture, and in a partial reform scenario, expansion of their protected domestic agriculture and food production leads to efficiency losses that are not compensated elsewhere.

To conclude—global agricultural trade reform generates a huge share of the gains to be made from merchandise trade reform. Market access into industrial countries provides significant gains, but a greater share of the gains for developing countries comes from agricultural trade reform among developing countries. Finally, reform in agriculture alone provides few benefits. It needs to be linked to reform in the processed food sectors.

Structural implications.   Accelerating integration is one of the key goals of trade reform. Beyond the efficiency gains that come from allocating resources to their best uses, integration is expected to bring productivity increases—scale economies, greater competitiveness, ability to import technology-laden intermediate goods and capital, greater market awareness, and access to networks.

The potential changes in trade from global reform of agriculture and food are large. World trade in these two sectors could jump by more than half a trillion dollars in 2015 (compared with the baseline), an increase of 74 percent (table 7.6).

Exports in agriculture and food from developing countries would jump $300 billion, an increase of more than 115 percent, with industrial-country exports increasing $220 billion, or 50 percent. On the flip side, imports from both industrial and developing countries would rise substantially. The net trade position of industrial countries would deteriorate marginally—from $50 billion in the baseline in 2015 to $48 billion after global reform of agriculture and food. The marginal improvement for developing countries decomposes into a boost of nearly $12 billion for low-income countries and deterioration for middle-income countries of nearly $10 billion.

If the reform is limited to industrial countries, the picture is modified significantly. First, the change in imports for industrial countries is almost identical under the two scenarios—$223 billion with full reform and $205 billion with industrial-country reform only (see table 7.6). Developing

TABLE 7.6   Impact of Global Agricultural and Food Reform on Agricultural and Food Trade: Change from 2015 Baseline

Country Grouping	Exports		Imports		Net Trade		
	Global	Industrial	Global	Industrial	Global	Industrial	2015 Baseline
Change in value (billions of 1997 US$)							
High-income countries	221.2	63.4	223.3	205.3	−2.1	−141.9	50.4
Low-income countries	41.0	20.9	29.2	−0.3	11.8	21.2	23.4
Middle-income countries	260.1	120.5	269.8	−0.2	−9.7	120.7	−73.8
Low-income countries, excluding India	33.8	17.5	21.9	0.1	11.8	17.5	22.2
Middle-income countries, including India	267.3	123.9	277.1	−0.5	−9.8	124.4	−72.7
Developing countries	301.1	141.4	299.0	−0.4	2.1	141.9	−50.4
World total	522.3	204.9	522.3	204.9	0.0	0.0	0
Percentage change							
High-income countries	50	14	57	52			
Low-income countries	74	38	92	−1			
Middle-income countries	125	58	96	0			
Low-income countries, excluding India	70	36	84	0			
Middle-income countries, including India	125	58	96	0			
Developing countries	115	54	95	0			
World total	74	29	74	29			

Note: The columns labeled *Global* refer to the impacts from global agriculture and food reform. The columns labeled *Industrial* refer to industrial-country only reform of agriculture and food.
Source: World Bank simulations with Linkage model, based on release 5.4 of the GTAP data.

countries see a significant rise in exports, but to industrial countries only, with little or no change in their own imports. Thus industrial countries would witness a much sharper deterioration in their net food bill, with net imports registering a change of $142 billion instead of $2 billion, as under the global reform scenario. The United States and Europe bear the brunt of the adjustment, with Canada, Australia, and New Zealand seeing little difference between the global and partial reform scenarios. In other words, these three countries reap much of the trade benefits from greater market access within industrial countries. Opening up of markets in developing countries significantly dampens the adjustment process for the United States and Europe, and the United States would reinforce its net exporting status significantly under a global reform scenario.

Most developing countries see a greater improvement in their net food trade with industrial-country-only reform than with global reform—but not all countries. Argentina, Brazil, and the rest of East Asia improve their net food trade more with global reform than with partial reform. They would gain additional market access from developing countries and reinforce their comparative advantage over more highly protected countries in East Asia. The biggest beneficiary in net terms would be China. While its (small) exports would not change much, removal of its own protection induces a huge shift in imports. The lack of reform under the partial reform scenario means that instead of its net food position deteriorating by $74 billion in the global reform, it sees a small improvement of $6 billion. On aggregate for developing countries the partial reform would generate an improvement in net trade of food of $142 billion.

The structural impacts described above are associated with global changes in the distribution of farm income. With global agriculture and food reform, farm incomes barely change at the global level (a loss of perhaps $10 billion,[12] or 0.6 percent of baseline 2015 farm income). Changes are much more significant at the regional level (figures 7.2 and 7.3). The largest absolute gains in farm income are in the Americas, Australia and New Zealand, and developing East Asia excluding China. Latin

FIGURE 7.2 Change in Rural Value Added from Baseline in 2015
(billions of 1997 $US)

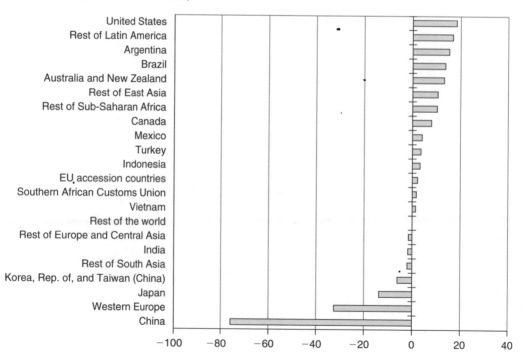

Source: World Bank simulations with Linkage model, based on release 5.4 of the GTAP data.

FIGURE 7.3 Percentage Change in Rural Value Added from Baseline in 2015

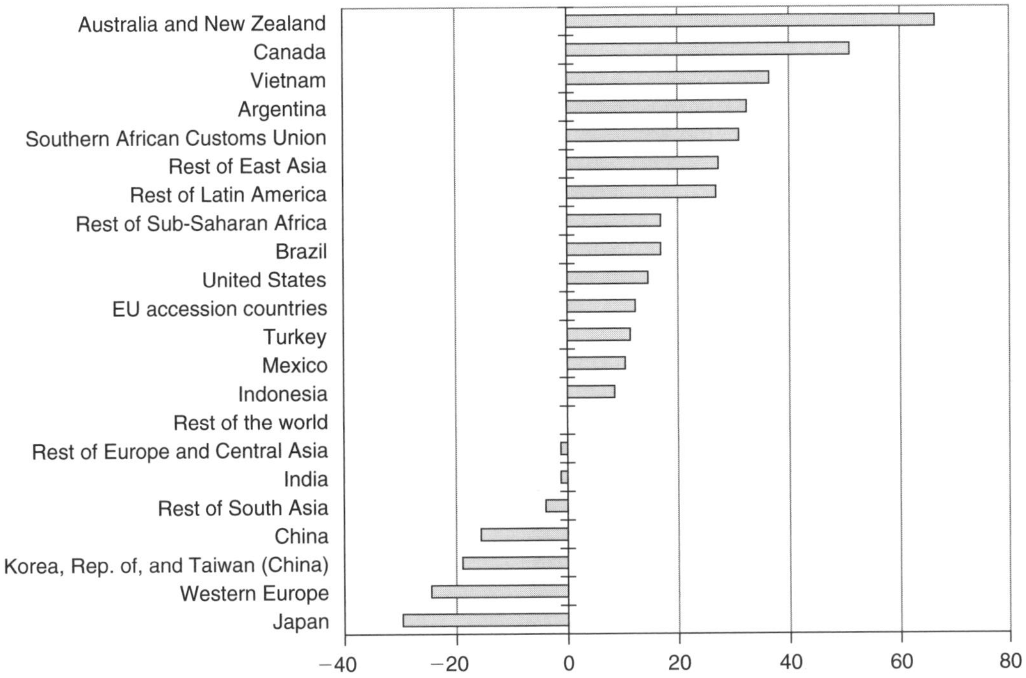

Source: World Bank simulations with Linkage model, based on release 5.4 of the GTAP data.

America would receive 40 percent of the total positive gains; Australia, Canada, and New Zealand 18 percent, and the United States 15 percent.

The relative position of regional gainers is somewhat different, however (see figure 7.3). Farmers in Australia, Canada, and New Zealand gain the most from global free trade in agriculture and food, with income gains of 50–65 percent. Farmers in a number of developing regions have gains of more than 25 percent—Vietnam, Argentina, countries of the Southern Africa Customs Union (SACU), the rest of East Asia (which includes Thailand, Malaysia, and the Philippines), and the rest of Latin America.

The farmers who lose most are in China, with potential losses of $75 billion in 2015 compared with the baseline scenario.[13] The next biggest losers are farmers in Western Europe and the developed East Asian economies—Japan, the Republic of Korea, and Taiwan (China). In percentage terms the biggest losses occur in Japan (30 percent) and Western Europe (24 percent), with China's losses down to about 15 percent because of its huge rural economy.

Most of the impact on rural incomes is generated by volume changes, not factor returns. Both labor and capital returns are determined essentially on national markets.[14] Thus wage changes are modest overall, with generally greater impacts in developing countries, where more labor is employed in agriculture (table 7.7). For example, wages for unskilled labor increase 8 percent in Argentina and Vietnam, and 5–6 percent in the rest of Latin America and the rest of Sub-Saharan Africa. Unskilled workers in Australia and New Zealand also benefit from these reforms. Unskilled workers in developing countries generally do better in relative terms than skilled workers, largely as a result of their concentration in agricultural sectors. China is a significant exception. Removal of its agricultural protection lowers demand for unskilled workers, and their wages decline. The impact on wages in the European Union and Japan is negligible, as agriculture employs a very small share of the national labor force.

As in the labor markets, the returns in capital market are determined mainly at the national level (table 7.8). Thus changes to income will largely be reflected in volume changes, not price changes. Direct payments to farmers, however, are implemented as an ad valorem subsidy on capital (and

TABLE 7.7 **Impact of Global Agriculture and Food Reform on Agricultural Employment and Wages: Change from 2015 Baseline**
(percent)

| Country or Region | Total Agriculture | | | Cereals and Sugar | | | Livestock and Dairy | | |
| | Employ-ment | Wages | | Employ-ment | Wages | | Employ-ment | Wages | |
		Unskilled	Skilled		Unskilled	Skilled		Unskilled	Skilled
Canada	8.5	1.0	0.8	30.4	1.0	0.8	−15.5	1.0	0.8
United States	0.4	0.6	0.6	−12.4	0.6	0.6	3.3	0.6	0.6
European Union with EFTA*	−23.7	−0.6	0.4	−57.7	−0.6	0.4	−28.0	−0.6	0.4
Australia and New Zealand	18.2	3.4	2.3	25.6	3.4	2.3	31.1	3.4	2.3
Japan	−26.8	−0.9	−0.1	−28.9	−0.9	−0.1	−46.2	−0.9	−0.1
Korea, Rep. of and Taiwan (China)	−13.8	−0.2	0.7	−3.9	−0.2	0.7	8.2	−0.2	0.7
Argentina	13.3	7.9	5.5	25.8	7.9	5.5	14.3	7.9	5.5
Brazil	12.5	3.4	3.0	25.8	3.4	3.0	11.7	3.4	3.0
China	−6.6	−3.1	0.0	−26.6	−3.1	0.0	8.6	−3.1	0.0
India	−0.3	0.0	0.2	0.7	0.0	0.2	1.1	0.0	0.2
Indonesia	4.3	1.4	−0.3	6.1	1.4	−0.3	−2.0	1.4	−0.3
Mexico	5.0	1.3	−0.2	1.3	1.3	−0.2	−4.8	1.3	−0.2
Southern African Customs Union	13.8	1.3	1.1	31.7	1.3	1.1	8.8	1.3	1.1
Turkey	5.2	3.0	0.5	−15.3	3.0	0.5	−18.7	3.0	0.5
Vietnam	17.0	7.8	3.0	63.1	7.8	3.0	−15.4	7.8	3.0
Rest of East Asia	11.6	2.7	0.9	72.0	2.7	0.9	−9.1	2.7	0.9
Rest of South Asia	−1.3	−0.2	0.0	1.1	−0.2	0.0	0.7	−0.2	0.0
EU accession countries	6.9	1.6	0.9	12.8	1.6	0.9	13.3	1.6	0.9
Rest of Europe and Central Asia	−0.4	−1.0	−0.3	0.3	−1.0	−0.3	−2.4	−1.0	−0.3
Rest of Sub-Saharan Africa	6.2	6.0	1.9	17.9	6.0	1.9	1.2	6.0	1.9
Rest of Latin America	6.2	5.4	3.4	17.9	5.4	3.4	42.6	5.4	3.4
Rest of the World including Middle East and North Africa	−0.1	−0.3	0.9	2.6	−0.3	0.9	−4.2	−0.3	0.9

*European Free Trade Association, (Austria, Finland, Iceland, Norway, Sweden, and Switzerland).
Source: World Bank simulations with LINKAGE model, based on release 5.4 of the GTAP data.

land), thus creating a wedge between the cost to farmers and the returns to owners. Removal of the capital subsidy has little effect on owners since the return is determined at the economywide level, but it raises the costs to farmers. For example, the cost of capital net of subsidies increases by almost 1 percent in the European Union, but the average cost to farmers increases by 22 percent—and even more for livestock producers (43 percent). Note that these capital subsidies are used mainly in industrial countries, so for most developing countries there is no difference between the owner return and the cost to farmers.

The changes in the contribution of land to agricultural incomes are driven largely by price movements—contrary to the case for labor and capital income (table 7.9). Land is essentially a fixed factor in agriculture, with some allowance for movements up and down the supply curve and for cross-sectoral shifts in land usage.[15] In Europe the average return to land drops 66 percent, with the supply of land falling 9 percent following global reform. Farmers gain some benefit in lower unit costs because of falling land prices. But removal of the direct subsidy does not allow farmers to reap the full cost gains from falling land prices. The average cost for farmers drops 57 percent, lower than the drop in the rental price of land (66 percent). And the change in the cost structure is highly sector specific. Thus cereal and grain farmers see a small drop in their net cost of land (5 percent); however, the drop in the price of land does not compensate for removal of the subsidies since the returns to owners falls by 74 percent. This is

TABLE 7.8 Impact of Global Agricultural and Food Trade Reform on Agricultural Capital: Change from 2015 Baseline
(percent)

Country or Region	Total Agriculture			Grains and Sugar			Livestock and Dairy		
	Volume	Owners' Return	Farmers' Cost	Volume	Owners' Return	Farmers' Cost	Volume	Owners' Return	Farmers' Cost
Canada	−4.9	−0.5	4.1	7.2	−0.5	3.1	−17.0	−0.5	7.1
United States	0.8	0.7	2.6	−19.2	0.7	2.6	4.5	0.7	6.5
European Union with EFTA	−32.9	0.7	21.8	−67.1	0.7	21.7	−29.2	0.8	43.1
Australia and New Zealand	40.2	0.6	1.2	3.0	0.7	1.3	123.5	0.6	1.7
Japan	−22.9	1.7	4.9	−25.0	1.7	7.6	−47.0	1.7	12.2
Korea, Rep. of and Taiwan (China)	−4.3	0.7	12.0	8.9	0.8	15.4	17.5	0.8	103.8
Hong Kong (China) and Singapore	9.8	0.7	0.7	75.4	0.7	0.7	−4.3	0.7	0.7
Argentina	6.0	4.2	4.2	9.0	4.2	4.2	17.9	4.2	4.2
Brazil	10.1	3.1	3.1	21.9	3.1	3.1	9.8	3.1	3.1
China	−2.7	3.2	3.2	−17.5	3.2	3.2	5.8	3.2	3.2
India	0.0	0.1	0.1	0.8	0.1	0.1	1.2	0.1	0.1
Indonesia	0.7	−0.2	−0.2	1.0	−0.2	−0.2	−0.9	−0.2	−0.2
Mexico	4.3	−0.1	3.7	2.3	−0.1	4.4	−7.5	−0.1	9.1
Southern African Customs Union	19.5	−0.6	−0.6	39.4	−0.6	−0.6	25.4	−0.6	−0.6
Turkey	0.2	−0.4	−0.2	−15.8	−0.4	0.5	−15.1	−0.4	−0.4
Vietnam	2.4	1.8	1.8	28.7	1.8	1.8	−13.3	1.8	1.8
Rest of East Asia	20.9	0.2	0.2	36.5	0.2	0.2	−8.6	0.2	0.2
Rest of South Asia	0.1	1.3	1.3	2.3	1.3	1.3	0.7	1.2	1.2
EU accession countries	−0.2	0.5	21.6	7.7	0.5	18.9	−6.3	0.5	67.6
Rest of Europe and Central Asia	−2.5	1.6	7.7	−1.9	1.6	8.3	−5.8	1.6	9.3
Rest of Sub-Saharan Africa	0.5	−1.1	−1.1	5.6	−1.1	−1.1	4.0	−1.1	−1.1
Rest of Latin America	6.2	1.8	1.8	15.9	1.8	1.8	41.1	1.8	1.8
Rest of the World including Middle East and North Africa	0.3	−0.2	−0.2	2.9	−0.2	−0.2	−3.7	−0.2	−0.2

Source: World Bank simulations with LINKAGE model, based on release 5.4 of the GTAP data.

not the case in the livestock sector, where subsidy payments are linked to capital (the herds) and not to land. The impacts in the United States are muted, with the overall return to landowners changing slightly—a decline of 5 percent—but costs to farmers increasing substantially—22 percent on average and more than 42 percent for cereal and sugar producers.

In most developing countries land prices increase substantially, except in China and in a few other regions. This may reduce to some extent the positive distributional impacts from relatively higher wages for unskilled labor since land ownership may not necessarily be congruent with the unskilled labor working the land. There are some interesting sectoral shifts. For example, China would see more land devoted to livestock and dairy and less to cereals, which would be imported from lower-cost sources.

Sensitivity Analysis

This section uses sensitivity analysis to explore how results change when some of the basic assumptions of the model change. It focuses on four areas:

- The agricultural productivity assumptions of the standard baseline scenario. Agricultural productivity is cut by 1 percentage point in developing countries and the results from global agriculture and food reform are compared with the results using the default productivity assumptions. In a separate analysis, productivity is increased for middle-income developing countries.

- The impacts of the mobility of agricultural capital. Agricultural capital is more closely tied to the sector, making it more difficult to shed and leading to a different transition when reform is undertaken.

TABLE 7.9   Impact of Global Agriculture and Food Reform on Agricultural Land: Change from 2015 Baseline
(percent)

Country or Region	Total Agriculture			Cereals and Sugar			Livestock and Dairy		
		Price			Price			Price	
	Land	Owner	Farmer	Land	Owner	Farmer	Land	Owner	Farmer
Canada	−6.4	69.5	133.8	6.6	76.9	192.8	−25.2	56.8	83.5
United States	2.4	−5.1	22.1	−19.0	−12.5	42.1	12.3	−0.2	9.1
European Union with EFTA	−9.4	−66.3	−57.0	−58.9	−74.1	−4.7	−3.5	−65.0	−59.7
Australia and New Zealand	6.2	197.8	219.1	1.9	197.0	224.0	34.8	219.6	252.4
Japan	−21.0	−44.9	−41.5	−24.0	−45.5	−34.6	−34.1	−48.9	−48.9
Korea, Rep. of and Taiwan (China)	−11.4	−27.6	−27.1	−0.2	−25.3	−24.6	4.1	−23.0	−20.9
Argentina	4.5	56.2	56.2	11.4	59.5	59.5	12.0	60.0	60.0
Brazil	9.9	18.0	18.0	23.8	22.9	22.9	8.6	17.6	17.6
China	−0.9	−25.7	−25.7	−21.1	−31.1	−31.1	7.6	−23.6	−23.6
India	0.0	−1.8	−1.8	0.8	−1.5	−1.5	1.4	−1.3	−1.3
Indonesia	0.7	10.9	10.9	2.1	11.4	11.4	−1.8	10.0	10.0
Mexico	2.7	0.6	13.1	−8.9	−3.6	52.1	−1.6	−0.6	0.8
Southern African Customs Union	8.0	86.4	86.4	26.4	95.2	95.2	4.5	84.9	84.9
Turkey	0.8	47.3	47.3	−14.9	39.0	39.0	−20.2	36.1	36.1
Vietnam	−0.3	44.6	44.6	33.2	60.3	60.3	−16.0	38.1	38.1
Rest of East Asia	−1.5	34.1	34.1	43.7	53.8	53.8	−9.6	32.7	32.7
Rest of South Asia	−0.1	−6.0	−6.0	3.2	−5.0	−5.0	1.3	−5.4	−5.4
EU accession countries	2.6	2.0	6.1	4.6	2.8	10.8	7.5	3.5	8.8
Rest of Europe and Central Asia	−1.5	−2.4	−2.4	−1.1	−2.3	−2.3	−1.2	−2.2	−2.2
Rest of Sub-Saharan Africa	−0.3	62.8	62.8	9.0	67.9	67.9	−2.4	61.7	61.7
Rest of Latin America	1.0	55.4	55.4	5.0	58.6	58.6	40.3	74.9	74.9
Rest of the World including Middle East and North Africa	0.0	0.1	0.1	2.7	0.8	0.8	−4.3	−1.2	−1.2

Source: World Bank simulations with LINKAGE model, based on release 5.4 of the GTAP data.

- Sensitivity of the results to supply rigidities in developing countries.
- Sensitivity of the results to the key trade elasticities.

Agricultural Productivity

Agricultural productivity is assumed to grow 2.5 percent a year globally in the standard baseline scenario based on existing evidence (Martin and Mitra 1996, 1999). This may be too optimistic for developing countries, particularly for low-income countries. This assumption may have an impact on long-term self-sufficiency rates, particularly of sensitive commodities. The more trade reform raises the world price of food, the more net food importers will be adversely affected by negative terms-of-trade shocks. To test the sensitivity of the trade results to agricultural productivity, a different

baseline was constructed with agricultural productivity improving at a slower 1.5 percent for developing countries, but remaining at 2.5 percent for industrial countries.

Trade impact.   Under the standard baseline, high-income countries go from a position of net food importers in 1997 to net food exporters in 2015 (table 7.10). Low-income countries improve their position significantly, going from a positive food balance of $12.5 billion in 1997 to $23 billion in 2015. The position of middle-income countries deteriorates, however. Under the low-productivity baseline, the net food trade position of industrial countries increases substantially—jumping to $151 billion in 2015 compared with only $50 billion in the standard baseline. Low-income countries still maintain a positive balance, but the balance is much closer to zero than it was in the previous

TABLE 7.10 Net Trade Impacts Assuming Lower Agricultural Productivity in Developing Countries
(billions of 1997 US$)

Country Grouping	1997	Standard Productivity		Low Productivity	
		Baseline 2015	Reform 2015	Baseline 2015	Reform 2015
High-income countries	−23.1	50.4	48.4	151.2	181.6
Low-income countries	12.5	23.4	35.2	0.9	4.5
Middle-income countries	10.5	−73.8	−83.6	−152.0	−186.1
Low-income countries, excluding India	7.4	22.2	34.1	8.5	17.2
Middle-income countries, including India	15.6	−72.7	−82.4	−159.7	−198.9
Developing countries	23.1	−50.4	−48.4	−151.2	−181.6

Source: World Bank simulations with LINKAGE model, based on release 5.4 of the GTAP data.

TABLE 7.11 Impacts on Output Assuming Lower Agricultural Productivity for Developing Countries

Country Grouping	Growth in 2000–15 (percent)		Baseline Difference in 2015		Difference between Baseline and Reform Scenario in 2015			
	Low Baseline	Standard Baseline	Value ($ billions)	Percentage Change	Low ($ billions)	Standard ($ billions)	Low (percent)	Standard (percent)
High-income countries	1.9	1.2	122.6	12.4	−100.0	−107.7	−9.0	−10.9
Low-income countries	2.8	3.6	−71.6	−11.4	8.7	12.1	1.6	1.9
Middle-income countries	2.6	3.2	−166.2	−9.4	27.0	37.2	1.7	2.1
Low-income countries, excluding India	3.0	3.7	−39.4	−11.6	10.3	12.3	3.4	3.6
Middle-income countries, including India	2.6	3.2	−198.4	−9.7	25.4	37.0	1.4	1.8
Developing countries	2.6	3.3	−237.8	−10.0	35.7	49.4	1.7	2.1
World total	2.4	2.6	−115.2	−3.4	−64.3	−58.3	−2.0	−1.7

Source: World Bank simulations with LINKAGE model, based on release 5.4 of the GTAP data.

baseline. And the net food trade situation of middle-income countries shows a greater dependence on world markets.

Whereas reform in the standard baseline positions low-income countries as net food exporters and has only a mild negative effect on the food balance of high- and middle-income countries, under the low-productivity assumption, the food trade balance of the high-income countries improves substantially—by $30 billion—largely because of an increased dependence on food imports by middle-income countries. The low-income countries still see an improvement in their trade balance,

but by a more modest $3.6 billion rather than the nearly $12 billion using the standard productivity assumptions.

Output impact. Average annual agricultural output growth in developing countries slows from 3.3 percent in the standard baseline to 2.6 percent in the low-productivity baseline (table 7.11). In industrial countries higher productivity provides an opportunity to gain market share, and higher world prices relative to the original baseline provide greater incentives to produce. World output under the alternative scenario declines 3.4 percent (higher prices lead to reduced demand), with a reallocation between industrial and developing countries. Industrial countries benefit from a 12 percent increase in output in 2015 compared with the standard baseline, whereas developing country output is reduced by some 10 percent.

With respect to output impacts following the trade reform scenario, the qualitative results of the different baseline assumptions of agricultural productivity are identical—trade reform of agriculture and food lead to a shift in agricultural production from industrial to developing countries. In the standard baseline, developing-country agricultural output increases more than 2 percent, whereas in the low-productivity baseline the increase is only 1.7 percent. The decline in industrial countries drops to 9 percent, from 11 percent in the standard baseline. The changes in output patterns across regions are identical, although the magnitudes differ.

Aggregate welfare. The change in the agricultural productivity assumption translates into modest changes in aggregate welfare (figure 7.4). Industrial countries see an improvement of $18 billion in 2015, a jump in gains of some 0.05 percentage point. Developing countries see a reduction in their welfare gains, with low-income countries seeing a drop of $1.4 billion (0.08 percentage point) and middle-income countries a drop of $17.8 billion (0.19 percentage point).

A high-productivity assumption. Many middle-income countries such as Argentina, Brazil, and Thailand have experienced rapid growth in agriculture, suggesting the potential for higher productivity growth than assumed in the standard baseline. To explore this, agricultural productivity growth was raised from 2.5 percent to 4.0 percent for middle-income countries (China, India, Indonesia, rest of East Asia, Vietnam, Argentina, Brazil, Mexico, rest of Latin America, the EU accession countries, rest of Europe and Central Asia, and Turkey).

Changes are as expected. Agricultural supply and exports expand for natural exporters such as Argentina and Brazil. China, the largest middle-income importer, reduces its deficit by about $18 billion (table 7.12). The middle-income group including India experiences a net surplus of $30 billion in 2015, whereas under the standard baseline it has a deficit of $19 billion. High-income countries experience a deterioration of their net agricultural trade of about $50 billion, compared with $3 billion in the standard baseline, and Europe's deficit increases to nearly $60 billion. Results for the food sector are qualitatively similar, but smaller in size,

FIGURE 7.4   Welfare Impacts of Productivity Changes

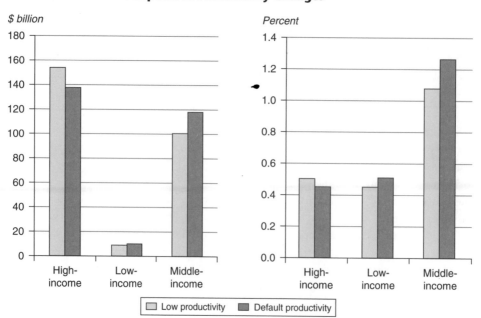

Source: World Bank simulations with Linkage model, based on release 5.4 of the GTAP data.

TABLE 7.12 Baseline Trends in Agriculture with Higher Agricultural Productivity in Middle-Income Countries

| Country Grouping | Average Annual Growth, 2000–15 (percent) | | | | Net Trade (billions of 1997 US$) | |
	Output	Demand	Imports	Exports	2000	2015
High-income countries	0.6	1.0	2.7	0.9	–24.3	–50.2
Low-income countries	3.9	3.8	4.0	6.2	9.9	25.2
Middle-income countries	3.7	3.6	7.5	7.2	14.4	24.9
Low-income countries, excluding India	3.8	3.5	4.0	6.2	7.2	19.1
Middle-income countries, including India	3.7	3.7	7.4	7.1	17.1	31.1
Developing countries	3.7	3.7	7.0	7.0	24.3	50.2

Note: Net trade is measured at f.o.b. prices (imports exclude international trade and transport margins).
Source: World Bank simulations with LINKAGE model, based on release 5.4 of the GTAP data.

TABLE 7.13 Baseline Trends in Food Processing with Higher Agricultural Productivity in Middle-Income Countries

| Country Grouping | Average Annual Growth, 2000–15 (percent) | | | | Net Trade (billions of 1997 US$) | |
	Output	Demand	Imports	Exports	2000	2015
High-income countries	1.1	1.0	1.4	2.0	7.7	36.2
Low-income countries	3.5	3.5	3.6	3.2	3.6	4.4
Middle-income countries	3.1	3.3	4.1	2.6	–11.3	–40.6
Low-income countries, excluding India	3.2	3.3	3.7	2.2	1.8	–0.1
Middle-income countries, including India	3.1	3.3	4.1	2.8	–9.5	–36.2
Developing countries	3.2	3.3	4.1	2.7	–7.7	–36.2

Note: Net trade is measured at f.o.b. prices (imports exclude international trade and transport margins).
Source: World Bank simulations with LINKAGE model, based on release 5.4 of the GTAP data.

with an increase in competitiveness of food processing in middle-income countries and a decrease in net trade by high-income countries relative to the standard baseline (table 7.13). These large changes show how sensitive baseline trajectories are to changes in assumptions about the future. They do not, however, affect the impact of the reform scenario measured in deviations from the baseline.

In conclusion, the baseline assumptions regarding productivity are important, although changes in the assumption would not yield substantially different results from agriculture and food trade reform for developing countries in terms of net benefits and agricultural output.[16] However, lower productivity will reduce the level of food self-sufficiency

among developing countries—particularly middle-income countries—and could lead to a different assessment of the direction of food self-sufficiency in the aftermath of reform.

Mobility of Agricultural Capital and the Transition in Industrial Countries

The focus so far has been mainly on the long-term impact of the removal of protection, with little attention to the transitional impacts. A key mechanism of the model is the vintage structure of capital. Sectors in decline have excess capital that will not readily be used in other sectors. This is certainly the case with agricultural capital, although some could be used for nonagricultural purposes, and other equipment could be used in nonprotected agricultural sectors.

Excess capital is released to other sectors following an upward-sloping supply curve. The value for the supply elasticity in the standard model is 4. To test the importance of this elasticity, the reform scenario is simulated again, but with a supply elasticity of 0.5. This makes excess supply much less mobile and, all else equal, will tend to increase supply relative to the same simulation with a higher supply elasticity.

Consider the case for the sugar sector in Europe. The starting point is 2004, since the trade reform starts in 2005. Under the baseline, sugar output in Europe increases modestly between 2004 and 2015 (figure 7.5). With the start of reform, output drops rapidly, and by 2015 output has fallen from about $42 billion to about $11 billion. The supply elasticity has an impact on the rate of decline of sugar output, but the final level is more or less identical. Thus with a low supply elasticity, the transition is drawn out over a longer period. The rate of decline between 2004 and 2010 is 18.4 percent using the standard elasticity and 16.5 percent with the lower elasticity.

There are only a handful of sectors in industrial countries where the supply elasticity has any noticeable impact: wheat and sugar in the United States; rice, wheat, other grains, oil seeds, and sugar in the European Union; and wheat and oil seeds in Japan. The aggregate impacts on agricultural production are negligible, at less than 1 percent over all industrial countries in any given year, and at most 0.3 percent for developing countries, but in the opposite direction. There are no discernible impacts on welfare.

In conclusion, lowering the supply elasticity will draw out the supply response during the transition phase but will have no discernible long-term impact on the results.

Supply Response in the Low-Income Countries

This section evaluates the impact of lowering the land supply response in three regions—rest of South Asia, the Southern Africa Customs Union region, and the rest of Sub-Saharan Africa—to examine whether low-income countries, with their potentially low supply response, will benefit from greater market access. This involves three parameters. First, the base year land supply elasticity was reduced from 1 to 0.25. Second, the land supply asymptote was reduced from 20 percent of the initial land supply to 10 percent.[17] These two parameters determine aggregate land supply. A third parameter moderates the degree of land mobility across sectors. The allocation of land across sectors is governed by a constant elasticity of transformation function.[18] The standard transformation elasticity is 3, a relatively elastic value. In the sensitivity simulation, the transformation elasticity for the three regions is set to 0.5.

The lower land supply elasticities affect the baseline scenario. For the three regions where changes

FIGURE 7.5   Sugar Output in Europe
(US$ billions)

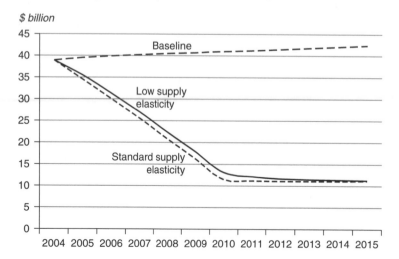

Source: World Bank simulations with Linkage model, based on release 5.4 of the GTAP data.

were made to supply elasticities, the overall rate of growth of agricultural output between 2000 and 2015 declines from 3.4 to 3.1 percent in rest of South Asia, from 4.0 to 3.8 percent in rest of Sub-Saharan Africa, and remains the same for SACU at 2.1 percent (table 7.14). In all three regions, the most affected crop is plant-based fibers. These three regions have a sizable market share at the

TABLE 7.14 Impact of Lower Land Supply Elasticities in Rest of South Asia and Sub-Saharan Africa
(percent)

| Commodity | Baseline Growth Rates 2000–15 | | Baseline Difference in 2015 | Impact of Trade Reform Standard | |
	Standard Supply Elasticity	Low Supply Elasticity		Standard Supply Elasticity	Low Supply Elasticity
Rest of South Asia					
Rice	2.8	2.7	−2.1	3.4	2.4
Wheat	2.7	2.6	−3.8	34.4	19.6
Other grains	3.8	3.6	−3.6	−2.4	−1.5
Oil seeds	4.1	3.5	−9.1	−10.0	−6.8
Sugar	3.8	3.3	−8.9	−17.2	−12.4
Plant-based fibers	4.5	3.7	−13.2	19.2	6.2
Other crops	3.6	3.2	−7.3	−8.0	−5.4
Cattle	4.0	3.7	−4.9	1.7	1.5
Other meats	4.1	3.6	−8.3	−1.0	−1.8
Raw milk	3.9	3.5	−6.1	1.3	1.3
Total	**3.4**	**3.1**	**−5.6**	**−0.2**	**−0.6**
Southern African Customs Union					
Rice	2.3	2.4	−1.7	8.8	8.4
Wheat	1.9	1.9	−0.5	0.0	0.5
Other grains	1.1	1.3	0.8	29.5	19.9
Oil seeds	1.6	1.8	−1.8	9.2	8.6
Sugar	1.3	1.4	−0.2	87.7	50.6
Plant-based fibers	6.0	3.8	−35.9	3.4	3.6
Other crops	2.4	2.4	−8.7	7.2	4.3
Cattle	2.2	2.2	0.0	24.2	23.0
Other meats	2.2	2.2	0.1	5.0	5.1
Raw milk	2.2	2.2	0.0	−2.7	−2.6
Total	**2.1**	**2.1**	**−2.9**	**18.4**	**14.0**
Rest of Sub-Saharan Africa					
Rice	3.2	3.2	−0.1	−1.2	−0.9
Wheat	3.4	3.5	0.4	0.3	3.0
Other grains	3.2	3.2	0.4	−0.1	3.0
Oil seeds	3.9	3.8	−0.8	51.0	37.7
Sugar	3.2	3.2	1.5	48.1	40.3
Plant-based fibers	8.1	6.5	−23.2	42.8	24.9
Other crops	4.5	4.2	−5.8	−3.6	0.0
Cattle	3.5	3.4	−1.4	4.6	3.5
Other meats	3.7	3.6	−1.9	−0.7	0.3
Raw milk	3.3	3.3	−1.1	1.7	1.2
Total	**4.0**	**3.8**	**−4.1**	**5.6**	**4.9**

Source: World Bank simulations with LINKAGE model, based on release 5.4 of the GTAP data.

global level in 1997 of 11.4 percent for plant-based fibers and 15 percent for rice. The demand for rice, however, is much less elastic than for plant-based fibers. The lower supply elasticity would make land relatively more costly, all else equal, and given the higher demand elasticities, the higher land prices will be reflected in lower demand from these three regions.

The impact of trade reform on agricultural output using both the standard and the lower land elasticities is broadly the same qualitatively, although lower in magnitude in general. Consider sugar again. Output increases 88 percent in SACU and 48 percent in the rest of Sub-Saharan Africa using the standard supply elasticity. Sugar output expansion drops to 51 percent in SACU and 40 percent in the rest of Sub-Saharan Africa when lower land supply elasticity is assumed.

The welfare impacts are modest, but measurable, and the results reflect only some of the possible supply constraints in low-income countries. For the three regions under question, aggregate welfare would decline $1.1 billion compared with the standard assumption and would drop from 1.2 percent to 1.1 percent of baseline income.

Trade Elasticities

The most critical parameter in trade reform scenarios is trade elasticities. There is ongoing debate about their size. Most econometric evidence suggests that the Armington elasticities (measuring the degree of substitutability between domestic and imported goods) are low, in the range of 1 to 2.[19] The studies are riddled with data problems—particularly the evaluation of unit values—and many trade economists downplay the empirical evidence, for two main reasons. First, low Armington elasticities lead to implausible terms-of-trade effects. And second, low elasticities would suggest high optimal tariffs. Trade studies fall into three groups—those with relatively low elasticities (1–3), those with middling elasticities (3–6), and those with very high elasticities (20–40). Examples of the first are the MONASH model (Dixon and Rimmer 2002) and the standard GTAP model (Hertel 1996). Recent World Bank work has been using the middling elasticities. High elasticities are mainly associated with the work of Harrison, Rutherford, and Tarr (for example, see Harrison, Rutherford, and Tarr 2003).

The impacts of the agriculture and food trade reform were reassessed using two alternative elasticities. A low scenario uses trade elasticities 50 percent lower than the standard, and a high scenario uses trade elasticities 50 percent higher than the standard (the standard values used in this study are shown in table A3 on the CD-ROM). Each set of assumptions requires two simulation runs. A new baseline is constructed each time—with all assumptions identical except for the trade elasticities—and the reform scenario is simulated. Thus the comparisons are between each individual baseline and each associated reform scenario.

Within this range of trade elasticities the model exhibits some modest nonlinearity, particularly on the upside (figure 7.6). For all three regions the 50 percent higher elasticities lead to a greater than 50 percent rise in real income gains—particularly for developing regions, where the rise is almost 75 percent. On the downside, both high- and low-income regions see an equiproportionate fall in the real income gains relative to the elasticities, with a fall to 40 percent of the standard gains in the case of the middle-income countries. The higher elasticities dampen the adverse terms-of-trade shocks from reforms, leading to the higher income gains. The global gains vary from a low of $126 billion to a high of $438 billion, with the gains at $265 billion using the standard elasticities.

For some countries and regions the range of results is much broader than at the aggregate level. For example, Mexico would lose some $1.2 billion with the low elasticities and gain $3 billion with the high elasticities compared with a gain of 0.9 with the standard elasticities. Several other regions show similar variation. The standard deviation of the index across all developing countries is 130 in the case of the high elasticities, whereas the weighted average is 170.

The impacts on trade are similar to the impacts on income but exhibit more nonlinearity (figure 7.7). At the global level, exports increase 80 percent using the high elasticities and decline 60 percent using the low elasticities (with export increases ranging from a low of $216 billion to nearly $1 trillion). There is also less variability across regions of the model than with the income results. In isolation the trade elasticities appear to have the greatest impact in determining the overall outcomes of trade reform, although other model changes—both in specification and in elasticities—combined may

FIGURE 7.6   Real Income and Trade Elasticities

Index relative to default elasticities in 2015

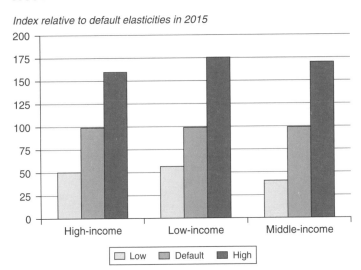

Source: World Bank simulations with Linkage model, based on release 5.4 of the GTAP data.

FIGURE 7.7   Exports and Trade Elasticities

Index relative to default elasticities in 2015

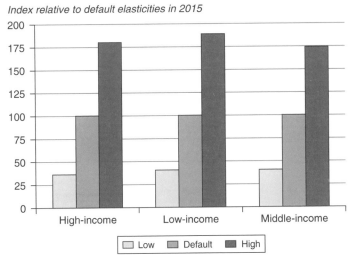

Source: World Bank simulations with Linkage model, based on release 5.4 of the GTAP data.

be at least as important in determining overall outcomes. This is an area of active research to better determine the bounds on the possible ranges for these elasticities. Better data would help, but there are still issues relating to model specification and aggregation that need to be thought through.

Conclusions

This quantitative assessment of the impact of agricultural and food market distortions on incomes, welfare, trade, and output shows that the changes in cross-regional patterns of output and trade tend to

be much larger than the more familiar gains to real income. A decomposition of the aggregate results across policy instruments and regions shows that reforms in agriculture and food account for a large share of the global gains of reforms of total merchandise trade. This result is driven by the relatively low protection levels in manufacturing sectors. Another major finding is that developing countries have more to gain from reforming their own support policies than from reforms in high-income countries. Symmetrically, high-income countries would experience larger welfare gains from their own reforms than from developing countries' reforms. These dimensions of the debate are often overlooked but are crucial. Global reform leads to additive results with aggregate gains close to the gains from reforms in each group. A third key finding is that agricultural reform alone in high-income countries would create moderate gains, about 10 times smaller than those of a combined reform of food and agricultural markets. Developing countries would be negatively affected as a group, because their own distortions would be exacerbated by the agricultural reforms in high-income countries.

The results are broadly robust to changing assumptions on future agricultural productivity in developing countries, supply constraints, and level of the trade elasticities, but the levels of the trade elasticities remain of foremost importance. The trade effects of reforms are also sensitive to assumptions about agricultural productivity gains in developing countries. Assuming low productivity gains leads to a reversal in the estimated impact of global liberalization for industrial countries, increasing their net food trade surplus as middle-income countries become much larger importers of food and agricultural products. Low-income countries experience an increase in net food trade surplus that is much smaller than under the higher productivity assumption. Hence, variations in productivity could lead to a different assessment of the direction of food self-sufficiency after reform. Supply constraints do not qualitatively affect the estimated impact of trade reform on agricultural output, although estimated changes tend to be smaller. Higher trade elasticities dampen the adverse terms-of-trade shocks from reforms, leading to higher income gains. The global gains vary from a low of $126 billion with low elasticities to a high of $438 billion with high elasticities, with the gains at $265 billion using the standard elasticities. There is also higher variation at the individual country level.

The changes in agricultural value added and factor prices are considerable in several cases. The estimated loss of rural value-added is large in Japan and the European Union, the Republic of Korea, Taiwan (China), and China. Thus, considerable adjustment and displacement of resources would take place to reflect these changes. Cairns Group countries and the United States experience sizable

gains in rural value-added as do SACU and the rest of Sub-Saharan Africa. Wages for unskilled labor in developing countries are moderately influenced by major policy reforms such as in China, where they decrease, but more significantly in Argentina, where they increase.

Notes

1. The model is based at the World Bank and uses the GTAP release 5.4 dataset (see van der Mensbrugghe 2003 for details). The details of the modeling and the results are given in the attached CD-ROM.

2. East Asia is divided into four economies—China, Indonesia, Vietnam, and the rest. South Asia has two components—India and the rest. Latin America has four economies—Argentina, Brazil, Mexico, and the rest. Europe and Central Asia is split into three components—the European Union accession countries, Turkey, and the rest. Sub-Saharan Africa has two components—the Southern African Customs Union countries and the rest, and the Rest of the World region has all other countries including those in the Middle East and North Africa.

3. Agricultural policies derived from the Agricultural Market Access Database (AMAD) reflect 1998–99 levels of support, except for cotton, for which International Cotton Advisory Committee data were used (see chapter 14 in this volume).

4. Income elasticities are held more or less constant over the time horizon. With China's rapid growth, one might anticipate a convergence of income elasticities toward levels in higher-income countries and thus a dampening of food growth over time relative to incomes.

5. Textile and apparel quotas that generate quota rents for exporters are converted to export taxes (for the country of origin). In the current simulations, these have not been eliminated.

6. Technically, it is a measure of the Hicksian equivalent variation. When comparing aggregate welfare measures across studies, it is important to convert them to similar scales. Thus $350 billion in 2015 is more or less equivalent to $250 billion in 2004 and $200 billion in 1997—assuming an average annual global growth rate of 3 percent in gross domestic product (all in 1997 US$, the base year of release 5 of the GTAP data set). Assuming a world inflation rate of 2.5 percent over the entire period, the measured $250 billion in 2004 in 1997 dollars becomes $300 billion in 2004 dollars.

7. The Mercosur preferential agreement is not incorporated in the standard GTAP dataset but is included in the dataset used for these simulations. Efforts were made to minimize distortions to the original social accounting matrix (SAM) while adjusting the original dataset.

8. There is also an issue regarding whether bound or applied tariffs are liberalized. Most developing countries have bound their tariffs at rates much higher than applied rates. Negotiations concern the bound tariffs; the reforms described here are relative to the applied tariffs. For a full reform scenario, it is not much of an issue, but for analyzing potential outcomes of a negotiation, it could be.

9. See *Global Economic Prospects 2002* and *2004* (World Bank 2001, 2003). The 2002 report notes *dynamic* gains of $830 billion compared with *static* gains of $350 billion, with a range of up to $1,340 billion depending on some key parameters (table 6.2, page 100).

10. Figure 7.1 shows output shares in the base year. One would assume that the agricultural and food shares are declining over time as income elasticities for food tend to be lower than for other goods and services.

11. While the model is highly nonlinear, the results to a close approximation are relatively additive.

12. Nominal values are measured with respect to the model's numéraire—the average export price of manufactured exports from industrial countries.

13. This should be considered an upper bound on China's potential loss since the baseline scenario does not include the impacts of China's accession to the WTO. Thus the reform scenario is capturing the combined gains from global reform and China's WTO accession, which include the gains to be had from reforming from 1998–99 base agricultural policies.

14. Sector-specific capital returns may be possible during the transition phase, as sectors in decline shed unwanted capital. The most mobile equipment will be shed first, and the return to the remaining capital may be priced lower than the national rate of return to capital.

15. In the default version of the model, cross-sectoral transformation elasticities are set to 3. Thus a 10 percent rise in the return in one sector (relative to the others) will lead to a 30 percent shift of land into that sector. Because of the finite transformation elasticity, land prices are sector specific.

16. Given the aggregate nature of the model, the impacts on vulnerable countries or sectors are harder to assess. In particular, Sub-Saharan Africa is a heterogeneous subcontinent that is not reflected in the level of aggregation of this study.

17. The land supply function is governed by a logistic curve. It is calibrated in the base year to an exogenously given elasticity and the value of the asymptote relative to the base supply level. Thus if the asymptote is set to 1.2, land supply can increase by at most 20 percent above its base level.

18. The elasticity measures the ease of shifting land from one activity to another when the relative price of these two activities changes.

19. More recent econometric work is resulting in higher estimates for the trade elasticities, and these are now being reflected in the forthcoming release of the GTAP dataset.

References

Dixon, P. B., and M. T. Rimmer. 2002. *Dynamic, General Equilibrium Modelling for Forecasting and Policy: A Practical Guide and Documentation of MONASH.* Boston: North-Holland.

Harrison, G. W., T. F. Rutherford, and D. Tarr. 2003. "Trade Liberalization, Poverty and Efficient Equity." *Journal of Development Economics* 71(1): 97–128.

Hertel, T. W. 1996. *Global Trade Analysis: Modeling and Applications.* Cambridge, U.K.: Cambridge University Press.

Martin, W., and D. Mitra. 1996. "Productivity Growth in Agriculture and Manufacturing." World Bank, International Economics Department, Washington, D.C.

———. 1999. "Productivity Growth and Convergence in Agriculture and Manufacturing." Country Economics Department Working Paper 2171. World Bank, Washington, D.C.

van der Mensbrugghe, D. 2003. "LINKAGE Technical Reference Document." Working Paper. World Bank, Economic Prospect Group, Washington, D.C.

World Bank. 2001. *Global Economic Prospects and the Developing Countries 2002: Making Trade Work for the Poor.* Washington, D.C.: World Bank.

———. 2003. *Global Economic Prospects 2004: Realizing the Development Promise of the Doha Agenda.* Washington, D.C.: World Bank.

PART II

THE COMMODITY STUDIES

8

SUGAR POLICIES: AN OPPORTUNITY FOR CHANGE

Donald O. Mitchell

Sugar protection dates back to at least the 1800s. It has been greatest in countries of the northern hemisphere that produce sugar beets. That is because sugar from beets is nearly twice as expensive to produce as sugar from cane, and most beet producers cannot survive without high protection. Over the years, high protection has led to lower consumption, reduced imports, and surplus production, which is disposed of in the world market at subsidized prices. Many other countries have been pressured by their producers for protection from heavily subsidized exports and depressed world market prices. The cycle of protection, subsidies, and more protection has run for decades.

The European Union (EU), Japan, and the United States are among the areas with the highest level of protection and therefore the most distorted import patterns. Since the early 1970s, U.S. sugar imports have declined from more than 5 million tons per year to slightly more than 1 million tons per year. The European Union was a net importer of about 2.5 million tons of sugar in the early 1970s, compared with net exports of about 5 million tons in recent years. Japan's sugar imports have

fallen from 2.5 million tons to 1.5 million tons over the past two decades. Thus, the three largest markets for sugar imports in the 1970s have been closing to competition after becoming largely self-sufficient, at least compared with the early 1970s, when their combined net imports accounted for half of the world's exports (figure 8.1).

Background

Sugar occurs naturally in most foods, but it is economically extracted from only a few crops such as sugar beets, sugar cane, and corn. Sugar beets are an annual root crop grown in temperate climates, while sugar cane is a tall perennial grass grown in tropical and semitropical climates. About 55 countries grow sugar beets, and 105 grow sugar cane. The process of producing sugar (sucrose) from sugar beets or sugar cane requires that the juice be extracted and processed in a factory near where the beet or cane is grown. The by-products of sugar cane are bagasse and molasses. Bagasse is the residue of cane, after the juice is extracted. It has some industrial uses and is often used to fuel the

---

The author wishes to express thanks for useful comments to Ataman Aksoy, John Beghin, Margaret Blamberg, Uri Dadush, Harry de Gorter, Stephen Haley, Steven Jaffee, Will Martin, John Nash, and Albert Viton.

FIGURE 8.1   World Sugar Exports and Net Imports of Selected Countries
(million of tons)

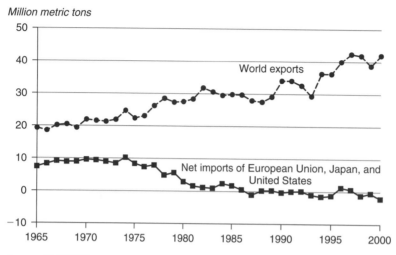

Source: FAOSTAT.

boilers in the sugar factory (also called a *sugar mill*). Molasses is an edible by-product as well as an animal feed. The by-products of sugar beets are beet tops, the leafy portion of the beet used for animal feed, and molasses, which is also used primarily as an animal feed. Once harvested, sugar cane is highly perishable and must be processed quickly. Sugar beets are less perishable than sugar cane but still must be processed soon after harvest. The high cost of transporting sugar beets or cane makes it impractical to locate the factory far from the producing areas.

Sugar growers and processors are economically interdependent and normally share in the value of total sugar and molasses sales according to a contractual agreement. Both can influence the value of total output since the volume and sugar content of sugar beets or cane is affected by input use and production practices, and the recovery of sugar from beets or cane is dependent on the technology and operation of the sugar factory. Various ownership arrangements exist in the industry—ranging from ownership by a single company of the factory and producing lands to independent growers who contract production with a factory. Some growers are members of cooperatives, which own and operate a sugar factory. State ownership of factories and lands is still common in developing countries, but substantial privatization has taken place in recent years.

Common sugar is sucrose. It is extracted in nearly pure, chemically identical form from sugar cane and sugar beets. Dextrose is a sugar derived synthetically from starch (most commonly corn starch). Fructose is a very sweet sugar derived from dextrose. High-fructose corn syrup (HFCS) is produced by the enzymatic conversion to fructose of a portion of the dextrose in corn syrup. It is chemically similar to sugar used in soft drinks, which is a mixture of equal parts of dextrose and fructose. The fact that identical or nearly identical sugars can be produced from different crops provides producers and consumers with a wide range of substitution possibilities. It also means, however, that sugar policies are often complex, as the different industries vie for support. For example, sugar producers in the European Union have been able to get legislated quotas on HFCS production. Japan also limits HFCS production to prevent it from further eroding sugar's market share. In the United States, HFCS producers benefit from high sugar prices and support current sugar policies.

High protection has led to the emergence of HFCS as a substitute for sugar in the United States and Japan. Because it is a nearly perfect substitute for sugar in uses such as soft drinks, HFCS and other corn syrups now account for 40 percent of caloric-sweetener use in Japan and more than half of U.S. caloric sweetener consumption (figure 8.2). The technique for commercial production of high-fructose corn syrup was discovered in the late 1960s and made profitable by high sugar prices in the protected Japanese and U.S. markets. But now,

FIGURE 8.2   U.S. Sugar and HFCS Consumption

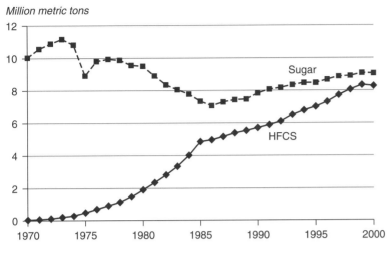

Source: USDA.

economies of scale, improvements in production techniques, and large installed production capacity (financed under high prices), have made corn syrups competitive with sugar from cane and less costly than sugar from beets.

Another product that can be produced from sugar beets, sugar cane, and corn (and some other crops) is ethanol—a clear colorless, flammable, oxygenated hydrocarbon that can be used for a number of purposes, including as a vehicle fuel, a use that accounts for about two-thirds of world ethanol consumption. It is normally more costly than petroleum-based fuels, however, and is used only when special incentives, such as environmental regulations or government subsidies encourage its production and use. Ethanol can be produced from crude oil, ethylene, and coal, or from agricultural products. Roughly 60 percent of global ethanol production comes from sugar cane and sugar beets. In Brazil, half of sugar cane production is used for ethanol production; government ethanol policies mandate the share of ethanol to be blended with gasoline.

The United States is a major producer and consumer of ethanol from corn. Ethanol has environmental advantages when used as a fuel, because it burns cleaner than gasoline and does not produce greenhouse gases. In 1990 amendments to the U.S. Clean Air Act required certain U.S. regions to use oxygenated, reformulated gasoline during certain high-smog months and stipulated that a certain percentage of oxygenates must be derived from

renewable sources such as corn. The legislation provided tax incentives for ethanol, amounting to $0.54 cents a gallon when blended with gasoline at a 10 percent rate. Some Midwestern states provide additional tax incentives.

The cost of ethanol production from corn is about $1.10 per gallon, but because ethanol contains less energy than gasoline, the comparable energy-equivalent cost is $1.65 per gallon (Oregon Office of Energy 2002). Thus, with the $0.54 tax incentive, ethanol is competitive with regular gasoline. In response to the incentive, U.S. ethanol production has been growing by about 6 percent per year (Berg 2001). Both HFCS and ethanol can be produced in the same facility by adding an ethanol unit to an HFCS facility, so the tax incentive on ethanol partly finances the facilities that produce HFCS. A seasonal complementarity between ethanol and HFCS production is also possible because ethanol is used for fuels primarily during the winter months, whereas the demand for HFCS in soft drinks increases during summer months. The U.S. ethanol policy contributes to production capacity, which also can be used for HFCS production, thereby reducing HFCS production costs and making HFCS more competitive with sugar.

Estimates of Production Costs

Although the costs of producing sugar vary among countries for a variety of reasons, it is cheaper to produce it from cane than from beets in all countries. LMC International, a London-based consulting firm, periodically estimates production costs for cane sugar, beet sugar, and HFCS. The firm's most recent estimates cover 41 beet-producing countries, 63 cane-producing countries, and 19 HFCS-producing countries (table 8.1). LMC bases its estimates on an engineering cost approach that accounts for the physical inputs of labor, machinery, fuel, chemicals, and fertilizers used in field and factory. The estimates are of actual average costs and include the impact of policies that protect producers in certain countries. Such cost estimates do not represent the supply curve normally estimated by economists, since they are not estimates of marginal costs. Nevertheless, they are useful for comparing the average costs of production of different products. Actual raw cane sugar prices are provided for comparison. The prices are f.o.b. (free

on board), while costs are exfactory; thus the prices should be higher.

The average cost of producing raw cane sugar by major exporters was 10.39 U.S. cents per pound in 1994–99, while the average cost of refined cane sugar was 14.25 cents per pound. Thus the raw-to-white spread averaged 3.86 cents per pound. Refined sugar from beets cost an average of 25.31 cents per pound—78 percent more than refined cane sugar. Among low-cost producers, the difference between refined cane and beet sugar was even wider. The average production cost for low-cost producers of refined cane sugar was 11.44 cents per pound, compared with 22.29 cents per pound for refined beet sugar—a difference of 95 percent. Based on this comparison, sugar from beets was not competitive with sugar from cane by either major exporters or low-cost producers. However, the wide

TABLE 8.1   Average Costs of Producing Cane Sugar, Beet Sugar, and High-Fructose Corn Syrup by Categories of Producers, and Actual Sugar Prices, 1994–1999

(nominal U.S. cents per pound[a])

Category	1994–95	1995–96	1996–97	1997–98	1998–99
Raw cane sugar					
Low cost producers[b]	7.43	8.10	8.18	7.78	7.58
Major exporters[c]	10.37	10.60	10.72	10.52	9.73
Cane sugar, white equiv.					
Low cost producers[b]	11.02	11.75	11.84	11.41	11.19
Major exporters[c]	14.23	14.48	14.61	14.38	13.53
Beet sugar, refined					
Low cost producers[d]	21.31	23.16	23.09	21.21	22.67
Major exporters[e]	25.47	26.87	25.90	23.56	24.75
High-fructose corn syrup[f]					
Major producers[g]	13.45	16.78	13.57	12.86	11.76
Actual market prices					
Raw cane sugar[h]	13.53	12.23	11.21	10.71	7.05

a. Exfactory basis.

b. Average of 5 producing regions (Australia, Brazil–Center/South, Guatemala, Zambia, and Zimbabwe).

c. Average of 7 countries (Australia, Brazil, Colombia, Cuba, Guatemala, South Africa, and Thailand).

d. Average of 7 countries (Belgium, Canada, Chile, France, Turkey, United Kingdom, and United States).

e. Average of 4 countries (Belgium, France, Germany, and Turkey).

f. HFCS-55, dry weight.

g. Average of 19 countries (Argentina, Belgium, Canada, Egypt, Finland, France, Germany, Hungary, Italy, Japan, Mexico, Netherlands, the Slovak Republic, the Republic of Korea, Spain, Taiwan (China), Turkey, United Kingdom, and United States).

h. Raw cane sugar price is U.S. cents per pound, July-June average of monthly prices, f.o.b. Caribbean ports.

Source: LMC International (1999). Actual market prices are from World Bank databases.

margin between refined sugar from beets and cane is partly a reflection of protection to sugar beet producers in the European Union and United States, which encourages production in marginal areas and contributes to higher average costs.

Production costs for HFCS-55 (55 percent fructose) averaged 13.68 cents per pound and were lower than white sugar from cane produced by major exporters in four of the five years. They exceeded the cost of cane sugar only when corn prices rose sharply in 1995–96. Thus, HFCS-55 can compete with refined cane sugar in the current policy environment, and perhaps even in a fully liberalized market environment, since many studies have suggested that raw sugar prices would rise more than corn prices under liberalization.

industry employee for those countries is estimated to range from 16.3 tons to 19.9 tons. In contrast, countries known to be high-cost producers such as Fiji, Kenya, and Mauritius have production of 7.0 to 8.3 tons of raw sugar per industry employee. Thus, one can reasonably conclude that an additional million tons of sugar production from a low-cost sugar-producing country would generate about 55,500 direct employment jobs. If the exports came from a high-cost producer, the same million tons of production would generate about 128,000 direct employment jobs. Additional indirect employment jobs would also be generated in transportation and related industries, but no attempt was made to estimate these jobs.

Employment

Data on employment in developing countries' sugar industries are not readily available but can be estimated from reports, surveys, and industry statements. Such estimates (table 8.2) show considerable cross-country consistency among high- and low-cost producers. For example, Brazil, Guyana, and South Africa are known to be among the lowest-cost producers; raw-sugar production per

The World Sugar Market

Brazil, the European Union, and India are the largest sugar producers, each accounting for roughly 14 percent of world production during 1999–2001 (table 8.3). They are followed by China and the United States, which each produce about 6 percent of the world's sugar. Sugar trade is dominated by Brazil and Russia, with Brazil accounting for about one-quarter of world net exports and Russia accounting for about 14 percent of world

TABLE 8.2 Raw Sugar Produced Annually per Sugar Industry Employee, Selected Developing Countries

Country	Direct Employment (Growers and Factory)	Tons of Raw Sugar Produced, Average 1999–2001	Tons of Raw Sugar Produced Per Employee
Low-cost producers			
Brazil	1,100,000	19,485,000	17.7
Guyana	18,000	293,072	16.3
South Africa	130,000	2,589,667	19.9
High-cost producers			
Fiji	40,500	336,333	8.3
Kenya	69,000	485,333	7.0
Mauritius	65,000	529,299	8.1
Other producers			
Malawi	17,000	200,667	11.8
Mexico	300,000	5,069,233	16.9

Note: Production is the three-year average of raw sugar production during 1999–2001 from FAOSTAT.
Source: Employment figures are derived from various sources and include total direct employment in sugar factories and plantations. Employment data for Brazil, Mexico, and South Africa are from OECD (2002a); Fiji, Guyana, and Mauritius data are from F. O. Licht (2002); Kenya data are from the Kenya Sugar Board; Malawi data are from the Malawi Ministry of Commerce and Industry.

TABLE 8.3 Major Sugar Producers, Net Exporters, and Net Importers, 1999–2001 Average

Producers		Net Exporters		Net Importers	
Country/Region	Millions of Tons	Country/Region	Millions of Tons	Country/Region	Millions of Tons
India	19.4	Brazil	9.3	Russia	5.2
European Union	18.6	European Union	4.2	Indonesia	1.7
Brazil	18.5	Australia	3.8	Japan	1.6
United States	7.9	Thailand	3.6	United States	1.4
China	7.8	Cuba	3.2	Korea, Rep. of	1.2
Thailand	5.4	South Africa	1.3	Canada	1.2
Mexico	5.1	Guatemala	1.1	Iran	1.0
Australia	4.9	Colombia	1.0	Malaysia	1.0
Cuba	3.8	Turkey	0.6	Algeria	0.9
Pakistan	3.0	Mauritius	0.5	Nigeria	0.7
All other	38.9	All other	10.3	All other	20.7
World	133.3	World	38.9	World	36.6

Note: Data are in raw sugar equivalents.
Source: USDA Production Supply and Distribution (PS&D) 2002.

net imports during 1999–2001. The European Union is the second largest net exporter, followed by Australia, Cuba, and Thailand, which each export about 8–10 percent of the world total. Net imports are widely dispersed after Russia, with the next largest net importer accounting for less than 5 percent of world imports. India is the largest sugar consumer, with about 15 percent of world consumption, followed by the European Union with 10 percent, and Brazil with 7 percent.

World HFCS production averaged 11.7 million tons (dry weight basis) during 1999–2001. Production in the United States alone averaged 9.2 million tons—79 percent of the world total. Japan was the second-largest producer, with an average of .78 million tons, followed by Argentina, Canada, European Union, Mexico, and Republic of Korea with between .3 and .4 tons each. HFCS is considered equivalent to sugar on a dry weight basis when used to produce products such as soft drinks.

World sugar prices have historically been characterized by periodic sharp increases followed by long periods of low or declining prices. This pattern has been caused, in large part, by policies in both developed and developing countries that isolated consumers and producers from international prices and diminished their price responsiveness. Since the early 1980s, however, some developing countries have reformed their policies. As the share of those countries in global consumption and imports has increased with population and income growth, the reformed policies have led to greater price responsiveness by sugar producers and consumers, likely reducing the severity of future price spikes. The collapse of the former Soviet Union also led to the abandonment of dedicated sugar imports from Cuba and increased trade at world market prices. Many developed countries still maintain highly protected sugar sectors and thus contribute to the likelihood of price spikes, but they now account for only one-third of consumption and one-half of imports—compared with slightly more than half of consumption and 60 percent of imports when the last sugar price spike occurred in 1980.

Despite some liberalization of sugar policies, roughly 80 percent of world sugar production and 60 percent of world sugar trade is at subsidized or protected prices. Only three major producers (Australia, Brazil, and Cuba) have sugar sectors that produce and operate at world market price levels.[1] These three producers account for a combined 20 percent of world production and 40 percent of world trade. The remaining 80 percent of world production and 60 percent of world trade relies on production subsidies, export subsidies, or preferential access to protected markets. The European

Union, Japan, and the United States account for 20 percent of world production; their average producer prices are more than double the world market. China and India account for another 20 percent of world production and protect producers with prices that are higher than world market prices. The remaining 40 percent of production is in countries that either produce for preferential markets (as is the case with Fiji, Mauritius, the Philippines, and many African and Caribbean countries) and thus receive prices higher than those of the world market, or they protect their domestic producers with policies that restrict imports to provide above-market prices.

The value of world sugar exports has remained relatively constant in nominal dollars ($11.8 billion during 1980–85; $11.6 billion during 1995–2000), and sugar has remained an important source of export earnings for some developing countries. However, the share of developing countries in total sugar exports declined from 71 percent during 1980–85 to 54 percent in 1995–2000, as developed-country exports increased and the share of higher-valued refined-sugar exports by developed countries increased. Twelve countries received 10 percent or more of their total export earnings from sugar during 1995–2000, and an additional five received 5–10 percent. In contrast, during 1980–85, ten countries received 20 percent or more of total exports from sugar, and nine additional countries received from 5–20 percent.

Sugar Policies in Selected Developing Countries

Although this chapter focuses on prospects for policy reform in the European Union, Japan, and the United States, it is useful to examine policies in other major sugar-producing and -trading countries to see how they would be affected by such reforms.

Brazil—the world's largest sugar exporter and generally considered to be its lowest-cost producer—would be a major beneficiary of increased world sugar trade and higher prices because it has the capacity to increase sugar production and exports substantially. The devaluation of the Brazilian *real* by 65 percent relative to the dollar since 1998 has contributed to the country's competitiveness. Despite its dominance, however,

exports are viewed as the third alternative for Brazilian sugar cane after production of fuel ethanol and sugar for the large domestic market. Only half of Brazil's sugar cane is used to produce sugar; the other half goes into ethanol for automotive fuel. Sugar cane can easily be divided between sugar and ethanol production depending on market conditions and government policies. If all of Brazil's sugar cane were used to produce sugar, production could roughly double (an increase of roughly 18.5 million tons per year). Most of the increase could be exported, subject to port and milling capacity.

The Brazilian government has pursued a biofuel policy since the 1970s, when concerns about the adequacy of petroleum supplies were high. These policies included tax incentives and direct subsidies for ethanol production and use, sugar price controls, and restrictions on sugar exports. Lower petroleum prices during the 1980s led to reduced ethanol subsidies and the removal of export and price controls on sugar beginning in 1990. Other controls on sugar were eased during the 1990s, and sugar exports increased from 1.5 million tons in 1990–91 to 11.3 million tons in 2000–01. Some subsidies remain on ethanol production and use, and the future of such subsidies can strongly influence the use of sugar cane for ethanol versus sugar production. Government mandates on the share of ethanol to be included in gasoline (currently 20–24 percent) can strongly influence demand for ethanol as automotive fuel and the supplies of sugar cane directed to sugar production. The future of the biofuel program depends on international petroleum prices as well as Brazilian policy. Recently marketed flex-fuel automobile engines that run equally well on gasoline or pure hydrous alcohol are expected to boost ethanol demand and direct some sugar cane production away from sugar production and exports.

Sugar cane production has increased rapidly in the center-south region of Brazil, where the climate is favorable, land is available, and sugar cane yields good returns relative to other crops. Further expansion of sugar cane production in the center-south region is possible and expected by most industry experts, but milling capacity will need to be expanded to allow significantly more sugar production. Sugar is also produced in the northeast region, where high-cost growers receive a small subsidy. The central government allocates Brazil's total annual quota of premium-priced U.S. imports to this region.

China was an occasional large sugar importer and exporter in the 1990s, but average net imports were about 400,000 tons during 1990–2000. Most of these imports came from Cuba under a long-term trade agreement. The government has followed a policy aimed at self-sufficiency by providing strong price incentives to producers, controlling imports, and accumulating and releasing government stocks to maintain high internal market prices. About 90 percent of China's sugar production comes from sugar cane and the remainder from sugar beets. A "guidance price" is provided to sugar refiners for sugar cane and beet, but market forces largely determine prices (Sheales and others 1999). The policy and strong demand growth kept sugar prices high during most of the 1990s, but prices fell sharply after the record 1998–99 crop, remaining low through 2000. Prices increased in 2001, with white wholesale sugar prices averaging about $0.22 per pound during the first half of 2001 (F. O. Licht 2002), more than double the world market price and similar to U.S. domestic prices. A record 2002–03 harvest caused prices to fall again.

Artificial sweeteners, mainly saccharin, are an important competitor to sugar in China and substitute for as much as 2.4 million tons. When China entered the World Trade Organization (WTO) in 2001, it agreed to a tariff rate quota of 1.6 million tons of sugar at a tariff rate of 20 percent, with an over-quota tariff of 76 percent. The quota is scheduled to increase to 1.945 million tons, and the over-quota rate to fall to 65 percent, by 2004. If China were to import the full amount specified by the tariff rate quota, imports would increase substantially over the levels of recent years. China's WTO tariff quota does not commit the country to import all of the quota tonnage, however, and China can choose among a number of different methods of administering the quota to influence its fill rate (Jolly 2001). For example, actual imports during 2001–02 were 1.15 million tons, according to the International Sugar Organization (2002), despite the tariff rate quota of 1.6 million tons. The Chinese sugar industry would undergo substantial adjustment if it were opened to international competition. A large number of small, high-cost sugar mills would become unprofitable, and production would likely decline.

India's sugar industry, heavily regulated under the Essential Commodities Act of 1955, is very politicized because of the large number of sugar cane growers (reportedly as many as 5 million) and the importance of sugar in Indian diets. The industry is largely self-sufficient, with occasional imports to offset domestic shortfalls. An import duty (currently 60 percent) is varied to maintain domestic prices above those of the world market. Large stocks of sugar currently burden the industry and can only be exported with substantial subsidies or at substantial losses. India provides an internal freight reimbursement and ocean freight subsidy to help export surplus production. State controls limit internal sugar movements, and licensing and stock-holding requirements for mills and shops contribute to industry inefficiencies. Sugar mills are small and inefficient, and high internal transport costs would limit export potential even if world prices were to rise above internal prices. Sugar millers and importers are required to sell a portion of their supplies to the Public Distribution System at below-market prices for resale to low-income consumers. Sugar-cane production is more profitable than most other crops, with prices that are about 50 percent higher than world market prices due to minimums established by the central government and higher prices advised by the states.

India has a small ethanol program, and there are government proposals to require ethanol to be blended with gasoline to reduce pollution. The government has announced plans to liberalize the sector, but past efforts at liberalization have been unsuccessful. Decades of regulation have also created complicated political interdependencies that will be difficult to disentangle. It is unlikely that India would emerge as a significant exporter even if policies in the European Union, Japan, and the United States were changed to allow greater imports.

Mexico privatized its sugar mills and partially deregulated its sugar industry in reforms that concluded in 1992 (Escandon 2002). It has maintained strong government regulation of the sector, however, by setting sugar-cane prices for its 150,000 growers. Mexico liberalized pricing and production of sugar in 1995 but simultaneously increased protection by increasing tariffs from 65 percent to 136 percent on raw sugar and from 73 percent to 127 percent on refined sugar. This led to a 60 percent increase in domestic sugar prices, a 50 percent increase in production, and a doubling of exports from 1992 to 2002.

The North American Free Trade Agreement (NAFTA) came into force on January 1, 1994. A 15-year adjustment period ending in 2008 was to be followed by free trade in sugar between Mexico and the United States. The implementation of NAFTA has been contentious because of a last-minute side-letter agreement on sugar added to ensure approval by the U.S. Congress. Although the side-letter agreement was never ratified by Mexico's Congress and is not recognized as valid by Mexico, the U.S. government administers NAFTA in accordance with its terms. Under NAFTA, the amount of Mexico's duty-free access to the U.S. sugar market depends on whether Mexico is a surplus sugar producer (sugar production minus sugar consumption). The side-letter agreement changed the definition of surplus producer to include HFCS consumption as well as sugar consumption. Using this definition, Mexico could export up to 25,000 tons per year of surplus sugar duty-free during the first 6 years of NAFTA. Beginning in year 7 (the 2000–01 marketing year), and until the end of the 15-year adjustment period, Mexico could export up to 250,000 tons of surplus sugar duty-free.

High prices for sugar in Mexico led to large imports and increased production of HFCS, which quickly displaced sugar in the soft-drinks industry and left Mexico with large sugar stocks that could not be exported duty-free to the United States because of the 25,000 ton limit. After the United States rejected a request to allow increased duty-free exports, Mexico charged that the United States was dumping HFCS in Mexico and initiated antidumping duties. Negotiations are continuing to resolve the trade and duties on HFCS.

Caught between the high prices that the government had established for sugar cane and the weak domestic and world market prices for sugar, many of Mexico's 60 sugar mills became insolvent. The government expropriated 27 mills with large and unpayable debts in September 2001. Public investments are being made to prepare these mills for resale to private investors.

Among the measures in Mexico's national sugar policy for 2002–2006, which is designed to make the sector profitable, is the formation of an export cooperative of all private and government-owned sugar mills. Mexico's sugar exports in the 2001–02

marketing year are estimated to total 650,000 tons, of which 148,000 tons were exported to the United States duty-free. Beginning in 2009, Mexico will have unlimited duty-free access to the U.S. sugar market and will likely increase exports substantially.

The Russian Federation is by far the world's largest sugar importer, with average annual imports of 5.2 million tons during 1999–2001, three times the amount of the next largest importer. Following the breakup of the Soviet Union, the Russian sugar sector faced an uncertain future, an unstable and confused policy structure, and a technically weak industry. Sugar production, all from beets, declined by about 45 percent from 1992 to 2000, while consumption declined by 17 percent and sugar imports increased by 35 percent. Low beet yields, poor factory recovery rates, outdated technology, and shortages of fuel and replacement parts hampered the adjustment of the Russian sugar industry to privatization. With trade policy changing frequently, high perceived risks discouraged foreign direct investment and slowed the modernization of the industry.

The government uses high tariffs to protect the domestic industry. To protect domestic sugar refiners, tariffs on white sugar are higher than on raw sugar. Seasonal tariffs are added during periods of peak domestic production to protect local producers and support prices. The import duty on raw cane sugar for 2003 has been set at $95 per ton ($.043 per pound). Russia is expected to remain a large importer as long as the investment climate remains uncertain and foreign companies are reluctant to invest. Even with foreign investment, Russia will likely remain a high-cost producer because its industry is based on beets.

Thailand is the world's fourth-largest sugar exporter, with net exports of 3.6 million tons during 1999–2001 (annual average). Thailand's sugar policy is patterned after that of the European Union, with high internal sugar prices maintained by quotas and import tariffs. The government uses production quotas, tax incentives, and subsidized credit to encourage exports. The tariff rate quota agreed under the WTO Agreement on Agriculture was 65 percent for in-quota imports in 1999 and 99 percent for outside-quota imports (Sheales and others 1999). Despite high protection, Thailand's costs of production are among the lowest in the world, roughly comparable to those of Australia

(Borrell and Pearce 1999). High protection and low costs have led to rapid growth of production and a more than tripling of exports over the past two decades.

This selective review of policies in major sugar-producing and -trading countries illustrates the significance of policy distortions in the world sugar market. India, the largest sugar producer, has a heavily regulated domestic sugar market and high import tariffs to protect local producers. China's import restrictions keep domestic sugar prices nearly as high as those in the United States. Russia, the largest net importer, has high tariffs to protect sugar-beet producers and additional tariffs on white sugar to protect local refiners. Brazil, the largest sugar exporter, has a sugar policy that is partly driven by its biofuel policies; until recently it restricted sugar exports. Thailand, the fourth-largest net exporter and a low-cost producer, has used high domestic prices, tax incentives, and sub-sidized credit to increase exports. Mexico's high domestic prices have stimulated production in anticipation of unlimited duty-free access to the U.S. sugar market beginning in 2009.

Sugar Policies in Selected OECD Countries

More than half of the value of sugar production in OECD (Organisation for Economic Co-operation and Development) countries during 1999–2001 came from government support or transfers from consumers. Such high support typically limits con-sumption through high prices and encourages pro-duction even when a country does not have a com-parative advantage in sugar production. Support to OECD sugar producers during 1999–2001 totaled $6.35 billion, more than half the value of world sugar trade (about $11.6 billion) and nearly equal to developing-country exports of about $6.5 bil-lion. The European Union provided the largest annual support, with $2.71 billion, while the United States provided $1.30 billion, and Japan provided $0.44 billion. Several developing coun-tries also provided high levels of support to sugar producers, including Mexico, Poland, and Turkey (table 8.4). Much of that support is provided through border protection.

The benefits of more liberalized trade in sugar and reduced domestic support, especially in OECD

TABLE 8.4   Government Support to Sugar Producers, 1999–2001

Country/Region	Producer Support (million US$)	Producer Nominal Assistance Coefficient	Support from Border Protection (percent)
OECD	6,351	2.11	n.a.
Australia	51	1.11	0.0
Czech Republic	16	1.25	47.6
European Union	2,713	2.11	91.7
Hungary	12	1.20	41.5
Japan	437	2.17	88.7
Mexico	713	2.10	83.9
Poland	176	2.28	92.9
Slovak Republic	16	1.94	54.7
Switzerland	86	4.36	73.0
Turkey	749	3.02	95.8
United States	1,302	2.37	84.3

n.a. Not applicable.

Note: Producer support was converted from local currency to U.S. dollars using period average annual exchange rates from the IMF's *International Financial Statistics,* May 2002. Producer nominal assistance coefficient is an indicator of the nominal rate of assistance to producers measuring the ratio between the value of gross farm receipts including support and gross farm receipts valued at world market prices without support. No calculations were made for Canada, Iceland, New Zealand, Norway, or the Republic of Korea.

Source: OECD 2002b.

countries, are substantial, according to several studies (Borrell and Pearce 1999; Devadoss and Kropf 1996; Elbehri and others 2000; El-Obeid and Beghin 2004; USGAO 1993 and 2000; Sheales and others 1999; USITC 2002; van der Mensbrugghe, Beghin, Mitchell 2003; Wohlgenant 1999). Study results differ because of different assumptions, methodologies, and scenarios, but the general conclusion is that reduced support to OECD sugar producers would result in lower production in those countries, lower domestic prices, increased consumption, and increased net imports. World sugar prices would increase and exports from developing countries, and some developed-country exporters, would rise. According to Sheales and others (1999), full liberalization of the world sugar market would result in a 41 percent increase in world sugar prices. Sugar imports would increase by 44 percent in the United States. Exports would decline by 34 percent in the European Union. Low-cost sugar-producing countries would increase exports, with Australia's exports rising 16 percent, Brazil's 23 percent, and Thailand's 22 percent. Removal of government support from domestic producers in the European Union, Japan, and the United States would save consumers $4.8 billion per year. A study by the U.S. General Accounting Office (USGAO 2000) concluded that the U.S. sugar program resulted in a net loss to the U.S. economy of $1 billion in 1998. Elbehri and others (2000) used the global trade analysis project (GTAP) multisectoral, multiregional general-equilibrium model to examine the impacts of partially liberalizing sugar tariff-rate-quota regimes, concluding that cutting the European Union's over-quota tariff by one-third would yield a global welfare gain of $568 million. Coordinated global reforms would result in the greatest benefits. Wohlgenant (1999) estimated that global sugar-trade liberalization would result in a 43 percent increase in world price.

Borrell and Pearce (1999) used a 24-region model of the global sweetener market to examine consumption, production, trade, price, and welfare effects for seven classes of sweeteners. A baseline projection that continued current protection was compared with a fully liberalized market with no trade protection or domestic support in any country or region. Under the fully liberalized scenario, sugar prices were projected to fall from the baseline by 65 percent in Japan; 40 percent in Western

Europe; 25 percent in Eastern Europe, Indonesia, Mexico, and the United States; and 10 percent in China, the Philippines, and Ukraine. Lower prices would lead to higher consumption, lower production, and increased imports of sugar in those countries that had trade protection. World prices would increase by 38 percent, and lower-cost producers would increase production and exports—however consumption decreased from the higher prices. In countries with the highest protection (Europe, Indonesia, Japan, the United States), net imports would increase by 15 million tons per year. Japan's production would drop by 44 percent, that of the United States by 32 percent, and Western Europe's by 21 percent. Among low-cost producers and exporters, Australia and Thailand would increase production by 25 percent, and Brazil, Cuba, and other Latin American countries (excluding Brazil, Mexico, and Cuba) would increase production by about 15 percent.

Global welfare gains from full liberalization are estimated by Borrell and Pearce (1999) to total $4.7 billion per year based on historical supply responses; gain could go as high as $6.3 billion per year if higher supply responses occur. Brazilian producers would gain the most from liberalization, at around $2.6 billion per year, but this would be offset by a loss of $1 billion to Brazilian consumers who would pay higher prices after liberalization—leaving a net gain of $1.6 billion for Brazil. Japan would enjoy a net gain of about $0.4 billion from lower consumer prices that would more than offset lower producer prices on the 40 percent of sugar that is domestically produced. The United States would have a small net gain of about $0.5 billion from full liberalization, with consumer gains slightly larger than producer losses. Western Europe would gain about $1.5 billion as consumer gains of about $4.8 billion exceeded producer losses of about $3.3 billion.

The exporting countries that now enjoy preferential access to European and U.S. sugar markets gain about $0.8 billion per year from prices that are more than twice world market prices on sales to the European Union, and 80 percent more than the world market price for sales to the United States. The value of the preferential access is less than it appears, however, because many of these producers have high production costs and would not produce as much at world market prices. Further, world

FIGURE 8.3   Sugar Prices, 1970–2003

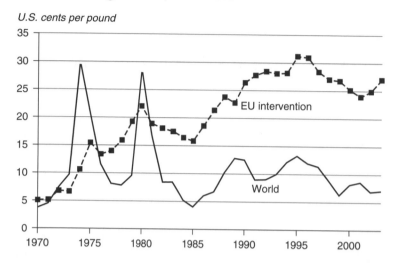

U.S. cents per pound

market prices would rise by an estimated 38 percent after full liberalization, partially offsetting the loss of high prices in preferential markets for producers. Borrell and Pearce (1999) estimate the net loss to these exporting countries from full liberalization at $0.45 billion. The cost to taxpayers in the European Union and United States of providing each $1 of preferential access is estimated to be more than $5. In a recent study of the Fijian economy (Levantis, Jotzo, and Tulpule 2003), alternative forms of aid were found to deliver much greater economic benefits and growth prospects.

Caribbean sugar producers are among the largest group of countries having preferential access to the European and U.S. sugar markets. A recent study (Mitchell 2004) found that most of the Caribbean producers cannot export profitably even to the European Union, which pays prices that are more than triple those of the world market. Many of these countries have abandoned their U.S. quotas because they do not produce enough to satisfy both their EU and U.S. quotas, and EU quotas have higher prices.

While the benefits to reform are not widely disputed, the opposition to reform within certain countries has been strong. The remainder of this section examines the sugar policies of the European Union, Japan, and the United States with an eye to the prospects for reform.

The European Union's Sugar Policy

The European Union's sugar policy uses production quotas, import controls, and export refunds

(subsidies) to support producer prices at levels well above international prices. The program is financed primarily by the European Union's consumers, who pay high prices for sugar. The sugar policy began in 1965 as part of the Common Agricultural Policy (CAP). Under the CAP, intervention sugar prices have been constant in nominal terms since 1984–85; however, they vary with exchange rates when expressed in U.S. dollars (figure 8.3). They have been more than double world market prices during most of the past 20 years. Import duties are used to prevent lower-priced imports from the world market, and export refunds are paid to exporters to cover the gap between the EU price and the generally lower world market prices when commodities are sold from intervention stocks.

Production quotas limit the amount of sugar eligible for price support. Quotas are divided into categories A and B, with different levels of price support. Sugar production in excess of quota is classed as C sugar and is not supported, but it can be carried over for use as quota sugar in the next year or exported at world market prices. The total of A and B quota sugar was 14.592 million tons in 2000–01, of which 11.983 million tons was for A quota and 2.611 million tons was for B quota (USDA 2003). The quotas have been declining to meet WTO commitments. The surplus of A and B quota sugar above domestic consumption is about 1.5 million tons; it is exported with subsidy. Excess quota (C sugar) averaged 1.59 million tons (white equivalent) between 1995–96 and 2000–01. Thus, the EU sugar program results in about 3.1 million tons of sugar exports per year (about 10 percent of world exports), and half of this is subsidized.[2] Critics of EU policy charge that A and B quota sugar is subsidizing the production and export of C sugar. Australia, Brazil, and Thailand have filed a complaint with the WTO to that effect.

Production levies are applied to all quota sugar production to cover the costs of export refunds. The levy on A quota sugar is 2 percent, whereas the levy on B quota varies from 30 percent to 37 percent depending on world market prices. An additional levy can be collected in the next marketing year to recover any shortfall in export refunds. Quotas are also set for some alternative sweeteners such as HFCS (known as isoglucose within the European Union) and inulin (produced from chicory and Jerusalem artichoke). The quota for production of HFCS is 303,000 tons; that for inulin is 323,000 tons.

The Uruguay Round commitments had little initial impact on the European Union's sugar regime. The variable import levy was replaced by a fixed duty plus a safeguard clause allowing for a variable additional duty with minimal impact on protection to sugar beet producers. The European Union agreed to reduce both the amount spent on export refunds and the volume of sugar exported with subsidy. Export refunds are also payable on sugar exported in the form of processed goods such as sugar confectionery, chocolate, biscuits, cakes, ice cream, soft drinks, and so on. The European Union amended legislation to allow changes in sugar-production quotas on an annual basis (rather than the previous five-year basis) to ensure that the limits on exports were met. The WTO commitment was to reduce only the subsidized exports net of preferential imports. This is a small proportion of total exports, and amounted to just 34 million tons from the 1986–90 base of 1.612 million tons per year.

Preferential access to the European Union's sugar market and its high prices are granted to the 46 countries from Africa, the Caribbean, and the Pacific (ACP) that signed the first Lomé Convention in 1975. The Lomé sugar protocol provided for imports of specified quantities of raw or white cane sugar originating in the ACP states at guaranteed prices. Unlike most articles of the Lomé Convention, the sugar protocol does not expire and cannot be changed unilaterally. The original quantities specified were 1,294,700 tons of white-sugar equivalent, with an additional amount allotted to India. The total import commitment was for 1,304,700 tons;

this amount has remained constant, with reallocation of quotas among existing members when a country did not fulfill its quota. The sugar imported under the Lomé Convention is known as "preference sugar." An additional import allocation of between 200,000 and 350,000 tons of sugar was made to ACP countries (primarily) in 1995. This allocation of "special preference sugar" is not permanent, and the quantity can vary based on import needs. The price specified for special preference sugar was 85 percent of the guaranteed price for the permanent preference sugar. In addition, the European Union took over the WTO import commitments of the new members joining the European Union in 1995. These included a tariff quota of 85,500 tons, mainly from Brazil, with an in-quota tariff rate of 98 ECU (European currency unit) per ton. The European Union has also granted several countries in the Balkans temporary access to its sugar market. Imports under this program totaled about 100,000 tons in 2001–02. In total, the EU permanent import commitment is 1.39 million tons (white sugar equivalent) plus additional quantities of up to 450,000 tons of temporary imports.

The European Union's Everything But Arms initiative (EBA), approved in 2001, allows duty-free access to the EU sugar market by the 48 least-developed countries (39 are ACP countries). It could become the largest of the European Union's commitments. Initially EBA imports will be limited by quotas, and the sugar imported will be counted against the quota of special preference sugar. The EBA quota will increase annually until full duty-free access for white and raw sugar is allowed in 2009. Safeguard clauses in the EBA initiative could be used to limit imports, but these would be difficult for the European Union to invoke because doing so would be seen in the least-developed countries as a policy reversal.

Imported sugar will eventually displace domestic EU production and could severely strain the EU sugar regime. The European Commission estimated the possible impact of the EBA on the EU sugar regime in 2000, concluding that sugar imports could increase by an additional 2.4 million tons and cost the EU budget about 1.05 billion euros. These imports would have to be offset by reduced domestic production quotas or used for ethanol (European Commission 2003).

A longer-term threat to the EU sugar program is the Commission's plan to offer, all 77 ACP countries the same conditions as the EBA countries under the Economic Partnership Agreements (EPAs). Negotiations, begun in September 2002, are expected to take five years. Under the EPAs, all ACP countries would have duty-free access to the EU market for all goods except arms. These countries currently produce 6.2 million tons of sugar. They could provide all of it to the European Union on short notice while covering their own demand from the world market. Taken together, EBA and ACP supplies could total 8.6 million tons. This is 60 percent of current EU production and would force major changes to the EU sugar program.

Enlargement of the European Union may also create new problems for its sugar regime. The 10 countries that joined in mid-2004 were Cyprus, the Czech Republic, Estonia, Hungary, Latvia, Lithuania, Malta, Poland, the Slovak Republic, and Slovenia. Bulgaria and Romania will likely join in the next several years; the last of the current round of accession countries, Turkey, may join several years later. Poland is the largest sugar producer of the 10 countries that joined in 2004, with nearly 60 percent of the group's total production. The first 10 accession countries produce about one-fifth as much sugar as the European Union, have higher per capita consumption, lower yields, and lower recovery rates than the European Union. They agreed to an A and B quota of 2.958 million tons, with 2.829 million tons of A quota and 0.129 million tons of B quota (European Commission 2003). Acceding producers will likely also produce C sugar,

as is done by current EU producers, and export it at world market prices. A 1998 EU Commission study of the 10 accession countries concluded that the group would add at least 200,000 tons to the European Union's export surplus.

The current EU sugar regime runs until June 2006, and the European Commission opened discussions on reform on September 23, 2003. However, unlike the other commodities scheduled for reform discussions—cotton, olive oil, and tobacco—specific reform proposals were not offered for sugar. Instead, three scenarios for reform were offered, ranging from an extension of the current sugar regime beyond 2006 to complete liberalization of the current regime. Complicating the reform discussions is an investigation launched by the WTO in August 2003 in response to the complaint by Australia, Brazil, and Thailand that the EU sugar regime illegally subsidizes the industry and depresses world prices. A negative finding against the EU by the WTO dispute-settlement body could force changes to the EU sugar regime.

Japan's Sugar Policy

Japan is the third-largest net sugar importer, after Russia and Indonesia, with average annual net imports of about 1.6 million tons of raw sugar during 1999–2001 (figure 8.4). Imports supply about two-thirds of domestic consumption; the remaining one-third is supplied by highly subsidized beet and cane production. Domestically produced

FIGURE 8.4   Japanese Sugar Trends, 1970–2000

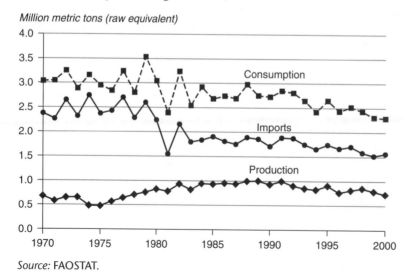

Million metric tons (raw equivalent)

Source: FAOSTAT.

HFCS accounts for about 40 percent of total caloric sweeteners. The government intervenes in the sugar market by establishing guaranteed minimum prices for sugar beets and cane, controls on raw sugar imports, prohibitive duties on refined sugar imports, high tariffs on imported products containing sugar, and quotas, tariffs, and other controls on sugar substitutes. The system results in retail sugar prices that are among the highest in the world ($.89 per pound in Tokyo in 2000) and producer prices for sugar beets and sugar cane that are roughly 10 times world market levels. Sugar consumption is gradually declining due to competition from HFCS, high sugar prices, slow economic growth, and dietary changes away from sweeteners. Consumption may actually be higher than reported, however, because sugar contained in imported products is not reported and is estimated to account for as much as an additional 10 percent of sugar consumption.

Japan's Ministry of Agriculture, Forestry, and Fisheries (MAFF) sets guaranteed minimum prices for sugar cane and sugar beets according to the Sugar Price Stabilization Law of 1965 and the Revised Sugar Price Adjustment Law of 2000 (Fukuda, Dyck, and Stout 2002). The minimum producer prices are set based on a formula comparing current agricultural input prices and consumer goods relative to prices that prevailed in 1950 and 1951. The minimum producer price for sugar beets during 1990–95 averaged $149 per ton, while the minimum producer price for sugar cane was $174 per ton. By comparison, U.S. sugar beet and cane producers received an average of $29 and $40 per ton, respectively, during the same period. Thus Japanese beet and cane producers received at least 10 times the world market prices.[3] For the 2001 marketing year, the minimum price was 17,040 yen per ton ($131 per ton) for sugar beets and 20,370 yen per ton for sugar cane ($157 per ton). Australian sugar cane producers, which receive no government price supports, received $16 per ton in the 2001 marketing year (Sheales 2002). The MAFF also sets the raw sugar price for domestic refiners, known as the "domestic sugar rationalization target price," at a level intended to allow restructured sugar refining firms to pay the guaranteed minimum price to sugar cane and beet producers and still recover costs. A subsidy is provided to sugar refiners to cover the difference between the domestic market price and the "target price." In marketing year 2001, the target price for raw sugar was 151,800 yen per ton ($1,168 per ton or $0.53 per pound), while the resale price on imported raw cane sugar was about $0.22 per pound (Fukuda, Dyck, and Stout 2002). The difference was made up by a subsidy financed by a surcharge on imported sugar, other surcharges, and funds from Japan's national budget. The current subsidy to refiners is 90 billion yen ($692 million) (Fukuda, Dyck, and Stout 2002). The government regulates the production and price of HFCS to limit competition with sugar and obtain funds to partially pay for the high support to sugar beet and cane producers.

Full liberalization of Japan's sugar and sweetener market would likely reduce domestic sugar production drastically—perhaps completely eliminating domestic production. Consumption would increase as consumers faced lower sugar prices. Imports would increase to meet consumer demand. HFCS consumption would likely increase without current controls but would not necessarily increase under full liberalization of the sugar and sweetener markets because of competition from imported sugar. The Australian Bureau of Agriculture and Resource Economics (see Sheales and others 1999) estimated that sugar imports would rise by 500,000 tons if Japan eliminated its tariffs, surcharges, and levies on sugar imports. The study assumed that domestic production would decline by just 22 percent because of other means of government support—this is probably an underestimate. The Economic Research Service of the U.S. Department of Agriculture (USDA) estimated that production would decline by 40 percent if Japan were to eliminate all border protection and trade-distorting domestic support. Consumer and producer prices in Japan would fall by 70 percent under the scenario, and imports would rise by as much as 735,000 tons (Fukuda, Dyck, and Stout 2002). Borrell and Pearce (1999) estimated that sugar prices would decline by 65 percent, production would decline by 44 percent, and net imports would increase by about 1.5 million tons.

The United States' Sugar Policy

U.S. sugar policy provides for a loan program for sugar beets and cane.[4] The nonrecourse loan program is reauthorized through fiscal 2007 at 18 cents per pound for raw cane sugar and 22.9 cents per pound for refined beet sugar. A Refined Sugar Reexport Program allows sugar cane refiners to purchase raw sugar at world prices, without duty, and export a like amount within 90 days. A similar program exists for manufacturers of sugar-containing products. A no-cost provision of the policy requires the secretary of agriculture to make every effort to operate the sugar program in a way that avoids forfeiture under the loan program. To avoid forfeitures, it is necessary to keep the domestic sugar price above the world market price. This is done by restricting sugar imports, first by quotas introduced in May 1982, and then by tariff rate quotas beginning in 1990 following a successful GATT (General Agreement on Tariffs and Trade) challenge.

Minimum import levels were approved in 1990 to allay concerns of quota-holding countries and cane processors. It provided for marketing allotments on domestically produced sugar if estimated imports were less than 1.25 million tons, raw value. The secretary of agriculture has the authority to impose marketing allotments in order to balance markets, avoid forfeitures, and comply with the U.S. sugar-import commitments under WTO and NAFTA. The allotments can be used only when sugar imports, excluding imports under the reexport program, are less than 1.532 million tons.[5] The USDA announced flexible marketing allotments for sugar for the 2002–03 marketing year (Haley and Suarez 2002).

In the Uruguay Round Agreement on Agriculture (URAA), the United States agreed to maintain minimum imports of 1.139 million metric tons of raw-value sugar imports (1.256 short tons). Of this, 22,000 metric tons were reserved for refined sugar. The tariff rate quota on raw cane sugar was allocated to 40 quota-holding countries based on their export shares during 1975–81, when trade was relatively unrestricted. The duty of 0.625 cents per pound, raw value, continues on quota imports. Most countries continue to avoid the duty because of programs under the Generalized System of Preferences and the Caribbean Basin Initiative. The duty on raw sugar above the tariff rate quota was 17.62 cents per pound beginning in January 1995 and declined by 0.45 cents per pound each year until it reached 15.36 cents per pound in 2000. The over-quota rate for refined sugar was 18.62 cents per pound in 1995 and declined by 0.48 per year

through 2000 to 16.21 cents per pound. The over-quota tariff will remain prohibitive at a world price of about 5 cents per pound (assuming a U.S. raw sugar market price of 22 cents per pound and a transportation cost of 1.5 cents per pound).

Under NAFTA most trade barriers between Canada, Mexico, and the United States were to be eliminated by 2009. As described previously, the treaty's sugar provisions were altered by a side-letter agreement prior to the start of NAFTA. But the side-letter agreement did not change other NAFTA provisions—such as the phased reduction in the United States over-quota tariff of 16 cents per pound by a total of 15 percent during the first six years, and then in a straight line to zero in calendar year 2008. The over-quota tariff on raw sugar, 7.6 cents per pound in 2003, drops about 1.5 cents per pound each year. If the world raw sugar prices are in the range of 7 cents per pound, and U.S. raw sugar prices are about 18 cents per pound, Mexican producers would benefit from exporting to the United States instead of to the world market (USDA 2002). Currently, Mexico does not have a large surplus of sugar to export, but increased production or reduced consumption could change that. In future years, the over-quota tariff will continue to decrease and could lead to large imports. A provision of the U.S. sugar legislation removes production quotas if imports exceed 1.5 million tons—a free-for-all if imports increase beyond certain limits. Under this alternative, the U.S. government could end up holding large stocks defaulted under the sugar loan program, and the sugar system would become more difficult to manage because of the no-net-cost provision. Mexico has increased sugar production from about 3.5 million tons during 1989–91 to 5.2 million during 2000–02, while consumption has increased from 4.0 to 4.5 million tons. Following the end of the NAFTA phase-in period, Mexico can ship unlimited quantities of sugar to the United States duty-free without the condition of being a net surplus producer. This will likely force changes to the U.S. sugar program. For example, Mexico could increase imports of HFCS for use in the soft drink industry, freeing sugar for export to the United States.

The effectiveness of the U.S. sugar program at keeping domestic prices above world prices since 1980 can be seen in figure 8.5. During this period, world prices have fallen sharply, but U.S. producers

FIGURE 8.5   U.S. Sugar Loan Rates, U.S. Prices, and World Prices, 1980–2002

U.S. cents per pound, raw cane sugar

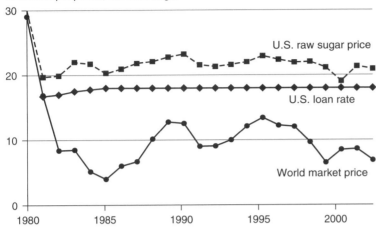

Source: USDA.

were protected. The sugar program, however, faces new challenges in the near future that could bring into conflict the no-cost provision of the sugar program, the minimum import commitment under the WTO, and the duty-free access provision to Mexican imports in 2009. The rapid growth of sweetener production compared with consumption could also destabilize the program. The growth rate of sweetener production during 1985–2000 was 3.2 percent, compared with consumption growth of 2.1 percent over the same period. If these growth rates are extended into the future, marketing allotments would be needed to prevent stock building. The problem is further exacerbated by the agreement under the URAA to import 1.139 million tons of sugar per year.

The U.S. sugar program, like that of the European Union, almost certainly will have to change. But although it benefits just 9,000 sugar beet producers and 1,000 sugar cane producers (Orden 2003), opposition to policy reform is strong, especially from sugar-cane producers, who average nearly 3,000 acres per producer (compared with 200 acres per beet producer). Florida accounts for one-quarter of U.S. sugar production, and two large corporations account for nearly 80 percent of the cane acreage in Florida. Such concentration of production suggests that reforming the U.S. sugar program will likely require compensation to existing producers.

A model to consider is the recent reform of the U.S. edible peanut program (Orden 2003). Under

that program domestic prices were supported at about double world prices, with quotas to limit production and tariff rate quotas to limit imports (see Diop, Beghin, and Sewadeh in this volume). And, like sugar, the edible peanut program faced the threat of increased imports due under WTO agreements and NAFTA. In the 2002 U.S. Farm Bill, the loan rate for edible peanuts was cut by half, compared with the mid-1990s, production quotas were eliminated, and direct cash payments were made to producers. The payments consisted of deficiency payments if prices fell below the new lower loan rates, decoupled direct payments, and countercyclical payments. In addition, quota holders were compensated with direct payments for their loss of quota rights. A similar program for sugar would be complicated by the loss of benefits by HFCS producers, who benefit from high sugar prices. Reform of the sugar program may also require compensating the industries that now depend on distorted sugar policies.

Conclusions

Sugar cane is an almost ideal commodity for some developing countries to grow for domestic consumption and export. It can be produced efficiently in tropical climates under a wide range of technologies, from low-input labor-intensive to high-input fully mechanized. Sugar is locally consumed in all producing countries and provides a substantial part of total calories in many countries. Processing can be varied to meet the needs of low-income domestic or high-income foreign consumers. Raw cane sugar stores well after initial processing. There are few problems in meeting sanitary and health standards because sugar cane juice is boiled during initial processing and raw cane sugar is boiled again when refined to produce white sugar. The biggest problems for producers are limited export opportunities and low world prices—caused partly by policies in OECD countries.

Support for current OECD sugar policies among beneficiaries is obviously strong, but problems are emerging that make change inevitable. The benefits of sugar policy reform are substantial, and the gains are greatest under multilateral reform. According to recent studies of the global sugar and sweetener markets, the global welfare gains of removing all trade distortions and domestic support are estimated to total as much as $4.7 billion per year. In countries with the highest protection (Europe, Indonesia, Japan, and the United States), net imports would increase by 15 million tons per year. World sugar prices would increase about 40 percent, while sugar prices in countries that heavily protect their markets would decline. The greatest price decline would occur in Japan, where sugar prices would fall 65 percent, followed by a 40 percent decline in Western Europe and a 25 percent decline in the United States. Brazilian producers would gain the most from liberalization, around $2.6 billion per year, offset by a loss of $1 billion to Brazilian consumers who would pay higher prices under liberalization. Employment in developing countries would increase by approximately 1 million workers if the 15 million ton increase in net imports that accompanied the removal of all trade distortions and domestic support were supplied by developing countries.

The exporting countries that currently have preferential access to European and U.S. sugar markets gain about $0.8 billion per year through prices that are more than double world market price. The value of the preference is less than it appears, however, because many of these protected producers have high production costs and would not produce at world market prices. Further, world market prices would rise by about 40 percent after full multilateral liberalization, partially offsetting the loss to producers of high prices in preferential markets. The net loss to these exporting countries from full liberalization is estimated to total $0.45 billion per year.

The nature of reforms can have very different consequences for developing countries. If existing EU and U.S. polices are adjusted to accommodate higher imports from countries in the EBA and NAFTA systems, low-cost producers such as Brazil will lose. Full multilateral liberalization of the world sugar market would allow efficient producers to expand production and exports, thereby benefiting consumers in protected markets. Coordinated multilateral liberalization also offers the advantage of somewhat higher world prices to soften the adjustment for producers in protected markets such as the European Union, Japan, and the United States.

Notes

1. Brazil's policies on ethanol indirectly affect sugar, but the government provides no direct subsidies to sugar producers. Other small sugar producers that produce at world market prices include Canada and Malaysia.

2. An additional 1.8 million tons of sugar is imported under the sugar protocol between the EU and the member countries of ACP (Africa, the Caribbean, and the Pacific) and reexported with subsidy after processing.

3. There appears to be an anomaly between the OECD's estimate of producer support in table 8.4 and the prices received by sugar beet and sugar cane producers in Japan. If sugar beet and cane producers in Japan receive five times the prices in the United States, then it appears the Producer Support Estimate (PSE) in percentage form should be higher rather than lower as reported in table 8.4.

4. Nonrecourse commodity loans are used by the government to support prices of many crops. Under the program, farmers who comply with the provisions of each commodity program are allowed to pledge their commodity as collateral and obtain a loan from the USDA's Commodity Credit Corporation at the specified loan rate per unit for the commodity. The borrower may elect to repay the loan with interest within a specified period and regain control of the commodity, or default on the loan as payment of the loan and interest. The farmer will normally default on the loan if the market price is below the level necessary to repay the loan and interest. Thus, the loan rate becomes the effective floor price.

5. This seems the opposite of what is required, but the logic is apparently that if imports exceed this amount then the sugar program has lost its ability to control imports and U.S. producers should be given unrestricted freedom to produce.

References

Berg, C. 2001. *World Ethanol Production 2001.* Ratzeburg, Germany: F.O. Licht.

Borrell, B., and D. Pearce. 1999. "Sugar: The Taste Test of Trade Liberalization." Center for International Economics, Canberra and Sydney, Australia. September.

Devadoss, S., and J. Kropf. 1996. "Impact of Trade Liberalization under the Uruguay Round on the World Sugar Market." *Agricultural Economics* 15: 83–96.

Diop, N., J.C. Beghin, and M. Sewadeh. 2004. "Groundnuts: Policies, Global Trade Dynamics, and the Impact of Trade Liberalization." In M.A. Aksoy and J.C. Beghin, eds., *Global Agricultural Trade and the Developing Countries*. World Bank, Chapter 12.

European Commission. 2003. "Reforming the European Union's sugar policy. Summary of impact assessment work." Commission Staff Working Paper. Brussels.

Elbehri, A., T. Hertel, M. Ingco, and K. Pearson. 2000. "Partial Liberalization of the World Sugar Market: A General Equilibrium Analysis of Tariff-Rate Quota Regimes." U.S. Department of Agriculture, Economic Research Service, Washington, D.C. August 25.

El-Obeid, A., and J.C. Beghin. 2004. "Multilateral Trade and Agricultural Policy Reforms in Sugar Markets," CARD Working Paper 04-WP 356, Iowa State University, Ames, Iowa.

Escandon, J. 2002. "Mexico: Sugar and Ethanol Don't Mix Well." *F. O. Licht's International Sugar and Sweetener Report*. Ratzeburg, Germany, June 27.

F. O. Licht. 2002. "India to Liberalize Its Sugar Market," *F. O. Licht's International Sugar and Sweetener Report*, March 4.

Fry, J. 1985. "Aspects of a Complex Commodity." World Bank Working Paper. Commodities Division, Washington, D.C.

Fukuda, H., J. Dyck, and J. Stout. 2002. "Sweetener Policies in Japan." Electronic Outlook Report SSS-234-01. U.S. Department of Agriculture, Economic Research Service, Washington, D.C. September.

Haley, S., and N.R. Suarez. 2002. *Sugar and Sweeteners Outlook*. U.S. Department of Agriculture, Economic Research Service, Washington, D.C. September 26.

International Sugar Organization. 2002. "Quarterly Market Outlook," September, London.

Jolly, L. 2001. "Will China Ever Fill its WTO Sugar Tariff Quota?" International Sugar Association, London. Processed.

Levantis, T., F. Jotzo, and V. Tulpule. 2003. "Ending of EU Sugar Trade Preferences: Potential Consequences for Fiji." *Current Issues* 3 (2). Australian Bureau of Agricultural and Resource Economics, Canberra.

LMC International. 1999. "Pricing Policy Reform—A Summary." *Sweetener Analysis*.

Mitchell, D. 2004. "Sugar in the Caribbean: Adjusting to Eroding Preferences." Policy Research Working Paper (forthcoming). World Bank, Washington, D.C.

Orden, D. 2003. "Sugar Policies and Implications: Integration into an FTAA." Paper presented at the conference on Agricultural Competitiveness and World Trade Liberalization: Implications of the WTO and FTAA, Fargo, North Dakota, May 29.

Oregon Office of Energy. 2002. "Biomass Energy: Cost of Production." Salem, Oregon.

Organisation for Economic Co-operation and Development (OECD). 2002a. Directorate for Food, Agriculture and Fisheries "Working Party on Agricultural Policies and Markets, Background Information on Selected Policy Issues in the Sugar Sector." Paris, June.

———. 2002b. *Agricultural Policies in OECD Countries. Monitoring and Evaluation*. Paris, June.

Sheales, T.C. 2002. "Australia's Sugar Industry: Operating in a Free-Market Environment," in A. Schmitz, T.H. Spreen, W. A. Messina and C.B. Moss, eds. *Sugar and Related Sweetener Markets: International Perspectives*. CABI Publishing, Wallingford, Oxfordshire.

Sheales, T.C., S. Gordon, A. Hafi, and C. Toyne. 1999. "Sugar International Policies Affecting Market Expansion," ABARE Research Report 99.14. Australian Bureau of Agricultural and Resource Economics, Canberra. November.

USDA. 2002. "Production, Supply, and Distribution" Foreign Agricultural Service (FAS). Washington D.C.

———. 2002. "Briefing Room Data for Sugar." Economic Research Service. Washington, D.C.

———. 2003. "European Union Sugar Annual", Global Agriculture Information Network Report, Foreign Agricultural Service (FAS). Washington D.C.

U.S. General Accounting Office (USGAO). 1993. "Sugar Program: Changing Domestic and International Conditions Require Program Changes." Report GAO/RCED-93-84, April, Washington, D.C.

———. 2000. "Sugar Program: Supporting Sugar Prices Has Increased Users' Cost While Benefiting Producers." Report GAO/RCED-00-126, June, Washington, D.C.

U.S. International Trade Commission (USITC). 2002. "The Economic Effects of Significant U.S. Import Restraints, Third Update 2002." Publication 3519. Washington, D.C. June.

van der Mensbrugghe, D., J.C. Beghin, and D. Mitchell. 2003. "Modeling Tariff Rate Quotas in a Global Context: The Case of Sugar Markets in OECD Countries." CARD Working Paper 03-WP 343. Iowa State University, Ames, Iowa.

Wohlgenant, M.K. 1999. "Effects of Trade Liberalization on the World Sugar Market." United Nations Food and Agriculture Organization, Rome.

9

DAIRY: ASSESSING WORLD MARKETS AND POLICY REFORMS: IMPLICATIONS FOR DEVELOPING COUNTRIES

Tom Cox and Yong Zhu

World dairy markets exhibit an extreme case of distortions traceable to a complex system of domestic and international trade barriers—including surplus disposal in the Quad countries (Canada, European Union, Japan, and the United States) and the Republic of Korea. Oceania (Australia and New Zealand)—which, with the Quad, dominates the export market—is a competitive exporter with few distortions. However, dairy interest groups in the Quad are entrenched, and prospects for policy reforms appear dim. Domestic price discrimination schemes in the Quad (minus Japan) rely heavily on the ability to close borders, suggesting that the emphasis in the Doha negotiations should be on commitments to lower border protection to force domestic reforms.

Despite the quagmire of distortions, dairy is a dynamic sector with much growth potential, especially in Asia, where dairy consumption has been propelled upward by income growth, urbanization, and westernization of diets. Dairy is also experiencing innovations in food processing, with value-added opportunities in traditional products and new dairy-based protein ingredients facing few trade barriers. Concentration and vertical integra-tion in industrialized countries are also important sources of economies in procurement, processing and logistics, and foreign direct investment.

Policy reforms leading to free markets would pitch consumers against producers in most countries because of the large transfers implied by current policies and their removal. In importing countries with high barriers (Asia), consumers' gains are larger than producers' losses because the dairy sector is small. In competitively producing countries, consumers currently benefit from depressed world dairy prices and low trade barriers and have much to lose in undistorted markets, whereas producers have much to gain. The largest net welfare gains would accrue in the Quad, however, because large consumer gains and reduced budgetary costs for support policies would be much larger than producers' losses. In most other countries, net efficiency gains would remain small because the gains to one group would be offset by losses to the other. Our simulations also show the production gains from trade liberalization are captured by dynamic reformers attracting foreign direct investment and overcoming supply constraints and technology transfers.[1]

Background on the World Dairy Sector

Milk Production and Dairy Product Manufacturing

Milk and dairy products are expensive to produce. Production of animal feed uses three to nine times more land than production of food plants that produce the same amount of protein (Bender 1992). When food sufficiency is a problem in a country, dairy is probably not an appropriate way to produce food, because the nutritional conversion rate from grains to animals is low. In most developed countries, milk is produced by feeding animals concentrates made from grains—these can be used directly as human foods. Livestock feed requires on average 7 kilocalories input for each kilocalorie generated. The range extends from 16 for beef production to 3 for broiler chickens, with milk somewhere in between (Bender 1992).

Animal food production does not always compete with other food production, however. Some animals, including sheep and cows, can be fed on inedible agricultural and industrial by-products (with limited alternative uses) to produce highly nutritional foods, or they can be grazed on marginal land. Marginal land suitable for grazing is often on small parcels in remote areas with low population density. Shipping perishable dairy products to urban consumers is expensive, as many developing countries face production and distribution challenges that constrain milk production, such as poor infrastructure and limited refrigeration facilities.

In Argentina, Australia, Ireland, and New Zealand, milk production occurs generally on large pastures within reach of relatively efficient transportation systems and with the support of better human capital and technology. These factors provide considerable advantage to these countries in producing milk and dairy products in free-trade environments. However, pasture-based milk farming is seasonal and vulnerable to weather and natural disasters.

Although raw animal milk is nutritious, only 5 to 10 percent of milk is consumed in raw form in most developed countries. Most raw milk is processed into derivative products in these countries (FAO various years). These processing sectors can be significant sources of income and employment to local economies. Derivative dairy products, or manufactured products, can be either in liquid form (standardized milk, pasteurized milk, cream, partly or totally skimmed milk, buttermilk), or products no longer liquid (cheese, butter, cream, condensed and evaporated milk, milk powder, casein).

Development of the dairy industry requires good infrastructure. A good transportation system, availability of low-cost refrigeration technology, and good packing technologies are all prerequisites for an advanced dairy manufacturing sector. Most developing countries have poor conditions for dairy manufacturing. In those that lack an adequate milk supply and infrastructure to process and distribute milk, people reconstitute milk powder and butter oil back to fluid form to meet daily consumption needs. In many countries, commercial milk combination, which reestablishes the product's specified fat-to-nonfat solids ratio and solids-to-water ratio, is widely used.

Overall, approximately one-third of world milk is consumed in fluid form. About one-fourth is used in cheese making. The joint production of butter, milk powder, and casein uses roughly one-fifth of all milk. The remainder is processed into soft or frozen products, condensed and evaporated milk, or other dairy products.

Derivative products satisfy specific consumption needs. Simple technologies for separating and recombining nutritional components of milk have lowered the cost of processing and made it possible to adjust fat content to different dietary needs. Cheese and butter do not require advanced technology. The production of milk protein concentrates and whey and lactose milk fractionations, however, is relatively new technology. Milk protein concentrates and whey and lactose products are important in the world dairy markets, where most buyers are developing countries, countries with low self-sufficiency in dairy production, and developed economies with relatively low trade barriers on these products.

Skim milk powder, whole milk powder, butter oil, and even butter are important inputs in a special dairy processing practice called milk reconstitution, a technology that converts milk powder, milk fat products, and other dairy products back to fluid milk for consumption or for making other dairy products. With the rapid development of dairy processing technology, milk reconstitution becomes commercially practical and desirable, even in more advanced dairy-producing countries where fresh milk is readily available.

Fluid milk is a major product of milk reconstitution in developing countries. In developed countries and countries with dairy foods in the traditional diet, "hard" dairy products, such as cheese, are produced through milk reconstitution. The recent growth of trade in milk powder and butter oil is partially attributable to the improvement in milk reconstitution technology in many dairy-importing countries. Milk reconstitution overcomes high transportation and storage costs. Trade distortions and investment decisions in the dairy manufacturing sector also make reconstitution desirable. Many developing countries reconstitute fluid milk based on cheap milk powder available in world markets. For example, Mexico makes cheese by reconstituting imported skim milk powder and adding vegetable oil (filled milk).

Besides technical difficulties and additional costs involved in milk reconstitution, other problems limit the practice of this technology. The reconstituted dairy products are often considered to be inferior substitutes for fresh-milk-based products. In addition, milk reconstitution from dried dairy ingredients often induces a loss of nutrients due to the heat required to condense and dry milk.

World Milk Production Trends

In the last decade, world milk production was between 445 million and 470 million metric tons. The Quad and Oceania's share of this production was around 42 percent, while the share from Eastern Europe and the Former Soviet Union (FSU) fell steadily from 27 percent to 16.8 percent. There is some reason to expect that the decline in the share of Eastern Europe and the FSU in world milk production may be reversed as several key milk-producing countries (Poland, Hungary, and Baltic countries join the European Union (EU) in 2004.

South Asia (India and other South Asian Countries) and Sub-Saharan Africa increased their share of world milk production slightly from just under 20 percent in 1990 to more than 20 percent by 2000. Similarly, other developing countries and

regions (China, Korea, other Southeast Asia, Middle East and North Africa, and Central and South America) increased their combined share from just over 10 percent in 1990 to almost 20 percent in 2000. These trends indicate significant changes in the production of milk in the developing regions. For example, growth in South Asia and the Middle East and North Africa was 3.8 percent annually, in sharp contrast to the negative growth of –3.5 percent recorded in Eastern Europe and the FSU.

About 25 percent of world milk was produced in Western Europe before the 1994 Uruguay Round Agreement on Agriculture (URAA) (FAO various years). After 1994 Western Europe's share of world milk production began to dip slowly, falling to 23 percent in 2000. Nevertheless, Western Europe remains a key factor in world dairy markets. The share of world milk production of the United States and Canada remained relatively constant at around 14 percent before (1989–1994) and after (1995–2000) the URAA. The share of Oceania in world milk production increased slightly, reaching 4 percent in 2000. Japan's share of world milk production remained relatively constant at around 1.5 percent over the same periods.

In China, Korea, and the rest of Southeast Asia, a steady increase in share occurred both before and after the URAA, reaching 2.8 percent in 2000. Much of the growth occurred in China and Korea. India, as well, showed a steady growth in share of world milk production before and after the URAA periods. That share stood at 13.8 percent in 2000. India appears to be expanding its activity in world export markets, particularly for butter fat products (butter, ghee/anhydrous milk fat). The share of other countries in South Asia reached 5.1 percent in 2000.

Central and South America showed strong growth in share of world milk production both before and after the URAA. Its share is now 10.5 percent. Expansion in this region is dominated by Argentina and, to a lesser extent, Uruguay, Brazil, and Mexico. Sub-Saharan Africa, including South Africa, has held relatively steady at around 3 percent of world milk production, suggesting that milk production and dairy processing are not expanding as rapidly in southern Africa as in other developing economies. Disparity in regional income growth likely plays a key role in this trend.

Trends in the World Dairy Trade

Dairy products exhibit two-way trade because they are differentiated products.[2] Over the 1989–2000 period, world dairy exports increased more or less steadily from 25.6 million to 39.1 million metric tons, with no difference between the pre- and post-URAA periods. World dairy exports are dominated by the developed economies (Quad and Oceania), but their share of the markets shrank from 87 percent in 1989 to 78 percent in 2000. Developed countries' share of world dairy exports grew an average 2.9 percent annually in 1989–2000. Exports represented 9.7 percent of the developed countries' total milk production in 1989; that share had grown to 12.4 percent by 2000. World dairy imports increased more or less steadily, from 26 million to 36 million metric tons (FAO, various years). World dairy imports in the pre-URAA period (1989–94) averaged 27 million metric tons, increasing to 33 million metric tons in 1995–2000 period.

Comparison of dairy exports as a share of total milk production before and after the URAA provides some informal evidence that the dairy trade liberalization during the Uruguay Round increased the importance of exports in the world's dairy economies. Developed countries' (Quad and Oceania) import market shares—16 percent (4 million metric tons) in 1989 and 20 percent (7 million metric tons) in 2000—grew an average 4.8 percent annually, but average annual growth was much faster after the URAA (7.3 percent). Japan is a large importer of high value-added dairy products, such as cheese and casein. Its demand for dairy products is driven by high incomes, more Westernized diets, and the inability of domestic supply to satisfy the demand growth despite protectionist policies.

Despite their decreased share of world milk production, Eastern Europe and the FSU increased their share in world dairy exports from 7.6 percent to 11.6 percent during the period under study. Those exports represented 1.3 percent of total milk production in the region in 1989 and increased more than three-fold, to 4.8 percent, by 2000. Eastern Europe and the FSU are relatively small importers, with imports fluctuating in the 3 million–4 million metric ton range. Import growth slowed in the years after the URAA (–5.9 percent). Low growth rates in gross domestic product (GDP),

rather than URAA-induced trade liberalization, are likely responsible for most of these changes.

Other developing economies (China, Korea, other Southeast Asia, Middle East and North Africa, and Central and South America almost doubled their share of world dairy exports from 5.3 percent in 1989 to 9.6 percent by 2000; much of the increase came from the Southern Cone (Argentina, Chile, and Uruguay), where exports represented 1.9 percent of total milk production in 1989 and 3.6 percent by 2000.

In South Asia (India and other South Asian countries) and Sub-Saharan Africa (including South Africa), which are primarily importers, exports represented less than 1 percent of total milk production in 1989–2000. The share of world dairy imports for these two regions was 9–10 percent (3 million metric tons) over the same period. The dominant countries in these regions (India and South Africa) are either self-sufficient or net exporters. Overall, the participation of South Asian countries in world dairy trade has been limited, because most countries in the region strive for self-sufficiency in food; both imports and exports of dairy products are restricted by the government. Imports consist of intermediate products such as butter oil, milk powder, and condensed milk, mostly obtained from food aid programs from Western countries.

The Middle East and North Africa are significant importers of dairy products, accounting for 21 percent of total world imports of dairy products. Lacking natural resources to expand their milk production, the countries of this region will continue to rely on imports to meet their increasing consumption needs.

Import substitution policies and economic hardship in Central and South America have prevented these countries from fully exploiting their significant comparative advantage in agriculture, though some South American countries increasingly participate in world and regional dairy trade. Under more stable macroeconomic environments and regional trade agreements, Latin American countries, have increased trade volume considerably. Latin America imports about 18 percent of world dairy trade while exporting 2 percent. Mexico is the world's largest importer of milk powder, accounting for some 10 percent of total world trade. Brazil is a significant importer of dairy products, most of which are imported from its Mercosur partners, Argentina and Uruguay. The European Union is also a big player in the Brazilian market, but Brazil's dependence on imports will likely change with the rapid adoption of new technology in domestic milk production and dairy processing.

Other African countries are net importers (mostly through food aid programs), accounting for about 6 percent of total world trade. Reduced government intervention in agriculture, propelled by the URAA and other factors, will result in reducing food aid to traditional recipients, including the Sub-Saharan countries. A significant proportion of food aid has been redirected to transitional economies. The affordability of commercial imports of dairy products (without current export subsidies) is questionable for many African countries.

Trade and Domestic Policy Regimes in Key Producing and Consuming Countries

Developed Economies: Quad and Oceania

Most developed countries intervene in their domestic dairy sectors with a wide variety of policy instruments. Intervention prices (price support programs) establish minimum domestic prices that are generally well above world market levels. This is true for butter and skim milk powder (SMP) in Canada and the European Union; for butter, cheese, and SMP in the United States, although SMP is priced near world-market levels.

Canada and the European Union use a system of milk production and marketing quotas to limit the production of milk and reduce the cost of protecting the domestic milk- and dairy-processing sectors. These policies have generated substantive "quota rents" to the holders of the quotas.

Canada and the United States use classified pricing schemes to enhance market returns for dairy farmers based on how their milk is used. Generally these are price-discrimination schemes that administer higher prices to less elastic, higher-value-added, and more perishable product markets (beverage milks, soft and frozen products). To the extent that these premium markets are nontradable, such schemes can help insulate domestic markets from world market forces. In addition, because they increase milk prices above the competitive

equilibrium price, more milk is generated, less premium milk is consumed (due to the higher administered prices), and the prices for manufactured milk are depressed relative to a competitive, non-distorted equilibrium. In a sense, these classified pricing schemes generate consumption cross-subsidies to manufactured products (and the consumers and processors who purchase these products) at the expense of the consumers of premium products. To the extent that these cross-subsidized manufactured products are exported, there is an open question as to whether the implicit, consumption cross-subsidies are in fact export subsidies.

In the case of Canada, several of the dairy classifications targeted to compete on export markets (the world or the U.S. market) have been deemed export subsidies generated by government intervention— hence countable against URAA export-subsidy commitments.

Canada, the European Union, and the United States also use a variety of other subsidies in production, marketing, and export financing. Among these are the European Union's consumption subsidies on butter (60 percent of EU butter is subsidized for use by the bakery sector) and skim milk powder (45 percent is subsidized for animal feed).

Market access under the URAA is controlled primarily by tariff rate quotas, a system of in-quota tariffs up to a negotiated limit, and a series of out-of-quota tariffs that are generally quite prohibitive. In addition, a variety of sanitary, phytosanitary, and technical trade restrictions (such as country-level standards of identity) act as nontariff barriers and impede global trade in dairy products.

Developed countries agreed in the URAA to increase their import quotas to 5 percent of consumption by 2000. Similarly, in- and out-of-quota tariffs were to be reduced 16 percent over six years, by 2000. Table 9.1 summarizes the URAA increases in dairy import quotas for the developed countries. Table 9.2 summarizes the URAA dairy product tariff reductions.

Under the URAA, the European Union and United States were obliged to make the greatest increases in access to their domestic markets, particularly for cheese, butter, butter oil, and skim milk powder. Australia, Canada, and Japan endured less market access change under the URAA since many of their dairy product imports were already in

TABLE 9.1   Dairy Import Quotas for the Developed Countries under the URAA
(1000 tons)

Country/Region	Policy Regime	Cheese	Butter, Butter Oil	Skim Milk Powder	Whole Milk Powder
Western Europe	BASE	37.0	79.5	41.2	0.7
	GATT 2000	123.1	91.3	69.2	1.1
	GATT 2005	194.7	101.0	92.6	1.5
Eastern Europe	BASE	6.9	12.6	10.5	3.0
	GATT 2000	8.8	20.9	19.0	5.0
	GATT 2005	10.4	27.8	26.1	6.7
Japan	BASE	na	3.5	99.8	0.0
	GATT 2000	na	3.5	99.8	0.0
	GATT 2005	na	3.5	99.8	0.0
Australia	BASE	11.5	na	na	na
	GATT 2000	11.5	na	na	na
	GATT 2005	11.5	na	na	na
Canada	BASE	20.4	2.0	0.9	0.0
	GATT 2000	20.4	3.3	0.9	0.0
	GATT 2005	20.4	4.4	0.9	0.0
United States	BASE	116.4	7.5	1.3	0.5
	GATT 2000	136.4	13.1	5.3	3.4
	GATT 2005	153.1	17.7	8.6	5.9

na — Not available

Data source: International Dairy Arrangement, Fifteenth Annual Report. November 1994.

BASE and GATT 2000 follow the URAA of the GATT (General Agreement on Tariffs and Trade), assume linear changes.

GATT 2005 projects the Uruguay Round Agreement linearly to 2005.

excess of the requirement of 5 percent of domestic consumption (by 2000). The level of most out-of-quota tariffs is prohibitive, with the result that tariff rate quotas act as pure import quotas for many products in developed countries.

The heavy intervention in domestic dairy markets by the developed countries often generates surplus production relative to domestic consumption requirements. Because the domestic policies usually keep domestic prices above world market levels, many developed countries—particularly Canada, the European Union, and the United States—are forced to export these surpluses with considerable subsidy. Those export subsidies depress world market prices, making cost-effective dairy production more difficult in many developing countries. While frustrating potential milk producers, consumers in these developing countries gain substantively from the transfer of wealth, which comes in the form of cheaper dairy imports.[3]

Since Australia substantially deregulated its domestic market in 2000–01, domestic market protection has been radically reduced. Currently, Australian dairy exports are without explicit export subsidies.

Eastern Europe and Baltics

Among World Trade Organization (WTO) members in Eastern Europe, only the Czech Republic and Estonia use Green Box policies to support their domestic dairy industry. These policies are limited. Under its Domestic Food Aid Plan, the Czech Republic donates milk to schools. The program's monetary value reached $0.74 million in 2000. At the same time, the Czech government paid $4.7 million in support to dairy cow herds through structural adjustment assistance provided through an investment aids plan. The monetary value of Estonia's school milk program value was small ($0.6 million in 2001) (Megli, Peng, and Soufi 2002).

The dairy industry is important in Eastern Europe. Many countries in the region use Amber Box policies to support its development. Some even

TABLE 9.2   Tariff Reductions for Dairy Products under the URAA, by Region
(US$/ton for specific duties, percent for ad valorem tariffs)

Country/ Region	Policy Regime	Policy Instrument	Cheese In-Q	Cheese Over-Q	Butter, Butter Oil In-Q	Butter, Butter Oil Over-Q	Skim Milk Powder In-Q	Skim Milk Powder Over-Q	Whole Milk Powder In-Q	Whole Milk Powder Over-Q
Western Europe	BASE	Specific duties	547	3,643	1,189	3,971	639	1,956	1,773	4,102
	GATT 2000		768	2,362	1,225	2,572	632	1,561	1,760	3,486
	GATT 2005		952	1,295	1,255	1,406	626	1,232	1,750	2,972
Eastern Europe	BASE	Ad valorem	53%	181%	39%	187%	67%	200%	40%	160%
	GATT 2000		59%	133%	39%	142%	66%	164%	40%	102%
	GATT 2005		65%	92%	39%	105%	65%	134%	40%	54%
Japan	BASE plus	Ad valorem	50%	50%	35%	35%	1.3%	15%	30%	30%
		Specific duties	0	0	0	13,406	0	4,954	0	10,228
	GATT 2000 plus	Ad valorem	32%	32%	35%	30%	13%	13%	30%	26%
		Specific duties	0	0	0	11,397	0	4,210	0	8,691
	GATT 2005 plus	Ad valorem	17%	17%	35%	25%	13%	11%	30%	22%
		Specific duties	0%	0%	0%	9,723	0	3,500	0	7,411
Australia	BASE	Specific duties	71	1,068	74	1%	37	1%	37	1%
	GATT 2000	or ad valorem	71	905	0	1%	0	1%	0	1%
	GATT 2005		71	769	0	1%	0	1%	0	1%
Canada	BASE	Specific duties	56	3,794	193	3,483	48	1,720	48	3,315
	GATT 2000		24	3,231	83	2,915	21	1,462	21	2,820
	GATT 2005		0	2,761	0	2,442	0	1,247	0	2,408
United States	BASE plus	Ad valorem	10.5%	0.0%	5.0%	5.0%	0.0%	0.0%	0.0%	0.0%
		Specific duties	0	1,924	62	2,004	33	1,018	68	1,320
	GATT 2000 plus	Ad valorem	10.5%	0.0%	4.3%	4.3%	0.0%	0.0%	0.0%	0.0%
		Specific duties	0	1,636	62	1,703	33	865	68	1,122
	GATT 2005 plus	Ad valorem	10.5%	0.0%	3.6%	3.6%	0.0%	0.0%	0.0%	0.0%
		Specific duties	0	1,395	62	1,453	33	738	68	957
Mexico	BASE	Ad valorem	50%	95%	35%	35%	0%	139%	0%	139%
	GATT 2000		49%	89%	31%	31%	0%	131%	0%	131%
	GATT 2005		47%	84%	27%	27%	0%	124%	0%	124%
South America, North	BASE	Ad valorem	56%	66%	59%	60%	65%	68%	49%	82%
	GATT 2000		49%	58%	56%	57%	59%	31%	46%	75%
	GATT 2005		44%	51%	53%	54%	54%	56%	43%	69%
South America, South	BASE	Ad valorem	37%	37%	37%	37%	36%	36%	36%	36%
	GATT 2000		36%	36%	35%	35%	35%	35%	34%	34%
	GATT 2005		36%	36%	34%	34%	33%	33%	32%	32%

Data source: International Dairy Arrangement, Fifteenth Annual Report, November 1994

BASE and GATT 2000 follow the URAA of the GATT (General Agreement on Tariff and Trade) and assume linear annual changes.

GATT 2005 projects the Uruguay Round Agreement linearly to 2005. "In q" and "over q" are in quota and above quota tariff rates respectively.

increased their support to the dairy industry during the WTO implementation period. Hungary increased its support for cow milk from $17.7 million in 1996 to $58.5 million in 1998 (nonspecific component of the aggregate measure of support). In 1995 and 1996 Slovenia spent $5.5 million on milk (increasing to $6.6 million in 1997 and 1998) and $9 million on ice cream in 1997 (decreasing to $0.8 million in 1998). Compared with negligible support before 1998, Poland increased its market support for butter to $6.5 million and $1.9 million in 1999 and 2000, respectively.

Some countries apply tariff rate quotas (TRQ) on dairy imports to protect their domestic markets. The Czech Republic applies TRQs to milk, cream, yogurt, butter, and ice cream. While the fill rate for ice cream and yogurt is relatively high, it is low for butter and even less for milk and cream (less than 1 percent). Similarly, the fill rates for butter in Slovenia and the Slovak Republic are quite low as they are for milk and cream in Hungary and Poland. The resulting reduction in market access contributes to distortions in world dairy markets, but the levels are small, reflecting the modest levels of both trade and support.

The countries of Eastern Europe use different methods to administer TRQs. The Czech Republic uses a first-come-first-served method to allocate them. Hungary uses licenses on demand. For milk and cream Poland applies licenses on demand; for other dairy products it uses the applied-tariff method. Slovenia and the Slovak Republic apply a license-on-demand method to allocate TRQs. No matter which method is used, additional import costs are incurred, and imports are restricted.

Milk powder, butter, cheese, casein, yogurt, creams, and some other dairy products receive export subsidy from the Czech Republic, Poland, and the Slovak Republic. The actual level of export subsidies is much lower than the commitment levels, however, and these levels have been decreasing over time.

Latin America

A major question regarding the future of dairy policy and trade agreements in South America is whether the Mercosur countries will join with the NAFTA countries in creating a Free Trade Area of the Americas, or FTAA. Initiated in 1994 with negotiations to be finished by 2005, the FTAA project is considered a single undertaking: nothing is agreed until all is agreed. If implemented, major changes can be expected for trade policies in South America, especially for the Mercosur countries (Megli 2002).

Current trade policies in South America revolve mainly around the Mercosur policies for the four main economies of Argentina, Brazil, Paraguay, and Uruguay. Negotiations are under way to bring Chile and Bolivia into full member status, and future negotiations are expected to take place for Colombia, Peru, and Venezuela.

The implementation of a set of common external tariffs and a substantive (if not total) elimination of internal tariffs and nontariff barriers in Mercosur countries began in 1995. Certain products or regions are exempted from these regulations until 2006. Mercosur has 11 different tariff levels bounded by 20 percent; exceptions can be greater than 20 percent but no more than 35 percent. As a result of this common market, trade among the member countries increased from $4.7 billion in 1991 to $18 billion in 1998.

Other trade agreements exist between countries in South America. The Andean Group consists of Bolivia, Chile, Colombia, Ecuador, and Peru, while the Group of Three is made up of Colombia, Mexico, and Venezuela. Bilateral agreements are also common (Bolivia-Mexico; Brazil-Argentina). Chile's tariff rates are around 8 percent for most dairy products. Peru has rates of 20 percent on most dairy products, with a surcharge of 5 percent. Both countries are members of the Asia Pacific Economic Cooperation (APEC). Argentina's agricultural sector enjoys export rebates that range from 1.4 to 10 percent. Brazil has a system of export credits and cash advances for exported products.

East Asia and South Asia

Income, price, tastes, age, and geography are main factors affecting dairy consumption in Asia.[4] China, India, Indonesia, Japan, the Republic of Korea, Malaysia, Philippines, Thailand, and Singapore—all WTO members—are the main dairy producers and consumers in the region. Because dairy products are not necessary products in Asia, income is the major factor affecting their consumption. When income goes up, dairy consumption will increase, as can be seen from the experience of China, Japan, and the Republic of Korea. Although the three countries show similar patterns of food consumption behavior, Japan's per capita GDP is much higher than those of Korea and China, and its per capita consumption of dairy products is 66 and 23 kilograms more, respectively.

In developed countries and cities of developing countries, dairy products represent a small portion of total expenditure. Thus, consumers' reaction to price change is not highly sensitive. In rural areas of developing countries, however, where dairy products are a luxury, consumption is highly sensitive to price changes.

Most of the dairy products consumed in Asia are fluid milk, yogurt, and milk powder. In 1999, for example, Asia's consumption of fluid milk and milk powder accounted for 97 percent of dairy consumption.

People in dairy-producing areas tend to consume more dairy products than in other regions, due to easy and convenient access. This may explain why per capita dairy consumption in South Asia is higher than in East Asia, even though its per capita GDP is much lower.

From countries' notifications to the WTO Agriculture Committee, we find that only Japan uses Green Box policies to support domestic dairy market in school-lunch programs. Another potential user of this policy may be China, which has begun a program to provide subsidized milk for school children in some cities and expects to expand it to the rest of the country.

With the exception of Japan and Korea, most countries in East Asia show a negative or de minimus aggregate level of support for agriculture (Amber Box policy). Japan uses price support programs for certain dairy products (mainly butter and skimmed milk powder), and also makes deficiency payments for calves and milk manufacturing. In 2000 Japan's milk-producer support estimate (PSE) reached $4.7 billion; the nominal protection coefficient for milk in 1999 was 364 percent (OECD 2001). Korea's milk producers receive more than three times the world price for milk. The PSE for Korean milk reached $0.8 billion in 2000; the nominal protection coefficient in 1999 was 225 percent. No Asian country uses blue-box policies to support their dairy sectors.

East Asia protects its dairy markets, and entry of many imports is governed by tariff rate quotas and high tariffs. The scale and scope of tariffs differ widely, however. China, India, Japan, and Korea impose relatively higher tariffs on dairy products than do Indonesia, the Philippines, Malaysia, and Singapore. Ten dairy exports to Japan, five to South Korea, two to Malaysia, and just one to Indonesia are subject to tariff rate quotas. Japan's and Korea's tariff rate quotas are allocated on a global basis. For whey and skim milk powder, Japan's tariff rate quotas are allocated to producers and producer organizations or sellers of mixed feed. For skim milk powder, whole milk powder, and other milk and cream, Korea's tariff rate quotas are allocated according to

the highest-price bidders at quota auctions held by the livestock products marketing organization. In Japan, the tariff rate quota fill rates for skimmed milk powder, whey, and butter are around 50 percent. South Korea and Malaysia have higher fill rates, but real imports are still lower than tariff rate quotas. Indonesia has out-of-quota imports, and the tariff rate quota fill rate is 100 percent.

World dairy trade liberalization would increase the region's imports.

The Middle East and North Africa

Dairy tariff levels in the Middle East and North Africa vary greatly among countries and products. They appear to be relatively high for nonconcentrated milk, cream, and yogurt, for example, and lower for milk powder and butter.[5] In addition to tariffs, countries implement regulations aimed at protecting dairy consumers from fraud. Such regulations impose technical requirements related to product composition and associated customs procedures such as sanitary certifications. There are various bilateral trade arrangements between the European Union and the countries of the region.

Import tariffs directly affect the supply of dairy products in the Middle East and North Africa. For instance, relatively high tariffs on milk powder tend to increase raw milk supply, while low tariffs on raw milk handicap local production. Also, low import tariffs on raw materials and equipment stimulate the production of processed dairy products and the derived demand for raw milk. Subsidies are not the main incentive tool used to encourage raw milk supply in the Middle East and North Africa. Where subsidies exist, they support production or transportation, but their level is not always effective.

The Impact of World Dairy Policy Reforms

Considerable scope remains for further removal of trade and domestic support policy distortions in the Doha Round. Even after full implementation of the URAA provisions by developed countries, almost 60 percent of world dairy trade will still be exported with subsidies (U.S. Dairy Export Council 1999). Market access provisions allow for tariff rate quotas with prohibitively high rates of out-of-quota duty (Griffin 1999). Also, special safeguards, low minimum-access requirements, and small tariff reduction requirements for individual commodities undermine the market access provisions of the URAA (Coleman 1998). Thus, even after full implementation, world dairy markets will continue to be characterized by highly subsidized exports, limited market access, and heavy government intervention.

As part of the URAA, countries agreed to begin new agricultural negotiations by the beginning of 2000, and dairy groups in several countries have detailed their policy objectives and positions for the Doha Round. U.S. dairy industry representatives outlined their negotiating priorities early on (U.S. Dairy Export Council 1999). Those priorities include gradual elimination of export subsidies, reduction and harmonization of high tariffs, and tightening disciplines on domestic supports. By eliminating export subsidies and reducing import barriers, it is assumed that world prices will rise sufficiently for the United States to be competitive in world markets (Kirkpatrick 1998). Countries of the Cairns Group (with the exception of Canada), which represents small- and medium-sized agricultural exporters, are pushing for measures that go even further toward freer markets and liberalized trade (Cairns Group Farm Ministers 1998). While the negotiating goals of the European Union are not yet articulated, their priorities will likely involve minimizing increases in import access and reductions in export subsidies, as well as maintaining the Blue Box and the Peace Clause (Oxford Analytica 1998).

The implications of alternative proposals on developed versus developing countries are not well researched. This chapter addresses these questions by simulating various dairy policy liberalization scenarios using the University of Wisconsin-Madison World Dairy Model (UW-WDM).[6] The results of the simulations provide insights into the tradeoffs between the heavily protected developed economies and the developing economies, providing quantitative measures of the impact of those tradeoffs on economic welfare and world trade.

World Dairy Deregulation Scenarios

A first scenario, discussed here in detail, contemplates full dairy sector liberalization: all trade and domestic support policies are removed between 2001 and 2005. Full world dairy sector liberaliza-

tion combines two other scenarios: free dairy trade, and no domestic support. The free-dairy-trade scenario considers the elimination of all trade distortions for 2001 through 2005. All export subsidies and import tariff rate quotas (quotas, in- and out-of-quota tariffs) are eliminated. Domestic support policies are maintained as in the base scenario. This should increase world trade, increase world market prices, and put considerable strain on several domestic support policies (intervention price programs, in particular) in the protected dairy sectors. The no-domestic-support scenario eliminates all domestic supports from 2001 to 2005. These measures include intervention prices for the European Union (SMP), Canada (butter and SMP), the United States (butter, SMP, cheese), and other countries; the elimination of classified pricing in the United States and Canada (modeled as a price premium for residual—fluid, soft, and frozen—products over manufactured products); and elimination of production and marketing quotas in the European Union and Canada.

Because the United States incurred large costs in the base year (2000) through its intervention/price support program (about $500 million in SMP purchases), domestic deregulation would have strong impacts on U.S. milk prices. Similarly, given the large levels of rents from milk-production quotas in the European Union and Canada (35 percent and 40 percent of the domestic milk prices, respectively), elimination of these policies would sharply increase these countries' competitiveness (no quota constraints and sharply reduced production costs). Hence milk production would increase sharply even as milk prices and revenues drop.

Domestic deregulation would lower prices in the protected dairy economies and thus lower world dairy prices, but it would not necessarily widen access to competitive exports—unless out-of-quota tariffs became less prohibitive at the lower market prices. Moreover, the increased milk production for the European Union and Canada would need to find a market, potentially beyond domestic consumption, and so would likely displace base-level imports by these dairy sectors and reduce other countries' potential for export-market growth.

We focus our presentation of the simulation results on the main scenario (full liberalization) and refer readers to the annex tables for the separate second and third scenarios.

Full world dairy sector liberalization. Developed economies with dairy sectors characterized by strong protection from domestic and trade policies would experience large changes from full liberalization, with large transfers from producers to consumers. In the absence of rents from milk production quotas, EU milk prices would fall 23 percent by 2005, generating a moderately competitive EU milk sector and expanded production (approximately 8 percent at prices roughly 20 percent less than base levels by 2005). The expansion implies a potentially radical restructuring of the EU milk sector toward more efficient farms. Dairy exports would increase 16 percent, while imports would fall 50 percent by 2005, suggesting that lower domestic prices (intervention price floors having been eliminated) and larger domestic milk availability at sharply lower prices (due to quota elimination) would cut imports. Currently competitive exporters, therefore, would suffer. The current producer surplus would take a massive hit of $8.1 billion by 2005, and the social and political costs of the implied radical restructuring of the milk production sector would be nontrivial. Consumers would be the big gainers from deregulation (due to falling prices), with large welfare gains of $8.1 billion. Total government costs would fall slightly (lost tariff revenues offset by reduced costs of domestic support and export subsidies). Consumer and treasury gains would offset producer losses, yielding net welfare gains of $1.1 billion.

The scenario would work similarly in Japan. By 2005 Japanese milk production would fall by 23 percent, milk prices by 54 percent, and the producer surplus by 61 percent (or $3.2 billion). The concurrent removal of domestic regulations would have little effect because trade barriers sustain most of the domestic programs. Imports would increase by 134 percent, bringing consumers a surplus of $4 billion. Net government revenues would fall by $21 million (lost tariff revenues net of smaller domestic policy savings). Consumer gains would offset producer and treasury losses to generate net welfare gains of $1.1 billion.

While the dairy sectors in Canada and the United States use both trade policies and domestic support programs, they derive more protection from the former (subsidized exports and limited market access due to import quotas and higher out-of-quota tariffs). Under the full liberalization sce-

nario, Canada's milk prices would drop by 44 percent and production by 4 percent, significantly more than under the no-domestic-support scenario. Dairy exports would fall by 6 percent, while imports would increase 215 percent (versus 80 percent export expansion and 5 percent contraction of imports, under the no-domestic-support scenario). Producer surpluses would be cut in half (to $1.4 billion) by 2005, but consumer welfare gains would be even greater at $1.6 billion (up 14 percent). Total government revenues would fall slightly (lost tariff revenues being not quite offset by gains from elimination of export subsidies, the intervention price program, and production and marketing subsidies). Consumer welfare gains would offset producer and treasury losses, yielding a net welfare gain of 2.7 percent ($385 million).

In the United States, milk production (–7 percent), prices (–12 percent), and producer surplus (–17 percent, –$2.7 billion) would fall sharply by 2005 under full liberalization, about three times more than under the no-domestic-support scenario. These relative impacts indicate that U.S producers enjoy substantive protection from current trade-policy distortions. U.S. exports would fall 61 percent (down 331,000 metric tons), while imports would more than double (130 percent, 510,000 metric tons) by 2005. U.S. consumers would gain $3.4 billion (4 percent); government costs would be reduced by $147 million (lost tariff revenues net of gains from eliminating intervention price and export subsidy costs). These gains would exceed producer losses by $2.7 billion to generate net welfare gains of $729 million (0.7 percent) by 2005.

As expected, Oceania's dairy producers and processors would gain under full liberalization, despite giving up large quota rents (especially New Zealand) associated with current preferential (quota) access to the protected developed-economy markets. As low-cost exporters, Australia and New Zealand would be able to fully exploit their comparative advantage in undistorted world dairy markets, increasing milk production by 6 percent, producer prices by 22 percent, and the producer surplus by 42 percent, or $1.1 billion, by 2005. Their exports would rise by 21 percent, or 429,000 metric tons, by 2005. The production and trade gains would be less than under the free-trade-alone scenario, because that scenario would not increase

TABLE 9.3 Full Liberalization of Trade and Domestic Support: Changes from 2005 Baseline

Country/Region	Milk Production (percentage change)	Milk Price (percentage change)	Producer Surplus $US M	% Change	Consumer Surplus $US M	% Change	Total Gov Rev/Costs ($US M)	Total Welfare $US M	% Change
Developing Economies, Potentially Competitive Exporters									
India	1.4	1.2	972	6.0	(993)	−1.3	(2)	(95)	−0.1
Other Eastern Europe	4.3	4.4	55	11.4	(66)	−2.9	(36)	(13)	−0.5
South America, South	6.5	8.6	60	1.7	(516)	−2.8	(2)	(18)	−0.1
China, Mongolia	0.4	14.3	498	17.4	(57)	−0.4	(74)	(33)	−0.2
Poland	3.3	10.4	247	13.1	(236)	−1.9	(0)	9	0.1
South African Republic	3.8	24.2	669	37.0	(692)	−7.0	1	(22)	−0.2
Total:	2.6	—	2,501	9.3	(2,560)	−1.9	(114)	(173)	−0.1
Developing Economies, Net Importers									
Former Soviet Union	4.0	−1.0	2,562	23.1	(2,574)	−4.0	(443)	(16)	0.0
South America, North	−5.7	−1.0	(1,445)	−18.0	1,707	3.3	(133)	129	0.2
Other South Asia	−0.1	−0.1	(12)	−0.2	171	0.5	(248)	(284)	−0.7
Middle East	−0.1	−30.4	(32)	−0.5	160	0.6	(163)	1	0.0
Rest of World	−0.3	−8.3	(334)	−12.4	300	2.2	(138)	(81)	−0.5
Mexico	−2.9	−8.9	(41)	−1.5	(48)	−0.4	(107)	(197)	−1.3
North Africa	−0.5	10.6	(125)	−11.9	237	5.0	(47)	(51)	−0.9
Central America, Caribbean	−3.3	−13.0	(302)	−43.3	(219)	−5.3	(34)	(387)	−7.8
Korea, Rep. of, Dem. People's Rep. of Korea	−6.7	18.6	80	15.0	416	14.4	(4)	80	2.2
Southeast Asia	3.5	−0.3	(64)	−1.2	372	1.5	(363)	(55)	−0.2
Total:	0.0	—	298	0.7	521	0.2	(1,680)	(861)	−0.3
Developed	1.1	−20.7	(14,472)	−25.3	17,464	6.8	1,184	4,176	1.3
Developing	1.1	2.7	2,797	4.1	(2,039)	−0.5	(1,795)	(1,037)	−0.2
World	1.1	−7.8	(11,675)	−9.3	15,425	2.5	(611)	3,139	0.4

— Not available

Source: University of Wisconsin-Madison World Dairy Model (UW-WDM).

production in Canada and the European Union. Consumer losses would pale in comparison to the substantive producer gains, generating net total welfare gains of 8.8 percent, or $1 billion, by 2005.

Developing-country exporters would enjoy the same benefits from full dairy sector liberalization as Oceania, but at slightly lower levels of gain and with larger transfers from consumers to producers (table 9.3). Wider access to developed-economy markets and elimination of export subsidies would generate aggregate increases in milk production (2.6 percent), prices (1–24 percent), and producer surpluses ($2.5 billion, or 9.3 percent), suggesting substantial import-substitution and export opportunities available in some of these countries. However, the aggregate consumer surplus in the developing countries would fall by $2.6 billion (1.9 percent) because of the loss of subsidized imports and higher domestic prices (except in Eastern European countries). Together with the loss of tariff revenues ($114 million), aggregate consumer and taxpayer losses would slightly dominate producer gains, generating modest welfare losses ($173 million, or 0.1 percent) by 2005. The political economy of dairy reform is complex even in developing countries, because consumer and producer interests are diametrically opposed. The poverty implications are also stark, pitching poor consumers (who benefit from the current regime) against the rural dairy sector, which would gain under free markets.

Consumers in net-importing regions would gain or lose depending on the tradeoffs between increased world import prices (a negative impact) and increased dairy trade (a positive impact). The loss of previously subsidized imports can be offset by gains from broadly expanding trade depending on the size, composition, and direction of import price increases. Many governments currently tax their consumers—removing those taxes could offset price increases. Although there may be some opportunity to expand domestic production to substitute for previously subsidized imports, the cost-competitiveness of scale-efficient exporters makes this less viable for many of these countries that would experience negative impacts on milk production, prices, and producer surpluses under full liberalization. These producer surplus losses could be offset by consumer gains, notably in South America (dominated by Brazil), where dismantling Mercosur common external import tariffs would

generate lower prices and large consumer gains ($1.7 billion, or 3.3 percent). Several regions would show substantive increases in production, price, and producer surplus, notably the FSU (with a producer surplus gain of $2.6 billion). Treasuries in all countries would suffer from lost tariff revenues. Aggregate treasury losses would amount to $1.7 billion exceeding modest aggregate producer gains of $298 million and consumer gains of $521 million. Net welfare losses would be $861 million by 2005.

Under full liberalization aggregate world milk production would rise by 1.1 percent by 2005. Average milk prices would decrease by 7.8 percent overall, falling 20.7 percent in the developed countries, while rising 2.7 percent in the developing countries, reflecting the modest loss to consumers in the latter countries on average. World dairy trade would expand by more than 2 million metric tons by 2005 as the impacts of domestic deregulation (chiefly quota removal) reinforced the impacts from the elimination of trade barriers. World producer surpluses would fall sharply in the developed countries (–$14.5 billion, –25 percent) while increasing in the developing countries ($2.8 million, 4.1 percent). Developed-country losses would be due primarily to the loss of quota value in the European Union and Canada, and to the removal of substantive domestic supports (in Japan and the United States).

Savings from elimination of domestic and export subsidies would exceed lost tariff revenues in the developed countries, generating a net treasury savings of $1.2 billion by 2005. In developing countries, where domestic supports are generally much smaller, their elimination would not offset the loss of tariff revenues, generating net increases in treasury costs of $1.8 billion, which could be an issue in some developing countries with few alternative fiscal sources. Aggregate world treasury revenues would fall nearly $611 million by 2005. Consumer welfare would increase by $17.5 billion in the developed countries, while falling $2 billion in the developing regions. In the developed countries, gains by consumers and taxpayers would exceed producer losses, generating $4.2 billion in net welfare gains by 2005. Just the opposite would occur in the developing regions, where producer gains would fail to offset consumer and treasury losses on average, yielding net welfare losses of $1 billion.

Because the markets of the developed countries are so much larger than those of the developing world, aggregate consumer gains would be larger (at $15.4 billion) than aggregate producer losses of $11.7 billion and treasury losses of $611 million, yielding net welfare gains for the world of $3.1 billion by 2005. These aggregate patterns hide the variability in individual country impacts and the large transfers at work between consumers and producers within many countries.

Other scenarios.   The free-trade scenario models the elimination in 2001 of export subsidies and all tariff rate quota barriers, while keeping substantive domestic supports in place. In the absence of changes in domestic support programs, free trade would decrease welfare overall, pointing to the fiscally unsustainable nature of domestic programs under conditions of free trade. Free trade would have the effect of stimulating domestic supports, possibly leading to violations of WTO ceilings on aggregate measure of support.

Under the scenario of free trade alone, trade-protected producers in developed economies would suffer substantive losses as their domestic consumers enjoyed world prices. In the protected developed countries, milk prices, exports, and producer surpluses would fall, while imports would climb. Elimination of export subsidies would not offset the loss of tariff revenues in Canada or the European Union, yielding net treasury and welfare losses in these countries. Exporting developing countries and Oceania's dairy producers and processors would realize strong gains due to free access to higher-priced, protected markets. Consumers in these countries would lose, but not as much as producers gain, resulting in net welfare gains. Consumers in net-importing dairy regions would gain or lose depending on the tradeoffs between increased import prices (a negative impact) and increased trade (a positive impact) from elimination of tariffs on imports into these regions.

In the last scenario, that in which domestic supports are eliminated but trade barriers remain, dairy producers in developed countries with strong domestic support and production controls would suffer as production quotas and associated rents were eliminated. Lower prices would lead inefficient producers to exit the market and nearly eliminate imports to these markets. In the European Union, producers would take a massive hit, offset

by strong consumer welfare gains. Total government costs would fall, yielding substantive net welfare gains of $4 billion, much larger than under full liberalization results ($1.1 billion). Similar forces would apply in Canada. Dairy sectors that were more protected by trade barriers than domestic subsidies (such as Japan) would not experience such losses. The United States would bear the full brunt of domestic policy deregulation, as U.S. milk prices, production, and producer surpluses all would fall sharply. Reduced government costs and massive consumer gains would offset producer losses, however, leading to a net welfare gain. In Oceania, New Zealand would gain and Australia would lose under the no-domestic-support scenario. Milk production, prices, and producer surplus would rise across most of the developing world, but consumers in unprotected markets would face higher prices. Impacts on net importers in the developing world would be quite similar to those for potential developing-country exporters, with the notable exception of the FSU, where consumer gains would barely exceed producer losses to generate a breakeven net welfare impact.

Conclusions

The world dairy sector is complex and characterized by multifaceted domestic and trade policy distortions. The results of our simulation model (detailed by commodity, policy, and region) provide a quantitative measure of the economic and welfare impacts of those distortions across regions, producers, consumers, and governments. While the usual limitations of sectoral simulation studies should be kept in mind, the simulations confirm what most standard economic policy analyses suggest—that the numerous and sizeable distortions induced by most developed economies to protect their domestic dairy sectors have large and generally negative spillover effects on competitive exporters and developing countries. Liberalization would lessen those spillovers, creating opportunities for growth in the domestic and potentially export-oriented portions of the dairy sectors in developing countries, but several caveats must be noted.

Liberalization would also cut into the large benefits that now accrue to consumers who enjoy access to subsidized dairy products on world markets thanks to the current protection regimes of the developed countries. Millions of these consumers live in poorer countries with low border protection and limited capacity to develop a dairy sector. The interests of these developing countries diverge starkly from those of others having an actual or potential dairy industry.

World Dairy Sector Growth: A Component Perspective

World product markets are increasingly driven by milk components (milk fat and fat fractionations; casein, whey, and other protein fractionations; and lactose). Current world growth trends are dominated by "industrial" demand for dairy-based ingredients—intermediate products, not consumer products. This growth in demand is driven by advances in food processing, both on the input side (fractionations of milk components) and the production side (processes that optimize cost and functionality using the evolving dairy-based ingredients), and by consumer demand for the final processed products. Shaping a competitive dairy sector in a world context will require producers to have component-based marketing plans, to organize incentive structures rewarding such plans, and to meet quality standards regimes. Making use of new dairy-based ingredients demands a moderately sophisticated food-processing sector and technology. Size and scale economies are important in many of these processes, suggesting differential advantages to larger firms and to firms with foreign direct investment backed by knowledge, expertise, and ready capital.

Prospects for World Dairy Policy Liberalization

Trends in dairy product development and markets occur in the context of current and evolving WTO agricultural trade negotiations. Short-term prospects for further dairy trade liberalization in developed markets may be somewhat limited, however. The heavily protected dairy sectors of Canada, the European Union, Japan, and the United States are not likely to open their markets before reducing subsidy levels. While the United States and Canada would likely support liberalization in grains, oilseeds, and livestock products, dairy remains an especially sensitive industry. Meanwhile, the

European Union is absorbed in its expansion to the East and the new 2003 CAP reforms, which leave dairy relatively unchanged.

U.S. dairy policy as articulated in the 2002 Farm Bill increases domestic subsidies through the Milk Income Loss Contract program. Meanwhile, low-cost dairy exporters (Australia, Argentina, and Eastern Europe) will likely continue pushing hard for additional market access through lower tariffs, lower export subsidies, and increased import quotas.

The fundamental question is, "Who has the bargaining power in dairy issues?" The WTO meeting in Cancún in 2003 changed this calculus by creating strong opportunities for expansion of regional trade agreements (as opposed to a difficult global agreement) that will limit access by nonmembers.

Expansion of the European Union will provide protected access to new members, benefiting the dairy sectors in several Eastern European countries. However, managing the EU's structural milk surplus will remain challenging in the face of existing WTO commitments, the integration of Eastern Europe, and the relatively strong entrenchment of protectionist farm lobbies. The interests and influence of EU dairy processors and consumers, both of whom would benefit in a liberalized market, compete directly with the established interests of the milk producers.

Prospects for Developing Economies

The potential for domestic market growth is driven by population and GDP. Population growth stimulates consumption of traditional dairy products; whereas increased incomes favor growth in new value-added products. Slow GDP growth will stall consumption of both types of products.

What firms will supply the demand of growing populations of more affluent consumers in the developing world? Will they be local or multinational firms? Will they use local milk supplies, imported dairy ingredients, or some combination of the two? Industry structure and infrastructure are crucial to answering these questions. Scale efficient (low-cost) and innovative processing firms are likely to have competitive advantages in meeting these potential growth markets. Local versus multinational ownership will be influenced by access to and the cost of capital and by the firms' marketing and procurement strategies. Foreign direct investment is often used to overcome market access limitations allowed by the current WTO agreement and regulations by countries that permit only domestically owned firms to import dairy products.

Export potential into the developed economies will be closely linked to further dairy trade liberalization characterized by increased market access and lower domestic subsidies. In this context, optimal world supply and demand will remain a crucial determinant of export prices and hence will define the competitive context of world trade. If recent trends continue, export markets should remain relatively competitive, with lower production costs and prices, but also with some structural weakness in demand due to macroeconomic factors. Discerning the differential potential for market growth in value-added products (which are sensitive to consumer income) versus bulk commodities (which are more responsive to price) will require careful consideration.

Overall, countries that are actual or potential dairy producers and exporters stand to gain from an unfettered market, but as liberalization occurs, special consideration should be given to poor consumers who are likely to suffer from higher consumer prices. Poor consumers in such countries will be hurt, at least in the short run, by a move to global free trade in dairy products unless special measures are taken.

Notes

1. The CD-ROM included with this volume contains an annex for this chapter presenting detailed market data and policy information by country, a description of the model used here, and additional tables of results of policy-reform simulations.

2. In this section all dairy products are expressed as total solids, milk equivalent, to facilitate comparisons.

3. The European Union and, to a lesser extent, Canada, and the United States have had substantive export subsidy allowances under the URAA and used them—a major impediment to the expansion of dairy production in many developing countries.

4. This discussion draws on Peng (2002).

5. See Soufi (2002) for further details.

6. The model is described on the CD-ROM that accompanies this volume. See also Zhu, Cox, and Chavaz (1999) and Cox and others (1999).

References

Bender, Arnold E. 1992. *Meat and Meat Products in Human Nutrition in Developing Countries.* Rome: Food and Agriculture Organization.

Cairns Group Farm Ministers. 1998. "Communiqué following talks on the upcoming WTO talks on agriculture." Sydney, Australia, April 2–3.

Coleman, J. R. 1998. "World Dairy Trade Overview: Trade Policy and the WTO." Paper presented at the Workshop for Dairy Economists and Policy Analysts, Cornell Program on Dairy Markets and Policy, Baltimore, October 26–27.

Cox, T. L., J. R. Coleman, J. P. Chavas, and Y. Zhu. 1999. "An Economic Analysis of the Effects on the World Dairy Sector of Extending Uruguay Round Agreement to 2005." *Canadian Journal of Agricultural Economics* 47: 169–183.

FAO (Food and Agriculture Organization of the United Nations). Various years. *FAO Yearbook: Production.* Rome.

———. "FAOSTAT PC: User Manual." Rome.

Griffin, M. 1999. "The Effects of Agricultural Trade Liberalization on Global Dairy Markets." Paper presented at the 4th Interleite Symposium on Intensive Dairy Production, Caxambu, Brazil, July 22–24.

Kirkpatrick, E. 1998. "Editorial comments." *Cheese Reporter,* July 10.

Megli, K., T. Peng, and W. Soufi. 2002. "Eastern Europe and Former Soviet Union Dairy: A Look at Policy, Country Groupings, and Income Elasticity." Agriculture and Applied Economics Working Paper, University of Wisconsin–Madison.

Megli, K. 2002. "South America in the UW World Dairy Model: Policy, Grouping, and Elasticity." Agriculture and Applied Economics Working Paper, University of Wisconsin–Madison.

Organisation for Economic Co-operation and Development (OECD). 2001. *Agricultural Policies in OECD Countries. Monitoring and Evaluation 2001.* June.

Oxford Analytica. 1998. "European Union: Farm Trade." *Daily Brief,* June 2.

Peng, T. 2002. "A Study of Income Effects on Dairy Consumption and Milk Supply Elasticity in Asia." Agriculture and Applied Economics Working Paper, University of Wisconsin–Madison.

Soufi, W. 2002. "North Africa and Middle East Dairy Supply and Consumption: Economic Policy, Disaggregation of the Area and Econometric Modeling." Agriculture and Applied Economics Working Paper, University of Wisconsin–Madison.

U.S. Dairy Export Council, International Dairy Food Association, National Milk Producers Federation, American Dairy Products Institute. 1999. "White Paper: Preparing for the Seattle Round: U.S. Dairy Industry Negotiating Priorities." July 21.

Zhu, Y., T. L Cox, and J. P. Chavas. 1999. "An Economic Analysis of the Effects of the Uruguay Round Agreement and Full Trade Liberalization on the World Dairy Sector." *Canadian Journal of Agricultural Economics* 47: 187–200.

10

RICE: GLOBAL TRADE, PROTECTIONIST POLICIES, AND THE IMPACT OF TRADE LIBERALIZATION

Eric J. Wailes

Rice is one of the most important food grains in the world, accounting for more than 20 percent of global calories consumed and 29 percent in low-income countries (table 10.1). Thus, policies that affect rice prices, production, and trade have a large impact on the poor.

Despite the importance of rice as a basic staple, global trade accounts for only 6.5 percent of consumption. That means that most countries are self-sufficient in rice and face increased price volatility in times of production shortfalls. By contrast, wheat trade accounts for 18 percent of consumption, corn for 12 percent, and soybeans for 35 percent (USDA PS&D 2003). The thinness of trade for rice stems primarily from the use of protectionist mechanisms to achieve national policy objectives of domestic food security and support for producer prices and incomes in major rice-producing and -consuming countries (box 10.1).

Jayne (1993) argues that the link between domestic stabilization policies and instability in world rice prices has been exaggerated, emphasizing instead the role of thin and fragmented markets. Clearly, however, domestic price stabilization policies have been pursued by restricting imports, in turn contributing substantially to international market thinness. Therefore, it is difficult to ignore the effect of domestic stabilization policies achieved through import and export restrictions as a significant cause of international rice price instability.

In addition to the thinness of rice trade, another important structural characteristic is the geographic concentration of production and consumption in Asia. More than 90 percent of production and consumption occur in Asia—nearly two-thirds of it in just three countries (China, India, and Indonesia). With as much as 40 percent of Asian rice cultivated under rain-fed systems, the monsoon weather effects are magnified on rice trade.

Finally, there is substantial market segmentation by rice type and quality. A key structural dimension is the degree of end-use differentiation. Substitution among rice types and qualities is limited by differences in taste preferences. Low substitutability

The author acknowledges the assistance of Frank Fuller and Alvaro Durand-Morat for model computations and expresses appreciation to John Beghin, Don Mitchell, and Kenneth Young for useful comments. The annex for chapter 10, on the CD-ROM, contains more extensive tables and figures on market data, policies, and simulation results.

TABLE 10.1   Share of Calories from Rice by Region and Income Level, 2000

Region	Total Calories Per Capita	Rice Calories Per Capita	Share of Calories from Rice (%)
World	2,805	576	20.5
Developed countries	3,260	118	3.6
Developing countries	2,679	703	26.2
Low-income countries	2,405	702	29.2
Low-income food-deficit countries	2,625	732	27.9
Africa	2,434	178	7.3
Asia	2,713	856	31.6
Sub-Saharan Africa	2,226	174	7.8
South America	2,838	315	11.1
North and Central America	3,411	117	3.4
Europe	3,250	45	1.4

Source: FAOSTAT.

BOX 10.1   Definitions of Rice Trade Flows in This Study

The international rice trade is differentiated by type, quality, degree of processing, and degree of milling. *Long-grain* varieties are typically longer than 6.2 millimeters , while *medium- and short-grain* varieties are 6.2 millimeters or less. Many factors enter into the designation of quality for long-grain rice, including share of broken kernels, seeds, chalkiness, and color. In this study *high quality* refers to grain that contains 10 percent or less of broken kernels and *low quality* to rice that contains more than 10 percent broken kernels. *Paddy rice* refers to rice as it is harvested in the field before the husk and bran layer are removed. *Brown rice,* also referred to as cargo or husked rice, has had the husk removed but retains the bran layer. *Milled rice,* also referred to as white rice, has had both the husk and bran layers removed. The *fragrant* rice varieties, basmati and jasmine, are generally considered long-grain types but are marketed and priced in global markets differently from unscented long-grain varieties.

---

for rice exists on both demand (mill and end-use) and supply sides. On the demand side, the closest substitute is wheat, particularly important in South Asia (India and Pakistan). In many Asian nations rice has become an inferior good, so that as incomes rise it is replaced by meats, fruits, and vegetables.

On the supply side, different rice varieties require different climatic conditions and production and milling technologies. This limits the ability of producers to respond to price incentives by switching the type of rice produced. Production benefits greatly from access to plentiful supplies of surface or ground water and soils with poor drainage that can maintain a flood condition. While these characteristics limit the potential rice production area, they also limit the production of other crops that cannot withstand flood conditions. Development of rice varieties that will be much less dependent on water will have the potential to greatly expand production areas suitable for cultivation, changing costs of production and geographic areas of comparative advantage and disadvantage. As the first major food crop to have its genomic structure fully described, rice genomics and biotechnology are progressing rapidly (Khush and Brar 2002).

Thus, the combination of high levels of domestic protection, geographic concentration, erratic weather, inelastic price responses in production and end-use markets, and relatively thinly traded volumes results in volatile prices and trade (Wailes 2002).

Rice Trade and Policies in the Major Producing and Consuming Nations

Because rice has been so highly protected in both industrial and developing nations, trade liberalization under the Uruguay Round Agreement on Agriculture is having a profound impact on the international rice market (Wailes 2002). Trade has essentially doubled in volume and as a share of consumption since the 1970s and 1980s (figure 10.1). The changes in protection have been modest, however, and rice remains one of the most protected food commodities in world trade.

As a result of the more limited and longer market access reforms required for developing countries under the Uruguay Round, rice policies in developing countries have not changed significantly since the early 1990s. This lack of rice policy reforms has intensified price volatility, placing a heavy burden on poor consumers and on governments to provide food distribution programs for the poor. The coefficient of variation of domestic prices in real terms over the past 20 years was 0.43 in India and 0.26 in Indonesia; it was 0.37 in China over the past 16 years. However, some price stability was achieved in these Asian countries in the 1990s because real world prices had fallen dramatically during this period as well as variability.

The major rice-producing countries are also the major rice-consuming countries and leading rice exporters and importers (tables 10.2 and 10.3 and annex table 1 on the CD-ROM).

China

China, the largest rice-producing and -consuming country, accounts for nearly a third of the global rice economy. Rice has been an important component of China's food grain security objectives and has been managed through procurement support prices to ensure stable supplies. Government rice stocks increased in the late 1990s to about 100 million metric tons, 73 percent of domestic use. In 1999 the government eliminated purchases of low-quality early season rice and lowered the procurement prices for its rice purchases. The area planted with rice has declined (USDA PS&D 2003), and rice stocks were reduced by more than 30 percent by the end of 2002, to 67.6 million metric tons. In some coastal provinces the government has since eliminated its procurement policy entirely, leaving producers to sell their rice in the open market (Wade and Junyang 2003). The government policy now emphasizes quality over quantity, and rice producers are quickly adopting improved quality varieties.

The rice tariff rate quota negotiated by China was initially 2.66 million metric tons in 2002,

FIGURE 10.1 World Rice Trade and Share of Total Use

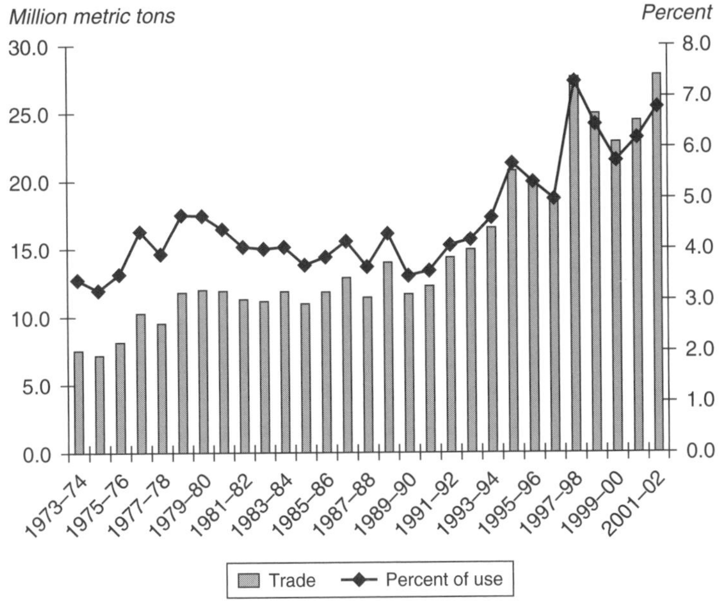

Source: USDA PS&D 2003.

TABLE 10.2 Leading Rice-Producing, -Consuming, -Exporting, and -Importing Countries

Rank	Producing	Consuming	Exporting	Importing
1	China	China	Thailand	Indonesia
2	India	India	India	Nigeria
3	Indonesia	Indonesia	Vietnam	Bangladesh
4	Bangladesh	Bangladesh	United States	Iran
5	Vietnam	Vietnam	China	Philippines
6	Thailand	Japan	Pakistan	Brazil
7	Japan	Thailand	Uruguay	Iraq
8	Myanmar	Myanmar	Argentina	Saudi Arabia
9	Philippines	Philippines	Egypt	European Union
10	Brazil	Brazil	Myanmar	Senegal
11	United States	Korea, Rep. of	Australia	China
12	Korea, Rep. of	United States	Japan	South Africa
13	Pakistan	Nigeria	European Union	Côte d'Ivoire
14	Egypt	Egypt	Guyana	Malaysia
15	Cambodia	Iran	Ecuador	Cuba

Source: USDA PS&D 2003.

equally divided between long-grain and medium- and short-grain or other rice (WTO 2001). Only 10 percent of the long-grain tariff rate quota and 50 percent of the medium-short grain quota are designated for private firms. The tariff rate quota rose to 3.78 million metric tons in 2003 and will increase to 5.32 million metric tons by 2004 (Sun and Branson 2002; Zhang, Matthews, and Branson 2002). Nearly all rice imports are fragrant jasmine rice, primarily from Thailand. Domestic production of fragrant rice is increasing, however, and displacing imports. Unless there is a significant adverse weather event, China is not expected to fill its rice tariff rate quota. In-quota tariffs are 1 percent for grains (including milled rice) and no more than 10 percent for partially processed grain products. Over-quota tariffs will be 76 percent initially, reduced to 65 percent in 2004 (WTO 2001).

China is a significant exporter of low-quality long-grain rice, with principal markets in Côte d'Ivoire, Cuba, and Indonesia. Medium-grain rice is exported competitively into Russia, Japan, the Republic of Korea, and the Democratic Republic of Korea (Hansen and others 2002). While the state trading agency handles most rice exports, export subsidies are not considered necessary for China's rice export shipments (except for out-of-condition stock liquidation).

India

As the second-largest rice producer, consumer, and exporter, India plays an important role in the global rice economy. India is a major supplier of low-quality long-grain rice and fragrant basmati rice. Like China, India views rice as a strategic commodity for food security based on grains (rice and wheat). Consequently, the government intervenes in the market through grain procurement, price supports, and export subsidies. In recent years the government has procured some 25 percent of the annual harvested crop to replenish government stocks. Since April 2001 the government has actively subsidized rice exports at 50 percent of procurement prices, underselling Pakistan, Thailand, and Vietnam in low-quality long-grain markets by $15–$20 a metric ton. Major markets for India's low-quality parboiled and regular long-grain rice include Bangladesh, Côte d'Ivoire, Indonesia, Nigeria, Philippines, and South Africa. Major markets for basmati rice include the European Union (EU), Iran, Kuwait, Saudi Arabia, and United Arab Emirates.

India bound its rice tariffs under the Uruguay Round at zero percent. Until May 1997 all rice was imported through the Food Corporation of India. Under an agreement to privatize the rice trade, the government negotiated higher import tariffs that

TABLE 10.3   Net Rice Trade, 1982–2002
(thousands of metric tons)

Countries by Trade Status	1982–83	1990–91	1995–96	2001–02
Net exporters	**9,167**	**12,041**	**17,415**	**24,522**
Thailand	4,111	4,432	5,249	7,468
India	−255	643	2,900	5,275
Vietnam	−65	1,481	3,183	3,685
United States	2,222	2,070	2,302	2,699
China	631	731	15	1,738
Pakistan	1,159	1,347	1,733	1,225
Myanmar	739	181	140	1,000
Uruguay	191	302	619	550
Egypt	43	184	269	350
Australia	286	534	567	310
Argentina	106	140	440	222.5
Net importers	**4,735**	**5,460**	**9,789**	**15,129**
Indonesia	744	366	960	3375
Nigeria	774	260	325	1803
Iran	715	938	1431	1,250
Iraq	364	408	489	1175
Philippines	−16	175	829	1,050
Saudi Arabia	507	553	716	919
Brazil	187	708	801	650
South Africa	152	339	466	650
Côte d'Ivoire	329	216	402	637.5
Malaysia	386	333	483	616.5
Japan	−135	18	461	525
European Union	321	33	492	525
Mexico	53	280	290	472
Bangladesh	249	25	593	387.5
Eastern Europe 10	0	163	311	367.5
Hong Kong (China)	369	398	345	320
Turkey	44	227	301	272.5
Canada	102	182	233	242.5
Taiwan (China)	−452	−150	−193	−54
Korea, Rep. of	44	−8	58	−55
Rest of the World	4,432	6,581	7,626	9,380

Source: USDA PS&D 2003.

become effective April 2000. Current tariffs are 80 percent on paddy, brown rice, and broken rice and 70 percent on milled rice.

Indonesia

The third-largest rice-producing and -consuming country, Indonesia is also the largest rice importer. Rice policy, particularly price stabilization policy, was historically implemented through quantitative management of imports by the state monopoly, the National Logistics Agency (BULOG). In late 1998, Indonesia agreed to liberalize the rice trade to private traders, but unable to sustain the domestic floor price, the government restored market powers to BULOG.

Following Indonesia's financial collapse and political instability in the late 1990s, the government sought to stabilize and support producer rice prices through a specific rice tariff of 430 rupiahs (Rp) per kilogram (equivalent to a 30 percent ad valorem tariff). Nontariff barriers and trader response to risks and regulation (including a 2002 requirement for an import license and redlining) have raised the effective rate of protection to 100 percent (Timmer 2002). Average border prices of milled rice were $200 per metric ton in 2002, while monthly retail prices in Jakarta averaged $377 per metric ton (Katial-Zemany and Alam 2003). It is believed that a significant share of imports in 2002 was smuggled into the country, thanks to a porous border and this large difference between world and domestic prices.

The tariff policy is currently under review, and producers are pressuring for an increase to Rp 510 per kilogram, equivalent to a 36 percent tariff but well below the WTO (World Trade Organization) bound rate of 160 percent until 2004 (Katial-Zemany and Alam 2003). Floor prices for paddy and milled rice were increased by 13 percent in 2003. In early 2003 BULOG's status was changed from a state agency to a state trading enterprise. It continues to distribute subsidized rice to low-income consumers. Current import and domestic price support policies clearly have negative consequences for Indonesia's consumers, especially poor consumers, and negative consequences on real wages and therefore economic growth.

Bangladesh

Bangladesh is the fourth-largest rice-producing and -consuming nation and an important but highly variable rice import market. Since much of the rice production in Bangladesh is dependent on monsoon weather, production can fluctuate greatly. In 1998 Bangladesh was the world's second largest importer at 2.5 million metric tons, but since 1998 it has imported an average of only 500,000 metric tons annually.

In 2000 Bangladesh imposed an import tariff of 5 percent on rice. The rate was raised to 25 percent in 2001, and a 10 percent regulatory duty was added mid-year, along with an advance income tax of 3 percent and a development surcharge of 2.5 percent. These import protections along with a crop shortfall in 2001 and a policy shift to distributing money instead of food grains in the national food distribution program resulted in a higher domestic price and a rise in smuggled imports from India. As

a result, the government withdrew the 10 percent regulatory duty in 2002 and more recently reduced letter-of-credit margins from 100 percent to 25 percent. Import restrictions that remained in 2003 include a tariff of 22.5 percent, an advance income tax of 3 percent, and a development surcharge of 3.5 percent. Bangladesh imposes no quantitative restrictions.

Vietnam

Vietnam produces the fifth-largest rice crop and is also the fifth-largest rice-consuming country. Following the adoption of the Doi Moi reform program in late 1986, Vietnam's rice economy recovered, and by the mid-1990s Vietnam had become the world's second-largest rice exporter. Vietnam exports both high- and low-quality long-grain rice. Important export destinations include Cuba, Indonesia, Iraq, Malaysia, and several African countries. Rice exports and prices are under the control of the Ministry of Trade and Vietnam's Food Association (Vinafood) (Young, Wailes, Cramer, and Tri Khiem 2002).

Vietnam has no significant production support policies or export subsidy programs. Vietnam and the other major Asian rice exporters (China, India, Pakistan, and Thailand) have discussed the formation of a rice export cartel in response to the low world prices for rice since 1999. India rejected the idea, but the others are developing the concept.

Thailand

Thailand has been the world's leading rice exporter for the past several decades. Private export companies supply world markets with a wide range of long-grain rice, including the fragrant jasmine rice. The primary government rice policy is the paddy mortgage scheme, a loan program operated under the Bank for Agriculture and Agricultural Cooperatives (BAAC). Participating farmers can obtain loans from BAAC using their crop as collateral. The loan price is set at 95 percent of a government-determined target price. In 2002 loan rice prices were $8 to $10 per metric ton higher than market prices (a 10 percent price support). Nearly a third of the Thai crop was pledged to the loan price support program. Government stocks increased as farmers defaulted on their loans. The government procured rice is milled and then exported through government-to-government arrangements.

Japan

Japan's rice economy is supported by the high prices paid by consumers. Japan controls rice imports through a tariff rate quota with a prohibitive over-quota tariff. As the traditional staple food, rice dominates the government's agricultural policy (Fukuda, Dyck, and Stout 2003).

In 1996 the government ended regulation of rice marketing, freeing up wholesale and retail markets from government supervision and licensing requirements. With market liberalization, farm-gate prices have declined. In 1998 the government adopted the Rice Farming Income Stabilization Program. When prices fall below a seven-year, moving-average standard rice price, producers are paid 80 percent of the difference between the current year price and the standard price. Payments are made from the Rice Farming Income Stabilization Fund, with 25 percent of contributions from rice producers and 75 percent from the government. Participation is voluntary, but participants must also enroll in the Production Adjustment Promotion Program, which diverts land from rice to other crops (wheat, barley, soybeans, forages, vegetables, and fruits). Since stabilization fund payments are tied to a diversion program, Japan claims Blue Box treatment (see chapter 3). Income stabilization payments to rice producers in 1999, the most recently reported year, were $815 million. Payments under the diversion program were $1.03 billion.

Before the Uruguay Round Agreement on Agriculture, Japan had banned rice imports for 30 years, except following the devastating production shortfall in 1993. Japan now imports 682,000 metric tons annually under a tariff rate quota, 7.2 percent of domestic consumption in the base period 1986–88. In-quota purchases are controlled exclusively by the Food Agency, for which a markup of up to ¥292 ($2.41 in 2001) per kilogram is allowed.

Imports are purchased through either ordinary market access or the simultaneous-buy-sell system. Under ordinary market access, which accounted for 85 percent of imports in 2001, the Food Agency imports rice and resells it into Japan's domestic market or donates it to food assistance programs. Under the simultaneous-buy-sell system, purchases are made through an auction at which importers sell rice to the Food Agency and simultaneously buy it back. The Food Agency selects bids that maximize the markup. They have averaged ¥100–¥200 per kilogram ($1,000 to $2,000 per metric ton). Over-quota tariffs are ¥341 per kilogram, ($2,842 per metric ton in 2003). The average successful bid price in December 2002 was $318 per metric ton. Summary measures of protection from the Organisation for Economic Co-operation and Development (OECD 2003) indicate that the average producer support estimate in Japan for 2000–02 was 86 percent and the nominal protection coefficient was 6.89.

Republic of Korea

The Republic of Korea also protected its rice sector with an import ban until 1995, when it agreed to a minimum market access import commitment in the Uruguay Round. In 2004, the final year of commitment, Korea will import 205,000 metric tons, 4 percent of domestic consumption in the 1986–88 base period. Consumption has been declining and, coupled with rising minimum market access imports, this has resulted in excessive stocks.

In April 2002 the government released "A Comprehensive Plan on the Rice Industry" to cope with the structural problem of oversupply and to prepare for future restructuring. The government had relied on a procurement program to support farm prices. In 2002 it procured 789,000 metric tons of a total production of 4.9 million metric tons at 2,097 won per kilogram ($1,667 per metric ton). Under the proposed comprehensive plan the government intends to decouple payments, moving from price supports to income support. In 2002 the government made a direct payment of 500,000 won ($398) per hectare in agricultural promotion areas and 400,000 won ($319) per hectare in nonpromotion areas. The program is similar to Japan's income stabilization program in that it will be linked to a production adjustment system to shift rice areas to other crops (soybeans, forages, and fallow) and therefore will claim Blue Box WTO status. In 2003 the government announced plans to keep rice land fallow by paying producers 3 million won ($2,531) per hectare on 27,500 hectares—2.6 percent of total rice area. OECD (2003) estimates an average producer subsidy equivalent to 82 percent and a nominal protection coefficient of 5.35 percent for Korean rice producers in 2000–02.

Imports are guided by the Uruguay Round minimum market access agreement and are assessed a 5 percent tariff under this tariff rate quota agreement. Imports, strictly controlled by the Ministry of Agriculture, have generally been of low-quality rice and are made available to end-users through controlled channels.

European Union

The European Union maintained an intervention price on paddy rice of €298.35 per metric ton. Since 1996 the European Union has accumulated intervention stocks as a result of increased production and imports. Direct payments were introduced in 1997, with payments up to a maximum guaranteed area of 433,123 hectares. The current direct payment rate is €325.70 per hectare. Based on average yields, the direct payment is equivalent to €52.65 per metric ton. Total support to rice producers, taking into account the intervention price and direct payment, is €351 per metric ton (Commission of the European Communities 2002).

Under the Uruguay Round agreement, the European Union agreed to convert variable levies to fixed tariffs and to reduce them by 26 percent by 2000. Current tariff levels are €211 per metric ton for paddy, €264 per metric ton for brown rice, and €416 per metric ton for milled rice. Import prices of brown rice were approximately €250 per metric ton in 2003, so the €264 tariff provides a protection rate of 105 percent. Tariff escalation makes the tariff rate on milled rice prohibitive.

A variety of tariff concessions and preferences for EU rice imports exist. Brown basmati imports from India and Pakistan are given a €250 per metric ton reduction, resulting in a tariff of €14 per metric ton. With the accession to the European Union of Austria, Finland, and Sweden in 1995, a tariff rate quota was negotiated with zero tariff per metric ton on imports of 63,000 metric tons of milled rice, €88 per metric ton on imports of 20,000 metric tons of brown rice, and €28 per metric ton on imports of 80,000 metric tons of broken rice. Egypt has an import concession for 39,000 metric tons at a 25 percent tariff reduction, and Bangladesh has a 4,000 metric ton concession for brown rice at a 50 percent tariff reduction. Preferences are given through a 110,000 metric ton quota to the African, Caribbean, and Pacific countries at a 35 percent tariff reduction and overseas countries and territories at zero percent duty. Beginning in 2007, tariffs on imports from the 48 least-developed countries will be progressively reduced to zero by 2009 under the Everything but Arms agreement negotiated in 2001.

The export regime for rice is based on Uruguay Round agreement commitments, which limit refunds to 133,400 metric tons of milled rice equivalent and a subsidy expenditure of no more than €36.8 million ($39.4 million). Export refunds are set by type of rice and destination. In 2003 export subsidies ranged from €111 to €165 ($119 to $177) per metric ton. The OECD (2003) estimates the producer subsidy equivalent at 31 percent and nominal protection coefficient at 1.24 for 2000–02.

United States

The United States is the world's fourth-largest rice exporter, exporting nearly 45 percent of its production. Under the 2002 Farm Bill, the U.S. government provides price supports through a market loan rate of $143 per metric ton of paddy rice. A market loan deficiency payment is made if the world reference price falls below the market loan rate. The 2002 crop received an average payment of $73 per metric ton.

Producers also receive income support through two payment programs, a fixed decoupled direct payment of $51.80 per metric ton and a decoupled countercyclical payment when the direct payment plus the market price or market loan rate (whichever is higher) are below a target price of $231.48 per metric ton.[1] When the market price is below the market loan rate, the maximum countercyclical payment is $36.68 per metric ton. Both direct payment and countercyclical payment are made on 85 percent of a fixed historical production level.

Rice imports are subject to tariffs of $14 per metric ton for milled rice, 11.2 percent ad valorem for parboiled, $21 per metric ton for brown, $8.30 per metric ton for basmati brown, and $18 per metric ton for paddy rice. In 2002, 10 percent of exports (380,000 metric tons) were funded by government programs, all food aid shipments. Export subsidies under the Export Enhancement Program have not been used for U.S. rice exports since 1996. The OECD (2003) estimates a producer subsidy equivalent of 50 percent and a nominal protection coefficient of 1.77 for 2000–02.

Magnitude of Policy Distortions in Key Rice Markets

The major distortions in world rice markets are caused by import tariffs and tariff rate quotas in key importing countries and price supports in key exporting countries. The global trade-weighted average tariff on all rice was 43.3 percent in 2000: 217 percent for medium- and short-grain rice and 21 percent for long-grain rice. Medium-grain rice markets are far more distorted than long-grain rice markets because of tariff rate quotas and quotas in the major medium-grain rice importing countries of Japan, the Republic of Korea, and Taiwan (China). OECD countries are a major source of distortions, with average annual producer support reaching $25 billion in 2000–02.

Trade protection is also provided for domestic milling industries. This protection is expressed in tariff escalation and is especially prevalent in Cen-

tral and South America and the European Union. EU tariffs are 46 percent for brown rice but 80 percent for milled rice (table 10.4). In Mexico, paddy rice imports pay a 10 percent tariff while brown and milled rice pay a 20 percent tariff.

The effect of tariff escalation is seen in trade flows. Most of the trade in milled high-quality long-grain rice goes to countries with low tariffs, while most of the trade in brown and paddy rice goes to countries with high tariff escalation. Trade-weighted average tariffs for high-quality long-grain rice are estimated at 4.3 percent for milled rice, 31.4 percent for brown rice, and 16.9 percent for paddy rice. Simple non-trade-weighted averages are 13.7 percent for milled rice, 18.7 percent for brown rice, and 25.4 percent for paddy.

The greatest degree of protection in world rice trade is in medium- and short-grain rice. Protection by Japan, the Republic of Korea, and Taiwan

TABLE 10.4   Schedule of Tariffs, Tariff Rate Quotas, and Quotas in Rice, 2002–03 Levels
(percent)

Country or Region	Long-Grain Milled Nonfragrant	Long-Grain Milled Fragrant	Brown	Paddy	Medium–Short Milled	Medium–Short Brown	Tariff Rate Quota (1,000 MetricTons)
Bangladesh	22.5	22.5	22.5	22.5	22.5	22.5	
Brazil	15.0	15.0	13.0	13.0	15.0	13.0	
Canada	0.0	0.0	0.0	0.0	0.0	0.0	
China	1.0	1.0	1.0	1.0	1.0	1.0	5,320
Costa Rica	35.0	35.0	35.0	20.0	35.0	35.0	
Côte d'Ivoire	32.0	32.0	12.0	7.0	32.0	12.0	
European Union	80.0	71.0	46.0	146.0	75.0	64.3	
India	70.0	70.0	80.0	80.0	70.0	80.0	
Indonesia	21.0	16.1	25.0	35.0	14.3	15.6	
Japan (yen/kg)	341	341	341	341	341	341	682
Korea, Rep. of	5.0	5.0	5.0	5.0	5.0	5.0	204*
Malaysia	0.0	0.0	0.0	0.0	0.0	0.0	
Mexico	20.0	20.0	20.0	10.0	20.0	20.0	
Nigeria	50.0	50.0	50.0	50.0	50.0	50.0	
Philippines	50.0	50.0	50.0	50.0	50.0	50.0	
Russia	5.0	5.0	5.0	5.0	5.0	5.0	
Senegal	12.7	12.7	12.7	12.7	12.7	12.7	
Taiwan (China)	0.0	210.0	0.0	0.0	210.0	229.4	
Turkey	35.0	27.0	35.0	27.0	35.0	35.0	
United States ($/metric ton)	14	14	21	18	14	21	

* The Republic of Korea uses a quota rather than a Tariff Rate Quota (TRQ).
Sources: AMAD (Agricultural Market Access Database), USDA, FAS GAIN reports.

(China) lowers world export prices by some 100 percent. Currently, very few rice exporting countries produce medium- and short-grain rice. The clear beneficiaries of trade liberalization in medium- and short-grain rice will be countries, especially China, with a competitive advantage in production costs and logistics relative to such other export competitors as Australia, Egypt, and the United States.

Trade liberalization would be expected to stimulate production of medium- and short-grain rice in other countries, but current varieties are suitable only for temperate climates. Thus South American exporters such as Argentina and Uruguay could develop adapted varieties more quickly. Many other developing countries have tropical or subtropical climates and would require a decade or more to develop varieties that would be competitive in liberalized medium- and short-grain rice markets. Production capacity in Australia and the United States and to some degree in China is increasingly constrained by lack of water.

Long-grain rice markets are far less protected. Tariffs in major low-quality rice-importing nations such as Indonesia and Bangladesh are estimated to reduce world prices by as much as 30 percent compared with full liberalization. The major impact is on consumers in these low-income developing countries and on producers of low-quality long-grain rice in exporting countries such as India, Pakistan, Thailand, and Vietnam. While tariffs are lower than on medium- and short-grain rice, tariff escalation is substantial, particularly in the European Union and several Central and South American countries. This pattern of protection depresses world prices for milled high-quality long-grain rice relative to brown and paddy rice, creating economic hardship for the milling industry in high-quality long-grain exporting countries such as Thailand, Vietnam, and the United States. Protection in high-quality long-grain milled rice markets is estimated to reduce prices by 10–20 percent.

Trade Flow and Price Impact of Rice Trade Liberalization

Estimates of the impact of the elimination of import tariffs and export subsidies using a spatial equilibrium model, RICEFLOW (Durand-Morat and Wailes 2003), show a significant expansion of rice trade and large price adjustments. An earlier version of the model was used to assess trade liberalization prior to the Uruguay Round (Cramer, Wailes, and Shui 1993; Cramer and others 1991). For the current study RICEFLOW was more completely disaggregated by rice type and degree of milling, and the baseline trade flows and elasticity estimates were updated through 2000. The results reflect the effects of trade liberalization applied to year 2000 trade flows and prices. Detailed analysis by quantities traded and prices are presented in table 10.5.

Complete liberalization in 2000 would have resulted in a significant expansion in global rice trade of nearly 3.5 million metric tons, a 15 percent increase in trade. Trade-weighted average export prices would be 32.8 percent higher and trade-weighted import prices would be 13.5 percent lower.

Trade in medium- and short-grain rice, where initial protection was highest, would increase by 73 percent. Producer export prices would rise 91 percent and import prices would decline 27 percent.[2] In the most protected medium- and short-grain brown rice markets, trade would increase 141 percent, export prices would increase 200 percent, and import prices would decrease 41 percent. Trade would expand 59 percent in milled medium- and short-grain rice markets, with export prices 71 percent higher and import prices 25 percent lower.

Because trade in high-quality, long-grain markets is subject to much less protection, trade liberalization results in only slight increases in volume traded—4 percent more for paddy rice, 7 percent for brown rice, and 3 percent for milled rice. Export prices increase only 2 percent but import prices fall 18 percent (10 percent for paddy, 31 percent for brown rice, and 4 percent for milled rice), improving consumer welfare in rice-importing countries. Most of the expansion in trade occurs in the low-quality markets, such as Bangladesh, Indonesia, and the Philippines. Traded volumes increase 13 percent and import prices fall 14 percent, improving consumer welfare in many low-income developing countries. Removing protection in these markets also improves producer welfare in developing countries as export prices rise 7 percent. In the fragrant rice market liberalization results in a 41.5 percent lower import price but only slight increases in the volume traded and the export price.

TABLE 10.5   Simulation Results for Rice Trade Liberalization Using RICEFLOW, 2000

Rice Type	Baseline	Free Trade	Change (%)
Long grain			
High-quality			
Paddy			
Quantity (metric tons)	1,035,320	1,081,254	4.4
Export price ($/metric ton)	149.21	154.67	3.7
Import price ($/metric ton)	185.51	166.89	−10.0
Brown			
Quantity (metric tons)	856,798	916,721	7.0
Export price ($/metric ton)	223.75	219.25	−2.0
Import price ($/metric ton)	363.32	250.64	−31.0
Milled			
Quantity (metric tons)	7,495,594	7,704,482	2.8
Export price ($/metric ton)	225.97	225.58	−0.2
Import price ($/metric ton)	262.06	252.16	−3.8
Low-quality			
Milled			
Quantity (metric tons)	8,084,093	9,149,728	13.2
Export price ($/metric ton)	177.05	188.70	6.6
Import price ($/metric ton)	248.19	213.09	−14.1
Fragrant			
Milled			
Quantity (metric tons)	2,449,711	2,467,502	0.7
Export price ($/metric ton)	265.24	267.07	0.7
Import price ($/metric ton)	511.20	299.07	−41.5
All long grain			
Quantity (metric tons)	19,921,516	21,319,687	7.0
Export price ($/metric ton)	206.87	210.68	1.8
Import price ($/metric ton)	287.45	236.43	−17.7
Medium and short grain			
Brown			
Quantity (metric tons)	483,063	1,162,478	140.6
Export price ($/metric ton)	271.80	814.47	199.7
Import price ($/metric ton)	1438.54	842.75	−41.4
Milled			
Quantity (metric tons)	2,487,760	3,946,170	58.6
Export price ($/metric ton)	367.71	628.92	71.0
Import price ($/metric ton)	855.89	645.69	−24.6
All medium and short grain			
Quantity (metric tons)	2,970,823	5,108,648	72.0
Export Price ($/metric ton)	352.11	671.14	90.6
Import Price ($/metric ton)	950.63	690.53	−27.4
All rice			
Quantity (metric tons)	22,892,339	26,428,335	15.4
Export Price ($/metric ton)	225.71	299.69	32.8
Import Price ($/metric ton)	373.51	322.97	−13.5

Source: Durand-Morat and Wailes 2003.

Welfare Impact of Rice Trade Liberalization

Global rice trade liberalization results in a total economic surplus gain of $7.4 billion annually.[3] Importing countries have a net gain of $5.4 billion and exporting countries a net gain of $2 billion. Gains vary considerably by country, rice type, and degree of milling.

Impact on Price Importers and Exporters

In most rice-importing countries, consumers gain ($32.8 billion for all importers), but producers lose ($27.2 billion). In some countries with large but not prohibitive tariffs, significant tax revenues evaporate under free trade ($2.9 billion in aggregate), while significant public savings occur with the removal of domestic support ($2.7 billion in aggregate).

In rice-exporting countries producers gain from higher prices and expanded output ($70.3 billion), while consumers lose ($68.8 billion). Among exporters, China accounts for the bulk of the producer gains and consumer losses. Behind the net gains are much larger transfers between producers and consumers. When these transfers are normalized by population to account for the large number of producers and consumers in China and some other countries, the transfers are much smaller and less daunting than they appear. Many households are involved in both production and consumption. The net buyers detached from production activities are the largest losers.

Impact by Type of Rice

This logic of large transfers between consumers and producers holds on examination of the impact of reforms by rice type. Reform of trade in medium-grain milled rice accounts for more than 60 percent of the total global welfare improvement, at $4.3 billion, with importers benefiting by $3.4 billion and exporters by $905 million. A breakdown by milling stage reveals that importers of medium-grain brown rice benefit by $1 billion and exporters by $449 million. Liberalization of long-grain rice trade generates improvements of $1.14 billion, with importers gaining $1.06 billion and exporters just $80 million. High-quality rice trade yields welfare gains of $218 million—$195 million to importers

and $23 million to exporters. Most of these gains are for high-quality milled rice ($69 million) and brown rice ($124 million). Liberalization of paddy rice trade improves the welfare of exporters by $2.4 million and of importers by $22.4 million. Liberalization of low-quality rice trade improves the welfare of importing countries by $315 million and exporters by $52 million.

Again these small net figures hide the large transfers at work between sellers and buyers of rice. Nearly all of the net gains are captured by developing countries. Reform of fragrant rice trade is estimated to improve the welfare of importers by $547 million, a result due primarily to Japan. Exporting countries (India, Pakistan, and Thailand) gain marginally in the net, although their producers do gain substantially.

Impact by Country

Results by country or region depend on the type of rice and degree of protection. The results discussed here are for some key countries that are highly protectionist or large traders of rice.

Asian importers. Among Asian importers, Japan, the most protectionist country in rice trade, would gain the most from liberalization. Medium-grain white rice prices would decline from $3,098 per metric ton to $656 per metric ton, while the volume of trade would increase from 392,000 metric tons to 2.18 million metric tons. This results in a welfare gain of $3.6 billion per year, with producers losing $19.2 billion and consumers gaining $24.2 billion. Savings from removing farm programs more than offset the loss in tariff revenue.

The patterns for the Republic of Korea and Taiwan (China) are similar. Border reform would triple Korean imports of medium-grain rice to 306,000 metric tons. Prices would decline from $1,952 per metric ton to $840 per metric ton. Korea also imports fragrant rice. With liberalization, the fragrant rice price would fall from $2,003 per metric ton to $288 per metric ton. Consumers would experience a net gain of $6.2 billion, while producers would lose $5.9 billion. Taiwan (China) shows trade and welfare patterns similar to those of Korea, but the welfare gains are of magnitude smaller.

The Philippines is a major low-quality, long-grain rice importer. Elimination of import tariffs would result in an increase of imports from 787,000 metric tons to 1.02 million metric tons, induced by price declines to $215 per metric tons. Consumers would gain $701 million annually, and producers lose from lower prices by $629 million.

The largest rice importer, Indonesia, would benefit from tariff reform of its low-quality long-grain rice imports. The volume of imports would increase from 1.3 million metric tons to 1.7 million metric tons. Prices would decline from $228 per metric ton to $196 per metric ton. Producers would lose $1.02 billion annually while consumers would gain $1.07 billion.

Asian exporters. China is the world's largest producer of medium-grain rice and would therefore be the largest export beneficiary of medium-grain rice trade liberalization. Exports would more than double, from 614,000 metric tons to 1.47 million metric tons. Export prices would increase from $270 per metric ton to $647 per metric ton. Brown medium-grain rice trade would increase from 113,000 metric tons to 403,000 metric tons, with prices rising from $233 per metric ton to $834 per metric ton. China is also a significant exporter of low-quality long-grain rice. With trade liberalization, exports would increase from 1.9 million metric tons to 2.3 million metric tons, and prices would increase from $178 per metric ton to $190 per ton. Producers would gain $64.2 billion in aggregate, and consumers would lose $63.6 billion, a large aggregate loss but less so when normalized by population.

Vietnam is the major low-quality long-grain rice exporter. Therefore tariff reform by importers of this type of rice would mostly benefit Vietnam. Exports would be expected to increase from 2.7 million metric tons to 3.1 million metric tons, and prices would rise moderately to $185 per metric ton. Vietnam has steadily increased its volume of high-quality milled long-grain rice. Trade reform would increase this volume moderately as well as its price. In aggregate, Vietnamese consumers would lose from higher prices by $210 million annually, but producers would gain $229 million.

Thailand is the world's dominant rice-exporting nation. All Thai exports are long grain, which is the least protected rice type in world trade. As a result, the benefits of rice trade liberalization are small for Thailand. Milled high-quality long-grain rice exports would increase from 3.3 million metric

tons to 3.4 million metric tons, milled low-quality long-grain exports from 1.6 million metric tons to 1.8 million metric tons, and fragrant rice exports from 1.21 million metric tons to 1.23 metric tons. Price increases would be modest and lead to small gains to producers of $123 million annually, while consumers would lose $101 million.

In India producers of long-grain rice would gain substantially ($973 million) but the gains would be almost offset by losses to consumers ($967 million). These figures are the results of moderate price changes applied to large volumes and represent moderate impacts per producer or consumer.

Other exporters. Among other exporters, the United States would be the next most important beneficiary of rice trade liberalization after China. Milled medium-grain rice exports would increase from 226,000 metric tons to 383,000 metric tons, with prices rising from $270 per metric ton to $617 per metric ton. Brown medium-grain exports would increase from 292,000 metric tons to 594,000 metric tons, and prices would rise from $296 per metric ton to $803 per metric ton. The United States is also a major exporter of high-quality long-grain rice. Summing across all rice imports and exports, the net gain to the United States would be $326 million annually, a result of higher total gains to producers of $2.2 billion and losses to consumers of $1.9 billion annually.

Australia is the third largest medium-grain producer and exporter and would also benefit greatly from rice trade liberalization. Exports of milled medium-grain rice would increase from 475,000 metric tons to 756,000 metric tons, with prices rising from $271 per metric ton to $615 per metric ton. The net welfare gain for milled medium-grain rice is $211 million. Brown medium-grain rice export prices would increase from $235 per metric ton to $805 per metric ton. Producers would gain $1.03 billion from higher prices, while consumers lose $745 million.

The fourth major medium-grain exporter is Egypt. Trade reform would result in an increase in exports of milled medium-grain rice from 326,000 metric tons to 448,000 metric tons and an increase in prices from $298 per metric ton to $629 per metric ton. Producers would gain $1.39 billion and consumers lose $1.26 billion, with a moderate aggregate net gain of $128 million.

Other importers. Among importers outside Asia, the European Union would have an overall net welfare gain from rice trade liberalization of $145 million annually. As an importer of high-quality long-grain brown rice, the European Union would increase imports from 451,000 metric tons to 588,000 metric tons, and prices would fall from $496 per metric ton to $260 per metric ton. The aggregate welfare gain for high-quality long-grain brown rice imports would be $138 million annually. This gain is offset by the higher prices that the European Union would pay for medium-grain imports, up from $372 per metric ton to $624 per metric ton. The volume of medium-grain imports would decline from 645,000 metric tons to 595,000 metric tons. The aggregate welfare change would be a gain to consumers of $254 million annually and a loss to producers of $109 million.

Africa. Nigeria became a major rice importer when it relaxed quantitative restrictions to rely primarily on tariffs. Nigeria imports milled high- and low-quality parboiled rice. High-quality imports would increase from 36,000 metric tons to 144,000 metric tons, and low-quality imports would increase from 682,000 metric tons to 877,000 metric tons. Prices would fall substantially for both. Rice producers would lose $186 million annually while consumers would gain $271 million. Several smaller African developing nations would gain similarly, with large gains to consumers partially offset by losses to producers.

North and Central America. Central American paddy rice importers would capture most of the gains associated with liberalization of paddy rice. On the export side the analysis does not change current rules in most countries, which ban paddy export. Only Argentina and the United States currently export paddy. The net gain to these two countries would be $2.4 million. Paddy rice importers—Costa Rica, El Salvador, Guatemala, Honduras, Mexico, and Nicaragua—would have a net gain of $22.4 million from lower import prices and increased imports. The expanded trade would benefit the domestic milling industries in the importing countries and rice consumers at the expense of rice producers.

Other countries. Several developing countries and regions would lose from rice trade liberalization.

These are countries that have been importing rice without trade barriers. In a sense they have benefited from protection by other importers since this protection has depressed export prices. Removing trade barriers would boost export prices for all rice types by degree of milling. This has negative consequences for countries that have had little or no import protection in rice. Most seriously affected would be Turkey, a major importer of medium-grain rice, which faces much higher export supply prices after global trade reform. The estimated net welfare loss for Turkey is $137 million. All importers of medium-grain rice, except Japan, the Republic of Korea, and Taiwan (China) lose as a result of significantly higher import prices after global reform. The same situation holds for long-grain rice importers that have little or no import protection. This includes Middle Eastern countries such as Iran, Iraq, and Saudi Arabia. Brazil, Canada, Hong Kong (China), Malaysia, Singapore, and South Africa would also not be expected to benefit from rice trade liberalization.

Dynamic Analysis of Rice Trade and Domestic Policy Reforms

The RICEFLOW model used for the trade and welfare analysis presented above is a static spatial equilibrium framework of excess supply and demand equations. It does not allow for analysis of domestic farm policies. For that, the Arkansas Global Rice Model (AGRM) was used. The AGRM is a partial equilibrium nonspatial dynamic econometric model of the global rice economy (Fuller, Wailes, and Djunaidi 2003; Wailes, Cramer, Chavez, and Hansen 2000). The AGRM structure is based on equations for supply (expressed for estimated area harvested and yields) and demand (domestic consumption, exports, imports, and ending stocks). Rice prices are endogenized, with world reference equilibrium prices for long-grain and medium-grain rice. The AGRM is used to generate baseline estimates for domestic and international rice for the FAPRI outlook (FAPRI 2004).

For this analysis, policy interventions in rice supply that are trade distorting (Amber Box in WTO parlance) were removed. The model was also simulated for the removal of import tariffs and export subsidies, to provide perspective. Finally AGRM was used to examine the net effect of complete policy reform including domestic support, import protection, and export subsidies.

The AGRM baseline global trade (sum of all exports) projections are 27.9 million metric tons in 2005 increasing to 33.6 million metric tons by 2012.[4] Long-grain rice prices in the baseline begin at $232 per metric ton in 2005 and increase to $277 per metric ton by 2012. Medium-grain prices rise from $332 per metric ton in 2005 to $406 per metric ton by 2012.

The removal of tariffs dominates all policy reform scenarios. Global rice trade increases by 3.5 million metric tons in 2005 and continues to expand to 5.3 million metric tons above the baseline. The removal of export subsidies reduces global rice trade in the short term by 720,000 metric tons, but the long-term effect is negligible. Taken together, the tariff effects swamp the export subsidy effects, and global trade is higher by 2.7 million metric tons in 2005 and by 5.2 million metric tons in 2012. Elimination of domestic supports in the United States, the European Union, and Japan reduces trade very slightly in the short term and not at all over the longer term. The combined effect of the removal of tariff barriers, export subsidies, and domestic supports increases trade by 2.4 million metric tons in 2005 and by 4.9 million metric tons in 2012. The 15 percent expansion of global rice trade given by the more aggregated but dynamic AGRM model is remarkably similar to the static results generated by the RICEFLOW model.

The impact on global export prices follows the impact on trade, with the dominant impact on prices resulting from removal of import tariffs. The long-grain export price is higher by $23 per metric ton in the short term and by $43 per metric ton in the longer term relative to the baseline level. In the more highly protected medium-grain rice market, tariff removal boosts prices by $291 per metric ton in 2005 and by $340 per metric ton in 2012. The impact of removal of export subsidies is important only in the short term, with long-grain rice export prices 6 percent higher and medium-grain prices 5 percent higher. The effect of removal of domestic support is negligible throughout the projection period. The aggregate effects of policy reforms, including tariffs, export subsidies, and domestic supports, is significant for both long-grain rice and medium-grain rice prices. Long-grain rice export prices are 18–22 percent higher. This result differs from the RICEFLOW model result. Medium-grain rice prices are higher than baseline projections by

70–80 percent, a result similar to the findings using the RICEFLOW model.

Policy Implications and Conclusions

Despite the importance of rice as a basic food staple, especially in developing countries, rice trade accounts for only 6.5 percent of consumption. Such limited trade is due partly to preferences for specific types and grades of rice, but also to protectionist policies based on food security objectives or price and income support for producers. The trade-weighted average import tariff on rice was 43 percent in 2000, and tariff escalation is common, to protect rice milling industries.

Several market and production characteristics make rice prices more volatile than the prices of most other commodities. Much of Asian rice production is subject to monsoon climates, resulting in uncertain yields. Global rice trade is highly segmented by rice type (long and medium), degree of processing (milled, brown, and paddy), and quality (generally pertaining to the percent of broken kernels). As a staple food, the demand for rice is not very responsive to price and income changes.

The combination of a high degree of protection, geographic concentration, market segmentation, inelastic supply response to price, and inelastic demand response to price and income results in volatile prices and volumes traded. Distortions in rice trade occur throughout the world. State trading enterprises are pervasive in rice trade, most notably in China, Indonesia, India, Japan, Republic of Korea, Vietnam, and Australia. State trading tends to result in a lack of transparency in pricing and trade competitiveness. Thailand is a clear exception, as rice trade is managed by a very competitive group of export companies.

Domestic policy distortions exist in a number of major rice trading nations, including Japan, the European Union, and the United States. In the United States and the European Union, domestic support results in implicit or direct export subsidies. In Japan the government's commitment to support rice prices is based on an aggressive rice land diversion program and a tightly managed tariff rate quota.

Policy reforms to eliminate protection in the global rice economy are estimated to boost economic welfare by more than $7.4 billion per year. But the real story is the large transfers between consumers and producers that lead to these net gains. Most of the gains can be achieved by eliminating tariffs on imports. In importing countries consumers gain $32.8 billion, while producers lose $27.2 billion. Governments lose $2.9 billion in tariff revenue but gain $2.7 billion by eliminating domestic supports. The net welfare gain to rice-importing countries is estimated at $5.4 billion. In exporting countries producers gain $70.2 billion, while consumers lose $68.8 billion. Imports by the exporting countries result in a loss of tariff revenue of $5.3 million while elimination of domestic supports saves $598 million. The net welfare gain in exporting countries is $2 billion.

With global policy reform, rice trade is estimated to increase by 10–15 percent. Prices received by exporters would be 25–35 percent higher. Prices paid by importers would be 10–40 percent lower, depending on the type of rice. Rice trade, despite the expansion, would remain relatively thin. Complete policy reform would result in an increase in rice trade from the current level of 6.5 percent of consumption to 8.4 percent by 2012. Thus, one of the major sources of world rice price instability is likely to remain after liberalization. Global rice stocks have declined by 30 percent between 2000 and 2003. Thus, the ability of stocks to buffer supply shocks has been markedly reduced. Global rice trade liberalization would make low-income, net-rice-importing countries more reliant on world rice trade, likely reducing political and food security.

Medium-grain rice is the most protected rice type. Consequently, policy reform would have its biggest impact on countries that export and import medium-grain rice. Japan is estimated to capture nearly 70 percent of the global economic welfare gains. Other industrial countries, such as Australia, the European Union, and the United States, that export medium-grain rice would also be significant beneficiaries of trade policy reform.

Countries that had little or no protection before reform are likely to be harmed by global policy reforms. This result is due to the large country impacts that increased imports in countries like Japan would have, increasing the demand for medium-grain rice and thereby boosting world prices. Countries like Turkey and Russia that have imported medium-grain rice with moderate or no

protection would experience higher prices as a result. The benefits of removing moderate levels of tariff protection, as in the case of Turkey, are swamped by the price effect of free and expanded trade in medium-grain rice.

Domestic policy reforms in the United States and the European Union are estimated to reduce rice exports by less than 5 percent in the initial years and to have little or no impact on trade in the longer term. Prices are estimated to be 5–10 percent higher initially, but the effect diminishes to zero over the longer term.

The multilateral and regional trade policy reforms adopted since the early 1990s have contributed to an expansion in rice trade and more stable prices. The achievements of the Uruguay Round Agreement on Agriculture include the opening of the previously closed Japanese and Korean markets. But the limits on domestic support and export subsidies have yet to have a significant impact. Regional agreements such as NAFTA (North American Free Trade Agreement) and Mercosur have increased rice trade in the Western Hemisphere. The prospects for the success of the Doha Round of the WTO hinge to a great extent on continuing the expansion of market access, reductions of tariffs, and limits on export subsidies required to achieve the benefits estimated here from global trade liberalization.

Notes

1. The direct payment is paid on a historical base production, decoupled from both current production and current market conditions. The countercyclical payment is also paid on a historical base production, and although payment is decoupled from current production, it is triggered by current market price conditions. The government claims both payments as Green Box in the WTO.

2. The large increase in the export prices for short- and medium-grain rice does not consider the likely supply responses by less-competitive producers that could enter the market and survive at that high price. Hence, this is an upper-bound estimate of the likely price increase.

3. Consumer and surplus gains and losses are estimated using the results of the baseline and free trade results of the RICEFLOW model. The welfare estimates for producers and consumers are detailed in annex table 3 on the CD-ROM. The results are reported for the major importing and exporting countries or regions by rice type and degree of milling. Annex table 4 on the CD-ROM includes the producer and consumer welfare estimates with the impact on government revenues lost due to tariff elimination and government expenditures eliminated because of the elimination of domestic support programs.

4. Results are presented in annex table 5 and annex figures 1–3 on the CD-ROM.

References

Agricultural Market Access Database. (AMAD). Online: http://www.amad.net/index.htm.

Childs, N. W., and L. Hoffman. 1999. "Upcoming World Trade Organization Negotiations: Issues for the U.S. Rice Sector." Rice Situation and Outlook. RCS-1999. U.S. Department of Agriculture, Economic Research Service, Washington, D.C.

Commission of the European Communities. 2002. "Rice: Markets, CMO and Medium Term Forecasts." Commission Staff Working Paper SEC(2002) 788. Brussels.

Cramer, G. L., E. J. Wailes, and S. Shui. 1993. "The Impacts of Liberalizing Trade in the World Rice Market." *American Journal of Agricultural Economics* 75 (February): 219–26.

Cramer, G. L., E. J. Wailes, J. Goroski, and S. Phillips. 1991. "The Impact of Liberalizing Trade on the World Rice Market: A Spatial Model Including Rice Quality." Arkansas Experiment Station Special Report 153. University of Arkansas, Fayetteville.

Durand-Morat, A., and E. J. Wailes. 2003. "RICEFLOW(R): A Spatial Equilibrium Model of World Rice Trade." Staff Paper SP 02 2003. University of Arkansas, Department of Agricultural Economics and Agribusiness, Division of Agriculture, Fayetteville.

Food and Agricultural Policy Research Institute (FAPRI). 2004. *FAPRI 2004 World Agricultural Outlook*, Iowa State University and University of Missouri, Ames, Iowa, Staff Report 1-04, ISSN 1534-4533.

Fukuda, H., J. Dyck, and J. Stout. 2003. "Rice Sector Policies in Japan." RCS-0202-01. U.S. Department of Agriculture, Economic Research Service, Washington, D.C.

Fuller, F., E. J. Wailes, and H. Djunaidi. 2003. "Revised Arkansas Global Rice Model." Staff Paper SP 01 2003. University of Arkansas, Department of Agricultural Economics and Agribusiness, Division of Agriculture, Fayetteville.

Hansen, J., F. Fuller, F. Gale, F. Crook, E. Wailes, and M. Moore. 2002. "China's Japonica Rice Market: Growth and Competitiveness." *Rice Situation and Outlook Yearbook*. RCS-2002. U.S. Department of Agriculture, Economic Research Service, Market and Trade Economics Division, Washington, D.C.

Jayne, T. S. 1993. "Sources and Effects of Instability in the World Rice Market." MSU International Development Paper 13. Michigan State University, Department of Agricultural Economics, East Lansing, Michigan.

Katial-Zemany, A., and N. S. Alam. 2003. "Indonesia Grain and Feed Annual, 2003." Foreign Agricultural Service GAIN Report ID3008. U.S. Department of Agriculture, Washington, D.C.

Khush, G. S., and D. S. Brar. 2002. "Biotechnology for Rice Breeding: Progress and Potential Impact." Presented at the 20th Session of the International Rice Commission, July 23–25, Bangkok, Thailand. www.fao.org/DOCREP/MEETING/004AC347E/AC347E00.HTM.

Nielsen, C. P. 2002. "Vietnam in the International Rice Market." Rapport 132. Fødevareøkonomisk Institut. Copenhagen.

OECD (Organisation for Economic Co-operation and Development). 2003. *Agricultural Policies in OECD Countries: Monitoring and Evaluation*. Paris.

Sun, X., and A. Branson. 2002. "Food and Agricultural Import Regulations and Standards, Interim Rules and Regulations of Tariff Rate Quota 2002." Foreign Agricultural Service GAIN Report CH2007. U.S. Department of Agriculture, Washington, D.C.

Timmer, C. P. 2002. "Food Security and Rice Price Policy in Indonesia: The Economics and Politics of the Food Price Dilemma." Indonesian Food Policy Program Working Paper 14. BAPPENAS/Department Pertanian/USAID/DAI Food Policy Advisory Team. Jakarta.

USDA PS&D (U.S. Department of Agriculture, Production, Supply and Distribution). 2003. PS&D Online. www.fas.usda.gov/psd.

USDA, FAS. "Rice. Annual". Various years and countries. Global Agricultural Information Network (GAIN) Reports, Foreign Agricultural Service (FAS), Washington, D.C.

Wade, J., and J. Junyang. 2003. "China Grain and Feed Annual 2003." Foreign Agricultural Service GAIN Report 3010. U.S. Department of Agriculture, Washington, D.C.

———. 2002. "Trade Liberalization in Rice." In P. Lynn Kennedy, ed., *Agricultural Trade Policies in the New Millennium*. New York: Haworth Press.

Wailes, E. J., G. Cramer, E. Chavez, and J. Hansen. 2000. "Arkansas Global Rice Model: International Baseline Projections for 2000–2010." Arkansas Agricultural Experiment Station Special Report 200. University of Arkansas, Fayetteville.

WTO (World Trade Organization). 2001. "Report of the Working Party on the Accession of China." WT/MIN(01)/3. Presented at the Fourth Session of the Ministerial Conference, November 9–14, Doha, Qatar.

Young, K. B., E. J. Wailes, G. L. Cramer, and N. Tri Khiem. 2002. "Vietnam's Rice Economy: Developments and Prospects." Arkansas Agricultural Experiment Station Research Report 968. University of Arkansas, Fayetteville.

Zhang, J., R. Matthews, and A. Branson. 2002. "Food and Agricultural Import Regulations and Standards, Implementation Measures for 2002 TRQ Allocation." Foreign Agricultural Service GAIN Report CH2008. U.S. Department of Agriculture, Washington, D.C.

11

WHEAT: THE GLOBAL MARKET, POLICIES, AND PRIORITIES

Donald O. Mitchell and Myles Mielke

Wheat is one of the most important food crops, providing nearly one-fifth of the world's calorie supplies. About 19 percent of the world's production is traded internationally, primarily as exports from the countries of the Organisation for Economic Co-operation and Development (OECD)—including Australia, Canada, the European Union (EU), and the United States—to developing countries to supply basic food needs and the growing demand for products made from wheat flour, such as bread, pasta, and noodles.[1] Wheat is also the food crop most commonly stored as a buffer against production shortfalls, with an average of 30 percent of the world's wheat production carried over from one crop year to the next. The global wheat situation and wheat policies of major actors are thus central to the food security and dietary preferences of many countries.

Major OECD wheat exporters, such as the European Union and the United States, support domestic production. The support policies often lead to surpluses, which are then exported with subsidies or donated as food aid that is not emergency related. Developing countries sometimes benefit from such surplus disposal programs because they pay lower import prices or receive food aid. However, countries are also harmed by such programs because they depress world prices and discourage local production. Competing exporters such as Argentina, Kazakhstan, the Russian Federation, and Ukraine are also harmed because they receive lower prices for their wheat. The surplus disposal programs are reduced during periods of low stocks and relative wheat shortages, thus contributing to global price volatility. In addition, many exporting countries have resorted to export restrictions to protect domestic consumers when prices are high, a practice that further adds to global price volatility. Such policies make it very difficult for importing countries to rely on the world wheat market to fulfill a significant portion of their needs because of the uncertainty of world supply. Consequently, many countries follow policies aimed at self-sufficiency and thus are deprived of the benefits of trade. Policy reforms that reduced global volatility in wheat prices, cut production subsidies, and improved access to exports during periods of high prices would reduce food security concerns.

This chapter discusses major trends and developments in the world wheat market and their impact on trade and food security. We begin by looking at the characteristics of wheat and trends in wheat production, use, trade, stocks, and prices. We then examine the policy environment, focusing especially on trade policy and domestic support.

Wheat Characteristics and Trends

Wheat is produced in 120 countries and accounts for about 19 percent of the world's calorie supplies. It is used primarily as flour for making bread, pastry, pasta, or noodles. It is also used to feed livestock, with feed use accounting for about 17 percent of global wheat consumption. In addition, the by-products from milling wheat into flour are used as feed. Wheat stores for several years without deterioration under proper conditions, making it well suited for use as a buffer against food shortages.

The many varieties of wheat have different protein levels and varying milling and baking characteristics. The protein levels range from about 8 to 18 percent. High-protein wheat is better suited to bread and pasta making, while lower protein wheat is better suited for pastry and noodles. There is substitution between wheat varieties and blending of different varieties to produce flour with specific characteristics. The demand for high-quality wheat and wheat with specific characteristics is increasing, as buyers become more sophisticated. Protein premiums have steadily increased since the early 1980s, as responsibility for import decisions has shifted to the private sector, which is better able to evaluate quality and more willing to pay premiums (Wilson and Dahl 1999). There has also been greater specificity in purchasing contracts. For example, the Australian Wheat Board offered 34 different segregations of wheat in the mid-

1990s, compared to just 2 in 1980 (Carter and Wilson 1999).

Production and Yields

Wheat is produced under a variety of climatic conditions using technologies ranging from fully mechanized production and harvesting on large tracts to manual planting and harvesting on small plots. About 61 percent of wheat is produced in non-OECD countries (table 11.1); this share has been increasing over time as production has grown more rapidly in developing countries than in OECD countries. The European Union, China, and India are the largest producers, with 18, 16, and 13 percent of global production, respectively.

Wheat yields have increased significantly since the middle of the 20th century. From 1961 (when data on many countries first became available) to 2000, world wheat yields increased by an average of 2.4 percent each year. The increase in yields in developing countries came from using more inputs (such as fertilizer) and high-yielding semi-dwarf seed varieties developed at the International Maize and Wheat Improvement Center (CIMMYT) in Mexico and released to developing countries in the mid-1960s in what is now known as the Green Revolution. These varieties, adapted to local conditions, were quickly adopted (Dalrymple 1974). As shown in figure 11.1, average yields in India are now very similar to those in the United States, at

TABLE 11.1   Wheat Production, Trade, and Growth Rates 1989–91 to 1999–2001, by Region

Region	Millions of Tons			Growth Rates (percent)		
	Production	Imports	Exports	Production	Imports	Exports
World	583	107	108	0.5	0.4	0.4
OECD	227	19	80	0.6	6.2	−1.1
Non-OECD	356	88	28	0.4	−0.5	5.4
Africa	17	26	0	1.3	3.3	9.7
Americas	111	25	58	−0.4	6.8	−0.3
Asia	199	27	4	1.7	−2.1	15.1
Europe	130	8	17	−1.0	−4.3	−2.2
FSU	75	6	9	−1.5	−12.2	4.8
Middle East	29	12	4	0.5	3.2	−6.3
Oceania	24	1	17	6.6	5.4	5.4

Note: Production, imports, and exports are the average for 1999–2001 crop years, which begin with harvest and vary by country. Growth rates are for the average of 1999–2001 compared with 1989–91.
Source: USDA PSD online database and USDA 2003.

FIGURE 11.1   Wheat Yields, U.S. and India, 1900–2000

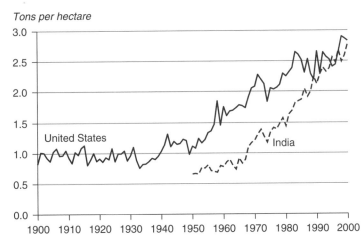

Source: USDA.

TABLE 11.2   Global Wheat and Wheat Products Exports, Selected Periods
(millions of US$)

Product	Average Value				Annual Percentage Increase		
	1970*	1980*	1990*	2000*	1970–80	1980–90	1990–2000
Wheat	3,146	15,502	15,572	14,399	17.3	0.0	−0.8
Bakery	227	1,362	3,913	8,108	19.6	11.1	7.6
Flour	408	1,889	1,748	1,763	16.6	−0.8	0.1
Pasta	39	285	841	1,508	21.9	11.4	6.0
Other	113	894	1,237	972	23.0	3.3	−2.4
Total wheat products	787	4,430	7,738	12,352	18.9	5.7	4.8

*Data is three-year average centered on year shown.
Note: Values are in nominal U.S. dollars. Bakery products include bread and pastry. Other products include gluten feed and meal, bran, germ, and whole meal bulgur.
Source: FAOSTAT.

about 2.8 tons per hectare, thanks largely to the Green Revolution. The annual increase in yields from 1950 to 2000 was 1.89 percent in the United States and 2.95 percent in India.[2]

While improvements in wheat yields have continued along historical trends, the growth of global wheat production has slowed to just 0.5 percent per year over the last decade (see table 11.1), largely because of slower consumption growth and the corresponding adjustment in production. Area planted with wheat declined by 5.5 percent from 1989–91 to 1999–2001, mostly as a result of land-diversion policies of major exporters such as the United States. Certain regions, such as Oceania, increased production and exports during this period because of favorable exchange rates and low production costs, while others, such as the former Soviet Union (FSU), reduced production because of reduced input use and lower domestic demand.

Trade

Trade of wheat is primarily from OECD to non-OECD countries, with about three-quarters of global wheat exports coming from OECD countries and 82 percent of imports absorbed by non-OECD countries (see table 11.1). Trade of wheat grew only 0.4 percent per year during the 1990s, while trade in processed products made from wheat (bakery products, flour, pasta, and other products) expanded more rapidly (table 11.2). This increase in wheat product trade has occurred despite tariff escalation with higher levels of processing. Most of the trade in processed products has been between developed countries. During 1999–2001 about 85 percent of global exports and 77 percent of global imports of processed wheat products were by developed countries. Developing countries primarily import wheat rather than products, with about 80 percent of total expenditures on wheat going for grain imports during 1999–2001. At the same time, developing countries have increased their wheat product exports from one-third of the average value of total wheat and product exports during 1979–81 to one-half the average value in 1999–2001.

Use

Wheat use has grown faster than population—at 2.5 percent per year since 1961, compared with population growth of 1.7 percent. More recently, however, use has slowed, and per capita food consumption has remained nearly constant for more than a decade in both developed and developing countries (figure 11.2). Feed use has shown strong growth among both developed and developing countries, but this growth has been offset by the dramatic drop in feed use in the countries of the FSU following the breakup of the Soviet Union. Global use of wheat for feed rose hardly at all during 1981–2001, compared with average annual growth of 7 percent during 1961–81. Among developing countries, feed use grew by 2.4 percent per year in 1981–2001, compared to 6 percent per year during the previous two decades. Developing coun-

tries tended to substitute wheat for other grains when prices were advantageous; this was particularly true for those Asian countries that are sensitive to prices of grain imports for feed rations. The demand for other uses of wheat, such as industrial uses and as a food additive (gluten, starches, and so on), also has been steady during the past four decades, growing at an average of 1.6 percent per year.[3]

Stocks

Wheat carryover, or ending-stocks, provide a buffer against wheat shortages during years of low production or rapid increases in demand. When stocks are high, prices tend to be low, and vice-versa. The level of global ending-stocks as a percentage of consumption and real wheat prices are shown in figure 11.3. The inverse relationship is readily apparent.

The share of global wheat stocks held by the five major exporters (Argentina, Australia, Canada, the European Union, and the United States), which together account for three-quarters of net exports, declined from 80 percent in 1960 to about 20 percent in 2002. This dramatic shift occurred for two main reasons. First, the share of global production of the five major exporters declined from a high of 46 percent in 1963 to 33 percent in 2002 as production in developing countries increased more rapidly than among major exporters. Second, policy changes in the major exporters reduced government-held stocks. The consequence has been a shrinking supply

FIGURE 11.2   Per Capita Food Consumption of Wheat

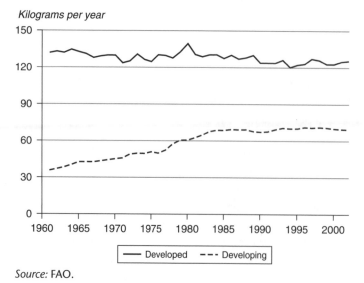

Source: FAO.

FIGURE 11.3   Wheat Ending-Stocks vs. Prices

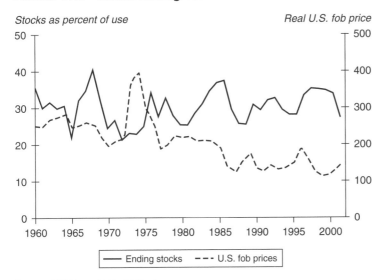

Source: USDA and World Bank.

FIGURE 11.4   U.S. Wheat Price

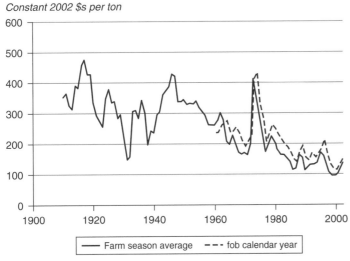

Source: USDA.

of exportable wheat supplies that could lead to more volatile prices in the future.

Prices

During most of the 20th century, real wheat prices fell (by about 75 percent since 1900 and by about half since 1970), while the policies of the major exporters (with the exception of Argentina) were aimed primarily at supporting prices, expanding exports, and restricting production through various schemes. A surge in wheat exports during the 1970s, combined with the oil-price shock, led to

sharp real price increases, but these were quickly reversed as production increased to meet the rising imports. By the end of the 20th century, real U.S. producer prices had declined by about 75 percent from the highs of the early 1900s (figure 11.4).

Overall Trends

The overall trends in wheat show that production has grown more rapidly than population since 1961, and that, in recent years, production and trade growth have slowed significantly because of slower consumption growth. Part of the recent slowdown in consumption has been due to the collapse of the FSU, but, in addition, per capita consumption of wheat as food has stopped increasing in both developed and developing countries. Trade in wheat products has grown more rapidly than grain trade, especially among developed countries. The steady decline in real wheat prices and the decline in stocks held by the major exporting countries as a share of world stocks could lead to greater price volatility.

Policy Environment

Under the Uruguay Round Agreement on Agriculture (URAA), member countries of the World Trade Organization (WTO) had to convert quantitative restrictions on imports into bound tariffs, reduce those tariffs over an implementation period, open their markets to imports under minimum access provisions, limit and reduce the most trade-distorting forms of domestic support, and cap and reduce subsidized wheat exports. Despite these significant achievements, the amount of trade liberalization achieved in wheat was modest because of the way the reforms were implemented. Many countries applied the Uruguay Round provisions so that they could protect producers in key sectors

from foreign competition. Applied tariffs were often set high, and bound tariffs even higher, leaving open the possibility of future increases in applied tariffs. Wheat export subsidies were reduced by the European Union and the United States—the countries with the largest export subsidies—but that was attributable more to budget constraints than to the URAA. Implementation of minimum access and tariff reductions have stalled as countries have introduced new measures to offset agreed commitments or to prevent them from taking effect.

Market Access

Most countries met the minimum market access requirements of the URAA by establishing tariff rate quotas (TRQs), which provided for reduced tariff rates on a specified volume of imports (table 11.3). Imports above these quotas faced higher tariffs. However, regional trading agreements often have provided even lower tariffs or duty-free access to regional trading partners. For example, Mexico established a TRQ for wheat of 605,000 tons at an in-quota tariff of 67 percent. Meanwhile, Canada and the United States receive a preferential tariff of 4.5 percent under the North

TABLE 11.3 Tariffs and Tariff Rate Quotas, by Country
(percent and millions of metric tons)

| Country | Year of Report | Bound Tariffs | | | Applied Tariffs | | Regional Trade Agreements |
		Final TRQ	In-Quota	Above-Quota	Average	Preferential	
Brazil	2001	750	0.0	55.0	12.5	0.0	Mercosur
Canada	2001	227	0.7	62.8	1.3	0.0	NAFTA
China	2001	7,884	1.0	74.0	—	—	—
Colombia	2001	692	124.0	130.0	12.5	—	Andean
Ecuador	1999	480	19.0	23.6	9.2	—	—
European Union	2001	350	0.0	58.9	12.8	0.0	Central Europe
Israel	2000	450	92.0	137.8	—	0.0	EU, U.S.
Japan	2001	5,740	249.2	414.3	—	—	—
Mexico	2001	605	50.0	67.0	67.0	4.5	NAFTA
Morocco	2001	1,555	144.0	198.4	30.1	2.5	EU
Poland	2000	280	25.0	64.0	20.0	0.0	EU
South Africa	2001	108	20.0	93.0	—	—	—
Tunisia	2000	900	17.0	86.7	20.0	—	EU
Venezuela	2000	1,317	24.0	117.0	11.0	—	—

— Not available.
Source: WTO, FAO, USDA, and ABARE 2002.

American Free Trade Agreement (NAFTA). Consequently, virtually all of Mexico's wheat imports come from Canada and the United States. Brazil's wheat imports are mostly supplied by Argentina, which has a comparative advantage in geographic proximity and in preferential treatment under the Mercosur regional trade agreement (Diaz-Bonilla 1999).

Turkey did not establish a TRQ for wheat, but instead relied on tariff-only protection with a bound tariff of 188 percent and an applied tariff of 55 percent. Because imports from the European Union receive a zero tariff under a regional trade agreement, however, most of Turkey's imports come from the European Union. The Russian Federation, which is not a member of the WTO, provides preferential access to several FSU countries. The European Union has protected its producers through variable import levies for many years as part of the Common Agricultural Policy, but it more recently resorted to TRQs on low- to medium-grade wheat to slow wheat imports from Ukraine and the Russian Federation.

Tariff escalation is a common practice that encourages trade in wheat grain rather than in wheat products (table 11.4). Tariffs generally escalate with the degree of processing of wheat products. Brazil, the largest wheat importer during the 1990s, imposed an average tariff on wheat imports of 6.3 percent, but the tariff on wheat flour was 13.5 percent, and those for pasta and bakery products were 18.5 and 20.5 percent, respectively. Because of the high tariffs on value-added products, most imports were in the form of grain or flour. Bangladesh, Costa Rica, Egypt, Guatemala, Jordan, the Philippines, and Uganda showed similar patterns, with most tariffs escalating with greater processing and larger imports of the products with the lower tariffs. Kenya, the Republic of Korea, Japan, and Mexico had different patterns that may reflect stronger protection to producers or specific processors. For example, Kenya had a 35 percent tariff on wheat imports, but a 25 percent tariff on flour, pasta, and bakery products. Korea had prohibitive tariffs on wheat flour imports, but much lower tariffs on wheat grain, pasta, and bakery products. Consequently, there have been almost no flour imports, while wheat, pasta, and bakery products have had large imports. The very low tariffs on wheat probably reflect the fact that

Korea produced less than 1 percent of its consumption but used high tariffs to protect flour millers. Japan has specific duties on wheat, flour, and pasta; Mexico had specific duties on bakery products. The relatively large imports of bakery products despite high tariffs suggest high demand or lack of competitiveness of local bakers.

Indonesia and Malaysia, which had low tariffs for wheat and all wheat products, provide an interesting case of imports without much distortion. There is still some tariff escalation, but the maximum tariff was a relatively low 6.3 percent on pasta imports in Malaysia and 5.0 percent on bakery products in Indonesia. Imports reflect these low tariffs, with wheat products accounting for almost half of the value of imports in Malaysia and for one-third in Indonesia. This suggests that without tariff escalation, wheat product trade would have increased significantly, benefiting consumers. Trade in processed wheat products is concentrated within free trade areas such as within the European Union and NAFTA. The shares of global trade occurring within these two regions alone during 2000–01 were 23, 36, 50, and 66 percent, respectively, for wheat, flour, pasta, and bakery products.

Some countries have used nontariff barriers (NTBs) to protect their domestic wheat markets. For example, the United States resorted to phytosanitary standards during the 1980s to block wheat imports from Mexico. At that time, durum wheat producers in the southwestern United States used the existence of Karnal bunt as a reason to block wheat imports from Mexico (Beattie and Biggerstaff 1999).[4] In an ironic twist, wheat imports from four southwestern states of the United States are currently banned by Mexico because of concerns about Karnal bunt (USDA 2004). U.S. wheat was also barred from three major wheat markets during the second half of the 1990s because of phytosanitary concerns. Brazil, China, and India banned the import of U.S. wheat, in particular from the Pacific Northwest, based on the possible presence of *tilletia controversa kuhn* (TCK) fungus and mycotoxins. While all three cases were resolved by the end of the decade, U.S. wheat exports to these markets have not recovered due to changing market conditions.

Several kinds of NTBs have also been administered by governments to control wheat imports— in many cases these have been lessened or

TABLE 11.4   Average Tariff Rates and Imports for Wheat and Wheat Products

Country	Year	Tariffs (percent)				Imports (million dollars)			
		Wheat	Flour	Pasta	Bakery	Wheat	Flour	Pasta	Bakery
Australia	2001	0.0	0.0	4.0	7.0	0	0	—	—
Bangladesh	1999	5.0	8.3	37.5	37.5	361	19	0	1
Brazil	2001	6.3	13.5	18.5	20.5	872	36	11	21
Bulgaria	2001	23.1	25.0	39.1	54.4	3	1	—	—
China	2001	74.0	98.8	24.1	24.0	319	20	—	—
Costa Rica	2001	0.0	6.0	14.0	14.0	36	3	1	8
Egypt, Arab Rep.	1998	1.0	8.3	40.0	40.0	816	25	1	3
European Union	2001	65.7	45.1	20.8	22.7	844	9	—	—
Guatemala	1999	0.0	10.0	15.0	15.0	56	1	3	19
Hungary	2001	25.0	38.4	38.4	34.7	0	0	—	—
India	2000	41.7	38.5	38.5	38.5	1	1	—	—
Indonesia	1999	0.8	2.5	5.0	5.0	404	68	3	8
Jordan	2000	0.0	12.5	26.7	25.6	68	2	1	5
Kenya	2001	35.0	25.0	25.0	25.4	46	2	3	2
Korea, Rep. of	2001	2.7	151.4	8.0	8.0	530	1	34	34
Malawi	2000	0.0	16.7	25.0	22.9	3	4	0	1
Malaysia	2001	0.0	0.0	6.3	3.3	206	4	19	24
Mexico	2001	67.0	11.7	12.0	10.0	423	8	11	56
Morocco	1997	33.6	71.3	59.5	50.0	366	0	3	3
Pakistan	2001	5	25	70		27	0	—	—
Philippines	2001	4.8	8.0	15.0	15.0	427	6	14	24
Romania	1999	232.9	206.3	261.5	225.0	1	5	—	—
Russia	2001	5.0	10.0			102	19	—	—
South Africa	2001	0.0	20.0	25.0	27.6	32	0	—	—
Togo	2001	5.0	13.3	20.0	20.0	23	0	3	1
Uganda	2001	0.0	15.0	15.0	15.0	11	1	0	0
United States	2001	1.1	0.7	4.6	0.8	300	56	—	—
Zimbabwe	2001	5.0	30.0	40.0	40.0	5	0	0	0
SITC Code	—	410	460	483	484	410	460	483	484

— Not available.

Note: Unless otherwise noted, the duties applied to 100 percent of the tariff lines. The exceptions are as follows: Mexico 83 percent of pasta tariff lines covered; South Africa 50, 67, 75, and 88 percent of tariff lines covered for wheat, flour, pasta, and bakery, respectively; Turkey had only 25 percent of pasta and 14 percent of bakery tariff lines covered; the European Union had 25, 0, 9, and 0 percent of tariff lines covered for wheat, flour, pasta, and bakery, respectively; the United States had only 33 percent of wheat and flour tariff lines covered.

Source: For Egypt's tariff data, TRAINS database. For Pakistan, all data from WTO tables. For all others: tariffs from WTO Integrated Database, MFN (most-favored-nation) Applied Duties; imports from FAOSTAT and COMTRADE.

eliminated following liberalization of domestic markets and international trade. Government import controls include the issuing of import licenses, quantity and quality restrictions, state trading, and bureaucratic red tape in general.[5] State trading is still practiced by many governments, but the private sector is responsible for a growing share of global wheat imports. Among large wheat importers, examples of greater private sector involvement can be found in Indonesia, Pakistan, the Philippines, and Turkey in Asia; Algeria, the Arab Republic of Egypt, and Morocco in Africa; and Brazil and Mexico in Latin America. However, many governments—among them those of China, the Islamic Republic of Iran, India, and Japan—still control wheat imports through various schemes.

Export promotion

The two largest providers of wheat export subsidies, the European Union and the United States, had largely eliminated export subsidies by 2001 as global prices rose and the European Union reduced intervention prices under its 1992 and Agenda 2000 policy reforms. The European Union agreed to reduce subsidized exports to 14.4 million tons by 2000 and thereafter under the URAA and has not reported export subsidies since the 2001–02 season.[6] The United States agreed to reduce subsidized wheat exports to 14.5 million tons by 2000 and thereafter under the URAA, although the U.S. primary export subsidy facility, the Export Enhancement Program, has not been used for wheat since 1995. Under URAA, however, both countries could revive their export subsidy programs and together could subsidize nearly one-quarter of global wheat exports. Export credits were still used by Australia, Canada, the European Union, and the United States as recently as 1998, the most recent period for which complete data were available (OECD 2000).

Food aid has been provided by many countries to respond to emergencies or persistent food shortages. It has often been charged, however, that food aid is partly used as a way to dispose of surplus production. This charge is supported by the fact that 85 percent of global wheat food aid during 1990–2000 was provided by four of the world's major wheat exporters. The United States provided 54 percent of world wheat food aid, the European Union 20 percent, Canada 8 percent, and Australia 3 percent (FAOSTAT). In total, wheat food aid accounted for about 6 percent of wheat trade during 1990–2000. Over a longer period, the United States provided an average of 3.3 million tons of wheat food aid from 1970 to 2000, averaging 10 percent of U.S. wheat exports. The level of food aid varied with price (figure 11.5), which suggests that it was partly surplus disposal.[7]

Food Security and Global Wheat Trade

Since wheat is the food grain most often used as a buffer against food shortages, any disruption of trade flows or sharp increases in prices causes food security concerns for importing countries. When real wheat export prices doubled from 1970 to 1974, for example, policymakers in wheat-importing countries were quick to raise concerns. These were further heightened when the United States imposed grain export embargoes in 1974 and 1975 to protect its own consumers from high prices.[8] Such actions likely contributed to the strong desire for food self-sufficiency in many food-importing countries. The United States again embargoed grain sales to the Soviet Union in 1980 as a foreign policy action motivated by the USSR's invasion of Afghanistan.

FIGURE 11.5   U.S. Wheat Food Aid vs. Prices

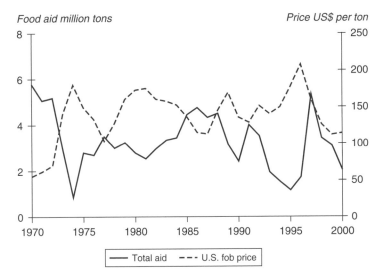

Source: USDA and World Bank.

The embargo lasted nearly 16 months and included a wide range of products. The European Union provoked anxiety over food security again in 1995, after it had become a wheat exporter, when it imposed an export tax of $35 per ton on wheat during 1995–96 to protect its consumers from high prices.[9] The Russian Federation recently took similar action by imposing an export tax on wheat of 25 euros per ton during the period from January 15 to May 1, 2004. Several other wheat exporters also imposed restrictions on wheat exports, including Hungary, India, and Ukraine. As with the previous actions, the policies were intended to protect domestic supplies and control prices. All came at times when world prices were rising and the availability of supplies was uncertain. Such actions send the signal that access to wheat exports cannot be relied upon during periods of shortages and high prices.

Domestic support

Because domestic support commitments under the URAA apply to the whole of agriculture rather than to individual commodities, countries have been able to protect their most politically sensitive sectors by keeping support high. According to OECD estimates, domestic support to OECD wheat producers averaged $17.3 billion per year during 1999–2001 (table 11.5), compared with $18.7 billion per year during the 1986–88 base period of the URAA. Domestic support in 1999–2001 accounted for 41 percent of the value of wheat production at farm-gate prices. The European Union and the United States provided the largest absolute support to wheat, amounting to $9.6 billion and $4.9 billion per year, respectively. However, support representing a higher percentage of the value of wheat

TABLE 11.5   Support to OECD Wheat Producers, 1999–2001

OECD Country/Region	Producer Support (millions of dollars)	PSE Percentage	Producer NPC	Producer NAC
OECD	17,331	41	1.16	1.70
Australia	119	5	1.01	1.05
Canada	358	15	1.01	1.17
Czech Republic	−10	−3	0.87	0.97
European Union	9,565	48	1.15	1.95
Hungary	53	13	1.06	1.15
Japan	822	86	6.38	7.20
Mexico	237	39	1.44	1.64
Norway	67	71	2.63	3.58
Poland	251	21	1.22	1.27
Slovak Republic	5	5	0.86	1.06
Switzerland	191	63	2.33	2.82
Turkey	551	26	1.30	1.41
United States	4,928	46	1.12	1.86

Note: Producer support was converted from local currency to U.S. dollars using period average annual exchange rates from International Monetary Fund's International Financial Statistics, 2002 Yearbook. PSE percentage is producer support estimate, an indicator of the annual monetary value of gross transfers from consumers and taxpayers to support agricultural producers, measured at farm-gate level as a percentage of the value of production arising from policy measures, regardless of their nature, objectives, or impact on farm production or income. Producer NPC is producer nominal protection coefficient, an indicator of the nominal rate of protection for producers measuring the ratio between the average price received by producers (at farm gate), including payments per ton of current output, and the border price (measured at farm-gate level). Producer NAC is producer nominal assistance coefficient, an indicator of the nominal rate of assistance to producers measuring the ratio between the value of gross farm receipts including support and gross farm receipts valued at world market prices without support. No calculations were made for Canada, Iceland, New Zealand, Norway, or the Republic of Korea.
Source: OECD 2002

TABLE 11.6   Major Wheat Exporters' Shares of Global Wheat Net Exports
(percent)

Exporter	1970–79	1980–89	1990–99
United States	40.9	36.1	27.1
Canada	19.5	18.4	17.9
Australia	12.1	12.8	12.0
European Union	0.0	7.8	9.9
Argentina	3.9	5.6	6.2
Total	76.4	80.7	73.1

Note: The average export shares were calculated on net exports because the European Union was both a large importer and exporter and net exports capture the net trade situation better than gross exports. When net exports were negative, a zero was assigned. The European Union was defined as the current 15 members even though not all of these countries were members during the entire period.
Source: FAOSTAT.

production was provided by Japan (86 percent), Norway (71 percent), and Switzerland (63 percent).

Major Wheat Exporters

Five countries accounted for about three-quarters of net global wheat exports in 1970–1999 (table 11.6). The United States was the largest net exporter over this period, but its share declined from nearly 41 percent during the 1970s to 27 percent during the 1990s. Canada was the second-largest net exporter with an 18–19 percent share. Australia maintained its 12 percent share throughout the period, and Argentina expanded its share from about 4 to 6 percent of global exports. The European Union exported 10 percent of global net exports during the 1990s after being a net importer of about 10 percent of global trade during the 1970s. The emergence of the European Union as a major exporter was attributable to highly subsidized production and exports under the Common Agricultural Policy (CAP) and was largely at the expense of U.S. exports.

Wheat support policies of the major exporters have changed since the early 1980s, with Australia and Canada significantly reducing support to their wheat producers, while the European Union and the United States have decreased support more moderately according to OECD estimates (table 11.7). Argentina, which is not an OECD country and does not have producer support estimates comparable to the other major exporters, has historically taxed rather than supported its wheat producers.

Canada made the largest reductions in wheat support among major exporters between 1986–88

TABLE 11.7   Producer Support Estimates, 1986–88 and 2000–02
(percent)

Exporter	1986–88	2000–02
Australia	9	5
Canada	45	16
European Union	52	46
United States	49	40

Source: OECD 2003.

and 2000–02, with total producer support declining from 45 percent of the value of production to 16 percent. The country largely abandoned direct price support to individual commodities in favor of income support in the early 1990s (Gardiner 1999). This led to reduced wheat production and reduced net exports by 13 percent between 1990–95 and 1996–2001 (table 11.8).

The European Union sharply reduced wheat intervention prices in the CAP reform of 1992 and implemented a mandatory land set-aside policy (Rayner and others 1999). Further reforms were taken in 2000 and 2003. However, total support did not decline significantly (see table 11.7), and production continued to increase (see table 11.8). Consumption increased because of the lower intervention prices, allowing net exports to fall by 41 percent between 1990–95 and 1996–2001.

The United States undertook major reforms in the 1980s, with the reduction in wheat loan rates and the introduction of the Conservation Reserve

TABLE 11.8 Percentage Change of Wheat Production, Area Harvested, Yields, and Net Exports of Major Exporters from 1990–95 to 1996–2001

Exporter	Production	Area Harvested	Yields	Net Exports
Argentina	47.2	28.0	14.7	53.8
Australia	66.2	37.5	21.7	61.9
Canada	−10.0	−13.4	4.0	−13.3
European Union	12.4	3.0	9.1	−40.8
United States	−2.0	−9.3	8.6	−16.7
Major exporters	10.2	1.4	8.6	−6.3

Source: Authors' calculations.

Program, which removed about 10 million acres of wheat land from production (15 percent of wheat area) (Hoffman, Schwartz, and Chomo 1995). Net exports declined by nearly 17 percent from 1990–95 to 1996–2001, as area declined 9.3 percent. The 2002 U.S. Farm Bill somewhat reversed previous reforms but did continue the large wheat-land diversion program begun in the 1980s.

The changes in Argentina led to large investments in the Argentine grain marketing system, more intensive input use, and a 50 percent increase in net exports from 1990–95 to 1996–2001 (Schneph, Dohlman, and Collins 2001). The financial crisis of 2002 contributed to the profitability of exportable agriculture, as the peso was devalued by 70 percent after being fixed to the U.S. dollar for 10 years. Export taxes of 20 percent were reinstated to offset windfall profits from the currency devaluation.

The combined impacts of reduced production support, lower export subsidies, and land set-asides are reflected in lower production and reduced net exports by Canada, the European Union, and the United States (see table 11.8). These declines were mostly offset, however, by larger exports from Argentina and Australia. On balance, the five major exporters reduced net wheat exports from 80 million tons during 1990–95 to 75 million tons during 1996–2001, a decline of 6.3 percent. The largest decline in producer support came in Canada, where lower support led to lower area planted, production, and net exports.

Major Wheat Importers

Global wheat imports have grown by just 1.2 percent per year since 1980, compared with nearly 6 percent per year between 1970 and 1980 (figure 11.6). The rapid increase in imports during the 1970s was caused by major economic and policy changes in several regions and countries. These include increased wheat imports by OPEC (Organization of Petroleum Exporting Countries), large net imports by the FSU and Eastern Europe because of poor production, and policy changes in China that led to large net imports. Most of these changes have either been reversed or had more moderate influences on wheat imports since 1980.

Imports by the FSU accounted for one-quarter of global imports at their peak in 1984 and then steadily declined to only 3 percent by 1995. Imports by Eastern European countries, while much smaller than those of the FSU, declined by 75 percent during the same period (FSU+Eastern European countries in figure 11.6). China's imports peaked at 16 million tons in 1989 (16 percent of global trade) and declined to 2 million tons in 2000 due to rapidly increasing domestic production following policy changes (see figure 11.6).

OPEC's import increases slowed during the 1980s as oil prices fell. Imports have only recently begun to increase with the recovery in oil prices that began in 1999. Thus the countries that fueled the large increase in wheat trade during the 1970s largely accounted for its stagnation after 1980. Offsetting these declines have been steady increases in imports by other developing countries (shown as Developing minus China in figure 11.6), but the increases were not large enough to raise global trade significantly. Imports by the developed countries have remained largely constant since 1980, with lower imports by Western Europe offsetting increases from high-income Asia.

Brazil, China, Egypt, Japan, and the Russian Federation were the largest importers during 1990–2000, each with 5–7 percent of global imports (figure 11.7). They were followed by Algeria,

FIGURE 11.6   Global Wheat Imports

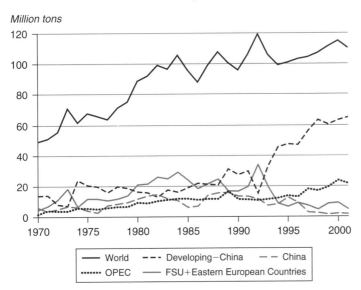

Million tons

Legend: World — ; Developing–China ---; China – –; OPEC ••••••; FSU+Eastern European Countries ——

Source: FAO.

FIGURE 11.7   Wheat Net Imports, Average for 1990–2000

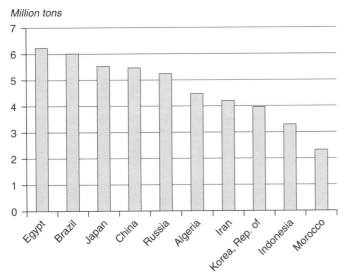

Million tons

Categories: Egypt, Brazil, Japan, China, Russia, Algeria, Iran, Korea, Rep. of, Indonesia, Morocco

Source: USDA.

Indonesia, Iran, and Korea, each with 2–5 percent of global imports. The 10 largest net importers during 1990–2000 accounted for 46 percent of global imports. Many of these large importers undertook policy reforms during the late 1980s or 1990s that removed government monopolies on imports.

Egypt was the largest importer during 1990–2000, with average imports of slightly more than six million tons per year. Wheat is considered a strategic commodity in Egypt, providing more than one-third of the daily caloric intake of Egyptian consumers and 45 percent of protein consumption. It is also the major staple crop produced in the country, occupying about one-third of the total winter crop area. The government's policy objectives in the agricultural sector have been to provide an adequate supply of food to all income groups, to promote greater self-sufficiency in crop production, and to increase farm income.

In the mid-1980s the widening food gap, stagnation of the agricultural sector, and the rising costs of the food subsidy system encouraged the government to reform agriculture and the wheat sector under the Agricultural Reform Program, initiated in 1987. In the first phase of the reform, prices, quotas, and marketing controls were partially liberalized. Import subsidies were reduced, and markets were opened to private investment. The second phase of the reform coincided with the launching of the Economic Reform and Structural Adjustment Program in 1991, which sought to shift Egypt from a state-controlled economy into a more market-oriented economy in which the private sector could play a major role (Kherallah and others 2000).

In 1992 the Egyptian government also began to liberalize the wheat-milling sector, which up to that time had maintained a monopoly over the importation of all types of wheat grain and flour. In addition, around 80 percent of all industrial wheat mills in the country belonged to the public sector—the rest were licensed to mill for the government under specific arrangements. The partial liberalization of wheat trading started in the flour market in 1992, when the government freed the prices of flour and bread and allowed the private sector to import wheat for the production of flour. Resale of wheat in excess of the milling needs for flour was not permitted. The government also allowed private traders to import flour directly. All the remaining restrictions on flour production and trading were removed in 1993, allowing both the public and private sectors to freely import, produce, distribute, and sell flour at free-market prices. The quotas of government-milled flour going to food-processing factories, shops, and bakeries were also eliminated, thus allowing these outlets to purchase their flour freely in the market.

Brazil was the second-largest importer during 1990–2000, with imports averaging 6 million tons per year. Before 1991 the Brazilian government heavily subsidized wheat flour, but consumer subsidies were removed in late 1991 along with other price controls, and the mill-quota system was eliminated (Brandão and Salazar 2003). Brazil now obtains nearly all of its wheat from Argentina with a zero import duty because of its membership in the regional trade group, Mercosur. In 2002, to reduce wheat imports, the government introduced a program to expand domestic wheat production to 50 percent of total consumption by 2004. The government operates a minimum-support-price system for wheat and other commodities. Other policies and programs to support domestic wheat

production include subsidized loan programs for farmers and processors to borrow against their products at below-market-interest rates while holding their products as collateral in accredited warehouses. Small producers are eligible for financing of production costs at subsidized interest rates under a program to strengthen family farms. Longer-term support for production and processing of agricultural products is available from the Brazilian Bank for Economic and Social Development and the Special Agency for Industrial Financing.

Japan was the third-largest wheat importer during 1990–2000, but unlike other importers it has not reduced import controls or significantly reduced producer support. Japan's agricultural policy is strongly influenced by concerns for food security and self-sufficiency. In addition, postwar land reforms created a very small-scale farm structure that is inefficient by global standards; thus income support for farmers is also a high priority. Wheat producers receive about $1,200 per ton for wheat—about 10 times the U.S. f.o.b. (free on board) price and 6 times the c.i.f. (cost, insurance, and freight) import price. Domestic wheat production is about 10 percent of domestic consumption, and the Japanese Food Agency imports about 6 million tons of wheat per year. Import policy has focused on food security and diversification of supplies in an effort to ensure guaranteed supplies rather than low import prices. Domestic producers are paid an administered purchase price for wheat, which is then resold at higher prices to the domestic milling industry. Imported wheat is resold to millers at prices that are about double the import price. A margin between the resale of domestic and imported wheat is necessary to adjust for quality differences between Japanese and imported wheat.

A new wheat policy was introduced in 1998 by the Japanese Food Agency, with implementation occurring during the 2000 to 2002 crop years. The Japanese Food Agency retained control over the pricing and marketing of domestic wheat, as well as the importing and pricing of foreign wheat. The new policy allows the private sector to import wheat, whereas the Japanese Food Agency had been the exclusive importer under the previous system. The new policy also introduced a new compensation system for domestic wheat producers. Other programs to improve quality allow continuous importation of wheat for food use by the Japanese Food Agency and a simultaneous-buy-and-sell system for imported feed wheat.

China was the fourth-largest importer during the 1990–2000 period, but it has undertaken major reforms in the past few years, lowering support prices to near world market levels and reducing imports by 90 percent (Crook 1996 and 1997; USDA 1998 and 2001a). The government's long-standing policy has been to approximate self-sufficiency in food staples, including wheat. This began in the 1950s with producer quotas, but the system changed significantly with the introduction of the Household Responsibility System in 1978. Under this system, local leaders began contracting production quotas with small work units and family farms instead of large collectives. China initiated the Governors' Grain-Bag Responsibility System in 1995, whereby provincial authorities were given the task of stimulating production, stabilizing prices, making provisions for adequate grain stocks, reducing imports, and ensuring supplies for urban areas and the military. These reforms led to an increase in wheat production of about 22 percent between 1990–92 and 1997–99 and to huge stocks by the end of the 1990s. Since the mid-1990s, the state grain procurement program has not been altered to any significant degree, although there have been revisions in some procurement procedures and efforts to improve wheat quality. In 2000 the government introduced new wheat standards to upgrade the average quality of the crop. Protected prices were removed from spring wheat in the north and winter wheat south of the Yangtze River. In 2001 market reforms eliminated protected prices in many provinces but not in the major producing regions.

One of the most significant consequences of China's domestic policies has been the shift in its cereal trade balances. The accumulation of large grain stocks caused average annual wheat imports to fall from 10 million tons in the early 1990s to below 1 million tons since 2000. China became a net exporter of wheat in 2002.

Other factors contributed to the decline in wheat imports, including local market conditions and government actions. China assessed a 13 percent value-added tax on imported wheat (while not collecting the tax on most domestic wheat production), and a 1 percent import duty, thus making imported wheat uncompetitive in some years. During the phase-in period after China's entry into the WTO in 2001, the volume of imports was regulated by a tariff rate quota system. The initial TRQ for wheat was 7.3 million tons in 2001; it rose to 9.64 million tons in 2004. China also agreed to expand the role of private traders after WTO accession, but state trading enterprises would still control 90 percent of the wheat TRQ. Notwithstanding China's WTO commitments, however, the fill rate of the wheat TRQ has been minimal—8 percent in 2002 and 5 percent in 2003, according to periodic reports from the Global Agricultural Information Network of the U.S. Department of Agriculture.

While many of the major importing countries have reformed policies, high protection is still evident in many countries, as shown by disparities between producer prices and U.S. fob prices (figure 11.8). Japan, has the highest producer prices, but several other countries also have high prices. Consumers in these countries have the most to gain from more liberal trade policies.

Emerging Wheat Exporters

China, India, Pakistan, and several countries of the FSU have emerged as wheat exporters. This is a shift from the past when these countries were either large regular importers or occasional importers.

Former Soviet Union

Several countries of the FSU have the potential to become large exporters—among them Kazakhstan, the Russian Federation, and Ukraine, which collectively moved from being net importers of 15 million tons of wheat in 1992 to net exporters of 23 million tons in 2002 (figure 11.9).

The emerging exporters of the FSU have many common problems, including weak marketing systems; inefficient storage, transport, and grain handling systems; lack of credit; and the challenge of making the transition from collective farms to private production systems. Policy reforms have been slow and only partially effective in stimulating private-sector initiative. Despite these problems, all of these countries have large land areas well suited to wheat production and low production costs. They also have an advantage in transporting wheat to importers in the Middle East compared with

FIGURE 11.8   Wheat Producer Prices in 2001 for Selected Countries

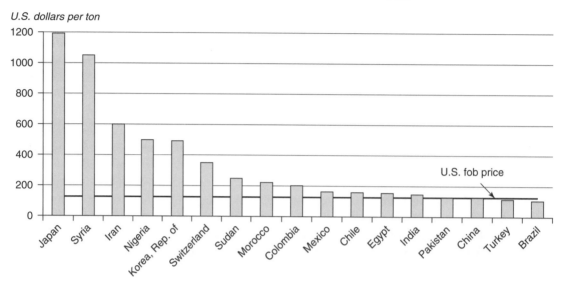

U.S. dollars per ton

Source: FAO.

FIGURE 11.9   Emerging Wheat Net Exports of Emerging Exporters in the FSU

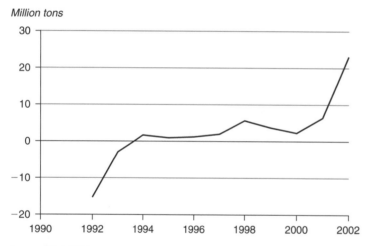

Million tons

Source: FAOSTAT.

major exporters such as Australia, Canada, and the United States.

Kazakhstan, a major wheat producer and exporter during the Soviet era, used intensive farming methods that relied on subsidized inputs. These intensive farming methods, which are not profitable without large subsidies, have been abandoned. The country has a large land area, however, with considerable potential for expanding wheat production and exports using low-input farming methods. Production remains constrained by high domestic marketing and transport costs traceable to a lack of competition and insufficient private

sector activity. Production is mostly high-protein spring wheat, which, with quality improvements, could compete with the best wheat from other exporters. Large investments during the Soviet era left the country with considerable infrastructure for grain transport and exports. If costs can be controlled and production increased, Kazakhstan could become a major wheat exporter (Longmire and Moldashev 1999).

Russia accounted for one-quarter of world wheat exports in the early years of the 20th century, when its yields were only slightly less than those of the United States. Whether the Russian Federation can return to its former role as a major exporter depends largely on policy developments. Input subsidies and price supports were largely dismantled in January 1992, when the transition toward a market economy began. Decreases in real incomes and changes in food prices led to substantial changes in food consumption and declines in feed use. Government procurement of wheat declined from nearly all before the reform to just 21 percent by 1995—in part because of lack of funds by the state procurement agency. Private grain-trading companies have largely replaced the state. Simultaneously, subsidies have been reversed and the agricultural sector (including wheat) are taxed. Grains are still produced on large farms and under the same management as before the reforms, but many of the farms have been converted into private stock companies. Regional authorities use wholesale and retail price controls, subsidies, and barriers to interregional trade to regulate prices and food stocks. The emerging private sector must deal with the high transaction costs of these interregional trade restrictions. Producers have considerable potential to increase yields if economic incentives improve. Efficient transportation and marketing systems could make the Russian Federation a net exporter (Goodwin and Grennes 1999).

Ukraine emerged from a decade of adjustment following the end of the Soviet era to become a significant wheat exporter. In 2002–03 the country exported about 6.6 million tons of wheat before a production slump in 2003–04 forced a return to imports. However, low production costs and shifts in resource use since the Soviet era suggest that wheat exports will likely increase in the future. During the Soviet era, Ukraine concentrated on livestock and poultry production, but soon after independence in 1991 poultry and livestock numbers declined by more than half. Wheat production fell as well (in part because of lower demand for animal feed) until 2000, rebounding in the two years before the severe drought of 2003. Production costs are estimated by the U.S. Department of Agriculture (USDA) to be $50 per ton (Thursland and Prikhodko 2002), offsetting inefficiencies in handling, storage, and transport.

Policy reforms began with price liberalization in 1992, but many agricultural subsidies were continued, resulting in budget deficits and inflation. Economywide price and trade reforms were fully implemented, but specific agricultural and institutional reforms were only partially implemented. Land reform has been slow to develop in the years since transfer and ownership legislation was passed in 1994 and 1995. The result has been a slow recovery of production (Debatisse and Chabot 2000).

Asia

Several Asian countries have become net wheat exporters in recent years because of large crops and stocks. It remains to be seen, however, whether they can sustain exports or will revert back to being net importers. Domestic policies in Asia remain aimed at self-sufficiency and self-reliance rather than on promoting surpluses for export.

India has followed a policy of self-sufficiency since independence, increasing crop output by expanding irrigation, improving crop yields through high-yielding varieties, and increasing land-use intensity with multiple cropping. Better yields were possible because of the Green Revolution, which provided the high-yielding varieties that were adopted with support from production and price policies. To increase yields, the public sector provided agricultural inputs, such as fertilizers, power, and water for irrigation at subsidized prices. The government also established a system of minimum support prices to procure wheat from farmers. Subsequently, India made substantial gains in food grain production, and over the past 30 years wheat production has grown by about 3.5 percent per year.

In the early 1980s, India cautiously began to liberalize trade, but only since 1991 has the process of liberalization picked up speed. In July 1991 India introduced radical policy reforms in various economic sectors, but trade restrictions on agricultural products were left largely untouched. Subsequent changes in trade policy gradually lifted restrictions on agricultural products. Bumper wheat crops starting in 1999 led to large accumulations of public stocks, which eventually prompted wheat exports, making India a net wheat exporter in 2000. In order to be competitive in the Asian markets, the government subsidized exports, displacing sales in the region by the United States and other traditional suppliers. Exports reached a record 6 million tons in 2002–03. Wheat exports were halted in August 2003 as stocks diminished following a poor crop in 2003.

China has been exporting wheat since 1992. Exports reached 1 million tons in 2002–03, making China a significant net wheat exporter for the first time. Despite stagnant domestic demand, however, domestic surpluses have been falling in recent years in line with policy-driven production declines. Rozelle and Huang (1999) argue that China will remain a net importer at the levels of the early to mid-1990s.

Pakistan has been a net wheat exporter since 2000–01, reaching 1 million tons in 2002–03, but reverted to being a net importer during the 2003–04 season.

The Impact of Liberalization

Various studies have estimated the impact of liberalizing trade and reducing domestic support on the world wheat market. Results vary and do not always consider the full range of reforms. The Food and Agricultural Policy Research Institute (FAPRI 2002) at Iowa State University and the University of Missouri recently evaluated the impacts of liberalization of agricultural markets using a multimarket global agricultural model. The results for wheat are reported here. The study considered two scenarios. The first, full liberalization, explored the probable effects of removing all agricultural distortions—domestic farm programs and border measures—including all TRQ schemes, tariffs, and direct export subsidies such as the European Union's CAP. The second investigated the effects of removing only border measures. The two scenarios allow the impact of domestic programs to be evaluated separately from border measures. The question of how to examine domestic programs without border measures was addressed by assuming that government payments would be used to provide producers with the difference between current domestic price floors and the lower prices that would result without border measures. The simulations did not include the 2002 U.S. Farm Bill but instead used an extension of the previous farm bill in the baseline simulation. Nor did they include the reforms to the European Union's CAP in mid-2003. The URAA was assumed to extend after 2004, when the final provisions are to be implemented. The results are presented as average percentage changes relative to the baseline simulation for the period from 2002 to 2011.

The FAPRI results show that wheat prices (U.S. fob Gulf) would rise from the baseline by an average of 4.8 percent under the full liberalization scenario and by 7.6 percent in the trade-only scenario. The price increase is lower under full liberalization because set-asides would be removed in the European Union and the United States, resulting in a substantial increase in production and exports that would dampen the price effect. Global wheat trade would increase by 7.9 percent under full liberalization and by 5.0 percent under the trade-only scenario, with the largest export increase going to the European Union once set-asides were removed. China would reduce imports under both scenarios because it would face slightly higher prices on wheat allowed under the low in-quota tariff in its wheat tariff rate quota. India would reduce exports and become a net importer, because export subsidies would no longer be allowed.

A USDA study (2001b) found a larger wheat price increase from elimination of all policy distortions. It concluded that wheat prices would rise by 18.1 percent from elimination of all policy distortions. Removal of global tariffs would raise prices 3.4 percent; elimination of OECD domestic subsidies would raise them 12.0 percent; and global elimination of export subsidies would raise them 2.0 percent. A recent FAO study (Poonyth and Sharma 2003) concluded that wheat prices would rise by 11.9 percent under the U.S.-proposed WTO reform, which is similar to the USDA's full-liberalization scenario.

The three studies provide a range of estimates—from 4.8 to 18.1 percent—of the increase in world prices that would result from eliminating all producer support and trade distortions.

Conclusions

The global wheat market has become less distorted since the early 1990s, as several countries have undertaken reforms unilaterally or as a consequence of commitments under the URAA. Governments in OECD countries still provide substantial support to producers, however. The effects of that support have been partially offset by land set-aside programs and by the way in which support is provided; however, support policies still distort trade and depress world prices. The European Union and the United States have not used export subsidies in recent years but still use other surplus disposal programs, such as nonemergency food aid and export credits. These programs make it more difficult for emerging exporters to compete with established exporters.

Most importing countries have reduced wheat tariffs or allowed duty-free imports from regional trading partners, thus benefiting from lower prices. A few countries, such as Japan, continue to apply extreme protection, with internal prices more than five times global market levels. Tariff escalation is a major problem for countries trying to diversify production and exports, with tariffs on flour well above those on wheat grain, and tariffs on bakery and pasta products even higher. Consequently, trade in wheat products is largely confined to free trade areas such as within the European Union or NAFTA.

A major concern for wheat-importing countries is the lack of assured access to wheat export markets during periods of supply shortages and high prices. Policies such as the U.S. grain export embargo of the 1970s, designed to protect domestic consumers, contribute to higher global wheat prices and increase the uncertainty of wheat-importing countries. The threat of such policy actions continues, with the European Union imposing export taxes on wheat in 1995 and the Russian Federation imposing export taxes in 2004—also to protect domestic consumers. Such actions reinforce the calls for food security through self-sufficiency in importing countries and deprive those countries of the benefits from trade.

Future reforms of the global wheat market should focus on reducing producer support in OECD countries, reducing protection in the remaining highly protected markets, reducing tariff escalation on wheat products, and ensuring access to exportable supplies during price spikes. Elimination of production subsidies and trade distortions could raise world wheat prices by 5–18 percent according to recent studies, but the large surplus capacity among major wheat exporters could boost production under policy reforms and prevent prices from rising further.

Notes

1. More detailed trade flow tables are given in the attached CD-ROM.

2. Note that the yields in India and the United States are not strictly comparable because a larger share of wheat area in India is irrigated than in the United States.

3. About 9 percent of global grain-based starch production comes from wheat (80 percent comes from maize). "Starch—Versatile and in Demand," *World Grain,* January 2004.

4. Karnal bunt is a wheat fungus that occurs during cool, rainy growing conditions. It is named after the city in India near where it was first reported in the 1930s. It is not harmful to humans or animals, but it causes an unpleasant odor in wheat flour.

5. Exchange rate controls are another means to regulate imports, but these are not normally commodity-specific.

6. Based on the use of wheat subsidies as reported to the WTO. Source: USDA, ERS WTO Agricultural Trade Policy Commitments Database.

7. Regressing wheat food aid (FA) on wheat prices (WP) shows a statistically significant relationship between the quantity of food aid and prices; as prices fall the quantity of food aid increases. The OLS regression estimated was FA = 6.487 − .023*WP. The R2 = .42 and the coefficient on prices was statistically significant at the 1 percent level of significance with $t = -4.6$.

8. The United States suspended grain exports in 1974 and again in 1975 because of low stocks, poor crop production prospects, and concern about the inflationary impacts of high grain prices. However, the action was directed only at the USSR in 1974 and at the USSR and Poland in 1975 since these countries were major buyers and perceived to be disrupting the markets (USDA 1986).

9. "EU Hits Grain Exporters, Steep New Tax Aims to Protect Supplies," *International Herald Tribune,* December 8, 1995. Most recently, however, the European Union declined to impose wheat export taxes following the 2003 production shortfall, but did temporarily suspend grain export licenses in August 2003. Reuters, July 31 and September 2, 2003.

References

ABARE. 2002. "Global Grains Policy and WTO Agricultural Negotiations." *Current Issues* 02.2 (January).

Beattie, B. R., and D. R. Biggerstaff. 1999. "Karnal Bunt: A Wimp of a Disease But an Irresistible Political Opportunity." *Choices* (2nd Quarter).

Brandão, A., and P. Salazar. 2003. "Brazil." In *FAO, WTO Agreement on Agriculture, The Implementation Experience.* Developing Country Case Studies, Rome.

Carter, C. A., and W.W. Wilson. 1999. "Emerging Differences in State Grain Trading: Australia and Canada." In J. M. Antle and V. H. Smith, eds., *The Economics of World Wheat Markets.* New York: CABI.

Crook, F. 1996. "China's Agricultural Policy Developments." China Situation and Outlook Series WRS-96-2, U.S. Department of Agriculture, Economic Research Service, Washington, D.C. June.

———. 1997. "Current Agricultural Policies Highlight Concerns About Food Security." China Situation and Outlook Series WRS-97-3, U.S. Department of Agriculture, Economic Research Service, Washington, D.C. June.

Dalrymple, D. G. 1974. "Development and Spread of High-Yielding Varieties of Wheat and Rice in the Less Developed Nations." Economic Research Service, U.S. Department of Agriculture, in Cooperation with the U.S. Agency for International Development, Washington, D.C.

Debatisse, Michel, and Philippe Chabot. 2000. "A Review of the Grain Marketing Sector in Kazakhstan and Ukraine." Environmentally and Socially Sustainable Development Working Paper 25, World Bank, Washington, D.C. June.

Diaz-Bonilla E. 1999. "South American Wheat Markets and MERCOSUR" in J. M. Antle and V. H. Smith, eds., *The Economics of World Wheat Markets.* New York: CABI.

FAOSTAT. Nutritional data: Food aid shipments. On line: http://faostat.fao.org/faostat/.

FAPRI (Food and Agricultural Policy Research Institute). 2002. "The Doha Round of the World Trade Organization: Appraising Further Liberalization of Agricultural Markets." Iowa State University CARD Working Paper 02-WP 317. November. Ames, Iowa.

Gardiner, Bruce L. 1999. "Canadian/U.S. Farm Policies and the Creation of a Single North American Grain Market." In J. M. Antle and V. H. Smith, eds., *The Economics of World Wheat Markets.* New York: CABI.

Goodwin, Barry K., and Thomas J. Grennes. 1999. "Russian Agriculture and World Grain Trade: Lessons from the Past and Implications for the Future." In J. M. Antle and V. H. Smith, eds., *The Economics of World Wheat Markets.* New York: CABI.

Hoffman, Linwood A., Sara Schwartz, and Grace V. Chomo. 1995. "Wheat Background for 1995 Farm Legislation." AER-712. U.S. Department of Agriculture, Economic Research Service, Washington, D.C. April.

Kherallah, Mylene, Hans Lofgren, Peter Gruhn, and Meyra M. Reeder. 2000. "Wheat Policy Reform in Egypt, Adjustment of Local Markets and Options for Future Reforms." IFPRI Research Report 115. International Food Policy Research Institute, Washington D.C.

Longmire, Jim, and Altynbeck Moldashev. 1999. "Changing Competitiveness of the Wheat Sector of Kazakhstan and Sources of Future Productivity Growth." Economics Working Paper 99-06. International Maize and Wheat Improvement Center (CIMMYT), Mexico.

OECD (Organisation for Economic Co-operation and Development). 2000. "An Analysis of Officially Supported Export Credits in Agriculture." Joint Working Party of the Committee for Agriculture and the Trade Committee, Directorate for Food, Agriculture and Fisheries, Paris. December 20.

———. 2002. *Agricultural Policies in OECD Countries, Monitoring and Evaluation.* Paris. June.

———. 2003. *Agricultural Policies in OECD Countries, Monitoring and Evaluation.* Paris.

Poonyth, Daneswar, and Ramesh Sharma. 2003. "The Impact of the WTO Negotiating Modalities in the Areas of Domestic Support, Market Access, and Export Competition on Developing Countries: Results from ATPSM." Paper prepared for the International Conference Agricultural Policy Reform and the WTO, Capri, Italy, June 23–26.

Rayner, Anthony, Robert Hine, Timothy Lloyd, Vincent H. Smith, and Robert Ackrill. 1999. "The European Union Common Agricultural Policy under the GATT." In J. M. Antle and V. H. Smith, eds., *The Economics of World Wheat Markets.* New York: CABI.

Rozelle, Scott D., and Jikun Huang. 1999. "Wheat in China: Supply Demand and Trade in the 21st Century." In J. M. Antle and V. H. Smith, eds., *The Economics of World Wheat Markets.* New York: CABI.

Schneph, Randall, Erik Dohlman, and Chris Collins. 2001. "Agriculture in Brazil and Argentina: Developments and Prospects for Major Field Crops." Agriculture and Trade Report WRS-01-3. U.S. Department of Agriculture, Economic Research Service, Washington, D.C. November.

Thursland, Marget E., and Dmitri Prikhodko. 2002. "Ukraine Grain and Feed: How Is Ukraine Grain Competitive?" U.S. Department of Agriculture, Global Agricultural Information Network, Washington, D.C. August 2.

USDA (U.S. Department of Agriculture). 1986. "Embargoes, Surplus Disposal, and U.S. Agriculture." AER 564. Economic Research Service, Washington, D.C. December.

———. 1998. "China: International Agriculture and Trade Report." WRS-98-3. Economic Research Service, Washington, D.C. August.

———. 2001a. "China: Agricultural in Transition." WRS-01-2. Economic Research Department, Washington, D.C. November.

———. 2001b. "The Road Ahead: Agricultural Policy Reform in the WTO—Summary Report." AER 797. Economic Research Department, Washington, D.C. January.

———. 2003. *Wheat Situation and Outlook Yearbook.* WHS-2003. Economic Research Service, Washington, D.C. March.

———. 2004. "Mexico Grain and Feed Annual Report." MX4033. Global Agricultural Information Network Foreign Agriculture Service, Washington, D.C. March.

Wilson, William W., and Bruce L. Dahl. 1999. "Grain Quality and North American Hard Wheat Exports." In J. M. Antle and V. H. Smith, eds., *The Economics of World Wheat Markets.* New York: CABI.

12

GROUNDNUT POLICIES, GLOBAL TRADE DYNAMICS, AND THE IMPACT OF TRADE LIBERALIZATION

Ndiame Diop, John C. Beghin, and Mirvat Sewadeh

Since the mid-1990s all major groundnut-exporting countries have been gradually liberalizing their groundnut sectors, in part to fulfill their commitments under World Trade Organization (WTO) agreements.[1] The results have been mixed, and trade in groundnut products remains heavily distorted. Both China and India have removed some import restrictions and allowed wider private-sector participation in importing groundnuts. However, tariffs on groundnut products remain very high in India and high in China. The large market size of both countries exacerbates these distortions and their effects on the world market.

In the United States the 2002 Farm Bill eliminated many unsustainable features of previous groundnut policies (such as the high support price and production quotas), but it introduced new distortions, such as countercyclical payments and the floor price mechanism. These policies subsidize U.S. groundnut exports when world prices are low, with the potential to depress world market prices.

Argentina still selectively subsidizes some processed groundnut products and exports and applies moderate export taxes on groundnuts. In Sub-Saharan Africa heavy producer taxation has ended, and unilateral liberalization efforts are continuing, although significant protection of processing remains.

The current situation raises many questions about the future of the sector and the prospects for various players. How will multilateral groundnut trade liberalization affect the competitive positions of different players? Which countries are likely to gain and which are likely to lose? How will small Sub-Saharan African producers be affected?

Groundnut Production

Groundnuts are a valuable source of protein, fat, energy, and minerals, and they generate cash income to many poor farmers in the developing world, especially in Sub-Saharan Africa and Asia. In Senegal, for instance, 70 percent of the rural labor force is employed in groundnut production, which accounts for 60 percent of households' agricultural income. Groundnut production and processing represent about 2 percent of gross domestic product and 9 percent of exports in Senegal.

This chapter is an abbreviated version of Diop, Beghin, and Sewadeh (2004), which is reproduced on the CD-ROM.

TABLE 12.1   Production, Use, and Export of Groundnuts, Average 1996–2001

Country	Area Harvested (1,000 ha)	Yield (mt/ha)	Production (1,000 mt)	Domestic Use (1,000 mt)	Edible Groundnuts (1,000 mt)	Crushed for Oil and Cake (1,000 mt)	Net Exports (1,000 mt)
World	21,452	1.4	29,997	29,896	12,416	14,590	169
Main producers and exporters							
China	4,234	2.9	12,204	11,777	4,753	6,140	427
India	7,902	0.9	7,176	7,082	534	5,581	94
United States	569	3.0	1,701	1,428	978	280	220
Argentina	280	1.5	403	191	21	155	213
Main producers in Africa							
Nigeria	1,187	1.1	1,340	1,340	636	427	0
Senegal	690	1.1	722	730	317	304	−6
South Africa	98	1.7	161	123	72	32	33
Malawi	117	0.9	103	101	78	18	2
Gambia, The	89	1.0	95	80	26	54	15
Main importers							
European Union	1	1.0	1	454	433	17	−449
Canada	0	0.0	0	115	115	0	−115
Japan	12	2.3	28	129	121	2	−103
Korea, Rep. of	7	2.2	15	30	30	0	−15

Note: The difference between production plus net exports and domestic utilization reflects stock variation and feed and seed use. Ending stocks are negligible for all countries except the United States, which had ending stocks of 28 percent of total production during 1996–2001.
Source: U.S. Department of Agriculture.

China is the world's largest groundnut producer, with 40 percent of world production in 2001. India accounts for 23 percent of worldwide production, a group of Sub-Saharan African countries produces 8.4 percent, and the United States produces 5.6 percent (table 12.1). Malawi, Nigeria, South Africa, and the United States produce shelled groundnuts, which are used as seed, consumed raw, or consumed after having been transformed into prepared (roasted, salted, flavored) groundnuts or groundnut butter or paste. In contrast, Argentina, China, India, and Senegal devote more than 60 percent of their production to crushing groundnuts for oil and meal.[2]

Groundnut production conditions vary considerably across countries, reflecting differences in technological development, access to modern inputs and irrigation, and farm management practices. Yields are highest in the United States and China and lowest in Sub-Saharan Africa (except South Africa) and India. The low yields in Africa and India are the result of limited use of modern inputs, including high-yielding seed varieties, and heavy dependence on rainfall.

Driven by tremendous growth in China, global shelled production grew 34 percent between 1981–85 and 1996–2000. Growth has been uneven across countries (figure A12.1 on the CD-Rom). China doubled its production between 1992 and 2000 by increasing its use of high-yielding varieties and agricultural inputs, including fertilizers, pesticides, mechanization, and irrigation (Colby and others 1992). In India production exhibited significant fluctuations, increasing between 1987 and 1998 before returning to the production levels of the 1970s (about 6 million tons). Production in Sub-Saharan Africa picked up in the early 1990s, after a long period of decline. Production has been stable since the early 1970s in the United States, which produces about 2 million tons a year, and in Argentina, which produces 300,000 tons.

The economic costs of groundnut production vary significantly across countries. In 1993 the average cost per acre was $694 in the United States, more than three times the average cost in China of $164 per acre (table 12.2). The higher economic costs per acre for U.S. groundnuts were attributed chiefly to production quota rent, land value, and

TABLE 12.2 Costs of and Revenues from Groundnuts in China and the United States
(US$ per acre)

Item	1992 United States	1992 China	1993 United States	1993 China
Variable costs				
Seed	70.32	43.83	71.18	45.96
Fertilizer	43.27	25.03	42.40	26.13
Chemicals	89.70	3.40	92.57	3.68
Labor	89.14	71.51	86.17	75.86
Other expenses	212.84	41.43	188.54	12.82
Subtotal	505.27	185.20	480.86	164.45
Fixed costs				
Land value	92.58	—	97.77	—
Quota rent	113.38	—	115.40	—
Total costs	711.23	185.20	694.03	164.45
Yield (pounds per acre)	2576	2520	1940	2135
Revenue (producer price times yield)	753.66	323.69	570.58	280.83

— Not available.

Note: More recent data are not available.

Source: Chen and others 1997.

the costs of using and maintaining farm equipment, fuel, electricity, repair, and capital replacement. Quota rent and land value are not costs for farmers in China, since there is no production quota and land is considered public property, belonging to local communities organized in groups of 30–40 households (Chen and others 1997).[3] Net returns for China and the United States are not significantly different if quota rent (irrelevant since the 2002 Farm Bill) is excluded from U.S. production costs. The U.S. cost disadvantage is, however, compensated for by higher producer prices brought about by the groundnut program and the higher quality of U.S. groundnuts. The elimination of quota production (and thus quota rent) in the 2002 Farm Bill reduces U.S. production costs. This development, as well as the high quality of U.S. groundnuts, which earn a high price premium in international markets, may well maintain U.S. competitiveness with China.[4]

Global Trade in Groundnuts

Domestic consumption of groundnuts is high, and only 5 percent of world production is sold in international markets. Of the three major groundnut products traded internationally (edible groundnuts, groundnut oil, and groundnut meal), edible groundnuts are the most traded, with a volume of 1.2 million tons in 2001; trade in groundnut oil was 250,000 tons (table 12.3). The global export of edible groundnuts has increased 2.2 percent a year since the early 1980s, while exports of groundnut oil declined 1 percent and meal exports fell 2.5 percent, despite growing global consumption of both products.

China is the world's largest exporter of edible groundnuts, accounting for 32 percent of world exports. The United States is the second-largest exporter, with 19 percent of the world market, followed by Argentina, at 10.5 percent. Sub-Saharan Africa (The Gambia, Malawi, Nigeria, Senegal, South Africa, and Sudan) has lost market share in international edible groundnut markets and accounts for only 5 percent of world trade. Senegal is the world's largest supplier of groundnut oil, but this market has declined as other vegetable oils are increasingly used as substitutes.

The European Union (EU) is the single largest groundnut market, accounting for 43 percent of world imports. The total value of net groundnut imports in the European Union was just below $500 million a year in 1996–2000. Canada, with 9 percent of world imports, is the second-largest market, followed by Japan, which imports 8.2 percent of world groundnuts.

TABLE 12.3   Value of Net Exports, by Groundnut Product, 1996–2000
(US$ millions)

Country	Edible Groundnut	Groundnut Oil	Prepared Groundnut	Total
EU-15	−378.47	−115.12	−4.54	−498.13
Japan	−44.00	−1.85	−71.46	−117.31
Canada	−76.67	−1.19	−3.31	−81.18
Korea, Rep. of	−4.55	0.01	−14.31	−18.86
Malawi	0.77	0.00	0.00	0.77
Nigeria	−3.29	4.64	0.00	1.35
Gambia, The	4.49	1.09	0.05	5.63
South Africa	16.01	4.68	0.27	20.95
Senegal	3.34	48.99	0.60	52.92
India	86.85	−0.13	7.27	93.99
United States	126.43	−12.77	28.26	141.92
Argentina	160.98	51.52	25.82	238.32
China	193.79	2.82	111.06	307.68

Note: Prepared groundnuts are roasted, salted, or flavored groundnuts. Peanut butter is not included.
Source: FAOSTAT.

Consistent with growth in world consumption, exports of raw edible groundnuts and prepared groundnuts have expanded rapidly since the mid-1980s (figures 12.1a–12.1d). Exports of edible groundnuts increased 8 percent in the 1990s, after a dramatic increase of more than 20 percent during the 1980s. The pattern of growth in prepared groundnut exports broadly mirrors that of edible groundnuts, signaling the highly integrated nature of these markets (figure 12.1c).

China has been the major beneficiary of this expansion (figure 12.1b). From barely 1 percent in 1976, its global market share in exports of edible groundnuts rose to 32 percent in 2001. During the same period, the U.S. market share dropped from 32 percent to 19 percent. The emergence of China as a leading exporter in the prepared groundnut market is even more impressive (figure 12.1d).

While the international edible groundnut market has become more concentrated (with 61 percent of exports controlled by China, the United States, and Argentina in 2001), the market for prepared groundnuts has become more fragmented. Concentration in the edible groundnut market partially reflects the significant decrease in Sub-Saharan Africa's share of prepared groundnuts, from 17 percent in 1976 to 5 percent in 2001. Africa's market countries (including The Gambia, Malawi, and Nigeria) enter the edible groundnut export market intermittently, depending on their crop quality and world market demand.

Figures 12.1e and 12.1f show the trends in exports and market shares of groundnut oil. Many countries, including Brazil and China, have exited the groundnut oil market since 1976 to focus on edible groundnuts and other vegetable oils. Other countries, such as the United States, have chosen to enter the market only when the quality of groundnuts harvested is too low for the nuts to be sold in the edible groundnut market. Senegal and Argentina remain the world's leading exporters of groundnut oil. The market has become significantly fragmented, however. Argentina, Brazil, Senegal, and the United States jointly supplied just 52 percent of total exports in 2001, down from 85 percent in 1976.

The decline in African countries' shares in global groundnut markets has significantly reduced the contribution of groundnut products to the export earnings of many Sub-Saharan African countries. The importance of groundnut products as a source of export earnings has declined dramatically in Malawi, Senegal, and South Africa since the early 1980s (table 12.4). The importance of groundnut products increased significantly only in The Gambia, where they accounted for 84 percent of total merchandise exports in 2000–02.

The volume of raw edible groundnuts exported decreased significantly in Malawi, Nigeria, and South Africa and stagnated in The Gambia and Senegal (table 12.4). As a result of declining and almost stagnant volumes, export earnings for

FIGURE 12.1   Global Groundnut Consumption, Exports, and Market Shares

(a) Global Exports and Consumption of Raw Edible Groundnuts, 1976–2002
(1,000 metric tons)

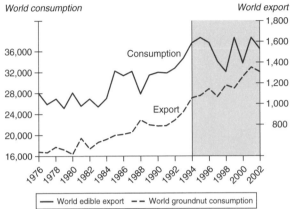

(b) Market Shares of Global Raw Edible Groundnut Exports, 1976–2002
(percent)

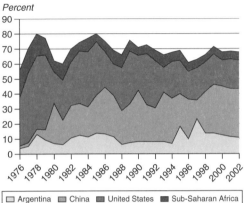

(c) Global Exports of Prepared Groundnuts, 1976–2002
(tons)

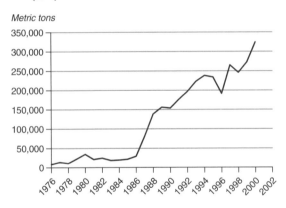

(d) Market Shares of Global Prepared Groundnut Exports, 1976–2002
(percent)

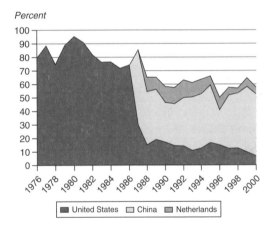

(e) Global Exports of Groundnut Oil
(1,000 metric tons)

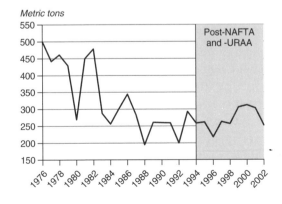

(f) Market Shares of Global Groundnut Oil Exports
(percent)

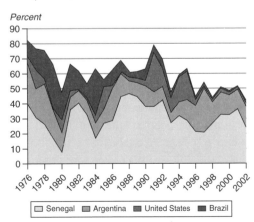

Source: FAOSTAT.

TABLE 12.4   Share of Groundnut Products in Total Merchandise Exports

Item	Period	The Gambia	Malawi	Nigeria	Senegal	South Africa
Shelled groundnut exports						
Volume (metric tons)	1980–82	27,333	14,867	1,026	2,725	41,333
	2000–02	27,939	662	412	2,915	34,830
Value (US$ thousands)	1980–82	11,743	12,333	400	2,145	29,730
	2000–02	5,763	436	204	1,371	22,875
Groundnut oil exports						
Volume (metric tons)	1980–82	7,651	0	0	82,693	22,667
	2000–02	8,633	0	1,287	98,879	1,519
Value (US$ thousands)	1980–82	6,400	0	0	60,285	14,071
	2000–02	6,333	0	797	63,007	1,053
Share of groundnuts in total exports (percent)	1980–82	59.62	4.65	0.003	16.17	0.21
	2000–02	84.64	0.10	0.006	8.16	0.08

Note: The share of groundnuts in total goods exports includes exports of groundnut meal.
Source: Production and groundnut exports data, FAOSTAT; total goods exports, World Bank.

shelled groundnuts dwindled. The extent of the decline suggests that unit values also decreased in The Gambia, Malawi, and Senegal.

International Prices of Groundnuts

Prices declined sharply in The Gambia and, to a lesser degree, in Senegal, while prices in South Africa remained higher (figure 12.2). The discount on groundnuts of Gambian and Senegalese origin reflects both their lower quality and stricter EU quality and technical standards. The European Union has become more demanding, from both a public health and a technical standpoint (size, uniformity).[5] Nigeria and Senegal increased the volume and value of their exports of groundnut oil, while South Africa exited the groundnut oil market.

International prices of edible groundnuts and groundnut oil in the Rotterdam market (the reference for groundnut trade) have exhibited two distinct patterns since 1970 (figure 12.3). During 1970–81 the prices of both products were increasing. Tests show no cointegration between edible groundnut and groundnut oil during this period (tables A12.1–A12.3 on the CD-ROM). Prices were high, and the world market was dominated by the United States, which supplied 45 percent of exports, and Sub-Saharan Africa, which supplied 18 percent. China exported no edible groundnuts or groundnut oil.

In sharp contrast with the 1970s, groundnut prices over the past 20 years have been stable, constantly reverting to their mean values following shocks (tables A12.4 and A12.5 on the CD-ROM). Two subperiods can be distinguished. Before 1994 prices of groundnuts displayed a higher level of volatility. The coefficient of variation of prices stood at 20 percent between 1980 and 1994, almost three times the 7 percent level witnessed between 1995 and 2001.

What are the main causes of this price variability? Is the change in price variability permanent? Revoredo and Fletcher (2002b) analyze both production instability (originating in exporting countries) and consumption instability (originating in importing countries). They find that the steady expansion of Chinese exports, which are negatively correlated with exports from Argentina and United States, was a stabilizing force in the second half of the 1990s. This stabilization occurred despite the fact that Argentina, India, and South Africa now transmit a higher proportion of their supply shocks to the world market.

Substitution between Chinese and U.S. groundnuts appears to have increased in recent years, although detailed data on substitution in world markets are not available.

In the groundnut oil market, the influence of Senegal on world prices remains significant. Senegal exported about 100,000 metric tons of groundnut

FIGURE 12.2 **Unit Price of Raw Edible Groundnuts Produced in The Gambia, Senegal, and South Africa**
(US$ per ton)

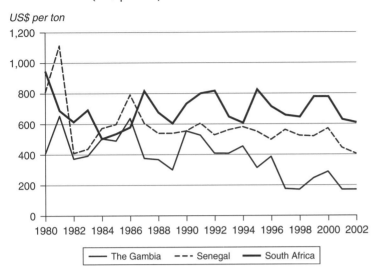

Source: FAOSTAT.

FIGURE 12.3 **Rotterdam Prices of Groundnuts, 1970–2000**
(cif, US$ per metric ton)

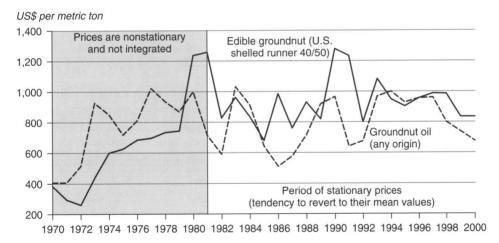

Source: Oil World, various issues.

oil in 2000–01, representing one-third of world exports and more than 60 percent of demand from the European Union, Senegal's main export market. While 2000–01 was an exceptional production year, econometric tests strongly indicate that variations in Senegal's exports were transmitted into the variability in international prices and that the reverse was not true.

Groundnut oil markets are broadly integrated with markets for other vegetable oils (soy oil, rapeseed oil, palm oil, and sunflower oil). Integration

seems to be much stronger for other oilseeds than for groundnuts, however.

Domestic Groundnut Policies of Major Countries in World Markets

Domestic producer support and taxation and trade policies determine excess supply and trade flows. It is important to examine these policies—in Argentina, China, India, Sub-Saharan Africa, and the United States—in some detail to anticipate the potential implications of policy changes on the distribution of gains and losses across countries.

Groundnut Policies in the United States

Groundnut products are a minor sector nationally, but they are a key component of agriculture and rural development in the southern part of the United States. Based on the U.S. Department of Agriculture (USDA) Census of Agriculture, many counties in the South derive 50–70 percent of their agricultural income from groundnuts. Shelling is performed locally, as are many groundnut product manufacturing activities (Fletcher 2001). Groundnut policies have played a major role in maintaining rural income in these counties.

The foundation of U.S. groundnut policy is the U.S. peanut program, which traces its roots to the 1930s. Until the enactment of the 2002 Farm Bill, the pillars of the system were production regulation through quotas, high producer support prices, and import control. The groundnut support program existed as a two-tier price support program. The support price for edible groundnuts was $610 per short ton paid for production under quota. Other groundnuts ("additionals"), which could be either exported at world prices or sold to the domestic crushed groundnut industry, were eligible for a lower support price ($132 in 2001). The quota farm-gate price tended to be higher than the prevailing export prices (table 12.5).

The average annual aggregate measure of support for U.S. groundnuts was estimated at $330 million during 2000–01, $31 million more than in 1996–2001. The average cost of aggregate support in 1996–01 stood at $206 per metric ton of groundnuts produced in the United States (table 12.6).

The 2002 Farm Bill eliminated groundnut production quotas (with a quota buyout), converted the price support program to a system of direct and countercyclical payments, and set a price floor with a production subsidy (nonrecourse loans, with marketing loan provisions). The key features of the new program include the following:

- All current groundnut producers have equal access to a marketing loan program under which producers can pledge their crops as collateral to obtain a marketing loan rate equal to $355 per short ton. Producers may repay the loan at a rate that is the lesser of the USDA–set repayment rate plus interest or the marketing loan rate plus interest, or they can forfeit the loan.

- For producers with a history of groundnut production, a new direct and fixed payment of $36 per short ton is available. Historic producers are those who were engaged in groundnut production between 1998 and 2001. Eligible production equals the product of average yields in the base period and 85 percent of base-period acres. These so-called decoupled payments are made regardless of current prices or the actual crop planted, as long as the farm remains in approved agricultural uses.

- Producers with a history of groundnut production are also eligible for a new countercyclical payment when market prices are below an established target price of $495 per short ton minus the $36 per ton direct payment. The payment rate is the difference between the target price ($495 per short ton) minus the direct fixed payment ($36 per ton) and the higher of the 12-month national average market price for the marketing year for groundnuts or the marketing

TABLE 12.5   U.S. Producer Support Prices for Groundnuts, 1993–94 to 1998–99
(US$ per pound)

Item	1993–94	1994–95	1995–96	1996–97	1997–98	1998–99
Quota price	0.388	0.339	0.339	0.305	0.305	0.305
"Additional" price	0.660	0.660	0.660	0.660	0.660	0.660
Average farm price	0.304	0.289	0.293	0.281	0.283	0.280
CCC[a] export price	0.200	0.200	0.200	0.200	0.200	0.200
Export unit value	0.330	0.286	0.292	0.322	0.327	0.328
Rotterdam cif price	0.371	0.292	0.336	0.316	0.360	0.290

a. Commodity Credit Corporation.
Source: Skinner 1999.

TABLE 12.6   U.S. Aggregate Support to Groundnuts, 1986–88 to 2000–01

Period	Aggregate Measure of Support (millions of US$)	Aggregate Measure of Support per Metric Ton of U.S. Production (US$)
1986–88	347.2	203.3
1995–96	414.6	264.1
1996–97	299.0	180.0
1997–98	305.8	190.5
1999–2000	300.0	172.7
2000–01	330.0	222.8

Source: Skinner 1999; Hart and Babcock 2002 for 2000–01 aggregate measure of support; USDA database for production data.

TABLE 12.7   U.S. Edible Groundnut Tariff Rate Quota Allocation, 1995–2008
(metric tons)

Year	Argentina Uruguay Round Tariff Rate Quota	Mexico NAFTA Tariff Rate Quota	Other Uruguay Round Tariff Rate Quota	Total NAFTA + Uruguay Round
1995	26,341	3,478	4,052	33,871
1996	29,853	3,582	5,043	38,478
1997	33,364	3,690	6,034	43,088
1998	36,877	3,801	7,024	47,702
1999	40,388	3,915	8,015	52,318
2000	43,901	4,032	9,005	56,938
2001	43,901	4,153	9,005	57,059
2002	43,901	4,278	9,005	57,184
2003–07	43,901	4,278	9,005	—
2008	43,901	unrestricted	9,005	—

— Not available.
Source: USDA.

assistance loan rate ($355 per short ton). The total countercyclical payment to each eligible producer is calculated as the product of the payment acres (85 percent of base acres), the base-year average yield, and the payment rate.

- Owners of groundnut quotas under the previous legislation receive compensation payments for the loss of quota asset value. Payments may be made in five annual installments of $220 per short ton during fiscal years 2002–06, or the quota owner may opt to take the outstanding payment due in a lump sum. These payments are based on quota owners' 2001 quota, as long as they owned a farm eligible for the groundnut quota (Wescott, Young, and Price 2002).

Beginning in 1994, under the Uruguay Round and NAFTA (North American Free Trade Agreement), the United States gradually increased the quantities of groundnut imports through a tariff rate quota system. For edible groundnuts the total tariff rate quota in 2001 was 57,059 metric tons, or 4 percent of domestic consumption, allocated first to historical importers and then on a first-come, first-served basis (table 12.7). In-quota tariffs for edible and prepared groundnuts range between $.066 and $.0935 per kilogram. Out-of-quota tariffs are very high (131.8–163.0 percent under the Uruguay Round; table 12.8).[6]

The phase-out of groundnut trade barriers under NAFTA and the Uruguay Round is limited in

TABLE 12.8   U.S. Over-Quota Tariffs, 1994–2008
(percent)

Year	NAFTA Edible and Prepared Groundnuts	Uruguay Round Prepared Groundnuts and Peanut Butter
Base[a]	123.1	155.0
1994	120.0	—
1995	116.9	151.1
1996	113.9	147.3
1997	110.8	143.4
1998	107.7	139.5
1999	104.6	135.7
2000	93.0	131.8
2001	81.4	131.8
2002	69.8	131.8
2008	0.0	—

a. Note: This indicates the base tariff levels from which the agreed cuts will be made.
— Not available.
Note: Prepared groundnuts are roasted, salted, or flavored groundnuts.
Source: USDA.

TABLE 12.9   U.S. Imports of Edible Groundnuts

Year	Argentina Imports	Argentina Quota	Mexico Imports	Mexico Quota	Total Imports	Total Quota	Over-the-Quota Imports
1996	38,270	29,853	4,710	3,583	57,000	38,478	18,522
1997	40,622	33,365	6,148	3,690	64,000	43,088	20,912
1998	34,465	36,875	4,834	3,801	70,000	47,702	22,298
1999	39,494	40,388	4,916	3,915	82,000	52,318	29,682
2000	72,230	43,901	4,864	4,032	97,000	56,938	40,062
2001	37,557	43,901	3,611	4,153	81,000	57,059	23,941
2002	29,927	43,901	4,406	4,278	46,795	57,184	Not filled
2003	4,692	43,901	292	4,278	5,698	57,184	Not filled

Source: USDA.

scope, but it continues to have a dramatic impact on U.S. imports. Edible groundnut imports by the United States—which were almost zero before 1994—have increased dramatically (table 12.9). Argentina's average fill rate was 87 percent and Mexico's, 77 percent, but out-of-quota imports were quite important, averaging 25,000 metric tons annually during 1996–2001. Edible groundnut imports represented 6 percent of U.S. groundnut consumption in 2001.

The initial impacts of the 2002 Farm Bill are also reflected in the collapse of imports in 2003 (see table 12.9). The elimination of production quotas decreased the price paid by U.S. processors, increasing domestic consumption of groundnuts (figure 12.4). It also removed the incentive to import edible groundnuts (Fletcher and Revoredo 2003; Revoredo and Fletcher 2002a).

Groundnut Policies in Argentina, China, and India

Since the mid-1990s Argentina, China, and India have gradually reduced potentially market-distorting direct government intervention in the production and marketing of groundnut products (table 12.10).

FIGURE 12.4   U.S. Domestic Groundnut Prices, 1993–2003
(US$ per metric ton)

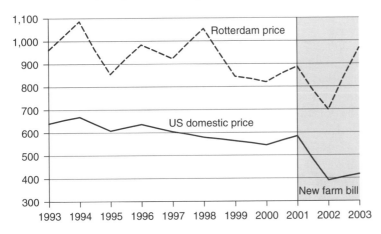

Source: USDA.

TABLE 12.10   Groundnut Trade Policy Distortions in Argentina, China, and India
(percent)

Country Product	Description	1999/2002
Argentina		
Edible groundnuts	Import tariff	5
Groundnut oil	Import tariff	13
Groundnut meal	Import tariff	8
Edible groundnuts	Export tax	3.5
Groundnut meal	Export rebate	3.2
Groundnut oil (refined)	Export rebate	2.3
China		
Raw edible groundnuts	Import tariff	15
Processed edible groundnuts	Import tariff	30
Groundnut oil	Import tariff	10
Groundnut meal	Import tariff	5
VAT on edible groundnuts and groundnut oil	VAT	17
India		
Edible groundnuts	Import tariff	45
Groundnut oil	Import tariff	35
Groundnut meal	Import tariff	45

Note: India raised its tariff on oil to 65 percent in 2002 and 85 percent in 2003. Raw edible groundnuts are raw, not roasted or cooked, in shell or shelled groundnuts. Processed groundnuts are bleached, preserved, or otherwise prepared groundnuts, including roasted, salted, and groundnut butter.
Source: WTO; WITS; USDA GAIN Report.

Argentina. Argentina's groundnut trade policy contrasts sharply with that of India and China, as almost all the distortions are associated with exports, which are subject to a 3.5 percent tax on raw groundnuts. With the peso devaluation of 2001, export tax retention on groundnut exports increased to 20 percent. This export tax may countervail the positive signal sent to groundnut exporters through the peso devaluation. Argentina maintains import tariffs on groundnut products, which exhibit some escalation (5 percent on edible groundnuts, 8 percent on groundnut meal, and

13 percent on groundnut oil). These tariffs are often redundant, since the country is a net exporter of groundnut products.

China. Like India, China liberalized groundnut trade to some degree in recent years. Before 1999 six public agencies were the only importers of groundnut products; today, private firms are free to import groundnuts. However, while the government has committed to cap and reduce trade-distorting domestic subsidies as part of its WTO accession commitments, guaranteed prices and government procurement schemes remain in place.[7] Furthermore, border protection remains high for processed groundnuts (30 percent). The tariff on raw groundnuts was only 15 percent in 2001, and many regions of China are natural exporters of groundnuts, making the tariff redundant. In-quota tariffs on groundnut oil (10 percent) and groundnut meal (5 percent) were much lower.

USDA attaché reports have repeatedly raised the issue of the uneven application of the Chinese value-added tax (VAT) on imported and domestic products. The VAT is significant, ranging from 13 to 17 percent, depending on the product, and there is ample room for tax evasion (USDA FASa, USDA FASb). The lack of uniformity in application prevents a more accurate measure of the impact. The quantitative policy analysis presented in the next section examines several cases with and without the VAT.

China's state trading imposes quantitative restrictions through quotas and licenses on groundnut oil imports, and it imposes tariff barriers on seeds, meal, and oil. These barriers create a wedge between domestic and world market prices. Domestic prices of most oils, including groundnut oil, are significantly higher than international market prices. Tariffs and rents on import licenses explain the price differentials.[8]

India. India removed most restrictions on domestic trade, storage, and export of groundnuts by 1998 and permitted trading in groundnut futures. However, import tariff levels remain very high for all three groundnut products. Moreover, in response to declines in prices, India has intensified its use of trade policy measures to protect its producers and processors. India is now the largest source of distortions in these product markets.

Tariffs on edible groundnuts and groundnut meal stood at 45 percent, while the tariff on groundnut oil was 35 percent in 2001 (see table 12.10). Since 2002 India has reversed its trade liberalization course on vegetable oil, increasing applied tariffs on groundnut oil to 65–75 percent in 2002–03 and 85 percent in 2003–04 (Gulati, Pursell, and Mullen, 2003; Pursell, 2003). The bound tariff is 100 percent.

Regulatory burdens increase domestic costs and prices. Producers are obligated to sell and purchase groundnuts only in the agricultural produce wholesale market.[9] The "small-scale reservation" policy in groundnut processing sets limits on fixed assets in plant and machinery, preventing the domestic processing industry from realizing economies of scale.

Groundnut Policies of Key African Exporters

After decades of extensive intervention in the groundnut sector, to varying degrees African countries underwent market reforms in the 1980s under structural adjustment plans. One of the main objectives of market reforms was to eliminate direct and indirect taxation of farmers that had undermined production incentives in the 1970s and early 1980s and led to underutilized processing capacities in many groundnut producing countries (Badiane and Kinteh 1994).

Reforms have been piecemeal and partial. Governments have generally withdrawn from input markets, making it difficult for producers to obtain certified seeds and fertilizer in countries such as The Gambia and Senegal, where there are market failures (in the credit market and elsewhere) and high transactions costs (Akobundu 1998). Governments have been reluctant to liberalize groundnut processing, for which privatization efforts started only recently (in The Gambia and Senegal). In The Gambia and Senegal producer prices are still set by the government.

African governments have traditionally used pricing policies as convenient levers to tax or subsidize farmers based on their industrial policies and political circumstances.[10] Taxation of groundnut farmers was high in the 1970s but has been reversed since the early 1990s in most countries, while real world prices have trended downward (Badiane and Kinteh 1994). In The Gambia and Senegal the main rationale for state intervention in the groundnut sector has been to safeguard the viability of state-owned processing mills. Consequently, the share of the export price to groundnut farmers has consistently been less than 60 percent in these countries. This policy has been counterproductive for the state-owned enterprises, since farmers have bypassed large public processing companies, creating excess capacity and financial difficulties.

Trade policies vary widely among traditional groundnut exporters in Africa. Malawi and Senegal apply high tariffs on processed groundnuts to encourage domestic processing or oil production (table 12.11). In contrast, The Gambia and Nigeria have liberal trade policies, with no tariffs or export taxes. South Africa's tariff structure exhibits a slight escalation, with processed groundnuts subject to a tariff of 6 percent while unprocessed groundnuts enter duty free. In The Gambia and Senegal unofficial cross-border trade is significant, with farmers frequently crossing the border depending mainly on producer prices and domestic supply levels in the two countries. Groundnut oil imports face a 20 percent tariff in Malawi, Senegal, and South Africa.

African countries are facing difficulties meeting EU standards on aflatoxin and stricter product and quality standards. In The Gambia and Senegal groundnut varieties were originally selected for oil production, which can accommodate lower-quality seeds, and raw groundnuts. A seed variety in Malawi proved successful in producing better yields, but it lacked commercially viable characteristics. Groundnuts exported from most African countries are sold at a discount relative to the high-quality groundnuts sold in the European Union.

African producers may be able to shift out of groundnut oil and upgrade the quality of their edible groundnuts. Unlike demand for groundnut oil and meal, demand for confectionery groundnut (the higher-quality edible groundnut) has been rising and is expected to continue to increase in the medium term. Confectionery groundnuts receive a price premium of as much as 100 percent over grades used for oil and meal. In Senegal 1 ton of first-grade confectionery groundnuts sells for $800–$900, equivalent to the price of groundnut oil. It takes three tons of unshelled groundnuts to produce 1 ton of oil. However, fob (free on board) prices of Gambian groundnuts are about $300 for crushing, $450 for birdfeed, and $600 for edible

TABLE 12.11 **Tariffs on Groundnut Products in The Gambia, Malawi, Nigeria, Senegal, and South Africa**
(percent)

Country Product	Tariff 1999–2002
Gambia, The	
Edible groundnuts	0
Groundnut meal	0
Groundnut oil (refined)	0
Malawi	
Raw edible groundnuts	5
Processed edible groundnuts	25
Groundnut meal	0
Groundnut oil (refined)	20
Nigeria	
Edible groundnuts	0
Groundnut meal	0
Groundnut oil (refined)	0
Senegal	
Raw edible groundnuts	5
Processed edible groundnuts	20
Groundnut meal	0
Groundnut oil (refined)	20
South Africa	
Raw edible groundnuts	0
Processed edible groundnuts	6
Groundnut meal	0
Groundnut oil (refined)	20

Note: Raw edible groundnuts are raw, not roasted or cooked, in-shell or shelled groundnuts. Processed groundnuts are bleached, preserved, or otherwise prepared groundnuts, including roasted and salted groundnuts and groundnut butter.
Source: World Trade Organization database.

groundnuts. Were The Gambia able to upgrade 50 percent of its 10,000 tons of exports from crushing to edible groundnuts, it would increase its revenues by $1.5 million.

Groundnut Trade Policies of High-Income Importers

Despite a general pattern of tariff escalation, trade barriers are not a major obstacle to high-income groundnut importers: the European Union and Canada have a zero tariff for unprocessed groundnuts and low tariffs for processed groundnut for

TABLE 12.12   Average Tariffs on Edible Unprocessed and Processed Groundnuts
(percent)

Importer	Most-Favored-Nation Tariffs		Generalized System of Preferences Tariffs		Low-Income Developing-Countries Tariffs	
	Unprocessed	Processed	Unprocessed	Processed	Unprocessed	Processed
Canada	0	4	0	4	0	3.2
European Union	0	13	0	9	0	0
Japan	3.7	19	3.7	19	3.7	15
Korea, Rep. of	243	65	243	65	243	65

Source: WTO.

generalized system of preferences (GSP) and low-income developing countries (table 12.12). Assessment of market access in these countries must, however, take into account the strict quality standards.

In contrast to the European Union and Canada, Japan and the Republic of Korea have high tariff regimes for groundnuts. Japan applies a high tariff on processed groundnuts and offers a very limited preference margin of 4 percent for groundnut exports from low-income developing countries. Korea has very high tariffs on both raw and processed groundnuts, with tariffs on raw groundnuts of more than 200 percent. This high tariff may reflect the government's desire to stimulate production, which has plummeted since the mid 1980s. In contrast to edible groundnuts, groundnut oils and meal enter all of these high-income countries duty free.

Impact of Groundnut Product Policy Reforms on World Prices, Trade Flows, and Welfare

Several key findings emerge from the quantitative analysis of distortions in groundnut markets. (For a full description of the model, see Beghin and others 2003.) The main results obtained under the most plausible assumptions underlying the model are presented first, followed by sensitivity analysis testing the effects of U.S. policy and uncertainty about protection by China (VAT and protection of processed groundnuts).

Policy Reform Scenarios

Several scenarios are analyzed:

- Full multilateral trade liberalization for groundnuts, meal, and oil, with and without elimina-

tion of the U.S. peanut program (FMTL&US and FMTL)
- Multilateral trade liberalization of groundnuts, with and without elimination of the U.S. peanut program (GMTL&US and GMTL)
- Full trade liberalization in the two largest and most distorted groundnut markets, China and India (CIFTL)

Summary results of these five scenarios are presented in tables 12.13 and 12.14. Detailed results for each scenario are presented in the longer report on the CD-ROM.

Analysis Results

In countries with high groundnut protection, the combined effect of the world price increase and elimination of their own protection is beneficial to final users of groundnuts, other things being equal. For countries with moderate or no protection before reform, tariff elimination and changes in the terms of trade result in an increase in domestic groundnut prices, handicapping groundnut users (consumers and crushers). A similar logic holds for groundnut oil and meal, for which the combined effect of world price increases and the elimination of tariffs has to be assessed. These substantial terms-of-trade effects have a significant impact on trade and welfare. Allocative efficiency gains in domestic markets can be offset by large price increases originating in postreform world markets.

In countries with high protection of groundnut oil or meal (such as India), tariff elimination, net of the world price hike, induces lower domestic prices and reduces margins on crushed groundnuts. As a result, the domestic excess supply of groundnuts

TABLE 12.13   Welfare Effects of Policy Scenarios, 1999–2001 Average
(millions of 1995 US$)

Country	FMTL&US	FMTL	GMTL&US	GMTL	CIFTL
Argentina	16.07	15.94	9.97	9.84	12.66
EU-15	−51.83	−51.27	−34.40	−33.82	−58.87
China	666.25	668.76	650.65	653.33	716.25
India	213.27	214.11	196.57	197.79	228.59
Rest of the world	−126.69	−127.06	−4.21	−4.86	−71.06
Canada	−5.94	−5.87	−4.88	−4.81	−4.59
Mexico	−7.43	−7.34	−6.11	−6.01	−5.73
Senegal	41.03	40.96	21.93	21.86	21.39
Nigeria	15.93	15.77	7.22	7.07	13.45
South Africa	2.30	2.28	2.19	2.17	0.53
Malawi	7.45	7.45	7.60	7.61	−1.06
The Gambia	0.43	0.42	0.24	0.24	0.36
USA	20.18	16.70	21.71	18.40	12.39
Africa-5 total[1]	67.14	66.89	39.18	38.95	34.67
Total	791.01	790.87	868.48	868.79	864.32

1. Denotes the aggregate of Senegal, Nigeria, South Africa, Malawi, and the Gambia.
Source: USDA.

crushed into oil and meal decreases, increasing imports. In contrast, countries with moderate or no protection in their oil and meal markets face a net price increase for oil and meal after full trade liberalization. Their final consumption of these value-added products decreases, and crushing increases, as the crush margin improves. Their excess supply of these products increase, and they increase exports.

The two full trade liberalization scenarios with and without the elimination of the U.S. farm policy (FMTL&US and FMTL) induce strong price increases for all three products: 10 percent for groundnuts, 18 percent for groundnut meal, and 27 percent for groundnut oil (see table 12.13). The welfare impact of the FMTL&US and FMTL reforms is influenced by the change in the groundnut oil price, which affects the crush margin. Crush margins narrow in the European Union and India, decreasing supply, but they may increase in China, The Gambia, Nigeria, Senegal, South Africa, and the United States.

Trade patterns change dramatically. China expands its exports of the three products. The large increase in the price of groundnut oil improves the crush margin, stimulating crushing in China. Higher prices for groundnut oil in world markets translate into larger exports. In India the lower

crush margin reduces groundnut oil production and meal production; lower consumer prices for all groundnut products stimulate groundnut oil production and increase demand and eventually imports. African producers expand their exports of value-added products. Malawi and Senegal decrease their exports of groundnuts because of increased domestic use, while India experiences a trade reversal, becoming a large importer of groundnut oil and meal. Aggregate trade in groundnuts increases 16 percent, and trade in value-added products more than doubles.

The aggregate net welfare effects of FMTL&US and FMTL amount to about $791 million at 1995 prices in each scenario (see table 12.14). China and India experience the largest welfare gains—not surprisingly, since they have the two largest and most distorted groundnut product markets. China's welfare gains are about $666 million, India's are about $213 million. The "moderate" magnitude of global welfare gains first comes from offsets—some countries gain in aggregate whereas some others, chiefly the European Union-15, lose. For many countries other than China and India, individual net gains and losses are moderate, mostly because of the small size of the groundnut markets and their price-inelastic nature, which produces large transfers but small deadweight losses. Indeed,

TABLE 12.14 Impact of Different Liberalization Scenarios on Groundnut Trade and Prices
(percent)

	FMTL&US	FMTL	GMTL&US	GMTL	CIFTL
		(percent except welfare)			
		for 3 years	for 3 years	for 3 years	
Peanuts Trade *(1,000 metric tons)*					
Net Exporters					
Argentina	7	6	22	22	−6
China	36	34	42	41	13
Gambia, The	11	11	31	30	3
India	−62	−64	−556	−557	−94
Malawi	−80	−82	−93	−95	84
Nigeria	3667	3564	7470	7358	1776
Senegal	−287	−298	−8	−20	−708
South Africa	22	22	20	20	14
United States	8	15	48	55	2
Total net exports	16	16	−17	−16	−4
Net Importers					
Canada	−5	−5	−4	−4	−4
European Union	−3	−3	−3	−3	−2
Mexico	−8	−8	−7	−7	−6
Rest of the world	63	65	−47	−45	−7
Residual	0	0	0	0	0
Total net imports	16	16	−17	−16	−4
Peanuts Price US Run.	10	10	8	8	8
40/50 cif Rotterdam $ per mt					
Peanut Meal Trade *(1,000 metric tons)*					
Net Exporters					
Argentina	13	13	−6	−6	18
China	741	739	−144	−146	759
Gambia, The	22	21	−2	−2	22
India	−1702	−1703	344	342	−1690
Malawi	9	8	1	1	46
Nigeria	2867	2862	−193	−196	2867
Senegal	5	5	−1	−1	14
South Africa	95	95	−7	−7	139
United States	484	487	−380	−376	563
Rest of World	499	499	−70	−69	385
Total Net Exports	−9	−9	0	0.4	−9
Net Importers					
European Union	−12	−12	1	1	−13
Residual	0	0	0	0	0
Total net imports	−9	−9	0	0	−9
Meal Price 48/50 cif	18	18	0	0	18
Rotterdam $ per mt					
Peanut Oil Trade *(1,000 metric tons)*					
Net exporters					
Argentina	11	11	−6	−6	16

TABLE 12.14 (Continued)

	FMTL&US	FMTL	GMTL&US	GMTL	CIFTL
		(percent except welfare)			
		for 3 years	for 3 years	for 3 years	
China	3469	3459	−705	−713	3354
Gambia, The	589	587	−5	−6	567
India	−24288	−24304	4591	4558	−24481
Malawi	43	43	0	0	185
Nigeria	123	123	−6	−6	120
Senegal	5	5	−1	−1	19
South Africa	49	49	−4	−4	224
United States	288	290	−194	−192	326
Rest of world	861	864	−103	−99	665
Total net exports	−6	−6	0	0	−8
Net importers					
European Union	−9	−9	0	0	−12
Residual	0	0	0	0	0
Total net imports	−6	−6	0	0	−8
Peanut Oil Price cif Rotterdam $ per mt	27	27	0	0	26
welfare(million dollars)	791	791	868	869	864
Argentina	16.07	15.94	9.97	9.84	12.66
EU-15	−51.83	−51.27	−34.40	−33.82	−58.87
China	666.25	668.76	650.65	653.33	716.25
India	213.27	214.11	196.57	197.79	228.59
Rest of world	−126.69	−127.06	−4.21	−4.86	−71.06
Canada	−5.94	−5.87	−4.88	−4.81	−4.59
Mexico	−7.43	−7.34	−6.11	−6.01	−5.73
Senegal	41.03	40.96	21.93	21.86	21.39
Nigeria	15.93	15.77	7.22	7.07	13.45
South Africa	2.30	2.28	2.19	2.17	0.53
Malawi	7.45	7.45	7.60	7.61	−1.06
Gambia, The	0.43	0.42	0.24	0.24	0.36
United States	20.18	16.70	21.71	18.40	12.39
Africa-5 total[a]	67.14	66.89	39.18	38.95	34.67
Total	**791.01**	**790.87**	**868.48**	**868.79**	**864.32**

Note: Table totals are average changes for three years totaled in each column. Results are percentage changes from the baseline. Baseline and simulations were run for three years (1999–2001) and averaged.

a. Totals are three-year averages.

Source: computed by the authors

a. Denotes the aggregate of Senegal, Nigeria, South Africa, Malawi, and The Gambia.

substantial offsetting transfers occur between consumers, crushers, and producers.

Price effects induced by the reforms have a similar impact large welfare transfer (rectangles) and small net welfare effects (triangles), even in countries with undistorted markets. In Nigeria, for example, following full multilateral trade liberalization without elimination of the U.S. peanut pro-

gram, groundnut producers gain $34 million in quasi-rents, consumers experience welfare losses of $65 million (because of higher oil and processed groundnut prices), crushers gain $51 million, and meal users (feed users) lose about $3 million. In aggregate the country is better off by $16 million.

Under multilateral trade liberalization for all three products, elimination of the U.S. program affects trade flows, terms of trade, and welfare. The strong price effects of trade liberalization invalidate the price floor established by the U.S. loan rate. The only remaining production-distorting element is the fixed payment (fully coupled to production in the model), which is small. Results under both scenarios (full trade liberalization with and without elimination of the U.S. peanut program) are qualitatively identical, except for the United States, which experiences additional welfare gains of $3.5 million (gains to U.S. taxpayers net of losses by U.S. producers) by eliminating its domestic distortions.

The world price impacts of the FMTL scenario are identical to those of FMTL&US (a 10 percent increase for groundnuts, an 18 percent increase for meal, and a 27 percent increase for groundnut oil). Trade flows are barely affected by the elimination of the U.S. domestic program under free trade. U.S. groundnut exports are about 15,000 metric tons lower in the FMTL&US scenario than in the FMTL scenario. Given that the parameterization of U.S. farm policy assumes full coupling to production for payments received by producers, the assessment provides an upper bound on the effect of the current U.S. peanut program.[11]

Many agricultural negotiations during the Doha Round of the WTO revolve around narrow issues of substantial importance to developing countries. Hence it is useful to assess what a narrow agricultural liberalization encompassing the value-added products of groundnut oil and meal would achieve relative to full trade liberalization.

The GMTL&US and GMTL scenarios consider these reforms and their impacts. Much is achieved by groundnut trade liberalization alone, but with a large second-best component, since distortions are present in the value-added markets. In these groundnut liberalization scenarios, the prices of meal and oil are little affected, and crush margins are driven primarily by changes in groundnut prices. Margins improve in India but deteriorate in countries with limited groundnut distortions.

Consumer welfare implications are also different in these trade scenarios. In highly protected groundnut oil markets, prices are higher under the groundnut trade (GMTL) scenarios than they are under all-product trade liberalization (FMTL scenarios). In countries with no oil distortions, prices remain roughly at their baseline level, and consumers do better under the groundnut trade liberalization than under the full liberalization

scenarios. The rest of the world fares much better under the groundnut trade liberalization scenarios than under the full liberalization scenarios. In contrast, African economies do much better under the full liberalization scenarios than with groundnut trade liberalization reforms. The potential welfare gains for Africa-5 (The Gambia, Malawi, Nigeria, Senegal, and South Africa) nearly double by moving from groundnut trade liberalization to full liberalization scenarios.

If China and India liberalized alone (the CIFTL scenario), the qualitative results of the full liberalization scenarios hold. What is striking in this last scenario is the importance of India's—and to a lesser extent China's—distortions and market size on welfare, trade, and price effects. As suggested by table 12.13, FMTL really hinges on the elimination of distortions in India and China. With liberalization in India and China, world prices would rise 8 percent for groundnuts, 18 percent for meal, and 26 percent for oil. The major welfare differences occur in the rest of the world, where consumers are worse off than they would be under the multilateral groundnut trade liberalization scenario, since groundnut oil prices are higher. Africa-5 improves its lot in aggregate but by less than it would under the full liberalization scenario, since groundnut prices are lower and distortions within Africa-5 remain in place.

Two key assumptions in the model—the prevailing groundnut market price in the U.S. market and the level of protection of the groundnut market in China—were investigated. The model was calibrated on 2002–03 U.S. prices ($389 per metric ton) to see if the new U.S. policy under the 2002 Farm Bill would have had a stronger impact on the world market under lower prevailing prices (farm prices in the United States were 25 percent lower in 2002–03 than in 2001–02). The loan rate, countercyclical payments, and fixed payments were eliminated (countercyclical payments and fixed payments are assumed to be fully coupled to provide an upper bound on the effect of the U.S. program), while all distortions in all other countries were retained. The price floor provided by the loan rate is effective under the lower 2002–03 farm price.

U.S. output decreases 7 percent under the new prices, and U.S. exports decrease 52 percent, inducing a 0.9 percent increase in the world price of groundnuts and negligible price impacts in the other markets. The aggregate net welfare effect is negligible and negative. Higher world prices exacerbate distortions in other markets or increase import costs in net importing countries. The United States gains about $22 million (program cost savings net of producer loss).

The same change was also tested with all other distortions removed in all countries (FMTL&US scenario). In this scenario the world price of groundnuts was 0.5 percent higher than under free trade plus the 2002 U.S. Farm Bill. The results suggest that removing the 2002 Farm Bill incentives in a free trade world would decrease U.S. production about 4 percent and exports about 31 percent. The aggregate welfare gains vary by less than $1 million. Hence the conclusion that the new U.S. groundnut policy is more benign than its predecessor remains unaltered under much lower prices.

The sensitivity analysis on China's protection structure is more pivotal to the conclusions reached, especially the protection of the groundnut sector. Protection of groundnut producers is now assumed to be 15 percent (the tariff is redundant in the original model). Without assistance the Chinese farm sector is no longer assumed to be a net exporter. Under this new assumption and following full trade liberalization (FMTL&US), China becomes a net importer of groundnuts, because demand for edible and crushed groundnuts increases. China's welfare gains are $1,029 million; aggregate welfare gains are $1,160 million. World prices increase 18 percent for groundnuts, 19 percent for meal, and 29 percent for oil.

A second sensitivity analysis examines the effect of providing baseline protection of processed groundnuts with a 15 percent ad valorem tariff (the original tariff was 30 percent and the VAT was 17 percent). Under this assumption welfare gains from FMTL are only $266 million in China, and aggregate gains are just $388 million. The world price of groundnuts increases 9 percent in this modified scenario, down from 10 percent under the original run. The major change in welfare occurs in China, because Chinese consumers gain much less from trade liberalization relative to the initial situation.

Conclusions and Policy Implications

The groundnut market has historically been distorted by heavy government intervention in both industrial and developing countries. In the United

States the 2002 Farm Bill eliminated some unsustainable features of earlier policies, but it introduced new distortions that have some limited potential to depress world market prices and subsidize U.S. groundnut exports. India and China have succeeded in stimulating production and exports, capturing a growing share of the international market. In India these gains have been artificial, because the groundnut industry relies on heavy protection. In contrast, in Sub-Saharan Africa and Argentina, government intervention has hurt the sector.

Unlike U.S. policy for cotton, dairy, rice, and sugar, the current U.S. domestic peanut program is now largely a domestic support program with some distortive impact. The scenario analysis suggests that developing countries would gain little by trying to negotiate further U.S. groundnut policy reform, as these changes would prove ineffective unless groundnut prices fell to very low levels. Only then would the countercyclical U.S. policy further destabilize world prices, sending the wrong market signal to U.S. producers. Under prevailing market conditions, U.S. producers would actually benefit from multilateral trade liberalization in groundnut product markets. Hence it would be rational for the United States to support foreign groundnut producers in their attempt to liberalize. As a bloc most OECD (Organisation for Economic Cooperation and Development) countries would experience welfare losses after trade liberalization, with moderate gains in the United States offset by losses in Canada, Mexico, and the European Union-15. Mexico, Canada, and the European Union-15 would lose from trade liberalization because there are few distortions in these markets, so consumers would be penalized by price increases for groundnut products.

Elimination of trade distortions by the two largest developing economies, India and China, is essential. The size of their markets—and the huge distortions in India—substantially depress world prices of the three globally traded groundnut products. Following elimination of these distortions, net buyers of these products would be worse off, but most Sub-Saharan African countries that export groundnuts would gain.

Full trade liberalization would increase world market prices about 10 percent for groundnuts, 18 percent for groundnut meal, and 27 percent for groundnut oil. Trade in groundnuts would increase 16 percent, and trade in oil and meal would more than double.

Although the net world welfare effects of liberalizing markets in the United States, China, and India are moderate, they remain significant for small agrarian economies in Sub-Saharan Africa. Liberalization would thus produce welfare gains in the countries in which they are most needed.

The simulations show that liberalization of the value-added markets is essential to achieve larger welfare gains in African countries. Although the bulk of the world welfare gains occur with groundnut trade liberalization, elimination of distortions in value-added markets doubles net welfare gains in Africa by yielding larger profits to producers and exporters of groundnuts and groundnut oil. African countries modeled in the trade liberalization analysis would experience aggregate welfare gains of $67 million, with Senegal and Nigeria reaping most of these gains. Groundnut and groundnut oil consumers in Africa tend to be urban, whereas groundnut production generates income in rural areas as a cash crop. African groundnut producers modeled in the analysis gain $50 million–$150 million of farm income, depending on the assumptions underlying the model. These figures are significant for small African economies and represent an important opportunity to expand rural development in these areas. In the scenarios tested, the rest of the world would fare worse under full trade liberalization, because consumers are required to pay higher groundnut product prices. Groundnuts are not without substitutes, however, and the price increase may induce increases in demand for other oils.

Recent changes present both challenges and opportunities for major countries in the market. The United States is likely to continue to dominate the high end of the international confectionery market under its new peanut program. Argentina and China have established strong groundnut sectors that can compete favorably under free market conditions. Chinese exports played a stabilizing role in world markets in the 1990s.

All developing countries except Argentina face the challenge of meeting the quality requirements of the expanding confectionery markets. This is particularly so for African countries, which are missing out on the opportunities and rewards created by the expansion of the edible groundnut exports market because of inadequate quality.

Notes

1. Groundnuts are also known as peanuts, earthnuts, goobers, pinders, and Manila nuts. The groundnut plant is a hairy, tap-rooted, annual legume that measures 1–1.5 feet in height.

2. Groundnut oil is an excellent cooking oil, with a high smoke point and neutral flavor and odor. Groundnut meal is used as animal feed.

3. Any grower in the group is eligible to farm a certain number of acres of land. Farmers who use the land are obligated, however, to pay agricultural tax in kind and sell a certain amount of their products to the state government at regulated prices.

4. Export markets reflect relatively high-quality premiums and discounts. Prices of U.S. groundnuts set a ceiling for international prices, because the quality is high. Edible U.S. groundnuts commanded a 40 percent premium on world markets over shelled Chinese groundnuts in 2000 (FAO 2002).

5. In 1998 the EU harmonized country regulations on the maximum permissible level of aflatoxin, setting levels at the lowest possible level (0.002 milligrams for B1 type aflatoxin for edible groundnuts). Aflatoxin is a cancer-causing chemical produced by species of aspergillus molds that can contaminate groundnuts. The spores of these molds, present anywhere in the air and the soil, require specific temperature, moisture, and nutrient substrates to germinate. Aflatoxin contamination of groundnuts can occur during cultivation in the field, as well as during harvesting, postharvesting, storage, or processing. While aflatoxin disappears with crushing, it remains in edible groundnuts and groundnut meal. Technical processes exist to reduce aflatoxin contamination (with ammoniac, for example, which Senegal uses on groundnut meal), but the best method is to improve farm practices through use of best-quality and resistant seeds, proper management of farms, and appropriate storage to avoid exposure to high temperature and humidity. See chapter 6 in this volume for a discussion of food safety and agricultural health standards.

6. The levels of quota and tariff for the period after 2003 are currently under negotiation.

7. According to the FAO (Food and Agriculture Organization), these policies provide little incentive to expand production due to unattractive administrative price levels and greater involvement of the private sector in marketing operations. Data on the magnitude of domestic support are not available.

8. The international price of groundnut oil in Hong Kong (China) was $728 a ton in 1998, and the wholesale price in China was 67.8 percent higher (Fang and Beghin 2002).

9. This regulation imposes a significant burden on farmers and processors. Even if they are located very close to one another, they have to travel to the wholesale market and pay an "agent commission" and other marketing fees before the transaction is processed.

10. Taxation of producers was direct (that is, marketing boards or similar agencies captured the rent, equal to the difference between the net world price and the producer price) or indirect (through appreciation of the real exchange rate). This taxation was generally mitigated by input subsidies and border protection.

11. Eliminating U.S. distortions under existing trade distortions produces a 0.13 percent increase in the world price of

groundnuts and virtually no increase in world cake and oil prices. U.S. groundnut exports decrease by 10 percent, or about 20,000 metric tons a year. Thus in contrast to the effect of U.S. subsidies on rice, cotton, and sugar, the impact of the current U.S. farm program on the world price of and trade in groundnuts is negligible.

References

Akobundu E. 1998. *Farm-Household Analysis of Policies Affecting Groundnut Production in Senegal.* MS Thesis, Virginia Polytechnic and State University.

Badiane, O., and Kinteh, S. 1994. "Trade Pessimism and Regionalism in African Countries: The Case of Groundnut Exporters." IFPRI Research Report 97. International Food Policy Research Institute, Washington, D.C.

Beghin, J., N. Diop, H. Matthey, and M. Sewadeh. 2003. "The Impact of Groundnut Trade Liberalization: Implication for the Doha Round." Presented at the 2003 American Agricultural Economics Association Annual Meeting, July 27–30, Montreal.

Chen, Changping, Stanley M. Fletcher, Ping Zhang, and Dale H. Carley. 1997. "Competitiveness in Peanuts: United States versus China." *Research Bulletin* 430. University of Georgia, Georgia Agricultural Experiment Station.

Colby, W. H., F. W. Crook, and S. Webb. 1992. *Agricultural Statistics of the People's Republic of China, 1949–1990.* SB-844, United States Department of Agriculture, Economic Research Service, December.

Diop, N., J. Beghin, and M. Sewadeh. 2004. "Groundnut Policies, Global Trade Dynamics and the Impact of Trade Liberalization," World Bank Policy Research Working Paper 322. Washington, D.C.

Gulati, A., G. Pursell, and K. Mullen. 2003. "Indian Agriculture since the Reforms: Performance, Policy Environment, and Incentives." World Bank, Washington, D.C.

Fang C., and J. Beghin. 2002. "Urban Demand for Edible Oils and Fats in China: Evidence from Household Survey Data." *Journal of Comparative Economics* 30(4): 732–53.

FAO (Food and Agriculture Organization of the United Nations) 2002. *FAO Yearbook. Trade.* Rome.

Fletcher, S. M. 2001. "Peanuts: Responding to Opportunities and Challenges from an Intertwined Trade and Domestic Policies." University of Georgia, National Center for Peanut Competitiveness, Griffin, Ga.

Fletcher, S. M., and C. L. Revoredo. 2003. "Does the United States Need the Groundnut Tariff Rate Quota Under the 2002 U.S. Farm Act?" Paper presented at the International Conference on Agricultural Policy and the WTO: Where Are We Heading, June 23–26, Capri, Italy.

Hart, C. and B. Babcock. 2002. "U.S. Farm Policy and the WTO: How Do They Match Up?" *The Estey Centre Journal of International Law and Trade Policy* 3:119–39.

Pursell, G. 2003. Private e-mail correspondence on India's groundnut protection, September.

Revoredo, C. L., and S. Fletcher. 2002a. "The U.S. 2002 Farm Act and the Effects on U.S. Groundnut Exports." University of Georgia, Griffin, Ga.

———. 2002b. "World Peanut Market: An Overview of the Last 30 Years." University of Georgia, Griffin, Ga.

Skinner, R. 1999. "Issues Facing the United States: Peanut Industry during the Seattle Round of the World Trade Organization." U.S. Department of Agriculture, Economic Research Service, Washington, D.C.

USDA FAS (U.S. Department of Agriculture, Foreign Agriculture Service). GAIN Reports, various years a. "China, People's Republic of. Oilseeds and Products. Oilseeds Update." Washington, D.C.

———. Various years b. "China, People's Republic of. Oilseeds and Products. Annual." Washington, D.C.

Wescott, P. C., C. E. Young, and J. M. Price. 2002. "The 2002 Farm Act Provisions and Implications for Commodity Markets." Agriculture Information Bulletin Number 778. U.S. Department of Agriculture, Economic Research Service, Washington, D.C.

13

FRUITS AND VEGETABLES: GLOBAL TRADE AND COMPETITION IN FRESH AND PROCESSED PRODUCT MARKETS

Ndiame Diop and Steven M. Jaffee

Trade in fruit and vegetable products has been among the most dynamic areas of international agricultural trade, stimulated by rising incomes and growing consumer interest in product variety, freshness, convenience, and year-round availability. Advances in production, postharvest handling, processing, and logistical technologies—along with increased levels of international investment—have played a facilitating role. For developing countries, trade in these products has been attractive in the face of highly volatile or declining long-term trends in the prices for many traditional export products. Although many developing-country suppliers have entered the field, relatively few have achieved significant, sustained success, reflecting the fact that the industry is highly competitive and rapidly changing.

Still, the aggregate picture is favorable. Fresh and processed fruit and vegetable products accounted for 16.7 percent of total agricultural exports from developing countries in 1980–81. By 2000–01, this share had increased to 21.8 percent. Only for one other product category—fish and fisheries products—are developing countries more significant exporters (see chapter 1). Fruit and vegetable exports from developing countries are now more than double exports for tropical beverages, three times exports of grains, three times exports of livestock products, five times

exports of sugar, and seven times exports of textile fibers.

This chapter highlights major global, regional, and product-specific trends in the trade in fruit and vegetable products, and examines the major policy and other factors that have affected this trade over the past two decades.[1] Particular attention is given to the performance and position of developing countries in this trade and the policies, institutions, and infrastructure they need to succeed.

Fruit and Vegetable Production and Trade Growth

For the purpose of this study, we group fruits and vegetables in four main categories: fresh fruits, fresh vegetables, processed fruits, and processed vegetables. These categories comprise all SITC (Standard International Trade Classification) Revision 1, Chapter 5 items except nuts, roots, and tubers. They correspond to most products in Chapter 7 (edible vegetables and certain roots and tubers), Chapter 8 (edible fruits and nuts; peel of citrus fruits or melons) and Chapter 20 (preparations of vegetables, fruit, nuts, or other parts of plants) of the Harmonized System (HS) nomenclature.

Trends in World Production and Trade

World production of fruit and vegetables grew by 30 percent between 1980 and 1990 and by 56 percent between 1990 and 2003, reaching 1,274 million tons by 2003. Much of this growth occurred in China, where production grew by 134 percent in the 1980s and by 200 percent in the 1990s. China is currently the world's largest producer of fruits and vegetables, with a share of 34 percent, followed by Latin America and the Caribbean (11 percent), India (10 percent), and Africa and the European Union (EU) (both at 9 percent) (figure 13.1).

The structure of world trade in fruits and vegetables does not fully mirror that of production. Many of the largest producers are not significant traders due to a combination of domestic demand and geographical and logistical factors. For example, in China and India, where strong domestic demand is fueled by growing income and a large and rapidly growing urban population, only a small percentage of fruit and vegetable production is exported. In contrast, Latin American countries (such as Mexico, Chile, and Costa Rica) are among the world's leading exporters of fruits and vegetables, mainly because of their proximity to the large U.S. market.

World trade in fruits and vegetables, fresh and processed, has increased by 30 percent since 1990, reaching $71.6 billion in 2001 (table 13.1). This followed even more robust growth in the 1980s, when trade in fruits and vegetables doubled. World trade in all categories of fruits and vegetables has grown strongly, with only slight changes in its broad composition. In 2001 fresh produce accounted for 63 percent of the total, whereas processed products accounted for 37 percent. The complexity of these definitions must be kept in mind, however. Both in Europe and the United States, one of the fastest-growing product segments is semi-prepared and packed fresh produce, including preassembled salads, vegetable dips, and sliced or mixed fruit products.

Taking all fruit and vegetable products combined, the value of world imports grew at 2–3 percent a year during the 1990s, a sharp deceleration from the 7–8 percent annual growth during the previous decade (figures 13.2–13.5). As elaborated below, the slower growth in world imports during the 1990s reflects two primary factors: a decline in world prices for many important fruit and vegetable products in the latter half of the 1990s, and stagnation in EU import demand due to market saturation.

Within the fresh fruit category, the deceleration has been sharpest for apples, grapes, and citrus (figure 13.2). Comparatively more dynamic trade has remained for various tropical fruits (especially papaya, mango, and pineapple), with average annual growth in the 1990s remaining at 8 percent.

FIGURE 13.1   Production of Fruit and Vegetables by Region
(million of tons)

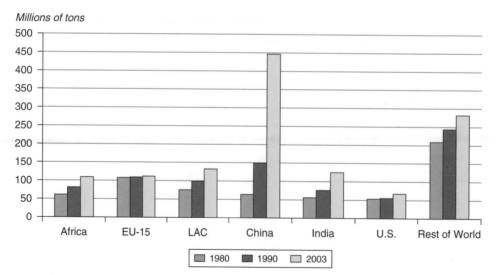

Source: United Nations Food and Agriculture Organization.

TABLE 13.1   World Fruit and Vegetable Imports, 1980–2001
(US$ millions)

Category	1980–81	Percent Share in Total	1990–91	Percent Share in Total	2000–01	Percent Share in Total
Fresh fruits	10,971	40	20,981	38	27,978	39
Processed fruits	4,441	16	9,916	18	13,176	18
Fresh vegetables	6,805	25	13,315	24	16,914	24
Processed vegetables	5,424	20	10,883	20	13,577	19
Total	27,641	100	55,094	100	71,644	100

Source: COMTRADE.

FIGURE 13.2   Annual Growth Rates of World Imports of Selected Fruits
(Value)

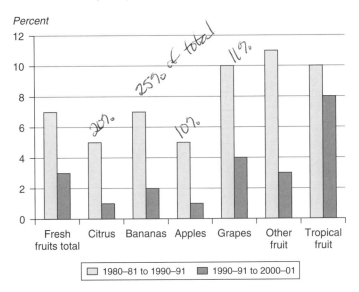

Source: COMTRADE.

Still, these latter products represent a relatively small proportion of world fresh fruit trade (7 percent in 2001), which is still heavily concentrated in particular lines, including bananas (25 percent of the total), citrus fruit (20 percent), grapes (11 percent), and apples (10 percent). A large number of other fresh fruits, not separated in the statistics, collectively represent 28 percent of world fresh fruit imports. Prominent items in this category include melons, various types of berries, and other temperate fruits.

World import values for fresh vegetables grew at 6.9 percent a year during the 1980s, yet decelerated to 2.4 percent a year in the 1990s (figure 13.3). The deceleration affected most individual commodities. World vegetable trade is fragmented among a large number of individual items. The largest single item

is tomatoes, which account for 17 percent of the total. The category of beans, peas, and lentils accounts for another 14 percent. Other relatively major commodities in the fresh vegetable trade include onions, potatoes, asparagus, mushrooms, and various types of sweet and pungent peppers.

The evolution of trade in processed fruit and vegetable products mirrors that for fresh produce. The annual growth rate in trade value was 8.3 percent a year during the 1980s, yet only 3 percent during the 1990s (figure 13.4). All categories of processed products saw a deceleration in trade expansion, although fruit and vegetable juices and preserved fruits and jams fell most sharply. Processed vegetables (such as canned mushrooms, dried mushrooms, and tomato paste) account for 55 percent of world trade in all these products, fruit

FIGURE 13.3   Annual World Import Growth Rates of Selected Vegetables

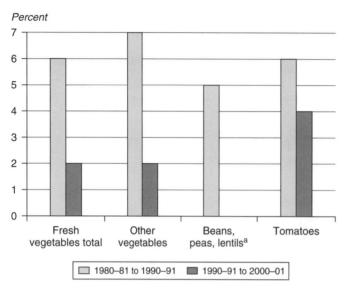

a. The corresponding value for 1990–91 to 2000–01 has the value of 0%.
Source: COMTRADE.

FIGURE 13.4   Annual Growth Rates of World Import of Major Processed Fruits and Vegetables

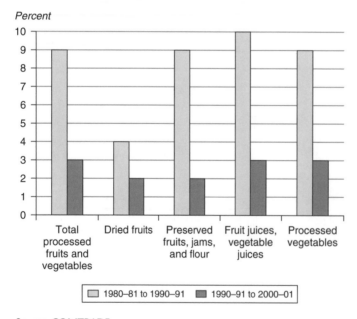

Source: COMTRADE.

and vegetable juices for some 20 percent, and several smaller categories for the balance.

Price played a role in the observed trends. The unit values of fresh fruit and of fresh and prepared vegetables dropped sharply in the second half of the 1990s after an extended period of increase dating from the early 1980s (figure 13.5). These trends suggest that price factors played a very significant role in the declining rate of growth in the value of

fruit and vegetable imports during the 1990s. Indeed, for each of the most important traded fresh fruits and vegetables, the rate of import volume growth was modestly higher in the 1990s than in the 1980s (table 13.2).

Part of the decline in world prices is a statistical matter. The data above are recorded in U.S. dollars. During the latter half of the 1990s, the U.S. dollar appreciated vis-à-vis the yen and most European

FIGURE 13.5   World Unit Values for Fresh Fruits, Fresh Vegetables, and Prepared Vegetables
(US$ per metric ton)

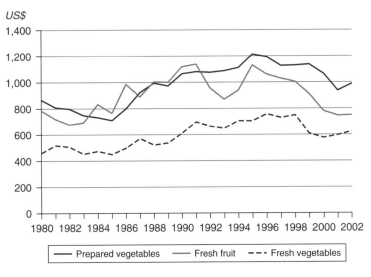

Source: FAOSTAT.

TABLE 13.2   Average Annual Growth Rates in World Import Volumes, 1980–2001

Commodity	1980–1991	1990–2001
Bananas	3.45	3.96
Oranges	1.11	1.68
Apples	1.42	2.33
Grapes	4.31	4.34
Tomatoes	3.11	4.45
Onions	3.50	4.17
Green beans	4.59	5.98

Source: FAOSTAT.

currencies, deflating Japanese and European import values upon conversion into U.S. dollars. For some commodities, however, the unit import values into Japan, Europe, and elsewhere actually did decline in local currency terms—in some cases substantially. For example, from 1996 to 2001, the average unit value of Japanese fresh vegetable imports fell by 25 percent, while that of processed vegetable imports fell by 8 percent.[2] A major factor in this decline was the rapidly expanding supply of low-cost production in China. During the 1990s China accounted for virtually all of the incremental expansion in Japan's vegetable trade, taking market share from other suppliers. Declining unit import values for various products in Europe can be attributed to at least three factors: the slow economic growth in the region (especially in Germany, the

leading importer); competitive and structural changes in fruit and vegetable distribution systems, which put downward pressures on trader and manufacturer margins; and greater availability of product and intensified international competition.

Sources and Destinations of Exported Fruits and Vegetables

The European Union, NAFTA (North American Free Trade Agreement), and a few middle-income countries dominate trade in fruits and vegetables (table 13.3). Eight categories of countries are distinguished. China, India, Japan, and the European Union are singled out. The United States, Canada, and Mexico are grouped together in the NAFTA category. The developing-country group minus China and India is split between low-income countries and middle-income ones.

Global Trade Patterns

The European Union is the world's largest market and supplier of fresh and processed fruits and vegetables. In 2001 its 15 member countries accounted for $37 billion in imports, or 51 percent of world imports, while exports stood at $28 billion, or 39.5 percent of world exports.[3] EU trade in fruits and vegetables is, however, largely intraregional. Intra-EU imports represent 64 percent of EU imports, while 83 percent of EU export trade occurs among its 15 member states. Still, with its affluent

TABLE 13.3   Import and Export of Fruits and Vegetables by Region or Country
(US$ billions)

Importers	Year	Low-Income	Middle-Income	Exporters European Union	Japan	NAFTA	Other Industrial	China	India	Total Imports
Low-income	1980–81	0.05	0.14	0.09	0.00	0.03	0.01	0.02	0.02	0.37
	1990–91	0.02	0.12	0.05	0.00	0.02	0.05	0.04	0.04	0.34
	2000–01	0.08	0.19	0.10	0.00	0.13	0.09	0.14	0.05	0.78
Middle-income	1980–81	0.10	2.24	0.88	0.18	0.84	0.21	0.39	0.09	4.94
	1990–91	0.14	2.77	0.91	0.10	1.12	0.33	0.79	0.12	6.27
	2000–01	0.44	4.69	2.22	0.05	1.88	0.58	1.04	0.17	11.08
European Union	1980–81	0.42	4.36	8.63	0.02	0.75	1.08	0.24	0.02	15.52
	1990–91	0.75	8.86	20.59	0.01	1.07	1.71	0.50	0.02	33.51
	2000–01	1.08	9.19	23.45	0.01	1.19	1.09	0.55	0.11	36.67
Japan	1980–81	0.02	0.68	0.05	0.00	0.49	0.07	0.13	0.00	1.43
	1990–91	0.01	1.49	0.17	0.00	1.21	0.25	0.56	0.00	3.69
	2000–01	0.04	1.49	0.25	0.00	1.69	0.36	1.93	0.00	5.76
NAFTA	1980–81	0.04	1.64	0.29	0.05	1.97	0.09	0.05	0.00	4.12
	1990–91	0.07	3.94	0.75	0.06	3.59	0.23	0.13	0.01	8.80
	2000–01	0.12	5.20	1.15	0.05	7.10	0.27	0.36	0.10	14.35
Other industrial	1980–81	0.01	0.31	0.61	0.00	0.13	0.11	0.02	0.00	1.20
	1990–91	0.03	0.55	1.16	0.00	0.17	0.21	0.04	0.01	2.17
	2000–01	0.03	0.56	1.10	0.00	0.23	0.21	0.08	0.01	2.22
China	1980–81	0.00	0.01	0.00	0.00	0.00	0.00	0.00	0.00	0.01
	1990–91	0.02	0.03	0.00	0.00	0.00	0.00	0.00	0.00	0.06
	2000–01	0.06	0.32	0.01	0.00	0.12	0.03	0.00	0.01	0.56
India	1980–81	0.02	0.04	0.00	0.00	0.00	0.00	0.00	0.00	0.06
	1990–91	0.08	0.10	0.00	0.00	0.02	0.04	0.00	0.00	0.24
	2000–01	0.10	0.03	0.00	0.00	0.08	0.02	0.00	0.00	0.23
Total exports	1980–81	0.65	9.41	10.55	0.25	4.21	1.58	0.85	0.13	27.64
	1990–91	1.12	17.86	23.62	0.18	7.22	2.83	2.06	0.20	55.09
	2000–01	1.95	21.66	28.29	0.12	12.41	2.65	4.10	0.45	71.64

Source: COMTRADE.

and aging population, its high factor costs, and its cold winters, this region represents one of the largest fruit and vegetable markets for non-EU countries ($13.2 billion), especially for low- and middle-income countries, which exported $1.08 and $9 billion, respectively, to the European Union in 2001. Major middle-income suppliers to the European Union market include banana-exporting countries (mainly Colombia, Costa Rica, Côte d'Ivoire, Ecuador, and Panama[4]) and counterseasonal-supplying countries such as Argentina, Chile, and South Africa. Led by South Africa, the latter three countries dominate exports of apples, grapes, and pears to the European Union.

Intraregional trade is also significant in NAFTA, the world's second-largest fruit and vegetable market. Trade between Mexico, Canada, and the United States accounted for 49 percent of NAFTA's imports and 53 percent of its exports in 2001. Intra-NAFTA trade is most important for fresh vegetables. For this commodity group, 90 percent of exports and 86 percent of imports occur within the trade group (Huang 2004). Still, middle-income countries (excluding Mexico) have a strong foothold in this market. By securing 71 percent of the $7.25 billion extra-NAFTA import market in 2001, middle-income countries are major players.

Interestingly, thanks to growing incomes in the 1990s, middle-income countries have seen their own market become a major destination of fruit and vegetable exports from other countries, with import demand totaling $11 billion in 2001. South-South trade—trade between developing countries, excluding China and India—totaled $5.4 billion in 2001, accounting for 45 percent of developing countries' imports. Japan has also emerged as a significant market for fruits and vegetables over the 1990s, with import demand culminating at $5.8 billion in 2001. China has emerged as a major supplier of horticulture to Japan with its market share doubling from 16 percent in the 1980s to 33 percent in the 1990s.

While import penetration increased in the United States and other regions, EU import demand grew little in the 1990s. As table 13.3 shows, a salient feature of world import dynamics is the sharp increase in imports of developing countries (6 percent a year) and NAFTA (5 percent a year), and the stagnation of EU imports (1 percent a year) over the 1990s. Focusing on the United States, the import penetration ratio has increased steadily over time for fresh produce (figure 13.6). In contrast, extra-EU import demand grew by just 0.2 percent a year between 1990 and 2001, indicating that the bulk of the small increase in the European Union's horticultural trade, shown in table 13.3, occurred internally. This is a major change from the 1980s, when EU imports almost doubled. Closer examination of the data shows that the European Union's import deceleration is largely driven by Germany, which represents 25 percent of the EU's fruit and vegetable market. Germany's imports dropped by

1.4 percent annually over the 1990s, reflecting its slow pace of economic growth during this decade.[5]

Income and population composition and dynamics are the major drivers of import demand. Demand for fruits and vegetables—derived from a combination of broad demand dynamics, domestic supply trends, and trade policies—is relatively income elastic. Higher incomes typically induce increased expenditures on a broader array of fresh and processed fruit and vegetable products. In addition to income, other important factors include the size, age, ethnic composition of the population, cultural and religious factors, lifestyle factors (including work patterns and urbanization), and consumer education about health matters.

Although not all of these factors can be examined statistically, we attempt here to quantify the importance of most of the factors that explain the observed cross-country differences in growth in imports of fresh fruits, fresh vegetables, and processed fruits over the 1990s. The analysis, based on a sample of 49 major importers, uses the standard imperfect substitutes model (Goldstein and Khan 1985), which assumes that imports are not perfect substitutes for domestic goods for the countries under consideration.[6]

It is well known that economic growth strongly stimulates imports of fruits and vegetables, whereas inflation reduces them (Goldstein and Khan 1985).[7]

FIGURE 13.6 Import Penetration Ratios in U.S. Fruit and Vegetable Markets, 1970–2001
(percent)

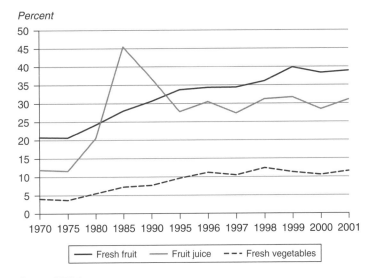

Source: USDA.

TABLE 13.4   Concentration of Fresh Fruit and Vegetable Exports among Developing Countries, 2001

Product	Leading Suppliers	Joint Percentage of World Exports (value)
Asparagus	Peru, Mexico, Thailand	94
Mangoes	Brazil, Mexico, Philippines	62
Pineapples	Costa Rica, Côte d'Ivoire	61
Bananas	Ecuador, Colombia, Costa Rica	60
Avocados	Chile, Mexico	53
Tomatoes	Mexico, Syria	52
Grapes	Chile, China, Mexico	38
Green beans	Jordan, Kenya, Mexico	49
Green peas	Guatemala, Kenya, Zimbabwe	38

Source: FAOSTAT.

But it is urbanization, not growth per se, that exercises the strongest and most significant influence on imports of fresh fruits (with the nuance that it plays a major role in developing countries only given the population shifts that are still occurring in these countries, see the Result Table A1 on the CD-ROM). Several factors could explain this relationship. First, urbanization helps to reduce the logistical and transaction costs to service demand from international sources, especially if the major cities are located in close vicinity to major ports or along efficient transport nodes. Second, with urbanization, there is greater demand for convenience in meeting food needs. Many fresh and processed fruit and vegetable products can be consumed with little or no further household preparation. Plus, these products feature heavily in menus of restaurants and catering services, most of which are in urban areas. Third, urban populations tend to be more heterogeneous in ethnic and other composition than is typical in any single rural setting. This mixing of populations increases consumer exposure to new or even exotic products, some of which may only be sourced in large quantities from abroad.

As expected, tariffs negatively affect fresh fruit trade, but the elasticity is not significantly different from zero. In sharp contrast, tariffs have a negative and statistically significant effect on processed fruit trade, highlighting the high degree of tariff escalation affecting trade in fruits and vegetables.

Developing Countries' Performance

Although many countries have entered the fresh fruit and vegetable export markets, only a few middle-income countries have succeeded on a sustained basis. The average shares of developing countries in world exports of fresh fruits and vegetables hide the heavy domination of trade by just a handful of middle-income countries. Between 1997 and 2001, just four Latin American countries—Chile, Costa Rica, Ecuador, and Mexico—accounted for 43 percent of developing-country exports of fresh fruit (FAO 2003). These countries are leading players in the most internationally traded fruit products (table 13.4). While exports of vegetables are similarly concentrated, the geographical distribution of exporters is wider. Mexico is the world's leading exporter of tomatoes, Kenya supplies 25 percent of the world's green beans, while Guatemala and Kenya jointly lead the world market for green peas.[8] Between 1997 and 2001, four suppliers—Argentina, China, Mexico, and the Syrian Arab Republic—accounted for 67 percent of fresh vegetable exports by developing countries (FAO 2003).[9]

A small number of medium-income countries have been successful in the processed segment of the export market, but as a group, developing countries account for a relatively low share in world exports of these products (36 percent in 2001). Chile, China, Thailand, and Turkey account for 58 percent of developing countries' exports of processed fruit and vegetable products (FAO 2003). Secondary, yet still significant exporters include Argentina, Indonesia, Mexico, and the Philippines (a combined 14 percent of developing countries' exports). Trade by developing countries in specific processed products is relatively highly concentrated (table 13.5).

TABLE 13.5   Concentration of Processed Fruit and Vegetable Exports among Developing Countries

Product	Leading Suppliers	Joint Percentage of World Exports (value)
Orange juice concentrated	Brazil	91
Canned pineapples	Indonesia, Philippines, Thailand	74
Canned mushrooms	China	52
Dried mushrooms	China	52
Dried fruits	Chile, China, Thailand	35
Tomato paste	Chile, China, Turkey	35
Apple juice, concentrated	Argentina, Chile, Turkey	31

Source: FAO 2003.

TABLE 13.6   Export Subsidy Expenditures for Horticultural Products

Country	Export Expenditure (US$ millions)	Total Horticultural Exports (US$ millions)	Export Expenditures as a Percent of Total Horticultural Export Value
European Union	40	5,301	0.8
Switzerland	14	69	20.6
Colombia	13	521	2.4
Turkey	11	2,348	0.0

Source: WTO 2000b and subsequent WTO notification updates. Export data from FAOSTAT.

Policy Factors Shaping International Trade Patterns

Domestic Support and Export Subsidies

Government interventions for fruits and vegetables are significantly lower than in other agricultural sectors. Consistently, domestic subsidies to producers are relatively low in OECD (Organisation for Economic Co-operation and Development) countries. Of the major industrialized regions, only the European Union reports an aggregate measure of support related specifically to several fruits and vegetables, while Japan and Canada indicate moderate levels of aggregate support for a few commodities.[10] The European Union's budgetary outlays for fruits and vegetables totaled $1.55 billion in 1999. Those expenditures covered compensation for surplus withdrawals; production aid to producers of bananas, peas, lentils, beans, pineapples, grapes, and stone fruits; and aid to producers of certain products intended for processing (tomatoes, peaches, pears) and to processors who pay producers at least the minimum price fixed each year (for dried figs and certain prunes, for example). Japan reported price support for starches ($179 million for potatoes and sweet potatoes in 1998) and direct payments to the vegetable and fruit sectors, but the aggregate measure of support was below the de minimis level. Similarly, in Canada, only its support for dry beans was above the de minimis levels (WTO 2000a).

Unlike in many other agricultural sectors, the use of export subsidies is not pervasive in horticulture. The export subsidy expenditures notified to the WTO in 2000 (WTO 2000b) (table 13.6) are well below those reported for other agricultural categories. In only one country, Switzerland, were expenditures large relative to horticultural exports, with export subsidies accounting for 21 percent of that country's exports. The European Union's export subsidies represented less than 1 percent of the value of its total exports. Although it did not supply information to the WTO, the United States indirectly subsidized horticultural exports, albeit to a very limited degree, through export credit guarantees.

Tariffs and Other Import Restrictions

Regulating market access is the main instrument used to protect the fruit and vegetable sector. The European Union, Japan, and the United States use, to varying degrees, similar protection tools: low but highly dispersed ad valorem tariffs, specific duties, seasonal tariffs, tariff escalation, and preferential access along with tariff-rate quotas. Tariffs for a specific range of products depend on numerous factors, including the date of entry (seasonality factor), the degree of processing (escalation phenomenon), and the relationships with exporting countries (preferential agreements and regional and bilateral free trade agreements—FTAs).

Average applied most-favored-nation (MFN) tariffs are very low in all countries of the Quad—Canada, the European Union, Japan, and the United States. These tariffs range between 0.9 percent for fresh fruits in Canada to 9.2 percent in the European Union for the same product category (table 13.7). The average tariffs, however, do not accurately reflect the level of actual protection caused by the wide dispersion in tariffs and the prevalence of high peaks. Closer examination of the tariff structure highlights the importance of tariff peaks, especially in the European Union and the

opacity of protection. Tariff peaks in the European Union, for example, can reach as high as 128 percent for fresh fruits and 132 percent for fresh vegetables.

Viewed in closer detail, the protection structure of several OECD countries is opaque. Canada, Japan, and the United States have the lowest tariffs, with, for instance, 85 percent of U.S. tariffs under 10 percent. In sharp contrast, the Republic of Korea and the European Union apply high tariffs on many products. For instance, in the Republic of Korea, 59 percent of fresh fruit and vegetable tariff lines lie between 20 and 50 percent and 37 percent of the lines are over 100 percent. Protection of fruits remains relatively nontransparent, as well, especially in Canada and the European Union (table 13.8). The percentage of fresh fruit tariff lines that are specific, compound, or mixed stands at 31 percent in Canada and 25 percent in the European Union.

Fresh vegetable exports face, in general, higher levels of protection, reflecting the fact that tariffs on temperate horticultural commodities are higher than they are for tropical commodities, dominated by fruits. The EU tariffs are particularly high for many commodities, as 60 percent of vegetable tariff lines are in the 20–50 percent range and 23 percent of the latter are greater than 50 percent. This reflects the large number of items that are subject to ad valorem tariffs (including seasonal) augmented by specific tariffs under the European Union's minimum entry price scheme (box 13.1).

TABLE 13.7   Applied MFN Tariffs for Fresh Fruit and Vegetables in the Quad Countries, 1999 and 2001

(percent)

Country		Average ad Valorem Rate	All Rates Average	Percentage of Lines Covered	Maximum	Standard Deviation	Number of Total Lines
European Union (1999)	Fruits	7.3	9.2	75.0	127.6	15.4	89
	Vegetables	5.5	6.8	98.0	131.8	10.7	200
United States (2001)	Fruits	6.1	4.6	100.0	29.8	7.0	70
	Vegetables	4.1	3.1	98.0	24.3	5.0	189
Japan (2001)	Fruits	8.7	8.7	100.0	32.0	6.8	56
	Vegetables	3.9	3.9	94.0	40.0	5.6	185
Canada (2001)	Fruits	0.9	0.9	72.0	8.5	2.5	67
	Vegetables	1.1	1.1	74.0	16.0	2.7	216

Source: WTO Integrated Data Base at the original tariff line level (6- to 11-digit tariff line depending on the country).

TABLE 13.8   Percentage of Tariff Lines on Fresh Fruits and Vegetables in Selected OECD Countries by Tariff Levels

Tariff Levels (percent)	Canada (2001)	United States (2001)	European Union (1999)	Japan (2001)	Korea, Rep. of (2001)
Fresh fruits					
Duty free	60	19	2	7	0
1–10	9	66	49	64	0
11–20	0	9	22	20	0
21–50	0	6	0	9	59
Over 50	0	0	1	0	37
Specific, compound, mixed	31	1	25	0	5
Fresh vegetables					
Duty free	47	16	0	10	3
1–10	7	59	11	69	42
11–20	1	14	1	11	47
21–50	0	1	60	7	1
Over 50	0	0	23	0	1
Specific, compound, mixed	45	9	5	2	5

Note: Average applied out-of-quota ad valorem and ad valorem equivalent of non-ad-valorem tariffs for those equivalent data reported.

Source: WTO IDB database.

BOX 13.1   The European Union's Entry Price Scheme: Hindering Cost-Based Competition in the EU Market

Current basic rules governing trade in fruits and vegetables were defined as part of the European Union's 1996 Common Market Organization (CMO) reform. One of the most prominent features of this reform is the "minimum entry price" system. This complex tariffication system applies to imports of a large number of fruits and vegetables, including fresh or chilled tomatoes, courgettes, cucumbers, apples, grapes, pears, peaches, plums, apricots, cherries, and citrus fruits. Under the system, the European Union calculates an entry price for each of the commodities covered by the program. The tariffs levied for each item depend on its import price compared with the calculated price.[11] Fruits and vegetables imported at prices equal to or greater than the established entry price are charged an ad valorem duty only. Commodities valued below the entry price are charged a specific tariff in addition to the ad valorem duty. In the latter case, two situations are distinguished: if the import price is more than 8 percent below the entry price, a large

specific tariff (called the maximum tariff equivalent) is levied against the shipment, most likely prohibiting its importation. If the entry price stands between 92 and 100 percent of the entry price, an additional specific duty is levied.

Through this system, applied tariffs are actually linked to the delivered price and the season. For instance, fresh tomatoes imported between June 1 and October 30 and priced 8 percent below the reference price of €52.6 per100 kilograms face tariffs amounting to 57 percent of the import price (Sallyards 2001). The entry prices are generally highest during the EU production season and lowest during the off-season, and the difference can be very large. The entry price for courgettes, for instance, increases from a base level of €450 a metric ton to €730 a metric ton in April and May. This system strongly restricts an exporter's ability to increase market shares in the European Union based on lower prices and efficiency, especially during the European production season.

TABLE 13.9   Percentage of Tariff Lines on Processed Fruits and Vegetables in Selected OECD Countries by Tariff Levels

Tariff Levels (percent)	Canada (2001)	United States (2001)	European Union (1999)	Japan (2001)	Korea, Rep. of (2001)
Processed fruits					
Duty free	35	1	0	7	1
1–10	43	14	0	62	2
11–20	20	43	0	24	44
21–50	0	34	47	4	40
Over 50	0	0	53	4	2
Specific, compound, mixed lines	2	7	0	0	10
Processed vegetables					
Duty free	22	3	0	8	3
1–10	31	39	6	65	6
11–20	40	50	0	24	76
21–50	0	6	88	3	5
Over 50	0	0	3	0	3
Specific, compound, mixed lines	7	2	3	0	8

Note: Average applied out-of-quota ad valorem and ad valorem equivalents of non-ad-valorem tariffs for those equivalent data reported.
Source: WTO IDB database.

The tariff structures of the European Union, Japan, the Republic of Korea, and the United States also feature a high degree of escalation. All EU processed fruit tariffs are above 20 percent, and the majority of processed fruit products entering the European Union face a tariff of greater than 50 percent (table 13.9). There is also tariff escalation in the European Union for processed vegetables, with 88 percent of these products facing a tariff in the range of 21–50 percent. The European Union's escalating tariffs for tomato and apple-based products inhibit a potentially large level of trade by nonmember countries. Tariffs facing most processed fruit and vegetable products entering Canada, Japan, Korea, and the United States are below 20 percent. These low tariffs do not exclude the use of high levels of protection for particular products, as illustrated by U.S. protection of its own orange juice industry (box 13.2).

In most middle-income countries, the tariff structure is more transparent than in the Quad, but average tariff levels are higher (table 13.10), posing a challenge to would-be external suppliers. Average applied MFN tariffs in Brazil, India, and Morocco, for example, are far higher than in the high-income

countries analyzed above. Ninety-four percent of MFN tariff lines for fresh fruits in India are between 21 and 50 percent, while all "MFN" fruits entering Morocco face a tariff of more than 50 percent. (In contrast, Indonesia and South Africa have tariff structures similar to those of Japan and the United States, with most tariff lines falling between zero and 10 percent.) The potential hindrance of these high tariffs to developing-country exports should not be underestimated. As seen above, South-South trade in fruits and vegetables is growing rapidly and now represents about one-fifth of developing countries' exports.

Preferential Market Access and Magnitude of Preference

The protection structure just described does not apply equally to all exporting countries. Many high-income countries maintain a complex system of preferential access (that is, better-than-MFN access) designed to provide privileged partners with favorable entry without undermining the protection of domestic producers. The product coverage of preferential access schemes is wide, but

BOX 13.2 The U.S.-Brazilian Trade Dispute over Orange Juice

The world market for orange juice is basically a duopolistic market structure, with only two players, the United States (mainly Florida) and Brazil, supplying roughly 85 percent of the world market. Over 95 percent of Brazil's production is exported, whereas more than 95 percent of U.S. orange juice is consumed domestically. Of the U.S. imports of concentrated orange juice, some 90 percent comes from Brazil. Imported orange juice is mixed with U.S. juice to improve its color and make up for seasonal supply shortfall. This trade pattern reflects Brazil's production cost advantages, which in turn mirror lower labor costs in Brazil, reinforced in recent years by the devaluation of the *real*. The United States levies a tariff of 7.85 cents per liter on Brazilian orange juice. In addition, an antidumping order remains in effect, with dumping duties ranging from 2 percent to 27 percent on imports of the Brazilian product.

Furthermore, Brazilian exporters pay a "Florida equalizing excise tax" on frozen orange juice concentrate, from which domestic producers in Arizona, California, and Texas whose juice is also blended with Florida orange juice are exempt. The proceeds of the tax are allocated by statute to the exclusive promotion of Florida-grown citrus products. According to one estimate, the combined tax and duty accounts for nearly 50 percent of the cost of a ton of Brazilian concentrate. This discrimination between imported and domestic products has prompted Brazil to initiate a dispute settlement process at the WTO. In March 2002 the government of Brazil requested bilateral consultations under WTO auspices with the United States regarding the "equalizing excise tax." Brazil argued that the incidence of the tax on imported processed citrus products and not on domestic products constitutes a de facto violation of most-favored-nation and national treatment provisions of GATT (General Agreement on Tariffs and Trade) (Articles II: 1(a), III.1 and III:2, GATT 1994).

Interestingly, the private sector has already taken pragmatic actions to deal with these problems, through joint investments and joint production. In an increasingly common tariff-jumping tactic, the Brazilian producers in the early 1990s began to invest directly in the Florida industry. It is estimated that foreign—mainly Brazilian—companies own as much as 40 percent of the Florida processing industry. The U.S. presence in Brazil's citrus industry started in the 1960s, when winter freezes prompted U.S. growers to seek out Brazil for planting.

Source: Thunder Lake Management 2002.

---

entry is often limited by quotas for "sensitive products" such as those put in special protocols (such as bananas).

The major EU preferential access schemes relevant to trade in fruits and vegetables include the Everything but Arms (EBA) initiative that benefits the 48 UN-defined least-developed countries (LDCs); the EU-ACP Lomé Conventions, under which the European Union grants unilateral preferential access to 75 African, Caribbean, and Pacific (ACP) countries, bilateral agreements such as the Euro-Med Agreements between the European Union and many Mediterranean countries, and the EU-South Africa free trade area; and the generalized system of preferences (GSP).

A large number of countries also enjoy preferential access to the United States through formal regional, bilateral, and preferential trade agreements. These include NAFTA, the African Growth Opportunity Act (AGOA), the Caribbean Basin Economic Recovery Act (CBERA), the Andean Trade Preference Act (ATPA), and free trade agreements with Israel and Chile. Since NAFTA was signed, tropical fruits shipped from Mexico (mangoes, guavas, avocados, and papayas) have been subject to steadily reduced tariffs. Since January 2003 they have entered the U.S. market free of duty.

While these different agreements are not always directly comparable, it is clear that they provide varied degrees of preference to the suppliers involved. Figure 13.7, adapted from Stevens and Kennan (2000), highlights the hierarchy of preferences within the European Union's fruit and vegetable import regime as of 2003. The major changes since 2000 include the promulgation of the EBA initiative and the multiplication of bilateral agreements, which erode the preferences of those on top of the pyramid. The ranking of preferences depends on the difference between preferential versus MFN tariffs (that is, the margin of preference), the breadth of product coverage, the extent of quota limitations, and the degree of certainty of

TABLE 13.10   Percentage of Tariff Lines at Different Levels in Selected Developing Countries, 2001

Tariff Levels (percent)	Brazil	India	Indonesia	Morocco	South Africa
Fresh fruits					
Duty free	0	0	0	0	15
1–10	0	0	100	0	47
11–20	100	3	0	0	29
21–50	0	94	0	0	9
Over 50	0	3	0	100	0
Specific, compound, mixed lines	0	0	0	0	0
Fresh vegetables					
Duty free	24	0	2	0	46
1–10	0	0	98	0	6
11–20	76	85	0	13	30
21–50	0	15	0	19	13
Over 50	0	0	0	68	0
Specific, compound, mixed lines	0	0	0	0	6

Note: Average applied out-of-quota ad valorem and ad valorem equivalents of non-ad-valorem tariffs for those equivalent data reported.
Source: WTO IDB database.

FIGURE 13.7   The Hierarchy of Preferences in the European Fruits and Vegetables Market

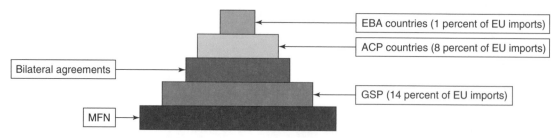

Source: Authors' calculations using COMTRADE data and based on Stevens and Kennan 2000.

preferences. The key characteristics of the European Union's preference system are:

- Duty-free and quota-free access for LDCs under the EBA initiative.[12] The beneficiary countries generally lack the capacity to provide reliable supplies, in part because of poor infrastructure and other behind-the-border constraints. Even with EBA, they accounted in 2002 for only 1 percent of the European Union's imports of fruits and vegetables from outside the EU.
- Generous access for ACP countries, accounting for 8 percent of the European Union's

third-country imports. Just a few countries—including Cameroon, Côte d'Ivoire, and Kenya—account for the bulk of this trade.

- ACP access for bananas is limited by quotas. ACP countries enjoy, within the allocated quota of 850,000 tons, duty-free access to the EU banana market (until 2008), whereas third-country suppliers face a duty of €75/ton.[13]
- Preferential access for many countries comes through bilateral agreements. The concessions granted under these agreements are typically restricted to certain tariff quotas or to certain periods of the year, depending on the EU season.

Tensions between opening markets for privileged partners and protecting domestic producers have led to a widespread use of tariff rate quotas (TRQs) in fruit and vegetable trade. In 2000 developed countries applied 355 TRQ schemes to imported fruits and vegetables, compared with 56 for tropical beverages and processed agricultural products (Jabati 2003). Quotas are typically set at low levels with low in-quota tariffs and prohibitive over-the-quota tariffs. A good example is that of winter seedless grapes, a product exported by some Southern Hemisphere suppliers, including South Africa and Namibia. Namibia may export only 900 tons per year to the European Union from November to end of January (Jabati 2003). Any over-the-quota export is subject to an import tariff of 16.4 percent. The tariff and period restrictions clearly constitute a constraint for Namibia if it wants to increase its exports.

Analysis of the value of ACP and AGOA preferences show heterogeneous situations among ACP countries, while South Africa stands out as the only country taking significant advantage of the AGOA preference. It has been argued that preferential treatment has contributed to the successful penetration of some developing countries into the EU market (Stevens and Kennan 2000). We examine here the effectiveness of ACP and AGOA preferences for fruits and vegetables exported to the European Union and United States, respectively. These indicators are preferred over changes in MFN tariffs, which do not capture the variety of specific trade regimes in the European Union and the United States that are relevant for many developing countries.

The value of an ACP preference can be defined as the product of the value of exports for which preferences have been requested and the preferential margin (figure 13.8). The value of the ACP preference in fruits and vegetables represented 12 percent of ACP country exports, with a great deal of variation around the average.[14] The ACP "rent" stood at less than 5 percent for Ethiopia, Madagascar, and Namibia, but between 28 and 42 percent for major banana producers such as Cameroon, the Caribbean islands, and Côte d'Ivoire.

In terms of scope, about 82 percent of ACP fruit and vegetable exports to the European Union are eligible for preference. Use of this preference is quite high, with an average 75 percent of eligible exports requesting preference. Use rates vary widely across ACP countries, however.

FIGURE 13.8 Value of Fruit and Vegetable Preference for Major ACP Exporters, 2002

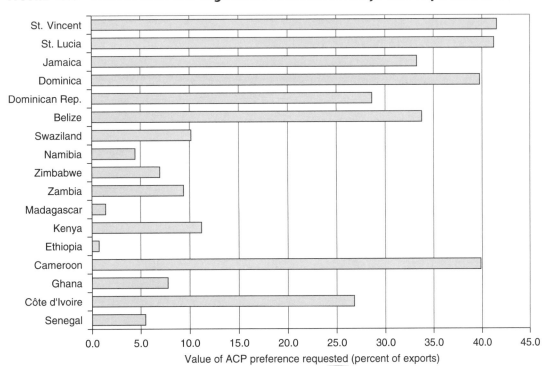

Source: World Bank staff calculations based on the EU Commission Database.

In sharp contrast with the ACP scheme, the use of the AGOA preference to export fruits and vegetables to the United States is not yet a widespread practice in Africa, since only 14 of 38 AGOA countries exported fruits and vegetables to the United States in 2002. Among those having done so, however, the use of the AGOA preference was high, averaging 73 percent (see annex table A3). The very small number of countries that have exported fruits and vegetables under AGOA is associated with the constrained logistics on African–U.S. trade in perishable products, the very limited degree of U.S. private investment in Africa in this field, and stringent U.S. phytosanitary requirements.

Not surprisingly, countries that have more advanced logistical systems and stronger international marketing ties (for example, South Africa) are better placed to benefit from AGOA. In fact, South Africa is the only AGOA country for which the preference "rent" represents a significant share of export values (74 percent) (figure 13.9). Few other African countries have a comparative advantage in servicing the U.S. market and, given comparative freight costs and availability, find the European market a more attractive outlet. We analyze these issues further in the next section.

As more and more countries are enjoying better-than-MFN access to the EU market, preferences are eroding and competition is stiffer—as illustrated by the experience of large middle-income exporters (figure 13.10). Morocco, South Africa, and Turkey are large exporters of fruits and vegetables that enter the European Union under bilateral agreements with limitations on some products.[15] Morocco, among the first countries to sign preferential agreements with the European Union in the late 1960s, has lost ground in the EU market to Turkey since Turkey's free-trade agreement with the European Union was signed in 1998. South Africa recently unseated Turkey in the EU market and is now the largest third-country supplier of fruits and vegetables to the European Union (with a 31 percent share). Turkey holds a slightly lower share (29 percent), while Morocco lags far behind (22 percent, down from 37 percent in 1980). In several products (citrus fruit, tomato products, dried fruit, and fruit juice), these suppliers have competed directly.

Determinants of Success in Fruit and Vegetable Export Markets

Many developing countries have sought to take advantage of emerging international markets for

FIGURE 13.9   Value of Fruit and Vegetable Preference under AGOA

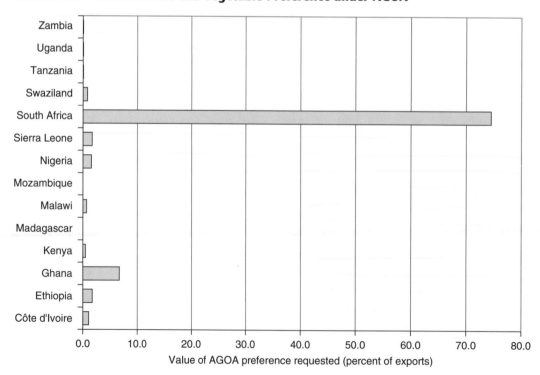

Source: World Bank staff calculations based on USITC Database.

FIGURE 13.10   EU–Third Country Imports and the Share of Key Exporters

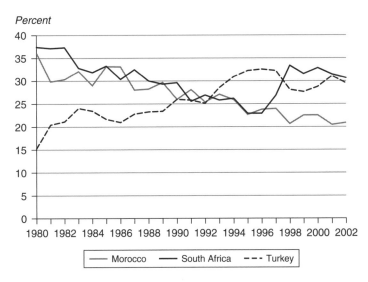

Source: COMTRADE.

fresh and processed fruit and vegetable products. Yet, as noted above, relatively few have achieved dominance in a range of such products. In Sub-Saharan Africa several dozen countries have participated in this trade, yet just three—Côte d'Ivoire, Kenya, South Africa—accounted for nearly 90 percent of the region's trade in recent decades. Only a few other countries in the region have been able to sustain growth in their horticultural trade over time; none has emerged as a major player in the international market.

Success Factors

To succeed in exporting fruits and vegetables, a country must have important assets that provide an initial comparative advantage. Among those assets are favorable agroclimatic conditions and ample and accessible land and water resources; a physical location on the sea or close to a major market; ample and relatively inexpensive labor; and a class of entrepreneurs with commercial experience. Many countries may possess some or even most of these assets. But translating them into a competitive horticultural industry that maintains or improves its competitiveness over time requires a distinctive set of investments and institutional structures, a range of facilitative government policies, and, usually, a bit of luck (Jaffee 2003; Gabre-Madhin and Minot 2003; FAO 2003; Huang 2004).

Jaffee (1993) examines the ingredients common to the initial growth and subsequent maturation of some of the developing world's leading fresh and processed fruit and vegetable success stories—among them Brazil, Chile, Kenya, Mexico, and Taiwan (China). In each case, the initial take-off occurred during a period of stable macroeconomic conditions and the presence of a favorable investment climate. Important initial catalysts for export growth included sudden shortfalls in major overseas markets, new foreign direct investment or strategic partnerships, and improvements in international logistics capacity. International technical and marketing partnerships provided a vehicle for the transfer of technology, for new market penetration, and for creating an identity for the products from the exporting country.

Many countries have experienced short-term spurts in horticultural exports; few have been able to consolidate their early gains. Those that have done so invested in research and adopted international technologies, expanded and upgraded logistical facilities, strengthened vertical supply chains, developed industry organizations for collective action, and built credible systems for quality assurance and food safety management. Industry expansion induced the development of associated industries, such as packaging, equipment supply, and technical consulting, which in turn contributed to the underlying competitiveness of the industries. Further investments were made in the industries' underlying assets, for example, through irrigation development and worker and management training. Synergies have generally developed between export horticulture and complementary industries such as domestic catering and tourism.

With certain historical exceptions, in most of the long-standing industries the private sector dominates the commercial dimensions of the business, while governments play a substantial and multidimensional facilitative role. In the early stages of industry development, the public sector has been critical in improving transportation and port/airport infrastructure, investing in research and farm advisory services, facilitating access by investors and farmers to suitable land, helping to transfer technologies and skills, and advancing the broad array of policies that make for a conducive investment climate (box 13.3). Over time, other important functions for government have emerged, notably sanitary and phytosanitary control, promotion of competi-

tion within the industry and in critical support services, negotiation of favorable international market access, and resolution of trade disputes.

Explaining Intercountry Differences in Export Performances

Focusing on the factors identified in the literature as influencing export performance, this section attempts to quantify their importance in determining the value of fruit and vegetable exports across a sample of 45 developing countries. The theoretical anchor of the empirical investigation is Redding and Venables' geographic and trade model (Redding and Venables 2002).[16]

The variables assumed to have a significant impact on the value of fresh and processed fruit and vegetable exports are grouped into supply-capacity

---

BOX 13.3 Peruvian Asparagus Exports—A Standard Success Story?

Once the leaders of Peru's asparagus industry and government specialists realized that it was in the best interest of the country, they worked together to bring national standards in line with international norms. The industry—and Peru—have greatly benefited as a result. Over the past decade, Peru has quickly risen to become one of the world's largest exporters of asparagus. In 2002 earnings reached $187 million, representing nearly 25 percent of Peru's total agricultural exports. Peru is able to produce quality asparagus year-round, yet because of high transportation costs, its exporters are unable to match prices with inexpensive asparagus from some other countries. Nonetheless, they have continued to increase exports and gain market share by growing asparagus of consistently higher quality that can be internationally certified. By meeting international standards, Peruvian exporters have increased production and worker efficiency, gained access to industrialized country markets, built customer loyalty, and drastically reduced the industry's risk of trade disruptions caused by poor quality, food safety hazards, and plant disease.

In 1997 Spanish health authorities asserted that two cases of botulism had been caused by consumption of canned Peruvian asparagus. Despite assurances from the Peruvian government and companies, press coverage of the botulism scare left an unfavorable impression among consumers in European markets, causing sales to slump in Peru's leading market. The

incident helped motivate the industry and government to take action, by reinforcing the fact that one careless exporter could disrupt markets.

Beginning in 1998, officials of the Peruvian Commission for Export Promotion (PROMPEX) convinced the asparagus industry to implement the Codex code of practice on food hygiene, not because it was the easiest but because it was the most appropriate. PROMPEX specialists worked closely with industry leaders and production managers to ensure proper implementation of good hygiene standards. The industry soon saw improved production methods, greater worker efficiency, and better product quality.

Thus, when the national fresh asparagus norms were published in early 2001, because the industry was already familiar with the concept of national standards, producers quickly complied with little argument. The first national norms—for fresh asparagus—established a quality and performance baseline for the industry that allowed many to generate the skills and experience needed to voluntarily certify under more stringent international standards, including HACCP (hazard analysis and critical control point), traceability systems, and Good Agricultural Practice (GAP) certification. Many large exporters have reached the level where they can now be certified under the even stricter EUREPGAP protocol.

Source: Tim O'Brien, Interamerican Institute for Cooperation in Agriculture.

variables and market-access variables. Supply-capacity variables include:

- Domestic market size, captured by the size of urban population.
- Infrastructure, proxied by the percentage of paved roads and access to telephones.
- Institutional quality and setting, captured by two variables: the number of days to enforce a contract and whether or not the country is a signatory of the International Plant Variety Protection Convention (a dummy variable).
- Human capital, captured by two separate variables: availability of semi-skilled labor, captured by the adult literacy rate, and managerial capacity, proxied here by the level of manufacturing exports.

Market-access variables include:

- Geographic variables: landlocked status (dummy), which increases distance and cost to reach markets.
- Volume of air transport freight (in millions of tons per kilometer). This variable attempts to capture freight space availability and the economies of scale in international transport (Clark, Dollar, and Micco 2002). The higher the volume of freight, the higher the economies of scale realized by shippers and the lower the transport cost.[17]
- Existence of a preferential agreement with the European Union or the United States (dummy variable).

Table 13.A2 (on the accompanying CD-ROM) reports our estimations of the equation for fresh fruit and vegetable exports and for processed fruits and vegetables. Common factors—notably distance (landlocked status) and the level of human capital—explain success in both fresh and processed export markets.

- Literacy and managerial capabilities exert a strong, robust, and statistically significant impact on export of fresh and processed fruits and vegetables. This result reflects two facts. First, horticulture is a knowledge-intensive business. Second, success in world markets requires the availability of a skillful class of entrepreneurs.

- Remoteness (that is, being landlocked) has a significant adverse effect on fruit and vegetable exports, corroborating the literature on geography and trade—for example, Frankel and Romer (1999), who showed that countries that are landlocked or remote from major markets tend to trade less than those that are not.
- Domestic market size comes out with a negative sign in almost all estimations (although at a statistically insignificant level), apparently contradicting the usual argument that exporting fruits and vegetables requires the prior or parallel development of domestic markets and experience in brand name merchandising (see, for example, Jaffee 1993).[18]

There are sharp differences in the factors explaining the intercountry performance in exports of fresh versus processed fruits and vegetables. Holding all else constant, the economies of scale obtained through large volumes of air freight are a key success factor for fresh fruit and vegetable exports but do not appear significant for processed horticultural exports (annex table A4 on the CD-ROM). This is because economies of scale translate into lower transportation costs, which claim a larger share of final value for fresh products than for processed products. Clearly, higher spoilage and handling costs make fresh produce much more expensive to transport, explaining why more countries tend to import fresh produce from the closest producers (Huang 2004). In contrast, because they are easier to handle and are almost universally shipped by sea, transport costs are smaller for processed products, making the geographical outreach of processed trade much larger.

The other factor that has a differentiated impact on fresh versus processed exports is the level of protection. While preferential access to the European Union or the United States has a positive and significant impact on export of processed horticultural products, it is not statistically significant at 5 percent for fresh product exports. This result is consistent with the structure of tariffs analyzed above, which features a high degree of escalation in OECD countries.

In conclusion, our estimations show the critical importance of proximity to major export markets and availability of human capital as common factors explaining success in exports of both fresh and processed horticultural products. They also indicate that countries wishing to boost exports of fresh products should invest in high-quality logistics, whereas those seeking success in processed markets need to develop or tie in with leading product brands and circumvent tariff escalation through preferential agreements with major trading partners or within the framework of multilateral negotiations.

Conclusion

This chapter has highlighted the major global, regional, and product-specific trends in fruit and vegetable products trade and examined major structural and policy factors that have affected this trade over the past two decades. Growth in world imports was 2–3 percent a year in the 1990s, representing a deceleration in the rate of growth from the 1980s. This slower growth in world trade in the 1990s was strongly affected by the European Union, which experienced relatively low growth in population and income during the decade and had many mature and saturated product markets. Adverse price movements for fresh and processed products from the mid-1990s onward also contributed substantially to the overall deceleration in the growth of trade values. Robust growth in trade has continued among NAFTA countries, for sales to high-income Asian countries, and between developing countries.

For developing countries, fresh and processed fruits and vegetables is now one of the most important categories for agro-food trade, accounting for about 22 percent of their exports in 2000–01. This is far larger than their current level of trade in many traditional commodities. Still, although many developing-country suppliers have entered this field, relatively few countries have achieved sustained success at a high level—testimony that the industry is highly competitive and rapidly changing, and that it requires sustained investments in infrastructure, human capital, technology, and good governance.

Unlike the situation in many other agricultural sectors, production and export subsidies are not common in horticulture. Instead, domestic fruit and vegetable producers are protected through regulation of market access. The European Union, Japan, and the United States use, to varying degrees, complex protection tools—among them highly dispersed ad valorem tariffs, specific duties, seasonal tariffs, tariff escalation, and preferential access along with tariff-rate quotas. A complex system of preferential access in many rich countries provides privileged partners with favorable entry without undermining protection of domestic producers. The product coverage of preferential access schemes is wide but quotas for "sensitive products" often limit entry. Tariff escalation for processed fruit and vegetable products is widespread, although its extent varies significantly between regions.

Because horticultural sectors throughout the world have traditionally seen a low level of direct government interventions, changes in domestic support cannot affect the sector broadly or significantly. Reductions in tariffs and other import restrictions, however, are critical in determining the impact of trade agreements and policies on world horticultural trade. Further tariff liberalization efforts would need to reduce tariff peaks, especially in the European Union and the Republic of Korea. Past trends suggest that the main beneficiaries from such reforms will be a limited number of middle-income countries that have developed strong production, postharvest processing, logistical marketing, and sanitary and phytosanitary management systems over the years and that continue to attract new investment. With only a few exceptions, low-income countries still face enormous supply-side challenges in taking advantage of existing and future international market opportunities.

Notes

1. More detailed tables on trade flows and tariffs are presented on the attached CD-ROM.

2. "Statistics on Foreign Trade of Vegetables." Vegetable Supply Stabilization Fund. Tokyo. October 2002.

3. This reflects the heavy influence of Spain, which is the global leader in fresh fruit exports (mainly oranges and clementines). Italy is also a significant exporter of grapes, apples, and peaches.

4. Bananas accounted for more than 80 percent of the fresh fruit imported by the European Union from these countries (Huang 2004).

5. Between 1993 and 2003, gross domestic product growth in Germany averaged 1.4 percent, the lowest among EU member states.

6. See box A1 in annex to this chapter in the CD-ROM.

7. Lacking a better alternative, food prices are considered here as a proxy for the prices of fruits and vegetables. The main caveat associated with this is that the range of goods covered in

the food-price index is wider than what a proper (and exogenous) fruits and vegetables import price index would cover.

8. Mexico remains the world's top exporter of many smaller vegetable products—among them asparagus, eggplant, and onions.

9. The bulk of Syria's trade is with other Middle Eastern countries; Argentina's is targeted primarily to other Latin American countries.

10. The aggregate measure of support was defined in the Uruguay Round Agreement on Agriculture as an aggregate subsidy measure, designed to quantify and compare countries' annual levels of domestic support. It aggregates the effects of all trade-distorting policies (direct subsidies plus implicit subsidies from border measures) into a single measure of support.

11. An importer can choose one of the three following methods to calculate entry price: the standard import value (SIV), calculated daily by product and by origin and published in EU's Official Journal; the f.o.b. price of the product in the country of origin; the effective resale value of the shipment concerned.

12. Bananas are the only exception in the fruit and vegetable category. For this product, duty-free access is phased in between 2002 and 2006 by a 20 percent yearly tariff reduction. This is unlikely to have a significant impact in the short run, however, as all LDCs producing bananas of export quality belong to the ACP group, which enjoys duty-free access.

13. This preferential access has allowed countries like Cameroon, Côte d'Ivoire, and Dominican Republic to compete with lower-cost Latin American suppliers (Costa Rica, Ecuador).

14. For more details regarding the definitions and estimations of these indicators, see chapter 4 of this volume.

15. A recent study has identified three categories of products that receive different treatments under the European Union and Mediterranean countries trade agreements: first, the products for which the preferential margin (tariff difference with MFN) is granted without quantitative restriction but with seasonal restrictions (such as tomatoes); second, the products for which the tariff reduction applies solely if the entry price is higher than a reference price in EU; and a third group for which the impact of tariff reductions are severely limited by quota restrictions (such as bananas and olives). Chahed and Drogué (2002).

16. The empirical model and its derivation from the Redding and Venables' theoretical model is described in box A2 of the annex to this chapter in the attached CD-ROM.

17. Lack of data prevented us from using the volume of maritime freight.

18. As noted earlier, a large and rapidly growing urban population (as in China and India) can absorb very large quantities of fruit and vegetables and lead entrepreneurs to focus on servicing the domestic market.

References

Chahed, Y., and S. Drogué. 2002. "Echanges agricoles et Accords Euromed, l'érosion des préférences en question." Department of Public Economics, INRA-INAPG, Paris-Grignon.

Clark, X., D. Dollar, and A. Micco. 2002. "Port Efficiency, Maritime Transport Costs and Bilateral Trade," NBER working paper 10353. National Bureau of Economic Research, Inc, Cambridge, MA.

FAO (United Nations Food and Agriculture Organization). 2003. "The Market for Nontraditional Agricultural Exports." Commodity and Trade Division. Rome.

FAOSTAT 2003. FAO Statistical Databases. Accessible at http://apps.fao.org/default.jsp.

Frankel, J., and D. Romer. 1999. "Does Trade Cause Growth?" *American Economic Review* 89(3), June, 379–399.

Gabre-Madhin, E., and N. Minot. 2003. "Successes and Challenges for Promoting African Horticulture Exports." World Bank, Washington, D.C. August.

Goldstein, M., and M. S. Khan. 1985. "Income and Price Effects in Foreign Trade." In R. W. Jones and P. B. Kenen, eds., *Handbook of International Economics*, vol. 2. New York: Elsevier Science Publications.

Huang, S. W., ed. 2004. "Global Trade Patterns in Fruits and Vegetables." Agriculture and Trade Report WRS-04-06. U.S. Department of Agriculture, Washington, D.C.

Jabati, M.C. 2003. "Market Access for Developing Countries of Africa: The Reality." AGSF Occasional Paper No. 1. United Nations Food and Agriculture Organization. Rome.

Jaffee, S. 1993. "Exporting High-Value Food Commodity: Success Stories From Developing Countries." World Bank Discussion Paper 198. Washington, D.C.

———. 2003. "From Challenge to Opportunity: Transforming Kenya's Fresh Vegetable Trade in the Context of Emerging Food Safety and Other Standards in Europe." Agriculture and Rural Development Discussion Paper 1. World Bank, Washington, D.C.

Redding, Stephen, and A. Venables. 2002. "The Economics of Isolation and Distance." *Nordic Journal of Political Economy* 28, Conference Volume, no. 2, pp. 93–108.

Sallyards, M. 2001. "European Union Agricultural Situation: EU Fruits and Vegetables Regime." GAIN Report E21058. U.S. Department of Agriculture, Washington, D.C.

Stevens, C., and Jane Kennan. 2000. "Will Africa's Participation in Horticulture Chains Survive Liberalization?" Working Paper 106. University of Sussex, Institute for Development Studies, Brighton, U.K.

Thunder Lake Management, Inc. 2002. "Florida-Brazil Citrus Case." *Trade Policy Monitor.* April. Online: http://www.thunderlake.com/brazil_oj.html.

Vegetable Supply Stabilization Fund. 2002. "Statistics on Foreign Trade of Vegetables." Tokyo.

WTO (World Trade Organization). 2000a. "Domestic Support: Background Paper by the Secretariat." G/AG/NG/8. May 26.

———. 2000b. "Export Subsidies: Background Paper by the Secretariat." G/AF/NG/S/1. April.

14

COTTON: MARKET SETTING, TRADE POLICIES, AND ISSUES

John Baffes

Cotton—by far the most common natural fiber of the 19th and 20th centuries—has been used as a raw material for clothing for at least 5,000 years. Its use expanded significantly after 1793, when the invention of the cotton gin introduced mechanical separation of lint from seed. The industrial revolution, which reduced the cost of producing textiles, accelerated cotton's progress.[1]

Cotton's most important competitors are natural and synthetic man-made fibers such as rayon and polyester.[2] Although large-scale commercial production of man-made fibers did not begin until after World War II, experimentation was taking place as early as the late 1800s. In 1925, rayon, a natural man-made fiber produced from cellulose, accounted for 1.6 percent of the world's total fiber consumption. Twenty years later, this share had increased to 11.8 percent. The share of all man-made fibers in total fiber consumption reached 22 percent in 1960 and now stands at about 57 percent.

As production of man-made fibers expanded, cotton's share fell (figure 14.1). Between 1960 and 2002, man-made fiber consumption grew at an annual rate of 4.7 percent, compared to just 1.8 percent for cotton.

Synthetic (noncellulose) man-made fibers such as polyester and nylon have traded at prices compa-rable to cotton's since the early 1970s. Between 1960 and 1972, the polyester price indicator declined from $12 to $2.50 per kilogram, mainly a reflection of the technological improvements (and consequent cost reductions) that took place in the chemical fiber industry. After reaching parity with cotton prices in 1972, the ratio of polyester to cotton prices has increased at an average rate of 1 percent per year, implying that while cotton and polyester are priced at similar levels, polyester has made small pricing gains (see figure 14.1).

The Global Cotton Balance

Cotton is produced in many countries, but the Northern Hemisphere accounts for 90 percent of global output. More than two-thirds of the world's cotton is produced by developing countries. Between 1960 and 2001, global cotton output doubled—from 10.2 million to 20 million tons. Most of this growth came from China and India, which tripled and doubled their production, respectively, during this 40 year period. Other countries that significantly increased their share of cotton production were Turkey, Greece, and Pakistan. Some new entrants also contributed. Australia, which produced only 2,000 tons of cotton

FIGURE 14.1   Cotton's Share in Total Fiber Consumption and Polyester to Cotton Price Ratio, 1960–2002

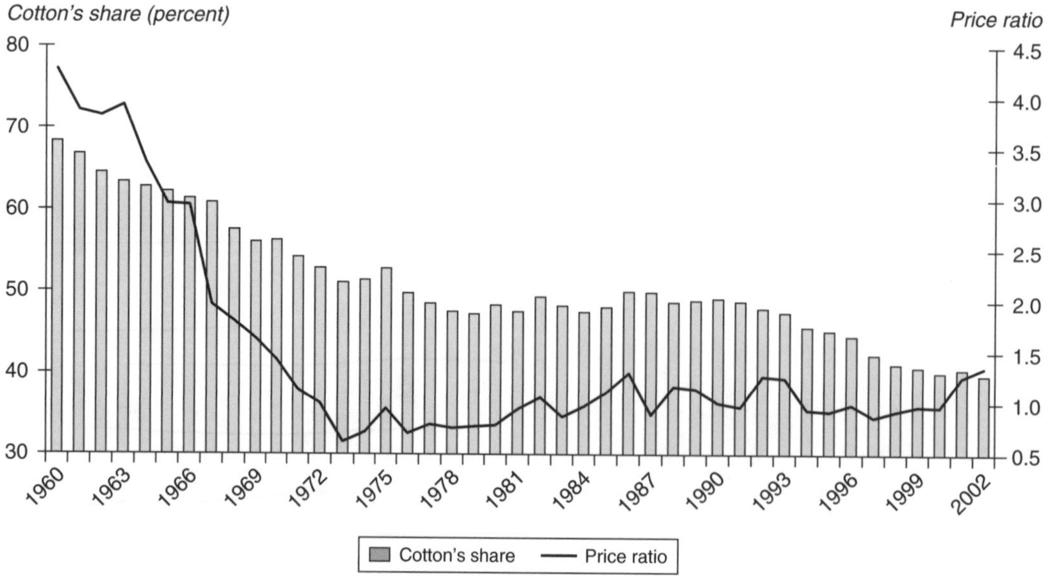

Source: International Rayon and Synthetic Fibers Committee.

in 1960, averaged 650,000 tons a year during the late 1990s. Francophone Africa, which produced less than 100,000 tons in the 1960s, now produces almost 1 million tons. The two dominant producers during the 1960s, the United States and the Central Asian republics of the Soviet Union, have maintained their output levels at about 3.5 million and 1.5 million tons, respectively, thereby halving their shares. Several Central American countries that used to produce almost 250,000 tons of cotton annually now produce almost none. The share of East African cotton producers, too, has declined considerably during this period.

The two largest cotton producers, China and the United States, each account for approximately 20 percent of world output, followed by India (12 percent), Pakistan (8 percent), and Uzbekistan (5 percent). Other significant cotton producers are the countries of Francophone Africa, Turkey, Brazil, Australia, and Greece, which account for a combined 18 percent of global output.

The consumption pattern of cotton is primarily determined by the size of the textile industries of the dominant cotton consumers. China, the leading textile producer, absorbed more than a quarter of global cotton output during the late 1990s. Other major textile producers (and hence major cotton consumers) are India, the United States, and Turkey, which, together with China, account for

three-quarters of global cotton consumption. Several East Asian countries have emerged recently as important cotton consumers. For example, Indonesia, Thailand, the Republic of Korea, and Taiwan (China) consumed only 130,000 tons in 1960 (1.2 percent of global consumption), but 1.5 million tons in 2002 (7.2 percent of global consumption).

Growth in the demand for cotton has been slow. Between 1960 and 2000, cotton demand grew at the same rate as population (1.8 percent a year), implying that per capita cotton consumption has remained stagnant.

Stocks, which historically have fluctuated between 20 and 50 percent of global output, have affected the cotton market considerably, especially in the area of price variability. The stockholding policies of the United States and China, the two major holders of cotton stocks, have affected the level and volatility of prices. Two major cotton destocking episodes are associated with periods of considerable price variability: the 1985 shift in U.S. policy from stockholding to price support and the 1999 reforms in China.

One-third of cotton production is traded internationally. The four dominant exporters—United States, Uzbekistan, Francophone Africa, and Australia—account for more than two-thirds of the world's exports. Four major producers, China,

India, Pakistan, and Turkey do not export cotton and occasionally import to supply their textile industries. Imports of cotton are more uniformly distributed than exports.

During the 2000–01 season, the eight largest importers (Indonesia, India, Mexico, Thailand, Turkey, Russia, Italy, Korea) accounted for more than one-half of world cotton imports. Apart from Russia (which before 1990 was considered a major producer but not an importer because Central Asian cotton production was considered internal trade), most of the remaining cotton importers are new in the sense that they have been importing cotton to supply newly developed textile industries. For example, four East Asian textile producers (Indonesia, Thailand, Taiwan, and Korea) accounted for less than 3 percent of world cotton imports in 1960, compared to 22 percent in 2002.

The International Cotton Advisory Committee (ICAC) collects data comparing costs of production among cotton producers. Its most recent 2001 survey, based on a questionnaire of 28 cotton-producing countries, suggests that West Africa (especially Benin, Mali, and Burkina Faso), Uganda, and Tanzania are among the lowest-cost cotton producers. High-cost producers are the United States, Israel, and Syria. The two European cotton producers, Greece and Spain, are probably the world's highest-cost cotton producers, although they did not participate in the survey. Calculating and comparing the costs of producing cotton in various countries is, admittedly, a difficult task, involving assumptions about the cost of land and capital as well as various hidden subsidies and distortions. The ICAC (2001) warns that its data must be used carefully: "Differences in production practices, variations in the input supply among countries, and direct and indirect technical and financial support to farmers in the form of free seed, technical advice, etc., make comparisons difficult among countries."

Population growth for the current decade is projected at 1.2 percent a year. In the absence of policy reforms by major players, ICAC (2003a and 2003b) projects that annual consumption growth during the decade will be about 1.8 percent, implying that by 2010 world cotton consumption will be 23.6 million tons. That may be optimistic, however, considering that for the last 15 years cotton consumption grew at an annual rate of just 0.7 percent.

Price Trends and Variability

Real cotton prices over the last two centuries have followed a declining pattern showing temporary spikes and troughs. The reasons for the long-term decline are similar to those behind the price declines in most primary commodities—reduction in the costs of production due to technological improvements, slow demand growth, and strong competition from substitutes (in this case, chemical fibers). The declining pattern of cotton prices has not been smooth, and it appears that a structural break took place in the mid-1980s. Between 1960 and 1984 real cotton prices averaged $2.62 per kilogram. Following a sharp decline in 1984 (from $2.45 per kilogram in 1984 to $1.83 in 1985 and $1.27 in 1986), they have been fluctuating around $1.49 per kilogram. Between 1985 and 2002, prices declined 0.9 percent a year (as opposed to just 0.2 percent a year during 1960–84).

Reductions in the costs of production stem primarily from yield increases—from 300 kilograms per hectare in the early 1960s to 600 kilograms per hectare in the late 1990s. The phenomenal yield growth is attributable to the introduction of improved cotton varieties, expansion of irrigation, use of chemicals and fertilizers, and mechanical harvesting. To these improvements one should add developments in genetically modified seed technology and precision farming during the late-1990s, which are expected to further reduce the costs of production. Innovations in transportation and information technology have lowered costs of transporting cotton and reduced the need to hold large inventories. Substantial technological improvements in the textile sectors have made it possible to obtain high-quality fabric from lower-quality cotton, a trend that holds for many products whose main input is a primary commodity.

The prime movers behind the 1984–85 decline in cotton prices were the structural shift in the support policy of the United States and the shift in China's trade policy (MacDonald 1997). During the 1950s the U.S. Commodity Credit Corporation bought and sold most American cotton. For example, between 1962 and 1966, it accounted for almost two-thirds of cotton stocks. Although its role was reduced after 1970, the United States still accounted for 35 percent of world cotton stocks (exclusive of Chinese stocks). Following enactment of the 1985

Farm Bill, support prices for cotton (that is, "loan rates," the equivalent of a floor price) were substantially reduced, and most of the U.S. stocks were released to the market, depressing the world prices. 1985 also marked the beginnings of large exports by China, which for the previous 20 years had been a net importer. In fact between 1980 and 1985, China went from the world's largest importer to the world's largest exporter.

Visual inspection of the 1984–85 price decline suggests a structural break in the series, something also supported by statistical tests. However, it may be argued that if the policy shift in the United States, which caused massive destocking, had been the main reason behind the price decline, a new stock equilibrium level would have brought a price increase, making the 1984–85 decline temporary. In reality, the U.S. policy shift accelerated a price decline that would have taken place even without it. Real cotton prices did rise somewhat after the shift but never reached pre-1984 levels.

While falling, cotton prices have been volatile. Admittedly, measuring volatility is a difficult (and often tricky) task precisely because prices have shown a long-term, nonlinear decline, making it difficult to isolate a meaningful average around which variability can be defined. Defining volatility as variability from one year to another shows that during 1985–2002 volatility was 2.5 times higher than in 1960–72 but only half of the level in 1973–84. Note that 1973 reflects the commodity price boom, while 1985 coincides with the U.S. change in cotton policy and the subsequent disposal of large cotton stocks. In summary, cotton prices were very stable before 1974, highly volatile until 1985, and then less volatile, but not as stable as before 1974.

Cotton and the Developing Countries

Although cotton trade is insignificant on a global scale—accounting for just 0.12 percent of total merchandise trade—it is an important cash crop for several developing countries at both the farm and national levels. Cotton accounted for between 30 and 44 percent for total merchandise exports in five West African countries (Burkina Faso, Benin, Chad, Mali, Togo) during 1998–99 (table 14.1). The corresponding figures for Uzbekistan, Tajikistan, and Turkmenistan are 32, 15, and 12 percent. Cotton's contribution to the gross domestic product (GDP) of these countries has been substantial, ranging between 3.6 percent

TABLE 14.1   Cotton's Importance to Developing and Transition Economies, 1989–99 Average

| Country[a] | Cotton Exports | | Percent of GDP | Merchandise Exports (millions of dollars) | Per Capita GDP[b] |
	Millions of Dollars	Percent of Merchandise Exports			
Burkina Faso	127	43.9	5.1	289	249
Benin	164	39.1	7.1	419	398
Uzbekistan	1,038	32.2	6.5	3,227	467
Chad	76	32.2	4.7	236	224
Mali	180	29.5	6.7	611	285
Togo	67	21.3	4.7	315	341
Tajikistan	97	15.1	8.2	643	352
Turkmenistan	110	12.3	3.6	891	1,126
Tanzania	44	7.6	0.5	576	185
Syrian Arab Rep.	214	6.7	1.4	3,177	858
Sudan	41	6.0	0.4	688	290

a. Countries ranked by decreasing order of cotton exports in merchandise exports; b. Constant 1995 U.S. dollars.
Source: FAOSTAT, and World Bank, World Development Indicators, various years.

(Turkmenistan) and 8.2 percent (Tajikistan). With the exception of Turkmenistan and Syria, the per capita annual GDP in these countries is well below $500. In most (especially in Africa), cotton is typically a smallholder crop and the main cash crop. It is grown in rain-fed land with minimal use of purchased inputs such as chemicals and fertilizers.

According to FAO (Food and Agriculture Organization) estimates, as many as 100 million rural households may have been involved in cotton production during 2001. In China, India, and Pakistan about 45, 10, and 7 million rural households, respectively, were engaged in cotton production. The total number of rural households depending on cotton in major African producing countries, including Nigeria, Benin, Togo, Mali, and Zimbabwe, was 6 million.

The high dependence on cotton in these countries has important ramifications for poverty, especially when prices change suddenly. In a study of Benin, Minot and Daniels (2002) estimated that a 40 percent reduction in farm-gate cotton prices—equivalent to the price decline that occurred between December 2000 and May 2002—implied a 7 percent reduction in rural per capita income in the short run and a 5–6 percent reduction in the long run. They also estimated that the incidence of poverty among cotton growers will rise in the short run from 37 percent to 59 percent, while the average incidence of rural poverty (among cotton growers and other farmers) will increase from 40 percent to 48 percent.

In terms of policy interventions, the cotton sector in developing countries has been traditionally taxed either explicitly through export taxes or implicitly through price-fixing arrangements or exchange-rate misalignments. The pattern, however, changed somewhat during the 1990s, as a number of cotton producers undertook policy reforms. However, several African and all Central Asian cotton producers still tax their cotton sectors.

Nonconventional Cotton Production

Recent trends in growing cotton focus on cost reductions through less intensive use of inputs, especially chemicals. These include the use of genetically modified seed technology and organic methods of production. Genetically modified

cotton (sometimes referred to as B_t cotton) has not faced the degree of opposition faced by genetically modified food crops, allowing more rapid adoption. Organic cotton has been embraced enthusiastically by environmental activists but not by consumers. Hence, while there is plenty of room for expanding genetically modified cotton, the scope for expanding organic cotton appears to be limited.

Genetically modified cotton, a result of technological developments of the 1990s, has the potential of reducing the cost of production and hence increasing profitability of the early adopters of this technology. Like other genetically modified products, it provides insurance against pests, insects, and weeds. Growers pay a premium for the resistant seed, as they would when buying insurance.

Genetically modified cotton was first grown in the United States in 1996. Among the cotton-producing countries that have introduced it since then are China, India, and Mexico in the Northern Hemisphere and Argentina, Australia, and South Africa in the Southern. Other countries are in the process of approval or at the trial stage, including Brazil, Indonesia, Israel, Pakistan, and Turkey. Major producers that had not used or approved genetically modified cotton as of 2003 were the European Union, Central Asia, and Francophone Africa (except Burkina Faso, which is conducting trials).

It is estimated that about 22 percent of the world's cotton plantings are now in genetically modified varieties, up from 2 percent in 1996–97. The largest user of such cotton is the United States, which during the 2003–04 season is estimated to have sown 70 percent of its cotton area with genetically modified varieties. In Australia about 44 percent of cotton area was sown to such varieties in 2002–03, up from 40 percent two years earlier. In China, which adopted the new technology at an experimental stage in 1996, more than 20 million hectares were planted with genetically modified varieties in 2002, corresponding to more than 20 percent of cotton acreage. In addition to the imported genetically modified varieties, China has developed 11 of its own varieties. According to Pray and others (2001), the major share of the benefits from growing B_t cotton in China went to farmers (most of whom are smallholders). In contrast, most of the benefits associated with genetically modified products in the other cotton-producing countries go to biotech and seed companies. They also found that the increased use of genetically modified cotton in China was associated with considerable positive health effects—notably fewer hospitalizations from pesticide poisoning. Farmers who did not use B_t cotton had to spray 12 times on average, whereas farmers who used B_t cotton had to spray only 3–4 times. If the conversion to genetically modified cotton varieties continues at rates experienced during the last few years, as much as half of the world's cotton (from 40 percent of total cotton acreage) will be of genetically modified origin within five years.

The second trend, organic cotton, may be a small market niche to be exploited by developing countries. Many developing countries can be classified as "organic" cotton producers without altering their current production practices because of their low reliance on chemicals and fertilizers. The potential for organic cotton appears to be limited, however. Organic cotton initiatives have taken place in many countries, including in Africa, but the scale is still insignificant compared to global production of conventional cotton. Myers and Stolton (1999) reported that in 1997, about 8,150 tons of certified organic cotton fiber was produced worldwide—2,600 tons was produced in the United States, 1,175 in India, 1,800 in Turkey, 1,570 in Africa, and 845 in Latin America.

Significant expansion of organic cotton faces difficulties on both the supply and demand sides. On the supply side, the certification process (especially in African cotton-producing countries where the majority of growers are smallholders) is costly to implement and monitor. On the consumption side, demand for organic cotton is not as strong as it is for other commodities such as coffee and tea. There are three reasons for this. First, there is a "distance" in the eyes of the consumer between the primary product (cotton) and the final product (cloth). Second, consumers of clothing (as opposed to consumers of, say, beverages) must pay attention to a host of factors before they make their purchasing decision. The decision involves brand, color, style, size, type of cotton (typically identified by its country of origin), content (for example, 80 percent cotton, 20 percent polyester), and care instructions. Adding to that already congested list information on whether the cotton is of organic origin is rather difficult. Note that this decision-making process compares unfavorably with much simpler labeling for, say, coffee or tea where something like "Organically grown from Costa Rica" or "Organic of Kenyan origin" is likely to suffice. Third, organic products are typically associated with health-related benefits that do not apply to nonfood products such as cotton.

Distortions in the Cotton Market

Cotton has been subject to various marketing and trade interventions. Townsend and Guitchounts (1994) estimated that in the early 1990s, more than two-thirds of cotton was produced in countries that had some type of government intervention, including taxation and subsidization policies. The ICAC (2002 and 2003), which has been monitoring the level of assistance to cotton production by major producers since 1997–98, found that eight countries provided direct support to cotton production—Brazil, China, Arab Republic of Egypt, Greece, Mexico, Spain, Turkey, and the United States (table 14.2). For 2001–02, direct government assistance to U.S. cotton producers reached $3.9 billion; China's support totaled $1.2 billion; and the European Union's was almost $1 billion. Producers in Brazil, Egypt, Mexico, and Turkey received a combined total of $150 million in support. India also supported its cotton sector in 2001–02 with an estimated $0.5 billion.

In addition to domestic support, some border restrictions apply, mainly in the form of import tariffs. Most countries that impose import quotas are cotton exporters, some with large textiles sectors. Import tariffs rates for 2003 were: Argentina (7.5 percent); Brazil (7.5 to 10 percent); China (3 percent within quota, 90 percent outside quota[3]); Egypt (5 percent); India (10 percent); United States (4.4 cents per kilogram within quota and 31.4 cents per kilogram outside quota[4]); Uzbekistan (10 percent); and Zimbabwe (15 percent duty plus 5 percent import tax).

The remainder of this section analyzes the structure and degree of interventions in the United States, European Union, and China. It also looks at Uzbekistan, a country that taxes its cotton sector.

United States

The main channels of support in the United States are decoupled payments (formerly known as

quota not binding

TABLE 14.2   Direct Government Assistance to Cotton Producers, 1997–98 to 2002–03
(US$ millions)

Country	1997–98	1998–99	1999–2000	2000–2001	2001–02	2002–03
United States	1,163	1,946	3,432	2,148	3,964	2,620
China	2,013	2,648	1,534	1,900	1,196	750
Greece	659	660	596	537	735	718
Spain	211	204	199	179	245	239
Turkey	—	220	199	106	59	57
Brazil	29	52	44	44	10	—
Mexico	13	15	28	23	18	7
Egypt, Arab Rep.	290	—	20	14	23	33

— Not available. Data for 2001–02 are preliminary.
Source: ICAC 2002 and 2003, U.S. Department of Agriculture, and European Union.

TABLE 14.3   Government Assistance to U.S. Cotton Producers, 1995–96 to 2002–03
(US$ millions)

Policy Instrument	1995–96	1996–97	1997–98	1998–99	1999–2000	2000–01	2001–02	2002–03
Coupled payments	3	0	28	535	1,613	563	2,507	248
PFC/DP	0	599	597	637	614	575	474	914
Emergency/CCP	0	0	0	316	613	613	524	1,264
Insurance	180	157	148	151	170	162	236	194
Step-2	34	3	390	308	422	236	196	—
Total	217	759	1,163	1,946	3,432	2,148	3,964	2,620

— Not available.
Note: PFC denotes production flexibility contracts, DP denotes direct payments, CCP denotes countercyclical payments.
Source: U.S. Department of Agriculture (assistance); International Cotton Advisory Committee (production); and author's calculations.

production flexibility contracts), loan deficiency payments (through the loan-rate mechanism), insurance, subsidies to domestic mills (the so-called Step-2 mechanism, also referred to as export subsidy), and emergency payments (introduced in 1998 to compensate for the loss of income caused by low commodity prices but made "permanent" under the 2002 Farm Bill) (table 14.3). Direct payments, predetermined annual payments based on historically enrolled areas of cotton, were introduced with the 1996 Farm Bill to compensate farmers for "losses" stemming from elimination of earlier loan deficiency payments. Market price payments are designed to compensate cotton growers for the difference between the world price and the loan rate (the target price) when the latter exceeds the former. Export subsidies, or Step-2 market payments, are made to eligible cotton exporters and domestic end users of cotton when domestic U.S. prices exceed c.i.f. (cost, insurance, and freight) prices in northern Europe by a certain level and the world price is within a certain level of the base loan rate. The objective of the Step-2 payment is to bridge the gap between higher U.S. domestic prices and world prices so that U.S. exporters and textile mills maintain their competitiveness.

In 2002 the U.S. Congress passed a farm bill that is expected to be in place for the next six years. The 2002 Farm Bill retained the earlier support through various loans, flexibility contracts, and insurance, as well as the Step-2 payment, while legitimizing emergency assistance under the term "countercyclical payments." If cotton prices remain at their

2001–02 levels, then U.S. support to its cotton sector is expected to be in the order of $3.5 billion to $4.0 billion for the next six years, implying the U.S. cotton producers will be receiving close to twice the world market price.

European Union

In the 1960s there were three cotton producers in Europe. Greece and Spain produced an average of 85,000 tons each; Bulgaria produced 25,000 tons. Throughout the 1970s Bulgaria's output declined, while that of Greece and Spain stayed at the levels seen during the 1960s. Cotton production by the three countries taken together declined by 0.4 percent a year between 1960 and 1982. With the European Union's expansion and the subsequent accession of Greece and Spain, cotton production grew by an annual average of 7.3 percent during the 1990s, averaging 325,000 and 78,000 tons in Greece and Spain, respectively.

Under the EU Common Agricultural Policy (CAP), support is given to cotton growers based on the difference between the market price and a guide (support) price. Advance payments are made to ginners based on estimates of seed cotton production. They pass the subsidy on to growers by paying higher prices. The policy also influences the quantity of cotton produced by setting a maximum guaranteed quantity of seed cotton for which assistance is provided—782,000 tons of seed cotton for Greece, and 249,000 for Spain, approximately equivalent to 255,000 and 82,000 tons of cotton lint.

The European Union reformed its cotton program in 1999 (European Commission 2000). While the guide price level and the maximum guaranteed quantity of seed cotton for which assistance is provided have been maintained, "penalties" (that is, reductions in subsidy) for excess production over the maximum guaranteed quantity increased. Under the reformed policy, for each 1 percent of excess production, the level of subsidy is lowered by 0.6 percent of the guide price as opposed to 0.5 percent prior to 1999. As production increases, the penalty becomes stiffer, effectively, putting an upper limit on the budgetary outlays to the cotton sector. It is important to note that this quantitative restriction (the so-called maximum quantity guaranteed) applies at the aggregate (that is, country)

level, implying that when this restriction is converted to individual basis, it creates not only administrative complexities but also leads to misallocation of resources (see chapter 5 on decoupling for more on this issue). Karagiannis and Pantzios (2002) found that the current system failed as a surplus containment mechanism and also resulted in farm income losses.

Between 1995–96 and 1999–2000 the budgetary expenditure on cotton aid ranged between €740 million and €903 million, implying that, on average, EU cotton producers received more than twice the world price of cotton. Note that even in periods of high prices, EU cotton producers would receive support since the amount allocated to the cotton sector had to be disbursed. In addition to output subsidies, EU cotton producers receive subsidies on inputs such as credit for machinery purchase, insurance, and publicly financed irrigation. On September 23, 2003, the EU Commission proposed to reform its cotton, sugar, and tobacco sectors (European Commission 2003). Under the cotton reform proposal, EU support to the cotton sector will consist of the following parts: a single farm payment scheme; a production aid scheme, granted as an area payment; and development measures.

China

China is currently the largest producer, consumer, and stockholder of cotton. China's cotton sector became fully government-controlled in 1953 after the introduction of the first Five-Year Plan (Zhong and Fang 2003). The central planning policies adopted then were similar to those of the Soviet Union and remained in place for the next 35 years. The central government set production targets and procurement quotas. This monopoly was easily exercised because all ginning facilities were owned by the cooperatives. A step to boost cotton production was taken in 1978 by increasing the price of cotton as well as supplying more fertilizer. A second boost came in 1980 with the partial abolition of the communal production system under the Household Responsibility System, which gave land use rights to individual farmers.

Evidence suggests that the government of China protects its cotton sector through support prices, import tariffs, export subsidies, and public stockholding. The government sets a reference price for cotton, typically above world prices. China also maintains tariffs on imports that bridge the gap between domestic and world prices. Following its WTO (World Trade Organization) accession arrangements the tariffs will be reduced to 15 percent, but at the same time a tariff-related quota system will be implemented to manage imports.

The International Cotton Advisory Committee found that support to the cotton sector in the six seasons beginning in 1997–98 ranged from $0.8 billion to $2.6 billion. Huang, Rozelle, and Chang (2004) estimated that during 2001 the nominal rate of protection for cotton averaged 17 percent. Fang and Beghin (2003), however, estimated that between 1997 and 2000, the nominal protection coefficient for cotton has averaged 0.80, implying that China taxes its cotton sector by 20 percent. The different views on the nature and degree of intervention, however, should not be surprising given the complexities of China's agricultural policies as well as the unreliability of the data.

In September 1999 the government of China announced reform measures which included the creation of a cotton exchange to facilitate domestic spot trading; the reduction of prices paid to producers; and a reduction in stocks. In some sense the reforms have worked: China's stocks declined from 4.1 million tons in 1998–99 to 2.3 million tons in 2000–01. In September 2001 further reforms were announced and are currently under way (Zhong and Fang 2003). First, the internal cotton market would be open to cross-regional trade. Second, various enterprises would be allowed to buy cotton directly from producers with approval granted by the provincial government. Third, ginning operations would be separated from marketing cooperatives, in effect making them commercial enterprises.

Uzbekistan

Uzbekistan, the world's fifth largest cotton producer and second largest cotton exporter, produces more than 1 million tons of cotton annually, most of which is exported. During 1998–99 cotton exports accounted for one-third of total merchandise exports, while the sector contributed an average of 6.4 percent to the country's GDP. Before 1991 all aspects of Uzbekistan's cotton sector were under state control (of the Soviet Union). Most cotton was either consumed by mills in Russia (then considered domestic trade) or shipped to Eastern European countries under barter arrangements. Following the collapse of the Soviet Union, Uzbekistan began exporting its cotton to Western countries in exchange for foreign currency (until 1996 some cotton still went to Russia in barter trade terms).

Although 12 years have passed since the change in the trade regime, most aspects of production, marketing, and trade of the sector closely resemble pre-1991 arrangements. Numerous entities are involved in all postproduction activities of cotton. The three most important ones are the state company handling ginning; the state trading organizations handling exports; and the Ministry of Foreign and Economic Relations, handling financial transactions.

All pre- and post-ginning operations of cotton are handled by UzKhlopkoprom/UzPakhtasanoitish (UKP), a state company that used to be a ministry. UKP is responsible for collecting, storing, ginning, and classifying cotton, making payments to growers, and providing inputs. UKP owns considerable assets, including all ginning and storage facilities as well as handling machinery and equipment.

The second important entities are the three state trading organizations (STOs) in charge of handling all aspects of cotton exports. The main responsibilities of these organizations include contracting cotton merchants for the sale of cotton, organizing the availability and shipment of cotton, receiving payments and converting them into local currency, and paying UKP. Although these organizations have a number of other responsibilities (such as purchasing machinery and equipment on behalf of the government), exporting cotton is their core activity. Because each organization has been allocated a quota of cotton to be exported, there is no competition involved in the export process.

The third important entity is the Ministry of Foreign Economic Relations, which reports directly to the government. Its main function is to manage cotton export operations, including setting prices, selecting buyers, and monitoring dollar receipts. Several other entities are involved in the sector including the state company responsible for domestic and international transportation of cotton, the organization responsible for quality monitoring, and the customs agency.

It appears that cotton growers are heavily taxed both directly through the lower price received by UKP (which, in turn, receives a fixed price from the STOs, as dictated by the Ministry) and indirectly through the exchange rate regime. A recent study (Uzbekistan 2003) found that at an ex-ginnery price of $1.03 a kilogram, the STOs receive the equivalent of $0.63 a kilogram (these calculations were based on a Cotlook A Index (price) of $1.24 a kilogram). With respect to the difference between $1.03 and $0.63 a kilogram, the study concluded: "It is not clear exactly where this profitability figure is allocated. It is alleged that, after a marketing fee is deducted, the balance is paid to the Ministry of Finance as an export duty." The declared price to be paid to farmers by UKP is 126,000 Sum per ton of seed cotton, which, at an exchange rate of 960 Sum per U.S. dollar and a 32 percent ginning out-turn ratio, implies a price of $0.41 a kilogram, about one-third of the A Index.

Perhaps, it is not unreasonable to conclude that even though cotton exports from Uzbekistan moved from a barter to a commercially oriented structure, the sector is still tightly controlled by the government. Moreover, growers are taxed heavily, receiving only about one-third of the export price of cotton.

Impact of Distortions and Prospects for Reform

The ICAC (2003a) concluded that in the absence of direct subsidies, average cotton prices during the 2000–01 and 2001–02 seasons would have been 17 and 31 cents a pound higher, respectively. If the United States alone removed its subsidies during these two seasons, world cotton prices would have been 6 and 11 cents higher, respectively. These figures imply cotton prices 30 and 71 percent higher than the actual averages of 57.2 and 41.8 cents a pound. The study, which is based on a short-run partial equilibrium analysis, does acknowledge that while removal of subsidies would result in lower production in the countries that receive them (and hence higher prices in the short term), such impact would be partially offset by shifting production to nonsubsidizing countries in the medium to longer terms; similarly higher prices are likely to reduce the growth of cotton consumption, making the long-run impact less striking.

Quirke (2002) estimated that removal of production and export subsidies by the United States and the European Union are likely to induce a 20 percent reduction in U.S. cotton production and a 50 percent reduction in U.S. cotton exports, with much higher figures for the European Union. He also estimated that if support was not in place, world cotton prices would be 10.7 percent higher compared to their 2001–02 levels.

Based on a partial equilibrium model, Tokarick (2003) found that multilateral trade liberalization in all agricultural markets (including cotton) is expected to induce a 2.8 percent increase in the world prices of cotton, with 0.8 percent coming from the removal of market price support and the remaining 2 percent coming from the removal of production subsidies (removal of market price support most likely applies to the United States Step-2 payment). Tokarick also calculated that global reforms would lead to $95 million in total change in welfare a year.

FAPRI (2002) found that under global liberalization (that is, removal of trade barriers and domestic support of all commodity sectors), the world cotton price would increase over the baseline scenario by an average of 12.7 percent over the 10-year period (table 14.4). The largest gains in trade would go to Africa, which would increase its exports by an average of 12.6 percent. Exports from Uzbekistan and Australia would increase by 6.0 and 2.7 percent, respectively, while exports from the United States would decline by 3.5 percent. The most dramatic impact is on the production side where the European Union's cotton output would decline by more than 70 percent. The latter outcome should not be a complete surprise, considering that the European Union's cotton output during the late 1990s was, on average, three times as much as it was before CAP took effect on the cotton sector.

Prospects for policy reforms by major producers subsidizing the sector are mixed. Support for cotton in the European Union is unlikely to increase for two reasons. First the countries expected to join the EU are not cotton producers and hence there will be no budgetary pressure. Second, the current support scheme is subject to an upper spending cap that appears to be a binding constraint; both Greece and Spain, being among the world's highest-cost cotton producers, are unlikely to

TABLE 14.4   Estimated Effect of Removal of Distortions
(percentage changes over baseline)

Variable	2003–04	2005–06	2007–08	2009–10	2011–12	Average[a]
World price	15.6	13.7	13.0	12.2	11.7	12.7
Exports						
Africa	12.1	15.1	14.0	13.1	12.3	12.6
Australia	3.9	3.0	2.7	2.3	2.1	2.7
United States	−8.4	−6.6	−4.0	−1.5	0.9	−3.5
Uzbekistan	5.4	6.9	6.7	6.4	6.2	6.0
World	3.9	5.6	6.2	6.7	7.3	5.8
Production						
Africa	4.5	7.5	7.1	6.7	6.3	6.0
European Union	−77.4	−77.7	−78.3	−78.8	−79.0	−70.5
United States	−18.3	−7.9	−5.9	−4.1	−2.3	−6.7
Uzbekistan	3.1	4.7	4.6	4.4	4.2	4.0

a. Average is taken over the 10-year period 2001–02 to 2010–11.
Source: FAPRI 2002.

increase production given the reduced support they would receive if they exceed the current output levels. At the same time, support is not expected to be eliminated because it supposedly goes to low-income areas and hence it is regarded as a poverty reduction program.

The nature of support is shifting away from direct price support toward partially decoupled payments. Beginning in 2006, the EU cotton sector will go through another reform. Under the Luxembourg Council's decisions of April 22, 2004 (which was based on the September 2003 proposal), an estimated €700 million will fund two support measures, with 65 percent of the total coming in the form of a single farm payment decoupled from current production decisions and the remaining 35 percent in the form of an area payment. Eligibility for the decoupled payment will be limited to growers who produced cotton during the three-year period from 1999 to 2001. The area payment will be given for a maximum area of 380,000 hectares in Greece, 85,000 hectares in Spain, and 360 hectares in Portugal and will be proportionately reduced if claims exceed the maximum area allocated to each country. To receive decoupled payments, cotton growers must keep the land in good agricultural use. To receive area payments they must plant (not necessarily produce) cotton. Karagiannis (2004) estimated that the reformed regime is likely to reduce EU cotton production between 10 and 25 percent (depending on the assumed elasticity of supply).

The United States took a step in the right direction with the replacement of the deficiency payment system by decoupled payments in 1996, but all progress was eliminated with the 2002 Farm Bill, which effectively legitimized emergency payments introduced in 1998–99 following the sharp decline in prices; renamed them as countercyclical payments; increased target prices; and made it more convenient for larger farmers to increase the support they receive. Historically, U.S. farm bills either give what they promise or give more than they promise (as the recent experience showed). Hence, if history is any guide, it is reasonable to expect that U.S. cotton farmers will be receiving generous support for the next six years, unless the support exceeds WTO commitments, in which case the U.S. secretary of agriculture has the discretion to intervene and reduce it.

A number of factors may induce some early reforms, however. First, the substantial increase of the support to the U.S. cotton sector along with 30-year record low prices and the fact that 10 percent of U.S. cotton growers receive 90 percent of the support (hence falsifying the claim that support preserves the small farm), is likely to put pressure for altering the nature of policy sooner. Second, Brazil's request for consultations at the WTO regarding U.S. cotton subsidies may create some pressure to lower subsidies (WTO 2002). Third, four West African cotton-producing countries (Benin, Burkina Faso, Chad, and Mali) pressed for removal of support to cotton sector through the WTO. In an unusual move, the president of Burkina Faso addressed the WTO on June 10, 2003, asking for financial compensation for cotton-producing low-income countries to offset the injury caused by support. This compensation, according to the request, should be in place for as long as subsidies are in place.

China appears to be the most promising case of reform. The reforms undertaken in 1999 and more recently in 2001 indicate that its cotton sector will be soon exposed to internal and external competition. China is also in the process of establishing a cotton futures exchange, indicating that market forces within the sector are likely to play a more significant role in the future (Shuhua 2003).

On the international side, while the phase-out of the Agreements on Textiles and Clothing (ATC) is supposed to end the distortions imposed on the location of the textile industries, it is uncertain whether the expected benefits will be fully realized.

- First, ATC is back-loaded, with most of the reforms expected to take place in the last year, thus increasing the risk of noncompliance.
- Second, a number of (mainly European Union) countries have repeatedly sought to impose antidumping duties on textile imports from Asia in recent years.
- Third, a number of provisions under the ATC allow for the imposition of temporary duties in the case that current domestic textiles suffer "significant damage" following the phaseout.

Reform Initiatives in Africa

During the 1990s, a number of African cotton-producing countries undertook substantial reforms. The reform process and its outcome have been studied extensively. See, for example, Kähkönen and Leathers (1997) for Zambia and Tanzania; Sabune (1996) and Lundbæk (2002) for Uganda; Larsen (2002) for Zimbabwe; Baffes (2001) for Uganda, Zimbabwe, and Tanzania; Baffes (2000), Badiane and others (2002), and Goreux and Macrae (2003) for Francophone Africa; Baffes (2004) and Gibbon (1999) for Tanzania. Poulton and others (2004) looked at the cotton sectors of six African countries, while Shepherd and Farolfi (1999) reviewed export commodity sectors for a number of sub-Saharan African countries.

Reforms in East African cotton-producing countries were in response to the inefficiencies faced by the parastatals that used to handle most (and in some occasions all) aspects of marketing and trade. For the most part, policy reforms meant elimination of the monopoly powers of the parastatals. Although the outcome of these reforms appears to have been mixed, if one considers that the countries that undertook reforms also faced the most difficulties, one may argue that reforms have been successful. For example, during the eight-year period staring in 1995–96, cotton output in Uganda has averaged 17,000 tons, an almost three-fold increase compared with the eight seasons before 1995–96. The corresponding world price average before 1995–96 was $1.56 a kilogram; after it was $1.40 a kilogram. The farmers' share in world prices rose from less than 50 percent to 70 percent after the reforms, while a number of new traders and exporters entered the sector. This success came despite the failure of most credit mechanisms that were launched after the reforms.

In Zimbabwe reforms appear to have been successful. First, cotton production is up substantially. During the eight seasons since 1995–96, cotton output has averaged 115,000 tons, 50 percent higher than the eight-year period average before 1995–96. Some 30 percent of the 1997–98 cotton harvest was marketed entirely by private entities. Private companies now transport most of the cotton. Competition has pushed the price farmers receive to close to 80 percent of international prices, and producers are being paid faster. Zimbabwe has also retained the premium for quality it used to receive in the world market.

The outcome of cotton reforms in Tanzania has been mixed. On the positive side, the share of producer prices increased to 51 percent (from 41 percent before the reforms). Furthermore, cotton growers receive payments quickly, a major achievement compared with the delays encountered before the reforms. Contrary to what many reports show, quality of cotton appears not to have suffered considerably. At the same time, cotton production since 1995–96 has averaged less than before reforms (55,000 after, compared with 61,000 tons before). On the policy side, the Cotton Board along with the two line ministries (Agriculture and Food Security, and Cooperatives) still play a major role in the sector that goes far beyond the regulatory role they are supposed to play. Collection and dissemination of data (as well as accuracy of statistics) are poor even by the government's own admission.

Reforms are also under way in West Africa. The World Bank has argued that the discipline and responsibility that a free-entry competitive system imposes on market participants would make for a more resilient, flexible, self-reliant, and innovative national cotton sector. Improved competition through market reforms offers important opportunities for regional trade and cooperation, the latter in areas such as research, phytosanitary regulations, and seed development and certification. Most important, improved sector performance would contribute to alleviating poverty by raising cotton prices to levels enjoyed by farmers elsewhere in the world.

Significant developments have taken place during the last few years, which indicate the future direction of institutional changes in the region's cotton sector. Three countries, Benin, Côte d'Ivoire, and Togo, have now opened their sector to private ginners. Benin and Côte d'Ivoire have eliminated the monopoly power of their national companies and transferred key responsibilities to the private sector.

Summary and Conclusions

Cotton is very important to a number of low-income African and Central Asian countries, in some cases contributing as much as 40 percent to merchandise exports and between 5 and 10 percent to GDP. Considering that in most countries cotton is a smallholder crop, the implications of price changes (either induced by market forces or policy interventions) as well as changes in market share are enormous. For example, a 40 percent reduction in price (the equivalent of the price decline that took place from December 2000 to May 2002) implies a 7 percent reduction in rural income in Benin—a typical cotton-producing country in West Africa. Cotton also faces intense competition from chemical fibers, especially following technological improvements in the early 1970s that brought their prices down to cotton price levels. Since 1975, polyester and cotton have been traded at roughly the same price levels. Currently, the share of cotton in total fiber consumption is 40 percent (down from 68 percent in 1960).

Although cotton faces minimal border restrictions, there is considerable domestic support.

Major subsidizers are the United States, $3.96 billion in 2001–02 and the European Union—Greece and Spain—$0.98 billion (compare this to $20 billion, the value of world's cotton production, evaluated at 2001 prices and quantities). This level of support implies that prices received by U.S. and EU cotton producers are 87 and 160 percent above world prices. China reportedly has been supporting its cotton sector during the last few seasons by an estimated $1.5 billion annually. Many cotton-producing countries have reacted to low prices by introducing offsetting support. Support in Turkey, Brazil, Mexico, Egypt, and India, totaled $0.6 billion during 2001–02. Further, Brazil initiated a WTO consultation process claiming losses to its cotton exports due to subsidies by the United States. WTO determined in its interim ruling that indeed the U.S. cotton program has violated the Agreement on Agriculture. Not only is this decision an important victory for Brazil, but it may also trigger similar cases, especially in view of the expiration of the Peace Clause in the Uruguay Round Agreement on Agriculture. More recently, four West African cotton-producing countries (Benin, Burkina Faso, Chad, and Mali) pressed for removal of support to the cotton sector through the WTO (the so-called "cotton initiative"). This compensation, according to the request, should be in place for as long as subsidies are in place.

Given the highly distorted nature of the cotton market and the fact that millions of rural poor households in developing countries depend on this commodity, what are the alternatives? As discussed earlier, a number of developing countries, especially in Sub-Saharan Africa have undertaken policy reforms during the 1990s. Setting aside the lively debate on the motives of the reforms, in many respects the reforms have been successful. For example, in the few cases reviewed here, cotton growers received a higher share of f.o.b. prices, they also received payments more promptly, and there was considerable supply response. In an environment of declining commodity prices, these are not trivial achievements. In a number of cases, however, the reform process has either not been completed (Tanzania), has been reversed (Zimbabwe), has been slow (West Africa), or has not even started (Uzbekistan). In these cases further reforms are the only feasible alternative.

A second issue that should receive attention is the enabling policy environment regarding the use of genetically modified cotton. In China for example, where genetically modified cotton is used extensively by smallholders, the costs of producing cotton declined by 20–25 percent. This cost reduction meant doubling the net income for cotton growers. One should also note that genetically modified cotton has not been subject to negative consumer reaction as has been the case with genetically modified food products.

A third issue (and one closely related to genetically modified cotton) is organic cotton. Producers of organic products typically command significant premiums. However, organic cotton production has not been as profitable as other organic crops (such as coffee and tea). The main reason is weak demand, which appears to be a reflection of the "distance" between the farm product—cotton—and the final product—cloth. It is because of this distance that genetically modified cotton has not faced resistance by the consumers, which further reinforces the conclusion that genetically modified cotton is something that developing countries should consider seriously.

The price prospects (and consequently the export shares of low-cost producers, including many African countries) can be improved considerably if support by developed countries is reduced substantially or eliminated altogether. Given the low probability of eliminating support, however, a second-best alternative would be for support to be given in a nondistortionary manner. A type of support with minimal distortionary effects—the so-called decoupled support mechanisms—has regained popularity recently. Income transfers under decoupled mechanisms are based on past production and prices and thus have no effect on current production decisions. What makes decoupled support in the cotton sector an interesting (and potentially applicable) alternative is that almost all support comes in the form of domestic measures. Therefore, changing the nature of support does not require changing the sources of funding, as it would in the case of border measures.

Notes

1. A more detailed version of this chapter is presented in Annex 14 of the attached CD-ROM.

2. Fibers include a wide variety of products that can be divided into two broad categories: natural and man-made. Natural fibers can be further divided into fibers of plant origin (such as cotton and linen) and fibers of animal origin (such as wool and silk). Likewise, man-made fibers can be further divided into inorganic and organic fibers. Inorganic fibers are materials such as ceramic, glass, and carbon (typically not used in garments.) Organic man-made fibers, on the other hand, are mostly used in garment production either as substitutes or as complements to natural fibers. Organic fibers are further subdivided into natural and synthetic polymers. Natural polymers (often called cellulosic) are made from wood. The most common natural polymer is viscose, also known as rayon. The synthetic polymers are made from crude oil. The most common synthetic polymers are polyester, acrylic, and polyamide (also known as nylon). Per capita chemical fiber consumption in 1960 and 2000 was 1.75 and 4.52 kilograms, respectively. China is the world's dominant producer of chemical fibers, accounting for 6.7 million tons each year.

3. China's 2003 tariff rate quota of 856,250 tons was exhausted.

4. The U.S. tariff rate quota for 2002 was 73,207 tons, while cotton imports totaled 6,295 tons.

References

Badiane, O., D. Ghura, L. Goreux, and P. Masson. 2002. "Cotton Sector Strategies in West and Central Africa." Policy Research Paper 2867. World Bank, Washington, D.C.

Baffes, John. 2000. "Cotton Reforms in West and Central Africa, and the World Bank." *Cotton Outlook, Special Issue: Cotton in the Franc Zone.* Liverpool: Cotlook Limited.

———. 2001. "Policy Reforms in the Cotton Market." In T. Akiyama, J. Baffes, D. Larson, and P. Varangis, eds., *Commodity Market Reforms: Lessons from Two Decades.* Regional and Sectoral Studies. Washington, D.C.: World Bank.

———. 2004. "Tanzania's Cotton Sector: Constraints and Challenges in a Global Environment." *Development Policy Review* 22 (January): 75–96.

European Commission. 2000. "Commission Analysis Paper: The Cotton Sector in the European Union." Brussels.

———. 2003. "Agricultural Reform Continued: Commission Proposes Sustainable Agricultural Model for Europe's Tobacco, Olive Oil and Cotton Sectors." Brussels.

Fang, C., and J. C. Beghin. 2003. "Protection and Comparative Advantage of Chinese Agriculture: Implications for Regional and National Specialization." In D. Sumner and S. Rozelle, eds., *Agricultural Trade and Policy in China: Issues, Analysis and Implications.* Aldershot, U.K.: Ashgate Press.

FAPRI (Food and Agricultural Policy Research Institute). 2002. "The Doha Round of the World Trade Organization: Liberalization of Agricultural Markets and its Impact on Developing Economies." Paper presented at the IATRC Winter Meetings, San Diego, CA.

Gibbon, P. 1999. "Free Competition without Sustainable Development? Tanzanian Cotton Sector Liberalization, 1994–95 to 1997–98." *Journal of Development Studies* 36:128–50.

Goreux, L., and J. Macrae. 2003. "Reforming the Cotton Sector in Sub-Saharan Africa." Africa Region Working Paper Series 47. World Bank, Washington, D.C. http://www.worldbank.org/afr/wps.

Huang, J., S. Rozelle, and M. Chang. 2004. "The Nature of Distortions to Agricultural Incentives in China and Implications of WTO Accession." In D. Bhattasali, S. Li, and W. Martin, eds. *China and the WTO: Accession, Policy Reform, and Poverty Reduction Strategies.* Washington, D.C.:World Bank, 2004, pp. 81–97.

ICAC (International Cotton Advisory Committee). 2001. *Survey of the Costs of Production of Raw Cotton.* Washington D.C.

———. 2002. Production and Trade Policies Affecting the Cotton Industry. Washington, D.C.

———. 2003a. Production and Trade Policies Affecting the Cotton Industry. Washington, D.C.

———. 2003b. *World Textile Demand*. Washington, D.C.

———. Various Issues. Cotton: Review of the World Situation. Washington, D.C.

Kähkönen, S., and H. Leathers. 1997. "Is There Life after Liberalization?: Transaction Costs Analysis of Maize and Cotton Marketing in Zambia and Tanzania." Prepared for the U.S. Agency of International Development. Center for International Reform and the Informal Sector, University of Maryland, College Park.

Karagiannis, G. 2004. "The EU Cotton Policy Regime and the Implications of the Proposed Changes for Producer Welfare." Report prepared for the Food and Agriculture Organization. University of Macedonia, Greece.

Karagiannis, G., and C. Pantzios. 2002. "To Comply or Not to Comply with Policy Regulation—the Case of Greek Cotton Farmers: A Note." *Journal of Agricultural Economics*, 53: 345–51.

Larsen, M. N. 2002. "Is Oligopoly a Condition of Successful Privatization? The Case of Cotton in Zimbabwe." *Journal of Agrarian Change* 2:185–205.

Lundbæk, J. 2002. *Privatization of Cotton Sub-Sector in Uganda: Market Mechanisms and Institutional Mechanisms to Overcome These*. Masters thesis, The Royal Veterinary and Agricultural University, Department of Economics and Natural Resources, Copenhagen, Denmark.

MacDonald, S.A. 1997. "Forecasting World Cotton Prices." In Debra E. Gerald, ed., *Federal Forecasters Conference—1997, Papers and Proceedings*. National Center for Education Statistics. http://nces.ed.gov/pubs98/98134.pdf (accessed December 9, 2002).

Minot, N., and L. Daniels. 2002. "Impact of Global Cotton Markets on Rural Poverty in Benin." International Food Policy Research Institute, Washington, D.C.

Myers, D., and S. Stolton. 1999. *Organic Cotton: From Field to Final Product*, London: ITDG Publishing .

Poulton, C., and others. 2004. "Competition and Coordination in Liberalized African Cotton Market Systems." *World Development* 32 (3): 519–36.

Pray, C., D. Ma, J. Huang, and F. Qiao. 2001. "Impact of B_t Cotton in China." *World Development* 29: 813–25.

Quirke, D. 2002. *Trade Distortions and Cotton Markets: Implications for Global Cotton Producers*. Canberra: Cotton Research and Development Corporation, Centre for International Economics.

Sabune, J. 1996. "Experiences of Uganda with Privatization of its Cotton Industry." Paper presented at the 55th Plenary Meeting of the International Cotton Advisory Committee, Tashkent, Uzbekistan.

Shepherd, A. W., and S. Farolfi. 1999. *Export Crop Liberalization in Africa: A Review*. Rome: Food and Agriculture Organization.

Shuhua, G. 2003. "Introduction to China's Cotton Futures Trading." *Cotton Outlook, Special Feature—China: The Future*. Liverpool: Cotlook Limited.

Tokarick, S. 2003. "Measuring the Impact of Distortions in Agricultural Trade in Partial and General Equilibrium." IMF Working Paper, WP/03/110. International Monetary Fund, Washington, D.C.

Townsend, T., and A. Guitchounts. 1994. "A Survey of Cotton Income and Price Support Programs." *Proceedings of the Beltwide Cotton Conferences*. National Cotton Council of America, Washington, D.C.

Uzbekistan. 2003. "Uzbekistan: Cotton Policy Note." Governmental publication. Processed.

WTO (World Trade Organization). 2002. United States—Subsidies on Upland Cotton: Request for Consultations by Brazil. WT/DS267/1. Geneva, October 3.

Zhong, F., and C. Fang. 2003. "China's Cotton Policy." Center for Agricultural and Rural Development, Iowa State University, Ames, IA. Processed.

15

SEAFOOD: TRADE LIBERALIZATION AND IMPACTS ON SUSTAINABILITY

Cathy A. Roheim

In many ways, fish as a commodity is treated differently from agricultural products. For one thing, it is not part of the agricultural negotiations of the World Trade Organization (WTO). That it continues to be treated as an industrial product in negotiations may be a mixed blessing—leading to lower trade protection but less discipline on domestic subsidies. Yet fish is the most important source of protein for many around the globe. Seafood constitutes the biggest category of food and agriculture exports from developing countries, at an annual average of $33 billion (2000–01), or 18 percent of exports—more than combined exports of coffee, cocoa, tea, spices and nuts, cotton, and sugar. Globally, per capita consumption of fish is estimated at 14.3 kilograms per year (Delgado and others 2003). Per capita consumption in 1997 was led by Japan, with 62.6 kilograms per year, and China, at 26.5 kilograms per year (up from 8.1 in 1985). The European Union (EU) consumes 23.6 kilograms per year per capita, and Southeast Asia 23 kilograms, up from 19.8 in 1985. By 2020 per capita consumption of fish is expected to rise to 35.9 kilograms per year in China and to 25.8 kilograms per year in Southeast Asia, whereas it will remain constant or decline in developed countries (Delgado and others 2003).

The goal of this chapter is to present the structure and important features of the global seafood market, including illustrations of the complexities of the market, followed by a discussion of the impacts of trade liberalization, with a particular focus on developing countries. Developing countries play a very important role in international seafood trade (FAO 2002b). Many rely on seafood for export earnings—among them the Maldives, Mozambique, Peru, Senegal, and Sierra Leone. Fisheries production, both caught and farmed, has doubled in the last 30 years, and most of that increase has come from developing countries. Over half of global fish exports by value come from Latin America and the Caribbean and the developing nations of Asia and Africa, and the majority of that production goes to developed nations.

With rapid growth in production and trade have come the overexploitation of fish stocks and a rapid

The author would like to thank Mirvat Sewadeh for her contributions to the trade policies and trade flows and Baris Sivri for his help with the data analysis. The CD-ROM accompanying this volume contains a longer version of this chapter with additional figures, tables, and boxes and an expanded narrative on fish and aquaculture production, value, trade, and policy matters.

expansion of aquaculture. Both have had severe impacts on the environment (FAO 2002c). Thus, the issue of trade liberalization in seafood markets relates directly to sustainability of fish production and, by implication, the sustainability of international trade in fish products.

Production

Production of fish (finfish, mollusks, and crustaceans) takes two forms, aquacultured (or farm raised) and captured. The vast majority of captured fish (by volume) are marine, while the majority of aquacultured fish are freshwater species. The fishing sector has expanded considerably in the past 50 years, with capture fisheries landing 19 million (metric) tons in 1950 to 98 million tons in 2000 (FAO 2002b). During this time the importance of developed countries in the fishing sector has declined relative to the developing nations because of overfishing of waters contiguous to developed countries and an increase in fishing in the developing world. Aquaculture has further expanded the seafood industry, increasing production from 2.5 million tons in 1970 to more than 35 million tons in 2000, with most of the increase occurring in developing nations (FAO 2002b). Production of carp and mollusks dominated aquaculture production during the 1990s, but shrimp have the highest value.

Thus, with the combination of capture fisheries and aquaculture, the volume of world production has doubled in the last 30 years. Most of the growth in aquaculture is occurring in developing countries, especially China, where it is destined predominantly for domestic consumption. Marine aquaculture has grown very slowly in developed countries, largely because of limited available shoreline.

China is the world's largest producer of captured fish, marine and inland, at 17 million tons (figure 15.1). Peru and Chile follow, primarily capturing anchoveta, largely used to produce meal and oil for industrial use. U.S. fleets catch large volumes of low-value pollock off Alaska. Most of the catch goes into surimi, a refined, stabilized fish protein concentrate used in making imitation crab meat and processed fish such as breaded fish sticks and patties.

China is the leading producer of carp. The majority of that harvest is retained for domestic consumption. Norway, Chile, Scotland, Ireland, and Canada are the leading producers of farmed salmon and trout, and most of that production is traded on the international market.

China and Thailand produce almost 50 percent of the world's supply of shrimp (figure 15.2), with other developing countries supplying most of the rest. Shrimp and prawns account for just 6.4 percent of the volume of the world fish trade but about 20 percent of its value (OECD 2003a). The global

FIGURE 15.1   Fish Catches by Leading Countries, 1991–2000
(millions of metric tons)

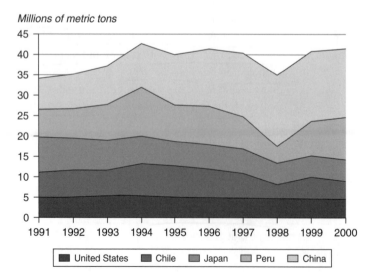

Source: FAO. Fishstat Database.

FIGURE 15.2 World Aquaculture Production of Shrimp, by Volume, 2000

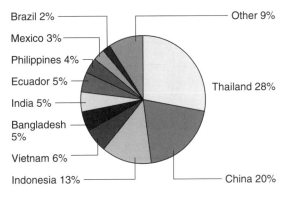

Source: FAO. Fishstat Database.

shrimp trade is valued at more than $10 billion annually.

It is estimated that more than 60 percent of Asia's mangroves have already been converted to aquaculture farms, primarily for the production of shrimp (ESCAP and ADB 2000), degrading habitats and land. Because shrimp is such an important export earner for Southeast Asia and South America and has such a marked negative effect on their environments, it is worthwhile to discuss its production in some detail.

Sustainable Shrimp Aquaculture in Bangladesh and Thailand

Subsistence fishermen have caught shrimp in Bangladesh for hundreds of years. But since the mid-1980s the cultivation of shrimp for export has grown significantly. In 1972–73 exports of captured shrimp were valued at $2.9 million. By 1985 exports had growth to $90 million, primarily from aquaculture. In 2000 the figure was $330 million (FAO 1999, 2002b).

Some of the credit for this rise goes to a structural adjustment program in which Bangladesh received a World Bank loan of $1.76 billion over the period 1979–96 (UNEP 1999b). Under the program, policies that had limited trade were replaced with new policies that encouraged exports. The changes created an environment in which private investments in shrimp culture, shrimp processing, and shrimp exports flourished.

Shrimp now accounts for almost 91 percent of fish exports from Bangladesh (FAO 2002b). It is

generally agreed, however, that this rapid expansion has had considerable environmental costs. The area under shrimp culture tripled in 10 years, from the mid-1980s to the mid-1990s, covering 130,000 hectares by 1999 (UNEP 1999a). In the process, mangroves have been removed and replaced by coastal ponds. The ponds have increased the salinity of adjacent land, jeopardizing its future productivity.

The costs of restoration would likely be very high. Disappearing mangroves have deprived the marine ecosystem of valuable habitat and nursery areas for fish reproduction. In addition, sustainable shrimp farming is threatened by its reliance on the collection of wild shrimp fry, which are then "grown out" to appropriate sizes for export, a practice that threatens the sustainability of wild shrimp stocks as well. Disease sometimes breaks out in shrimp ponds and may spread to the wild shrimp population. Finally, the feed for cultured shrimp is based on fish meal, which is produced from fully used, if not overused, stocks of anchovies, herring, menhaden, and sardines.

Recognizing the negative externalities caused by shrimp culture in Bangladesh, the U.N. Environment Programme (UNEP) recommended that effective environmental policies with proper enforcement should be implemented to ensure that trade liberalization did not lead to externalities that reduced overall welfare (UNEP 1999a).

Thailand is the world's largest producer of shrimp, with approximately 23,413 farms covering an area of 72,663 hectares (in 1996) (FAO 2000). By 2000, Thailand was exporting 249,638 metric tons of shrimp, valued at some $2.7 billion, to the world market. Shrimp production in India, Indonesia, and Vietnam combined equal what Thailand produces in export value. The same environmental issues highlighted for Bangladesh apply to Thailand—satisfying the huge export market for cultivated shrimp has led to significant environmental damage.

The Shrimp Industry in Madagascar

Madagascar's shrimp industry is the country's leading foreign exchange earner. Exports grew from $20 million in 1980 to $102 million in 1999 and now account for 7 percent of gross domestic product (GDP). Approximately one-half of the shrimp produced are from capture fisheries, the other half from aquaculture. The industry provides direct employment for approximately 53,000 people and indirectly for another 30,000 people (World Bank 2003).

In the shrimp capture industry, there are three types of fisheries: traditional, artisanal, and industrial. The bulk of employment occurs in traditional fisheries, in which fishers have no motorized equipment. Entry into the fishery is open; no license is required. Most of the catch of traditional fishermen is consumed domestically. Production was about 3,400 tons in 2000 (World Bank 2003).

The cost of the license required to ply the artisanal fisheries depends on the power of the fishing boat's motor. Most artisanal boats belong to a company rather than being individually owned. Industrial trawlers that fish in Madagascar's waters are mostly foreign owned and have processing facilities on board. In 2000, approximately 8,200 tons of shrimp were captured by artisanal and industrial fisheries, which directly employed some 10,500 people. Virtually all of the shrimp captured in these two fisheries are exported, with France and Japan being the primary markets (World Bank 2003).

Industrial Products

Developing countries are important exporters and importers of fish meal. Fishmeal and oil are derived from small, wild-caught pelagic fish such as capelin from the North Atlantic, anchovies from the South

Pacific, and other species such as menhaden and herring found around the globe. In processing the fish are cooked, pressed, dried, and milled. The dry remainder is fishmeal; oil is extracted from pressing.

Fishmeal and fish oil, used in animal feeds (for both terrestrial livestock and aquacultured fish) but not for human consumption, are industrial products. Demand for fish meal from the farmed fish industry has increased dramatically in the last 20 years. Growing poultry and pig industries in China and Southeast Asia also create strong demand for fish meal.

The primary producer of fish meal has long been Latin America, with a total of 2.8 million tons produced in 1997 and an annual growth rate of 1.7 percent between 1985–97 (Delgado and others 2003). Much of that production, from Chile and Peru, is susceptible to the vagaries of El Niño. The most heavily exploited fish is the Peruvian anchoveta (figure 15.3). World production in 1997 was 6.1 million tons, with the balance after Latin America made up primarily by China, Southeast Asia, Japan, and the European Union.

If world markets and production do not change substantially over the next 17 years, fish meal prices are projected to rise by 18 percent (Delgado and others 2003). Conversely, if aquaculture expands by 50 percent, then the price of fish meal will increase by 42 percent. Greater efficiency in the use of fish meal in animal feed could push prices down. In the

FIGURE 15.3   World Aquaculture Production by Value, 1991–2000

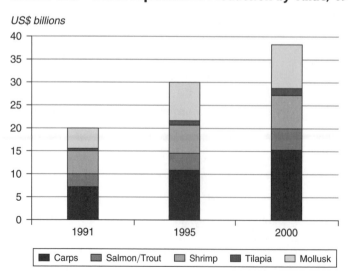

Source: FAO. Fishstat Database.

worst-case scenario, in which the world experiences an ecological collapse in fisheries yielding fishmeal and oil, the price will rise by 134 percent (Delgado and others 2003). Any of these potential price changes would dramatically affect livestock production in developing countries.

International Markets

Fish is one of the most traded food commodities in the world. The value of world imports of fish products was $60 billion in 2000, greater than international trade in many agricultural products (figure 15.4). The most valuable component of seafood trade is shrimp, with world trade in 2000 valued at more than $10 billion (FAO 2002b).

A myriad of issues underlies fisheries and aquaculture production. Capture fisheries still supply the majority of fish production, but fully 60 percent of the world's fisheries are already being fished at or over capacity (Grainger and Garcia 1996). Even with the establishment of 200-mile exclusive economic zones (EEZs) in 1977, which brought one-third of the world's oceans under the jurisdiction of coastal states, most fisheries management plans have not achieved their stated goal of maintaining sustainable fisheries. Many countries, mostly developing, do not have management policies or lack resources to enforce them.

Fish and fish products have not always been major internationally traded products. Several influences led to the rapid expansion in international trade beginning in 1975. Certainly the passing of the International Law of the Sea and the institution of the 200-mile EEZ in 1977 had a large impact. The establishment of the EEZs effectively created importers out of countries, such as Japan, with very large distant water fleets, and created exporters out of those countries, such as the United States, that had large marine resources and relatively low domestic demand.

The most important trade commodities in order of their value in 2000 are shrimp ($10.8 billion), salmon and trout ($5.2 billion), tuna ($4.8 billion), groundfish ($4.4 billion), crabs and lobsters ($3.8 billion), mollusks ($2.8 billion), cephalopods ($2.7 billion), fish meal ($2.1 billion), small pelagics ($1.6 billion), large pelagics ($1.1 billion) and flatfish ($1.1 billion) (Anderson 2003).

Thailand is the world's top exporter of food fish in the world, followed by China, Norway, and the United States (see figure 15.4). Seventy-four percent of Africa's exports are destined for the European Union, while exports from Central and South America go primarily to the United States, Canada, and the European Union.

The major importing nations are the European Union ($19.5 billion), Japan ($15.5 billion), and the

FIGURE 15.4 Food Fish Exports by Top Countries, 2000

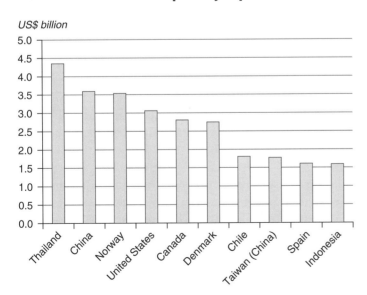

US$ billion

FIGURE 15.5 World Food Fish Exports by Value of Major Commodity Group, 2000

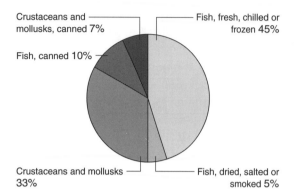

Crustaceans and mollusks, canned 7%

Fish, canned 10%

Crustaceans and mollusks 33%

Fish, fresh, chilled or frozen 45%

Fish, dried, salted or smoked 5%

Source: FAO 2002b.

United States ($10.4 billion). Within the European Union, imports go to Spain ($3.35 billion), France ($3.0 billion), Italy ($2.5 billion), Germany ($2.3 billion), the United Kingdom ($2.2 billion), and Denmark ($1.8 billion) (FAO 2002b).

Crustaceans account for 19 percent of the weight of exports but 33 percent of the value. Finfish, by contrast, contribute 63 percent of volume but only 45 percent of value (figure 15.5). The most widely traded processed seafood products are items such as canned tuna, canned crab and lobster meats, canned herring and sardines, roe (such as caviar), shelled and deveined shrimp, and dried or salted finfish.

Significant reexporting occurs in the world seafood markets. Thailand, for example, imports a significant amount of the world's tuna catches, processes it into cans, and then exports it. Similarly, China is a major reprocessing market for U.S. and Norwegian seafood.

For low-income, food-deficit countries, exports are far larger in value than imports. When fish meal and oil are excluded from export values, the picture changes only slightly, since their value is not high and many of these countries do not participate in fish meal or fish oil production. Among the developing countries that rely on exports of seafood as a primary source for export earnings are the Maldives, Mozambique, Peru, Senegal, and Sierra Leone (FAO 2002b). Thus, reductions in the stocks of fish in developing countries because of poor management have the potential to jeopardize the food supply while reducing household incomes and export earnings.

Institutional Influences on International Trade in Fishery Products

Even though most caught, farmed, and traded fish are clearly food products, no fish is included in the WTO Uruguay Round Agreement on Agriculture (URAA). The concern among some nations is that fishing as an industry involves not only market access, but also *resource access* on a scale unprecedented in other areas of agriculture. Therefore, negotiations regarding trade liberalization for fish have proceeded far differently from those on agricultural commodities.

Tariffs on fish products, in contrast to those on agricultural products, have been reduced with every successive trade round. And international agreements on sanitary and phytosanitary measures, technical barriers to trade, antidumping, rules of origin, import licensing, and safeguards have all been applied to trade in fish. Subsidies in the fishing industry fall under the GATT (General Agreement on Tariffs and Trade) Agreement on Subsidies, whereas in agriculture they fall under the URAA.

This section of the chapter discussed the domestic and international policies and institutions most relevant to global trade in fish and fish products. The domestic policy interventions are fisheries management policies, fishing subsidies, and trade barriers, including tariffs, technical barriers to trade, sanitary and phytosanitary measures, and antidumping and countervailing measures.

Fisheries Management Policies

To fully understand the impact of trade liberalization on fishery products, one first must understand the factors influencing supply. The impacts of trade liberalization will differ depending on several factors, including production method (capture or aquaculture) and domestic fisheries management policies.

Fish in capture fisheries belong to a common pool. Before 1977 jurisdiction of most nations over fishing grounds extended only 12 nautical miles from shore. Expansion to 200-mile EEZs was discussed and agreed to in 1977 by nations at the Third Law of the Sea Convention (UNCLOS-III, 1973–1982) (Hannesson 1996). EEZs cover 40 percent of the world's oceans and 90 percent of its living marine resources (Deere 2000).

UNCLOS assigns the exclusive right to coastal states to manage and exploit marine living resources and to regulate fisheries resources through a comprehensive management system. There is considerable debate over the effectiveness with which coastal nations have managed their EEZs with respect to the sustainability of production. Creating an EEZ does not remove the common-pool property of the resource; it simply redistributes the use of the resource to new (domestic) market entrants. Many nations, especially developed nations, encouraged expansion of the domestic fleet to increase the national capacity to catch fish that foreign nations would have caught in the past. Catches quickly grew as the number and size of fishing boats increased. In ensuing years, however, supplies in many fisheries decreased drastically as fish stocks were reduced beyond the sustainable limit and the remaining fish became harder to find.

An often-quoted statistic is that fully 60 percent of the world's major fisheries resources are already being exploited at or above capacity (Grainger and Garcia 1996). Fish stocks in OECD (Organisation for Economic Co-operation and Development) countries, in particular, have been subject to large fishing pressure over the years and are mostly overfished (OECD 2003b). The problem derives not from a lack of regulations per se, but rather from a lack of effective regulations.

In a fishery where there is no restriction on entry into fishing, the management system (or lack of it) is referred to as *open access*. It is well known from economic theory and experience that open access will lead to overexploitation of the fish stock, as individual fishermen have little incentive to restrain their fishing efforts to promote a sustainable fishery, because the fish forgone by one fisherman will simply be captured by someone else (box 15.1). Most fisheries in the United States and European Union operate under some form of limited access or limited harvest.

Management policies can be categorized as being either an input or output control. Input controls, the oldest type of fishery management tool, are designed to limit either the number of people fishing or the efficiency of fishing (National Research Council 1999). Input controls generally lead to inefficient outcomes. They raise the cost of fishing but generally do not reduce effort or capacity.

Output controls are designed to limit directly the volume of the catch from a given fishery. The critical necessity for this form of management is the ability to monitor the catch. In some fisheries, managers may have personnel at the dockside to count the number (or weight) of fish caught as they are landed. In other cases, on-board observers may monitor the catch. In either case, once the total allowable catch (TAC) is reached, the fishery is generally closed for the season.

Management by TAC has at least three shortcomings. First, it induces fishers to compete to catch as much as possible before the TAC is reached. Second, as fishers become more intensively capitalized, the TAC is reached in a shorter time, leading to a backlog of fish for processors that pushes down fishermen's prices and reduces product quality. Third, idle vessels may move to fish in another fishery, leading to overcapitalization in yet additional fisheries (Conrad 1999).

The management systems of fisheries have caused vexing trade and environment issues, and several cases have landed before dispute panels discussions with the WTO and format GATT. The disputes below (drawn from Robb 2001) were directly related to fisheries management policies.

- *Canada v. U.S.*—Prohibition of Imports of Tuna and Tuna Products from Canada, 1982.
- *Canada v U.S.*—Measures Affecting Exports of Unprocessed Herring and Salmon, 1988.
- *Mexico v. U.S.*—Restrictions on Imports of Tuna (Tuna/Dolphin I), 1991.
- *European Economic Community and Netherlands v. U.S.*—Restrictions on Imports of Tuna (Tuna/Dolphin II), 1994.
- *India, Malaysia, Pakistan, and Thailand v. U.S.*—Import Prohibitions of Certain Shrimp and Shrimp Products—1998.

Because of poor management and other factors, the status of fish stocks worldwide is alarming. The implications of trade liberalization for capture fisheries are many, but the most obvious implication is that the current level of catches from capture fisheries is unsustainable. Should trade liberalization provide incentives to fishermen to catch even more fish, it would simply speed up the overfishing and depletion process, leading to unsustainable international markets as well. This is not to say that further

---

BOX 15.1 Impacts of Trade Liberalization in Uganda's Fishing Industry

Economywide liberalization and reforms in Uganda's trade regimes have made the fisheries industry one of the country's most important in terms of employment and export earnings. The fisheries sector is Uganda's second-largest national export producer, with export values growing from $1.4 million in 1990 to $78 million by 2001 (UNEP 2002a). More than 1 million workers are directly engaged in harvesting, transporting, processing, distributing, and marketing fish (UNEP 1999b).

With success have come problems common to fishing industries elsewhere. Uganda's fish come from the country's many lakes and rivers. Current legislation allows open access to lake fishing. There are relatively few restrictions on who may fish, and few technical measures to control fishing mortality. Poor data make it difficult to determine the amount of fish that can be taken without depleting the stocks beyond a sustainable level, particularly in Lake Victoria, which borders not only Uganda but also Kenya and Tanzania. Thus it has been difficult to establish harvest limits. The U.N. Environment Programme recommends that Uganda should determine the level of fish stocks it currently has, establish a total allowable catch that is in line with sustainable harvests in each of the major water bodies, and implement an individual transferable quota system.

Overfishing is not the only problem in Uganda. According to UNEP, unsustainable fish-

ing practices are on the rise, as the catch of native fish has declined. For example, exotic species are being introduced to lakes and rivers. In another example, poisons are being used, illegally, to stun the fish, bringing them to the surface, making them easy to scoop up in nets. The poisoning has led the European Union to impose a ban on fish exports from Uganda due to food safety concerns.

Other issues related to food safety include a lack of refrigeration facilities to preserve fish after harvest. Transportation to processing facilities is made difficult and slow by poor road conditions, further degrading the quality and safety of the fish prior to processing.

Other environmental concerns include effluent pollution from fish-processing industries. Raw, untreated waste is dumped directly into the very rivers and lakes from which the fish are being pulled, contaminating the environments for tomorrow's catch.

Social problems also threaten the fishing industry, as most of the products are destined for export markets, where they fetch higher prices. Much of the local population can afford only fish rejected by processors for the export market. Food security concerns have been raised, as well, as Nile perch feed heavily on freshwater shrimp that are also caught and used as animal feed.

Source: UNEP 1999b.

---

liberalization should not occur, but rather that overfishing and other externalities must be considered in free-trade discussions.

Fishing Subsidies

The most sensitive issue related to capture fisheries before the WTO Committee on Trade and the Environment (CTE) is fishing subsidies. Subsidies exist in the fishing sector globally and have come to be recognized as having a significant impact on the quantities of fish traded, largely because they lead to unsustainable fishing practices. At the WTO High-Level Symposium on Trade and Environment in March 1999, five WTO member nations (Australia, Iceland, New Zealand, the Philippines, and the United States) submitted a joint statement on the need to eliminate "environmentally damaging and

trade-distorting subsidies" in the fisheries sector (WTO 1999, 2000, 2001). In 2001, at the Fourth Ministerial Conference in Doha, Qatar, the WTO explicitly included fisheries subsidies in the negotiating agenda to improve current discipline on subsidies—this as a result of discussions in the CTE. The Doha Declaration states that the need to "clarify and improve WTO disciplines on fisheries subsidies, taking into the account the importance of this sector to developing countries" (WTO 2003a: 28).

In an excellent review of fisheries subsidies, Schrank (2003: 49) cites three implications.

Three implications are noted: (1) countries that do not subsidize and that restrain total catch to maintain the resource lose the extra catch to countries that subsidize and do not restrain total catch; (2) competition from subsidized distant water fleets can make it economically unviable for developing countries to develop their own fisheries and therefore to realize the benefits of their own 200-mile zones of fishery jurisdiction; (3) subsidies can contribute to stock depletion, with negative economic, trade, and environmental effects for other countries that have an interest in the stock.

The greatest contrast to agricultural subsidies is the effect noted in Schrank's first point. Fishing subsidies create not only a trade distortion in the markets, but also, in the case of straddling or migratory fish stocks, a negative externality on the nation competing to capture the fish.

The relationship between fisheries subsidies and their environmental and social impacts is obviously complex. According to Hussein Abaza, who heads UNEP's Economics and Trade Branch, "It is becoming clear that developing countries stand to gain a great deal from trade in fisheries products, but only if trade and fisheries policies are reformed to support sustainable management of these resources" (UNEP 2002a). The policy recommendation is simple—eliminate trade and domestic distortions while adopting environmental policies that address overfishing. But the implementation of sound environmental management is the real policy challenge.

Fishing Access

In a form of fishing subsidies, the European Union signed its first fishing access agreement with Senegal in 1979, shortly after nations exercised their rights to the 200-mile EEZ. Since many developing nations with EEZs did not have the capacity to make use of their resources, they opted to sell access to these resources to third parties. The European Union has been predominant in negotiating these agreements on behalf of its member countries and has been paying the access fees.

Most fishing access agreements have been reached between the European Union and African countries and a few other nations. In these access agreements, an amount is negotiated to guarantee access to foreign waters by portions of the EU industrial fishing fleet. During 1999–2000, the European Union had agreements with 20 different

nations for a total value of more than €400 million. The countries with the largest negotiated fees in 2000 were Morocco (€114 million), Mauritania (€54 million, box 15.2), Argentina (€16 million), Angola (€13 million), and Senegal (€12 million) (OECD 2003a). The primary beneficiaries of the access agreements are Spain and France. Portugal, Italy, and Greece have also benefited.

The agreements are very controversial. Fishing access agreements have been seen as a way to reduce capacity in the European Union while securing employment and supplies of fish for the European market (Institute for European Environmental Policy 2002b). On the environmental side, catch limits are either not imposed on the foreign fleets or the limits are not enforced, and so the sustainability of stocks of fish in accessed waters is in doubt in many nations.

Trade Barriers: Tariffs

Tariffs in OECD member countries are important barriers to the developing nations that export to them. But a good deal of South-South trade is also affected by tariffs.[1]

Tariffs on seafood in developing countries are generally higher and more transparent than those in OECD countries. The structures of the tariff regimes, however, differ considerably among developing countries. Among developing countries, Thailand has the highest tariff levels on seafood products (60 percent across all product forms), followed by India, whereas Chile and Malaysia generally apply the lowest duty rates. Yet all developing countries for which detailed tariff schedules are available implement transparent tariff structures with all product lines subject only to ad valorem duties.

After the Uruguay Round, average weighted import tariffs on fish products in developed countries were reduced to around 4.5 percent (Lem 2003). This average hides a number of tariff issues, however, including some tariff escalation and tariffs on specific items (such as canned tuna in the United States). The European Union and the Republic of Korea have the highest tariffs (ranging from 4 percent to 33 percent), whereas the United States and Canada have the lowest (0–5 percent) (figure 15.6).

But despite their relatively high tariffs, both Korea and the European Union have very transparent tariff

---

BOX 15.2   Foreign Fishing Access Agreements Involving Mauritania

The fishing sector in Mauritania accounts for more than 40 percent of exports and about 6 percent of gross domestic product. The only major export items are squid and octopus, with an export value of $68 million in 2000 (FAO 2002b). Only $639,000 were fish products exported in processed form and that was for dried, salted, or smoked products. Total fish product exports were $74 million.

The primary source of earnings from the fishery sector in Mauritania is not from exports but from access fees. The European Union pays for its fleet to fish in Mauritanian waters. In a sense one might say that Mauritania exports its fish resources, while they are still in their habitat, directly to the European Union fishing fleet. Eighty percent of fish in Mauritania, or 450,000 tons, were landed by industrial vessels in 2001 (WWF 2003). A new agreement on fishing access by The European Union was enacted in 2001 and is effective until August 2006. The European Union is paying €430 million, creating access to Mauritanian water for 248 vessels, targeting hake, squid, crawfish, and tuna. The EU vessels are predominately from Spain and France, but also from Italy, Portugal, Greece, the Netherlands, Germany and, to a minor extent, Ireland.

In addition to the access fees, vessel owners are required to pay €29 per ton of catch taken by freezer tuna seiners, and €19 per ton for catches from pelagic fish trawlers. A license fee is also payable, based on tonnage per year in some cases and a flat annual fee for tuna vessels.

In response to critics, the European Union has begun to increase the value of the access payments (for Mauritania up 61 percent over the previous agreement) and to work toward agreements that promote sustainable development of the fisheries in the target nations. To that end, the agreements, by design, allow the Mauritanian authorities to inspect and control fishing activities—requiring a daily log of catches by the foreign vessels and setting up a system of observers on board vessels. These opportunities for Mauritania are not fully taken advantage of. Restricted fishing zones have increased in size. There remain no catch limits.

Determining economic benefits for either party to the agreement is uncertain, as there is little information on catch statistics. However, based on the previous agreement between the European Union and Mauritania, for each euro paid to Mauritania in 1996, the value of the catch was two times greater. In 1997, the value of the catch was three times greater than the cost of access. Little of the access money appears to be utilized to build within Mauritania a domestic infrastructure to nationalize its resources rather than selling foreign access. In addition, reports from nongovernmental organizations, such as the World Wildlife Fund, indicate that the agreements have negative effects on local communities and on sustainable development.

Source: Institute for European Environmental Policy (2002a and b);
www.integratedframework.org.

---

structures. All tariffs applied on seafood products are ad valorem duties. In comparison, Japan and the United States implement more complex tariff structures. In Japan about 20 percent of the tariff lines on intermediate seafood products are either per-unit-specific or compound duties. Similarly, 38 percent of U.S. tariff lines on intermediate seafood products are per-unit-specific or compound. The U.S. tariffs do not seem to be aimed at concealing protection, since their average ad valorem equivalent is only a little more than 2 percent. At the same time, the products that receive tariff protection in the United States, such as canned tuna, are protected only through high ad valorem tariffs.

Most industrial countries offer preferential access to developing countries' seafood exports.

The European Union offers free access to all seafood products from the least-developed countries and partial tariff exemption to most of seafood exports from Africa-Caribbean-Pacific (ACP) countries and other developing countries. The United States grants free access for all developing countries for all seafood products. Japan also grants free access to some seafood imports from the least-developed countries and maintains only one seafood tariff line for other developing countries (table 15.1).

Table 15.1 shows that the trade-weighted tariff averages across the OECD countries exhibit some trade escalation for imports from developing countries and all other countries, but not for the least-developed countries. However, in the context of

FIGURE 15.6   Tariff Structure by Level of Processing, (1998–2001)

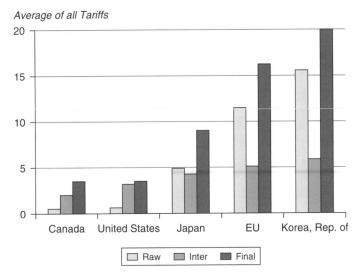

Average of all Tariffs

Legend: ☐ Raw   ◩ Inter   ■ Final

Source: WTO IDB database.

TABLE 15.1   Trade-Weighted Tariff Averages for Developing Countries' Fish Product Exports to OECD Countries, by Processing State
(percent)

Level of Processing	Least-Developed	Developing	All Other
All	2.5	2.9	3.2
Unprocessed	2.5	2.5	2.5
Fillets	2.8	2.5	2.0
Semi-processed	0.5	1.9	1.4
Processed	1.7	4.3	8.0
Total value (US$ millions)	437	10,689	21,992

Source: OECD 2003a.

tariffs on agricultural goods, tariffs in seafood products are lower and the level of tariff escalation is very moderate.

Trade Barriers: Technical Barriers

In recent years, there has been a large increase in policies that could potentially come under the heading of technical barriers to trade. Among them are labeling programs and the resultant tracing capability they require. The programs are typically found in developed countries but can have potentially large impacts on developing countries.

Among the labeling programs are ecolabeling, country-of-origin labeling, and other labeling related to the production process, such as "organic."

A great deal of regulatory activity concerning country-of-origin labels is occurring in the United States and European Union. Ecolabeling and organic labeling are voluntary programs, but the WTO is interested in whether such labels constitute a nontariff trade barrier. Currently, these labels are not considered to be trade barriers as long as they are nondiscriminatory (WTO 2003b).

Trade Barriers: Sanitary and Phytosanitary Measures

Import regulations based on hazard-analysis, critical-control-point (HACCP) principles, adopted by many of the major importing nations, are regarded as nontariff barriers by many developing countries, as the investment required to bring processing plants up to code can be substantial (Filhol 2000). During 1997–98, the European Union imposed bans on the import of seafood from India, Bangladesh, Kenya, Madagascar, Mozambique, Tanzania, and Uganda, citing food safety concerns both in processing and in possible contamination prior to catch in both capture fisheries and aquaculture (Filhol 2000).

For example, most of the fish caught in Kenya are from Lake Victoria; the majority of that catch is Nile perch (FAO 2002b).[2] Nile perch are also the main export from Kenya, earning about $50 million annually. Of the 18 fish processing and exporting firms now in Kenya, 10 specialize in Nile perch and 8 in marine products such as shrimp, other crustaceans, and tuna. In 1997 the European Union became concerned about the safety of fish from Kenya when Spain and Italy both banned fish imports because of the presence of salmonella. Some other members of the European Union continued to import from Kenya, but exports declined by 34 percent between 1996 and 1997. In 1998 the European Union banned imports of fish from Kenya because of a cholera outbreak, causing a 66 percent drop in fish exports to the European Union. In 1999 the European Union banned fish from Lake Victoria yet again, this time because of the presence of pesticides, causing another 68 percent decline in fish exports. In 1997 Kenyan exports were $52 million, in 1998 $39 million, and in 1999 $32 million. In 2000 they were back up to $39 million (FAO 2002a).

In response to the requirement for a HACCP program to export to many nations, Kenya has instituted stringent quality control procedures. The Fisheries Department controls quality though provisions of the Kenya Fisheries Act and the Fish Quality Assurance Regulation of 2000. However, fish quality comes at a cost. There are strict regulations on production, handling, processing, packaging, and transportation of fishery products. In addition, strict regulations govern construction of buildings, equipment, purification tanks, and storage facilities. Costs were incurred to train workers in hygiene related to fish handling. There is also the additional cost of electricity to maintain strict temperature controls. Finally, the cost to fishermen is significant. They must invest in newer boats that have chillers to maintain the quality of caught fish.

Kenya has adapted to the new realities by restricting the number of facilities handling fish to be exported. Only five fishing villages (out of nearly 300) are authorized to handle fish landings. This causes fishermen from elsewhere to incur higher transportation costs to land their catch.

The costs of exporting to nations with strict quality controls are not trivial, but Kenya has had to incur those costs to remain in the international market. As long as Nile perch continues to be in demand in the world market, it is likely that Kenyan producers can more than cover their costs. Should the prices rise too far, however, other white-fleshed fish will become competitive substitutes. The international seafood market in white-fleshed fish is very competitive, particularly now that farmed tilapia and catfish are available in large quantities.

Trade Barriers: Antidumping and Countervailing Measures

As tariff barriers have been relaxed and the aquaculture industry has boomed globally, more and more fishing industries in the United States have found themselves competing with lower-priced imports. Thus, the United States in particular has been quite active in pursuing antidumping and countervailing duty suits against foreign competitors. The United States brought antidumping and countervailing charges against imports of Norwegian farmed salmon in 1990, Chilean farmed salmon in 1997, crawfish from China in 1997, and farmed catfish from Vietnam in 2003. A petition was filed with the U.S. International Trade Commission (USITC) in December 2003 against six exporters of farmed shrimp. Details on several of these cases follow.

Crawfish from China.   The imported product was defined as freshwater crawfish tail meat in all its forms, grades, and sizes. China supplied 62 percent of all imports by the United States in 1997 and 92 percent in 2001. U.S. production of crawfish in 1996 was 12.5 million pounds; in 1997, 23 million pounds (U.S. Department of Commerce 1997). Meanwhile imports of crawfish from China were 2.6 million pounds in 1996 and 5.8 million pounds in 1998.[3] The average value per pound of imports from China was $1.85 in 1997, compared with $5.82 per pound for the domestically produced product. As a result, antidumping duties of

223.01 percent were imposed (USITC 2003b). However, Chinese crawfish continue to dominate imports to the U.S. market, with sales of 8 million pounds in 2001 and 7.5 million pounds in 2002, worth a total of $38.7 million in 2001 and $22.2 million in 2002. The ruling was reviewed in 2003, and it was determined that the antidumping duties should remain in place.

Catfish from Vietnam. In 2002, independent processors and the Catfish Farmers of America, a trade association of U.S. catfish farmers and processors, brought a petition to the USITC regarding dumping of frozen catfish fillets into the U.S. market by Vietnam. Catfish farming is the largest aquaculture industry in the United States. Production in 2000 was 150.6 million pounds (USITC 2003a). The primary producing states are Mississippi, Arkansas, Louisiana, and Alabama. Prior to 1999 imports were largely absent from the U.S. market. In 1999, Vietnam exported fewer than 2 million pounds of what the Vietnamese call catfish into the U.S. market. By 2001 that number had increased to 15.9 million pounds. Although the Vietnamese product was successfully labeled and marketed as catfish, the Latin names of the imported species were *Pangasius bocurti, Pangasius pangasius,* and *Pangasius micronemus.* American catfish are from the *Ictaluridae* family.

A problem in world markets for fish is that once fish is processed, it is very difficult to determine its species. Some fish marketed as red snapper are not, in fact, red snapper, a high-value fish. Due to many cases of intentional and unintentional fraud in seafood markets, in which consumers were falsely led to believe that they were buying a certain product or confused by the same product being marketed under different names, the U.S. Food and Drug Administration has become more rigorous in its regulations of appropriate names for fish.

Vietnam is now required to label its fish not as catfish, but instead as *basa* and *tra.*[1] However, Vietnamese basa and tra are still considered similar enough to American catfish to be subject to antidumping measures. Producers have had to pay antidumping duties of between 36.84 percent and 63.88 percent.

Shrimp from some developing countries. As of December 2003, the Southern Shrimp Alliance

(SSA), a group of shrimp harvesters and processors in the United States, filed antidumping petitions with the USITC, alleging that Brazil, China, Ecuador, India, Thailand, and Vietnam were dumping shrimp (primarily farmed) with an approximate annual value of $2.4 billion into the U.S. market. The SSA is petitioning for tariffs on imports of shrimp from these countries ranging from 30 percent to 267 percent. It argued that "a variety of financial incentives provided by *national governments and international institutions* over a number of years have overstimulated the infrastructure and production of farm-raised shrimp in these countries" (emphasis added) (McGovern 2003). Thus it seems that the investment by organizations such as the World Bank and others in helping build an export industry in some of these countries is perceived to have created unfair subsidies for these shrimp-exporting nations.

Impacts of Trade and Domestic Policy Reforms

The previous section makes clear that the primary trade barriers for capture and aquaculture fisheries are tariffs, countervailing and antidumping measures, and the discriminatory potential of ecolabeling, country-of-origin labeling, and sanitary and phytosanitary measures for seafood safety.

To analyze the impacts of trade liberalization on trade in seafood, particularly on seafood from developing countries, one must distinguish between the impacts of trade liberalization on seafood derived from capture fisheries and on seafood from aquaculture. This is because of their distinct attributes. Capture fisheries are generally ill-managed. As such, changes in trade policies may create changes in welfare that differ between the short and long run because of the sustainability of fish stocks. With respect to the effects of trade liberalization, aquaculture is more similar to agriculture. However, to the extent that aquaculture is dependent on feed derived from capture fisheries or seed stock from wild fisheries, trade liberalization may have a different effect on aquaculture than on agriculture.

Whereas the research literature on markets for fish is extensive (Wessells and Anderson 1992; Kinnucan and Wessells 1997), there has been little empirical analysis of the impacts of trade liberalization through tariff reductions related to fish and fish products. This is partly because of the complex nature of the global seafood market, partly because of a lack of data, and partly because of a governmental and academic focus diverted away from seafood markets toward the economics of management of capture fisheries. In addition, although nongovernmental organizations and international development agencies have produced many studies on trade liberalization and its impacts on the agricultural sector in developing countries, there is a spectacular lack of quantitative information on the impacts of trade liberalization for developing countries with respect to fish.

The study by Cox, Stubbs, and Davies (2000) is the notable exception. This section begins by discussing its findings on trade liberalization in Asia Pacific Economic Cooperation (APEC) countries.

Trade Liberalization in APEC Countries

Cox, Stubbs, and Davies (2000) investigate the short-run effects of trade liberalization on seafood products in the APEC countries. These countries maintain a tariff and other trade barriers against fish and fish products. With the conclusion of the Uruguay Round, WTO member nations agreed to lower tariff rates. However, the APEC agenda was more ambitious. Under the 1994 Bogor Declaration, APEC made a commitment to fully liberalize all markets by 2020, with 2010 as the deadline for developed countries. This was followed by "early, voluntary sectoral-liberalization" (EVSL) proposals in which nine sectors, including fisheries, would accelerate tariff removals beyond the Bogor Declaration. Rather than having 2010 and 2020 as deadlines for developed and developing countries, respectively, the timeline was moved to December 31, 2005.

Cox, Stubbs, and Davies (2000) developed a simulation model to evaluate the impact of seafood tariff removals under the Bogor Declaration, EVSL, and another scenario wherein only the developed countries in APEC would remove their tariffs while those of developing countries remained the same. The model included all the APEC countries and the rest of the world as sources and destinations. Seafood products were generally grouped together except for a focus on species particularly important to Australia such as tuna, lobsters, and shellfish.

As expected the results show that there would be significant increases in export volumes (and prices) under the Bogor Declaration and the ESVL relative to the baseline. If only the developed countries removed their tariffs, the simulation shows that there would be little difference from the baseline because developed-country tariffs are generally small. The greatest change would occur under the EVSL scenario, at least initially. By 2020 the effects of the Bogor and EVSL agreements would be the same (tables 15.2 and 15.3).

Significant benefits from import tariff reductions accrue to the "Other APEC" countries of Brunei, Indonesia, Malaysia, Mexico, New Zealand, Papua New Guinea, the Philippines, the Russian Federation, Singapore, and Vietnam.

Removing Subsidies in Capture Fisheries

The previous section discussed the types of subsidies found in the fishing sector and the concern of the WTO CTE about fishing subsidies as a potential distorter of trade and contributor to unsustainability of fish stocks around the globe. To analyze the trade impacts of these subsidies, a logical place to begin may be to calculate producer subsidy equivalents (PSEs). According to the OECD, "the PSE is an indicator of the value of the transfers from domestic consumers and taxpayers to the producers resulting from a given set of agricultural policies at a point in time" (FAO 2003).

The PSE also may be useful in assessing the advantages of producer subsidies in the fisheries sector. The complicating factor is management. In agriculture, it is assumed that subsidies are compared to a subsidy-free world characterized by economically efficient allocation of goods at various prices. However, if the fishery is managed under an open-access system, for example, then the subsidy-free world is not economically efficient, because that system does not lead to efficient allocation. To be truly efficient, the subsidies would not exist *and* there would be perfect management of fish stocks so that all negative externalities were incorporated into the price of each fish. PSEs for fisheries products have not been calculated because fish are highly heterogeneous and reference prices to measure market-price support are hard to pin down.

TABLE 15.2 Simulated Changes in the Real Value of World Exports in 1995 Prices
(percent)

Type of Export	Annual Growth in Base (1995–2020)	EVSL 2010	EVSL 2020	Bogor 2010	Bogor 2020	Developed APEC Countries 2010	Developed APEC Countries 2020
Unprocessed							
Tuna	1.3	5.0	4.8	1.5	4.8	1.6	1.5
Other fish	8.2	32.4	28.0	0.4	28.0	−1.9	−1.9
Rock lobster	1.4	1.5	1.5	0.7	1.5	0.7	0.7
Prawns	2.6	11.3	15.5	0.4	15.5	0.4	0.4
Other crustaceans	7.1	38.5	51.2	1.3	51.2	1.3	0.7
Abalone	3.4	20.2	21.9	2.6	21.9	2.6	2.0
Scallops	6.2	15.5	23.5	0.5	23.5	0.6	0.1
Other mollusks	3.9	22.5	23.7	1.3	23.7	1.3	1.4
Processed							
Tuna	2.4	0.4	0.8	0.3	0.8	0.3	0.3
Other fish	4.4	11.7	17.0	2.6	17.0	2.6	1.5
Rock lobster	0.4	0.0	0.0	0.1	0.0	0.1	0.0
Prawns	1.2	0.6	0.7	0.3	0.7	0.3	0.3
Other crustaceans	1.6	0.4	0.4	0.4	0.4	0.4	0.4
Mollusks	3.0	8.4	9.4	4.0	9.4	4.0	3.9
Total	5.1	20.4	24.1	1.0	24.1	0.2	−0.4

Source: Cox, Stubbs, and Davies 2000.

TABLE 15.3 Simulated Benefits from Tariff Reductions, by Country
(percent)

Country	Growth in Base (1995–2020)	EVSL 2010	Bogor 2010	Developed APEC Countries 2010	EVSL and Bogor 2010	Developed APEC Countries 2010
Australia	2.7	0.0	0.1	0.1	0.7	0.1
Canada	2.4	1.9	0.1	0.0	5.9	0.1
Chile/Peru	0.2	0.0	0.0	0.0	0.4	0.0
China	9.1	0.0	0.0	0.0	−0.3	0.0
Hong Kong (China)	4.8	−0.3	0.0	0.0	−1.4	0.1
Japan	1.9	−0.3	−0.2	−0.2	0.0	−0.3
Korea, Rep. of	3.7	1.1	0.1	0.0	2.5	0.0
United States	1.7	0.6	0.0	0.0	2.9	−0.1
Other APEC	4.6	1.0	0.0	−0.1	0.9	−0.2
Total APEC	5.4	0.2	0.0	0.0	0.2	−0.1
Non-APEC	1.8	0.2	0.0	0.0	0.7	0.0
World	4.0	0.2	0.0	0.0	0.4	0.0

Note: These benefits represent changes in the sum of consumer surplus, producer surplus, and import tariff revenue.
Source: Cox, Stubbs, and Davies 2000.

The impact of removing subsidies may be analyzed according to the type of subsidy. For subsidies that lower the costs of production (such as government-paid fishing access fees, low-cost vessel construction loans, and tax exemptions), removal will increase costs of production. A large portion of the world's subsidized fishing fleet is from the European Union, Japan, Russia, China, and other nations that subsidize (Milazzo 1998). A reduction in these subsidies would almost certainly benefit fish stocks—as well as decreasing trade.

Milazzo (1998) provides an excellent summary of the benefits to developing nations of removing subsidies.

- Subsidies that pay for access arrangements support continued operations primarily by European and East Asian distant-water fleets off Africa and in the Western Pacific. These subsidized operations reduce the fishing opportunities available to local fishermen. In most cases, the payments probably do not compensate adequately for the full economic value of the resources.
- There is scattered evidence that subsidized access arrangements are beginning to compromise local food needs.
- The combination of developed countries' subsidies to their distant-water fleets and to their domestic (coastal) fleets minimizes to some extent trade opportunities that should be available to developing countries.
- Fishing subsidies are highly nontransparent in the sense that more than three-quarters of the subsidies are not budgeted, and a good share of budgeted subsidies are controlled by governmental agencies other than those responsible for fisheries.
- Environmentally harmful subsidies outweigh the effect of subsidies that are environmentally benign or positive. Milazzo's estimates show that possibly no more than 5 percent of all subsidies support conservation.

Influence of Management Regime on Effects of Trade Liberalization in Capture Fisheries

An alternative means of looking at impacts of trade liberalization is to assess their implications under different management programs. Rögnvaldur Hannesson (OECD 2003a) has investigated the effects of liberalizing trade in fish, fishing services, and investments in fishing vessels. Three styles of fisheries management are defined: open access, catch control, and efficient management. As we saw earlier, under open access fishermen are free to respond to prices by increasing or decreasing their catch. Increased prices will invite entry into the fishery by more participants, so that in the long run the fishery will be overfished. Under catch control and efficient management, total supplies are fixed and will not change with changes in prices. This is because a TAC will have been set to guide the fishing effort and guarantee a sustainable fishery. The difference between catch control and efficient management is that the TAC catch control imposes no constraint on each fisherman, who retains the incentive to catch as much as he can, as fast as he can, before the TAC is reached and the fishery closed. Catch control alone is economically inefficient because it allows too many fishermen in the fishery, and the capitalization and effort are too high.

If trade barriers are removed—that is, if fish-importing countries lift their barriers—prices decline in the importing country and rise in the exporting country to a global equilibrium (accounting for transportation costs). What are the impacts of such a development, assuming adequate management measures? Table 15.4 shows the expected outcome.

The "double dividend" refers to the gain in the importing country from getting fish at a lower price and redirecting resources from the domestic fishing industry to higher-value uses. Although there is no reason to assume that both the importing and exporting countries share the same type of management regime, if both have an effective regime then the results will be very similar to the classic outcome of agricultural trade liberalization.

With open access and catch control, under which a change in prices induces increased effort in the exporting country, it is conceivable that a country could end up worse off with trade liberalization (Brander and Taylor 1997a, 1997b, 1998; Hannesson 2000). This is because the total quantity caught in the open-access fishery will increase at first but then decline as the fishery becomes overfished. With a decline in prices resulting from the elimination of import barriers, however, the effort

TABLE 15.4 Effects of Relaxing Trade Barriers

Regime	Fish-Exporting Country			Fish-Importing Country		
	Open Access	Catch Control	Efficient Management	Open Access	Catch Control	Efficient Management
Short-term effects	Increased effort, larger catches, more trade gains from trade	Increased effort, no change in catch, higher profit gains from trade	No change in effort unless higher allowed catch, gains from trade, higher market value of quotas and licenses	Lower effort, smaller catches, more trade, gains from trade	Lower effort, no change in catch, lower profits, gains from trade	No change in effort unless smaller allowed catch, gains from trade, lower market value of quotas and licenses
Long-term effects	Fish stocks decline, catch may decline, possibly loss from trade	Increased investment in fishing boats, no change in catch, small gains from trade	Same as above	Fish stocks recover, catch may increase, double dividend from trade	Reduction of fishing fleets, no change in catch, double dividend from trade	Same as above

Source: OECD 2003a: 170.

in the importing country would be likely to decline, giving fish stocks a chance to recover. This is not necessarily the predicted outcome. Indeed, in many cases, as the price of fish has decreased, fishermen have actually increased their effort to maintain total revenue, at least in the short run.

The results above were premised on two separate stocks of fish—one in the importing country and one in the exporting country. The discussion can be made much more complicated by assuming that several countries share the resource.

Consider the European Union and Uganda as trading partners. Much of Uganda's fisheries products come from Lake Victoria and are exported to the European Union. Uganda has an open-access management regime on Lake Victoria and shares the lake with Kenya and Tanzania. If trade were to be liberalized, the amount traded would increase. Fishing pressure on Lake Victoria and its stock of Nile perch would increase, putting further pressure on the fish stock from both Uganda and Kenya. The price of the fish would rise as fewer and fewer fish were found. Food security would decline as the local community found it increasingly difficult to afford Nile perch. Unless some type of enforcement management regime were set up to limit total catch from the lake, this source of export earnings might be short-lived. Holding all else constant, trade liberalization would deplete stocks in Lake Victoria more quickly than if trade were not liberalized.

Impact of Trade Liberalization in Aquaculture

The implications of trade liberalization in aquaculture would likely be very similar to those in agriculture, because aquaculture shares many of the resource constraints and externalities of agriculture (tables 15.5 and 15.6). Certainly, if tariffs in the European Union, the Republic of Korea, and Japan were reduced, the quantity of aquacultured products sold to those countries would grow.

The concern among many is that increased trade in cultivated shrimp has had a large and negative effect on the environment and that the effect rises with production and exports. The same is true for salmon farming. Chile, Norway, Scotland, Canada, and Ireland are the largest producers of farmed salmon, with Chile and Norway being by far the largest. Environmental groups are concerned not only about pollution but also about effects on the genetic diversity of wild fish from escaped farmed fish that may not be indigenous to the area (Porter 2003).

Both salmon and shrimp production rely on fish meal for feed. Any increase in aquaculture production of either species will have an impact on demand for fish meal. I have already discussed the various issues associated with fish meal production, including the growing concern that the stocks of fish from which fish meal is produced (herring, anchovies, capelin, menhaden) are themselves

TABLE 15.5   **Effects of a Rise in the Price of Cultivated Fish on Aquaculture Output and Fisheries Catch If Feed Is Held Constant**

Management Regime in Capture Fisheries	Effect on Output in Aquaculture	Effect on Output in Capture Fisheries for Consumption Fish
Open access	Output rise for sufficiently low prices, but as the price of feed fish increases, the stocks will ultimately be exploited beyond MSY[a], supply of feed falls, and aquaculture output falls	Lower stocks of feed fish lead to less growth of consumption fish. Higher price of consumption fish leads to less supply as stocks are pushed beyond MSY
Capture fisheries for feed fish and consumption fish managed separately	Output rise and flattens out as supply of feed cannot be further augmented	Output of consumption fish falls as the price exceeds a certain level
All capture fisheries managed as a whole	As above, but aquaculture is initiated at a higher price	As above, but output of capture fisheries continues to rise with price longer before starting to fall.

a. Maximum Sustainable Yield.
Source: OECD 2003a: 204.

TABLE 15.6   **Effects on Price and Quantities of Market Liberalization: Relaxing Border Measures in the Importing Country**
(two-country situation)

	Exporter	Importer
Fishery managed by TAC set without reference to economic factors	Increase price, no change in quantity	Decrease price, no change in quantity
Open access		
a) Stock above MSY	Increase price and quantity	Decrease price and quantity
b) Stock at MSY	Increase price, decrease quantity	Decrease price and quantity
c) Stock less than MSY	Increase price, decrease quantity	Decrease price, increase quantity
Aquaculture		
a) Feed available without significant price rise	Increase price and quantity	Decrease price and quantity
b) Managed fishery for captured feed fish	Increase price and increase or leave unchanged quantity	Decrease price and decrease or leave unchanged quantity
c) Open access fishery for captured feed fish	Same as open access above	Same as open access above

Source: OECD 2003a, page 200.

overfished. Unless effective management of the total catch in those fisheries is instituted, the sustainability of aquaculture may not be possible until an alternative to fish meal is developed.

This section has focused so far on carnivorous fish (salmon and shrimp), and the impact of trade liberalization on the source of feed. However, a large portion of the world's aquaculture production consists of herbivores such as carp. Carp contribute significantly to food security in China and other nations, particularly as they tend not to be found on the export market, so trade liberalization is likely to have little impact.

The other face of aquaculture is farmed shellfish, which makes up a good proportion of aquaculture production worldwide. In Thailand production of green mussels, blood cockle, oysters, and other shellfish doubled from 73,976 million tons in 1988 to 138,202 million tons in 2000 valued at approximately $47 million (Chalermwat, Szuster, and Flaherty 2003). Because the primary concern with these products is the placement of the farms in unpolluted areas, the WTO Agreement on Sanitary and Phytosanitary Measures is likely to have the largest effect on this sector. Table 15.6 summarizes the discussion in this section.

Conclusions

Global seafood markets are truly international. Production, consumption, imports, and exports cover the globe, just as several species of fish migrate around the globe. Because the global market for fish and fish products has specific dynamics and issues separate from global agriculture, understanding the impacts of trade liberalization on seafood and fishery products requires an understanding of the differentiated markets for the various products.

Key aspects of trade liberalization on global seafood, fish meal, and fish oil markets have emerged from the discussion. Impacts of trade liberalization on the welfare of countries depends critically on the fisheries management systems of the producing countries, since negative externalities in global seafood markets are much larger and more detrimental than those specific to agriculture. Open access, the management regime in many developing countries, invariably leads to overfishing. Any event that raises prices for fish from exporting developing countries creates incentives to fish even more, exacerbating overfishing and leading quickly to collapses in stocks. Even trade liberalization in the aquaculture industries is not immune from the effects of fisheries management regimes to the extent that the feed for that production is derived from a poorly managed capture fishery.

Increased trade in aquacultured products, independent of issues with feed, can lead to increased environmental degradation from conversion of land from benign agricultural use to less benign aquacultural use. Little has so far been done to internalize the negative externalities caused by excess fishing, unintended trapping of other marine life, or water pollution from aquaculture operations.

As stocks in developed countries have declined, their fleets have gone elsewhere to capture fish. The governments of the European Union, for example, have paid several developing countries for access to their fishing territory. While the developing nations gain access fees, enforcement of fish-management policies to limit the catches of the foreign fleets are minimal, resulting in an overfishing of these fish stocks. Thus, developing countries derive a short-term gain by allowing foreign fleets to fish in their waters; that value disappears in the long run.

Removing foreign access from developing countries' waters may not be the complete answer, even though foreign access is usually subsidized by the foreign fleets' governments. Developing countries have fisheries resources within their exclusive economic zones. Removing foreign fleets from those waters is good for the fish stocks, but if the country itself has no means to capture the value of the resource, it gains little else. Two options present themselves under such circumstances: first, to negotiate better access agreements to ensure that the true value of the resource is being paid to the developing country, and, second, to invest in the developing country's fishing capacity so that it can take advantage of its rightful resource. It should go without saying that in either case an effective management system must be put in place to prevent overfishing.

Tariffs in global seafood markets have come down significantly and may no longer be a prime trade barrier, except perhaps in South-South trade. In the United States, as the markets for certain seafood species has become more competitive, industries in the United States have increasingly turned to antidumping and countervailing duty measures to protect themselves from competition from developing countries.

The WTO has the opportunity to use its purview over subsidies through the Agreements on Subsidies and Countervailing Measures to encourage members to drop fishing subsidies and thus to cure the trade distortions caused by the subsidies while encouraging sustainability of fish stocks globally. In addition, from the developing countries' perspective, an important focus in WTO negotiations must be the Agreement on Technical Barriers to Trade and the Agreement on Sanitary and Phytosanitary Measures. The processes by which developed countries impose technical barriers to trade must be transparent and demonstrably nonarbitrary. Developing countries need resources to assist them to meet current sanitary and phytosanitary measures by building infrastructure that permits them to meet the requirements and training workers to maintain the proper measures.

Finally, international trade in fish and fish products also has an impact on food security. Often the domestic market in exporting developing countries retains only the inferior fish, while the better, more valuable fish are sold abroad. A collapse in the stock of the fish consumed domestically may lead to significant food security problems. Similarly, if fish meal prices were to rise for any reason, the increase would have an impact on the ability of some nations to feed terrestrial livestock.

Everyone has an interest in ensuring that fisheries and aquaculture are managed in a sustainable way. As externalities are internalized into the production process and their value incorporated into the prices of fish products, then it is likely that trade liberalization will bring about a net benefit to trading partners. The distribution of benefits across countries, producers, and consumers can best be judged after effective management measures are in place. That distribution is not easily judged today.

Notes

1. The primary source for the material in this section is Abila 2003.

2. www.st.nmfs.gov/webpls.

3. The Farm Security and Rural Investment Act of 2002 (Farm Bill) states that for the purposes of the Federal Food, Drug, and Cosmetic Act, "the term 'catfish' may only be considered to be a common or usual name (or part thereof) for fish classified within the family *Ictaluridae*" (USITC 2003a).

References

Abila, Richard. 2003. "Food Safety in Food Security and Food Trade, Case Study of Kenyan Exports." International Food Policy Research Institute, Washington, D.C. September.

Anderson, J. L. 2003. *The International Seafood Trade.* Oxford: Woodhead.

Brander, J. A., and M. S. Taylor. 1997a. "International Trade and Open-Access Renewable Resources: The Small Open Economy Case." *Canadian Journal of Economics* 30: 526–52.

———. 1997b. "International Trade between Consumer and Conservationist Countries." *Resource and Energy Economics* 19: 267–98.

———. 1998. "Open Access Renewable Resources Trade and Trade Policy in a Two-country Model." *Journal of International Economics* 44: 181–210.

Chalermwat, K., B. W. Szuster, and M. Flaherty. 2003. "Shellfish Aquaculture in Thailand." *Aquaculture Economics and Management* 7: 249–61.

Conrad, J. M. 1999. *Resource Economics.* Cambridge: Cambridge University Press.

Cox, Anthony, Matthew Stubbs, and Luke Davies. 2000. *Southern Bluefin Tuna and CITES: An Economic Perspective.* Report prepared for the Fisheries Resource Research Fund and Environment Australia, ABARE Research Report 99.2, Canberra.

Deere, C. 2000. "Net Gains: Linking Fisheries Management, International Trade and Sustainable Development." International Union for Conservation of Nature and Natural Resources (IUCN), Washington, D.C.

Delgado, C. L., N. Wada, M. W. Rosengrant, S. Meijer, and M. Ahmed. 2003. *Fish to 2020: Supply and Demand in Changing Global Markets.* Washington, D.C.: International Food Policy Research Institute.

ESCAP and ADB. 2000. *State of the Environment in Asia and Pacific 2000.* Economic and Social Commission for Asia and the Pacific and Asian Development Bank. New York: United Nations. www.usepscap.org/enrd/environ/soe.htm.

FAO (U.N. Food and Agriculture Organization). 1999. "Country Profile: The People's Republic of Bangladesh." Rome. August.

———. 2000. "Country Profile: The Kingdom of Thailand." Rome. May.

———. 2002a. *FAO Yearbook—Fisheries Statistics, Aquaculture Production.* volume 90/2. Rome.

———. 2002b. *FAO Yearbook—Fisheries Statistics, Commodities.* vol. 91. Rome.

———. 2002c. *The State of World Fisheries and Aquaculture.* Rome.

———. 2003. "Report of the Expert Consultation on Identifying, Assessing and Reporting on Subsidies in the Fishing Industry." FAO Fisheries Report 698. Rome.

Filhol, Agnes. 2000. "Effect of World Trade Organization's Regulation on World Fish Trade." *GLOBEFISH* 65 (February). Rome.

Grainger, R. J. R., and S. M. Garcia. 1996. "Chronicles of Marine Fishery Landings (1950–94): Trend Analysis and Fisheries Potential." FAO Fisheries Technical Paper 359. Rome.

Hannesson, Rögnvaldur. 1996. *Fisheries Mismanagement: The Case of the North Atlantic Cod.* Oxford: Fishing News Books.

———. 2000. "Renewable Resources and the Gains from Trade." *Canadian Journal of Economics* 33: 122–32.

Institute for European Environmental Policy. 2002a. "Subsidies to the European Union Fisheries Sector." London. October.

———. 2002b. "Fisheries Agreements with Third Countries—Is the EU Moving Towards Sustainable Development?" London. November.

Kinnucan, H., and C. R. Wessells. 1997. "Marketing Research Paradigms for Aquaculture." *Aquaculture Economics and Management* 1: 73–86.

Lem, Audun. 2003. *The WTO Doha Round and Fisheries: What's at Stake.* FAO Fact Sheet for WTO Ministerial Conference in Cancún, Mexico. July.

McGovern, Dan. 2003. "SSA Files 6 Shrimp Antidumping Petitions; Alleges Dumping Margins of Over 200 Percent." *The Wave News Network,* December 31.

Milazzo, Matteo. 1998. "Subsidies in World Fisheries: A Reexamination." World Bank Technical Paper. Washington, D.C.

National Research Council. 1999. *Sustaining Marine Fisheries.* Washington, D.C.: National Academy Press.

OECD (Organisation for Economic Co-operation and Development). 2003a. *Liberalising Fisheries Markets: Scope and Effects.* Paris.

———. 2003b. *Review of Fisheries in OECD Countries: Country Statistics 1999–2001.* Paris.

Porter, G. 2003. "Protecting Wild Atlantic Salmon from Imports of Salmon Aquaculture: A Country-by-Country Progress Report." www.worldwildlife.org. May.

Robb, Cairo. 2001. *International Environmental Law Reports,* vol. 2, *Trade and the Environment.* Cambridge: Cambridge University Press.

Schrank, W. 2003. "Introducing Fisheries Subsidies." FAO Fisheries Technical Paper 437. Rome.

UNEP (United Nations Environment Programme). 1999a. Environmental Impacts of Trade Liberalization and Policies for the Sustainable Management of Natural Resources: A Case Study of Bangladesh's Shrimp Farming Industry. UNEP: New York.

———. 1999b. "Environmental Impacts of Trade Liberalization and Policies for the Sustainable Management of Natural Resources: A Case Study of Uganda's Fisheries Sector." New York.

———. 2002a. "Africa Environment Outlook: Past, Present and Future Perspectives." www.unep.org/aeo.

———. 2002b. "Well Managed Fisheries Vital for Environmentally Friendly Development in Poor Parts of the Globe." Press release. New York. March.

U.S. Department of Commerce. 1997. "Fisheries of the United States, 1997." National Marine Fisheries Service, Washington, D.C.

USITC (United States International Trade Commission). 2003a. "Certain Frozen Fish Fillets from Vietnam." Investigation No. 731-TA-1012 (Final). Publication 3617. August. Washington, D.C.

———. 2003b. "Crawfish Tail Meat from China." Investigation 731-TA-752 (Review). Publication 3614. July. Washington, D.C.

Wessells, C. R., and J. Anderson. 1992. "Innovations and Progress in Seafood Demand and Market Analysis." *Marine Resource Economics* 7: 209–28.

World Bank. 2003. "Madagascar Diagnostic Trade Integration Study." Prepared for the Integrated Framework for Trade-Related Technical Assistance to Least Developed Countries, Washington, D.C.

WTO (World Trade Organization). 1999. "Benefits of Eliminating Trade Distorting and Environmentally Damaging Subsidies in the Fisheries Sector." WT/CTE/W/121. Geneva.

———. 2000. "Environmental Benefits of Removing Trade Restrictions and Distortions: The Fisheries Sector." WT/CTE/W/167. Geneva.

———. 2001. "Environmental Benefits of Removing Trade Restrictions and Distortions: The Fisheries Sector—Addendum." WT/CTE/W/167/Add.1. Geneva.

———. 2003a. "Possible Approaches to Improved Disciplines on Fisheries Subsidies." TN/RL/W/77. Geneva.

———. 2003b. "Understanding the WTO." Third Edition. September. www.wto.org. WWF (World Wildlife Fund). 2003. "WWF Fact Sheet: West African Marine Ecoregion." Dakar, Senegal.

16

COFFEE: MARKET SETTING AND POLICIES

John Baffes, Bryan Lewin, and Panos Varangis

All coffee is produced in the tropics, primarily by smallholders. Most is consumed in high-income countries. Latin America accounts for 60 percent of global output, followed by Asia (24 percent), and Africa (16 percent). More than half of global coffee output is accounted for by the three dominant producers: Brazil (33 percent), Colombia (10 percent), and Vietnam (10 percent). Some other African and Latin American countries, however, are heavily dependent on their exports of coffee, despite their low share in global output. For example, coffee accounts for more than half of total merchandise exports in Burundi, Rwanda, and Ethiopia and more than 20 percent in Guatemala, Honduras, and Nicaragua. More than 80 percent of coffee production is traded internationally. Historically, coffee is the second most traded primary commodity after crude oil, generating more than $15 billion in export revenue (evaluated at 1997–98 average prices and volumes). Overall, consumption volumes have stagnated in the mature markets, in which the United States accounts for about 18 percent, followed by Brazil (10 percent), Germany (9 percent), Japan (6 percent), and France and Italy (5 percent each). However, consumption has been increasing in some new (especially transition) markets.

There are two types of coffee. Arabica, grown at high altitudes in Latin America (including Brazil) and northeastern Africa, accounts for two-thirds of total world output. It has a strong aroma and low level of caffeine. Robusta, with a much stronger taste than arabica, is grown in humid areas at low altitudes in Asia, western and southern Africa, and Brazil. During the last decade, production of robusta, which is particularly suitable for instant coffee, has increased (table 16.1).[1]

During the last decade, the coffee market has gone through a number of structural changes. On the supply side, Brazil's production capacity expanded enormously, with new plantations in the north that are less affected by frosts and, because of irrigation, not affected by droughts. Vietnam entered the coffee market in a major way in the 1980s—it currently supplies more than 12 million bags, making it the world's second-largest coffee exporter. On the demand side, consumption of specialty coffees has expanded, currently accounting for an estimated 6–8 percent of total consumption. Demand for low-quality coffee beans has also increased, primarily reflecting new technologies that enable roasters to remove the harsh taste of robustas for normal coffee while continuing to

The authors thank Ataman Aksoy and Harry de Gorter for helpful comments and suggestions on earlier drafts.

TABLE 16.1   The Changing Structure of the Coffee Market
(thousands of 60-kg bags)

| Year | Arabica | | | | Robusta | Total |
	Colombian Milds	Other Milds	Naturals	Subtotal		
1992	16,959	25,122	23,317	65,398	27,291	92,689
1993	13,256	23,398	28,555	65,209	26,989	92,198
1994	15,059	24,582	29,300	68,941	27,901	96,842
1995	15,503	27,525	18,545	61,573	27,193	88,766
1996	12,489	27,040	27,126	66,655	37,033	103,688
1997	13,498	27,965	23,436	64,899	32,753	97,652
1998	12,509	27,380	35,024	74,913	33,506	108,419
1999	11,821	31,698	30,178	73,697	39,706	113,403
2000	12,026	28,480	30,717	71,223	45,638	116,861
2001	13,229	26,123	28,540	67,892	42,834	110,726
2002	13,179	25,585	43,667	82,431	41,720	124,151
2003	13,352	26,318	26,217	65,887	39,945	105,232
Market share (percent)						
1992	18	27	25	71	29	100
1993	14	25	31	71	29	100
1994	16	25	30	71	29	100
1995	17	31	21	69	31	100
1996	12	26	26	64	36	100
1997	14	29	24	66	34	100
1998	12	25	32	69	31	100
1999	10	28	27	65	35	100
2000	10	24	26	61	39	100
2001	12	24	26	61	39	100
2002	11	21	25	66	34	100
2003	13	25	25	63	37	100

Source: U.S. Department of Agriculture.

meet the increasing demand for instant and flavored coffees, which primarily use robusta coffees.

For most of the 20th century the coffee market has been subject to various supply-control schemes. The most important were the price-stabilization schemes implemented by Brazil at the beginning of the century, the Inter-American Coffee Agreements implemented during and after the Second World War, the agreements administered by the International Coffee Organization (ICO) from 1962 to 1989, and more recent attempts by the Association of Coffee Producing Countries (ACPC). Although the stated objective of these arrangements was to stabilize prices, prices often ended up being higher than they would have been in the absence of the arrangements. The most influential of these schemes were the International Coffee Agreements

(ICAs) under the auspices of the ICO, the last of which collapsed in 1989. Government intervention in domestic markets was also prevalent in many countries through parastatals that controlled marketing and trade in the coffee industry. Following the collapse of the last ICA, most parastatals were either dismantled or their roles diminished. Currently, the global coffee market is, to a large extent, a distortion-free market. On the trade side, import restrictions are nonexistent, except some tariff escalation in coffee products (such as instant coffee).

Global Balance and Price Trends

Brazil, by far the largest coffee producer and exporter and the second-largest consumer, accounts for one-third of global output and

TABLE 16.2 Coffee Production, Selected Years
(thousands of 60-kg bags)

Country	1960	1970	1980	1990	2000	2002	2004
Brazil	29,800	11,000	21,500	31,000	34,100	51,600	42,400
Vietnam	53	39	77	1,200	15,333	11,167	12,000
Colombia	7,260	8,000	13,500	14,500	10,500	11,712	11,600
Indonesia	1,327	2,327	5,365	7,480	6,495	6,140	5,750
India	1,225	1,914	1,977	2,970	5,020	4,588	4,835
Mexico	2,100	3,200	3,862	4,550	4,800	4,350	4,500
Ethiopia	1,687	2,589	3,264	3,500	3,683	3,693	4,000
Guatemala	1,500	1,965	2,702	3,282	4,564	3,802	3,671
Uganda	1,925	2,667	2,133	2,700	3,205	2,910	3,200
Peru	598	1,114	1,170	1,170	2,824	2,760	2,980
Honduras	291	545	1,265	1,685	2,821	2,661	2,753
Costa Rica	951	1,295	2,140	2,565	2,502	2,207	2,050
Nicaragua	437	641	971	460	1,610	997	1,500
Côte d'Ivoire	0	4,414	3,973	4,734	5,700	3,568	1,444
El Salvador	1,452	2,054	2,940	2,603	1,624	1,351	1,285
Papua New Guinea	61	426	889	969	1,051	1,118	1,210
Cameroon	855	1,180	1,860	1,450	1,113	801	1,100
Kenya	566	999	1,568	1,455	864	926	1,085
Thailand	1	19	201	785	1,692	757	950
Ecuador	594	1,255	1,517	1,830	1,005	790	750
Total	64,999	58,838	85,738	99,911	116,861	124,151	117,650

Source: U.S. Department of Agriculture.

produces both arabica and robusta coffee. It is followed by Colombia (arabica) and Vietnam (robusta), each accounting for about 10 percent of global output. Other significant producers are Indonesia and Mexico (6 percent each) and India (4 percent) (table 16.2).

The technology of coffee production has changed significantly in the past 30 years, but not all countries have shared equally in the changes. Average yields in Asia are double those in Sub-Saharan Africa, and yields in Latin America are 60 percent higher than in Africa. Annual yield growth during the 1990s was 2.6 percent in Asia, 1.7 percent in Latin America, and 1.1 percent in Sub-Saharan Africa, according to data from the U.N. Food and Agriculture Organization (FAO).

On the demand side, the United States consumes about 18 percent of global output, followed by Brazil (10 percent), Germany (9 percent), Japan (6 percent), France and Italy (5 percent each). On a per capita basis, Scandinavian countries consume about 10 kilograms a year, followed by Germany (8 kilograms), and France, Italy, and Spain with

approximately 5.5 kilograms each. U.S. per capita consumption fluctuates between 4 and 5.5 kilograms; in the United Kingdom and Japan it is between 2.5 and 3 kilograms. Only five coffee producers consume a substantial portion of their output: Brazil and Ethiopia (30 percent each), Indonesia (23 percent), Mexico (19 percent), and Colombia (11 percent), which together account for about 20 percent of global output; the remaining 80 percent is internationally traded.

Vietnam's emergence as a major robusta producer altered the landscape of the global coffee market in a permanent way. In 1980 Vietnam produced 77,000 bags—less than 0.1 percent of world production. In 2000, it exceeded 15 million bags—more than 13 percent of world production. Vietnam entered the coffee market in response to a series of policy reforms in the early 1990s that changed the balance of incentives toward export crops. These reforms facilitated land ownership and liberalized input and output markets. Following the reforms, for example, fertilizer prices declined by almost 50 percent. Other reforms (known as Doi Moi) encouraged internal migration to the Central Highlands because of easy access to new land (eventually to be used for coffee production). These reforms, combined with the 1994 coffee price spike, made Vietnam an important player in the coffee market. It is worth noting that Vietnam's coffee expansion took place without assistance from either national or multilateral funding. However, some help came from the Soviet Union and Eastern European countries in the form of technical assistance during the early 1980s. Because neither Vietnam nor these countries were ICO members, and hence not bound by any quota obligations, they could expand coffee production and trade without any restriction. The expansion was also aided by the desire of the Soviet Union and Eastern European countries to have access to coffee without paying hard currency.

Brazil has been able to maintain unprecedented output levels, averaging more than 35 million bags during the last four seasons. Extensive mechanization of coffee harvesting, along with the development of high-yielding varieties, has reduced costs of production, while shifting production to the north, away from the frost-prone areas of the south, has reduced the likelihood of weather-related supply disruptions. Extensive use of irrigation in areas such as Bahia and the Cerrado has stabilized and sustained yields. Another significant development in Brazil is emergence of semi-washed arabicas; a process that makes better coffee. About 3 million bags of semi-washed arabicas compete directly with higher-quality coffee from Central America.

Given that both Vietnam and Brazil are low-cost producers, they are unlikely to reduce coffee production. Consequently production cutbacks to restore the balance of supply and demand are now coming from the higher-cost African and Central American producers. In Central America, for example, production of the lower-altitude, lower-quality coffees that can be easily replaced in commercial blends by Brazilian arabicas have fallen sharply.[2]

While Latin America and Asia have increased their shares in global coffee output, Africa's share has declined from 33 percent in 1970 to 18 percent in 2000. Africa's coffee output has never surpassed its peak in 1972. After remaining almost constant at 20 million bags for two decades following that peak, it has been in slow decline since then.

Numerous studies have identified several factors that are likely to further influence coffee processing and consumption patterns (see, for example, IADB/USAID/World Bank 2002, and Lewin, Giovannucci, and Varangis 2004). First, roasters are able to work with a lower level of stocks. Second, new technology enables them to remove the harsh taste of robustas, achieving the same level of quality with lower-quality beans. Third, roasters have been more flexible in their ability to make short-term switches between coffee types, implying that the premiums commanded by certain types of coffee cannot be retained for long. Finally, a small segment of the market has emerged that focuses on product differentiation, such as organic, gourmet, and shade coffee. The implication of all this is that the demand outlook is likely to be different for different coffee producers. Specifically, if any expansion in coffee demand takes place, it is likely to be at the two ends of the spectrum: lower-quality beans (reflecting improved technology and increased demand for soluble coffee) and specialty coffees (reflecting expansion to niche markets).[3] Efforts to increase coffee consumption may also come at the expense of tea consumption, a commodity produced mainly by low-income (and often coffee-producing) countries.

Coffee prices are highly volatile. (figures 16.1a through d). During the 1990s arabica prices ranged from $1.17 a kilogram in August 1992 to $5.89 a kilogram in May 1997. Robusta prices ranged from $0.82 a kilogram in June 1992 to $4.03 a kilogram in September 1994. The price volatility stems in part from weather conditions in Brazil, where frost affects crops every five to six years and severe droughts also occur periodically. While short-selling and buying by hedge funds are sometimes cited as a reason for the high volatility of coffee prices, this activity probably contributes only to short-term volatility.[4]

Coffee prices have declined considerably since 1998 (figure 16.1). In January 2002 robusta dropped to $0.50 a kilogram (the lowest nominal level since the $0.49 a kilogram price of May 1965 and 86 percent below its high four years earlier), while in October 2001 arabica averaged $1.24 a kilogram, a nine-year low and 76 percent below its high four years earlier. The combination of increased availability from Vietnam and Brazil, as well as domestic policies in many producing countries that retard

FIGURE 16.1(a) **Nominal Coffee Prices, 1990–2003**
(US$ per kilogram)

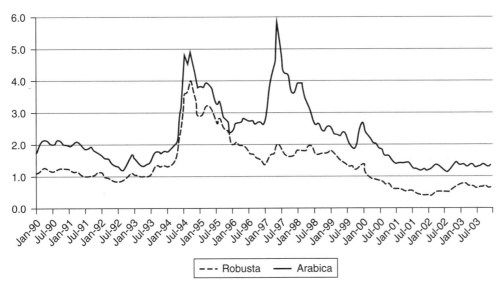

Source: World Bank.

(b) **Real Coffee Prices, 1960–2003**
(US$ per kilogram)

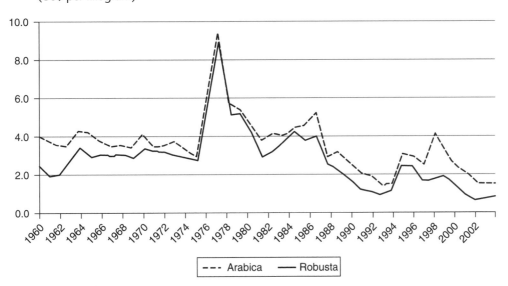

Source: World Bank.

exit from the market of uncompetitive producers, led to these historically low prices, which, in the absence of any international supply control mechanism, gave rise to the so-called coffee crisis and probably prolonged its length.

Exports from small coffee producers are a minuscule proportion of global trade in coffee but can loom large in the exporters' economies. For example, three African countries (Burundi, Rwanda, and Ethiopia) derive more than half of their total merchandise exports from coffee. The

poverty implications of coffee in these countries are enormous—in seven coffee-dependent African countries, per capita gross domestic product (GDP) ranged between $112 and $336 (table 16.3).

Areas with relatively high labor costs and large farms that are heavily dependent on seasonal labor, especially in Central America, can feel the effects of changing prices in a significant way (Lewin, Giovannucci, and Varangis 2004). For example, the rural labor employed in the coffee sectors of five Central American countries represented, on

(c) Nominal Price Indexes for Coffee and Other Commodities, 1990–2002
(August 2002 = 1.0)

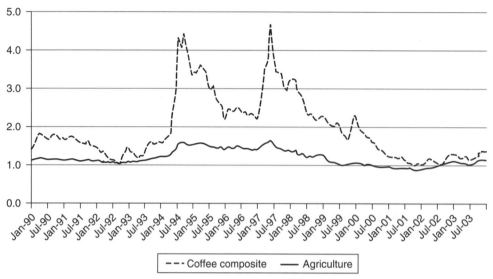

Source: World Bank.

(d) Real Price Indexes for Coffee and Other Commodities, 1960–2003
(2001 = 1.0)

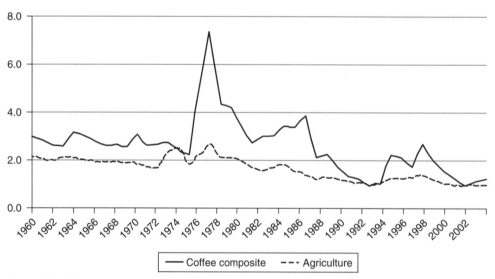

Source: World Bank.

average, 28 percent of the labor force in those countries (Nicaragua, 42 percent; Guatemala, 31 percent; Costa Rica, 28 percent; Honduras, 26 percent; El Salvador, 17 percent).

The Policy Environment

The coffee market has been subject to considerable intervention at the international and national levels. Those interventions are the subject of the next two subsections.

The International Environment

Regulation of coffee supplies at the international level has a long history (box 16.1). Calls for supply controls were made as early as 1902 following price declines due to Brazil's oversupply (Hutchinson 1909). At least three successful stabilization schemes took place in Brazil between 1905 and 1921. However, the coffee market became depressed following the crash of 1929. Attempts by Brazil to convince other coffee producers to coordinate

BOX 16.1   Coffee Supply Controls in the Twentieth Century

Calls for supply controls in the coffee market came as early as 1902 at an (unsuccessful) International Coffee Conference held in New York following price declines due to Brazil's oversupply (Hutchinson 1909). At the time, Brazil accounted for more than 85 percent of world's coffee output of 18.2 million bags. Chronic oversupplies prompted the state of São Paulo, which accounted for three-quarters of Brazil's coffee, to initiate a price stabilization scheme in 1905—called *valorization*—and to prohibit new plantings. The stockholding mechanism that regulated sales of coffee was financed by the federal government and several foreign banks. The scheme not only stabilized prices but also kept them at levels higher than demand and supply would have supported. A second valorization was undertaken in 1917 (following the disruption of coffee consumption in Europe during World War I), and a third in 1921. These schemes were very profitable for their promoters. However, greater stability in the coffee market arising from the supply controls encouraged the rapid extension of new plantings in Brazil and led to new calls for even more state intervention (Wickizer 1943: 143). Thus, São Paulo's coffee problem became Brazil's coffee problem.

Following the success of the valorization schemes, a permanent supply-control scheme was envisaged for the newly created São Paulo Coffee Institute. The institute began buying coffee after the 1927–28 bumper crop and convinced other states that had become important suppliers to join in. It withdrew from coffee purchasing after the crash of October 1929, when coffee consumption plummeted and financing dried up. The Brazilian government then attempted to convince other Latin American coffee producers (which had increased their market shares considerably) to find ways to regulate exports. Two Pan-American Coffee conferences (in Bogotá in 1936 and Havana in 1937) ended with no agreement. In the meantime, several coffee destruction schemes were undertaken by Brazil using public funds. During 1931–38, a total of 68.7 million bags were destroyed—twice the world's annual coffee output. Following inaction by other coffee producers (not surprisingly, since they were enjoying the benefit of controls), Brazil abandoned restrictions in favor

of free entry and competition. However, 30 years of controls had taken a toll: Brazil's share in the export market of coffee had fallen from 87 percent in 1905 to 55 percent in 1940. Brazil's coffee problem had become Latin America's coffee problem.

Weak demand from Europe during the Second World War, coupled with the desire of the United States to keep Latin America on the side of the Alliance, led to the formation of the Inter-American Coffee Agreement. Its membership consisted of the two dominant coffee producers (Brazil and Colombia) and several smaller producers in Central America (Wickizer 1943). A second agreement was negotiated after the war. The two agreements had the same outcome. Supply restrictions and investment activity by European countries in their colonies brought African producers into the market. Latin America's coffee problem became the Western world's coffee problem.

In 1962 coffee-producing countries accounting for 90 percent of global output and almost all developed consuming countries formed the International Coffee Organization and signed the International Coffee Agreements (ICAs). The objective of the ICAs was to stabilize coffee prices through mandatory export quotas. The United States enthusiastically backed the agreement, considering it a means of increasing the income of Central American coffee producers, hoping that this would contain the spread of communism. Consumer-country support for export quotas was also encouraged by large importers, who benefited from export-tax rebates offered by the Instituto Brazilieno de Café in return for high-volume purchase commitments. Western European countries viewed the ICAs with sympathy, believing that high coffee prices were a good way to aid their former colonies (Bates 1997). To satisfy their quota obligations, governments of coffee producers bought stocks using part of their coffee tax revenues. The export-quota system, first implemented in 1963, continued intermittently until 1989.

After Vietnam entered the world market in the 1980s, with assistance from the Soviet Union, the West's coffee problem became the world's coffee problem.

TABLE 16.3   Coffee's Importance to Developing Countries, 1997–2000 Averages

Country	Percent of Merchandise Exports	Merchandise Exports (millions of current US$)	Per Capita GDP (constant 1995 US$)
Burundi	72.2	64	143
Rwanda	58.1	65	227
Ethiopia	51.5	520	112
Uganda	40.1	509	336
Sierra Leone	29.7	11	161
Nicaragua	25.4	613	435
Honduras	21.7	1,398	715
Guatemala	20.2	2,505	1,535
El Salvador	18.2	2,580	1,737
Tanzania	13.4	637	185
Madagascar	11.1	616	241

Source: International Coffee Organization.

supply-containing mechanisms failed. Brazil then introduced a number of coffee destruction schemes. Between 1931 and 1938, a total of 68.7 million bags were destroyed—twice the world's annual global coffee output. Following years of weak demand from Europe during the Second World War, Brazil negotiated two agreements with other producing countries in Latin America. Those agreements were largely unsuccessful. The countries that agreed to restrict their exports in return for Brazil's coffee stock destruction did not respect their commitments.

In the early 1960s most coffee-producing countries (accounting for 90 percent of global output) and almost all developed coffee-consuming countries formed the ICO, which attempted to stabilize coffee prices through mandatory export quotas under the International Coffee Agreements. The export quota system, first implemented in 1963, was temporarily suspended in 1972 as coffee prices soared. Quotas were restored in 1980 and suspended again in 1986 due to soaring prices. They were reintroduced in 1987 and suspended indefinitely in 1989. These agreements kept coffee prices higher than they otherwise would have been (Gilbert 1995).

Following the collapse of the last International Coffee Agreement, several coffee producers—including Brazil and Colombia but not Vietnam and Mexico—formed the Association of Coffee Producing Countries in September 1993. In the following year, export restrictions did contribute to the price increase already under way, but the agreements were overtaken by the price rises that followed the Brazilian frosts in 1994. During 2000 and 2001 the ACPC worked to persuade coffee-producing countries to retain part of their exports so as to staunch the decline in coffee prices that had started in 1998 and accelerated in 2000. Following some initial enthusiasm, ACPC's efforts failed, and the association was dissolved in February 2002, one month after robusta prices reached their historic low. The ACPC failed for several reasons, but a principal one was that in a liberalized market, the institutional structure necessary to ensure compliance in the member countries—a single-desk marketing agency—had been dismantled. There was also the problem of free-riding by nonmembers. The ICO attempted once again in 2002 to reduce coffee availability in a new agreement under which coffee producers are to remove low-quality beans from the market. Regulation 407 of the ICO states minimum specifications for export qualities, but it will depend entirely on voluntary compliance for its success.

A final consequence of the ICAs was that they gave rise to rent-seeking behavior by governments and marketing boards. The extent of this problem was revealed in the late 1980s, shortly before the collapse of the last ICA, when the Instituto Brazilieno de Café decided to auction 10 percent of its export quotas. The very high prices exporters paid for the quotas revealed to the entire domestic coffee industry the extent of the rents being extracted. A common consequence in many countries of the end of the ICA was an end to opportunities for rent seeking—this led to significant shifts in domestic support policies in several producing countries.

Domestic Policies

Since the collapse of the ICAs, domestic policies of coffee producers have focused on the reform and liberalization of marketing systems, and more recently on helping producers survive periods of low prices, sometimes through state intervention.

Akiyama (2001) reported that only 15 of the world's 51 coffee-producing countries had private marketing systems in 1985. Twenty-five countries sold coffee through state-owned enterprises, including marketing boards and stabilization funds, and another 11 countries had mixed state and private-sector marketing bodies. Most aspects of coffee marketing and trade, especially in Sub-Saharan Africa, were handled by government-controlled agencies, which typically resulted in heavy taxation of the sector. Although the reasons behind the tax policies varied, the main ones were low price elasticity of short-run supply, implying minimal impact of taxation on supply; less social and political resistance to taxation for cash crops than for food crops; the relative simplicity of tax collection, facilitated by the single marketing channel; and support for the government budget and balance of payments through foreign exchange earnings.

Many coffee-producing countries undertook reforms during the 1990s by removing or redefining the role of the parastatals. A combination of falling prices and rent-seeking activities by some of the marketing boards led several countries to reform their coffee sectors altogether. The outcome of these reforms has been mixed and mirrors the outcome of similar efforts in other export crop sectors (Akiyama and others 2003; Shepherd and Farolfi 1999). Bohman, Jarvis, and Barichello (1996) showed that in many cases, prices paid to growers were lower under the ICAs compared with what they would have been under a free market. Krueger (1990) showed that this was the case for other commodities as well. Krivonos (2003), who evaluated the impact of reforms undertaken in 14 coffee-producing countries during the late 1980s and early 1990s, concluded that in most cases

domestic prices adjusted faster after the reforms than they did before the reforms. In addition to higher prices, considerable private investment in the marketing, processing, and transportation sectors took place. Increased supply response also took place in most occasions.

At the same time, the gap created by the withdrawal of the state has not been filled in all cases—the quality of public-sector services has deteriorated. It has been often argued that the quality of coffee declined after the reforms, but this cannot be substantiated from the data. Quality may have declined after the collapse of the ICAs, since during the coffee agreements, quality improvements were the only means of increasing revenue.[5]

Uganda undertook sweeping reforms in 1990 (Akiyama 2001). An overvalued exchange rate, the inefficiencies of the country's Coffee Board, political instability, and the price decline of 1989 made reform the only viable alternative. Under the reforms, producer prices rose from 40–50 percent of export prices to 70–80 percent. The supply response has been considerable, and many entrepreneurs have entered the market. Regulation, quality control, and promotion issues were assigned to the newly established Uganda Coffee Development Authority. In addition to increased output, Uganda regained its reputation as a reliable robusta producer, commanding a premium for its exports.

Reforms in neighboring Tanzania have been less successful. Before 1990 the Tanzania Marketing Board and the cooperative unions handled all marketing (including input provision, transportation, and processing) and trade aspects of the sector. The cooperatives were also responsible for managing the large estates nationalized in the early 1970s. Some reforms were introduced in 1990, but they affected only inputs, price announcements, and retention of export earnings. More comprehensive reforms begun in 1994 allowed private traders to purchase coffee directly from growers and process it in their own factories for the first time in more than 30 years. The outcome of these reforms has been mixed. Growers receive a higher share of f.o.b. (free on board) prices, they are paid promptly, and entrepreneurial activity has increased enormously. But the Tanzanian coffee sector is still plagued by over-regulation (including mandatory auction), high taxation, and ad hoc decisions by the Tanzanian Coffee Board (Baffes forthcoming).

Domestic policies in producing countries remain sensitive to international developments as well as to local pressures, and consequently distortionary domestic policies appear in many countries. Although coffee prices have been in long-term decline, the volatility discussed above can make it difficult to determine whether price changes are temporary or a genuine shift in market fundamentals. Under such circumstances it is equally difficult to determine the correct policy response. An additional complication is that the shift to lower-cost producers has been paralleled by the fact that those countries with greater market power have lower dependency on coffee export volumes. This makes defensive policymaking difficult for countries with greater dependency.

The approaches taken to recent domestic policymaking are varied. Among the larger producing countries, Brazil has long had a policy of preferential credit access but more recently has been auctioning put options to farmers at well below fair value; these options are exercisable as sales of coffee to the government. In Central America governments have bailed out the banks that had lent heavily to the coffee sector, but because most loans had been made to larger, more creditworthy farmers, the bailout failed to have much impact on the poorest, except by maintaining employment in larger estates.

Niche Markets and Changing Patterns of Consumption

The last decade has witnessed the emergence of nontraditional channels of production, marketing, and consumption of "new coffees"—gourmet (or specialty[6]), organic, fair trade, eco-friendly (shade-grown or bird-friendly), and other certified coffees. Lewin, Giovannucci, and Varangis (2004: 99) make the following distinction between differentiated and mainstream coffees:

"Differentiated coffees are those that can be clearly distinguished because of distinct origin, defined processes, or exceptional characteristics such as superior taste or zero defects. In contrast, mainstream coffees are nearly always preground blends that are often unidentified in terms of origin. These are usually, though not always, distributed through mainstream chan-

nels such as supermarkets, foodservice, and other institutions and they compete strongly on the basis of price. Differentiated coffees are often distinguished by a closer and sometimes direct relationship with a roaster or buyer rather than being traded in bulk or via the commodity markets.

Differentiated coffees can help the coffee industry compete with other beverages by leveraging unique characteristics that include: (1) geographic indications of origin (appellations); (2) gourmet and specialty; (3) organic; (4) fair trade; (5) eco-friendly or shade-grown; (6) private or corporate standards."

The expansion of differentiated coffees has two, often overlapping, dimensions. The first is social. Rising consumption of fair-traded, eco-friendly, shade-grown, or bird-friendly coffees is driven by social concerns. Consumers wish to ensure that coffee growers receive higher prices (fair trade) or to improve the effects of coffee growing on the environment (shade-grown or bird-friendly coffee). The second dimension relates to taste or preference. Here, increasing consumption derives from geographic indications of origin as well as gourmet and specialty coffees (such as Kona coffee or Kilimanjaro coffee). Consumers are willing to pay a premium for these coffees because of their superior characteristics. Quite often these two dimensions overlap in the sense that consumers may demand specialty coffee that also satisfies certain social criteria.

Certification of nontraditional coffees is complicated and often contentious. Currently, no government agency or international organization has the official mandate to certify nontraditional coffees. With the exception of organic coffee, all certification comes from nongovernmental organizations—hence some of the value of the certified coffee rests with the reputation of the certifying organization. Organic coffee carrying a legally protected trademark is regulated in the European Union, Japan, and the United States.

The rise of self-certification by large supermarket chains, often with standards below those set by the independent certification agencies, raises the issue of credibility and thus of the further expansion of niche markets. Parallel to the question of self-certification is the emergence of institutional buyers that require producers to meet certain sustainability criteria but do not offer a price premium for doing so.

Firm estimates of the market share of differentiated coffee do not exist, but the figure is probably between 6 and 8 percent of global coffee consumption. Organic consumption in major consuming countries reached 700,000 bags in 2002–03 (or about 0.6 percent of global coffee consumption). In terms of market share the highest rates of consumption were in Denmark (2.8 percent), Switzerland (2.3 percent), Austria (2.0 percent), and Germany (1.2 percent), followed by the United States and Canada (1.1 percent each). Japan's share was 0.5 percent. In the fair-trade coffee market about 240,000 bags were traded in 2001, 43 percent of which were consumed by Germany and the Netherlands.

To summarize, several characteristics of these "new" markets must be highlighted. First, the phenomenal growth of these markets reflects, in part, a low base—implying that as a share of global output, niche markets are small. Second, supply and demand conditions will soon saturate these markets—there is increasing evidence of falling premiums for these coffees in some markets. Third, the benefits usually accrue to producers with some organizational structure, who are usually not the poorest.

Synthesis

The coffee market may have been subject to supply controls longer than any other important commodity. Apart from stabilizing (and perhaps raising) prices in the short term, these agreements brought new entrants into the coffee market. With few exceptions, the trade and marketing regimes of coffee-producing countries are largely free of domestic support or taxation measures. At the international level, there are no tariffs or quantitative restrictions, with the exception of some tariff escalation on coffee products (such as soluble coffee). This escalation is very small compared to other commodities, however.

During the 1990s Brazil expanded its coffee output to less frost-prone areas, thus reducing the probability of weather-induced supply disruptions. Vietnam emerged as the dominant supplier of robusta coffee; it now produces as much coffee as Colombia. At the same time, numerous niche markets have emerged. Currently 6 to 8 percent of coffee output is traded outside traditional marketing channels. On the other hand, new technologies have enabled roasters to be more flexible in their ability to make short-term switches among coffee types, implying that premiums for certain types of coffee cannot be retained for long.

Given the inability of the various supply-control measures to arrest the decline in coffee prices, and in the absence of any new international initiative or distorting domestic policies by dominant producers, the outlook for the coffee market rests entirely on supply and demand. Neither the supply nor the demand outlook favors a reversal of the events that shaped the coffee market during the last decade.

Per capita coffee consumption in high-income countries, where more than three-quarters of coffee is consumed, has remained virtually unchanged over the past decade, implying a near-zero income elasticity for coffee. According to recent International Coffee Organization calculations, per capita coffee consumption in Western Europe declined from 5.8 kilograms a year in 1993 to 5.5 kilograms in 1999 and in the United States from 4.5 kilograms a year to 4.2 kilograms (table 16.4). That is the same as the 1910–20 average. Annual per capita coffee consumption in the United States peaked at about 8 kilograms after World War II and declined to 6.5 kilograms during the 1960s, before returning to its 1910–20 average (Pan-American Coffee Bureau 1970).

Like tea, coffee faces strong competition from the soft drink industry. In 1970 annual per capita consumption of soft drinks in the United States was 86 liters; in 1999 it exceeded 200 liters, according to the U.S. Department of Agriculture. With the exception of a few coffee producers, low-income countries that have high income growth potential and high income elasticities for food do not consume much coffee. Efforts to penetrate new markets (China and Russia, for example) have only recently begun. Even if such efforts succeed, two points must be made. First, success is likely to come at the expense of tea consumption, which is often produced by the same countries that produce coffee (the tea industry has also engaged in efforts to increase consumption). Second, any increase in coffee consumption by developing countries is likely to come in the form of soluble coffee, which, as mentioned earlier, requires lower quality beans.

TABLE 16.4   Per Capita Coffee Consumption of Major Consumers, 1993–99
(kilograms per year)

Country	1993	1994	1995	1996	1997	1998	1999
European Union							
Germany	7.93	7.53	7.37	7.16	7.22	7.01	7.46
France	5.73	5.30	5.48	5.69	5.68	5.39	5.52
Italy	5.18	5.00	4.86	4.95	5.08	5.16	5.16
Spain	4.19	4.28	4.21	4.49	4.63	4.68	5.15
United Kingdom	2.61	2.71	2.25	2.43	2.46	2.62	2.30
EU average	5.76	5.57	5.33	5.57	5.56	5.51	5.52
Japan	2.83	2.92	2.98	2.83	2.90	2.91	3.01
United States	4.50	4.01	3.98	4.10	4.00	4.14	4.24
Average	4.88	4.64	4.51	4.64	4.59	4.62	4.69

Source: International Coffee Organization.

With the aggressive production prospects of major Asian producers, especially Vietnam; with Brazil's expansion, considerable efficiency gains, and reduced likelihood of frosts; and with weak demand prospects due to low income elasticity and strong competition from soft drinks, the outlook for the coffee market is poor. While prices are expected to recover from their current lows when the downward adjustment of supply takes place, prices are unlikely to reach the highs experienced during the boom years of the late 1970s or the mid-1990s.

Notes

1. Arabica typically commands a highly volatile premium over robusta. However, a bivariate time series error-correction model that examined the comovement of arabica and robusta prices using monthly data from January 1983 to September 2001 found extremely low comovement. In the 1990s, for example, the price differential fluctuated between 13 percent in October 1995 and 156 percent in August 1997.

2. The concentration of coffee production has increased (from 0.11 in 1970 to 0.14 in 2000), mainly reflecting the increased shares of Brazil and Vietnam. The concentration index, also known as the Herfindahl index, is defined as the squared sum of production shares of all countries. A value of unity indicates that a single country accounts for the entire production. Values close to zero indicate that a large number of countries have equal shares.

3. There has been some concern that the increasing concentration of the coffee industry has allowed for rent-seeking by the coffee industry. Evidence cited includes the very high profits made by the coffee industry in times of low prices and the "stickiness" of retail prices, which do not fall as fast as world green coffee prices. It is claimed that this reduces final demand because of higher-than-necessary retail prices, thus holding down world demand for any given level of supply. Although recent work by

RIAS (2002) found no evidence of collusion or a cartel, it is also the case that the coffee industry wishes to sell the volume that maximizes profits, which appears not to be the highest possible volume.

4. Highly liquid coffee futures contracts, where the hedge fund activity takes place, are traded at the New York Board of Trade for arabica and at the London International Financial Futures and Options Exchange for robusta. Less liquid coffee contracts are traded at the São Paulo Commodity Exchange, Singapore Commodity Exchange, Bangalore Commodity Exchange, and Tokyo Grains Exchange.

5. Quality deterioration has been presented as a negative consequence of policy reforms. However, the two studies that have looked at the issue in some detail, albeit for different commodities found little or no evidence of lower quality of cocoa in Cameroon (Gilbert and Tollens 2003) and cotton in Tanzania (Baffes 2004) after the reforms.

6. UNCTAD (2002: 65) describes specialty coffees: "It is fair to say that 'specialty coffee' has become a generic label covering a range of different coffees, which either command a premium price over other coffees or are perceived by consumers as being different from widely available mainstream brands of coffee. The term has become so broad that there is no universally accepted definition of what constitutes 'specialty coffee', and it frequently means different things to different people. Given this lack of precision in definition it is extremely difficult to describe the market in a global way."

References

Akiyama, T. 2001. "Coffee Market Liberalization since 1990." In Takamasa Akiyama, John Baffes, Donald Larson, and Panos Varangis, eds., *Commodity Market Reforms: Lessons from Two Decades*. Regional and Sectoral Studies. Washington, D.C.: World Bank.

Akiyama, T., J. Baffes, D. Larson, and P. Varangis. 2003. "Commodity Market Reform in Africa: Some Recent Experience." *Economic Systems* 27: 83–115.

Baffes, J. (forthcoming) "Tanzania's Coffee Sector: Constraints and Challenges." *Journal of International Development.*

Baffes, J. 2004. "Tanzania's Cotton Sector: Reforms, Constraints and Challenges." *Development Policy Review* 22: 75–96.

Bates, R. H. 1997. *Open-Economy Politics: The Political Economy of the World Coffee Trade.* Princeton, N.J.: Princeton University Press.

Bohman M., Lovell Jarvis, and R. Barichello. 1996. "Rent Seeking and International Commodity Agreements: The Case of Coffee." *Economic Development and Cultural Change* 44(2): 379–404.

Gilbert, C. L. 1995. "International Commodity Control: Retrospect and Prospect." Policy Research Working Paper 1545. World Bank, International Economics Department, Commodity and Policy Analysis Unit, Washington, D.C.

Gilbert C. L., and E. F. Tollens. 2003. "Does Market Liberalisation Jeopardise Export Quality? Cameroonian Cocoa, 1988–2000," *Journal of African Economies* 12: 303–342.

Hutchinson, L. 1909. "Coffee 'Valorization' in Brazil." *Quarterly Journal of Economics* 23(3): 528–35.

IADB/USAID/WB (Inter-American Development Bank, U.S. Agency for International Development, World Bank). 2002. "Managing the Competitive Transition of the Coffee Sector in Central America." Paper presented at the Regional Workshop "The Coffee Crisis and its Impact in Central America: Situation and Lines of Action," Antigua, Guatemala, April 3–5.

Kreuger A. O. 1990. *The Political Economy of Controls. Public Policy and Development: Essays in honor of Ian Little.* Oxford: Oxford University Press.

Krivonos, Ekaterina. 2003. "The Impact of Coffee Market Reforms on Producers' Prices and Price Transmission." Development Prospects Group, World Bank, Washington, D.C.

Lewin, B., D. Giovannucci, and P. Varangis. 2004. "Coffee Markets: New Paradigms in Global Supply and Demand." Agriculture and Rural Development Internal Report, World Bank, Washington, D.C.

Pan-American Coffee Bureau. 1970. *Annual Coffee Statistics.* No. 34. New York.

RIAS (Rabo International Advisory Services). 2002. "Raising the Income of Coffee Growers." Paper prepared for the Ministry of Foreign Affairs, The Netherlands.

Shepherd, A. W., and S. Farolfi. 1999. *Export Crop Liberalization in Africa: A Review.* Rome: United Nations Food and Agriculture Organization.

UNCTAD (U.N. Conference on Trade and Development). 2002. *Product and Market Development—Coffee: An Exporter's Guide.* International Trade Center, Geneva.

Wickizer, V. D. 1943. *The World Coffee Economy with Special Reference to Control Schemes.* Palo Alto, Calif.: Stanford University Press.

INDEX